# NOT MY PARTY

---

The *The* **RISE** *and* **FALL** *of*

**CANADIAN TORIES,**

*from* **ROBERT STANFIELD**

*to* **STEPHEN HARPER**

---

# Tom McMillan

**NIMBUS**
PUBLISHING

Nimbus Publishing Limited
3731 Mackintosh St, Halifax, NS, B3K 5A5
(902) 455-4286 nimbus.ca

Printed and bound in Canada

NB1265

Cover and interior design: Jenn Embree

Library and Archives Canada Cataloguing in Publication

McMillan, Tom, 1945-, author
Not my party : the rise and fall of Canadian Tories, from Robert Stanfield to
Stephen Harper / Tom McMillan.
Issued in print and electronic formats.
ISBN 978-1-77108-423-9 (paperback).—ISBN 978-1-77108-424-6 (html)
1. Conservatism—Canada. 2. Conservative Party of Canada. 3. McMillan,
Tom, 1945-. 4. Harper, Stephen, 1959-. 5. Canada--Politics and government—
20th century. 6. Canada—Politics and government—2006-2015. I. Title.

FC641.M36A3 2016                971.06                C2016-903751-7
                                                      C2016-903752-5

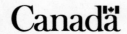 

Canada Council    Conseil des arts
for the Arts      du Canada

Nimbus Publishing acknowledges the financial support for its publishing activities from the Government of Canada through the Canada Book Fund (CBF) and the Canada Council for the Arts, and from the Province of Nova Scotia. We are pleased to work in partnership with the Province of Nova Scotia to develop and promote our creative industries for the benefit of all Nova Scotians.

*For Kelly, Becky, and Emily*
in loving memory of
*Eileen (McMillan) Fulford*

*Politics is more difficult than physics.*
— Albert Einstein

# CONTENTS

PART I

## Searching for Progressive Conservatism:
## The Robert Stanfield Years

PART II

## Inside Looking Out:
## Progressive Conservatism in Action

PART III

# Outside Looking In: Conservatism from a New Perspective

# INTRODUCTION

This book is a memoir of my life in politics: first as a political operative, then as an elected politician, later as a non-career diplomat, and finally as a candidate for office yet again before retiring from the game altogether. But the book is not just a memoir. I also discuss my personal search for the meaning of Canadian conservatism throughout a long public career in which I both observed and practised it.

The story first focuses on two men: a Tory leader, Robert Stanfield; and a university president, Tom Symons. It tells how, in the 1960s and 1970s, they quietly and discreetly, but steadily and undeniably, transformed and modernized the policies and image of the Progressive Conservative Party of Canada. Their work followed a decade of erratic, and often reactionary, leadership by John Diefenbaker, with his increasingly anachronistic brand of prairie populism. Diefenbaker's biographer, Denis Smith, characterized his subject as a "rogue," a leader whose personality and stands on issues constituted a marked departure for the PCs. By restoring the party to its pre-Diefenbaker leadership and policy traditions, Stanfield, in partnership with Symons, engaged in what I call a "counter-revolution." In telling that story, I discuss my own relationship with the two men who led it. My role was principal functionary in the PC leader's extraparliamentary policy process. It gave me a ringside seat to witness one of the most extraordinary partnerships in the history of party politics in Canada.

I am especially interested in the Stanfield-Symons legacy in the context of the Conservative Party's 2003 marriage to the Reform/Canadian Alliance Party and the new identity the party adopted, under Stephen Harper's leadership, following that merger. Was Harper committed to the rich heritage and historic values of the grand old party of Sir John A. Macdonald and Georges-Étienne Cartier, to the Conservative/Liberal coalition tradition they launched in the 1850s, before Canada was even born? That tradition survived long after the coalition itself dissolved. Or, instead, did Harper perpetrate a hostile takeover of this great national institution, then render it but a shadow of its former self—and a very dark shadow at that? To me, those questions have gained relevance since the October 2015 federal election, when "anyone but Harper" strategic voting coalesced behind Justin Trudeau's Liberals to oust Stephen Harper from power, just as a bar's security guard would evict an unruly patron: on his backside.

Harper's abrupt resignation as party leader, the PCs' need to find a new one, and their return to the familiar role of official opposition in Parliament inevitably will force the party to address fundamental questions—two, in particular. First, should the Conservative Party continue as the kind of national political party many people think it became after Harper orchestrated the 2003 merger in concert with then-PC leader Peter MacKay? Critics of the merger believe it caused the historic Conservative Party to morph from a progressive party that embraced economic and social values rooted in Canadian tradition into a US Republican-style or "neoconservative" party foreign to that tradition. Second, if those critics are correct, and in light of the 2015 election results, does the Conservative Party now need to chart a far different course: more centrist, less ideological, less religiously directed, and one much closer to that which it followed for almost a century and a half before the merger?

In the post-Harper era, I believe the Conservative Party needs to embrace the kinds of progressive policies—and the values that underpinned them—for which Robert Stanfield stood. While writing the book, I found it illuminating to contrast Stanfield's leadership, including his temperament and management style, with Brian Mulroney's to help explain why Stanfield and Symons worked so well as a policy team. I was PC deputy House leader the entire time Mulroney was opposition leader (1983–84). In that role, I soon got a clear view of how Mulroney's policy mind and political instincts operated. My fraternal twin, Charley, was Mulroney's chief policy advisor from the time Mulroney first sought the PC leadership in 1976 to well into his time as prime minister about a decade later. Both at the time and long afterwards, Charley shared with me his insights into Mulroney's political and governing style and, indeed, into the man himself. I weave many of Charley's insights into the narrative. I also provide my own reflections on Mulroney, underscoring his deep roots in, and self-identification with, the Maritimes and the region's impact on the man's politics and personal growth. No doubt, this "twin" perspective about Canada's eighteenth prime minister is unique.

Throughout the book, I draw heavily on my political experiences in Prince Edward Island, because that is where my electoral career was mostly based. I also sometimes focus on the Island because, small as it is, PEI—and Atlantic Canada more generally—practises a type of politics that can teach valuable lessons not restricted by either geography or the particular periods discussed. The role of the media in political campaigns—specifically as partisan actors, whether journalists acknowledge it or not—is a case in point. This book concerns much more than Atlantic Canadian politics, though that is its rudder. It is also about national politics, albeit through the eyes of a former politician steeped, virtually from birth, in a distinct political culture indigenous to the region.

The book is not a work of scholarship. But I am a political scientist—at least in education, if not as a lifelong practitioner. As such, I am confident that the story breaks new ground on two important fronts. First, it fills a gap in the history of the PC Party, still a barren land in Canadian studies, particularly relating to Atlantic Canada. Robert Stanfield inarguably was the most outstanding and widely respected national public figure to emerge from this region in the last half of the twentieth century. I find it strange, therefore, that no one has yet written a biography covering this towering figure's full public career, merely parts of it. This book is not that comprehensive biography. I have, however, tried to fill some of the void. I stress Stanfield's "politics of thoughtfulness" legacy and the impact various factors have had on it, for good or ill, over the years since then. Those factors include both the actions and policies of subsequent PC leaders and certain changes in the political culture more generally, among them the growing influence of television (especially House of Commons Question Period coverage) and of social media. The second new ground the book ploughs is its demonstration and analysis of how one of our three major national political parties developed and used policy and, in doing so, profoundly influenced laws and government practices in Canada to this day. I also hope to shed light on certain dimensions of Canadian politics more generally. Some countries, notably the United Kingdom, have a long and rich tradition in which former politicians reflect on and write about their experiences in government and in politics. Such a tradition is not nearly as strong in our own country. It is weakest of all outside central Canada, and particularly in Atlantic Canada. I seek to add to that tradition. Although the main reach of the book is not historical but contemporary—what the Conservative Party of Canada is today and where it is headed—my emphasis on the party's past reflects my strong belief that therein lies the marker for the party's future. Indeed, I worry about whether it has any future at all as the distinguished national institution it once was.

The core of the book concerns how Canada's Conservatives—by various names over time—have influenced the country, from either the government or the opposition benches, under diverse leaders from Stanfield to Harper. To advance that narrative, I identify (and, in some cases, detail) the party's policies in defining areas over the generations. I focus on the Stanfield period, particularly in the early chapters, for two reasons. First, this was when I was active in the affairs of the party at the very centre of its decision-making, prior to my parliamentary and Cabinet career. Second, I believe that the highly innovative policy process that Stanfield and Symons created for their party, almost five decades ago, could well serve in contemporary times as a model for all political parties, not just the Conservatives. The fundamentals are as valid and germane today as they were then. Such a policy process would especially help opposition parties address issues and develop policies in a more thoughtful, evidence-based, and responsible way than any of them typically has done, either at the federal or the provincial level, with the exception of the Stanfield experience, ever since political parties began to operate in our country. (The party in power can access the public service for this purpose.) As the national Conservative Party seeks new leadership—and, I hope, a fresh start—the Stanfield-Symons policy process could serve as a blueprint.

In Harper's time as leader, the Conservative Party, like the Republican Party in the United States today, demonstrated hostility to science and objective facts—as opposed to extreme ideology, ersatz moral values, and exclusionary religious beliefs—as guideposts for public policy. Conservatives need to remedy the extent to which, since the 2003 merger, their party has subjugated evidence to emotion in forging a distinct agenda for the country. Otherwise, the party will continue to alienate a large swath of the electorate, especially the educated, the young, the urban, and the non-religious. Such voters are much more interested in practical solutions to everyday problems than battles between conflicting ideologies or sets of sectarian beliefs that originated centuries before their time. This is a challenge that Robert Stanfield faced—quite successfully—when he inherited the Progressive Conservative Party leadership from an emotion-driven, anti-intellectual John Diefenbaker five decades ago. The tension between evidence and emotion in developing public policy is a recurring theme of the book, particularly in the context of such pressing and complex issues as the environment. I had to address this tension head-on as federal environment minister, after my Tory predecessor, Suzanne Blais-Grenier, almost wrecked the federal environment portfolio by placing rigid ideology and mean-spirited partisanship above the essentially scientific mission of the department. A political party that is a stranger to science cannot easily make friends with the truth. Neither will it likely bond with Canadians who want their elected officials to respond to their concerns based on objective facts, rather than on personal feelings. When politicians justify their positions based on religious or sectarian values or absolute principles of any other kind and conduct partisan warfare against those who do not share their beliefs, they operate in the realm of emotion, not objectivity. And emotions—however valid and useful in one's personal life—are a primitive compass with which to chart a practical course of government action. In this book, I argue for a more reliable direction finder for the Conservative Party—and for the nation.

I hope, above all, that the book proves a good read—a fix, so to speak—for other political junkies.

# A CHANCE ENCOUNTER

L ouis St-Laurent has a lot to answer for. He got me hooked on politics, and I have been a junkie ever since, beyond any hope of redemption. May he pay for his sin. Certainly, I have been paying for mine from that day on.

I met the seventy-five-year-old Liberal prime minister from Quebec in the dying days of the June 1957 federal election campaign. I was eleven years old, in grade six at Queen's Square School in Charlottetown, PEI. The old red-brick school, now long gone, squatted directly across the street from Canada's most sacred heritage site, Province House. There, the Fathers of Confederation gathered in September 1864 to give birth to Canada, and there the Island's Legislative Assembly has met from the day the classical structure was completed in 1847.

I remember every detail of my chance encounter with the aging prime minister that June afternoon more than half a century ago. A retentive memory for minutiae is, perhaps, the only piston I inherited from the formidable high-performance engine that was my father's mind. It was equipped with so much horsepower that he was remembered at McGill University's medical school long after he graduated in 1938 with all the gold.

In a scene that could not happen in today's world of supertight security, Prime Minister St-Laurent was standing all alone staring at the south side of Province House. Now close to the end, the election campaign had pummelled him. Like the criminal lawyer he had been, Tory leader John George Diefenbaker, a fiery orator, had excoriated the Liberal government in Parliament. Now he was doing the same on the hustings. The issue was the so-called TransCanada Pipeline scandal concerning efforts by the St-Laurent government to ram through legislation to authorize the building of the controversial, much-opposed infrastructure to transport natural gas from Alberta to the east. The prime minister was exhausted and wounded from the savage beating his government had received at the hands of not only the Tories but also the Co-operative Commonwealth Federation (CCF), forerunners of today's New Democratic Party. The two opposition parties had coordinated their parliamentary strategies to inflict maximum damage on the government's reputation on the eve of the election.

By that day in Charlottetown, in front of Province House, the septuagenarian St-Laurent was a dead man walking. Had his handlers and security detail taken pity and kept their distance, so the old man could be alone with his thoughts for a brief spell? Had he asked to be taken to this most sacred of ground, in the last lap of the campaign? Was it to derive inspiration and strength from the ghosts who, through dint of courage and vision, had "builded better than they knew"? Those are the words on the historic plaque at Province House that so eloquently describe the statecraft that Sir John A. Macdonald and Georges-Étienne Cartier and the other Fathers of Confederation had exercised in the hallowed halls there nearly a century earlier. Why else would the leader of the country, at the climax of an election campaign that would seal his fate, find himself alone in front of this historic shrine on a tranquil, overcast mid-afternoon in June in the country's tiniest capital, in its tiniest province…and with tiniest me?

I had no idea who the spectator was, but I walked up to him, thinking he was just an old man lost. "Can I help you, Sir?" I asked, in the Good Samaritan way we Islanders have wired into our DNA when seeing someone who looks "from away." And this gentleman of distinguished bearing in a grey pinstriped suit certainly appeared from away to a young schoolboy who had taken a shortcut from Queen's Square School through the Province House grounds en route home.

The old man smiled warmly, but with a touch of wan. In a soft, but rich and quiet avuncular voice, he said, "No, thank you. I'm fine. What's your name?" When I told him, he asked, with no hint of braggadocio, "Young man, do you know who *I* am?" "No, Sir, I'm afraid I don't. Who *are* you?" I responded. "Well, Tommy," he replied, "I am Louis St-Laurent, prime minister of Canada." And, with haunting words fraught with meaning even for this young lad, he added something that has stuck with me to this day. I can still hear the old man's words with the same clarity that I can see the fine web of blue veins on his sunken, pale-purplish cheeks: "No matter what happens to me in a few days, son, you can always say you met the prime minister of Canada." He then said goodbye and vanished, as though a ghost of a Father of Confederation himself. All the way home I kept saying to myself: "He knows he is not going to be prime minister in a few days. He knows the end is near. He wanted *me* to know he was prime minister when I met him because he won't be for long."

As it turned out, a few days later Louis Stephen St-Laurent *was* no longer prime minister of Canada. The June 1957 election sent 112 Conservative, 105 Liberal, 25 CCF, 19 Social Credit, and 4 independent members to the House of Commons. But St-Laurent's Liberals had prevailed in the popular vote (40.75 percent versus 38.81 percent for the PCs). They had also led in most of the public opinion polls leading up to the election; indeed, *Maclean's* magazine went to print reporting a Liberal triumph over the Tories. Instead, the election result was a historic upset. Virtually no one expected St-Laurent's defeat. And yet, an eleven-year-old schoolboy in Charlottetown did. Someone had, in effect, forewarned him—Louis St-Laurent himself.

# Part I

# SEARCHING FOR PROGRESSIVE CONSERVATISM: THE ROBERT STANFIELD YEARS

*It must be remembered that there is nothing more difficult to plan, more uncertain of success, nor more dangerous to manage than the creation of a new order of things. For the initiator has the enmity of all who profit by the presentation of the old institutions, and merely the lukewarm defenders in those who would gain by the new ones.*

—Machiavelli, *The Prince*

# Chapter 1

# POLITICS
# IN THE BLOOD

M y chance encounter with Louis St-Laurent made me the first non-Tory on either
side of my family (McMillan or McQuaid) since paleolithic times. It would be
an understatement akin to calling Niagara Falls a drip to say neither of my parents
was thrilled by the unabashed enthusiasm with which St-Laurent had unwittingly
caused me to discover my Inner Liberal. This apostasy occurred in an era when, on
Prince Edward Island, as elsewhere in the Maritimes, one's political label was as pivotal as one's religion.

The first of our direct forebears in Prince Edward Island, Captain Alexander
McMillan, came to the Island in 1778 as a Tory United Empire Loyalist from Carlisle,
Pennsylvania. There, he and his brother Charles had been shipbuilders. Our ances-
tor had received a land grant in PEI from King George III for his loyalty to the
Crown, having fought, as a British officer against the rebels, in the American War of
Independence. The king gave "us" more than a thousand acres in all, over time—
about half in the area now known as Rocky Point, across the Hillsborough River from
Charlottetown, and the other half in Belfast, about thirty miles east of the capital.
More than a thousand acres from the king was a huge estate in a small colony later
dubbed "the million-acre farm."

My mother's people, the McQuaids, were comparative newcomers to the Island.
The earliest McQuaid on record in PEI is George, a tailor from Donagh Parish, County
Monaghan, Ireland. He and his illiterate wife Sarah (née McNally), from the same
parish, and their nine children emigrated in August 1849 from Ireland to Elmira, at
the most easterly tip of the Island. Later moving with only part of his family to Kelly's
Cross—still rural but much closer to Charlottetown—George was said to be "the
proudest, dandiest man of the parish." From their roots in Ireland, the McQuaids
were as rock-ribbed Tory as the McMillans, albeit in a distinctly Irish tradition.

Unfortunately, within a year, George McQuaid collapsed and died in his wife's
arms from a self-inflicted razor wound. Whether the man was overwhelmed by trying
to survive with a wife and nine children in a new and strange land or by some other
factor is anyone's guess. Many other McQuaids from the same branch of the family
moved to PEI from Ireland after George and his family arrived. Despite the tragic
circumstances surrounding his demise, they early on established a reputation for
probity and community service that has remained their hallmark through the generations to this very day. Ironically, given George McQuaid's flamboyance and eventual
suicide, the prevailing distinguishing characteristics of the broader McQuaid tribe
on the Island have been sobriety, dignity, and reserve.

For his part, Captain Alexander McMillan is reputed to have used his land and
attendant economic clout on the Island, not to mention a close relationship with the

PEI governor's clique, for unfair gain. He was also considered a bully and a generally unpleasant man. Fortunately, Captain McMillan's "ship" was soon righted by his heirs. Like the McQuaids, the McMillans gained much respect locally and beyond both for their personal qualities and for their community-mindedness—even if not always with quite the same degree of sobriety demonstrated by my mother's people. Somebody had to sustain the Celts' reputation for love of the cup!

---

If, as William Wordsworth wrote, "The Child is father of the Man," in no other facet of life is that truer than in politics. Politicians, more than any others who toil for a living, are engaged in a one-product enterprise: marketing themselves as individuals and doing so with every decision they make, every action they take, every breath they draw. Even a politician's choice of spouse or lover can seal his or her fate. The politician is inseparable from who the individual is and how he or she became that person.

I am not sufficiently introspective to know why I entered such a punishing business. It was not exactly the family business—that was medicine. But, at home, politics was closer to the kitchen table than cutlery. So we four boys and two girls grew up exposed to animated political talk over meals and in every other family circumstance. My father was often under intense pressure from Progressive Conservative pooh-bahs to run for the party in one election or another, both federal and provincial. And, certainly, Dad would have liked to do so. Mother, however, was dead set against it—literally, for she feared the effects on his health, given the several heart attacks he had suffered, beginning when he was only in his forties. In any event, I do know that upbringing had much to do with my choosing politics and, even more profoundly, with my progressive Tory DNA. It can be rightly assumed Dad and Mom were major influences in both cases.

My father, Dr. Joseph Alexander McMillan, was a towering figure in PEI, especially to the Island's Roman Catholic community. He was a revered medical doctor whom journalist Barbara MacAndrew would later characterize, in *Maclean's* magazine, as the province's Joseph P. Kennedy (patriarch of the American political family dynasty).[1] Dad had become a local television star as the public face of the 1957 Tory federal election campaign across the Island while endorsing the four PC candidates in celebrated party-sponsored appearances in the new medium. One of the four candidates (all of them ultimately elected) would later describe those appearances as "brilliant and eloquent performances."[2] Dad would play that TV role in subsequent national elections throughout the leadership of John Diefenbaker, to whom he was fanatically devoted.

My father possessed legendary brainpower, a near-photographic memory, and four university degrees, not to mention advanced training and certification in surgery in Montreal and Boston. In addition to being a surgeon, Dad was a theologian/philosopher, with a master's degree in that field from Université Laval. He had spent four years at the Grand Seminary in Quebec City, but stopped short of ordination when he decided to pursue medicine instead. More accurately, the Bishop of Charlottetown decreed that the archdiocese needed a brilliant lay-Catholic medical doctor in the flock more than yet another parish priest. It was an era when every good Catholic family was expected to—and usually did—give up at least one son to the "calling." Dad's own family had already done so in his brother Ken. The third and youngest, Frank, became a urologist.

I know my social consciousness, in particular, was instilled in me at a young age by that of my parents, especially my father. Dad was nothing if not a Good Samaritan—almost to a fault. It used to exasperate Mother that, despite a life-threatening heart condition, when spotting people struggling with heavy luggage in an airport terminal, he would insist on helping them—at the risk of his life. Little wonder, then, that he gravitated first to the priesthood and finally to medicine. No doubt remembering my late father's saintly devotion to his own Hippocratic Oath, Mother once laid out in lavender a young local doctor who had failed to rush to help another player in sudden serious medical stress on the fairway at Charlottetown's Belvedere Golf and Country Club, where she had been the first woman president. "You're unworthy of the title 'doctor!'" she scolded him in a voice that could be heard all the way to the clubhouse—if not to Greece.

Education and training, more than any other factors, explain Dad's uncommon concern for the poor in very practical terms, not just theoretical. The last thing he did on Christmas Eve, after finishing "rounds" at the hospital, was to drop by Catholic Social Services to see Sister Mary Henry. The big husky head of the Sisters of St. Martha, she ran the operation with the competence and authority of a fleet commander. Dad had to ensure himself that all the needy families of the Catholic Diocese had been taken care of with Christmas hampers, to which he already had generously contributed both money and supplies.

Inarguably, my father's moral compass was bolted to his Catholicism. He attended Catholic primary and secondary schools, and graduated from no fewer than three Catholic-affiliated universities before studying medicine at heretical McGill. At each of the three then-sectarian universities, he was steeped in Catholic social teaching. This was especially the case at St. Francis Xavier in Antigonish, Nova Scotia, where the doctrine of social justice on poverty and wealth is as integral a part of the institution's identity as football at Notre Dame. Its social justice ethos had a profound impact on the lives and careers of graduates such as Brian Mulroney and Cape Breton political titan Allan J. MacEachen, just as it had on my father till the day he died, more than four decades after graduating. For his part, MacEachen, who once taught economics at "X," served as a senior minister in successive federal Liberal governments, including as deputy prime minister under Pierre Trudeau. He fought tenaciously for many of Canada's most important national antipoverty programs, including medicare. In the same spirit, my father pioneered prepaid private medical insurance in the Maritimes through Blue Cross/Blue Shield in the pre-medicare years. He was passionately committed to many of the same values Allan MacEachen championed, even as he fought for them from a substantially different ideological command post.

Nowhere else in Brian Mulroney's one-thousand-page *Memoirs* does he make a stronger link between his performance as prime minister and his formative years than in those passages in which he discusses the impact that St. Francis Xavier University had on him both as a man and as a politician. He says Dr. Moses Coady, founder of the Antigonish Movement, had an especially strong influence on him. Dr. Coady instilled in his followers the belief that everyone is morally obliged to help the poor both at home and throughout the world. "That influence," Mulroney states, "stayed with me." The former prime minister reveals: "For the next nine years, the government I led placed Dr. Coady and his principles at the forefront of government policy and decision-making."[3]

The overarching themes of the Catholic social teaching that helped mould the character of my father and that of so many others schooled in this tradition were rooted in the writings of towering Catholic thinkers, most notably St. Thomas Aquinas and St. Augustine of Hippo, along with concepts articulated in the Bible. This intellectual and spiritual tradition stresses the intrinsic dignity of all human beings, the fundamental importance of solidarity and community "among all God's children," and the principle of "subsidiarity"—the concept that holds that spirituality and justice are grounded in the dignity and freedom of individuals participating in society at the closest-possible community level. This perspective, in turn, is rooted in a profound concern about the stifling of these values by a big, impersonal national government operating in a moral vacuum. It is telling that Dad, like Mulroney and MacEachen and others of their ilk, strongly believed that the state needed to foster and defend vigorously the broad, though not necessarily Catholic, social-justice values to which he was committed as a private citizen—a mindset typically associated with the "left." Yet, Dad believed equally passionately that overreaching government was the biggest threat to human rights and personal liberties—a concern typically associated with the "right." Fears about government overreach were the main reason Dad publicly opposed medicare's launch in the mid-1960s, despite having done so much to help protect people from health care costs through prepaid private insurance. The apparent contradiction, or at least paradox, of these dual perspectives vanishes, however, when viewed and understood in the light of Social Catholicism, whose intellectual and moral framework reconciles them, or at least tries mightily. On practical issues such as poverty and health care, it succeeded for Catholics such as Mulroney, MacEachen, my father, and—dare I say it in such superior company—for me as well.

I have nothing close to my father's grounding or capacity in Catholic philosophy—or in most other fields, for that matter. But before going to graduate school at heathen Queen's University in Kingston, Ontario, I grew up and studied in this same tradition in Charlottetown, from Queen's Square School to Birchwood Junior High to St. Dunstan's High School—farm teams for the Big League: St. Dunstan's University, later part of the University of Prince Edward Island. Every local Catholic boy and girl in my time was expected to aspire to attend SDU, which, with St. Dunstan's Basilica—a neo-Gothic behemoth whose twin spires reach almost to Heaven— was the centre of the Catholic Diocese on the Island. Central to the Catholic tradition in which I grew up was St. Thomas Aquinas's insight that "[o]ne solitary man cannot discover everything for himself. He must combine in a team, so that one may help another and different men be reasonably engaged in different jobs, one in medicine, another in this, another in that."[4] For my father, that job *was* medicine. For me, as for Mulroney and MacEachern, it was politics.

In the mid-1950s, the school system in PEI, as elsewhere, expanded like a powerlifter on steroids as the children of Second World War vets—the "baby boomers"—came of school age. The need for teachers with university accreditation grew correspondingly across the Island. In a dark chapter of the province's history, the Protestant-dominated provincial legislature tried to block efforts by Catholics to help meet the dire need for more teachers. "Dr. Joe," as everyone called my Dad, used his considerable oratorical skills to rally people of all faiths against the legislature's action. The controversy raged over a bill proposed by the province's Liberal government to grant the Island's only degree-granting institution legal authority to certify teachers. The fly in the ointment was that St. Dunstan's University was Catholic. In PEI at the time, when religion enflamed the hottest passions, that fly was not an insect but a pterodactyl.

Dad's peroration on the floor of the legislature came at the climax of Islanders' passions on the explosive issue. He spoke as a private citizen for Island Catholics in the public debate on the proposed law conducted at the legislative committee stage. With the connivance of a Catholic member of the Liberal government Caucus (Eugene Cullen), Dad had been held in reserve as the Catholics' ace of spades, with spades trump if the card needed to be played. It was. In high drama, the prestigious doctor was brought into the legislature as the last speaker. He followed the Protestants' final salvo by the Shriners, then, unlike now, virulently anti-Catholic in PEI. Dad's powerful and eloquent address stopped the juggernaut against the beleaguered Catholic university. Many elderly Islanders still recount the performance more than fifty years later.

Heath Macquarrie, a Protestant, always believed that my father's endorsement in high-profile TV appearances turned the tide, especially among Catholics, who were half the total vote, in Heath's tight first run for Parliament in 1957 in the dual constituency of Queen's (later "Hillsborough," now "Charlottetown"). Heath was desperate for the blessing of the Island's pre-eminent Catholic layman. Though a wily politician, the first-time candidate had done something that risked knocking him off his horse before he even mounted—literally: he had ridden a white steed in the Orange Parade, a red flag for Catholics. Certainly, it was a disastrous colour combination for a Protestant eager to convince Catholics to vote Tory blue. It didn't help that most voters, not just Catholics, were already suspicious of this recently repatriated Islander. Although only thirty-seven at the time, Heath had long wispy white hair (what little he had of it), a bald dome, a substantial girth, a broad and jowly and ruddy Scottish face, and, even on a cold winter's day, a fondness for donning a beret and kilt, not to mention a taste for Appleton rum (mother's milk to him). To boot, Heath had been living off the Island for a long time. He had pursued a politics PhD at McGill (itself cause for grave suspicion for some) and then taught political science at Brandon University in Manitoba. So, the "Scottish laird" was virtually unknown in PEI. To Islanders, anyone without red soil on his boots is "from away." Heath Macquarrie struck many as not just from away, but from another planet—an eccentric, if not an apparition. He was hardly their idea of a homegrown parliamentary fighter for the Island's cause in Ottawa. To many Catholics in the 1950s, this Scottish Presbyterian was suspect on religious grounds alone. But now, Heath Macquarrie was receiving the benediction of Dr. Joe McMillan, a fifth-generation Islander and Knights of Columbus luminary, riding high on the heels of religious heroism in the provincial legislature. Short of the pope's endorsement, that was as good as it got. Catholics voted for Macquarrie in droves and, consequently, he emerged victorious. The margin was 926 (10,651 for him; 9,725 for his nearest opponent, Liberal Neil Matheson). Heath went to his grave believing that "Dr. Joe" had made the 926-vote difference and more.

———————

Right after the war, my father built an imposing seven-bedroom house on an elevated piece of land in the prosperous Charlottetown neighbourhood of Brighton at 45 Greenfield Avenue. The edifice was designed by the distinguished Toronto architectural firm of Page & Steele, which did some of its best work for the University of Toronto. The mansion, as locals viewed it, had more firsts for a private PEI residence than the Island had potatoes. Among others, it was the first brick structure built on the Island after the war, the first with baseboard heating, and the first with an inside incinerator. The firsts also included an electric kitchen-sink "garburator" to grind peelings from those potatoes, and other such organic matter, when the "spuds from the bright red mud" arrived at our house. And, in this pre-medicare era, so they did—in truckloads, along with all the lobsters and other foodstuffs grateful farmers and fishermen would deliver to our door when not otherwise able to pay Dad for removing a gallbladder or tonsils or a cancerous tumour or for delivering their babies.

The house at 45 Greenfield Avenue was not enormous by today's "McMansion" standards, but it was the largest built in Charlottetown, and likely on the whole Island, since the start of the Great Depression in 1929. Charlottetown school principal Frank Costello, grandmaster of the local Boy Scouts and Cubs, always called it "the palace." TV broadcaster Mike Duffy, a senator from PEI, grew up down the street and over from us on Villa Avenue. From the outside, one would never have guessed the spaciousness, let alone elegance, inside—no doubt, reflecting Dad and Mother's insistence on public understatement. From the time the house began to rise from its foundation, however, locals marvelled at the grandeur unfolding brick by brick. My parents saw it as a home, everyone else as an Egyptian pyramid.

My mother, Dorothy Eileen McQuaid—always "Eileen"—of Souris, joined Dad in many of the activities he was engaged in as one of the country's most prominent medical leaders. Our home, for example, hosted the Royal Commission on Health Services (the Emmett Hall Commission) when it visited Charlottetown as part of countrywide consultations to prepare its 1964 landmark report. Mom also volunteered for a wide variety of local charities and other community causes and organizations, of which she invariably became the executive head. Like her own mother, Mom was not just one but a couple of generations before her time. As a young girl she had trekked from her home in Cranbrook, British Columbia, to Quebec City to study with the Ursuline nuns and learn French. She acquired a university degree (in home economics from St. Francis Xavier) in an era when women were not encouraged to finish high school, let alone go to college, still less to graduate. Before marrying Dad, she had an independent career managing Macy's, a well-known Montreal restaurant and pharmacy, part of a locally owned small chain in the city (and no connection to the namesake New York-based department store chain). At Macy's, Mom became a virtual daughter to Jacob Jassby, her wealthy employer and patron, whom she always described to us as "the smartest man I ever met except for your father." Jassby, who was Jewish, was denied entry to many private clubs and social affairs in Montreal in that era, but he nevertheless paid for Dad and Mom to go to places from which he himself was barred. To the day my mother died, she opposed all forms of discrimination, and her tales about Mr. Jassby—and about my parents' personal struggles as Catholics after they moved back to Charlottetown—shaped my own zero tolerance for discrimination against anyone on any ground.

Both my parents had lived and worked or studied for years in Quebec. My father spoke French flawlessly, after years at Université Laval and in the Quebec City seminary, studying the classics. This facility surprised and impressed francophone tourists from Quebec, New Brunswick, and the Magdalen Islands to whom he gave directions on the streets of Charlottetown, typically in French more polished than their own. Quebec newspapers, in English and French alike, were as familiar in our household as skates and baseball bats. The now-defunct *Montreal Star* had precedence even over Charlottetown's own *Guardian*. One never opposed two things in Dad's presence: John Diefenbaker and the Montreal Canadiens. They were equally sacrosanct.

My father once hired a car and guide to give me and my brother Charley a private tour of Montreal. The tour guide, in awe, soon clammed up; Dad knew more about the city, including obscure back alleys, than the professional himself. In many such ways, notably his fluency in French, Dad was as much a Quebecer and quasi-franco-phone as he was a Prince Edward Islander and anglophone. He took enormous pride in the French Quebec influences in his life. Mom felt similarly about her own years living, studying, and working in Quebec. Admittedly, though, she had mixed views, to say the least, about the Ursuline nuns who taught her in Quebec City, some of whom she considered cold and cruel.

In short, our parents raised us to believe that the country's English/French duality was culturally integral to the *idea* of Canada.


## Twins and a Second Mother

My twin brother, Charley, and I were born on October 15, 1945. Our birth followed that of first-born Colin, three years our senior, and of Eileen, only thirteen months before us. Four children all under the age of four in four years—even for a good Catholic family, that was a challenge. Later, two more arrived: Maura and John, respectively six and seven years junior to "the twins."

Charley and I have always been referred to as though we were a single unit. We both miraculously survived a highly contagious form of intestinal enteritis that struck the Charlottetown Hospital, our birthplace, like a monsoon. Even the priests weren't allowed in to give Last Rites to the many babies dropping dead faster than hospital personnel could process the death certificates. To a Catholic, slamming the door on a priest was tantamount to turning away God. But Dad was hospital chief of staff, so he ferreted Charley and me out of that den of death and brought us home to the modest white clapboard house on equally unprepossess-ing Churchill Avenue in which we then lived. In the heart of Brighton, the house of Dad and Mother's real dreams was being constructed with tens of thousands of bricks transported by barge from Montreal. The high drama to save the lives of "the twins" was played out with round-the-clock nurses under the direction of Mary Bradley, Dad's head nurse, whose devotion to duty was exceeded only by the military efficiency and medical knowledge and aptitude of a Norman Bethune. Whether thanks to prayer or Dad and Mary Bradley's Herculean medical efforts or both, Charley and I survived the near-deadly crisis. Appropriately, in gratitude for her pivotal role in the "Miracle on Churchill Avenue," Dad set Mary up for life, with her husband, Bob, in the funeral business (the Charlottetown Funeral Home). And then, as if the gods had not blessed the McMillans enough by sending Mary Bradley to Earth, they sent us Helen.

Helen Doyle, who virtually raised me, is a large part of why I am the person I became. She will loom large in different parts of my narrative as a moral complement of Robert Stanfield writ humble beginnings. It's important, therefore, that the reader come to know her. Helen's real name was Elizabeth Ann Doyle. But in our family, "Helen" was a one-word moniker like that reserved for deities such as Cleopatra and Jackie (or Madonna, if you will). Helen's celestial talent was people. And she applied that talent almost exclusively to the McMillan family, to which she came as a housekeeper—she loathed "maid"—as the day approached when Charley and I were to be born.

Dad hired Helen, a patient's daughter, from a convent in Rustico, where she had been working as a chambermaid. Helen, in fact, had aspired to be a nun, but a doctor had erroneously identified a disqualifying heart problem in her pre-entrance medical exam. It was not the only time the gods of fortune would intercept the plans of mere mortals concerning Helen's place in the universe. So apparently naïve was this would-be religious postulant that she had no idea that Mom was even pregnant, much less twin-bearing, when hired late in the pregnancy.

Helen was born on December 6, 1910, in the tiny Acadian fishing village of Tignish, about as far west of Charlottetown as it's possible to get on the Island. She had more than a dozen siblings, and her father, John, was a blacksmith and some-time breeder of sulky racehorses. Helen was as short as a thimble, nowhere near five feet. We boys teased her about it mercilessly, to mutual enjoyment, especially hers. She had a terrific sense of humour, which the gods must have decided to throw in when running out of other gifts to bestow on her. Not that beauty was one of them: her Roman nose was as large as her chin was prominent. (Had the gods given Joe Clark such a chin, he might well have remained prime minister a lot longer; a big chin didn't hurt Brian Mulroney.) Helen was family, and stayed with us McMillans in her own quarters at one end of the house until she retired a quarter-century later. Helen kept the sprawling red-brick house on Greenfield Avenue spotless, but she did much more than that. She washed our clothes, darned our socks. And she baked. And baked and baked. Her specialties were bread and rolls and donuts and apple or lemon pies and, at Christmas, an Acadian chicken-and-pork pâté for which French revolutionaries would have guillotined. My personal favourite was her multilayered strawberry or raspberry shortcake, depending on the season. They were created with wild berries that she and I alone picked together in the countryside near the family's summer cottage. All these delights were made with flour spread fine, and a wooden rolling pin pushed hard, on a pullout breadboard as large as a runway tarmac. Towards the end of Helen's life, my younger sister Maura decided that, if the gods insisted on taking Helen from us, they weren't also going to get her recipes. She would extract the recipes from Helen in the hope of replicating her wonders in the kitchen. But the gods outsmarted her. There *were* no recipes. Helen, it turned out, always baked from memory.

Most important of all, Helen—a devout Roman Catholic, born of an Irish father and an Acadian mother—was the resident family moralist. "Don't you dare do anything to disgrace your father," she would lecture us boys, usually about our gal squeezes. Evidently, Mother's reputation was either beyond reproach or of no concern. It was more the latter. Helen did not so much tolerate another woman in the house as act as though there was none. Her order "not to disgrace your father" had the moral authority of a papal encyclical. Still, Helen had an unlimited capacity to bend her strict Moral Code concerning both us children and even our respective Significant Others. In those days on the Island, particularly for someone as fanatically religious as Helen, a Catholic's marrying outside the faith was like abandoning one's citizenship: it was just not done. Through the years, however, only my sister Maura among the six of us siblings married a Catholic. And yet, Helen treated every one of our respective spouses as if he or she were a candidate for papal beatification. She showered them with love and baking, and always viewed them as her new children, infidels though they all be but one.

Upon her retirement, with the big house sold, Dad set Helen up in a comfortable apartment, where her innumerable perpetually blooming African violets were, like Helen herself, bright and colourful and good and full of life. She spent much of her retirement knitting woollen stocking caps, mittens, and boot-weight socks for the McMillan children and for the Charlottetown Diocese Catholic Social Welfare Bureau, run by the Sisters of St. Martha. When she died, she left behind a steamer trunk packed with her handiwork, but just a tiny fraction of what the woman had made and donated to us and charity.

Helen eventually moved into a Charlottetown provincial senior citizens' home. And then, after she contracted terminal breast cancer, as her illness started taking its toll on her strength, but never her spirits, she had to move into a palliative-care hospice just two blocks from the house that, as chatelaine, she had tended with love and devotion. At "the San," Helen, though sicker and often weaker than many of the other residents, served as the principal emotional caregiver and source of high spirits to everyone, patients and staff alike, all the while continuing to knit her masterful woollies. Helen Elizabeth Ann Doyle passed away in her sleep in her eightieth year, on a warm August day in 1989. The gods knew what they were doing. They wanted this Special Person back for themselves. Could anyone blame them?

Helen was not formally educated, but she was extraordinarily shrewd. On her own, she had engaged a lawyer to prepare a Last Will and Testament. All of us McMillans got a massive shock—Helen left a small fortune: tens of thousands of dollars scattered in bank and credit union accounts throughout Charlottetown. Apparently, such wealth is what accrues when one never has to spend a penny of one's wages over many years while being cared for by a loving family. But a fortune, even if nowhere near Howard Hughes's league? How did Helen do it—this woman who couldn't sign a cheque, still less a bank deposit slip, unassisted? Nobody in the family knows. The mystery remains. Less mysterious is that Helen, appearances to the contrary, was no simple country bumpkin. Never was it truer than with Helen Elizabeth Ann Doyle of Tignish, out of Rustico, that one makes a colossal mistake when judging a book by its cover.

# Nature or Nurture?

How substantially do genes affect—perhaps even dictate—one's political beliefs and allegiances? It's a question of steadily increasing interest to psychologists. A respected American psychologist once told me something that has stuck with me ever since: "Tom, we psychologists have long held that an individual's psychological makeup is the product of complex genetic and environmental factors that often reinforce one another in a way that's almost impossible to deconstruct." But, she said, "the longer I am a parent and observe my own children and their friends, the more I think genetics, not environmental factors, define who and what a person is—not just physically, but emotionally as well." And then she added: "Frankly, whatever they might feel compelled to say officially, most of my colleagues believe the same thing."

Psychiatrist and historian Anthony Storr, known for his psychoanalytical portraits of historical figures, echoes this school of thought. While acknowledging "a man's cast of mind is largely influenced by the way he is brought up and educated [nurture]," he links character traits and personality to physique, saying they are "intimately connected." He argues that, although "physical endowment" is modifiable to some extent, it "is more likely to be a datum of heredity [nature]."[5] I can't help but believe that genetics partially explain the man I have become, and perhaps always was—in particular, my being a Tory and, more specifically, a Stanfield/Symons Tory. Almost everything about my family points in that direction. Surely, there must be something to the idea of the powerful role of genetics across the spectrum of an individual's makeup, both positive and negative. Studies of identical twins separated at birth but discovered later to have made very similar life choices—including even the types of people they married—lend credence to this.[6]

And yet I know Helen Doyle, though unrelated to me, influenced my emotional composition and major life choices almost as much as my parents did. Nearly three decades after she died, I find myself doing even the simplest things (like cleaning my apartment) precisely the way she would have. I still have to discipline myself not to say the word "good" as though it rhymes with "food," the way she pronounced it in her Tignish Irish/Acadian dialect. As if not to be eclipsed, my father habitually held his right hand gently to the throat when reading or just ruminating, as though he were in the early stages of strangling himself. A weird habit, yet I find myself doing the exact same thing in similar circumstances. Are all my father's traits, good and bad, embedded in my DNA? Nature or nurture—does it really matter if an individual is imprisoned by one but not the other, or by both and not either exclusively? The person is still incarcerated in one of life's unsolved mysteries.

Will science ever be able to reveal the answer? In my experience, politicians are the hardest people to figure out in these terms. This is especially true when it is they themselves who are trying to do the figuring. I am no exception. Walter Jones was premier of Prince Edward Island from 1943 to 1953. A brilliant McGill-trained agronomist, he was instrumental in introducing, in the mid-1930s, the potato crop to PEI, now a staple of the provincial economy. In 1935, he received the King George V medal as the best farmer in the province. As outspoken as he was knowledgeable about all phenomena agricultural—"Farmer Jones," he was called by everybody—the premier once publicly stated that humans were no different from cows: in both species, genes tell everything.

I can remember my father saying that precise thing. He believed strongly, in those pre-feminist days, that a man made a huge mistake by marrying a stupid or physically weak woman because their children risked being the same. I assume he felt similarly about women marrying genetically flawed men. He certainly practised what he preached when marrying Dorothy Eileen McQuaid of Souris, my mother, whom he idolized, rightly, as top of the gene pool.

---

In those pre-Internet days, a young boy in tiny Charlottetown found the world a much bigger place and himself a much smaller person than that same kid would experience today. It is not because his city is much bigger— it isn't. But technology has shrunk the world. Now, with the click of a mouse or tap of a finger, today's kid can transport himself or herself to any real or virtual reality imaginable. In my boyhood days—I can remember them as though they were yesterday—I would be glued to the radio in my bedroom listening to *Amos 'n' Andy*. I did not see a television screen until I was about ten years old, around 1955 or 1956.

A fancy French-Canadian family, the Alberts (pronounced "Albears"), had just moved into a brand new house they had built up the street from us on the corner of Greenfield and McGill. Their house was the first ranch-style split level built on the

Island, a style that was a great source of controversy all across town. Most found it peculiar, though today the Albert house seems to be just a standard urban bungalow among all the others that dot the entire province. Like the house, the family that lived in it was considered exotic. The Alberts were Quebecers, a type we Islanders then saw only during the summer, as tourists. Now, a family of them was living among us. More than that, they had a TV set! Their son Danny and I became fast friends, and in an instant I was catapulted into the television age: *I Love Lucy, The Lone Ranger, The Adventures of Wild Bill Hickok, Leave It To Beaver*—all this was a much bigger world than a Charlottetown boy could enter by paying twenty-five cents to see *Old Yeller* at the Capitol movie theatre downtown.

Such was the tiny world I lived in until practically an adult. In 1956, my Dad, an inveterate (and not always wise) investor in real estate, bought the Chandler House, an elegant, turreted, three-story Queen Anne Revival home adjacent to the Charlottetown Hotel. He thought it only a matter of time before the hotel would need the property to expand, or just to increase parking, and thus the purchase seemed a good "flip" investment. It never happened, so he converted the gracious home into a country-style housekeeping ("efficiency") inn. He calculated the new establishment would be rendered more appealing with a modern-sounding appellation: the Dundee Motel & Efficiencies.

Motels were all the rage as he and Mother went on their annual mid-winter trips to Florida in the early 1950s (and long afterwards), but they were unknown on the Island except for the Kirkwood, a sprawling, snake-like motel on Elm (now University) Avenue, in what was then the outskirts of the city. It had just been built by aviation pioneer Carl Burke, who founded Maritime Central Airways (later Eastern Provincial Airways, now part of Air Canada).[7] He, like Dad, was a visionary and heavy investor in the future. Burke was also the Island's wealthiest resident. His wife, Florence, gave her name to the Kirkwood's dining room: the Florentine Room. She drove a silver Rolls-Royce, the only one on the Island at the time and for long afterwards. As I recall, the vehicle was licensed in Florida, where the Burkes lived part of the year.

Dad added ten fairly luxurious but more conventional motel-style units to his own operation as a separate stand-alone annex in 1964. This two-level complex was designed by Alfred Hennessey, one of the pre-eminent Charlottetown architects of the day, while the units were decorated in avant-garde colours and fabrics by a young interior designer Hennessey had recruited from off-Island. Dad later would add another "motel," the Dundee West, about twelve blocks away, to his growing real estate portfolio. This time, he had the place built from scratch, close to the Charlottetown Hospital, where my father did his surgery, and to his own Charlottetown Clinic next door. Dad figured the travelling prescription drug salesmen he had so generously patronized over the years owed it to him to stay there. These days, it is a multi-unit elders' residence, but the original Dundee Motel still operates, transformed (though not expanded) by various new owners since the family sold it in 1972, after Dad died of a fourth heart attack. The Dundee Arms Inn, as it is now more felicitously called, has become one of the finest places to stay and dine in Charlottetown.[8] As a teenager, I worked at the Dundee and the Dundee West, both at the front desk and as a maintenance boy most summers and, occasionally, on weekends.

Then there was the Keppoch Beach Hotel. Our family summer cottage in Keppoch was but a stone's throw from that summer resort. We cottage kids, mostly from Charlottetown, made the hotel part of our world, befriending kids our own age vacationing with their parents. Much later, as a teen, I landed a summer job at the hotel as a groundskeeper and all-round handyman. I soon learned a simple but valuable truth: a smile and flattery and an endearing quip paid big dividends both in tips and in "here's something a little extra" at the end of a family's vacation. By the end of the summer, I had learned to be very charming, indeed. Practice does make perfect. My fledgling bank account was flush with cash when September arrived. I was getting hands-on training and education at the Dundee and at the Keppoch Beach Hotel in how the wheels of tourism spun. Those wheels were to spin a lot faster for me as Canada's tourism minister.

---

My early idol Louis St-Laurent left politics after his defeat in the 1957 federal election. Nobel Peace Prize–winning diplomat Lester B. Pearson replaced him as Liberal Party leader. Only then was the family able to herd the Black Sheep back into its political fold. The conversion transpired when two things happened. First, I became enthralled by John Diefenbaker's vision for Canada, and by his oratory and charisma, in the run-off election in 1958. Second, I became captivated, in 1959, by Walter R. Shaw, elected PC premier that year on the Island at age seventy-two, having long served as the province's deputy agriculture minister. His vision for PEI and the soaring eloquence with which he expressed it roped me in. The *Toronto Star* once characterized Shaw, an imposing, heavy-set man, as the only politician in all Canada capable of upstaging John Diefenbaker at the podium. If Diefenbaker's oratory had not been enough to lead me back to the family's traditional political path, Walter Shaw's would certainly have done so. The double-whammy clinched it. I saw the light. And I reverted to a White Sheep, never to change colours again.

The power of the inertia towards being a Tory on both sides of the family is illustrated by an incident that involved my brother Charley, who later became Brian Mulroney's chief policy advisor, in opposition and in government. Like me, Charley was a student leader at PEI's St. Dunstan's University. In our senior year, he was the student union president, I the editor of the student newspaper. Though, like me, congenitally a Conservative, Charley found himself rescuing two of the Island's Liberal candidates during the 1965 federal general election, running together in the dual riding of Queen's against the incumbents, Tory running mates Angus MacLean and Heath Macquarrie. One of the two Liberals was brilliant legal scholar Mark MacGuigan, who lived three houses down from us on Greenfield Avenue in Charlottetown. Mark became a senior Trudeau Cabinet minister after moving to Windsor, Ontario, to be dean of law at the University of Windsor. The other Liberal candidate Charley rescued that day was potato farmer Ira Lewis.

The two Liberal candidates had arrived for a student forum at St. Dunstan's, unaccompanied, unrecognized, and adrift. Good Samaritan that he was (shades of my offering to help Louis St-Laurent), Charley brought the two campaigners to the front of the assembly hall and introduced them to the student body. In the process, my twin unwittingly found himself the next day in a photograph on the front page of the Charlottetown *Guardian*. There, in all his glory and spread across six columns, was Charley flanked by the two Grit candidates with a large Liberal banner in the background. In our family, being caught on camera in a "house of the rising sun" would have carried less stigma, and been considered a less serious mortal sin. One of our most partisan relatives, in a highly partisan extended family, was Aunt Mary McQuaid, who is said to have choked and almost died on her cream of wheat when, first thing in the morning, she saw the photo of Charley, front and centre, at the Liberal rally. Like most other families on the Island, we took our politics very seriously—and, preferably, our breakfast without evidence that one of our own had crossed over to the other side.

By the time I entered St. Dunstan's University in 1964, I had become a militant Tory activist, not only organizing campus events for the party, but also participating in provincial and federal election campaigns. From then on, I attended every manner of partisan conference or meeting at home and farther afield. And I participated, as a voting delegate, in every national party leadership convention right up until recent times. In 1970, following graduate school, I became full-time policy secretary for national PC Party leader Robert Stanfield. In 1978, I was nominated to run for Parliament in my home constituency of Hillsborough (mostly Charlottetown), succeeding Heath Macquarrie. I was elected in the subsequent general election in 1979, then re-elected twice, in 1980 and 1984. By late 1988, when I was defeated in the Liberal sweep of Atlantic Canada during the hysteria over the Canada-United States free trade deal, I had served almost a half-decade in Cabinet, first in the tourism portfolio, as a junior minister of state under the senior minister of regional industrial expansion, then as minister of the environment, at a time when environmental issues had reached the centre of the government's agenda, and were never far from national and parliamentary controversy. I ran in two other elections: in 1993 in Hillsborough again, and in 1997 in Peterborough, Ontario, but failed to be elected—the first time because of the near-total collapse of the PC Party nationally, and the second partly because of the divided conservative vote after the emergence of the Reform Party under Preston Manning. I nevertheless remained a Tory partisan long after electoral politics lost its charm for me.

# Chapter 2

# AN UNLIKELY POLITICAL STAR: THE ASCENT OF ROBERT STANFIELD

In late July 1969, I was at my family's summer cottage in Keppoch, on PEI's South Shore, taking a break from graduate studies at Queen's University, when I received a phone call from the local federal Tory Member of Parliament, Heath Macquarrie, in whose first election campaign back in 1957 Dad had played a key role.

"There's someone eager to meet you," Heath's stentorian voice informed me, in an intonation that suggested the suitor was either the pope or the queen. "He is the president of Trent University in Peterborough. His name is Professor T. H. B. Symons. He has heard all about you." Translation from Macquarrie-speak: *This man is a real comer. I think you should meet him and hitch your wagon to his star.* Symons had been searching for a second young person to help him organize a policy conference for the federal Progressive Conservative Party. Symons was taking a short break at Shaw's Hotel, at Brackley Beach on the Island's North Shore. The Trent president and Island Tory MP, who knew each other, had crossed paths a few days earlier. Symons had asked Heath whether there might be a "bright young person" in the MP's own political circles suitable for the conference job. Macquarrie mentioned me—a little like saying the pope mentioned prayer, the queen duty. Heath was phoning me to arrange an interview with Tom Symons in the subterfuge of a social visit. The visit was to change my summer—and my life.

To understand the background to Heath Macquarrie's telephone call on that warm July evening in 1969, we need to go back to September 1965.

The Liberals are in power in Canada under Prime Minister Lester Pearson. They hold 129 of the 264 seats in Parliament, a minority government. Savaged by the Opposition for months over a string of scandals, Pearson is eager to exploit a recent spike in his party's public-opinion poll numbers by calling a snap federal general election. He longs to win a majority government, as much to free himself of the toxic political climate in Parliament as to gain the power needed to complete his ambitious plans, especially for social reform. The writ is dropped, the election set for November 8. The politicians are off to the hustings.

The Progressive Conservatives panic, though not their leader. He is former prime minister John George Diefenbaker, the spellbinding prairie orator under whose erratic leadership the Tories squandered the largest parliamentary majority in Canadian history, amassed in 1958. Reduced to a minority government in the 1962 election, the PCs are currently out of office altogether after their 1963 defeat in Parliament on two Opposition non-confidence motions and the election those motions forced that year. The PCs must now conduct an election campaign sagging in the polls, bitterly divided over leadership, and without a platform—none whatsoever. It is bad enough the policy cupboard is bare. Worse, there is no cupboard.

What are they to do? To patch together something—any policy at all—former Diefenbaker agriculture minister Alvin Hamilton and PC Party director James Johnston frantically cull snippets from speeches by Diefenbaker and Hamilton himself, a Saskatchewan populist MP with an intellectual bent. The policy stew is heavy on grand phrase-making: "One Canada" masquerades as federal-provincial relations policy; "unhyphenated Canadianism" claims the way to national unity; "a great national conference on Confederation" substitutes for substance on constitutional reform; a commitment to rid the country of the "galaxy of wrongdoers" heralds the answer to the political corruption and scandal that continue to hound the Pearson government. In all such areas, including the economy, Diefenbaker and the PCs, in the words of one journalist, "scatter jelly-like promises across the campaign trail."[1]

What policy Hamilton and Johnston cannot stitch together virtually from whole cloth, national PC campaign chairman Eddie Goodman, a high-powered Toronto lawyer and backroom party heavyweight, scratches out "on the coffee table of his suite at the Château Laurier Hotel or pirates from other sources."[2] The Tories' entire science policy is lifted holus-bolus from a speech British Labour Leader Harold Wilson made two years earlier.[3] What an irony, given that the Diefenbaker majority government had begun to disintegrate over a science and technology issue: its decision to cancel the job-intensive Avro Arrow supersonic fighter-plane contract based in the vote-rich Toronto area.

As predicted, the PCs lose the 1965 election, but not nearly as badly as even they had expected. The Tories, in fact, win four more seats than in 1963. The credit belongs to the indomitable spirit of John Diefenbaker, whose blazing oratory and irrepressible campaigning rob Pearson of his coveted majority. The election outcome reinforces the Tory chief's reputation as the greatest stump campaigner in the country's history. The party's survival with a slight increase in its parliamentary standing, however, is despite its election platform, not because of it, for the party had, in the searing words of journalist Geoffrey Stevens, "no party policy worthy of the name."[4]

Fast forward two years to September 1967. The Tories now have a new leader, elected at the most exciting leadership convention in Canadian history. There, Diefenbaker, at the last moment, in high drama, throws his hat into the ring to succeed himself in order to save the party, he claims, from those who would divide the country with the *deux nations* concept making the rounds in Tory circles. But the old stump magic fails him this time, and in the end the party abandons the aging warrior in favour of Robert Lorne Stanfield, premier of Nova Scotia.

Each of the two Tory titans, Diefenbaker and Stanfield, is the subject of a first-rate biography: Diefenbaker's (*Rogue Tory*) is by political scientist Denis Smith; Stanfield's (titled simply *Stanfield*) is by journalist Geoffrey Stevens. Smith's book, though an academic tome, reads like a fast-paced novel whose protagonist seems too wildly unbelievable, even for fiction, for the manuscript to have survived beyond a publisher's first read, but the narrative is all true. Stevens's *Stanfield* is based partly on hours of private interviews with the subject. It is much shorter than Smith's, covering as it does the subject's life only up to the 1972 election. But, while journalistic in style, as befits the author's *métier*, the Stanfield biography has a heft, and an insider's credibility, that earns the book a place on the same shelf as that of the award-winning Diefenbaker treatise. Each author paints a portrait of his subject that could not be more different from the other's if the two biographers had collaborated to achieve this sole purpose.

# John Diefenbaker

In Denis Smith's account, Diefenbaker is tumultuous, anachronistic, "never fully in control of his emotions," suspicious, bitter, vindictive, petty, stubborn, and even manic; someone who, at a young age, became a romantic and an iconoclast through parental influence and who, later, was ill-at-ease, in time and place, in mid-twentieth-century Ottawa.[5]

I was to discover first-hand how accurate Smith's portrait was of John Diefenbaker when, in the spring of 1969, I interviewed the former Tory leader for almost an hour for my Queen's University political studies master's thesis. The venue was his office in the Centre Block of the Parliament buildings. My thesis topic was the 1956 PC leadership convention that elected him Tory leader. The interview had been arranged for me by my MP, Heath Macquarrie, ironically one of John Diefenbaker's "termites" (the term Diefenbaker used for anyone in the party who opposed him). To get the interview for me, I knew how heavily Heath would have had to spread the manure about my father's active role in Tory campaigns on the Island during Diefenbaker's leadership. So I brought along my twin brother, Charley, for an extra measure of family value. I had already interviewed all the other principals surrounding the convention that elected Diefenbaker leader—not just his detractors (for example, erstwhile national PC Party president Dalton Camp), but also charter loyalists such as Toronto advertising guru Allister Grosart, who had masterminded Diefenbaker's marketing and media strategy for the Tories' victories in both 1957 and 1958, the latter the greatest in Canadian history until Brian Mulroney routed John Turner in 1984.

Alas, not a single substantive thing John Diefenbaker told me about my thesis topic in my nearly hour-long interview with him was true. And a lot of the rest had dubious veracity, at best. He merely imposed his latter-day prejudices and personal hatreds and resentments, retrospectively, on the events and personalities at play during the leadership campaign and convention more than a decade earlier. He reserved especially pungent bile for veteran Ontario MP George Hees, famous for his Hollywood good looks, dazzling smile, lady-killer charm, and dapper dress—later one of Diefenbaker's biggest "termites." The former party leader dismissed Hees as irrelevant not just to the convention but also to the party as a whole at the time, even though Hees had been PC Party president since 1953. Moreover, as Denis Smith notes in his biography, Hees was, along with Manitoba MP Gordon Churchill and agents of Ontario premier Leslie Frost, one of "the most significant elements in [Diefenbaker's leadership] organization."[6] Without a doubt, Diefenbaker's perspective on his leadership win had more to do, in this case, with Cabinet colleague Hees's having abandoned him over defence policy in 1963 than with any objective reality circa 1956.

Charley has never been at a loss for words, especially ones with four letters. As I left the interview, my brother let out a litany of expletives unsuitable for paraphrasing, let alone direct quotation. The experience had been a waste of time, except for the perverse entertainment quotient. Was the former prime minister deliberately lying to me? Or had he convinced himself that his version of history was actually true? Did he think I was so gullible that I would take his word at face value without checking with other principals? Or was he in such a world of his own that, in his mind, there were no other principals? Is it possible he thought the very act of his saying something about himself made the statement true? After all, who would know more about the subject than the subject himself? For his part, Smith notes that, as far back as the time of the convention, there were "whispered doubts about Diefenbaker's health and mental balance."[7] I will say only that Charley and I walked away from the experience thinking the old man was, in a word, nuts. Charming, welcoming, eloquent, physically imposing, colourful, witty, generous with his time, but nuts. And yet, we had been raised in a household in which John Diefenbaker had roughly equal status with John Kennedy and the Blessed Virgin Mary and the Christ Child—in that precise order of divinity—in the affections of our former-seminarian father. For my thesis, however, I was not able to cite a single statement from the thirteenth prime minister of Canada—clearly, "thirteen" an unlucky number for me—just the fact that I had interviewed him, thus compounding the academic absurdity. Whatever my abilities as a scholar, I learned that John George Diefenbaker was one very strange man.

# The New PC Leader

In Robert Stanfield, by contrast, Geoffrey Stevens sees a calm, reflective, intelligent, highly disciplined, and humane gentleman of the Old School, eager to work with others, a man of wry humour and good nature. Moreover, "[Stanfield] possessed qualities that were shared by everyone in the Stanfield family: common sense, patience, *the determination to see a difficult job through to completion*...[qualities] bred into him, nurtured by his parents, and refined by his education."[8]

It should surprise no one that the qualities that made these two Tory leaders so different from each other personally—the mercurial loner versus the cool-headed team player—rendered their respective approaches to party and public policy utterly different as well. It is as though the two leaders had not led the same party at all. In Diefenbaker's case, policy per se was of no interest. It was merely what a political warrior used in battle cries to rally supporters and bludgeon enemies, real or perceived, not only in other parties but also in his own (the "termites"). For the "Chief," as supporters fondly called him, Opposition policy was not devised carefully, step by step, to advance an agenda as an alternative to the government's program. Nor was policy needed to prepare the party for office in the event of electoral victory. Instead, policy was a matter of identifying issues that could stir the emotions and mobilize the voters through rhetoric and sloganeering, rather than detailed exposition. As Peter Newman puts it, "[d]uring the long stewardship of John Diefenbaker, policy was regarded as a sub-branch of rhetoric and given the very lowest priority."[9] Diefenbaker was the grandmaster of what today would be called "bumper sticker" politics: "policy" as polemics or, as practised by Diefenbaker and his school, demagoguery.

Under Diefenbaker's leadership, the PC Party's stand on an issue was typically what the Chief felt at the moment. It was often based on no more than gut political instinct as to how best to destroy a foe. As prime minister, Diefenbaker once told his principal secretary, Vancouver lawyer Gowan Guest, that the content of his speeches was not important, whereas "sound cadences" were.[10] Diefenbaker revealed to Guest the priority he gave to oratory over policy, to style over substance, to dazzling an audience over informing or enlightening it. Little wonder, then, that, as Canadians headed to the polls in 1963 following the Tories' defeat in Parliament, Diefenbaker had no reasonable policies for electors to judge. According to the reliably Tory Toronto newspaper the *Telegram,* he had "no budget…no Government defence policy…no long-range economic plans; no tax reforms; no…trade policies… no comprehensive role for Canada in world affairs."[11] Even after the 1963 electoral defeat, the party continued to lack a detailed official policy on a single issue or, truth be known, the vaguest idea of where it wanted to take the country. The new leader, Robert Lorne Stanfield, was determined to change all that.

To understand how Robert Stanfield revolutionized the national PC Party's policy and, in the process, transformed its public image, one must understand how he rebuilt the Tory party of Nova Scotia from the ground up. His approach to seemingly insurmountable challenges—that he would take them on at all—was rooted in the nature of the man himself. Both the choice of destination and the mode of travel were inseparable from the traveller. The revolution and the revolutionary were inextricably linked.

When Robert Stanfield became national PC leader, he had been premier of Nova Scotia for eleven years, the most successful politician in the province's long history. His ascent to the premiership, however, had not been easy. He was elected leader of the provincial Tories in November 1948, at a time when, for an entire generation, legendary premier Angus L. Macdonald had kept the Liberals in office and banished the PCs to the political wilderness. The PCs, in fact, did not hold a single seat in the provincial legislature. Stanfield had not won the provincial party leadership by default, but there was an element of desperation in Tory backrooms. Certainly, his was thought to be a loser's, if not a fool's, errand. Virtually no one gave this Ichabod Crane–like figure a chance to make any inroads against the charismatic orator Macdonald and the mighty Grit political machine.

Soon after Stanfield was elected party leader, "Angus L.," as Macdonald was affectionately known, called a snap provincial election. In the 1949 spring campaign, Stanfield focused like a laser on every policy and organizational detail, no matter how minor; visited every nook and cranny of the province, no matter how remote; and made speeches to every audience he could locate, no matter how small or uninterested. As the campaign wore on, astute observers began to notice something strange: Nova Scotians were beginning to take to this odd new species of politician. The Tories' own huge gamble in choosing such a singular individual as leader paid off. Not initially in spades or even hearts, but certainly in clubs or diamonds: the PCs emerged election night with eight seats to the Liberals' twenty-seven. It was enough for Robert Stanfield to form a real Opposition—and to launch the Stanfield era.

Indeed, by 1956, with Angus L. retired from politics, Stanfield was sitting in the premier's chair. Now it was the Liberals' turn to be banished to the wilderness, exiled by the man they had so sorely underestimated. In fact, Stanfield's popularity, and corresponding numbers in the legislature, soared ever higher with each election. By 1963, the PCs' popular vote under Stanfield exceeded anything political giant Angus L. Macdonald had ever attained for the Liberals at the height of his popularity. In Stanfield's last provincial election, in 1967, on the eve of his becoming national Tory leader, the PCs won all but 6 of the legislature's 46 seats. From 0 to 8 to 12 to 24 to 27 to 39 to 40 seats in six consecutive elections.

No previous democratic government leader had ever accomplished this kind of electoral trajectory anywhere in the western world. Robert Lorne Stanfield proved to be no conventional politician.

Stanfield achieved all this electoral success by doing exactly what he was about to do as national PC leader, including—and I would argue *especially*—in policy development. Hard work and tireless attention to detail were everything. Conventional political skills of the sort John Diefenbaker possessed naturally could not be counted on. After all, unlike the Chief, Stanfield was not a great—nor, early in his political career, even a good—public speaker. Undeniably, as Dalton Camp once said famously, "he's not pretty." Nor, with people, did Stanfield possess the affected ease, the *faux bonhomie*, the ready glibness of most successful politicians—among them, quintessentially, the man who would succeed Stanfield two leaders later, Brian Mulroney.

I was to learn first-hand how desperately unconventional Robert Stanfield's political skills were. One example should suffice. By 1972, Stanfield knew me well personally. I had been working on his staff for over three years, spending countless hours with him at party policy meetings. In early January, he phoned to console me on the death of my father. In Stanfield's condolences—which, given his taciturn and reserved nature, would have been awkward at the best of times—he assumed my father had been the son of the late, near-mythic (and near namesake) W. Joseph P. MacMillan (different spelling). Like my father, a well-known PEI doctor, "WJP," as he was called, had been the Island's Tory premier in the 1930s. "I knew your grandfather well," he intoned sympathetically. No, Stanfield had not—mistaken identity. But, between the many "ah's" and "um's," his essential goodness shone through like a powerful beacon. I felt like consoling *him*. But it did not matter. The sheer goodness of the man radiated from every halting syllable more brightly than a conventional politician's glibness could ever have done.

It was this personal quality, a sincerity that politicians who do not possess it naturally just cannot fake, that endeared Robert Stanfield to Nova Scotians. It was the content of his character, a certain indescribable authenticity, especially a penchant for steadiness and diligence, that was to enable him to prepare the Progressive Conservative Party of Canada—both for Opposition and, it was hoped, for government—more carefully, and to better effect, than any previous Tory leader had ever done before or has done since. On the policy front and in the party's organization, the need for steady leadership could not have been more dire. To the surprise of everyone except those of his admirers who knew him best, he rose masterfully to the challenge. True to his character, he did what he had always done: exceed expectations.

# A New Policy Approach

To build a policy cupboard and lead a team to develop policy to fill it, Stanfield initially turned to the man who had run third behind himself and Manitoba premier Duff Roblin at the September 1967 leadership convention. That man was E. Davie Fulton. Such an ecumenical choice was partly in Stanfield's management style, akin to Abraham Lincoln's "team of rivals," as Doris Kearns Goodwin called it in her well-known 2005 book of that name.[12] Indeed, many Canadians likened Stanfield to Lincoln, not just because both men were tall, craggy-faced, and bony, or because each possessed a gentle manner, but also because their respective political styles were similar. It was no coincidence that one was called "Honest Abe," the other "Honest Bob." Historical parallels are always imperfect, but, like Lincoln a century earlier, Stanfield believed passionately in the value of reaching out to, and trusting, opponents and critics to build the kind of team he thought necessary to achieve great goals.

Stanfield's choice of Fulton as his chief policy leader made excellent sense by any standard. A brilliant and scholarly man, Fulton was the son of a former MP and grandson of a former premier. The British Columbia native had been a Rhodes Scholar at Oxford, and was first elected to Parliament in 1945 when only twenty-nine. Throughout his political career, which included a failed run for the PC leadership against Diefenbaker in 1956, the majestically bilingual lawyer distinguished himself as one of the great House of Commons orators and debaters of his generation. He seemed—like the Liberals' John Turner later—always the Prince of Wales, in line and impatiently waiting to be crowned king. Although it never happened for Fulton, his name will be forever attached to the Fulton-Favreau Formula, a valiant, unsuccessful effort at constitutional reform and patriation in which he provided inspired leadership as justice minister in the Diefenbaker government. That formula became the basis for Pierre Trudeau's own constitution-making and patriation formula in the early 1980s. If Trudeau was the father of Canada's new Constitution, Fulton was its midwife.

Unfortunately for Stanfield, however, Fulton was a spent force, both politically and physically, by the time he agreed to become the new PC leader's policy committee chair.[13] Despite fits and starts—a memo here, a meeting there, a few efforts to reach out to intellectuals beyond party ranks—Fulton just did not get the policy job done, and Stanfield had to reach out to a successor. This time, however, and with Fulton's encouragement, it would be someone far outside Caucus. Meanwhile, as Anthony Westell, Ottawa editor of the *Toronto Star*, noted, "[d]uring the barren Diefenbaker years, the party was shut out of the academic world."[14]

# Chapter 3

# STUMBLES, FUMBLES, AND BUMBLES

Even if E. Davie Fulton had been effective, the PCs, under their new leader, would not have had time to create a full-scale policy-development process before Robert Stanfield's first national electoral test. Closely paralleling his experience as the new Nova Scotia Tory leader two decades earlier, he found himself thrust into battle almost before he could don a helmet. There was but a seven-month period between his leadership win and Pierre Trudeau's calling of an election for June 1968.

The PC Party did not totally ignore policy in the period leading up to the 1968 election. In August 1967, on the eve of the leadership convention, the Tories held a "Thinkers' Conference" near Montmorency Falls, Quebec. There, the party dealt with a resolution that seemed at the time to state an historic fact as innocuous as it was irrefutable: "That Canada is composed of two founding peoples (*deux nations*) with historic rights who have been joined by people from many lands. That the constitution should be such as to permit and encourage their full and harmonious growth and development in equality throughout Canada." Unassailable boilerplate, it would seem in hindsight now, but in politics nothing is ever truly unassailable in real time.[1] It was the "*deux nations*" French equivalence of the English phrase "two founding peoples" that constituted the Trojan horse from which warriors emerged to confront Stanfield. The first battle occurred at the leadership convention, where Diefenbaker used the party's apparent embrace of "two nations"—an inflammatory English translation of a French translation of an English phrase—to justify his dramatic eleventh-hour entry into the leadership race. It was a contest most people knew he had intended to enter all along on one pretext or another. I was a delegate to the convention, as were many of my friends and some relatives, and we all took it for granted "Dief" would be a candidate. No one in my political circle was surprised when he announced; the surprise would have come had he not done so.

The second policy battle against Stanfield struck during the 1968 election campaign itself. Trudeau and the Liberals ruthlessly exploited the inability of most English-Canadian voters to grasp the subtlety of the French meaning of the word "*nation*"—or, for that matter, even the sociological meaning of the word, as opposed to its political connotation, in their own language. The sense of Canada as a community of parts organically linked both to one another and to the whole is a quintessentially Tory vision of the country. By expressing that vision with the phrase *deux nations* in the context of Quebec, Tories of the era were being true not only to their political souls, but also to the very nature of the country itself. In the campaign, however, the Liberals tied the "two nations" concept to the Tory leader in a message that was as lethal as it was wrong: "Stanfield will split the country in two." Seven words—the perfect bumper sticker. Intellectual dishonesty of this kind was the stock-in-trade of John Diefenbaker and his followers still in the party. For it to have come from Pierre Trudeau, an intellectual of solid standing, demonstrated that, when it came to sloganeering and demagoguery and sheer sophistry, he was equal to the banished Tory leader.

If Robert Stanfield failed to learn from the *deux nations* experience the Ninth Beatitude—"Blessed are those who don't let down their policy guard"—he certainly did from another issue in the 1968 campaign that would stick with him long afterwards: the so-called Guaranteed Minimum Income (GMI). Stanfield was to become the first—and to this day one of the few—major Canadian politicians to endorse the concept. How he came to it says much about both Stanfield's policy-development approach and the man himself, especially his vision, pioneering spirit, and moral values.

In the absence of anything then resembling a Tory think tank, Stanfield's major 1968 campaign speech in London, Ontario, on the GMI reflected mostly his own thinking. He had started his university studies in economics at Dalhousie University. There, he became the protégé and lifelong friend of W. Russell Maxwell, head of the Economics Department (after whom Stanfield's only son, Max, was named). The Dalhousie economics professor looms large in this narrative. It was Maxwell who later steered Stanfield towards law at Harvard University and away from economics at the London School of Economics, where the young student himself was eager to go instead. But Stanfield never lost a keen interest in his preferred field. He read voraciously the writings of everyone from Fabian socialist G. D. Cole to liberal economist John Maynard Keynes, just as he was to devour the books of conservative guru Milton Friedman and liberal original thinker Paul Samuelson in later years. He was the most economically literate national party leader in the country's history, except for Mackenzie King.[2]

For us Atlantic Canadians, it is a cherished principle, bordering on a right of citizenship, that no region of Canada should be denied the fiscal capacity to provide residents with the public services necessary to avoid the area's falling below a certain living standard relative to that of the rest of the country. This principle girds a wide range of regional-development programs sponsored by successive federal governments, Liberal and PC alike. The most notable is equalization payments to the so-called have-not provinces. Launched by Louis St-Laurent in 1956, that federal program has done as much as any other to solidify the Canadian federation. The program redistributes tax dollars from the wealthier parts of Canada to the poorer ones through the central government by a complex formula set in law. In a nutshell, provinces that earn more than the national average pay into the equalization program each year, while those that fall below the average receive money from the program to help narrow the disparity. Stanfield had long believed that, if this principle were valid for regions—and, as a Maritimer, he strongly felt it was—the same principle applied with equal validity to individuals. Put simply, he thought no Canadian, least of all the working poor, should have to live without a certain minimum level of income necessary to pay for food, shelter, clothing, medicines, and other basics. It was a revolutionary idea at the time. Alas, for policy-makers, it is still too revolutionary. For Robert Stanfield, though, it was and would remain an important principle throughout his public life. Nowhere else were Stanfield's communitarian values more in evidence than in the views he expressed on the GMI. It is those values that most sharply define him as a classic conservative, one who puts the community first, in stark contrast to the "conservative"—really, the old-fashioned limited-government liberal—who puts the individual first. This latter type populated the ranks of the Reform/Canadian Alliance Party and constitutes the core of the Conservative Party in the post-2003 merger era. (The distinction between classic conservative and classic liberal looms also large in this narrative.)

Stanfield did not see the GMI as just another, even if ambitious, entitlement program. But neither did he see it as wild-eyed socialism. Rather, he viewed it as sound public policy that made sense by every reasonable management standard, including "conservatism" and common sense, the most uncommon of all standards. For him, the GMI was the way to integrate, and to rationalize in one overall program, most other safety-net and income-support programs. These would include, potentially, everything from Old Age Security to Canada Pension Plan benefits to unemployment insurance payouts and even to provincial and municipal welfare. The PC leader was motivated by compassion for the poor. But he also thought the GMI would make the entire entitlement system more efficient and cost-effective. As a premier, Stanfield had seen first-hand how the system had been allowed to grow like Topsy and become wildly ineffective and extravagantly expensive over many decades. He believed that a fundamentally new approach would introduce the principle of incentives to the system by *supplementing* a poor worker's earned income with government payments, rather than *substituting* public welfare for earned income, as typically happened under traditional income support. Able-bodied workers could often receive as much—and, in some cases, more—money from government programs such as unemployment insurance by not working as they could earn by working. So why work? Criticism that his plan would undermine the work ethic puzzled and offended the PC leader. He thought the GMI, with its emphasis on incentives, would fortify the work ethic, not threaten it. To his mind, the real threat was working Canadians being unable to participate fully in Canadian economic and social life for lack of adequate income. He saw his plan as the best way to address that threat.

To Stanfield, the existing public income-support system was, as I once heard him put it, "damn crazy." But like so much else about the 1968 PC election campaign—organization was no better than policy—Stanfield's efforts to explain the Guaranteed Minimum Income idea beyond general principles were a disaster. There just had not been enough time to research, and prepare answers to, such questions as: who would qualify? how much income would a recipient get? what would be the standard of basic services? how would the program be paid for? who would administer it? what would be the federal-provincial cost split? and so forth. In this policy area, as in others, Geoffrey Stevens writes, "Stanfield was stumbling from town to town giving the impression of a man reading pronouncements he did not understand."[3]

# Policy and Television

The problem was not that Stanfield was ignorant about policy. Although new to federal politics, the Nova Scotian revelled in issues and policy detail, and always kept himself well informed. In today's parlance, he was a "policy wonk." At worst, he had a barely good enough grasp of the facts; at best, an expert's grasp, depending on the issue. But he lacked more fundamentally a set of integrated well-researched policies on a wide variety of issues that he and his party could draw on, both in the heat of a campaign and in the relative calm of government should they win. Without this resource, the leader was forced to rely largely on his own knowledge, albeit considerable, and on the brains of others he could pick, literally on the fly, under the brutal pressures of a tight campaign schedule. He often then had to communicate this policy hash in fifteen-second TV sound bites.

Television was by definition never the ideal medium through which to explain complex policy ideas, much less for a slow and deliberate speaker such as Stanfield. The days of duelling mass rally podiums were fast giving way to the battle of pithy sound bites, yet sound-bite politics challenged the man. His halting speaking style, whether expressing condolences or giving a media interview, ill-equipped him for it. Podium politics had given the fire-breathing Diefenbaker a huge advantage over the lisping and cerebral Lester Pearson in their various electoral contests over the years. In the sound-bite political culture, Stanfield was not even on the same battlefield as the ever-quotable Trudeau. More than any other politician of the era, John Kennedy had pioneered the application of Hollywood-style glamour and media savvy to retail politics, especially on television. His legacy was permanent. Pierre Trudeau applied—and, I would argue, perfected—the formula in a distinctly Canadian idiom. Stanfield was never able to master this particular performance art.

The Tory leader did, however, have the advantage of being more "cool" than "hot," to use media guru Marshall McLuhan's famous terms. McLuhan explained how a certain type of individual's "cool," laid-back presence and manner projected better through the TV lens into the viewer's living room than another type's "hot," edgy personality. Stanfield was anything but edgy: the man was calm to the point of motionless. Plus, the PC leader had a deep, manly voice. And the craggy face, while not handsome by any conventional standard, projected character. Still, the "small screen" was not nearly large enough to capture such an extraordinary man's full dimensions. McLuhan taught that, no matter how much attention a political leader or party might devote to policy, ultimately "the medium is the message."[4] By that he meant the medium—in particular, television—influences how the message is perceived. The medium embeds itself in the message, creating a symbiotic relationship. Robert Stanfield stepped onto the national stage just when television was beginning to revolutionize politics in ways that did not reward his strongest qualities, thoughtfulness and personal integrity, while rewarding those he lacked, sex appeal and a silver tongue. Form was trumping content as never before. No amount of pre-camera cosmetology could have neutralized Stanfield's natural disadvantages against Trudeau, just as it could not have for Richard Nixon against John Kennedy in almost the same era. Stanfield's "Honest Abe" image did resonate well with Canadians. Unfortunately for him, voters were in the market for something else in the heady days of the 1968 election: sex appeal and glamour and excitement and rhetorical flourish of the Kennedy kind—form, not substance.

Canada in the late 1960s was caught up in post-Centennial, post–Expo 67 fever. In the US, the assassinated president's brother, Robert, made a strong run for the Democratic presidential nomination until he himself was assassinated the night of his California primary triumph on June 5, twenty days before the 1968 Canadian election. The PC leader was well aware of the impact of the assassination on the mood of the Canadian electorate. The 1968 election was the first national one in Canada during which a leaders' debate was held. The June 9 debate saw Trudeau, Stanfield, NDP leader Tommy Douglas, and (in the latter part) Social Credit leader

Réal Caouette battle it out. In the debate, only Stanfield raised Robert F. Kennedy's assassination, paying tribute to the man whose tragic death Stanfield knew would be fresh on voters' minds. Both Kennedy's upbeat primary campaign and his untimely death gave many Canadian voters nostalgia for his brother's "Camelot." In Trudeau, not Stanfield, the voters found what they wanted: a red rose, not a yellow banana. Content's turn would have to wait.

# A Vision for the Long Haul

In the face of the Trudeaumania that swept every part of the country except Stanfield's own region, the Tory leader could have been Moses descending Mount Sinai with the Decalogue raised high in hand, but he still would not have been able to turn back the Liberal tide. No amount of sound policy would have made much difference. On election night, Stanfield, scarred but not downcast, watched the results from his gracious vintage home, "The Oaks," in Halifax (now part of Saint Mary's University). His party elected only 72 MPs to the Liberals' 154. The NDP won 22, the Créditistes 8. It was the Tories' most dismal result since 1953. Stanfield won 25 fewer seats than John Diefenbaker had salvaged in his last hurrah, in 1965, with even less policy.

Stanfield, though, had always been a man for the long haul, and he was determined to rebuild the PC Party for the next time. He was now a veteran of one federal election and a two-decade veteran of provincial politics, including eleven years as premier. From growing experience, the PC leader believed voters tended to defeat governments, rather than elect parties or, more often than not, governments defeated themselves. He had seen the Nova Scotia Liberals lose despite their favourable odds when he first became premier. And the newly selected national Tory chief had watched his own party blow a Nova Scotia election he and a lot of other people thought it should have won following his own departure from the provincial scene. So, the very day after the 1968 election, Robert Stanfield started to plot a strategy to exploit his opportunity should the Trudeau government founder, as he felt in his bones it would.

The PC leader's first priority was to unite the party behind him. This was no mean feat. A large number of the MPs who survived the 1968 election—at least a third of the new parliamentary Caucus, principally from the West and rural Ontario—were Diefenbaker loyalists, and Diefenbaker himself had been re-elected in his own Saskatchewan riding. Many of those members were now gunning for Stanfield to avenge their fallen chieftain. In his biography, Denis Smith characterizes Diefenbaker as a vindictive man. True to this portrait, the embittered former Tory leader, like the man's followers in Caucus, was out for his successor's blood. But Stanfield was determined to do everything he could to win them over. His other top priority was equally clear: he must modernize the party based on sound policies for the times and the future, and especially for the next election.

The heart of the problem facing Stanfield thumped loudly from the ballot box on 1968 election night. Under Diefenbaker in the 1960s, the party's base had steadily shrunk to older, rural, poorer, and less-educated voters in an era when those likely to vote in by far the largest numbers were, increasingly, the mirror opposite: the young, the city dweller, the more successful, and the better educated. Trudeau's hip Hollywood appeal, contrasted with Stanfield's staid, long-underwear public persona, had reinforced the trend. In an analysis of the 1968 election results, political scientist John Meisel wrote: "The Conservative Party of 1968 was marching to a different drummer than the majority of the Canadian people."[5] If the party did not begin to appeal to those segments of society that decided elections, it would not win elections. Robert Stanfield knew this simple truth, and was eager to act on it. The PC leader also knew, intuitively, that he could not compete with Pierre Trudeau on form or style in the razzle-dazzle of the TV-era political game pioneered by John Kennedy. He believed innovative and progressive policy was the best way to level the playing field. The goal was to present himself and the party in a more modern and appealing light.

By "modernizing" the party, the PC leader meant rendering its policies more directly relevant to contemporary problems and conditions of greatest concern to Canadians at large—not just the party's supporters, much less only its traditional hardcore base. Stanfield was especially sensitive to the economic challenges facing Canadians. The need to foster mass employment while restraining inflation was a high priority of his, as was promoting national unity. He was eager to explore, understand, and push the party to respond to the burden Canadians bore in their everyday lives. He considered it important, as well, that the party have ideas for managing challenges to the country's future well-being, such as heightened international trade competition and foreign investment and control, domestic unrest (principally in Quebec, with an increasingly militant separatist movement), and inadequate national preparedness in basic scientific research, education, and training, among other things. Stanfield was determined that the party's policies to address such issues be rooted in evidence, not in ideology; be pragmatic and workable, not unduly theoretical or abstract; and, as important as anything else, be developed and kept up to date with the best information and most informed counsel available, from within the party and outside alike. For many party members, though, this last perspective in particular was all too "modern."

Stanfield believed the party had relied much too heavily in the previous decade on policy thinking and expertise within its own ranks to the exclusion of insights from outside sources able to bring fresh perspectives and specific innovative policy ideas to bear on both familiar problems (such as joblessness) and emerging issues (such as industrial pollution, population congestion, and urban sprawl). The leader thought that the party needed to be "ahead of the game" in identifying the problems Canadians faced in their daily lives *and* in developing proposals to solve those problems. So, for him, modernizing the party was a matter of not just changing, in some cases, what it said on particular issues, but also choosing more wisely than it had often done before which issues to highlight in the first place. He was determined to ensure both thrusts were, to the maximum extent practicable, in sync with where Canadians themselves stood. To this end, Stanfield wanted Progressive Conservatives to think creatively, unimpeded by outdated party orthodoxy or untested conventional wisdom in society generally. The leader himself was open to unorthodox thinking, but he also had a keen sense of which policy ideas were not merely trendy or fashionable and yet of real substance. For him, "modern" did not always mean better nor did "traditional" necessarily mean outdated. He was deeply concerned, however, that the party had allowed itself to become caricatured as out of step with the times, if not altogether anachronistic, even crusty. The party's opposition to Canada's having a distinct flag was, to Stanfield in retrospect, an especially egregious example of its tone-deafness. The man himself was imbued with virtually none of the qualities most commonly associated with the party's out-of-date image—quite the opposite. Sober personality and staid public image notwithstanding, Robert Stanfield was a thoroughly modern man in the subjects that interested him, in the way he thought about them, in the sources of information he pursued about them, and in his openness to pioneering approaches to addressing them. The leader was determined to transform his party, especially its public agenda and policies, in kind. He thought his own image with voters would be "modernized" following suit. (He was proven largely right.)

For Stanfield, modernizing the party's image or his own was neither an end in itself nor even just a means to making the party and himself more popular across the land—though that, of course, was his main partisan tactical goal. More fundamentally, he sought to ensure that the party under his leadership acted as an instrument for *progress*, particularly should it win a national election and form a government—a *progressive* government. This goal was central to Stanfield's leadership. To him, "progressive" meant, basically, improving the economic conditions of all Canadians and of the country as a whole through the state, typically in concert with the private sector as the senior partner. In a nutshell, for Stanfield, "progressive" entailed a belief that an activist government sufficiently constrained by factors built into the total political and economic and social system— Parliament, the media, the courts, and, above all, the ballot box—could help solve the big, complex economic and social problems the country faced. Those problems could not be addressed adequately, Stanfield held, unless government played its legitimate role in the affairs of the nation, and did so wisely. Stanfield believed his party had fallen far short of embracing this activist view of government in the positions it had taken, however vaguely, over the previous decade under John Diefenbaker's leadership. The new leader was determined to correct the PC Party's course to ensure that it led to where most Canadians were at the time.

The Nova Scotian was most concerned about the plight of the working poor, which he was profoundly committed to ameliorating through an activist, but judiciously constrained, government. A wealthy man himself, he did not believe money was the root of all evil—far from it. Rather, he believed the lack of income, especially enough to meet basic needs, accounted for many of the social problems facing the country. The PC leader was well aware, for example, that crime was typically rooted in poverty. The man believed passionately that government had both a capacity and a moral obligation to help improve the lives of all Canadians, particularly the disadvantaged, not only by helping to create the overall conditions for prosperity, but also by aiding people directly through specific state programs.

Robert Stanfield's most strident Caucus critics to the contrary, the man respected and valued the free-market economy and private enterprise. Geoffrey Stevens quotes journalist Richard Gwyn's comment that Stanfield was an "aristocratic socialist."[6] If, in any reasonable sense, Stanfield was a socialist, the man was no firebrand. After all, his family's fortune had been made in the private sector with no government help, only his grandfather's brilliance and tenacity and vision and hard work—qualities Stanfield himself both admired and possessed. Accordingly, the PC leader shared the view that prevailed within his party—right across the ideological spectrum, from Red Tories to arch-conservatives—that small and medium-sized businesses constituted the engine of economic growth and job creation. To him, the role of government was, at a minimum, to do no harm, and at its most activist to partner with private enterprise to create wealth and jobs while cushioning people who fell between the cracks through no fault of their own. Later in his public life, Stanfield was one of the first major Canadian political figures to muse openly about whether the state had become, or was becoming, too big; whether it had taken on so many responsibilities that it was too unwieldy to be competently managed and effective; and whether, in particular, the welfare state might be crushed under the weight of its own excesses. He was not, therefore, in any way romantic about government and its possibilities. Though the Tory leader thought government had an important role to play, he also had a very real sense of the inherent limits of what government could accomplish or handle well.

All this said, Stanfield did not believe Adam Smith's "invisible hand"—the self-regulation of the marketplace—could be relied upon to advance everyone's economic lot, least of all that of the poor and underprivileged. To him, the state was necessary to ensure everyone benefited from the country's wealth. He was especially eager to see that no one got squashed as powerful interests sought to maximize their own gains. From the time Stanfield entered politics in Nova Scotia until the very end of his life, this was a central theme of his. An article he wrote on conservative principles and philosophy a decade after leaving the PC leadership stressed the value of free enterprise and social order. But the article also underscored how important it was for a "decent civilized society" to respond through the state to address poverty and the plight of the less fortunate.[7]

For Robert Stanfield, "progressivism" entailed a large measure of government activism in the interests of the Canadian community and every member of it, both living and yet born. In that sense, Stanfield, though not an ideologue, was a classic conservative. At the same time, he qualified as a reformer and a progressive, not just by the standards of the time, but by today's as well. Stanfield's zeitgeist was, fundamentally, a search for the balanced, the practical, the doable, and (through consensus-building) the broadly acceptable. And yet, as we shall see, he was not risk-averse. That this essentially cautious man often proved willing to take "the road not taken"—in Robert Frost's immortal phrase—was itself a measure of the duality, to say nothing of the complexity, of the man's ideas and of the man himself. In his intellectual sophistication, Robert Lorne Stanfield was a rarity in politics—indeed, among people: someone who could see the pros and cons of every possible course all at the same time and still retain the capacity to act decisively when it mattered, more often than not wisely. Politics is hardly ever simple. Stanfield, the politician and the man, never was. In "Song of Myself," from *Leaves of Grass*, Walt Whitman says of himself: "Do I contradict myself? / Very well then, I contradict myself. / I am large, I contain multitudes." Robert Stanfield was large. He contained multitudes.

The new PC leader recognized that a policy or program that worked well in an earlier era, however "progressive" at the time, might fail in his own time. By the same token, he also knew that what might be viewed as progressive in his own time might be rightly perceived as wholly inappropriate, even reactionary, at some future time. He was, in that way, as in others, not an absolutist but a principled pragmatist. Self-styled progressive Gore Vidal said that, because societies change, "[l]ast year's wisdom is this year's folly."[8] Throughout his political career, Robert Stanfield sought to separate folly from wisdom and apply the latter while shunning the former. He did not believe any political philosophy or politician had a monopoly on wisdom or immunity from folly. He applied this realism to his search for practical solutions to problems Canadians faced in their daily lives. To Stanfield, the status quo for most Canadians was unacceptable, and so it was for him. Stanfield to this day symbolizes for many Conservatives—certainly me—the progressive values for which the grand old Tory Party at its best has always stood.

The Tory leader applied his progressive mind and instincts not just to economic policy, but also to social affairs, notably on official languages, on Canadian federalism, on Quebec in particular, and (under the influence of his chief policy advisor later) Aboriginal, education, and training issues, among many others. On all such policy challenges, Stanfield was contemporary and innovative while remaining true to basic values and proven solutions. He embraced technological change while appreciating its limits and potential dangers. He was open to change more broadly while shunning change for change's sake, particularly change he considered bad or questionable, however fashionable it might be or valid it might appear. He championed economic and social justice and equity, not as an impractical romantic or incurable idealist, but as one committed to making society fairer in real ways. He tried to anticipate history as it was being made in his own time, and wanted to be on the right side of it as long as the "right side" was truly right, not just widely deemed right. No one dimension alone constituted Robert Stanfield's progressivism or defined his modernity. Stanfield's world view was a highly textured mosaic, not a flat solitary tile. Yet, on the national stage, he alone could not lead his party in this direction. He needed a partner.

# Chapter 4

# THE POLITICIAN AND THE ACADEMIC

Enter stage right—or, more accurately, left of centre—the new chair of Robert Stanfield's Policy Advisory Committee, to whom Stanfield turned to play the starring role in a show the director knew required not only a new script but also new players. E. Davie Fulton had bowed out of Stanfield's policy committee chair by amicable agreement. Indeed, there had not been much of a committee to chair, nor much policy generated, either. Stanfield now wanted a bona fide member of the academic community—somebody likely outside the traditional ranks of the party— for this pivotal policy role. He sought an individual of unimpeachable stature who had broad contacts and could reach out beyond the party to knowledgeable people in diverse fields.

What Stanfield sought, as well, was a person with whom he would be personally comfortable and who, in turn, would be at ease with him, as he contemplated they would be spending a great deal of time with each other. The new chair needed to be contemporary enough in his thinking to help lead the party on a new policy course, yet sufficiently sensitive to the party's rich history and heritage and diverse grass-roots makeup to avoid undermining Stanfield's other priority: unifying his Caucus behind him. So, although that individual did not need to be a rabid Tory, he could not be a card-carrying member of the Communist Party of Canada, either—or, at least, not part of its Revolutionary Guard. Someone who would be true to Tory traditions while able to help blaze a new trail for the party—that was the individual Stanfield sought. It was a tall order. But Stanfield knew exactly the man he wanted for the challenge. Who better to fill such requirements than one of the fastest-rising stars in Canadian academe, a man who, less than a decade before, at the young age of thirty-two, had become founding president of the country's most exciting new university, an institution whose very character bespoke the precious value of blending the old with the new? That institution was Trent University. That man was Thomas Henry Bull Symons.

Tom Symons's rise to academic stardom was as meteoric as Stanfield's political ascendancy. He had been a history instructor and dean of Devonshire House at the University of Toronto. There, the University of Toronto- and Oxford-educated historian was earning a growing reputation as an educator and administrator. At the same time, a group of municipal leaders and citizens in Peterborough, Ontario, was laying the groundwork for a new university in their community 145 kilometres northeast of Toronto, on the rim of the Canadian Shield. From the day Symons accepted their invitation to run the university, he helped guide this community-spirited but inexperienced group of local enthusiasts through the ABCs, and eventually the XYZs, of the harsh realities of launching the ambitious academic enterprise, which bore fruit when the university was formally established in 1961. It was the same methodical way he would later guide Robert Stanfield in his ambitious policy enterprise.[1]

The young, pipe-smoking Symons, of substantial frame, stooped shoulders, courtly manner, and fatherly demeanour, exuded the aura of the academician and the Ivory Tower—and of the political *éminence grise* he would become. By the time the first students enrolled at Trent in 1964, the choice of Symons as president seemed as divined by the gods as the location of the campus itself: the west bank of the Otonabee River, which winds through the valley that gives Trent its elegant name. The institution and the man are inextricably linked to this day, a half-dozen Trent presidents and a half-century later. The link between Robert Stanfield and Tom Symons in Progressive Conservative policy was to become just as unbreakable.

If Stanfield had been looking for a symbol to capture his vision of the kind of party he was determined to lead—futuristic, but traditional; all-inclusive, but sensitive to every individual's concern; contemporary and appealing, but grounded in the tried and the true—he had to look no farther than the institution Tom Symons was cultivating like a bed of rare orchids in the Trent Valley. The university was modelled on the great residential colleges of Europe, at the drawing board of brilliant British Columbia master architect Ron Thom. The all-grey buildings, with their modern, clean lines, but old-seeming rubble-aggregate construction and surfaces, earned Trent not only top design awards, but also the popular epitaph "Oxford on the Otonabee." Under Tom Symons's nurturing, Trent University exuded, as one wag put it, "instant antiquity." It even had a bell tower. And the bell appeared to be chiming for Robert Lorne Stanfield.

The bell that rang in Stanfield's own mind in recruiting Trent University's founding president as his new policy chair was not struck by any strong connection Tom Symons had forged with the PC Party. As an undergraduate at the University of Toronto, however, he had been the founding president of the Macdonald-Cartier Club, a group whose orientation was very much in the progressive traditions of the party. Clearly, Stanfield had an eye out for just such an orientation.

The chairmanship of the party's Policy Advisory Committee and the role of chief policy advisor to the leader were to become fused, throughout Robert Stanfield's time as leader, in the person of Tom Symons, who served in both capacities. The committee was, technically, a creature of the party through its Executive Committee (commonly called the "National Executive"), mandated by the party's constitution to establish such structures. The advisory role, by contrast, was not a party appointment but a leader appointment and, therefore, not strictly partisan. Stanfield was eager that this leader-focused advisory role—and, by extension, the role of the more party-focused Policy Advisory Committee—not be seen as unduly partisan. The new leader expected both roles to focus on outreach to people who did not necessarily identify with the party, but who were open to helping it become, through progressive policies, more welcoming to this very category of people. A progressive Tory in the Macdonald/Cartier, Conservative/Liberal coalition tradition—Symons, Stanfield thought, would be just what the doctor (or, more appropriately, the spirit of the Old Chieftain) ordered.

# Robert Lorne Stanfield

The policy partnership between Robert Stanfield and Tom Symons was based on two personalities both very similar and very different. Deceased, Robert Stanfield now "belongs to the ages." Stanfield's distinguishing qualities are well known to any Canadian of a certain age. He was a patrician—many Maritimers might even say an aristocrat. Bostonians would have regarded him as a certified "Brahmin,"[2] and one cannot fully appreciate what made Stanfield tick without grasping the similarity between him and the class of New England bluebloods to whom that term is commonly applied.

His biographer does not stress the cross-border similarity, but it is vital. He was a member of an illustrious family and a wealthy man by any standard. Stanfield would have been as comfortable in a Boston Brahmin's front parlour as a Prince Edward Island farmer in an Idaho potato field. He had the same elite Yankee-style ethic: hard work, a sense of duty, an aversion to ostentation, a penchant for understatement to the point of muteness, and, most characteristic of all, a belief embedded in his DNA that, in biblical terms, "to whom much is given, much is expected." In a phrase, noblesse oblige.

Before Confederation, the Maritimes' connections to New England were closer than ties with Upper and Lower Canada. The connections weakened, but did not die, when Sir John A. Macdonald's "National Policy" forced the Maritime provinces to trade westward, within the new Dominion, instead of with their Yankee neighbours to the south—the traditional, closer, and, therefore, more rational market for their goods. On both sides of the border, these bluebloods, like Stanfield himself, are Protestant, socially progressive, and fiscally responsible. Upstanding citizens, they are imbued with probity and a powerful sense of moral obligation derived from privilege.

As a Maritime "Brahmin," Robert Stanfield was the grandson of the founder of the Stanfield underwear industrial empire, Charles E. Stanfield, to whom the younger man has often been likened by those who know the family best. Charles established the business in 1856 in Tryon, Prince Edward Island, and operated it as Tryon Woollen Mills until 1870, when the enterprise was moved to Truro, Nova Scotia.[3] Renowned in the industry for its innovation, the business sold many different types of heavy woollen underwear, famously worn by prospectors during the Klondike Gold Rush in the late 1890s. In 1898, the company developed Stanfield's "Unshrinkable Underwear," and in 1915 it introduced and patented an adjustable two-piece design. To this day, Stanfield's is widely known as "the Underwear Company." Charles E. Stanfield made his fortune the same way his grandson was to rebuild the shattered Nova Scotia Conservative Party and, later, the national Tory party following the mess in which Diefenbaker had left it: through "slow determination and unswerving attention to detail."[4] Like the product that bears his family name, Robert Stanfield the politician would prove both innovative and durable.

Starting his schooling in Truro, Bob Stanfield finished his secondary education at Ashbury College, an elite boarding school in the affluent Ottawa suburb of Rockcliffe Park.[5] He then went off to Dalhousie University in Halifax and, finally, Harvard Law School in Boston. At both universities, he was a stellar student, graduating *magna cum laude* in each case. At Harvard, Stanfield made the prestigious *Harvard Law Review* editorial team, and was the first Canadian to serve as its editor.

Outside a structured speech, especially in media interviews, Stanfield was a halting speaker, with a tendency to think through every possible nuance of an issue before pronouncing on it. His characteristic pauses—not only between sentences, but, indeed, within sentences—became fodder for satire by others and for his own amusing, sometimes hilarious, self-deprecation. Television interviews after Question Period in Stanfield's era were conducted in Room 130-S in the Centre Block basement of Parliament Hill. Former Stanfield press secretary Rod McQueen tells the story of Stanfield's standing in front of a row of cameras waiting patiently while a technician fixed a problem. Veteran NDP parliamentarian Stanley Knowles entered the room, lingered at the back amid the silence, and finally said: "Speak up, Bob; we can't hear you." Quipped Stanfield, "I'm in the middle of one of my pauses." As often happened, the leader's rapid-fire wit brought down the house.[6]

By objective standards of reasoning and exposition, the practice of careful deliberation before and while speaking is commendable. But it is heavily penalized in the modern political and media world of the snappy fifteen-second sound bite. What too often counts is not the content of a politician's message but how crisply he or she says it on TV. "Drill, baby, drill!" gets more points and media attention than a detailed policy on national energy; "Zap, you're frozen!" more votes than a courageous policy of wage-and-price controls. This fact of political life was to plague Robert Stanfield throughout his time in federal politics, for he lacked the oratorical skills of a John Diefenbaker at the podium to compensate. The role and impact of policy in the political process are not independent of such human and institutional factors.

# Thomas Henry Bull Symons

Tom Symons was fifteen years younger than the Tory leader, but seemed much older than his actual years. Nevertheless, the cloth he was cut from was similar to Robert Stanfield's, even if blue serge in contrast to Stanfield's Harris Tweed. Symons's father was writer and humourist Harry Lutz Symons, winner of the 1947 Stephen Leacock Award for *Ojibway Melody*. His mother, Dorothy Sarah Bull, was a certified grande dame of Toronto's Rosedale. Tom's brother Scott had distinguished himself as an author (most controversially with *Place d'Armes*, in 1967), an authority and writer on cultural property, and as a latter-day Oscar Wilde bon vivant, aesthete, and dandy. Contrary to mythology, Thomas Henry Bull Symons was not strictly of old Upper Canada Family Compact stock. Nor, unlike Stanfield, had he inherited substantial family wealth. His maternal grandfather, William Perkins Bull, however, had been prosperous in law and real estate and even cattle breeding. With or without real wealth, the entire family (father's and mother's sides alike) exuded Old World class and values and high style. Indeed, in most people's eyes, if Tom Symons's own blood had been any bluer, he would have had to be treated for hemophilia. Like Stanfield, moreover, Symons was elite-educated: Upper Canada College, University of Toronto, Oxford University (reading History) and, later, more honorary degrees than Dr. Williams had "pink pills for pale people." As significant as anything else, Tom Symons, like Robert Stanfield, carried noblesse oblige in his soul, as though personally ordered by God to carry out His command that "faith without works is dead." (James 2:14–26.) Both Stanfield and Symons were preternaturally disposed to public service. And, now, motivated by the same spirit, the two men were linked in the service of the Progressive Conservative Party of Canada.

In other respects, the two men were very different. Stanfield was reserved, almost shy—awkward and uncomfortable both in social settings and with individuals, painfully inarticulate when not surprisingly eloquent if required to rise to the occasion, as he often was. And yet, ironically, Stanfield's *bon mots* frequently left colleagues and staffers buckled over in laughter, even stunned when, as sometimes happened, the repartee entered the profane. "I'm busier than a two-hundred-dollar-an-hour whore working two beds!" he once told me at the end of a particularly long policy meeting that competed with a zillion other things on his agenda that day. So much for Yankee-style understatement and reserve! Long after Stanfield vacated the Tory leadership, when I was in Cabinet, I ran into him and his perky wife, Anne, at an Ottawa Airport luggage carousel as they and I awaited bags from our trips. I knew Anne (née Austin) well from her time as president of the Don Valley PC Riding Association before the two became romantically involved (and married in 1978—Bob was twice-widowed). Anne remarked that she and Bob had just returned from a speaking engagement, not of his, but of hers, for which "I was actually paid," said she with exaggerated mock pride. To which, without missing a beat, Stanfield shot back: "Oh, yes, she has never been above selling herself."

No one, least of all Nova Scotia Liberals, ever made any money predicting what this man would or would not do—or say. Stanfield had a hilarious stand-up comedy act. It was scripted, and regularly adapted to meet the requirements of the occasion, by staffer Bill Grogan. The PC leader's performance always brought down the house, and upstaged Pierre Trudeau, in every appearance at annual black-tie Parliamentary Press Gallery Dinners. At this strictly off-the-record affair, the media hosts expect the Ottawa politicians they invite to let down their guard and their dignity, but not, even at this raucous affair, their pants.[7] Grogan, a former Winnipeg broadcaster and freelance writer widely admired for his quick wit and comedic talents, was recruited as a speech writer and special assistant for the PC leader. His main job was to help expose Canadians more widely to Stanfield's own dry but considerable sense of humour. Grogan's most effective contributions typically involved injecting levity into the leader's formal policy addresses, most often at the beginning. But some of Stanfield's best and most memorable one-liners came spontaneously from the man himself, delivered with pitch-perfect comedic timing. Coming from such a dour-looking, taciturn, and formal man—more like the butler at a grand English estate than a stand-up comedian—Stanfield's humour was all the funnier for being so incongruous.

Symons, by marked contrast, oozes charm with every invisible pore. He has an uncommon gift of putting at ease the most insecure Nervous Nellie and a silver tongue in conversation and public forums alike that would require a Brink's truck for security if ever converted to hard currency. Moreover, the man possesses a sense of humour that, in contrast to Stanfield's drollness, is counterintuitively outlandish and mischievous, often at his own expense. He once tucked condoms in crevices of my Mercury Cougar coupe's back seat. They weren't discovered until weeks later—by two Catholic nuns whom I was driving home from a politics class I was teaching part-time at Peterborough's Sir Sandford Fleming College. It was not easy in that era for a Catholic lad to explain away the prophylactics when, as today, the Vatican considered birth control a gateway to Hell. "They came with the car" didn't quite do it.

Physically, Bob Stanfield and Tom Symons could not have been more different from each other had the former been born a blue heron, the latter an Arctic owl. *Stanfield*: bald, of craggy face and pallid complexion, gangly height, long neck, arms, and legs, and boniness. *Symons*: greying black hair, strong patrician profile, a shorter, somewhat stooped man as though weighed down by a heavy academic gown, stocky, waistcoated and pocket watch-chained, skin slightly swarthy and satin-smooth. Not birds of a feather, to be sure!

And yet, these two markedly different men—bound more by a shared sense of privilege and attendant commitment to public service than by partisan label—were to form one of the most remarkable partnerships in the history of party politics in Canada. That partnership was consummated at the Priorities for Canada Conference in the city of marital partnerships, Niagara Falls, in October 1969.

*Chapter 5*

# HONEYMOONING IN NIAGARA

That evening in July 1969 when I received Heath Macquarrie's phone call, I drove the forty kilometres from my family's cottage at Keppoch, PEI, to Shaw's Hotel at Brackley Beach. And there, for the first time, I met Thomas Henry Bull Symons. Until then, I knew nothing about the man, much less that he was about to change my life.

Symons greeted me warmly and invited me to join him in the hotel's rustic bar. Over drinks, unbeknownst to me in my naiveté, he sized me up as though vetting for the highest rank at the Vatican or the Court of Saint James. As we sat together awaiting our order, my first response was one of awe. To this callow youth (a mere twenty-four), Tom Symons, though still only in his late thirties himself, looked more like he could be the chairman of a Scottish bank than the president of a small Ontario university. He dressed the part, in an informal but subtly elegant seersucker ensemble so different from what I was used to seeing academics wear at the three universities I had attended, classy Queen's included. The thing I noticed right off were his brown brogue shoes, which colour the sartorial trendsetting Duke of Windsor had, in the 1930s, given men of a certain social standing His Royal Highness's imprimatur to wear with grey or blue trousers. Symons was wearing the brown brogues with grey trousers. Clearly, the person whose presence I was in that night was a Grand Gentleman.

While the pale amber flowed, I learned many of the fundamentals of the zeitgeist that Tom Symons would infuse in PC Party policy (directly or indirectly) throughout Robert Stanfield's leadership. Indeed, this spirit—virtually identical to Stanfield's own, I would later discover—constituted the broad orthodoxy the two men would draw on to reshape the party in the new leader's image. I learned that Symons was a committed Stanfield man and progressive Tory, but no rabid partisan. He taught me that one is not small-"c" conservative, but progressive and enlightened, to believe, as I volunteered I did, that the monarchy helped Canadians preserve our distinctiveness from Americans; that the separation of political power and symbolic head of state through the Crown was highly desirable both towards the same end and on principle. For Symons, true conservatism meant a commitment to others in the spirit of community, not a blind or slavish allegiance to private enterprise or rugged US-style individualism. Government was not an evil, but an instrument for good, Symons said, doing necessary things for society that private interests refused to do or could not do or could not do as well. He was proud of government-created institutions such as the Canadian Pacific Railway, Canadian National, the CBC, the Bank of Canada, and the Canadian Wheat Board—all established under Tory prime ministers—and that these "connectors of social cohesion," as he put it," were not the product of socialist excesses, but instead "part of the yarn that knitted the country together." Successive

Tory prime ministers, from Sir John A. Macdonald to John Diefenbaker, had not only "bought some of that yarn, but also fingered the darning needles that wove the knitting with equal measures of pride and devotion to duty." The country's cultural and heritage property, he continued, expressed both Canadians' inherent values as a people and their sense of commune with generations past and yet born. *Conservatism*, he said, was a hollow value system if it did not contain a firm commitment to the *conservation* of the natural environment; the natural and built environments were inextricably linked, so heritage principles ought to be applied to the dual parts of humanity's habitat if planet Earth was to be much more than a place to do penance for Original Sin (at least, that is how this Irish-Catholic lad interpreted his remarks). Symons reminded me that human, civil, and Aboriginal rights, and individual dignity were among the highest of Canadian values, and that a state's essential role in maintaining law and order did not justify its taking a human life, for no one had yet proved capital punishment deterred crime. He maintained that the Commonwealth was not merely a vestige of British imperialism, but also a modern opportunity for Canada as a "middle power" to advance its own economic interests and values and to help other Commonwealth members in a way otherwise denied a country of Canada's small population. "Foreign aid," he pointed out, was a ten-, not a four-, letter word. He insisted that multiculturalism and pluralism were at the heart of Canada's national identity, and should be proudly fostered, that the French Fact and official bilingualism enriched all our lives while opening economic and cultural doors for Canada to other French-speaking countries. Above all, he averred that I was dead wrong when I said it wouldn't make a "pisser's bit of difference" (that was the scotch talking) where one took undergraduate studies because, proffered I pompously, "it is only professional and graduate schools that count in the end"— an indelicate comment given that my audience was himself an undergraduate university president.

Symons pushed back gently, choosing his words with the care of a diamond merchant selecting precious gems from a seller's tray for a royal wedding engagement. His response was an exercise in diplomatic dexterity that, in many different circumstances throughout the PC policy process, I would later see him employ so often, and so deftly, to save others from the deep hole they had dug for themselves, as I myself had just done. "Well, yes, I get your point," he said, "but...." And then he tactfully shot down my argument with the precision of a heat-seeking missile. A quality undergraduate liberal arts or science education was vital to a youth's personal development and future, he told me emphatically, but it could not be obtained at just any university. Attention to the needs of the individual student through small teacher-student ratios was central to quality learning, he said with particular passion. "Throwing students to the wolves in mega-classes where teaching assistants, rather than first-rank scholars, did the real work is not what quality education is all about." "Quite right, Sir," I retreated, "Trent being an obvious case of how to do it right." Good save! Or, at least, the scotch seemed to think so. We did agree, though, that Stanfield's speech on the Guaranteed Minimum Income in London, Ontario, in the previous election had been magnificent and, therefore, we were both enlightened fellows. And what's more....

Well, I could drink only so much, even as my drinking partner showed no signs of wear himself. But none of it mattered: Tom Symons had me at hello. More relevant, he was impressed with my "interview." Following character and academic checks I subsequently learned the Trent president had made with my professors at Queen's, Symons phoned me on the Island several days later from Peterborough. He asked me to help organize the PC Party's policy conference in Niagara Falls throughout the rest of the summer right up until it was held in early October 1969. And thus began a professional relationship, and friendship, that has lasted almost five decades. And so, too, was formed, over time, the two-man team that directed the Policy Advisory Committee while serving as the secretariat of the party's separate Policy Coordinating Committee (as I explain in the next chapter). We were to perform this dual function together (I very much the junior partner) until Robert Stanfield quit as leader in 1976. But, effectively, our work was finished after the 1974 election, when the party set its sights, not on policy, but on finding a new boss to replace the one we ourselves had worked so hard to elect leader of the country.

## Solid Policy Planning

"The Niagara Policy Conference," as the more formally titled "Priorities for Canada Conference" entered the history books, was the brainchild of more than one father.[1] Funding and all other relevant mundane matters were duly vetted and approved by the PC Party's representative Executive Committee, whose mandate it was to convene such a conference. The committee's responsibilities under the party constitution for conferences of this sort were similar to those it had, on behalf of the party as a whole, for creating committees and other mechanisms to develop policy. But the idea of the conference itself was conceived primarily by Robert Stanfield in the embrace of Tom Symons. The latter's sense of moment as a historian made him well aware of how spectacularly successful the Liberals had been in 1960 with their landmark Kingston Policy Conference, held, in one of history's practical jokes on the Tory party, in the Ontario city of Sir John A. Macdonald.[2] The Grit policy conference, convened at Queen's University in early September, sparked the fire that gave badly needed new life to the Liberals under Lester Pearson's floundering leadership. At the time, the Diefenbaker government was competing with its enemies for evermore innovative ways to destroy itself. The Kingston Conference generated the ideas that produced the policies that led to the laws that created the national social revolution that made the five-year Pearson government in the mid-1960s among the most progressive and visionary in the country's history. Milestone social programs such as the Canada Pension Plan and medicare were born in Sir John A.'s hometown. Red Tory that he was, the Old Chieftain would have been in on the joke.[3]

The lack of policy in the Conservative Party Robert Stanfield inherited from John Diefenbaker, however, was not at all funny. Stanfield and Symons saw the Niagara Conference in the manner the Liberals had seen their Kingston Conference: the first major step towards reshaping the party's policies. In the Tories' case, new approaches were needed not only in the social field, but in a wide variety of others as well—from taxation to poverty to foreign investment to external affairs and foreign aid to federal-provincial relations to the environment to parliamentary reform... even to marijuana laws, the liberalization of which the delegates were to come within a puff of supporting. The conference was to showcase the party's progressive thinkers, expose to the public a more modern and attractive side of Tories, present the party as serious about issues Canadians cared about, and launch a continuing process to generate the policies that would convince voters this was a party they could trust.[4]

Among the more than four hundred delegates to the conference were Tory MPs and senators and provincial legislators, a few given key roles to chair sessions or present papers organized around eight main policy streams. It was also attended by rank-and-file Progressive Conservatives from across the country interested in policy. More vital to the main rationale for the conference, some sixty individuals with expertise and reputations in specialized fields were invited, provided with travel allowances and per diems, asked to prepare papers for discussion, and put front and centre in the proceedings. The stars of the conference were chosen for their box office appeal with as much care as David O. Selznick had taken to fill the role of Scarlett O'Hara in *Gone with the Wind*. Stanfield, like Selznick, intended no ordinary show: PC headquarters claimed that the conference was to be "the largest and most widely representative political gathering to study policies that has ever been held in Canada."[5] MPs and other party notables or wannabes who sensed an opportunity to steal a scene or two for themselves in Niagara were, instead, discreetly diverted to the director's trailer for cocktails.

Although all this struck some party traditionalists as inappropriate for their grand old political home—Woodstock meets Niagara—Stanfield was prepared to shake the home to its very rafters if that was what it took to modernize the plumbing and electricity to get Canadian voters to come through the front door. In Tom Symons, he had found the ideal butler to welcome them. Over the course of the summer, Symons had recruited not only me but also Paul Gardner, a York University history grad student, to help him plan the policy conference. Our job was to compile and pour over lists of potential resource people; investigate their credentials and political leanings as carefully as the RCMP would a candidate for highest security clearance; court scores of experts thought suitable to the task with the resolve of stags in rut; try repeatedly, in the face of many more rejections than acceptances, to get the courted to reconsider; and prepare multipage fact sheets, in that pre-computer era, with more entries—of names and bios and notations about each individual's suitability or reachability or attendance status—than a New York City phone book.

At one point, in mid-summer, the complaints from party headquarters about steadily rising costs and the apparent futility of it all outnumbered the experts whom Symons had been able to draw to Stanfield's side on this seemingly *Titanic* folly as it headed full steam towards the iceberg. The party's national director, Malcolm Wickson, and executive secretary Robert Bédard—both often caustically critical of Symons (the latter in four-letter words)—aged a decade that summer. I myself tried to get a former professor of mine at St. Dunstan's University, in Charlottetown, to accept the Trent president's invitation to attend the conference as a resource person. A unilingual English-speaking historian, he rejected the invitation by saying "*ça n'est pas possible*." Invitees were finding ever more creative ways to say no.

But, as the heat of the summer declined, the number of acceptances from invited resource people began to increase. The special-guest travel and hotel confirmations soon began to gain the scale of an international Shriners' convention in the eyes of us two hard-working grad students. We had been particularly discouraged by our lack of progress in this category. Only a few short weeks earlier, the worst party sceptics, including paymasters at PC headquarters, had become convinced our Symons operation was pie-eyed and doomed. Now, even they had to admit that "God-damned crazy egghead up in Peterborough" (Bédard's exact words to describe Symons) might know what he was doing after all. They had been running out of vulgarities to express how they felt about his process and, indeed, about the man himself, including to his face. Those vulgarities were now being replaced with words of praise, even if, at this point, still grudgingly.

Finally, on the appointed day, the Priorities for Canada Conference opened. And Stanfield could not have been more delighted with the new curtains in the living room as the butler led him to the place of honour by the fireplace in the newly renovated political home the Tory leader had so recently shaken to the rafters. The egghead had not been so crazy after all.

The PC leader was much more than an honoured guest at the conference; he was its chairman (Symons was, officially, chairman of the Program Committee). Stanfield also chaired the major session on fiscal federalism, a subject he knew as well as anyone in the country. The leader's substantial involvement could not have contrasted more with Diefenbaker's participation in an admirable but unproductive conference that his later nemesis, Dalton Camp, had organized for the party in September 1964 in Fredericton, New Brunswick. That conference assembled a politically diverse group of politicians, academics, and political analysts such as media guru Marshall McLuhan, Montreal newspaper editor Claude Ryan, future Trudeau finance minister Marc Lalonde, and Trent University historian W. L. Morton.[6] The conference offered, said Denis Smith, "a feast of ideas, but little evidence of a clear direction for the Conservative Party"; Diefenbaker "attended briefly to insist upon his friendship for intellectuals."[7] Tellingly, Stanfield was the only PC premier or provincial party leader to attend. His attendance presaged the high premium he would place on policy as national party leader three years later.

Over the decades, the Conservative Party had lacked a strong policy-conference track record. There had not been a brand-name conference on a broad range of issues since the Port Hope Conference in 1942, a generation earlier, the Conservatives' 1967 Montmorency Falls "thinkers' conference" having been dominated by constitutional issues. At the Port Hope Conference, in an effort to modernize the party's policy program, delegates agreed to resolutions that supported full employment, low-cost housing, trade union rights, and a government-financed medicare system, among other progressive stances. In correspondence with me, retired senator Lowell Murray said that the Port Hope Conference "really broke a lot of important new ground, and its conclusions formed in my opinion the inspiration and the foundation for all progressive conservative parties/governments in the future—whether they realized it or not." I do not disagree. But the party was in transition at the time. The on-again, off-again party leader, Arthur Meighen, failed in his comeback attempt to win a House of Commons seat in a February 1942 by-election in Toronto's York South riding. Before long, the party was focused on finding a new leader—eventually John Bracken, who would bring to the leadership a markedly different background and policy agenda from that associated with the party previously, except at the Port Hope Conference. So, whatever progress the Conservatives made at Port Hope, it did not advance the party nearly far enough to redress years of approaching policy on a helter-skelter, hit-or-miss basis. Still less did it help build a base for organic policy development in future months and years. Robert Stanfield saw the need for a far different approach. Ad hoc-ery was to be replaced by an ongoing process. The aim was to generate policy ideas and positions on a sustained basis over the long term.

At Niagara, Stanfield, unlike Diefenbaker at his Fredericton policy conference, was not just interested in being seen in the company of intellectuals to burnish his own image. He was eager to pick their brains, to cultivate a connection with them for future purposes, to associate them with the party, however indirectly, both in fact and in public perception, to extract from them as many policy ideas as he could, not only at the conference, but (again) in the future, and to encourage them to stay in contact with one another, so the party could have its own self-cultivating community of experts as a resource for both the leader and the parliamentary Caucus. Concerning this last objective, Stanfield succeeded spectacularly in the case of a future prime minister, Brian Mulroney. The Quebecer participated actively in the Niagara Conference, as did his future Opposition and government chief policy advisor, Japanese management expert Dr. Charles McMillan, who then, as now, was with York University's Faculty of Administrative Studies. L. Ian MacDonald, in his book, *Mulroney: The Making of the Prime Minister*, cites *Montreal Gazette* journalist Hubert Bauch's description of McMillan as "Mulroney's Intellectual Bodyguard," and notes that Mulroney and McMillan first connected at the Niagara Conference.[8] This notable relationship, like many others forged at the conference (including my own with Tom Symons), probably would never have happened had it not been for Niagara.

## Substantive Issues, Progressive Policies

The Niagara Policy Conference succeeded well beyond Stanfield's most optimistic expectations. He never doubted Symons could pull it off, even as some underlings had carped and complained from the time the planning began. Stanfield's biographer Geoffrey Stevens writes: "[The conference] nailed together a party platform that, if not daring, at least brought the Conservative Party into the mainstream of Canadian opinion."[9] Here, however, I take substantive issue with the author. It is not true the party got a platform from the conference, although the deliberations, and the substantial media attention they received, did wonders for the party's policy image, the overall improvement of which was one of the goals Stanfield and Symons had set for the confab. A party platform, however, was not. Indeed, the two men had never intended the delegates to vote on individual issues, but to seek a more informal consensus through discussion and reports prepared by a *rapporteur* assigned to each session. This process was designed to give the leader and Caucus, and the party as a whole, a sense of direction on issues—not, as Stevens noted, hard-and-fast policy, let alone dogma. The leader stressed this point in a news statement and conference on September 4, 1969, in the lead-up to the Niagara Conference. He said the conference was to be one stage of a "continuing process" whose purpose was to propose "the direction of Progressive Conservative policy rather than to hammer out a platform."[10] In a few particular sessions, though, something akin to a vote—a virtual vote, as it were—was conducted, making it clear the relevant session, and the plenary that approved its report, favoured progressive stances on a range of issues. One of the progressive stands taken was support for the introduction of a capital gains tax to render the total taxation system more equitable and to increase public revenue, particularly for social security. The delegates supported this position three years before the federal Liberal government introduced such a tax for those very purposes.

On the Guaranteed Minimum Income (GMI) that Stanfield had supported in general terms in the 1968 election, he had not given up. It would be an enduring theme with him, no matter how lukewarm some party members were towards it. Opponents in the party, including at Niagara, feared the policy would be an easy target for political foes to misrepresent. Candidates in other parties already had done so in the 1968 election. Before the conference, Stanfield had asked research staff to flesh out his GMI plan. They proposed, for example, a $2,030 annual income floor for a family of four, equivalent to $12,635 in today's inflation-adjusted terms.[11] A Senate inquiry in 1969, the year of the conference, revealed that one in four Canadians lived below the poverty line, and that close to two million of these were the working poor whose income from employment was insufficient to lift them above the poverty line, which the report defined as $5,000 ($31,600 today) for a family of four.[12] The PC Research Office's proposal for a $2,030 annual income floor for a family of this size was, thus, not extravagant relative to what the senators considered necessary to live on. But the PC leader made only limited progress in convincing the more cautious party members at Niagara to go along with even this modest proposal. Opponents were concerned about its alleged threat to the "work ethic," a phrase coming into vogue at the time. A compromise, however, was achieved when the party accepted the principle of a basic income floor for people unable to work and job incentives for able-bodied individuals who could. Always a hard worker himself, Stanfield found it difficult to credit the concerns certain party members had about destroying the work ethic. He believed most people do work hard, with or without actual jobs. He thought, given a choice between earning income for themselves and their families and relying on government support, most people would be motivated by pride alone to choose work. He saw the GMI as a way to ensure that, in the face of bad luck and other circumstances beyond some people's control, the disadvantaged had the income support they needed to meet at least basic needs. He bristled at the idea that such a fundamental notion of decency somehow threatened any Canadian traditional value—noblesse oblige in train, no doubt. Tom Symons kept in touch with the specialists who had participated most actively in the GMI discussions at Niagara, and asked a few to provide him with further ideas on the issue. He then prepared a memorandum synthesizing their thoughts, forwarded it to Stanfield, and told the leader he planned to discuss the matter with him later—as, indeed, he did, and at length.

On the other issue that had plagued Stanfield in the 1968 election, *deux nations,* delegates were less interested in taking a stand, for or against, than having it just disappear. An article in Halifax's *Mail-Star* reflected the way most people, both within the party and without, viewed the outcome: "The controversial '*deux nations*' concept of Canadian society...was quietly laid to rest [at the conference]."[13] However eager many Conservatives were to avoid controversy over the issue, Stanfield himself never wavered in recognizing Canada's linguistic duality. He was not prepared to allow the setting aside of a mere phrase to change either his views or political tactics on the nature of the country. Both publicly and privately, he remained firm, a position that stuck yet another burr under the saddle of John Diefenbaker and his Caucus loyalists, particularly from the West. For them, "bilingualism" and "biculturalism" (but also "multiculturalism") were incendiary terms. They believed Stanfield's support for these values undermined their own fundamental view of the country. That view continued to be captured in Diefenbaker's dual mantra from the 1967 Conservative leadership convention: "One Canada" and "Unhyphenated Canadians," early seeds for the sprouting of the western-based Reform Party in the 1990s by disgruntled Tories of this very sort. Clearly, the new leader of the party of Sir John A. Macdonald and Georges-Étienne Cartier was much more open to the view of Canada represented by the controversial *deux nations* phrase than were many others in the party at the time (and still more would be later). Influenced by the still-meddlesome Diefenbaker, those Conservatives became convinced that the phrase contained hidden meaning, that the concept posed a threat to *l'ancien régime*. In the best sense, it did. Stanfield and Symons were eager to reach out to French-speaking Canadians, make a new home for them in the party, restore the federal *bleu* tradition in Quebec, and rebuild, within the party, the English-French partnership that Macdonald and Cartier had embodied. The two new Conservative partners in this cause, Stanfield and Symons, were not averse to a revolution in the party's more recent incarnation if they thought such a drastic step would reshape the party and its image, especially in the eyes of francophones.

Robert Stanfield and Tom Symons were quintessential WASPs. It might surprise students of Canadian history now, almost half a century after the fact, that two such men embraced so readily the centrality of the French Fact to Canada's national identity, and were so committed to ensuring that dimension of the country became once again an integral part of their political party's own identity. Biography alone would suggest the two were unlikely beacons for this enlightenment. Stanfield did not begin learning to speak French until after he became Tory leader, when well into his fifties. For all practical purposes, Symons was unilingual. He could understand spoken and written French, but never learned to speak it. The obvious, however, does not always direct history. Nor do people who make history always reflect the obvious. The idea of Canada itself was not obvious to anyone but inspired visionaries back in the mid-nineteenth century. The vast empty spaces, the geographic isolation of the colonies from one another, the paucity of transportation links throughout the territories, the absence of anything resembling a common political culture or community, the powerful pull of the capacious republic to the south, and the petty rivalries and jealousies among the colonies (PEI would attend the founding 1864 Conference in Charlottetown only if it could host!): all such centrifugal forces rendered Canada highly unlikely by the laws of nature. What made the centripetal forces stronger, and Canada possible despite the powerful forces against it, was political leadership, the vision and sheer doggedness and political skills of some three dozen men who were not prepared to let the strength of nature prevail over the spirit of man. Statecraft is not the application of the obvious to the inevitable, but the act of linking vision to the seemingly impossible. Robert Stanfield and Tom Symons were statesmen. They were engaged in statecraft.

In Stanfield's original notes, personally annotated in his handwriting, for the kickoff to the subsequent federal general election in 1972, one paragraph (in French, but translated as follows) demonstrates how committed the PC leader was to connecting with francophones—Quebecers, in particular: "I sincerely expect to obtain strong support in the province of Quebec in this election. *I would be very unhappy if we had to form the next government without adequate representation from Quebec.* I will stress it throughout the campaign" [emphasis added]. Meanwhile, the PC leader stressed the need to reflect sensitivity to the French Fact in all the party's policies. As we shall see, he was prepared to have every single policy statement redrafted if, in his judgment, that objective was not met. And, on his instructions, many of the policy statements had to be substantially reworked accordingly. This was his overarching priority in the policy process. It was no less a priority for Tom Symons, in his own right and as the person most responsible for ensuring that the leader's overall policy direction and specific instructions were followed.

Apart from any consensus achieved on particular issues—such as the proposed tax on capital gains (positive); the GMI and *deux nations* (not so much)—all the papers presented by resource people for discussion in the various sessions at the

Niagara Conference were impressive, a few outstanding. Among the best was that of David Slater, dean of graduate studies at Queen's University, on "the Canadian Economy in the 1970s." The PC Research Office prepared an internal summary and analysis of "Editorial and Press Comment" during and after the conference. It noted that the Slater paper "obviously made a strong impression on Mr. Stanfield." The impression lasted a long time. Now, these many years later, Slater's paper strikes one as eerily prescient, as though he had kept secret from Symons and his assistants that he was a clairvoyant on the side. In retrospect, it is not surprising that the man's contribution at the conference was so impressive. Within a year, Slater, who had a PhD in economics from the University of Chicago, would become York University's second president. From 1978 to 1985, he was the director and then chairman of the Economic Council of Canada. As head of the body that represented all graduate students in residence at Queen's University on the students' council, I dealt directly with Dean Slater for many purposes. He was one of the most impressive men I have ever known personally—brilliant but practical, businesslike but personable, tough but fair. For the PC leader and his chief policy advisor to have attracted people with this kind of brainpower and expertise and public stature to Niagara to help the party on policy was a formidable achievement. Dalton Camp contrasted Stanfield's constructive, expertise-based approach to issues with Diefenbaker's use of "policy" merely to attack political foes: "Mr. Stanfield has introduced his party to the power of positive thinking. In doing so, we have, for the first time in a long time, an Opposition party whose policies are more specific than general platitudes and more positive than the customary catalogue of complaint."[14]

So many individuals and organizations outside the party requested copies not only of Slater's *tour de force* but also of many other papers presented at Niagara that a publisher prevailed on Tom Symons to allow him to provide them in book form. Symons also agreed to serve as editor. He did do a lot of preliminary editorial work on the book, mostly with his own funds. I handled all the administrative details, including negotiations with the various authors. Unfortunately for posterity, and Canadian studies in particular, the Trent University president was unable to complete the project. Pressures to prepare for the next election, scarce party research and editing resources, and logistical and legal complexities surrounding the collection and publishing of reworked texts—all such factors conspired against the project from the beginning. It was worth the effort, though. The fact the PC Party even tried to publish an intellectually weighty book of this sort shouted from the rooftops how high the party had climbed to shed its Luddite image—nay, reality—that Stanfield and Symons were striving to change. Fortunately, a few of the individual authors published their papers independently. Excellence, like nature, abhors a vacuum.

With or without a book to show for it, Robert Stanfield emerged from the Niagara Conference much stronger than before. It was, writes Stevens, "a major move towards modernizing the party's image and overcoming the anti-intellectualism in the party that had long blocked attempts at reform."[15] Stanfield was beginning to succeed in remaking the party in his own image, replacing John Diefenbaker's prairie populism with something more acceptable to contemporary voters. Charisma had not suddenly seized Stanfield, but, in that era of Nixon, Vietnam, and Watergate, with politicians on both sides of the border increasingly seen as corrupt, if not evil, homespun Nova Scotian noblesse oblige was starting to look darn good to a lot of Canadians.

# Chapter 6

# PLANNED AND PROCESSED POLICY

An Opposition party, even one with the high-sounding appellation "Her Majesty's Loyal Opposition," is at a distinct disadvantage in competing for voters' support, or even attention, against the party in office it strives to replace. The incumbent party has, at its beck and call, all the resources of the permanent public service—what former Conservative senator Hugh Segal called at one time the "Liberals' perpetual government machine."[1] By contrast, Opposition parties have only the personnel and policy and other resources they can afford themselves. They depend, primarily, on their own fundraising, sometimes with more hope than success. Admittedly, the effort is indirectly subsidized by taxpayers through tax-deductibility provisions in the donations-related parts of income tax laws. But the imbalance is huge, nevertheless.

In a burst of rhetorical energy, if not a lot of follow-up, Pierre Trudeau trumpeted as one of his bumper-sticker policies in the election campaign of 1968 a commitment to "participatory democracy." This promise, however, foundered on the shoals of reality once Trudeau was prime minister for a while. On one occasion, the PM, with all the moral certitude of the pope unfurling a Papal Bull, labelled MPs "nobodies" when fifty metres off Parliament Hill. Another time, in the Commons, he told a heckling Opposition MP to "fuddle duddle" (or so he claimed, though many heard a stronger two-word "f" expletive). Towards voters he was sometimes no more respectful. Agriculture minister Alvin Hamilton and trade minister George Hees in the Diefenbaker government had aggressively, and effectively, promoted western Canadian wheat sales to China. Confronted by western farmers worried about plunging grain sales to China years later, Trudeau replied with a haughtiness that would have shocked Marie Antoinette: "Why should I sell your wheat?" Such a mindset should make historians wonder whether "participatory democracy" was not a lot of "Bull" in the first place.

To his great credit, Pierre Trudeau did do something remarkable in the name of participatory democracy. It was worthy of his own considerable intellectual powers and of the intellectualism he tried to apply to government programs and policies. In the Speech from the Throne opening the Twenty-Eighth Parliament on September 12, 1968, only three months after the election, the Trudeau government announced plans to fund Opposition party research offices. The offices were to have their own research staff paralleling the government's, albeit on a much smaller scale. The staff, in each case, was technically to be employed by the House of Commons. The chief appointment, that of director, would be made by the Speaker of the House on the recommendation of the party leader. The initial budget for the PC operation was $125,000 annually (worth around $790,000 today). It was a start. The budget would increase substantially over the years.

The Progressive Conservative Party's Research Office was established in May 1969. The first director was Dr. E. R. Black, forty, a Canadian federalism expert recruited by Stanfield from Queen's University's political studies department. Black, who took a leave of absence from Queen's to accept the post, was to report to the leader directly. The new director's first team had ten professional researchers and three support staff. With all the ironic symbolism one finds only in politics, they operated from the Hope Building, in the Sparks Street Mall, just minutes on foot from Parliament Hill. In this period, the PC Party had not much more than hope going for it; and not a lot of that, either. Each researcher reported to a Caucus committee chair in his or her area. That committee, in turn, corresponded to the relevant parliamentary committee. Among its many mundane functions, this operation prepared a daily booklet of subjects on which PC MPs were urged to query the government in Question Period. It identified and developed issues that Caucus members could run with, both in Parliament and on the stump, to catch the media's attention, hold the government in check, and place the party in a good public light. It prepared background material for MPs on politically salient subjects that staff believed could be exploited in the longer term. And it provided them up-to-date facts and statistics on such matters as employment and inflation for all these diverse purposes, particularly for the day-to-day skirmishes in Parliament. Much of the spadework for Stanfield's detailed proposals for a broad range of tax cuts, for example, was done by the PC Research Office.

The high-quality professionals Black recruited included Robert Batt, a long-time Commons and Senate legal counsel and expert on parliamentary procedure. Another recruit was Dennis Roberts, who had headed Simon Fraser University's information office and, with a journalism background, had a good nose for the communications value of the office's work. Later, Leslie Horswill was hired to brief the Caucus each morning in preparation for Question Period. Only twenty-five when recruited, Horswill had earned a master's degree in history from the University of British Columbia. He soon gained a reputation throughout parliamentary circles, including among researchers in the other political parties, as one of the brightest and most knowledgeable policy specialists in Ottawa. The PC Research Office's resources were Lilliputian compared to those available to the government party through the public service. The new resources did, however, boost the Official Opposition party's capacity to develop policy, whether for the day-to-day skirmishes in Parliament or for the longer term. In the process, the party gained a little more hope. The other parties benefited similarly from their new research offices. Many in Trudeau's own parliamentary Caucus opposed the innovation. They believed it was tantamount to arming the enemy. They were dead right.

For this enlightened measure, especially in the face of hostility from within his own ranks, Trudeau received too little credit from instant historians and the Opposition parties themselves. Stanfield, however, true to his magnanimous character, expressed his own appreciation on the floor of the House of Commons. The government, he said, could not function without expert assistance. For the same reason, neither should the Opposition be expected to do so. "I express my personal thanks and the thanks of this party for the constructive measure that the prime minister has taken in this regard."[2] Whether Trudeau knew it or not at the time, the establishment of the PC Research Office was to Robert Stanfield what a good horse was to a cavalryman: the surest and fastest way to invade enemy territory.

Soon after becoming director of the Research Office, Dr. Black wrote an important strategic memo to future prime minister Joe Clark, then on Stanfield's senior staff.

In the memo, Black proposed a policy-development process with several dimensions. The process would both deal with "specific matters that need attention" and develop general themes to help "define" the party. He contemplated the party would focus on areas "we want to discuss because we might find attractive new approaches" and on "those [areas] we have to discuss [only] to touch bases." He contemplated, as well, that the party would hold "several" policy conferences towards these ends. Clearly, the Niagara Policy Conference was in the spirit of the Black memo, leaning more towards the "defining" objective than to "specific matters that need attention."

In the news release issued on the eve of the Niagara Conference, Stanfield said: "I am not satisfied that this [PC] Party, or any Canadian party, has yet become an adequate instrument of either an understanding or agreement [concerning public policy]. I intend to request our National Association to call subsequent policy conferences on a national and regional basis." At the news conference that followed, the leader called on the Niagara Conference "to recommend the machinery we can establish within the Party to allow a wide range of Canadian citizens to examine and understand a wide range of public questions." In accordance with this exhortation from its leader, the PCs did much more than begin developing policy and rebranding itself in October 1969: the Niagara Conference produced a mechanism to formulate party policy after the gathering. In one of the few actual votes taken, the conference, at Stanfield's urging, approved, and the party's Executive Committee later endorsed, a formal motion to establish a Policy Coordinating Committee (PCC) "whereby the policies of the [party] can be given continued study and examination." How overdue this mechanism was is stressed in an internal memo written by PC headquarters research director Peter McCreath immediately following the Niagara Conference: "In the present decade, the Progressive Conservative Party has held two policy conferences, a leadership convention, and several Annual Meetings, yet has never managed to develop either well-defined policy positions or the machinery for the co-ordination and development of policy positions between such major events or, indeed, elections. The Policy Coordinating Committee is designed to be this mechanism."[3]

It is incomprehensible that any of the three major national political parties in Canada would have operated for so long in such an ad hoc fashion on the policy front. And yet, the record of all three major parties in developing policy systematically over time when not in government and able to rely on the public service in this area is spotty at best, appalling at worst. Most of the time, it has been the latter. As political scientist James Farney has put it, Canadian political parties have given "only a minimal role in making policy to ordinary members or even backbench MPs."[4] The Reform Party was supposedly a populist organization, stressing grassroots participation rather than control from above. But, says Farney, its leader, Preston Manning, "was undoubtedly more dominant [over policy and strategy] than usual, even compared to [the leaders] of other Canadian parties."[5] There is, in fact, no exact or even close parallel with the Stanfield-Symons policy partnership and process in the Liberal Party, the NDP, or the PC Party itself in prior or subsequent eras. Before forming governments, Lester Pearson, for example, had corporate accountant giant Walter Gordon by his side and Jean Chrétien had academic and intellectual Chaviva Hosek by his. These two other party leader-advisor partnerships, however, were fundamentally different from the Stanfield-Symons model. The Chrétien-Hosek model is instructive.[6]

Chaviva Hosek earned a doctorate in English language and literature from Harvard University. She taught in the English Department of Victoria College, at the University of Toronto, prior to serving for seven years as director of policy and research in the Prime Minister's Office from 1993 to 2000, when Chrétien was in power. Between 1990 and 1993, Hosek ran the Liberal Caucus Research Bureau and was "senior policy advisor" to Chrétien as Leader of the Opposition. During that period, together with front-bench MP Paul Martin, who succeeded Chrétien as PM, she was responsible for directing research for and the production of the Liberal Party's 1993 election platform, "Creating Opportunity," commonly known as the *Red Book*.

Chrétien-Hosek is likely the closest parallel with Stanfield-Symons as a partnership model to develop policy for both the leader and his party. But Hosek's relationship with Chrétien in the Opposition period was as a full-time paid functionary of the Liberal Party's Research Office. As such, her role with Chrétien was closer to that of PC research director E. R. Black's with Robert Stanfield, in an earlier period, than to Tom Symons's role with Stanfield. Symons was an academic who donated his services on a voluntary basis and without remuneration. Moreover, the Liberal Party's policy process under Chrétien-Martin-Hosek was primarily *parliamentary* and only secondarily *extraparliamentary*. The PC Party's policy process under Stanfield-Symons was primarily *extraparliamentary* and only secondarily *parliamentary*. The two operations were mirror images of each other. But in democratic values, the image was disfigured, as in a children's play-park distortion mirror, in favour of the PC Party's process. It was far more complex and ambitious, produced stronger policy, had a longer-lasting impact, involved many more party members, and cast a much wider net to tap outside expertise.

Notwithstanding the low priority John Diefenbaker attached to policy development, he did recruit economist Dr. Merril Menzies as his policy advisor for the 1957 and 1958 elections. Menzies accompanied Diefenbaker on the campaign trail and generated a raft of memos for the leader's speeches, often literally on the fly. The PC leader's "vision" for northern development—and specific measures the Diefenbaker government later took based on it—came largely from this idea source. Menzies would continue as an informal advisor to Diefenbaker in government, but he eventually resigned in frustration for having been unable to convince the prime minister of "the need for long-term planning from a Conservative perspective," as Denis Smith puts it.[7] So, the Diefenbaker-Menzie relationship—it could hardly be characterized as a partnership—did not fit the Stanfield-Symons mould, either.

The policy work Dr. Reva Gerstein did for Joe Clark while he was opposition leader might seem a bit closer to the Stanfield-Symons partnership. But the reality was far different. A respected psychologist and educator, Gerstein headed a policy council for Joe Clark that comprised five members of Caucus, an equal number from various PC associations, and ten outside specialists in various fields. In announcing this body, Clark said it was "an integral part of the Progressive Conservative Party's process of preparation for forming a new government." I have no doubt that, as a former member of his predecessor's staff, Clark tried to model his policy process after Stanfield's. Indeed, Clark's policy advisory council resembled Stanfield's Policy Coordinating Committee in structure and membership. The truth is, however, in light of the colossal failure of the Tories' wage-and-price controls program in the previous election, the new PC leader viewed policy at this point the same way most members of his Caucus did: being too specific was a time-tested prescription for electoral disaster. As the 1979 election approached, therefore, Clark and the PC Party stressed general themes on select issues, rather than detailed policies on a broad range of topics. Among the rare specifics were, notably, commitments to privatize Petro-Canada and to move the Canadian embassy in Israel from Tel Aviv to Jerusalem. Those aside, as a (successful) PC candidate in that election, I was struck by the paucity of specific policies available to us Tory aspirants on the hustings compared to what PC candidates had been equipped with in the Stanfield era after the 1968 election. The overarching theme of the PC campaign in 1979 was, in effect, "Let's get rid of Trudeau." It was almost enough to produce a majority government. After our defeat in the 1980 election, we were back in Opposition. Clark then found himself too embroiled in both party leadership battles and parliamentary confrontations (including over the restored Trudeau government's constitutional reform measures) to have the time for or interest in extraparliamentary policy development, much less the elaborate Stanfield-Symons process mode. The substantial amount of work my fellow Conservative MPs John Fraser and Stan Darling and I did together for the party on the environment (acid rain, in particular), for example, was conducted almost totally without involvement by PC partisans outside Caucus. It is inconceivable that would have been the case when Stanfield was leader, especially after Tom Symons became his chief policy advisor and established a complex extraparliamentary policy process for the party.

As we shall see, the Trudeau government implemented more of Robert Stanfield's policies in the 1972–76 period than the Chrétien government would ever implement from its own *Red Books*. Stanfield's policies legislated by Trudeau included tax and pension indexation, wage-and-price controls, and (arguably) the introduction of the capital gains tax, which the Tory leader supported publicly well before the Liberals did officially and then made it law. The most substantive promise in the 1993 Liberal platform was to repeal the 7 percent goods and services tax (GST) introduced by the Mulroney government. But the Chrétien government retained the GST once it won the election based partly on that commitment. Like the GST cancellation promise, much of the rest of the 1993 *Red Book* was utter demagoguery, including the other two most attention-getting and popular planks in the document: the Liberals' commitment to renegotiate the Mulroney government's Canada-United States Free Trade Agreement (by then the North American Free Trade Agreement, NAFTA, involving Mexico as well), and their promise to cancel the Kim Campbell government's plans to replace the country's aging and increasingly crash-prone Sea King helicopters.

Repeal the necessary (the GST), renegotiate the non-renegotiable (NAFTA), and cancel the advisable (new helicopter procurement): that was, basically, Liberal Party policy. With it, the Liberals under Jean Chrétien won the 1993 election in a landside (177 Commons seats). The new finance minister was Paul Martin, who was widely quoted as having said (supposedly off the record): "Don't tell me about the *Red Book*. I wrote the damn thing, and I know that it is a lot of crap!" Much of the 112-page *Red Book* of 1993 *was* "crap." If not for its artful hocus-pocus detail and politically calculated Orwellian double-speak, the demagoguery that reeked from this document could have come from John Diefenbaker circa 1963–65 ("Ah, they're all against me but the people!"). The two subsequent *Red Books* contained many fewer specific promises than the 1993 version. Once in government, the Liberals felt haunted by the 1993 platform (concerning the GST, free trade, and helicopters, in particular). So, in future, they were determined to avoid making specific promises on the campaign trail. Liberal policies would be made so general, and so dull, that the party could not be held accountable for them in government in the likely event they were re-elected. Accordingly, their 1997 and 2000 election *Red Books* were not so much crap as pabulum. If the Liberals had been defensive about their 1993 *Red Book*, they were—with good reason—

paranoid about the subsequent *Red Books* even as they promoted them with as much energy and swagger as they had done the first edition. As part of his shtick, the famous Berlin-born juggler and humourist Hilby liked to draw attention to the fact he spoke English with a heavy German accent. Once asked why, he replied, "If you can't hide something ugly, paint it red." In the 1997 and 2000 federal elections, the Liberals could not hide their ugly dearth of detailed policy. How appropriate, then, that, just as they had done in 1993, the Grits called their campaign policy books *Red*.

That the PC Party itself had long functioned pre-Stanfield-Symons without any kind of continuing systematic policy-development process is mind-boggling. So is the party's failure to create any kind of permanent mechanism to mobilize extraparliamentary personnel and resources to develop policy, not just for elections but also between elections. No wonder the PCs were denied power for most of the previous three decades and then blew it when, almost by default under Diefenbaker in 1957, they finally won. Wasn't a political party supposed to be a vehicle to bring together people of like minds, on principles and on specific issues, so the electorate could compare their shared perspectives and positions with those of the alternative parties and vote accordingly? Robert Stanfield and Tom Symons thought the PC Party's chaotic and capricious approach to policy had to end. They believed the party needed to apply modern management principles to the task if it was to have any credibility with those voters for whom policy was important and whom the two men were eager to court. Otherwise, they knew the party would have no chance against the Liberals, in particular, with the vast policy resources and mechanisms and specialists at their disposal, as the governing party, through the public service. In Stanfield and Symons's view, the PCs had to replace rank amateurism with professionalism of the highest order. That many party members considered this perspective rebellious was a measure of the challenge they faced. The Policy Coordinating Committee was intended to be the principal mechanism to meet that challenge.

# The Byzantine Formalities

The PC Party provided Symons with a full-time assistant both to help him personally as the leader's senior policy advisor and to serve as the secretary of the PCC. After helping Symons organize the Niagara Conference while a young graduate student, I myself became that assistant. My title was "Executive Assistant to Mr. Stanfield's Policy Advisory Committee." National Headquarters paid my salary, but, for strategic reasons detailed later, I was to operate under Mr. Stanfield's wing, not from Headquarters.

The Niagara Falls resolution that established the PCC mandated Headquarters to be its secretariat, and the "appointment of such a secretariat would be the responsibility of the National Director" (that is, the party's chief officer). Under successive national directors of the party, however, from the beginning of the PCC's work, everyone assumed that, with funding and administrative support from Headquarters, Tom Symons and his assistant would fulfill this role. And we did. Political circumstances, rather than the strict letter of the "law," dictated practical arrangements.

The membership of the PCC was to include, notably, "the National leader or his representative." The qualifier "or his representative" was to prove academic, for Stanfield attended virtually every meeting, sometimes leaving urgent business elsewhere to do so. In addition to the leader, the PCC was also to consist of the chairman of the Policy Advisory Committee, the national chairman of organization, the PC national president, the National Headquarters director, the Caucus chairman, the House leader, three Caucus members, and the presidents of the PC Women's Association, the PC Students' Federation, and the Young PCs Association. In a telling provision, which Stanfield himself not only approved but also urged, the chairman of the party's new mechanism to establish policy was to be the leader himself or, in his absence—equally telling—the chairman of the Policy Advisory Committee (Tom Symons). If Niagara Falls had been the policy honeymoon, the resolution that established the PCC was, in a reversal of the usual chronology, the marriage licence. The hard slogging to make the marriage work was about to begin.

It is necessary to distinguish between two structures: the *Policy Advisory Committee* (PAC) and the *Policy Coordinating Committee*. In a letter dated April 15, 1968—sent widely, in effect, "to whomever it may concern"—Tom Symons informed recipients that "Mr. Stanfield and the members of the Policy Advisory Committee, at their recent meeting, have asked if I would undertake the chairmanship of the Committee." The PC Party was a little like the British governmental system, which operates without a single discrete written constitution.[8] The party did have a multipage, detailed, and highly legalistic constitutional document, for the institution was technically a major non-profit corporation. The document governed most of the party's operations concerning membership, election of officers, the holding of general and other meetings, fundraising, the establishment of committees thereof, the role of functionaries, and most important of all, the selection of party leader and his/her relationship with all the above. In some important respects, however, the party operated outside any written legal framework, including its constitution. This is the specific respect in which the parallel with the British system of government applies: despite the legal nomenclature, the PAC under Stanfield's leadership was not a *committee* at all. Rather, it was a *process* directed by Tom Symons. That process was devised to recruit a wide variety of people in a host of different ways to do a host of different things for a host of different purposes at a host of different times. All of this had one ultimate objective: the formulation of a body of integrated and thoroughly researched policies on a wide range of public issues well before the next election. The policies were intended to help the leader and Caucus, both on a continuing basis (in Parliament and elsewhere) and in the election, while also assisting party candidates and their active supporters in the campaign. To the extent the PAC was a real committee, it consisted of Tom Symons and his assistant (me), who acted as a virtual two-man steering committee to make the PCC's mandate happen.

The party's constitution authorized, among other things, meetings at which structures were sometimes created. This happened at the Niagara Conference when the PCC was established. But the PC Party was like the Government of Canada itself, reflecting the same broader political culture. On the one hand, Canada's system is not as formally legalistic as the US system, with its fetish for checks and balances, defining everything short of where the president's White House washroom must go. Unlike Americans, Canadians did not have even a constitution-based charter of rights until, under Pierre Trudeau, we got one in the early 1980s, more than a century after the birth of the nation. On the other hand, the Canadian system is not as custom-based as the British one, either. In true Canadian fashion, our bargain was somewhere in the middle. Canada is a middle power in more ways than one.

Accordingly, the PC policy process was never burdened unduly by party constitutional strictures. Not once did anyone say the PCC lacked authority or jurisdiction to do something. And that was not because the committee was particularly careful to respect its legal boundaries—it often was not, sometimes not at all. Neither the party president nor the Headquarters director ever reined in the committee on such grounds. Certainly, the leader did not. Costs, however, were invariably a major issue, especially between Symons's Peterborough operation and paymasters at Headquarters. The Trent president periodically had to plead with them to pay the bills incurred at his end. It was not uncommon for Symons to have to dip into his own pocket to meet costs when the paymasters were especially parsimonious or simply wanted to demonstrate who they thought was really boss: themselves. Symons himself had no time for such petty games, and refused to play them. In the worst cases, he would just hold his nose and pay up personally. For his part, Stanfield was mostly kept blissfully unaware of these games and of the patience of Job required of Symons to cope. I say "mostly" because the PC leader was impossible to keep wholly in the dark about anything that mattered. If he didn't have extrasensory perception, the five senses he did have were keener than those of anyone around him concerning every facet of the party—and virtually everything else, too. Regarding intraparty tensions, I discovered the leader did, in fact, know the basics, despite everyone's efforts to hide them from him for his own peace of mind. In a personal note to me of May 13, 1973—otherwise quoted later here in a different context—Stanfield wrote: "I wondered...whether you sometimes question whether your labours are always fully appreciated...because there have been frequently some difficulties involved in our mutual operation"—that is, PC Headquarters and the PAC headed by Tom Symons out of Peterborough. Extrasensory perception, indeed! As a Cabinet minister years later, I would witness this same "the man knows everything" phenomenon when anyone tried to shield Brian Mulroney from uncomfortable truths. As with Stanfield, he always seemed to have a way of finding out. That's why such individuals are able to clear much higher bars than most other people can: they're born to leap like Olympic high jumpers.

For my part, I periodically had to work without a paycheque. How Tom Symons survived all this—set aside my own frustration—still confounds me. The feudal manner in which certain party functionaries operated versus how Symons ran Trent University was like comparing a sundial to a Swiss watch. For Symons, it was not so much a culture shock as an electrocution. With all the personal uncertainty, I looked forward to payday—and my monthly car payments and rent—as one would anticipate his last meal: with trepidation. Just as Stanfield was largely (but, again, not totally) unaware of Symons's situation, I doubt Symons was fully aware of mine, either. I never raised the matter. Otherwise, I knew he would be too quick to write yet more cheques from his own desk drawer. I did not want that. As it was, he was making more than enough personal sacrifice for the cause—in time, in absence from his wife and three young children, in labour, in talent, and in cash. The way the entire process worked in practice had more to do with such human elements than formal structures or legalities. Extraordinarily gifted and giving operators—Stanfield and Symons, in particular—helped overcome both the human and the institutional limitations of the system. But, alas, not entirely. No system is perfect, and for sure this one wasn't. And yet, on the policy front, it was the best the party would ever have.

The leader of the Progressive Conservative Party of Canada was bound by certain legal and constitutional arrangements. But unless he egregiously abused his authority, party members typically gave him wide latitude to lead them how he wanted. Accordingly, the PCC operated under Stanfield's leadership in an almost extralegal manner in most respects. The leader derived his authority from being elected by the party membership at a leadership convention under the terms of the PC constitution. Once elected, he had two primary functions. The first, by definition, was to head the party as an aggregate of individuals and groups committed to a common cause: principally, to obtain or retain government power. In theory, the leader and party members operated as a team based on shared vision and policies. The other role of the leader was to head the party's parliamentary Caucus, whether in Opposition or government. Among other functions, policy linked these dual roles

As Caucus head, the PC leader could pursue almost any channel and set up almost any structure he wished to develop policy for himself and his parliamentary followers. As party head, though, he was subject, at least in theory, to the party's constitution. And under that legal framework, it was the party itself—through its Executive Committee ("National Executive")—that was authorized to establish structures to develop policy both for the membership and for the Caucus to the extent that body felt like part of the institution from which it derived its political label. In practice, the National Executive established a policy committee, but invariably it was the leader who appointed its chairman, and the policy committee's operations revolved around him, although it technically reported to the body whose authority it was to establish it. Thus, Tom Symons's policy work pivoted around Robert Stanfield; it did not operate as part of the party's bureaucracy, however much it depended on Headquarters for administrative support and funding. The Symons operation worked closely with the PC Research Office, a partner in the overall policy process. The two operations, however, were distinct in sponsorship, mandate, personnel, and function.

# The Membership

The membership of the PCC, as detailed above, was defined by a resolution passed by the party at a duly constituted policy conference mandated by the party's National Executive (the Niagara Conference). In practice, however, the membership was fluid, again reflecting the human factor. Some people were invited to attend from time to time as the need arose; others attended routinely by virtue of office. Even in this category (*ex officio*), attendance was fluid. Some *ex officio* members attended regularly for a while but not other times, depending on personal circumstances. Some attended hardly at all, even though they had the right. (The first time I met Brian Mulroney, my future boss and Cabinet colleague, was at a PCC meeting. To my knowledge, he attended only that one time, though he always participated actively in policy in other ways—for example, at policy conferences and in Annual Meetings.) A few people who, technically, had the right to attend only if invited got invited so often that, after a while, they and other members took their attendance for granted to the point where no invitation was deemed necessary. They became de facto members, the same as ex officio members. Indeed, many de facto members attended more regularly than *de jure* ones. All this must seem Byzantine, but the process worked because, in practice, the rule was simple: if the committee wanted you to attend or you wanted to attend, you did attend. Stanfield, as PCC chairman, almost always attended. He took his policy role seriously and, following his example, most others did theirs, too.

Robert Stanfield was eager that francophones be well represented on the PCC. At its first meeting, he lamented the absence of "the French-speaking element of the Party." He noted that the PCC could not change its "terms of reference" (his term), but he insisted that the committee redress the imbalance anyway. So much for the rules. Stanfield instructed that the following be invited to join the PCC: Senator Jacques Flynn, leader of the Opposition in the Senate; Fernand Alie, president of the PC Federal Association of Quebec; André Lalonde, chairman of the PC Policy Committee of Quebec; and Claude Dupras, vice-president of the PC Federal Association of Quebec. All responded positively. Lalonde and Dupras took their membership seriously, just as everyone else took them seriously. Senator Flynn's political antenna was unerring, especially concerning Quebec—a political warhorse of the old stable.

The francophone members participated seamlessly in French and English. Although some members understood only English (none only French), language was never a barrier, even without simultaneous translation. Stanfield, as chairman, ensured no one felt excluded from the discussion, even if he sometimes needed to translate. (Again, Tom Symons, though not bilingual, could follow spoken French without difficulty.) What other country could practise "participatory democracy" so splendidly or produce a political leader with such sensitivity to the language and culture of others? Sir John A. Macdonald said of French Canadians: "Treat them as a nation and they will act as a free people do—generously. Call them a faction and they will become factious."[9] Stanfield treated French Canadians in the spirit of this wisdom. In the Policy Coordinating Committee, they responded in kind.

I had never before been prouder to be a Tory, or a Canadian, than I was in these circumstances. Seeing the English-French dynamics at play in the PCC under Robert Stanfield's skilful and enlightened chairmanship left a lasting impression on me. My parents had raised me and my siblings to appreciate that the French Fact was integral to the *idea* of Canada. The particular dynamic at the PCC just described was, for me, the *practice*. There could be no starker contrast between Stanfield's and Diefenbaker's respective approaches to political leadership than the way the former responded generously to the country's French Fact, including in the private conclaves of the party, while the latter, to the end, continued to view the country's linguistic duality as a national and personal threat. It is a pity many of Stanfield's shiniest qualities were hidden from public view. They would have set a tremendous example. Had that example been displayed, rather than kept behind closed doors, it would have been as precious as sterling. It is still precious to all of us who had the privilege to see it, even if only in a private vault. Rod McQueen said: "Who knows how voters' perceptions of Stanfield might have changed for the better had they been able to see him in action for themselves."[10] I had that opportunity for several years, and my perceptions could not have been more positive.

# Modus Operandi

The Policy Coordinating Committee held its first meeting at the PC Research Office on November 26, 1969. The committee usually met thereafter in the boardroom at National Headquarters. Meetings of the PCC were all about business, not socializing. The Headquarters building was owned by the party under the Bracken Trust.

Its principal tenant was the prestigious clothing retailer Holt Renfrew, as if to symbolize the contrast between the fine-thread leaders who sometimes led the PC Party (including, now, the Maritime aristocrat) and the more homespun variety. In the latter category was John Bracken, who not only gave his name to the trust, but also gave the Progressive Conservative Party the first part of its dual name. He had been with the Progressives, a prairie agrarian protest movement, and insisted on the name change before agreeing to be drafted national Conservative leader in 1942. The challenge ahead for Stanfield's PCC was to follow its new leader in the spirit of the "progressive" half of the party's name. From the very beginning, the new PC leader signalled that was the direction in which he intended to nudge the party. And he did, unfailingly.

Unless required by the length of the meeting, food was not routinely served. Nor, as I recall, was much else, either—certainly never alcohol. When Stanfield arrived, almost always punctually, the meeting began. Introductions of newcomers were short and perfunctory. Significantly, Stanfield, without a hint of condescension, always noted the presence of francophones with special warmth and extra words of welcome (in French). And, it seemed to me, he did so with genuine appreciation. By the same token, the leader went out of his way to encourage francophones to participate, and subtly acknowledged, in both French and English, his keen interest in their remarks when they did. Minutes of a previous meeting, routinely kept, were deemed approved unless corrections were thought advisable—not usually the case, because I wrote them! Tom Symons sat to the right of the leader at the end of a long board table. It was like placing all the cargo on one side of a ship. Rather than list, however, the ship was navigated a lot more smoothly that way—for, in this case, the practice set a classy and businesslike pace. (That is, provided Stanfield was not sending the meeting into gales of laughter, as he periodically did, with witty interjections of the most unexpected and sometimes profane sort. I resisted, but barely, the temptation to include the leader's witticisms in the minutes, both for posterity and for my own continued amusement.)

There was, invariably, a formal agenda, containing about a half-dozen to a dozen items, most of them easily dispatched. If the primary task was to review draft policy, as it usually was, members began detailed line-by-line analysis and started to share ideas. The party's Research Office provided a staff member or two as resource people, and its director almost always attended and participated actively in the discussions. People knew Stanfield was a man of business and few words. Consequently, no one needed to be admonished about being too long-winded or unduly argumentative. Everyone was an equal, but, as at any meeting, members gained respect by contributing well. Stanfield, however, was clearly "first among equals" and Symons a close second, no matter who else was in the room. Both Stanfield and Symons exuded an aura of "we're doing something important" that ensured important things actually got done. With pipe in hand, whether smoked or not—a different era then—and a water-tower-sized tea thermos always at the ready, Symons projected an image of gentlemanly informality while telegraphing, consciously or not, the likelihood that the meeting was not going to end any time soon. And it scarcely ever did. A meeting never lasted less than an entire afternoon or evening, sometimes the two combined, a few even well into the next day. Again, people were there to work, not enjoy camaraderie. As people got to know one another better, though, the atmosphere got ever more congenial.

Stanfield rarely dominated the discussion, seldom took sides in a heated debate, and never discouraged disagreement. But he would become impatient when wheels were spun and progress was delayed, particularly due to any one person's dogmatism. Draft policy—whether from a conference, the Opposition Research Office, the PCC itself, a study group, or some other outside source—was not likely to recommend either a general direction or a specific turn wildly far from what the leader, Caucus, or party as a whole would find potentially acceptable or, at least, debatable. After all, it was not as though anyone would have proposed selling Nova Scotia to the Sultan of Brunei to help pay down Canada's national debt. Most participants were able to find common ground, no matter how vigorously details (large or small) might be debated. When agreement was just not possible (say, because of principle) or practical (say, given time constraints) or desirable (say, in the face of looming political sensitivity) or some other reason (say, nobody gave a damn about the subject), the item would be held over or simply set aside, never to be seen again.

The leader periodically—but not routinely—would dig in his heels if he thought an idea was particularly dumb politics or plain dumb, period. When that happened, no one in the room would have doubted how he felt: the man made it abundantly clear. The leader was extraordinarily sensitive to proposals that would affect Quebec or francophones more generally. He was hostile to almost anything that seriously grated on provincial sensitivities, as though still a provincial premier himself. A particular foreign-investment proposal close to being agreed upon, for example, was taken off the table until the views of the affected province (Ontario) could be investigated. In all such cases, one standard was pre-eminent: could the leader sell the idea to his parliamentary Caucus? Party members' views were important to him, but less so than those of Caucus. Stanfield calculated that, if he could not get a certain policy proposal through his Caucus, how members across the country felt about it would be academic; the proposal would go nowhere, anyway.

Stanfield took notes, though not copiously. He was not like the student in class recording, *figuratively*, every morsel of wisdom from a professor's mouth. He was more like the Duchess of Windsor, who was known to keep a tiny gold pen and pad discreetly under the rim of a dinner charger to note, *literally*, any morsel served wrong at her elegant dinner parties lest the chef ever again put too much vinegar in the vinaigrette. In the innumerable hours I spent in his company in policy discussions, I never saw him visibly angry—frustrated, tired, confused, disappointed, impatient, uneasy, uncomfortable...all those things, certainly—but never expressly angry. In all the meetings and conversations to which I was a party or witness over the years, only once did I see the vaguest hint of tension between Stanfield (a non-smoker) and Symons (then a pipe smoker, though not now, and not for an eon). The incident concerned Symons's pipe. ("Mind my pipe, Sir?" he always said deferentially to the leader.) The Trent president had been experimenting with an unusually fragrant tobacco that even I, with a high tolerance, found challenging. Looks might not kill, but in this instance Stanfield's stern look and comment—"What's *that* you're smoking?"—killed any chance of the offending weed's ever again finding its way into a Symons bong in the leader's presence.

Tom Symons, too, took notes. As discussions proceeded, he invariably jotted down thoughts with a ballpoint pen. Thank God, not his black-and-gold submarine-sized fountain pen! The man used it exclusively for formal letters in which the instrument wrote so broadly, and with so much ink, that the Trent president would cover a single leaf of deckle-edged parchment with scarcely a half-dozen short sentences. By contrast, the policy-meeting notes were written in Symons's neat and precise and distinct hieroglyphics on just a few sheets, each hardly bigger than a Post-It.

The cryptic "etchings" could fill the entire eleven-volume set of Will and Ariel Durant's history of the world when converted to my orders. At least, that's how I viewed it at the time.

All told, the PCC had its own dynamics. Stanfield was chairman, or "skipper," as Heath Macquarrie called him, especially when fuelled by the Appleton rum. Symons was not so much "vice-skipper" as *éminence grise*. Even if the man on the throne did not always like his pipe tobacco.

# The Art of Policy Chairing

Personality is a crucial factor in whether or not an individual succeeds in politics. It also determines if the relationship between a politician and a senior advisor works. Indeed, this factor is more important than shared party label or ideology.

Robert Stanfield lacked many of the personal traits required of a national party leader to succeed in retail politics countrywide, however popular he was in his own province and region. But his personal qualities were ideal for rebuilding the Progressive Conservative Party after John Diefenbaker almost destroyed it. Stanfield knew how to recruit talent, build a team, create structures, set goals, devise strategies, execute tactics, manage his own time, delegate authority, accept and process criticism, and change course if necessary in light of setbacks. His were the skills of a first-rate manager. Equally important, he had the temperament to persevere in the face of obstacles until the job got done. His interest in public policy and his intellectual capacity for it were unmatched within the party in his era. Management and policy skills and a good temperament were a powerful combination. A leader with that combination of traits could not have been chosen by the PC Party at a better time. Stanfield applied those skills and personal strengths to the elaborate policy process he developed and managed in partnership with Tom Symons. It required a person of Stanfield's competence and character to transform the national PC Party from an organization with virtually no policy when he became leader to one whose strongest suit was policy by the time he fought his second national election five years later.

Setting aside the PC leader's mixed electoral record, on the policy front he was the ideal leader for the party at this juncture in its history. No other Tory in modern times could have done what Stanfield was able to do in this area. That includes Brian Mulroney, the only PC to lead his party to two consecutive majority governments in peacetime in the twentieth century. (Robert Borden won two majorities in a row, but he achieved his second win as head of the wartime Unionist government party, with Liberal participation, in 1917.) The skill set and personal qualities required to win an election, however, are not necessarily those needed to transform and manage a large organization like a national political party, let alone govern a country. In 1958, Diefenbaker won the largest federal electoral victory in Canada at that point in history. Within four years, his government was in shambles; within five, it lost power. In 1968, Trudeau took the country by storm. In four years, his government, in disarray, came within a parliamentary seat of being tossed on the scrap heap of history.

Even Brian Mulroney would not have been able to do what Robert Stanfield did with the party in policy development. Without question, Mulroney had the intelligence and management and people skills required for the task. He was a first-rate labour lawyer, businessman, and party organizer in Quebec before becoming party leader.

His record as a private citizen speaks for itself. So does his record in government. Whatever might be said about his policies or programs, nobody can doubt he ran a tight ship as both prime minister and party leader. But Mulroney did not have the temperament, especially patience, that Stanfield brought to the PC Party policy process he launched and administered with Symons. The countless long meetings, the innumerable policy drafts, the tedious line-by-line examinations, the exhaustive (and exhausting) discussions, the widespread consultations, the difficult compromises, the careful consensus-building, the redrafting to completion and then constant updating of policy materials, the numerous national and regional and local policy conferences, in a never-ending cycle—these would have driven Mulroney insane. That he attended only one meeting of the PCC is evidence of his little interest in, or patience for, such a tedious and time-consuming policy process.

When I first met Brian Mulroney, around this time, his reputation had preceded him: the man was already a legend in the making in PC Party circles across the country, not just in Quebec. I remember the occasion well. He sat directly across from me at a PCC meeting. I could tell he was impatient—if not totally bored—with the process. In fact, he left early, and said little before doing so. I was to see the same demeanour at Cabinet. Not that he was ever bored there. But, as chair, he made sure every item was managed with maximum dispatch. Everyone knew better than to be long-winded or ill-prepared with him in charge. It was no different in private one-on-one meetings. Even when meeting with him to be appointed to Cabinet or reshuffled to a different portfolio, one faced a man uninterested in anything but the business at hand. Focus was all.

In contrast, the attributes that made Stanfield an ideal steward of the PC Party's policy-development process in the late 1960s and early 1970s were likely the very ones that made him an unexciting alternative to Pierre Trudeau on the campaign trail: in Geoffrey Stevens's words, quoted earlier, "common sense, patience, the determination to see a difficult job through to completion,"[11] qualities the PC leader applied brilliantly to the PCC's deliberations. For most voters, however, they meant "boring."

Great men and women have great flaws. Not much about them is undersized. As Winston Churchill demonstrated, the qualities that make some individuals great are the very ones that render them less than ideal parents or spouses or friends or colleagues. Churchill's self-confidence, sensitivity, noble principles, vision, resolve, genius, and indomitability were at the heart of his greatness. But the flip side was that Churchill was egomaniacal, stubborn, volatile, obsessive, intellectually arrogant, mean-spirited, and even cruel—not to mention alcoholic. Renowned psychiatrist and historian Anthony Storr has proffered that, "had [Churchill] been a stable and equable man, he could never have inspired the nation. In 1940, when all the odds were against Britain, a leader of sober judgment might well have concluded that we were finished."[12] By the same token, had Stanfield been a more exciting politician on the campaign stump, perhaps he would not have been as ideally suited for the steady-as-she-goes policy leadership role he played with such spectacular success in concert with Tom Symons. Charisma, so powerful a force on the campaign trail, is—virtually by definition—incompatible with the even-keeled frame of mind the leader of a long-term policy-development process must possess "to see a difficult job through to completion." The two sets of leadership qualities rarely coexist in the same politician. As with the actual animal species, a political workhorse isn't, and can't be, easily a show horse. The political leader who possesses all the ideal leadership qualities is as rare as a white rhinoceros—and, even then, is far from perfect. Winston Churchill, the greatest English-speaking human being of the twentieth century, was not. Certainly Robert Stanfield was not, and neither was Brian Mulroney. The political animal is born a human being, not a god.

One of Brian Mulroney's greatest strengths as leader was his extraordinary capacity to rally his Cabinet and Caucus colleagues in the face of imminent disaster. He inspired his troops with soaring oratory. He projected (often faked) absolute confidence. He laid on the Irish charm. He used humour to great effect. If all else failed, he resorted to sheer dogged wilfulness. The last stratagem tended to be not only infectious but also self-fulfilling. In the 1988 free-trade election campaign, Tory fortunes plunged overnight after the leaders' English-language debate. In it, the PC leader was generally thought to have been trounced by Liberal leader John Turner on the central issue of the campaign. The next day, Mulroney hit the campaign trail, and within days he almost single-handedly reversed party spirits and polls. With the possible exception of Laurier, a unique breed, John Diefenbaker was the sole party leader in the country's history who could rival Mulroney as a stump campaigner and orator. And only one other major national party leader in Canadian history was a better "military" strategist than Mulroney: Mackenzie King, in a class by himself.

But what made Brian Mulroney such an inspiring general or admiral on the battlefield made him less than an ideal chairman of the war room. Every Cabinet or Caucus meeting is, at its core, a debate. By speaking too often and too long himself, and telegraphing too early in a debate his own strong views on an issue, Mulroney sometimes (unwittingly, I'm sure) discouraged others from expressing contrary views. This practice reflected Mulroney's seemingly psychological need to hear his own opinions to the exclusion of others' views. It tended to thwart a more natural process of consensus-building in which colleagues clash and resolve their differences in a free and open forum. I was not the only colleague who sometimes felt, at Cabinet or Caucus, more like an audience for a Mulroney oration than a peer joined in common effort to tackle a problem by talking it through. To be fair, the situation may well have been different in smaller forums of the government such as the *Priorities and Planning* and *Operations Committees*. I was not a member of those powerful committees and attended only when invited for specific reasons concerning my programs or legislation. There, I found the PM focused and helpful to my causes, as though he were a crypto ally. Was Mulroney's domination of debate a way of erecting a firewall to protect himself from painful and inconvenient truths that might have weakened his confidence and thereby threatened his ability to lead? Alternatively, as a natural actor, was the man perhaps just unable to resist the urge to perform before a larger audience?

The irony is that Mulroney would not have tolerated loquaciousness from others, least of all at Cabinet meetings. It is likely he had been told by staff how some Cabinet ministers felt. At one meeting of the full Cabinet, towards the end of his first term as prime minister, right out of the blue he uncharacteristically called on several members not usually active in discussions—I remember Public Works Minister Stewart McInnes was one of them—to raise any issue of concern to them. Put on the spot, each responded in some way—more, it seemed to me, because they were expected to than because this was a genuine opportunity to participate in Cabinet, let alone redress the previous imbalance. By the same token, whether the party was in Opposition or in government, the dynamics of Caucus were substantially different under Mulroney's leadership from what they had been under Joe Clark's.

The difference was almost totally attributable to the two men's markedly different ways of performing personally in that fairly large forum (very large in Mulroney's case, following the 1984 landslide).

When he was party leader, Joe Clark lacked Mulroney's natural gifts to inspire. Moreover, he was a well-meaning but inept strategist. How else to explain the imploding of his strong minority government (short of a majority by only six seats) in just seven months? In Caucus and other forums, however, Clark, with astonishing skill, used a meeting to advance an agenda, rather than serve—as a Mulroney meeting too often did—as an echo chamber for the leader's own thoughts. Joe Clark's modus operandi was more like Robert Stanfield's, just as the latter's was like Tom Symons's. Clark fostered debate. He encouraged others' views. He listened carefully to, and absorbed, what was said. He nudged discussion in one direction or another, if necessary, but never dominated. He sought common ground. And, at the end, he synthesized everyone's opinion into a consensus. Clark used this technique to reach a decision. Yet, almost as important for Clark, he did so to make people feel part not only of the process, but also of the decision itself. Had Clark, as a senior Stanfield staffer, learned this modus operandi from his boss, just as his boss had learned it from his Dalhousie University mentor, Russell Maxwell? Or did the method stem from Clark's personality? Or was it all the above? I believe Tom Symons's uncommon skills as a discussion leader and consensus-builder were natural, then honed at the University of Toronto and Oxford. Certainly Trent University's teaching ethos, under his leadership, put a high premium on the Socratic approach, of which he was a grandmaster.

For his part, Robert Stanfield valued teamwork, discussion, consensus-building, and collective decision-making. His management style was the exact opposite of John Diefenbaker's. The latter's was based on the "cult of personality" model. In Tom Symons, Stanfield had found the ideal team-builder. Team-building is Symons's greatest strength. He had few equals at the time. The man could make a community out of two people, a nation out of three, an international alliance out of scarcely more. Where does such magic come from? The fact that the party leader and the Trent University president saw eye to eye not only on the goal, but also on the management method to achieve it, was the principal reason they worked well together as a formidable PC Party policy team. Personal compatibility was more important to their success than any particular set of policies, let alone any individual policy, still less any underlying ideology they might have wished to advance in concert.

How, and why, did the two men's policy partnership work? And what might be required to replicate their kind of partnership and policy success by all political parties, not just the Conservative Party, now or in the future? Tom Symons's management style relied heavily on the personal touch, on hospitality, and on inclusiveness. As such, it was labour-intensive, time-consuming, and, truth be known, expensive. His almost obsessive attention to detail ensured that deadlines sometimes took a back seat to perfection. Of no one else was it truer than of Symons that "perfection is the enemy of the good." Bob Stanfield was more amused than frustrated by his chief policy advisor's genteel (some would say anachronistic) management and personal relations mode. That mode could hardly have been more different from Stanfield's: businesslike, frugal, impersonal, focused, goal-oriented, and time-efficient. But Stanfield's management style was also successful, just in a completely different way.

It is impossible for me to envision a Tom Symons type as Brian Mulroney's chief policy advisor. It would not have worked. Their personalities were too vastly different, their methods too diametrically opposite. Mulroney's thoughtfulness, especially towards friends or colleagues experiencing adversity—late-night phone calls, personal notes, sympathetic inquiries in person—is legendary. As someone who has benefited from his kindness, I know it is sincere. But, as a manager, the Brian Mulroney I saw at close range was direct to the point of curt, determined to the point of impatient, economical (particularly with time) to the point of parsimonious. He placed a high premium on getting the job done right, but just as high a value on getting it done right now, if not yesterday.

Tom Symons's modus operandi—more circuitous and ponderous and with little sense of urgency—was effective in its own way. But it was far different from how Mulroney himself operated or expected others to conduct themselves with him. The Trent University president would have driven the former heavy drinker, now teetotaller, back to the bottle. Stanfield, who enjoyed a drink, was more sanguine than Mulroney in the face of others' personal idiosyncrasies. Stanfield not only tolerated his chief policy advisor's "individualities"—critics might say "peculiarities"—he quite enjoyed them. Some he shared—for example, Old World manners, even if his were not nearly as courtly as those of his senior advisor.

Symons tended to surround himself with colleagues and staff with whom he felt viscerally simpatico. This practice would continue long after the Trent-Stanfield period, no matter the field in which he was engaged. Symons sought out, and kept if he could, individuals who he thought met the highest professional standards by conventional measure—brains and managerial competence and reliability chief among them. But the individuals also had to have something else, too: good judgment and common sense, and moral and personal balance and affability, among other qualities. This latter set of qualities is not always quantifiable, or even discernible except by exemplars themselves, including, needless to say, Tom Symons himself. Symons is a shrewd judge of talent and character. He seeks out people who can help him make the world go round. And go forward, as he and Stanfield tried to drag the PC Party into a more modern era.

# Resource People

Drawing on the contacts with, and the goodwill generated among, the policy experts who, in some cases, had been conscripted at the Niagara Conference, Tom Symons began immediately to put such people to work to help the party. Former Diefenbaker election campaign manger E. A. ("Eddie") Goodman, a top-flight Toronto lawyer and political heavyweight involved in politics since Methuselah was in the womb, wrote to the Trent University president on November 4, 1969, soon after the conference. He said: "At no time have we had better liaison and cooperation between members of the academic world and a political party, in my memory." This comment was both astute and revealing. No other words could have captured more succinctly, and more truthfully, the marked contrast between Diefenbaker's and Stanfield's respective approaches to public policy, management styles, and personalities. That contrast reflected the anti-intellectualism instilled in Diefenbaker by his parents and his rearing in western Canada. Stanfield's style did not appear to have come from external influences, as in Diefenbaker's case. Rather, it seemed bred into his very fibre as though the product of generations of genetic evolution that had blessed both sides of the Stanfield family—notably, but not exclusively, the PC leader and his grandfather, Charles. If some members of the Stanfield family were not as palpably intellectual as Bob, most, including his mother, Sarah Emma (née Thomas), were at least uncommonly thoughtful. Clearly, Goodman thought the Stanfield-Symons approach to policy was a lot more intellectual and thoughtful than his own for the 1965 election. It was not an easy road for Stanfield and Symons. They often had to haul the former Diefenbaker party kicking and screaming in the more modern direction they thought necessary if the party were to be both relevant and successful at the ballot box.

Jean Casselman Wadds was certified party royalty, with a long and rich Tory pedigree. Wadds was the daughter of Earl Rowe, who served in the House of Commons from 1937 until 1962. On two occasions (1954–55 and 1956), Rowe served as acting leader of the Official Opposition. (From 1958 to 1962, he and Jean were the only father and daughter ever to sit together in Parliament.) Jean's first husband, Arza Clair Casselman, represented rural Ontario's Grenville–Dundas riding in the Commons until his death in 1958. She was elected to the same seat later that year. Still later, as high commissioner for Canada in London (1979–83), appointed by Joe Clark, this uniquely gifted power broker became a strong ally of Prime Minister Pierre Trudeau. At both Buckingham Palace and Westminster, she helped pave the way for the British Parliament's passage of his Charter of Rights and Freedoms and "patriation formula" constitutional reforms. Jean Wadds was one of the great Tory Party progressives of the era. In the subsequent period, Flora MacDonald would pick up her baton as conscience of the party, on Guaranteed Minimum Income (GMI)-type issues, in particular.

I knew Jean Wadds personally and was periodically a guest at her baronial family home in Prescott, Ontario. Jean was defeated in the Trudeaumania sweep of 1968, but she continued to be revered throughout the party in all parts of the country as a shrewd strategist and future-oriented thinker, to say nothing of the woman's stunning looks and winning personality. Bob Stanfield and Tom Symons both thought highly of this regal party doyenne. With the leader's blessing, Symons placed her prominently in the Niagara Conference program. Indeed, she was asked to chair one of the most important, and certainly most politically sensitive, sessions. It handled welfare policy, including the Guaranteed Minimum Income plan dear to Stanfield and to her and other Tory reformers. Wadds, however, was frustrated with her session. She believed the delegates' compromise on a GMI weighed too heavily on the side of reactionaries within the party. Quoted by journalist W. A. Wilson in the *Toronto Daily Star* following that session, she lamented: "Mr. Stanfield has been trying to lead his party into a genuinely progressive position…but, in the welfare debate [at Niagara], the conservatives made it inescapably clear…there is a hard core that wants the party to be the voice of reaction."[13] Though made in a specific context, her comment spoke to a broader and continuing truth: the forces hostile to a more progressive and contemporary policy direction for the party remained strong throughout Stanfield's time as leader. But with the help of party luminaries such as Jean Wadds and Flora MacDonald—and, among others, Dalton Camp, Lowell Murray, Richard Hatfield, Roy McMurtry, Libby Burnham, Brian Mulroney, John Fraser, Hugh Segal, Michael Meighen, and Jean Bazin—Stanfield made steady progress.

Neither Stanfield nor Symons was deterred by setbacks of the kind they experienced on the GMI proposal. They were engaged in the process for the long haul. On the brighter side, before long not a single policy specialist turned Symons down because of the party's anti-intellectual image, as many had done in the

Niagara Conference planning. The roster of informed people willing to help with the process climbed steadily: within a year of the conference, the number of volunteers far exceeded that of conscripts. Despite defeats of the sort that alarmed Jean Wadds and other party progressives and reformers whom she symbolized, it was beginning to look like a war that could be won.

As valuable as outside specialists were to the process, many PCC members themselves brought a lot of expertise to it—obvious examples being Symons and Stanfield. Some individuals might have been part of the formal PCC process at one point or another, but contributed most valuably outside the committee structure. Michael Meighen (Prime Minister Arthur Meighen's grandson) and Hugh Segal (both later appointed senators) are cases in point. Such individuals brought to the process not only expertise in particular areas, but also, just as important, political noses keenly sensitive to what the party would accept and the voters would find appealing. MPs and senators are too often underrated for the policy experience and expertise they accumulate over the years in the individual areas of special interest to them, and their informed input on committees is invaluable. In Stanfield's time, this was also true of the leader's own staff and of many others who participated from within the party. All the while, these insiders became better informed—indeed, more expert— by participating in what was an intensive learning experience. How could it not be with Stanfield and Symons directing it?

The process, for me, was like participating in the best seminar or tutorial at graduate school on a never-ending loop. I learned an enormous amount both about process and about specialized topics, often without being fully aware until much later. I know from talking to others that everyone else felt similarly about the experience. Just as everybody brought something different to the table, so we also all gained from one another's talents and expertise and perspectives. I was once taken aback when Symons told me, approvingly, that he was struck by how much he thought my Catholic education was reflected in some of the initial policy drafts I had prepared for his editing. The entire process involved a continuous exchange of knowledge and ideas and (as in this case) idiosyncrasies among all the participants.

There is no way of knowing for certain what, in his most private thoughts, Robert Stanfield originally expected of the PCC. Did he believe the committee would generate policy proposals that he and his Caucus would find of practical value, given the dire need? Or was the committee to be primarily an exercise in intraparty democracy, given that, in that era, "participatory democracy" was the politics *du jour*? Or was the PCC devised to help unify the party, given that, by the leader's order, the committee's membership tilted heavily towards representative office holders? Or did Stanfield view the PCC, from the start, as a private forum in which he could safely test his own policy views before he risked making them public, given his cautious nature? Or did he just have a comfort level with the Socratic method and think the committee might prove useful for ill-defined policy-related purposes, given his commitment to that kind of process? Maybe, originally, it was a combination of all such considerations. No matter the case, it did not take Stanfield long to judge the process worth his own heavy investment of time and intellectual capital. The PCC soon became, for him, the party's principal extraparliamentary forum in which to consider policy proposals and reach consensus on them, in concert with Caucus. The evidence of this is his almost perfect attendance record, the importance he attached to his role as chairman, the large amount of funding and other party resources (including personnel) he authorized for the process, and how attentive he was to every policy detail the committee considered. There was nothing perfunctory about either the process or the leader's involvement in it. For Stanfield, as for Symons, this was serious business.

Robert Stanfield, encouraged and aided by Tom Symons, was not finished shaking up the political home that many Diefenbaker loyalists, and some others in the PC Party, continued to find quite comfortable just as it was, thanks very much. On June 29, 1970, the leader announced a round of "Policy Probes" struck on a number of specific issues and chaired or co-chaired by well-informed individuals: Employment and Economic Growth (Dr. James Gillies of the Faculty of Administrative Studies, York University, later an MP); Urban Affairs (former agriculture minister Alvin Hamilton and MP Vince Danser, former president of the Canadian Federation of Mayors and Municipalities); Consumer Affairs (Heward Grafftey, Quebec lawyer, former MP, and well-known and respected consumer advocate, and Jill Armstrong, formerly of the Canadian Liberties Association and Oxfam); Pollution (Ontario MP and lawyer Gordon Aiken and lawyer and future fisheries minister and House of Commons Speaker John Fraser of Vancouver, who would long continue to serve as a progressive influence in the party on environmental matters, even from the Speaker's throne); and Housing (first-ever black MP Lincoln Alexander of Hamilton, later lieutenant governor of Ontario, who involved or consulted a wide variety of community activists and specialists, especially from major cities such as Vancouver and Toronto).

Reports from all these Policy Probes—enriched by the party Research Office's own work and guided by Symons at a discreet distance—were fed into the fast-developing policy discussion mix. They also added to the growing image of the party as serious about public policy. Geoffrey Stevens says of the housing probe, for example: "[It] served to remind the public that there was a party called the Progressive Conservative Party, and that it, too, was concerned about the problems of the cities."[14] Other approaches included study groups that took a particular issue, but tackled it in a broader context. This innovative approach gave the party a store of ideas across a range of subjects in an integrated way. Typically, the membership was selected so a specific facet would benefit from knowledge and insights from an individual expert in the relevant area. This approach did more than help the party cover a larger number of "bases," in PC Research Office director E. R. Black's term. It also gave the party wider perspectives than would have been possible had the pertinent issues been studied separately, if at all. A case in point was a far-ranging study of economic and cultural facets of Canadian sovereignty, including foreign investment. It was headed by former Manitoba attorney general Sterling Lyon, who also helped with both legal and political dimensions. The group involved, as well, international business professor I. A. Litvak and economics professor C. J. Maule, both from McMaster University, who handled the purely economic aspects, law professor Robert Kerr of the University of New Brunswick (legal), and politics professor William Neville of Trent University (cultural).

The Lyon group produced one of the best, and most substantial, sets of ideas and proposals for the party while Robert Stanfield was leader. Stanfield was to draw heavily from its work, including in a major speech in the House of Commons in response to government legislation on foreign investment. As we shall see, a number of the group's specific proposals were slotted into the subsequent 1972 PC election platform. Some were used word for word—for example, requiring "majority Canadian membership on boards of Canadian subsidiaries of foreign corporations." However anachronistic this kind of policy idea might seem to some observers decades after the fact, in light of today's circumstances—economic globalization, in particular—it was deemed fresh and forward-looking at the time. That quality, not just the idea's inherent soundness, was important to the PC leader as he sought to ensure that his party's policies were relevant to Canadians' contemporary concerns and priorities. For the sovereignty working group, as for others in greater or lesser amounts, the party provided funding—in this case, $1,000, equivalent to about $6,000 in today's dollars. As secretary of this working group, I served as liaison with the PC Research Office, made the administrative arrangements, actively participated in meetings, kept a record of the content as it proceeded step by step, and helped write policy drafts. For me, it was a crash course in the diverse subjects being studied. I could have had no better teachers. The group's report recommended an aggressive approach to growing concerns across the country about US economic and cultural influence on Canada in certain sensitive sectors. The group's work, like that of others, was fed into the policy mix to be considered by the PCC. Around this time, syndicated journalist Anthony Westell wrote that "Canadian politics are entering an era of wide-open policy debate and renewed national soul-searching as the major parties seek to identify the great issues of the seventies."[15] The truth of his insight could not have been more applicable to what, under Tom Symons's guidance, the PC Party was doing, and would continue to do, in policy subgroups.

The policy-development pace accelerated in the lead-up to the party's pivotal 1971 Annual Meeting. Meanwhile, for Robert Stanfield, it was essential that the party explore not only possible approaches to specific issues, but also the overall direction in which, through policy, it wanted to lead the country. To that end, the PC leader asked his chief policy advisor to host a special gathering, the subject of the next chapter.

# Chapter 7

# "A ROSE BY ANY OTHER NAME"

Robert Stanfield wanted to explore the Progressive Conservative Party's fundamental beliefs and how they related to both the present and the future. Stanfield had headed a government for over a decade in Nova Scotia, so he knew that the burning issues of the moment chill with time, and that the time can be short, even for issues that inflame passions the most. People move on to the next problem, the next issue, and forget the last one. In politics, everyone has Attention Deficit Disorder.

Starting as a young man, Stanfield wrestled with the ultimate question: What is it all about? He was keenly interested in the root causes of things. He wanted to know more than just *what* those things were and *how* they impacted people; he wanted to know *why*. The Great Depression especially fascinated him. *Why* did this happen? That's the rub. Others might ask *what* happened and *to whom*; he wanted to know something more basic. Richard Clippingdale, former director of Canadian Studies at Carleton University and Tom Symons's successor as the senior policy advisor to the PC leader—in his case, Joe Clark—published a slim but elegant book on what he called Stanfield's "perspectives." The book, *Robert Stanfield's Canada*—which the Criminal Code should require every student of Canadian politics to read or face execution—is filled with insights into Stanfield's mind. Among the author's most insightful comments is that "Stanfield's mind was most engaged with the challenge of Canada writ large."[1]

It was in that spirit that Stanfield asked Tom Symons to assemble a group of people to think out loud with him, and with one another—in an off-the-record, informal, and non-partisan way, in a private secluded setting—about Canada, in effect, "writ large." Stanfield wanted to know what his party's view was beyond particular issues of the day and from a larger perspective of Canada and its place in the world. To the extent that the discussion would be structured, the subject would be less "whither conservatism?" than "what is conservatism?" or "does conservatism exist at all?" or "for what reason, to what end?" In short, are there certain constants? If so, what are they? And how can they inform, and thereby improve, decisions and actions in contemporary times with a view to not only the present, but also the future?

There was, of course, an agenda of sorts. I say "of course" because a Symons meeting without an agenda would be like one without his elephantine thermos of tea: against the laws of both man and God. The seminar was held at Trent University. Tom Symons hosted, and Robert Stanfield's role was a cross between discussion leader and guest of honour—though it was not in the spirit and dynamics of the occasion to have rankings at all, much less Stanfield at the top. The idea was that good, open conversation would be conducted by good company in a good setting with good food and good wine so that all could have a good time. It was not to be all work: relaxation would be conducive to good thought. Goodness prevailed.

In his Stanfield biography, Geoffrey Stevens stresses how, when an undergraduate at Dalhousie University, the future PC leader came under the spell of his economics professor and lifelong mentor, Russell Maxwell, who Stanfield said was the best teacher he had ever had. The PC leader told Stevens that Maxwell's method was classically Socratic: raising points, asking questions, subtly leading, not forcing the flow of ideas, letting the truth will out naturally through the airing of conflicting views.[2] Was this behind Stanfield's idea for the seminar? It seemed like it to me. The process also resembled the leader's approach at policy work sessions: he was not heavy-handed but resolute, diplomatic but firm, congenial but businesslike, not close-minded but decidedly goal-oriented, and, most important of all, committed to the *process* not as an end in itself but as a means towards an end: the Socratic Method.

A small group of diverse people met. Almost all were outright Tories: *Robert Stanfield*, quasi-chairman; *Tom Symons*, gracious host; *John Fraser* (he of the PC pollution probe), defeated PC candidate in Vancouver (1968), future MP, and fisheries minister under Mulroney, and (later) Commons Speaker; *Tom Sloan*, senior Stanfield aide and former Université Laval journalism director; *Sterling Lyon*, former Manitoba attorney general (and sovereignty working group head); and *Serge Gagnon*, University of Ottawa historian. *Ralph Heintzman* attended as a rising bilingual history scholar and intellectual who, it was hoped, would help keep the discussion elevated and lively—as, indeed, he did. Heintzman was the lone total outsider, having had no previous association with Stanfield or the party. The young historian, scion of the piano company family, was still in no danger of becoming a Conservative; it was a peril he has been able to avoid, without much effort, to this day. As if to atone for inviting such an infidel, we also invited *Alexander Brady*, a renowned University of Toronto political scientist, one of God's gentle souls. Distinguished and aging, but still powerfully productive, Brady was an expert on the Commonwealth. His secondary role in the seminar was to demonstrate, as his very presence did, that one could be shorter and slighter than a tulip and still stand taller and stronger than an oak. And, finally, there was Trent University political scientist *Denis Smith*, later to write the authoritative Diefenbaker biography *Rogue Tory*, cited often here. Smith, if not a certified Conservative, did greatly admire the party Mr. Stanfield was working valiantly to reshape in his own image. He had become an outspoken critic of what he viewed as Pierre Trudeau's "presidentialization" of Canada's office of prime minister and of the country's overall political culture; he remains a vocal critic on such matters. My own role in the seminar was to sit in awe of the sheer brainpower Tom Symons had surrounded the PC leader with at Trent University that weekend. I performed my role magnificently.

It was to be a three-day seminar. Specific issues were discussed, but in the context of the general objective: exploring whether mundane approaches to public policy should be, or could ever be, rooted in an underlying small-"c" conservative ethos. Participants knew that the group's target—indeed, whether there was a target at all, let alone a hittable one—was elusive, at best. Saturday and Sunday were devoted to broad areas of public policy, but in the aforesaid larger context, with each discussion led by a different participant: *regional and urban problems* (Lyon); *constitutional issues* (Brady); *language and culture* (Gagnon); *Canadian–US relations* (Smith). The opening session, Friday night, focused on *A Possible Conservative Approach to Issues of the 1970s*. Stanfield led the discussion.

The purpose here is not to summarize, much less detail, what was said and by whom. No broad consensus was achieved, in any event. The PC leader mostly listened—intently indeed—so there is nothing to report at length about his interventions. Two points, however, are worth stressing. First, that Stanfield convened an occasion of this kind speaks volumes about the premium he placed on thoughtfulness—actually thinking, or at least trying to think, deeply about problems and issues and policy, in contrast to approaching them, as some politicians do, merely to win votes, get voters off their backs, impress someone, build a record for history, or some other such self-focused motivation or combination thereof. Stanfield was intellectually curious, intellectually restive, intellectually inclined. He *was* an intellectual. Heath Macquarrie, a scholar himself, called Stanfield "a brilliant scholar."[3] That accolade was, perhaps, a stretch, but the leader was brilliant, for sure—and, doubtless, scholarly, if not technically a scholar. Stanfield believed ideas counted. And he thought public people should value ideas and have ideas—or, at least, try to have them. He himself did value ideas, did have ideas, and did try to generate more ideas of his own. The Socratic Method was at the heart and soul of Trent University's own approach to learning. Indeed, the very architecture of the institution reflects this fact: lots of small tutorial rooms, few amphitheatres. The Socratic approach characterized the teaching modus operandi of its founding president, who had arranged for the PC leader to experience it in a distinctly Trent form that weekend.

## Conservatism and Liberalism

The second point that needs to be stressed is as follows. Ralph Heintzman summarized what he considered the tenets of classic conservatism and liberalism. He argued that both "conservative" and "liberal" mean, in modern times, the opposite of what they meant in the late seventeenth or early eighteenth century. In that bygone era, conservatism meant an emphasis on the value of tradition ahead of freedom of thought and speech and on supporting the total interests of society over those of individual members. This orientation, in turn, implied a predisposition towards the state's playing a strong role in advancing the commonweal: the community as a whole. By contrast, liberalism meant strongly supporting individual freedom and civil liberties while insisting on a limited role for government in one's life lest these values be jeopardized. Heintzman's analysis provoked the most heated debate of the weekend. Tom Sloan, the senior Stanfield staff member, could hardly contain his disagreement with what he thought—wrongly, I believe—Heintzman had implied: that the two sets of values were mutually exclusive.

The more conservative members of the PC parliamentary Caucus always believed that Tom Sloan was to the left of the Bolshevik Revolution, if not its architect. In truth, Sloan was simply a progressive Tory. A native of Hamilton, he had spent much of his working life in Quebec City, first as the *Globe and Mail*'s correspondent and then as a columnist with the *Montreal Star*. Sloan had a master's degree in philosophy from the University of Toronto, had studied at the London School of Economics and the Université de Paris, won a Nieman Fellowship to study communications and international politics at Harvard, and ended up being asked to establish a journalism department at Université Laval. Sloan was as much an intellectual as any of the hundreds of policy specialists Symons had recruited to help make Stanfield prime minister.

He was deeply committed to individual freedoms against all forms of arbitrariness. A strong Canadian federalist, he believed that *québécois* nationalism was a constructive force. He wrote prolifically in opposition to Pierre Trudeau's tough, confrontational style of dealing with Quebec. And now he was equally offended by Ralph Heintzman's remarks at the Trent seminar. "As a Tory I will not cede one inch of territory to liberals on the personal freedom and human rights front," he bellowed. "Liberals don't have a lock on those values. Who are you to tell me, Heintzman, I, as a conservative, cannot have them? How dare you!" Tom Sloan's presence on Robert Stanfield's staff, as senior speech writer, showed that the PC leader liked to surround himself with brilliant people who possessed the spunk and abilities to defend their deeply held principles against all challengers—including, as I saw on many occasions, the leader himself.

The verbal fisticuffs—as Heintzman had, no doubt, intended—did provoke a vigorous debate on the popular versus the traditional meanings of the words "conservative" and "liberal," on the extent to which each word retains or rejects its original meaning now, on whether either word has sufficient currency in modern times that it can be applied to contemporary politicians and approaches, and on how much crossover there might be between the corresponding two sets of values. In such circumstances, including Policy Coordinating Committee meetings, Stanfield did not generally preside over arguments like a judge settling a lawsuit, and he played no such mediating role in this case.[4] But he relished the debate, listened to every word with rapt attention, and took discreet notes. It was obvious to me that the PC leader enjoyed the spectacle of his senior staff member's verbally jostling in an arena in which he was challenged on high intellectual ground by someone as mentally and verbally adroit as that staff member himself. Most important of all, in understanding this complex man, Stanfield nodded approvingly when Sloan insisted that modern conservatism must be strongly committed to human freedoms, while *also* embracing the legitimate and necessary role of government in advancing the interests of the community.

Stanfield's own remarks to this gathering, at the opening, had grazed the same theme. It was evident that, despite the similarities in their perspectives, Stanfield and Sloan had not coordinated their thinking or remarks and had not even discussed the matter previously. In fact, Sloan told me at the time that the leader had prepared his own notes for the occasion. Stanfield obviously had given the question at hand a great deal of thought privately, and was eager to give it even more thought, preferably in the presence of others through a Socratic process. Russell Maxwell and Socrates would have been pleased. As for me, I was never again able to view in quite the same way as before the PC leader's policy-development process. Clearly, the rest of us were his Socratic partners. What was not as clear to me at the time, however, was the answer to this question: Who did Stanfield consider the Socrates in that process, himself or Symons? With the leader's strong commitment to such a process, it could have been he. With Symons's undoubted mastery of that same process—gentle prodder of the truth through discussion and debate that he was—maybe the Trent president was Stanfield's Socrates. Perhaps, in 1968, Stanfield had sought, and in Symons found, his new Russell Maxwell. For me at the time, the jury—or, expressed more aptly in this context, "the thinking group"—was still out on that question. But upon intense reflection these past few years, the jury (or group) has reached its verdict: Tom Symons was guilty as sin on all counts, as charged.

We live in an era of mega-mergers when everything from banks to movie studios to telecommunications companies is consolidated at a frenetic speed, in dizzying combinations, with a confusing array of ever-changing names, identities, images, slogans, and logos. With the 2003 Reform/Canadian Alliance/Progressive Conservative Party merger, the Conservative Party of Canada has not escaped this phenomenon. Indeed, since its very founding in the mid-nineteenth century, the party has been the product of different alliances with names as diverse as "Liberal-Conservative"—or, as I prefer here, "Conservative-Liberal"—"Conservative," "Union Government" (in the First World War), "Progressive Conservative," and currently "Conservative" again. The most recent incarnation was executed only a year before the party needed to fight a national election, in 2004. It was much too short a time for the new party to sort out what should be retained from the traditional Conservative Party's philosophical and policy heritage, even if the new guard were inclined to undertake the task—a questionable assumption, at best. In the decade or so since, the party has yet to reflect systematically on its historic values and how those might be usefully applied in contemporary times or whether they could or should be. In the current rebuilding process, following the party's October 2015 federal election defeat, those in charge should ask themselves this question: Wasn't Robert Stanfield onto something when he insisted that the future direction of Canadian Conservatism be based on more than, at either extreme, a narrow catechism or a blinkered focus on what the most recent public opinion poll numbers mean for the election around the corner? At this critical time, the party would be wise to examine Stanfield's example in thinking "writ large."

As leader of a major national political party, Bob Stanfield did not view policy as mere fodder for electioneering, in the mode of John Diefenbaker; still less as red meat to energize the party's electoral base. Rather, the Tory leader thought it important that the party have a broader, more fundamental vision. The man had the intellectual firepower and confidence to challenge himself, and to allow other good minds to challenge him, on a higher plain. For Stanfield, none of this was ethereal. It was all rooted in reality—specifically, the party's need to clarify what, in the event of electoral success, it would actually do with power within a framework much bigger than the dimensions of individual problems or issues at a given time, however major they might seem then. The PC leader had an eye to a future considerably more distant than the likely date of the next election. In focusing in this way, he sought to be guided both by classical thinking and by the party's own history and record, in addition to what made sense by less cerebral markers. Clearly, for Stanfield, party policy had to be planted in soil that ran deeper than just objective facts and raw data and the application of logic and clear thinking to those matters, as important as they are to the research and drafting process. The philosophical dimension of the process was important to him, but not for its own sake. He believed that, as a practical matter in public policy, as in life in general, answers should be considered right only if the right questions are asked.

# Ideology versus Pragmatism

Few enterprises waste more time and effort than trying to draw stark boundaries around a politician's ideology. It is a mug's game. Does anybody know what "conservative" and "liberal" really mean? The Stanfield seminar at Trent University reached no consensus, despite the best efforts of first-rate intellects to reach one. The same words can mean different things to different people. And, as Ralph Heintzman underscored, a meaning can change, even from its original to its opposite, over time. Food experts can't agree on what constitutes "natural" when applied to grocery product ingredients; why would anyone think political theorists could do better with the content of politicians' minds?

Even assuming agreed-upon definitions do exist, a Canadian politician's "conservatism" or "liberalism" (or any other political "ism") traditionally has often depended on the issue or the timing or the vagaries of personalities and events, never simple at the best of times. The same politician might have been a "fiscal conservative" but a "social liberal," or the converse, or some combination thereof, at one time and its opposite the next, even in closely comparable circumstances. In Canada, it typically boils down to whether one's party is in government or in Opposition. What might be considered a Deadly Sin for a politician on one side of the Speaker's throne can soon became a Cardinal Virtue when that person crosses the floor to the other side, only two sword-lengths apart. An election and a political defection have one thing in common: they can change the laws of God pretty darn fast. As the saying goes, "Where you stand is where you sit." Was that any longer true in the Stephen Harper era? It certainly was in my time in Parliament, to say nothing of Stanfield's.

As Canada's environment minister, I managed one of the most contentious issues the Mulroney government faced: establishing a national park reserve in South Moresby (Gwaii Haanas), now part of the country's natural treasury. The park is in Haida Gwaii (formerly known as the Queen Charlotte Islands), off the west coast of British Columbia. As we shall see later, the issue pitted environmentalists and Aboriginal people against loggers and miners, the federal government against the BC government, members of the federal Cabinet against the Caucus, Caucus members against one another—and, it seemed for a while, me against the known world. And we Progressive Conservatives were supposed to have the same political label! Politics, like life in general, is not easily categorized.

My *Canadian Environmental Protection Act* (CEPA) needed final Cabinet approval before a crucial parliamentary vote. The lone holdout was, of all people, the most "leftist" of all members: Energy Minister Marcel Masse, from Quebec. Masse was the closest Cabinet had to a Renaissance Man. He made James Bond look like Austin Powers. Marcel was one of my Cabinet colleagues with whom I conspired most to advance progressive measures—in his case, for Quebec. Masse was obsessed with getting funds from my department to acquire and restore the baronial 1850 Queen Anne Revival residence of Louis-Joseph Papineau in Montebello, halfway between Ottawa and Montreal. Masse idolized Papineau, one of our country's most important nineteenth-century political figures. If I got one dollar for every minute I spent with Marcel concerning that matter alone, on which he had no stronger ally than me, I could have bought myself as grand a residence as Manoir Papineau. Even *in* Quebec, the most "liberal" of all provinces, had Marcel Masse been any farther "left" he would have qualified for a Cuban passport. And yet, I had to lobby and court him hard to approve my "left-wing" package of environmental reforms in, surely, the reddest of all federal Cabinet portfolios—mine. I did get his approval, finally. But I did so only minutes before months of my own, and my department's, hard labour was about to flush down the drain as Cabinet sat prepared to wash itself of the whole matter if consensus between the two battling ministers could not be achieved.

With Cabinet colleagues, sometimes getting down on one's knees and begging, both to the gods above and to the self-declared ones below, works. Pleading ideological kinship does not. If all else fails, alternative strategies do exist. But I refuse to confirm the rumour that, committed as I was, I threatened to scrap, for lack of funding, my department's plans to pursue Marcel's beloved Manoir Papineau. After all, should a minister be held personally responsible when, out of nowhere, a mysterious departmental memo suddenly appears to that effect? In the end, with Marcel's blessing, Cabinet approved, and then Parliament passed, CEPA. Manoir Papineau was formally designated a national historic site, not for its eccentric but fascinating mid-nineteenth-century country-estate architecture, but for its "physical manifestation of the personality of Louis-Joseph Papineau"—Marcel's hero. Soon thereafter, Parks Canada accelerated plans to acquire the property from Canadian Pacific. In 1993, the federal government took full ownership and restored the entire estate. It is now one of the gems in our country's cultural property heritage necklace. The credit belongs primarily to Marcel Masse—not to shared political label or ideological kinship. As for that rumour....

One can never be sure where a politician's heart, and vote, might land. It is often in the most unexpected of places, as was the case with Marcel Masse on CEPA. A politician's upbringing, education, religion, moral values, vested interests, back-home political realities, political and personal insecurities, hidden agendas, peer pressure, vendettas, or (too rarely) personal vision and courage—all such factors can come into play. A complex combination of influences shapes a politician's decision, consciously or subconsciously—typically both. Under our system of responsible government, party discipline, enforced by a whip, is a major factor. So also is the principle of collective ministerial responsibility, in the case of Cabinet members. Sometimes, though, it just comes down to how the politician's spouse or son or daughter felt about the issue over breakfast. Or a politician decides based on nothing more complex than which side of the bed he or she got up on that morning.

At a policy meeting, PC Research Office director Geoffrey Molyneux, who respected Robert Stanfield, once told me privately how strange he thought it was that the PC leader scarcely ever asked individual staff members about anything personal, whether their health or family well-being or even just, on a Monday, what they had done over the previous weekend. Brian Mulroney, a decade later, was a far different kind of politician: a master of such small talk and minor but important symbolic gestures. In neither Mulroney's case nor Stanfield's, though, does any of this reflect on his character, only on his personality. Stanfield and Mulroney were fundamentally dissimilar individuals, however much they shared a commitment to public service through the same political party. To slap a political label on either of them, let alone one that applied to both, other than Progressive Conservative—and, arguably, both "progressive" and "conservative"—would be misleading at best, and at worst dead wrong.

## Stanfield and Symons's "Ideology"

I thus make no effort to label the political philosophy or ideological bent of Robert Stanfield or Tom Symons, beyond what I have already done, except for the following. Both were public-spirited men unmotivated by personal gain in any narrow sense. They had already been blessed (in Stanfield's case, at birth) with all the creature comforts and social status either of them felt they needed in life. With rare exceptions, neither was absolutist or categorical about any matter, political or otherwise.

Each did have a set of principles, not necessarily identical to the other man's. Essentially, "what worked" in the real world of the "here and now" was more important to them than "how would this be judged?" in the Hereafter. The Stanfield and Symons families shared a religion: Anglicanism. And both men were spiritual, each in his own way, but not particularly religious—Symons less so than Stanfield, for sure. They were practical men doing their life's work in the best way they knew how to achieve goals or solve problems, whether chosen or thrust upon them. For neither man was there a rule book—sectarian or secular—against which every decision had to be tested. What is the problem? What are the objective facts? What are the options? Would this approach work? Who would be affected, for good or ill, and how? Is there a better solution? No? Then, let's do it. On to the next problem. Although no doubt oversimplified, the dynamic I have described is much closer to the truth than the belief that either man would ever have consciously asked himself, "Is this conservative enough?" before choosing a solution. Nor would he have done so subconsciously, either. Both were too deliberate, too strategic, and too self-aware when making decisions for Freud to have prevailed over Descartes. Charles McMillan has been famously quoted as saying, over a hotel room-service breakfast: "You know, [Brian Mulroney] is about as ideological as that coffee pot."[5] I participated for uncountable hours in policy meetings with Stanfield and Symons as they laboured over policy drafts or detailed thoughts for drafts about to be written. From this vantage, I am certain that neither man would have taken great exception, or offence, if someone were to have said he, too, was as ideological as a coffee pot.

Stanfield was much more interested in economic than social questions, Symons the converse, though each had his own hobby horse in the other's corral. Stanfield, for example, saw the Guaranteed Minimum Income proposal as a social issue as much as an economic one. For his part, Symons viewed, say, the Aboriginal issue from an economic perspective as much as from a social one. What is an economic issue or a social issue and not the other, anyway? Not a single environmental issue I had to address as environment minister (to wit: South Moresby) was without a profound economic dimension, even though my portfolio was considered a social field and, accordingly, was slotted into the Social Affairs Committee of Cabinet. The same could be said, in converse, of the "economic" issues I dealt with, stemming from colleagues' "economic" portfolios, which, true to formula, were slotted into Cabinet's Economics and Regional Development Committee. In government, as in partisan politics, no well-defined boundaries exist naturally, only huge messes that have to be sliced and diced to render them more manageable. Most often, the names given to the slices are arbitrary, even capricious. Just as life is not fair, it is not simple, either. Categories were created by the gods so that mortals would find life less confusing, and so that philosophers and political scientists hell-bent on giving those categories labels would have something to do with their time. The gods did a fine job, because the labellers have been busy ever since. Individuals like Stanfield and Symons typically duck and bob and weave to thwart the name-stickers as they bolt their way towards them, reams of labels held high in hand. Sir John A. Macdonald, no mean ducker himself, founded a nation without the need to be labelled—except as a drunk. And that label did not make his creation one drop of gin less grand. He once said voters preferred him drunk to *Globe* editor George Brown sober. Voters have a way of discounting labels.

When it came time to release the first batch of policy papers for the PC Party's 1971 Annual Meeting, the Policy Coordinating Committee considered giving the package a catchy title—or bumper sticker, if you will. At one point, "Compassionate

Conservatism," of all things, was bandied about as the label of choice, three decades before George W. Bush used the exact same phrase as his bumper-sticker slogan against Al Gore in the 2000 US presidential election. Unlike Bush, however, Stanfield vetoed the slogan because he thought "compassionate" reeked of condescension. To him, it implied superiors extending pity to inferiors, and he did not see either himself or the unfortunate that way. The disadvantaged, he argued, deserved more than sentiment. They needed help. Accordingly, he dismissed the recommendation virtually out of hand, ordered the policies released without a label, and said he did not want to hear any more about the subject. Nor did he.

# "Red Tory" and Other Labels

It is difficult to discuss a politician or administration without a hold on one handle or another, and so one should not discard "conservative" and "liberal" altogether. In context, especially at the extremes, they have their value as political markers, as do some other such terms. Distinguished political scientist Gad Horowitz of the University of Toronto is credited with coining the term "Red Tory" in a groundbreaking application of Louis Hartz's "fragment theory" to Canadian political culture and ideological development. In a pioneering essay, "Conservatism, Liberalism and Socialism in Canada: An Interpretation,"[6] Horowitz advanced the idea that, in the context of both Europe and Canada (but *not* the United States), ideology is not a straight line or linear progression, such that "left" (socialist) and "right" (Tory) are at polar extremes. Rather, ideology is more like a circle, with "left" and "right" joined at the ends, around the circle, in how they see, essentially in the same way, the fundamental role of government: acceptance of state enterprises, the welfare state, and other public institutions as instruments to advance the commonweal and express national character. Horowitz could have been thinking of Robert Stanfield and Tom Symons. This is, at its root, how both men viewed the role of the state and the function of public policy that expresses it.

For Stanfield, as for Symons, "Red Tory" would have done the trick, though the former never applied it to himself within my earshot. "Progressive" would have been more both men's cup of tea or, in Charley McMillan's words, "coffee pot." "Reformer" would have done just fine with them, too, for they were both progressive reformers, above all else. Stanfield demonstrated that as premier of Nova Scotia. His administration was not only reformist; it was, indeed, pioneering. In industrial development, the province led the country in new techniques and structures, most notably the Nova Scotia Industrial Development Corporation. Prince Edward Island premier Walter R. Shaw (1959–66), for example, modelled his government's aggressive strategy for promoting small-scale industry largely on Nova Scotia's innovations. (Food processing, in particular, was Shaw's priority.) Presaging the policy-development approach Robert Stanfield was to take with Tom Symons and the PC Party at the national level, Premier Stanfield crafted Nova Scotia's Industrial Development Corporation on ideas generated by some five hundred specialists the premier and his administration had consulted outside government, ranging from fishermen and farmers to mining executives and university scientists. As Geoffrey Stevens puts it, "Stanfield bought to the task [of reforming the industrial base of the province] hard work in overcoming any obstacle, and the willingness of a reformer to seek out ways of attacking old problems."

In education, Stevens says, "[Stanfield] did more...in the province than any leader since Sir Charles Tupper introduced free schooling before Confederation." The biographer quotes Stanfield's agriculture minister, Ed Haliburton, to summarize the premier's overall approach to issues: "Stanfield is not doctrinaire, not dogmatic; his ideas are not rooted in the past."[7] Hugh Segal has described Robert Stanfield as a "man of ideas and reflection," but of "equilibrium," not of "narrow ideology of the right or left."[8] This is the same Stanfield who, with Symons, transformed the policies and public image of the political party he inherited from John Diefenbaker.

Premier Stanfield did not apply dogma or ideology to the task of governing Nova Scotia, let alone what could be described as "conservatism" in the contemporary meaning of the word. He had no such mindset. Indeed, as Stevens notes, following hours of interviews with him, Stanfield did not know if he was even a large-"C" Conservative, let alone a small-"c" conservative, despite the rich family tradition in politics—his brother Frank, for example, had been a federal Tory MP—until well into adulthood.[9] He had flirted with socialism while an undergraduate at Dalhousie until finally, over the years, settling into a political philosophy no more complex, and therefore needing no more complex a label, than "Common Sense": what is the job at hand, and what must we do to get it done? That is not to say Robert Stanfield ignored opportunities to fit his "common sense" approach into a broader vision, as we saw at the beginning of this chapter. Stanfield asked Symons to organize the Trent University seminar for that very purpose. But it was not in his nature to allow himself to be blinded or limited by absolutist values. Put simply, he was not a fundamentalist, but, rather, a principled pragmatist who weighed all the options before deciding to act.

## Stanfield and Symons's Conservatism

Hugh Segal, former president of the Institute for Research on Public Policy, a Montreal-based think tank, a senator from 2005 to 2013, and now head of the University of Toronto's Massey College, was an aide to Robert Stanfield in the early 1970s, a two-time federal Tory candidate (1972, 1974), and (briefly) Brian Mulroney's chief of staff, a position he also held earlier with Tory premier Bill Davis of Ontario. In his book *The Right Balance*, the self-styled Red Tory stresses that Canadian conservatism is indigenous, rooted in our own history, and distinct from the US variety. Theirs, he says, reflects "an American economic and social system that is very much about competition, the primacy of accumulating wealth and...a commitment to outcomes—economic, social and political."[10] Segal states that Canadian conservatism, by contrast, takes a more "communitarian"—that is, community-oriented—route, a fusion of our French and British heritages. "Together, these two streams moulded the foundations of the Tory brand in Canada." To Segal, that fusion is about balance: a system of political beliefs "in which fairness and compassion are not threatening to enterprise, profit, growth or freedom." He argues "[f]airness and compassion are, in fact, the very foundations of a society within which the reality of a durable freedom can rest and prosper. That is a central ingredient of the right balance within the Tory mainstream and not...a quaint Red Tory indulgence."[11]

This priority given to community over individual ambition ("communitarianism"), in a proper balance, goes to the heart of Robert Stanfield's approach to governance and public policy. He expressed it in his first address as a candidate at the

1967 leadership convention. As we shall see, the address resonated so powerfully with delegates that it shot him, from far behind, to the top of the race and helped him win the leadership. Segal writes that a Tory argues "that the whole is greater than the sum of the parts, providing that the parts are not diminished or excluded from the identity that defines the greater whole."[12] This statement captures the essence of Stanfield's vision. The vision shaped his record as premier of Nova Scotia and guided his approach to policy-making as national PC leader. Segal associates the politics of Sir John A. Macdonald with a "sense of democratic noblesse oblige."[13] The penniless son of a failed and impoverished merchant/shopkeeper/miller, Macdonald was not n aristocrat, but in his mind much had been given to him, so a great deal was expected. Again, it is a value system many of us Maritimers associate with Bob Stanfield, who was a provincial aristocrat. Segal attributes, for example, Stanfield's embrace of Quebec as a *nation* and of Canada as *deux nations* to the Tory leader's fundamental view of Canada as a "framework of respect for a people [as a] constituent foundation of the make-up of Canada itself" in the tradition of Macdonald. The very essence of a distinctly Canadian approach to "communitarian conservatism," he says, is about "common interest conservatism" versus "special interest conservatism."[14] Segal notes that "Stanfield's conservatism was characterized by its equilibrium, which is far more important than narrow ideology of the right or the left," and that he "tolerated no excessiveness in either government or ideology."[15]

Everything Hugh Segal says about Robert Stanfield accords with what I observed close-up in the innumerable hours I spent in the leader's company while working with him on party policy. As Segal has stressed, Stanfield was not so ideologically hidebound, or so restricted in any other way, that he denied himself maximum freedom to act in a thoughtful, practical, goal-oriented manner characteristic of the man he was. As individuals, Robert Stanfield and Sir John A. Macdonald could hardly have been more different—a sober aristocrat from the Maritimes versus a hard-drinking plebeian from Upper Canada. How ironic, then, that these two men shared the same personal characteristic that most strongly influenced the way each performed in the domain for which they both made their mark: politics and public service. That distinguishing characteristic was pragmatism. As Segal said of Macdonald, just as the former senator said of Stanfield in almost identical words, he "was a man unrestricted by left or right, even as they were defined in his day."[16] How many Conservative politicians in Canada today, federal or provincial, share this characteristic with two of their greatest former leaders? Does anyone in his or her right mind believe that, as prime minister, Stephen Harper did? Or that most—or even any—of his Cabinet ministers did, either? If the answers are no, was embracing absolutist ideology and eschewing political pragmatism the reason greatness eluded all the Harperites, including their cult leader, both as individuals and as a government? It is hard to believe otherwise.

Robert Stanfield's support for Quebec, at the core of his policy thinking, was mostly rooted in practicality, not federal-provincial ideology, in contrast to the mindset Pierre Trudeau brought to Canadian federalism. Quebec was then one of Canada's five "have-not" provinces, along with the four Atlantic provinces. Moreover, Quebec was contiguous with Atlantic Canada and, indeed, the region's only proximate Canadian neighbour. As such, Quebec's economic interests were overwhelmingly congruent with those of Stanfield's own province and region. Federal regional-development and equalization programs were the fiscal lifeblood of all five of these provinces at the time. In that sense, disadvantaged Quebec had a closer kinship with Stanfield's impoverished region than with wealthy Ontario, then the milk cow of Confederation, even though the two behemoths were "central Canada's" regional sisters. The PC leader believed Canada could not be strong and united if major economic disparities existed among the country's regions and provinces, especially when language and culture were thrown into the mix. There needed to be, in Segal's word, "balance." Stanfield lacked a distinct ideology, still less one easily labelled. But on the fundamental nature and direction of the country—such as, notably, Quebec's relationship with the rest of Canada—his thoughts were unfailingly consistent over the years. As a mature man, he applied those thoughts to political action and decision-making within a mostly unchangeable, cohesive, and coherently expressed intellectual framework. Within it, moderation and balance were the distinguishing features. His intellectual guideposts did not, together, constitute an ideology, but were a practical substitute for it. His view of Quebec's place in Confederation remained constant from the time the *deux nations* controversy erupted in the 1960s to his support and public championing of the Meech Lake Accord decades later, long after retiring as Conservative leader. Just as a non-ideologue can be *thoughtful*, so also can an ideologue be *thoughtless*. Stanfield was thoughtful in both senses of the word—on issues concerning French Canada and Quebec most of all.

# Tory Kindred Spirits

In Tom Symons, Robert Stanfield found a kindred spirit—a man with passionate views, to be sure, but one who, like him, was a prisoner of neither ideology nor dogma. As with Stanfield, Symons was a problem-solver, not an ideologue. The challenge they faced, as policy partners, was how to restore the PC Party's soul. In all the years I worked as a junior partner with Symons on policy, we did not once discuss party dogma. We frequently did discuss what it meant to be a Tory in the best traditions of the party—the party of Sir John A. Macdonald and Georges-Étienne Cartier, and now, for Symons, of Robert Stanfield. To him, Stanfield embodied those best traditions. The Trent University president was eager to ensure it would continue to be the party of Macdonald and Cartier and Stanfield—and not of those who would leg-iron it to the heavy ball on its darkest side. Symons's anger, usually kept in a locked box, had special fury for the Diefenbakers and the Jack Horners when they used labels such as "true Conservative" or "Red Tory" or "socialist PC," not as tools to inform, but as weapons to incite. To Symons, their real purpose was often just to consolidate their own standing in the party or across the land, not to advance the public interest. And they seemed willing to act in this reckless way even at the risk of destroying the party that Sir John A. had crafted so magnificently with values that were, in the context at hand, exactly the opposite of theirs. For Symons, Stanfield was the gold standard for political integrity and public virtue, values Symons himself embodied. In that sense, Symons was, for the lack of any other way of saying it, a "Stanfield Conservative." Indeed, it was the label he always used to describe himself. That is all the labelling he wanted, all he felt he needed. It's what he calls himself still: "A Stanfield Tory." It sounds just about right. In the same spirit, Symons, like Stanfield, refused to reject outright individuals of other political stripes, no matter what labels they applied to themselves, provided, as the Trent president put it, "their heart is in the right place."

Just as Tom Symons never discussed political dogma with me, he also never told me, nor did I ever ask him, how he voted. But knowing the man as well as I do, I am sure he cast ballots for Liberals and New Democrats he admired, though not likely federally (and, therefore, against Stanfield) in the 1968–74 period. Among those he supported, with votes or money, certainly would have been Ontario MPP Walter Pitman, who represented the NDP in Peterborough. Pitman was the kind of politician in the other camp Symons respected. The Trent president would have seen such a person as a "Stanfield Man"—a term he often used—whether or not he thought that individual ever actually supported Stanfield or likely ever would. To Symons, it was the individual's character and values that counted, not how he or she voted or the party to which the person belonged. Without question, Symons did not vote for, or support in any way, certain Conservative Party politicians whose character or positions he found odious. (He was privately outspoken with me about such people, individually naming them with contempt.) Many Roman Catholics—I include myself—select from their faith what serves a spiritual need, while rejecting official Church dogma that conflicts with deep-seated personal beliefs. In my own case, against Church doctrine I support, for example, a woman's right to choose to terminate a pregnancy, in consultation with her doctor. I also believe in marriage equality for the LGBT community. In an analogous way, during my most active period working with him, Symons chose from the Progressive Conservative Party the candidates and policies he felt he could support in the interests of the broader community while rejecting those he disrespected. Symons had earned the right to be selective. When, over many years, a man has paid the amount of tithes he did to the institution, it is not likely many ushers at the front door would deny him a pew.

Whether Stanfield or Symons was the more liberal or conservative, the more progressive or traditional, the more modern or hidebound—all that sort of political metaphysics makes for an interesting parlour game on a cold winter's night, but it does nothing to keep flames on the hearth. Stanfield was more a Conservative by accident—of birth, of family, of geography, of timing, of opportunity—than Symons. The Trent president was more a Conservative "by design." He might have arrived there by family heritage and other such influences—I'm not certain. But I do know he stayed a Conservative, to the extent he did, which was not always, because he felt most at home in that party. "Progressive," "reformer," "Red Tory," on the one hand; "Conservative" or "conservative," "traditionalist," even "romantic," on the other: each of these verbal constructs applied to him except when it did not. "Stanfield Tory" is the one label that he thought always applied. And it still fits him like a latex glove on a surgeon's hand.

Throughout my time with Stanfield and Symons together (the summer of 1969 to the leader's retirement in 1976), the two men did not argue once on a substantive issue. Nor, to my knowledge, did they do so on a lesser one, either. While Tom Symons was chairman, the Ontario Human Rights Commission published a landmark report, *Life Together,* under his direction.[17] The report recommended a broad range of reforms, including adding "sexual orientation" to the protected grounds— religion, nationality, place of national origin, colour, race, and so on—on which discrimination was prohibited by law. I was an executive officer of the commission when the report was prepared, and I helped write it. I was in a position to know, therefore, how instrumental Symons was in the controversial decision to add sexual orientation to the other protected grounds. He also wrote much of the report himself. Sometimes, but not always, he used drafts that I (or others) had prepared for him. For his part, Stanfield supported much of Pierre Trudeau's progressive legislation, including the

*Official Languages Act*, even as some in his Caucus did not support him in the relevant parliamentary votes. In 1967–68, while justice minister, Trudeau introduced to Parliament a courageous but highly controversial package of Criminal Code reforms on everything from abortion and contraception to gambling to gun control to drunk driving. Among the amendments was one to decriminalize homosexuality. It was the only reform in the total package that Stanfield voted against. This example aside, one would be hard pressed to see much light between Stanfield and Symons on issues. On gay rights, the sun was on Symons's side of the tree, the shade on Stanfield's, but the Tory leader had more than a fair share of sunshine on his Criminal Code votes as a whole. Sometimes, even on a sunny day, a leader, too, can get up on the wrong side of the bed.

# THE COURT
# AND KEEPER OF
# THE KEYS

The Progressive Conservative Party's policy mix was to get much richer at the party's 1971 Annual Meeting in the first week of December. Towards the end of 1970, Robert Stanfield released a formal statement in which he described the progress of the party's policy process as the New Year approached: "We are well along the path towards formulating a comprehensive and integrated policy program to present to the Canadian people when it next chooses a government. That has been our task this year, and *it will continue to be our major challenge in the year to come.*"[1] The meeting would challenge Tom Symons's policy operation as never before.

For the PC Party, the formal constitutional term "Annual Meeting" is a misnomer. In the Stanfield era, "Annual Meetings" were not always held even biennially. After the new leader was elected in September 1967, it would be two years before the party held its first one, in March 1969. And that meeting followed a three-year period when none was held at all. So the 1971 Annual Meeting was a big deal. After it, another one would not be held until 1974, Stanfield's last, rendering the trend closer to triennial than annual in the 1960s and 1970s.

The Annual Meeting this time was to be, if not the "Annual" Meeting to end all Annual Meetings, then at least one that would end any foolish suggestion that Stanfield and Symons did not mean business on the policy front. It was an occasion, as all such meetings are, for the party to conduct the prosaic affairs that make any big institution, political or otherwise, work: election of officers; approval of budgets; constitutional amendments; reports of committees; speeches from senior officers, including the head; regional caucuses; meetings of this, that, or another subgroup; receptions, parties, and other celebrations. A political party's general meeting can be the most tiresome gathering of *Homo sapiens* since a candidate for executive office last practised a nomination speech before a mirror alone. When, as rarely happens, there is genuine excitement at an Annual Meeting, the leader can be sure it's because someone is up to no good.

At the 1971 Annual Meeting, Stanfield was not looking for excitement. If, in life, no news is good news, in politics no excitement is no news. And Stanfield was prepared to have "no news" the media's verdict as it covered the meeting. While he prepared for the coming federal election, the leader was not looking for fireworks, least of all with him in the midst of the flare. Around the time of the previous Annual Meeting, in 1969, Stanfield had survived, but barely, a palace revolt on a parliamentary vote. It concerned the *Official Languages Act,* on which seventeen Diefenbaker Caucus rebels, including the embittered former leader himself, perversely voted against not only the legislation, but, in effect, the new leader. Stanfield had been eager to project a unified and progressive front on the issue. The Diefenbaker insurgents ensured he did not get it. At the 1971 national gathering, Stanfield was decidedly not eager to have another cabal within the palace throwing china at its principal occupant: himself. The meeting presented Stanfield with an especially heavy challenge, for it was the PC leader himself who had insisted the occasion be largely about policy. Like china, policy is a cupboard's content a leader does not want hurled at him as he mingles among his most militant partisans. In this case, the venue was the ballroom of Ottawa's Château Laurier Hotel. Tom Symons's job included ensuring that participants did not hurl plates at Stanfield, or missed the target if they did.

The policy deliberations focused on the individual resolutions prepared by National Headquarters based on the work of the Policy Coordinating Committee (PCC) over many months. Headquarters had mailed to each delegate, beforehand, a preliminary policy questionnaire, vetted by the PCC. It asked delegates to rate the relative importance they attached to a range of issues from the environment to urban affairs to the economy to federal-provincial relations to taxation to income-support programs to foreign affairs to many others. Recipients were asked such questions as: "Should the federal government establish a Ministry of Housing?" and "Should the federal government be involved in urban affairs at all?" Some months earlier (May 8–9, 1970), the party had held a pilot project conference in Toronto on these kinds of urban issues, which the party needed to address if it were to have any realistic hope of breaking into the big cities, a strategy central to making inroads against the Liberals and NDP in the coming election. The questionnaire Headquarters subsequently sent out to delegates at the Annual Meeting was based partly on the concerns raised, and the consensus reached, at that Toronto conference. Questionnaire items across the board were based on policy work done by others within, or for, the party at the grassroots level. In certain categories, such as defence, the questionnaire asked party members to rank priorities numerically from among a range of specific options. The resolutions to be voted on at the Annual Meeting, in turn, paralleled the questions mailed out earlier.

By August 1970, Geoffrey Molyneux had replaced Dr. E. R. Black as director of the PC Research Office. British-born Molyneux, who spoke with a proper, but man-of-the-people, English accent, was a bright, down-to-earth former journalist from British Columbia. The scruffily bearded and often dishevelled Molyneux had been recommended for the post by Tom Symons. His varied career as a journalist included stints on the news desk of the *Daily Express* and the *Evening Standard* in London. In Vancouver, Molyneaux had worked for the *Sun* and the *Province*. With a Woodrow Wilson fellowship, he then completed a master's degree in English at the University of Toronto. Molyneux proceeded to teach at Simon Fraser University, where he became Assistant Dean of Arts. He was a dean at Centennial College in Scarborough, Ontario, when recruited as PC Research Office director. Geoffrey Molyneux transformed how the Research Office operated throughout the rest of Robert Stanfield's leadership and for long afterwards. I both admired and liked him, as did most people familiar with his work for the party—not least Tom Symons. Molyneux's greatest strength was an ability to balance the various competing policy orientations within the PC Caucus and other quarters of the party. That ability not only prevented the Research Office from becoming a tool of any one ideological faction; it also advanced the cause of producing cohesive party policy generally acceptable to everybody. Apart from writing elegantly, the man had a sensitive political nose more characteristic of a politician than a functionary. To see Tom Symons sitting near Geoffrey Molyneux at a PCC meeting—the former the quintessence of Old-World style and comportment; the latter the stereotypical hard-nosed "tell it like it is" beat reporter that he had once been—was to appreciate how big a tent the PC Party had become in such policy conclaves under Robert Stanfield's leadership.

Under Molyneux's direction, research staff prepared so-called *Blue Papers*, a play on the party's official colour and on the term "White Papers" traditionally used by the federal government for policies it periodically releases for public discussion as trial balloons, not established public policy. The *Blue Papers* dealt with such issues as taxation, pollution, federal-provincial relations, and more specialized issues—for example, agriculture in eastern Canada. A party policy conference in Quebec City (May 21–23, 1971) was one of many regional meetings held to discuss policy, often using the *Blue Papers* as a point of departure. Regional policy meetings were also held in Peterborough, Toronto, and Calgary, among other places. Athenian democracy was running amok in the Tory party! It was a far cry from when party policy constituted what John Diefenbaker decreed it was. The Stanfield-Symons counter-revolution was almost as much about process as about policy per se. But the two were inextricably linked: a "form follows function" sort of thing.

Diefenbaker continued to retain the affections and support of many Canadians, not only in the party but among voters at large as well. This was especially the case in western and Atlantic Canada, mostly in rural areas and small towns. It's amazing, though, how strong an appeal the old man had for many different types of Canadians, not all of them hidebound traditionalists. My father thought the sun rose and set on John Diefenbaker. He admired the former PC leader's championing of civil rights and the "little guy." A child of the Great Depression, Dad saw in Diefenbaker a kindred spirit in concern for the disadvantaged. The fact this westerner attached so much importance to issues of particular concern to Atlantic Canada— narrowing regional disparities, in particular—further endeared the man to my father. Dief remained a hero for Dad until the latter died. Coincidentally, John Diefenbaker himself died in 1979 on my father's birthday, August 16. Because of Diefenbaker's residual (even if dwindling) following, the old man's capacity for mischief could not be ignored by his successor. Diefenbaker loyalists, especially in Caucus, were no less menacing for being in the minority. As much to humiliate Stanfield as to try to get the party not to change its old ways—but that, too—a PC Party western Canada regional conference held in Saskatoon in late August rejected, in some instances outright, policy positions proposed by the national party even just for discussion. It was not exactly a palace revolt, more like plate-throwing among kitchen staff. The PC leader's urging Tories not to fight with one another so the party could present a united policy front was like a temperance crusader demanding that an Irish pub close early lest anyone get drunk—ain't gonna happen. This particular skirmish presaged much more serious trouble for the party, not so much during the rest of Stanfield's leadership as farther down the road.

# Genesis of the Reform Party

The reader might be sensing a pattern in the opposition demonstrated by some western Canadian elements of the PC Party towards Robert Stanfield himself and against the progressive direction in which he and Tom Symons were attempting to lead the party.

At the time, no one could have predicted where this phenomenon would eventually lead. But, in retrospect, it is clear that spores were being germinated in the late 1960s and early 1970s by these types of Conservative Party members for what would sprout, in the 1990s, as the Reform Party. At the outset, the embryonic organism was as much an ideological cause as a traditional political party in the making. The early development of Reform had antecedents in western Canada–based protest movements in the 1920s and 1930s. One such movement was the Progressives, who rose to prominence after the First World War. This movement was rooted in widespread agrarian discontent with the policies of both major national political parties of the era. The Progressive Conservative Party gained the first half of its dual name, in 1942, from the Progressive Party that had stemmed from the Progressive movement. The Progressive Party was tied to provincial United Farmers parties in several provinces, not just in the West but also in Ontario. The Progressive Party emerged from the refusal by the First World War Union coalition government, headed by the Conservative prime minister Robert Borden, to change a tariff structure that farmers blamed for devastating agriculture in large parts of the country. To protest the tariffs and demonstrate their unhappiness with the government's policies more generally, the farmers became increasingly radicalized. They organized themselves, entered politics, drew heavily from the ranks of established political parties, and soon controlled provincial governments in Ontario, Alberta, and Manitoba. Those governments were all loosely aligned with labour and socialist groups. In 1921, the federal Progressive Party won sixty-four seats west of Quebec (but only one in the Maritimes). The formation of the Reform Party in the late 1980s from bits and pieces of more traditional political parties—both national and provincial—had clear precedents in the way the earlier protest parties emerged from, and opposed, the established order. Even the number of federal parliamentary seats won by the Progressive and Reform Parties, in completely different eras, was approximately the same.

The Reform/Canadian Alliance Party from 1987 to 2003—which, in turn, gave rise to the current Conservative Party—would be formed from two main aggregates. The first group was traditional *federal* Tory supporters whose conservative ideology I have mentioned here in the context of the PC Party's 1971 Annual Meeting. These partisans supported the kinds of stands John Diefenbaker had taken on the issues, particularly as Opposition leader after the defeat of his government in 1963. Most of them lived in western Canada and (in smaller numbers at first) in rural and small-town Ontario. The second aggregate that gave birth to the Reform/Canadian Alliance Party consisted of political activists of the same general ideological ilk as those in the first category. But they had not been involved primarily, or in some cases at all, in any federal party, including the Progressive Conservative Party. Many in this second category were *provincial* Social Credit members or voters, primarily in Alberta and British Columbia. In these two provinces, Social Credit had held power for decades under, respectively, premiers Ernest Manning and W. A. C. ("Wacky") Bennett, the second- and sixth-longest-serving premiers in Canadian history. So, we're talking about a long and well-established base of both political professionals and politically experienced rank-and-file workers and sympathizers at the provincial level. As such, they were eminently capable of helping to launch a new federal political party based on shared values. Their values were mostly negative. They opposed both specific policies of the kind Robert Stanfield had supported two decades earlier (principally bilingualism) and the perceived ideological direction that underpinned those policies—in a word, "leftist." It would oversimplify things to say that the

Reform/Canadian Alliance Party was formed to protest, and provide an alternative to, what its founders considered the socialist character of the three major national political parties at the time (Progressive Conservative, Liberal, and NDP). But that interpretation would not be far off the mark.

It would also be generally accurate to attribute the rise of this new protest party to the widespread belief in certain parts of the country, especially the West, that federal policies continually favoured Quebec at the expense of those other parts. Western resentment and alienation based on that factor climaxed when, in 1986, the Mulroney government awarded the country's rich CF-18 fighter-plane maintenance contract to Quebec-based Bombardier, rather than to Winnipeg's Bristol Aerospace, whose bid was both cheaper and stronger. (As a member of Cabinet at the time, I well remember the regional politics that dominated the issue.) Indeed, the Reform Party was launched the next year. Large swaths of western Canada saw the Mulroney government's "Meech Lake" package of constitutional reforms, around this very time, in the same light: as favouritism to Quebec. Most Canadians who bolted to the Reform/ Canadian Alliance Party in this spirit, particularly in the West, believed that Brian Mulroney, a Quebecer, embodied everything that was wrong with the government and political party systems. But, on similar grounds, many traditional Progressive Conservative partisans of this sort had also viewed with suspicion the two Red Tory leaders who preceded Mulroney: Robert Stanfield and Joe Clark, though the latter was an Albertan. In mindset and specific policies, Stanfield and Clark, too, were thought to have been in Quebec's pocket but westerners' pocketbook. No one such factor alone explains the Reform/Canadian Alliance Party's rocket rise and the earthquake with which it would shake the country's political landscape upon takeoff. Each factor reinforced the others to foster a growing belief among voters of a certain type that, for years and years, the country's power wielders had been failing them and their part of the country.

The Reform/Canadian Alliance Party, therefore, did not just burst onto the political scene like mushrooms sprouting across verdant grass on a warm day after a spring rain. The "mushrooms" had been thriving in the meadow for many seasons. It's just that no one had previously noticed the little fungi, picked them, gathered them together, placed them in one big basket, given them a spiffy new name, and taken them to market. Now, someone was beginning to do so. And he was one of the best mushroom harvesters to emerge from western Canada in a long time. Indeed, he was the best since his father exploited fundamentalist religion and discontent with traditional political parties in his province to construct one of the longest-surviving political dynasties in the history of Canada. That mushroom harvester was Preston Manning, spawn of the self-same Social Credit premier Ernest Manning of Alberta mentioned above. The son revealed to the type of westerners enamoured of his father's brand of conservative politics that the fungi he was collecting in the meadow were magic mushrooms. And, before long, the little edibles became the rage.

In ten years—the time it typically takes to begin university and complete a doctoral degree—the Reform Party of Canada shot from zero seats in the Canadian House of Commons to forming (in 1997) the Official Opposition. It took the New Democratic Party (founded in 1961) a half-century to achieve that status (in 2011). Two factors help explain the Reform/Canadian Alliance Party's rapid-fire electoral success. First, a broad swath of the *electorate* already had an appetite for what the party was offering: the "mushrooms." As with the political professionals and partisan activists profiled above, these mainstreet voters were typically very conservative (in the contemporary sense of the word). And they, too, resided in western Canada, outside major cities in Ontario, and, to a much lesser extent, in Atlantic Canada. Second, there was not only the skilled and motivated professional political class required to harvest the "crop," but also the *political infrastructure* needed for this purpose. It did not have to be built from the ground up. The professionals at the top and experienced activists on the ground just had to integrate different federal and provincial political organizations across the country. In building the new federal party, western Canadian Social Credit partisans were joined by, for example, supporters of Alberta PC premier Ralph Klein (1992–2006) and Ontario PC premier Mike Harris (1995–2002). Both Klein and Harris were "neoconservatives"—or, more accurately, "neoliberals," in the classical sense. (The latter term is generally favoured nowadays by political scientists.) These two premiers championed the very kinds of policies associated with the Reform/Canadian Alliance Party and, later, the Conservative government of Stephen Harper: fiscal restraint, slashing taxes, hostility to state-funded social programs, privatization of major government assets, deregulation, and reliance on the private market for job growth. The Harris and Klein administrations were hostile to government intervention in society, except in a few areas—notably law enforcement and fostering "family values." All such people had a strong pro-market, anti-statist governing ethos. They believed the spoils of the free enterprise system should go overwhelmingly to the fittest competitors—not to "freeloaders," as they tended to perceive recipients of public assistance. These American-style right-wing ideologues—and, for sure, that's what they were—demonstrated a take-responsibility-for-your-own-welfare moralistic mindset towards the individual citizen. They did not spare even the struggling poor, including full-time, low-paid workers (the "working poor"), who were of prime concern to Robert Stanfield.

The shift by Ralph Klein away from Peter Lougheed's modernizing technocratic but humane governing approach in Alberta, and by Mike Harris away from the Drew/Frost/Robarts/Davis centrist, or Red Tory, modus operandi in Ontario, is all of a piece with the formation of the new Conservative Party in 2003. Indeed, in 2002, after retiring from provincial politics, Harris joined the Fraser Institute, a US-type right-wing/libertarian think tank. As a "senior fellow," he became involved with followers of Preston Manning both federally and provincially, particularly in Alberta. His so-called Common Sense Revolution in Ontario had been virtually indistinguishable from the agenda of Ralph Klein's government. Klein's agenda included militant opposition to the Kyoto Protocol on climate change and almost maniacal resistance to same-sex marriage. The pre-eminent characteristic shared by the architects and supporters of the post-2003 Conservative Party was a free-market-centred individualism—again, essentially, classic liberalism. It contrasts with traditional Canadian Toryism, or classic conservatism, with the latter's emphasis on the "whole," rather than the former's on the "parts." Individualism replaced communitarianism, a you're-on-your-own self-reliance ethic replaced a belief in state or collectivist activism, and a conservative party in the US Republican mould replaced a "progressive conservative" party in the Canadian/British Tory tradition. Put simply, fidelity to governance no longer characterized the Canadian Conservative Party's prevailing ethos. Reverence for this ethos became heretical.

Whether or not anyone this far back either planned it that way or had any idea it would happen as it did, the Reform/Canadian Alliance Party got its first spores in opposition to Robert Stanfield when he was national PC Party leader. Stanfield was attempting to redirect the party, with academic Tom Symons at his side, towards a fundamentally different policy path from the one John Diefenbaker had followed. A western Canadian, Diefenbaker was far more "conservative" than Stanfield, in the contemporary sense. Stanfield's immediate successors, Joe Clark and then Brian Mulroney, followed Stanfield's direction, not Diefenbaker's. Eventually, resistance within the Progressive Conservative Party to the Stanfield/Clark/Mulroney direction contributed to the formation and breakneck success of the Reform Party and, shortly afterwards, its replacement, the Canadian Alliance Party. It bears repeating that the resistance also came from people of like mind outside the traditional ranks of the PC Party. These "conservative" parties merged only a decade after the PC Party was booted from power in the 1993 federal election, reduced to two parliamentary seats, and then denied official party status in the House of Commons for lack of the qualifying twelve members. Greatly weakened, in both numbers and spirit, the party was "ripe for the picking."

The walkway from western Canadian discontent with Stanfield's perceived philosophical direction and particular policies in the late 1960s and early 1970s to the formation of the Reform/Canadian Alliance Party a generation later might have been indirect and winding. But there were few actual detours. The first bricks for that walkway were laid around the time the PC Party held its 1971 Annual Meeting. The bricklaying was done by Conservative Party members who hated the road Robert Stanfield had chosen for the party. Not able to block that road initially, they eventually decided to choose a road of their own and to recruit many more fellow travellers eager to follow it with them. The new road was utterly unlike Robert Stanfield's. Indeed, it diverged from the party's historic course, except for the Diefenbaker "rogue" period, particularly in the late stages of Opposition. Its mappers viewed the state's role in Canadian society far differently from how traditional Tories had. In core values, the old Conservative Party and the emerging new one were as inherently different from each other as orange marmalade is from strawberry jam. The incipient new party merely appropriated the old one's name and recruited, by persuasion or default, many of the latter's members and then expanded the ranks. The PC Party's 1971 Annual Meeting needs to be seen in light of the aforementioned political topography, for that meeting—unintentionally, as far as the main planners were concerned—helped chart it. I know whereof I speak because, over many months, I was the principal draftsman and record keeper for every single policy planning meeting. At every stage, all of us involved in trying to modernize the party through policy had to struggle against the forces of reaction. Policies aimed at improving our standing in French Canada, of such importance to the leader himself, met with especially strong resistance. The leader's support for official bilingualism was but one object of their ire. At the time, the term "Red Tory" was entering the political vocabulary of the country. So, "red flag"—and, for sure, bilingualism was that to these party elements—took on a whole new meaning.


# A New Policy-Development Model

All the policy work conducted by or for the PC Party over the preceding months—the policy papers, especially—influenced the content of the 250 issues resolutions to be debated and voted on at the party's 1971 Annual Meeting. The total policy content was drawn from the numerous sources the party had cultivated since the spring of

1968 under Symons's direction, and included not only the resolutions themselves, but also discussion papers, background materials, summaries, bullet-form fact sheets, question-and-answer handouts, and media packages. At each stage in the process, the party had asked policy specialists to prepare or vet drafts, and consulted them even on technical terms that appeared in particular resolutions. Symons scrutinized every detail, considering none too minor to merit his attention. Neither Stanfield nor Symons wanted the party to pull policy material out of thin air, as it had so often done—typically at the eleventh hour—for general meetings under Diefenbaker and in a long line of party leaders before him. This time, the situation would be completely different. Never before the 1971 Annual Meeting had the party been better prepared on policy matters for a national gathering. Indeed, this meeting constituted the apogee of the party's policy preparedness throughout the period Stanfield was leader and Symons his policy impresario. The only subsequent Annual Meeting held while Stanfield was leader, in 1974, applied the same formula.

The thoughtful, deliberate, painstaking manner in which Stanfield developed policy for the PC Party could have served as a model both for successive Tory leaders and for leaders of other parties, federal and provincial alike. Opposition parties, which don't have government bureaucracies to help them develop policy, would have benefited the most from his example. But all parties, including the Conservative Party itself afterwards, whether in government or Opposition, have largely ignored the policy process Stanfield and Symons devised. The country has paid the price. Opposition political parties still tend to develop policy the scatterbrained way they did more than four decades ago, when Stanfield said, in effect, "Enough, already!" Then, for the first time in history, a major national Opposition party began applying thoroughly modern management principles to its policy development. It did so on a full range of issues to ensure its positions were well researched, evidence-based, specific, thoughtful, and contemporary—if not ahead of their time (as, in fact, many of Stanfield's policies were)—on a continuing organic basis. When an Opposition party wins power without having developed a substantive agenda beforehand, it must rely on government officials (the permanent public service) to recommend one. That's an atrocious way to operate a democracy, let alone ensure the best policy course is taken. It is not too late for all political parties—not just in Opposition—to rip whole pages from the Stanfield-Symons playbook. The issues, the technology, and the players might have changed since that era, but the principles on which the two men operated to modernize the PC Party through policy remain relevant and, therefore, potentially helpful to the national interest to this day. To Stanfield, the most important of those principles was the need to maximize the number of informed people involved in the process. These included policy specialists not necessarily self-identified as Conservatives, but nonetheless committed to the PC leader's goals. Even more than at the Niagara Conference, that principle was made real at the PC Party's 1971 Annual Meeting in Ottawa.

As the Conservative Party tries to rebound from its stunning defeat in the October 2015 federal election, Tories would be wise to examine how Robert Stanfield, as national PC Party leader, rebuilt the party after Canadians threw it from power in the early 1960s for reasons similar to those that explain the defeat of the Stephen Harper government. Not the least of those reasons was the widespread belief that the government of the day had lost touch with Canadians' problems and priorities in favour of pursuing an agenda of import only, or primarily, to those in charge. In Diefenbaker's case, the agenda was not supported even by many of his own ministers—thus, for example, on defence matters, George Hees resigned from Cabinet and, for a while, from politics altogether. In Harper's case, the agenda was ideology-driven, not grassroots-crafted. And, as evidenced by the 2015 election results, neither was it broadly supported in the country at large or possibly even by elements within the party itself.

---

After the PCC processed the policy papers prepared for the 1971 Annual Meeting, to be held on December 5, 6, and 7, PC Headquarters released them with great fanfare to the media and then, almost simultaneously, to party riding presidents and secretaries across the country. Headquarters next distributed them to delegates as soon as they became elected or otherwise chosen at the local level. The papers were distributed, with news releases and summaries, in batches, rather than individually, so as to maximize both media coverage and general public interest. This way, too, the delegates had an opportunity, well before the meeting, to study each policy paper in the context of others, as did anyone else interested in them.

At the meeting—party president Nathan Nurgitz of Manitoba presiding—Tom Symons outlined for delegates the procedure for discussing and voting on policy. Delegates debated the 250 policy resolutions in three concurrent sessions organized around distinct groupings of related issues. The rules permitted delegates to strike a resolution from the ballot or add to it, but only by unanimous agreement. Just three were removed; not many more were added. The individual policy streams were masters of their own discussion, subject to the overall rules. No plenary debate was scheduled. Quebec's place in Confederation was hotly debated, as it had been at the Niagara Conference and would be long afterwards. The *deux nations* controversy, however, was discreetly avoided. Whether delegates reached consensus on such individual issues, in individual sessions, depended on the session and on the issue, not to mention one's interpretation of what constituted consensus.

Critics argued that the rules had been set to minimize controversy. They were mostly right. Again, Stanfield was not keen on broken palace china, least of all with shards fired into his own hide. Symons was of the same mind. Just as Symons had done with the policy content, he oversaw every convention logistical detail as though the fate of the entire kingdom rested on the scurrying of the tiniest field mouse. Dogmatic positions on rocky issues would not have made for smooth sailing for the leader as he skippered his warships towards the looming federal election battle. The delegates knew and generally accepted this fact. Nevertheless, throughout the proceedings, debate was heated; on some issues, such as economic independence, it was scorching. Esteemed political scientist Stephen Clarkson, an Ontario Liberal Party senior policy advisor (and Toronto mayoralty candidate in 1969), attended the meeting as an official observer. In a hotel corridor at the convention, he cornered Symons and tried to nail him—good luck with that!—on the likelihood the rules would cause the delegates to produce contradictory policy results and, therefore, less danger for Stanfield. "Oh," he quoted Symons as saying—'with a mischievous glint appearing through a puff of [pipe] smoke'—"can you promise?"[2] Clarkson needed to make Symons no such promise, because Symons had kept a virtual promise to Stanfield: no plate would be thrown, no china broken, no shards scattered, no leader hit. The field mice would scurry *around* the plate stacks.

Tom Symons had held tightly to the keys to the policy cupboard; there are, after all, limits to noblesse oblige. But these limits did not prevent something remarkable from happening: the assemblage rose as one to cheer Symons. All his hard work had paid off—not just in policy preparation, but also in unsought esteem and affection afforded Symons by party delegates and staff. The latter included individuals who had referred to him, not long before, as that "god-damned crazy egghead up in Peterborough" and a lot worse. In a journal article, Clarkson wrote: "While it was not surprising that Stanfield received a standing ovation, what impressed this observer was the ovation accorded [Symons] when the policy chairman gave his report to the same meeting." As for Symons's selfless labours for the party in the preceding period, Clarkson said the delegates were "struck" by the sheer magnitude of what he had achieved.[3] Once, Symons had been the object of abuse and even expletives in some quarters; now, the party rose in unison in thunderous ovation as he took a discreet bow. The *éminence grise* had done well for the party; it now paid homage in kind.

# A Successful Policy Model

To make the kind of policy process Robert Stanfield launched and actively participated in as PC Party leader work took many factors: substantial party resources (both funding and staff); plenty of volunteers, with nothing to motivate them but loyalty to the cause and political passion; first-rate policy specialists recruited within and outside the party to provide intellectual heft and public credibility; a strong commitment by MPs, senators, and senior party officials to direct and work with rank-and-file members from across the country at every stage; and a judiciously selected team of policy professionals (the PC Research Office) to give all this a solid technical foundation. More fundamentally, the party's broad membership—not just its brass—needed to believe that policy development was central to election preparedness, right up there with fundraising, candidate recruitment, grassroots organizing, and marketing. This belief could not be taken for granted. Nor did it spread overnight. Stanfield, with Tom Symons's help, worked hard and long to instill it. And then it happened. "Give me a couple of years, and I'll make that actress an overnight success," movie mogul Samuel Goldwyn famously said. Stanfield's "overnight success" took four years in all.

A major party's national gathering, whether focused on policy or not, is a colossal undertaking. It cost a ton of money to pull off without a hitch. And, again, the enterprise requires untold hours of labour from professionals and civilians alike—"sweat equity." Moreover, the occasion is a major news story, covered massively by every important media outlet in the country. Failure is not an option. Success is imperative, as the stakes are so high. The party leader has the most to win if the enterprise succeeds, and everything to lose if it fails. Stumble, and the entire country watches—and long remembers. The media and other political parties have ways to perpetuate the humiliation. Such is the harsh reality of politics. Stanfield did not want to stumble at the 1971 national gathering of his party; after all, the next federal election was just around the corner.

When a major political party's national gathering is focused on policy— as opposed to electing a new leader or campaign planning, typically the case with the PC Party on previous occasions—it does not take much to ruin the event. The whole thing can be derailed by a small, extremist faction. If enough members are unhappy with the leader's overall performance, personal style, or policy direction—or all three, in the case of the Diefenbaker militants opposed to Stanfield—the potential for disaster can enter the Twilight Zone. John Diefenbaker himself discovered this fact at the party's national gathering in Ottawa in November 1966, a meeting that set the stage for his downfall less than a year later. The leader and his closest advisors, therefore, must take a big hand in planning every stage of a national gathering to ensure it reflects his priorities and protects his interests. The task can't be totally delegated to others except at great risk. Stanfield refused to take a hands-off approach. (I myself was on the receiving end of many an inquiry the leader made about important details.) Moreover, the leader must play a starring role at the meeting itself. It's his show. Otherwise, nothing noteworthy happens, the media largely ignore the event, and the public at large couldn't care less about it—unless things get out of control. All the more reason the leader needs to take the occasion seriously, from initial planning to the very end. Such a national party gathering is as scripted as anything you will ever see on TV. That's because the event is essentially a television show, is intended to be, and is planned accordingly. Every "actor" and all parts of the "script" are considered important and, therefore, potentially grist for the critics' venom. All that said, a national party gathering focused on policy requires one person—a director, as it were—to provide the inspiration and intellectual firepower and managerial competence at ground level to make the occasion a success, or at least prevent it from failing. Typically, neither the leader himself nor anyone on his staff, however senior he or she might be, is equipped to do this pivotal creative and micromanagement job. Nor do they have the time, for too many other matters demand their attention.

At no other time in the entire period that Bob Stanfield and Tom Symons worked together were the stakes higher for them as a policy team than during the 1971 Annual Meeting. The occasion was close to the next election—likely Stanfield's last if he foundered. The PC leader saw the event as the best opportunity he and the party would have to stake out their positions on the issues for the campaign ahead. He knew the nation's attention would be focused on the meeting—his own performance, in particular. The event gave him a national platform leading up to the election to convince Canadians he was an acceptable alternative to Pierre Trudeau as prime minister and the PC Party a better choice than the Liberals to run the country. In an ideal world, Stanfield would not have wanted to face a national gathering of his party so close to the election. The risks of discord and mischief, especially from the Diefenbaker faction, were high. A single issue could ignite a firestorm—official languages and the Guaranteed Minimum Income (GMI) proposal were among the most inflammable. But Stanfield was well aware that the meeting was overdue, and it was a matter of making the proverbial silk purse out of a sow's ear. For him, that purse needed to be of the finest fabric. Except for the Diefenbaker insurgents, delegates fortified Stanfield's hand as the 1972 election fast approached. Had he stumbled then, he would have been severely handicapped entering the campaign. Stanfield did not stumble. On the contrary, he was at the top of his game.

## Policy Voting, Counting

The PCC directed me, as policy secretary, to tabulate and compile the 1971 Annual Meeting policy voting results. It was no easy task in that pre-computer era, when all the data had to be managed with manual calculators. I was not looking forward to the monumental task. And yet, everybody attached great importance to the results, for the election was looming and those results might affect it. The media were especially eager to learn whether, perhaps deep in the voting numbers, a time bomb lurked to blow the party apart on some issue. For his part, the PC leader was concerned a particular vote might throw him and the party on the defensive as they entered the campaign. He had experienced quite enough of that in the 1968 election on a number of issues, especially *deux nations*. The challenge for me, as the principal ballot counter, was compounded by my never before having done anything remotely like it. I was no whiz with a calculator or, for that matter, with anything else that had a cord and plug. It was not as though the PC Party itself was experienced, either. In *Party Democracy in Canada*, Queen's University political scientist George Perlin writes: "Whether in government or in opposition, both [the Liberal Party and the PC Party] have accorded a role in policy discussion to their extra-parliamentary memberships. In fact, the biennial meetings of the national Liberal party are now formally described as policy conventions and are organized around formal processes of policy debate which culminate in votes on policy resolutions. The Conservative party holds policy conventions from time to time, *but Conservative biennial meetings have no routinized structures for policy discussions and rarely take votes on policy resolutions.*"[4] Perlin does acknowledge that, despite the aforementioned difference between the two parties, "the results of this form of extra-parliamentary activity have been substantially the same."[5] He means in neither party is the leader bound by convention resolution; rather, both leaders reserve to themselves the right to declare policy—a right, in the PC Party, Diefenbaker exercised in the extreme, Stanfield only in moderation and sometimes not at all.

The contrasts between the two PC leaders' approaches towards policy in this respect, as in most others, could not have been starker. As he demonstrated at the 1971 Annual Meeting and on many other occasions starting with the Niagara Conference, Bob Stanfield placed a high premium on consulting the party about policy before deciding on a particular major course. He also did everything he could to reach beyond the membership to enrich official positions. From the beginning of his leadership, John Diefenbaker dismissed such approaches outright. Heath Macquarrie notes in his memoirs: "One of...Diefenbaker's first acts after assuming the leadership in 1956 was to discard, and indeed destroy, the elaborate policy statement worked out so assiduously at the 1956 convention."[6] So much for party democracy! Stanfield's and Diefenbaker's approaches were as different from each other as Athenian democracy is from dictatorship. Some six decades after Diefenbaker's "book burning," the Conservative Party under Stephen Harper regressed to handling policy in much the same way it had under the Chief. As Tom Flanagan described it at the time, "[t]here is an official policy manual, but the leader is free to adopt virtually any policy he wishes for strategic purposes."[7] The situation Flanagan details—in which "the party is focused on election readiness rather than policy development"—is almost exactly as it was under Diefenbaker, absent the message discipline and military precision that Flanagan says Harper applied to the "permanent campaign."[8]

The PC Party's lack of much experience with policy voting fell heavily on my shoulders, for I was mandated to supervise a small team of hard-working and congenial temporary workers, all of them women, assembled by Headquarters to help with the laborious and tedious task of counting and recording votes. My Fine Ladies and I examined each ballot and tabulated the totals with scrupulous attention, as it would have been your humble servant's neck in the noose if anything went seriously wrong. As it, of course, did. It was around this time, I think, that Murphy's Law was renamed

McMillan's Law: "Anything that can go wrong will go wrong." On each ballot question, the percentage of votes for or against or otherwise was supposed to total 100—say, 58 percent in support, 35 percent against, 7 percent undecided or no opinion. But a technical glitch threw the results out of whack by about 1 or 2 percent on every vote: either above 100 percent or below, usually the latter.

Some Headquarters snitch reported the discrepancy to Stanfield senior staffer Tom Sloan before we were able to solve the problem. Much concerned, Sloan phoned me to inquire about the snafu. He acted as though the voting tabulation was the formula required to release the entire human population from a life sentence in Purgatory. Chastened, My Fine Ladies and I continued to slave away, with hardly a break to eat, much less rest. The party had contemplated being able to release the voting results by early January 1972, a month after the meeting. Stephen Clarkson noted that Liberals, with both more complex voting procedures and more delegates, had been able to make available policy voting results within hours after their policy convention the previous year.[9] But I had not been responsible for tabulating those results; or, else, given my limited technical competence, they would likely have remained uncounted to this very day.

The sheer number of votes we had to tabulate, not to mention technical misfires, caused one further delay after another. The delays, in turn, caused the media dogs to bay at Stanfield with louder and louder barks at every successive news conference and media scrum. Mr. Stanfield, was the party hiding a deep dark secret? Discomfiting results on the Guaranteed Minimum Income, perhaps? Had the delegates voted yes to legalize marijuana and, by law, require parents to include a joint in the school lunch of every kindergarten kid in the country? Well, it was not that extreme—but close to it. The media ascribed any number of sinister motives to the delay and secrecy. The real story was that My Fine Ladies and I were still unable to get all the darn percentages to add up precisely. Mankind would just have to remain in Purgatory a while longer.

Finally, in frustration, Stanfield himself called me at Headquarters: "Tom…um, ah, um, ah, Tom, um…about the voting…." With fewer words, or halts, than needed to tell a lost tourist that Parliament Hill was the next block over on the left, the leader made his point: he was not angry, just impatient. Anger was not imprinted in his DNA, at least not in bold script. It immediately became clear to me that Stanfield's impatience had less to do with the delay itself than with his anxiety about the Guaranteed Minimum Income vote. He, in fact, asked: "um, ah, um…Tom, you know that question on the…." Shades of his condolences on the death of my father. "Yes, Bob," I felt like telling him, to prevent any further delay in the results he and his staff were so impatient to obtain, "the damned thing passed by 13.7468 percent." As, indeed, it had. Clearly, My Fine Ladies and I had now gotten the methodology down not only to a science, but also to the last decimal point. Like a kid eager to know what was inside a particularly tempting Christmas package, Stanfield just had to know the GMI results. When I told him—albeit, in tamer words—the kid was delighted.

Despite technical glitches that delayed the vote counting, the job did finally get done, the results did get released, and the media, true to character, did get to fuss about one thing or another. But the results contained nothing troublesome for the party leader or his senior policy advisor. On the GMI, in particular, Stanfield had dodged not just a plate but a bullet. Notwithstanding the delays and frustrations for all concerned, including the leader, word soon spread throughout the party network in Ottawa that I had accomplished the job with considerable competence and aplomb. Accordingly—unbeknownst to Tom Symons—the brass at National Headquarters discreetly asked me to quit my service with the policy head and accept a senior management post there.

If I deserved any credit for productivity and high morale among workers, hadn't I learned that skill from Tom Symons? His personnel and management ways make it difficult to answer the question. Do the style and values of a Tom Symons colleague or staffer seem like those of Symons himself because Symons has moulded him or her in the master's own image? Or is he or she that way anyway, and Symons has recruited the individual partly because he had already seen something important of himself in that person? I suspect it is both, but more the latter than the former.

In a sense, I was already employed by Headquarters. The Niagara Conference had mandated Headquarters to be the secretariat of the conference-created PCC, and I was the committee secretary, my salary in that role paid by that office. I was not, technically, Tom Symons's employee—not directly. I was his assistant in the work he was doing for the PCC as chairman of the Policy Advisory Committee and as chief policy advisor to Stanfield. In practice, as noted earlier, Symons and I together served as the PCC's secretariat, with Headquarters providing valuable administrative support.

All such Byzantine bureaucracy aside, Tom Symons and I were, de facto, a duo, albeit a highly asymmetrical one in which the heavy weight (including literally) was on his side. Stanfield was eager that the public not view Symons's policy leadership role in the party as overtly partisan. We did not require experts courted by the party to be card-carrying members of the Progressive Conservative Party of Canada. They had only to be independent of another party and, preferably, sympathetic to ours to whatever degree. It would have been more difficult for us to recruit policy specialists if those people saw me as a political hack. By association, the perception would have undermined Symons's standing as a public service–minded citizen trying to make one of the major national political parties more progressive and its policies better grounded in research and analysis. This was, in fact, who Tom Symons was and what he was doing. The Trent University president was a rare and valuable resource. So no one in the party wanted him exposed to circumstances or associations that would tarnish his public image, as the "political hack" label would have done. I was no political hack, anyway. And, most certainly, Symons was not. The PC Party telegraphed this "public message" by associating me with Stanfield's operation, rather than with National Headquarters. And it did so with all due respect for the vital work Headquarters and its employees were also doing for both the party and the country.

# Policy Specialists

Some of our policy experts, or specialists, were proudly committed Tories from the outset. Among many others were Oxford-educated historian Robert Page at Trent University (whom I appointed chair of my Environmental Advisory Council when I later became federal environment minister); Canadian Studies specialist Richard Clippingdale at Carleton University (later Opposition Leader Joe Clark's senior policy advisor and Sir Wilfrid Laurier biographer); and law professor Ron Atkey of Osgoode Hall (later elected MP for St. Paul's and appointed Joe Clark's minister of employment and immigration).

Elizabeth ("Libby") Burnham, Toronto corporate and commercial lawyer but New Brunswick native, served as senior advisor to that province's premier Richard Hatfield. Burnham was not an academic, but she brought to the policy process a combination of professional expertise, knowledge of how government and politics function in the real world, and first-rate political smarts. We could not have accessed her kind of talent at universities or think tanks had we raided every one of them in the country. (As I write, Libby is currently chancellor of Acadia University, in Wolfville, Nova Scotia.)

The same applies to Ottawa's Jean Pigott, president and CEO of her family's business, Morrison-Lamothe Bakery. One of only three women CEOs in Canada in the 1970s, Jean would win a House of Commons seat in Ottawa–Carleton in 1976, only to lose it in the 1979 general election. Later, Prime Minister Brian Mulroney appointed her chair of the National Capital Commission, from which she transformed the Ottawa/Hull district. Meanwhile, Jean brought to the Stanfield-Symons policy process business expertise and experience we would have had to pay a small fortune to obtain from a consulting company, even assuming it could be found there. Instead, we got it gratis from within our own ranks.

Another in-house specialist who provided invaluable service to the policy process was Roy McMurtry. Later Ontario attorney general (1975–85) and solicitor general (1978–82), he helped broker Pierre Trudeau's patriation and Charter of Rights and Freedoms constitutional reforms in the early 1980s. As external affairs minister, Joe Clark appointed him Canada's high commissioner to the United Kingdom in 1985. Currently retired as chief justice of Ontario (appointed in 1996), McMurtry was yet another partisan whose expertise was linked to keen political instincts not readily available to us from academe.

We had a rich roster of such individuals. They were either actively involved in the continuing policy process or on call, without notice, to help on a particular matter, or both—typically both. Never before in its history had the PC Party had at its disposal anything like this organized team of professionals to assist it in a systematic way with policy and issues. And, outside government, the party has not had it since. It would have been one thing for the party to be able to tap into a wealth of policy ideas in universities and think tanks. But no matter how brilliant or innovative or interesting those ideas might have been, if politically tone-deaf they would have been useless to us. Policy specialists within our own walls helped ensure PC policy was not only smart and evidence-based, but also focused and practical, and, most important of all, politically marketable. Scores of people like those mentioned above helped plan the policy program of the 1971 Annual Meeting and make it a success. Many of them participated as delegates themselves. And most continued to help formulate policy to the end of Stanfield's leadership and well beyond, under other leaders. Tom Symons's "Black Book" contained the names and multiple addresses and private phone numbers of literally hundreds of such people. In-house and outside specialists, together, went a long way—but, of course, not all the way—towards bridging the gap between our policy operation and that which the governing Liberals had available to them through the public service. The gap had never been narrower under any previous Tory leader than it was under Robert Stanfield. Now, for the first time, the party was within shooting distance of hitting its target: competing with the governing Liberals on policy, issue by issue. For sure, it was not because the Liberals were any weaker than before. We had upped our game.

Increasing numbers of specialists not inclined to identify themselves publicly with the party or its leader, especially right after the Diefenbaker era, became less of this mind as the party's image acquired a more "Stanfieldian feel," to coin a phrase. Some in this category became not only less nervous, but, indeed, utterly comfortable—though not always willing to make the full leap, at least not yet, by becoming official party members. All the while, the Symons policy operation made anti-intellectualism no longer acceptable to most Progressive Conservatives. The thunderous ovation Symons received as policy head from every quarter of the ballroom at the 1971 Annual Meeting reflected this fact. That response would not have happened even two years earlier, at the 1969 national party gathering, much less under Diefenbaker. The PC Party's transformation from anti-intellectual to pro-intellectual was the Trent University president's most important, and enduring, contribution to the party as senior policy advisor to Stanfield.

The PC Party's new pro-intellectual direction closely paralleled an end to the party's knee-jerk impulse to oppose government policies for mere opposition's sake when Diefenbaker was leader of the Opposition. Under Stanfield, the party took a far more selective—and, therefore, constructive—approach to opposing the government. No longer did it automatically oppose policies simply because the government or Liberals had advanced them. The Criminal Code amendments and the *Official Languages Act* were notable examples of progressive government measures the PC Opposition largely supported. Stanfield led his party in all such policy directions, knowing full well the attendant electoral risks he was taking in certain parts of the country and the deep fissures those stands would cause within his own ranks, particularly out West and in Caucus. And yet, the leader was prepared to pay the price, both on principle and in an effort to broaden the party's and his own appeal beyond traditional Tory strongholds and reliable types of supporters. To him, the role of an Opposition party was not just to oppose government measures, or to oppose them at all when he thought they were right for the country. Least of all would he have tried to pander to, just to harvest the votes of, the angry mob that any skilled demagogue can incite against government measures such as Trudeau's language and justice reforms, which were deemed personally threatening to a certain type of voter. Stanfield believed the party needed to propose worthy alternatives to whatever government measures he found deficient. He was especially eager to have the party develop counter-policies that would equip it with an agenda should the PCs win power—one that the country as a whole, not just the party's core supporters, could support. He believed Conservatives needed to make an affirmative case for themselves, not simply convince the public the Liberals were wrong, let alone (as Diefenbaker would have it) "scoundrels." History owes Stanfield a gold star, if not sainthood, for the courage, vision, noble instincts, and sheer patriotism he applied to managing the PC Party's affairs and fulfilling his role as Official Opposition leader in this responsible and civic-minded way. Not only was he advancing the PC Party's interests; he was also wilfully and strategically helping to unite the country through what political scientists call "brokerage politics."

Robert Stanfield led Progressive Conservatives in this fundamentally new direction in three main ways. First, he placed policy development at the centre of PC Party planning for parliamentary and electoral purposes alike. And he ensured that the party found and applied the funds and personnel necessary to make this priority real, not simply a lofty principle embraced without conviction and touted without substance. Second, Stanfield devoted an enormous amount of his own time and physical and intellectual energies both to the policy-development process and to specific issues and policies he considered important to modernizing the party and making it more relevant to the needs of everyday Canadians. As crucial as Tom Symons was to that policy process, the leader himself was its principal patron and participant. As such, he inspired and motivated his Caucus and the broad membership of the party, equally, to take policy as seriously as he did. Third, and by no mean least, Stanfield personally projected an image of superior intelligence and thoughtfulness, to say nothing of his elite education from childhood to adulthood, his solid professional credentials as a lawyer via Harvard, and his undisputed status as a former premier of the first rank.

Robert Lorne Stanfield's very persona gave credibility to the policy process the PC Party devised and employed under his leadership. And the same factor caused Canadians to give greater credence to the product of that process than would ever have been the case had they not generally deemed the Tory leader an extraordinary individual in his own right, independent of the high office he held. Put simply, Canadians took the message seriously because they considered its principal messenger a heavyweight—not a demagogue, a shyster, a charlatan, or a flake. The man and what he publicly stood for rhymed. And to a steadily growing number of both opinion leaders and everyday Canadians, Stanfield's message was music to the ear. Truly, Stanfield was remaking the national PC Party in his own image. To a broad range of Canadians, that image rang true to the values associated with the best of the leaders the Conservative Party had had over the generations, beginning with Sir John A. Macdonald. This was *his* most important and enduring contribution to the institution. The party was transformed by the process, substantially for the better. The transformation was enduring, but, alas, under Stephen Harper, not permanent.

Despite the efforts to ensure I was identified with Stanfield and not directly with National Headquarters, I still had one foot in the HQ sandbox. From time to time, I worked for brief periods there—to wit: the 1971 policy resolution vote counting— apart from attending PCC meetings in the Headquarters boardroom. Neither fish nor fowl in this respect, I was like some rare and exotic amphibian not yet classified by zoologists. But I was much more a "Stanfieldian" than a "Headquartersonian" both in job role and in personal preference. And that was the way I was eager to remain. In Tom Symons, I had found somebody I liked and admired and enjoyed working with, and from whom I was learning an enormous amount. It was akin to having my own private university president as personal mentor and academic advisor and father confessor and political kindred spirit and counsellor all rolled into one. I intended to continue both swimming in his ocean and flying in his sky. I thought: let the zoologists figure it all out in their good time; I have already figured it out in mine. To Headquarters' generous offer to quit Symons and join them, I thus said no. Besides, weren't *they* some of the same people who had called that egghead up in Peterborough crazy a while back? Well, *he* now happened to be my friend.

# Chapter 9

# COUNTDOWN TO D-DAY: THE 1972 NATIONAL GENERAL ELECTION

For Robert Stanfield, policy was not an end in itself. Unlike Tom Symons, he was not an academic but a politician. In personal interests, reading choices, and nature, however, he was the closest the party had ever had to a bona fide intellectual among all its leaders over the years except for Arthur Meighen. Had Stanfield not gone into politics, he likely would have chosen academe, perhaps becoming a dean of law or economics professor or faculty head. In any event, he would have risen to the top. With humans, as with horses, bloodline and fire in the belly usually win, though not necessarily in politics. Stanfield himself had always crossed the finish line first, and this was one set of odds where a ticket on the Stanfield stallion—no gelding he— would have been almost a sure bet.

With the 1972 election looming, the leader embarked on a schedule of work and travel more backbreaking than that of any previous Tory leader. He became dispirited, though, when Pierre Trudeau invoked the *War Measures Act* in October 1970 against Quebec terrorists, the first time it had ever been employed in peacetime. Ironically, this unprecedented show of force by the federal government against its own citizens caused the Liberals' popularity to soar and the PC Party's to plummet (59 percent versus 22 percent at the worst point). It appeared to Stanfield that, no matter how hard he worked to prepare the party—or how committed he was to dragging it from antediluvian to modern—it didn't count. Events and Pierre Trudeau and the Liberals (with all the government levers at their disposal) conspired against him. Like a car bomb detonated under a freshly restored Model T Ford, in one swipe they wiped away the precious gains he had made. Were all those hours of body work with the Symons crew for naught? Wouldn't he have been better off, or at least no worse off, just staying home, reading Milton Friedman and Paul Samuelson in the enjoyment of his own solitude? It seemed so.

For the first time in my close-up experience with the PC leader, the toll politics was taking showed both in his demeanour and on his face. I felt like consoling him, just as he had tried to console me, however awkwardly, when my father died. But Stanfield was not a man for the maudlin. It is not in the Stanfields' DNA.

Gone were the wit and humour, the wry and the droll. All those hours filling rust holes and applying new paint on the Tory Tin Lizzie were now up in smoke with one lit fuse. Had it been worth all that bodywork, anyway? Was it just an aging jalopy that, under its previous owner, made a great deal of noise when running, but would have gone faster if pushed from behind with the motor off? At least John Diefenbaker had driven with flair—enough to distract the Tory passengers from noticing the Tin Lizzie was going nowhere fast, just noisily. Stanfield, due to events beyond his control, seemed, in this dark period, unable to get the car out of the driveway.

Stanfield's hurt was compounded when he learned, in November 1970, from an authoritative and unimpeachable source located by Tom Symons, a shocking truth. It was a truth Stanfield was not at liberty to reveal publicly. The source could not have been closer to the prime minister had Pierre Trudeau personally authorized the informant to share with Stanfield the state secret (he did not). The information concerned the real reasons Trudeau had invoked the *War Measures Act*. It was not, as the prime minister had claimed, because government intelligence had revealed an "apprehended insurrection" in Quebec when British diplomat James Cross was kidnapped. Indeed, there had been no such intelligence. The truth was, the government had a woeful lack of intelligence. Civil liberties taken for granted for centuries in Canada's tradition of governance had been summarily suspended in Quebec during the so-called October Crisis because Trudeau felt he needed the powers under the *War Measures Act* to *get* the intelligence. It was a fishing expedition! Quebec labour minister Pierre Laporte would later be strangled and stuffed in a car trunk. His murder, however, was not a reason for the government's invoking the act but, rather, a consequence; it happened after the act was invoked. More explosive, if ever revealed, was that the federal Liberal government had invoked the act also because it lacked confidence in Quebec Liberal premier Robert Bourassa's ability to manage the crisis, even with all the powers and resources the federal government made available to him.

For Stanfield, Trudeau's popularity soared on the wings of an untruth. At the core, it was as mendacious as the rationale US president George W. Bush would use three decades later to justify invading Iraq on similar specious grounds of perceived imminent threat to the domestic citizenry. If patriotism is the last refuge of a scoundrel, national security is its next-to-last refuge. In both cases, truth is the first casualty. Stanfield had an enormous tolerance for people's shortcomings because, in his heart, though not by any objective standard, he felt he had so many of his own. But truth-stretching was totally foreign to his character. *That* was not in his DNA. Just as it had not been in the DNA of his saintly grandfather Charles, from whom he had inherited so much of it. In fond remembrances of Robert Stanfield, his former press secretary Rod McQueen stresses the permanent scar the *War Measures Act* issue had left on Stanfield's psyche. Giving the Trudeau government "the benefit of the doubt" on the act's invocation, McQueen says, was "Stanfield's only regret in a long political life."[1]

---

Sometimes in life, bloodline and fire in the belly are just not enough. One needs luck. And Stanfield's luck was just about to change…big time.

Politicians in Nova Scotia did not always fight under Marquess of Queensberry Rules when Robert Stanfield was in the boxing ring there. He had taken a few sucker punches of his own, and punched right back. He was no lily-livered coward hovering by the water cooler while the Big Boys fought to unconsciousness to hide insecurities about their manhood. But neither was he in the ring for that purpose. Whatever Stanfield might have doubted about others of his qualities, manliness was not one of them. As he sometimes joked later in life, after a scotch and water or two, he had bedded three women in the bonds of matrimony, the self-styled Casanova Trudeau only one. In an atmosphere of national crisis, however, Stanfield was at an enormous disadvantage against his Liberal opponent even before Trudeau converted to bare-knuckles politics in 1974. For Trudeau, a gentler fight two years earlier had almost lost him the government. Even intellectuals such as Stanfield and Trudeau learn the ropes if able to stay on their feet long enough.

And so it was that Stanfield picked himself up from the mat after a period of deep anxiety and frustration and (I sensed) depression. He would continue the good fight leading up to the 1972 election. As before, policy was central to his preparation. From the time the Policy Coordinating Committee was established in October 1969 up to the October 1972 federal election, sixteen meetings of the PCC were held—thirty-six months, sixteen full-scale meetings; one approximately every two months. In that period, up to the 1971 Annual General Meeting in December, twelve "official" meetings were also held by a special Working Committee of the PCC— for all practical purposes, a slightly smaller version of the full PCC—set up to plan the policy sessions and prepare policy papers to be discussed and, through resolutions based on those papers, voted on at the meeting. Numerous unofficial meetings were also held, the main difference being that minutes were kept of the former. A fast pace.

The Working Committee operated in a more informal manner than did the whole PCC to allow maximum flexibility in membership and modus operandi. The actual membership, though, did not vary markedly between the two. The leader attended Working Committee meetings, but, unlike Symons, less regularly than he did the PCC per se. When not there himself, however, Stanfield followed its progress as a securities broker would examine tallies at trading day's end at the stock exchange—he had a lot riding on the "market." One should view the PCC and the Working Committee as one and the same, except for the above qualifications. All told, between the sixteen meetings of the PCC and the twelve of the Working Committee, twenty-eight policy meetings were held in a thirty-six-month period. That was about once every month when holidays and parliamentary recesses and other such blank-out dates are excluded. The Working Committee met a number of times, as well, during the Annual Meeting itself. No minutes were recorded then. If included, the total would be even more impressive.

As underscored earlier, the membership of the PCC was fluid, ebbing and flowing depending on people's schedules, the arrival and departure of individuals whose membership was tied to office, and other such variables. Nobody left for lack of interest—not a single one. People sought to join. After all, the leader would be there. If he says this is important, it makes a difference. He *said* it was important. It *made* a difference. At the time of the 1972 election, the members of the PCC were as follows: Robert Stanfield (leader); Tom Symons (Policy Advisory Committee chair); Tom McMillan (PCC secretary); MPs Ged Baldwin, George Hees, Paul Yewchuk, and Wallace Nesbitt; Senators Jacques Flynn and Martial Asselin; National Headquarters Director Liam O'Brian; Research Director Geoffrey Molyneux; Stanfield staff members Graham Scott and Tom Sloan; Headquarters staff member Bruce Douglas; Research Office staff member Les Horswill; Quebec PC organizer Claude Dupras; University of New Brunswick law professor Robert Kerr; women's president Isabel MacAulay (succeeded soon by Alene Holt); and Quebec PC president Claude Nolin. Clearly, the membership had a strong political component. Much of the intellectual content came to the party from elsewhere through this body. The content was getting steadily richer with each passing meeting.

In the lead-up to the 1972 election, twenty-five policy pamphlets—of varying lengths, depending on the subject's importance or political salience—were prepared by the PCC for MPs and candidates and their workers and supporters. The papers drew heavily on: the policy background and discussion papers prepared for the 1971 Annual Meeting, revised and updated as needed; reports of the various regional and local conferences and seminars held across the country; policy work by probes and study groups and pilot projects; individual research or policy ideas commissioned by the party and carried out by its resource specialists on specific questions, sometimes of a technical nature—for example, on the Guaranteed Minimum Income (GMI); as well as other sources, not the least the continuing research conducted by the party's Research Office, very much the PCC's partner, under Molyneux's energetic direction.

Throughout this period between October 1969 and October 1972, the Policy Advisory Committee (again, Symons and I, acting as the secretariat of the PCC) amassed thirty-five full-sized cabinet drawers of files. We also compiled a roster of specialists at the service of the party that numbered 555 by late October 1972 before peaking at some 620 by 1974. A huge Black Book! Was Symons conspiring with fellow historians to make work for themselves later? As the dark-haired kid who needed to manage all this material, I certainly thought so at the time. As now the aging, grey-haired man who needed to research it all for this book, I am glad Symons was such a pack rat. But, as I laboured, sometimes late into the night and on weekends and even some "holidays," to help amass the material originally, I occasionally thought he was just a rat, period. The thought, however, never lasted long. The "crazy egghead up there in Peterborough" had method to his madness. Few people at the time—me included, Stanfield *always* excluded—fully appreciated it back then. I realize now, with the wisdom of hindsight, this fact: on the policy front, only Robert Stanfield and Tom Symons, together, had the Big Picture fully on the radar. The role of the rest of us was to help them sharpen the image and make it real.

# The 1972 PC Party Platform

On September 12, 1972, at the outset of the campaign leading to the October 30 general election, Stanfield released his priorities for a Progressive Conservative government. Some of the main campaign issues were as follows.

*Unemployment*: From an average of 6.3 percent, considered worrisomely high at the time, it would rise to 6.6 percent a week before the vote.

*Inflation:* An emerging problem, at 5.19 percent (year over year) at the time of the election. Stanfield thought the issue needed to be addressed, and he did address it in the campaign with a qualified wage-and-price controls approach—controls if necessary, but not necessarily controls (shades of Mackenzie King—both economists at heart, the latter literally). In even more urgent economic circumstances, in the 1974 election, Stanfield would sharpen his plan to great detriment to the party's electoral fortunes, as we shall see.

*Taxes:* Stanfield promised to reduce them on personal income and on corporations to stimulate job growth, and to abolish them on family-farm capital gains to boost agriculture and protect rural culture. He would also introduce a constant-dollar approach to taxation to prevent taxpayers from having to pay extra tax on income increases due to inflation, as opposed to real increases (a revolutionary idea then). Specifically, he would index tax brackets to the cost of living. Old Age Security payments would also be tied to the cost of living, a practice taken for granted nowadays, but not then.

*Sovereignty:* The PC leader promised to place curbs on foreign ownership of Canadian corporations and require foreign-owned companies operating in Canada to have a majority of Canadians on their board of directors. (These nationalist ideas were taken directly from the Sterling Lyon study group, as was the principle, if not the leader's specific campaign promise, to adjust tariffs to encourage secondary processing in Canada of the country's natural resources.) In the same vein, Stanfield said a government he headed would declare "unqualified Canadian sovereignty" over Arctic waters. This was two decades before the matter would emerge as a major concern to Canadians or even to policy specialists. It is yet another example, among many, of the PC leader's visionary thinking.

*Industrial growth:* Stanfield said a PC government would launch a national economic strategy in concert with the provinces. (It was later characterized as "industrial strategy," with ideas from the Science Council of Canada, many of them shared with Stanfield or his representatives *sub rosa*.)

*Urban affairs:* Right out of the party's housing conferences and study group was a commitment to establish residential land banks to reduce the cost of housing and also to eliminate the 11 percent sales tax on building materials towards the same end.

*Labour and workers:* The PC leader embraced the controversial, but in many parts of the country popular, policy to ban strikes in essential services. Stanfield addressed the need to rationalize the income-support system and provide help and incentives for the working poor and retraining for the unemployed. But, to minimize controversy, he did not allude to the GMI plan directly or by name (most of this from the Niagara Conference consensus).

*Energy policy:* Reflecting the leader's strong provincial-rights sensitivity, the platform promised to turn over to the provinces 100 percent of offshore mineral-rights proceeds. This position sharply contrasted with the Liberals' stance, which, within a decade, was to prove so explosive, especially in the West—and, more particularly, in Alberta concerning oil—with the launch of Trudeau's National Energy Program. Had Robert Stanfield's visionary mind foreseen that, down the road, energy could risk blowing the country apart? As I reflect on some of the things he said in the privacy of the PCC conclave, I think, in hindsight, he had.

Stanfield stressed a range of other policies, including detailed ones to support small Canadian-owned businesses. The centrepiece here was a $300 million Canadian Investment Credit Incentive plan to provide tax credits to support this sector. He also promised to overhaul government management and planning. One of his most specific promises regarding government operations was to increase the power of the auditor general to fight waste and inefficiency (motherhood now, but innovative then). The leader also promised to create a Ministry of State to coordinate economic planning of all government departments to ensure that the measures of one did not undermine those of another. Many of the policies of this sort reflected the leader's own ideas based on his experience as a premier. They expressed, as well, his Maritimes/New England Brahmin sense of frugality and discipline. It was in this spirit that Stanfield said that, in the name of government and political reform, he would require all his ministers to disclose their personal holdings (de rigueur in contemporary times, but not then). Meanwhile, years before the practice was made mandatory in many jurisdictions, Stanfield placed his personal assets in a blind trust. The leader's promise to ameliorate the needs of specific disadvantaged groups was grounded in noblesse oblige concern about so much poverty thriving amidst wealth and plenty.

The party's specific proposals to combat poverty came from PCC study groups, resource people, individual Caucus members, and the Research Office. Many staffers were social reform zealots in the progressive Tory tradition, notable among them Maureen McTeer—future wife of Prime Minister Joe Clark[2]—whose politics were substantially of the Jean Wadds (and, later, Flora MacDonald) sort: preoccupied with the plight of the disadvantaged and disenfranchised. The Research Office director himself, Geoffrey Molyneux, was the reddest of Red Tories. Among the disadvantaged groups the PC Party promised to help were Aboriginal peoples, to whose plight and heritage Symons was especially sensitive. The party promised, for instance, to recognize Aboriginal claims and treaty rights.

If "town and gown" means anything, "gown and Tory" sure did in this case. With Symons hovering about, it usually did. "Okay, if he *insists*." He *does* insist. In such social policy areas, the platform had Symons's name written all over it—in calligraphy. Stanfield and Tom Symons alone were not responsible for this impressive, detailed, and, on many issues, visionary election platform. But the two men were its architects, even as it took many builders and carpenters over a four-year period to construct the edifice. Just as the PC leader valued team work above all else in election planning, and the Trent University president was a team-builder above all else in management style and method, so also the 1972 election platform was a team effort. Both the way the platform was built and the platform itself reflected who these two particular men were as individuals and as partners. The platform was impressive because the two main designers themselves were impressive.

For reasons I don't know, I have in my personal files the original final draft (before retyping) of notes Stanfield used when launching the campaign and policy platform. (I hadn't yet become a kleptomaniac, so that can't be it.) The leader heavily edited the staff-drafted notes before he delivered them. Typically, when a speech writer included a statement such as, in this case, "a decent government must feel compassion," Stanfield would add words such as the following ones he actually did tack onto the text for the 1972 launch: "and offer adequate help where it is needed." For Stanfield, it was not good enough just to preach the gospel of compassion; the gospel had to be acted on. Faith *combined* with good works. Noblesse oblige, formerly in rolled-up sleeves in the policy workshop, was now in sneakers on the campaign trail.

# Election Shocker

Few historic facts are as certain as this one: from the time the Conservative Party was just a twinkle in the eye of founding leader Sir John A. Macdonald to Robert Stanfield's leadership more than a hundred years later, no Tory leader had prepared his party for an election and for government with the care and commitment and thoughtfulness that Stanfield applied to the policy task in the lead-up to the 1972 election. And none has done so since, either. This view is not only my own; it is a subtext in the last part of Geoffrey Stevens's *Stanfield* biography. A measure of how successful Robert Stanfield and Tom Symons were in modernizing the PC Party, both in policy and in image, came when the passionately Liberal *Toronto Star*—the virtual house organ of the Liberal Party's left wing and the largest-circulation daily newspaper in the country—endorsed the Progressive Conservative Party and its platform for the first time in its long and storied history.

But the question in the air remained: would Stanfield, the man who made all this happen, reap any temporal rewards for his labours? Or would he have to await indulgences in Heaven reserved for those who laboured by the divine dictum, and personal noblesse oblige ethic, that "faith without good works is dead"? By the night of the election, Stanfield, with Symons's help and blessing, had done his good works. And now he would have to await the results with faith alone. Stanfield *was* rewarded in this temporal world with at least a nod of approbation from Above. It was almost enough to make him prime minister of Canada.

On election night, as the returns rolled in, the results stunned the nation: it was a near dead heat, with the PCs taking the lead in parliamentary seats 109 to 107. Later, the ratio flipped to the Liberals by the same margin, but for a while it looked like Robert Stanfield would become prime minister and the Tories would form the government.[3] Robert Stanfield out-campaigned the man who, only four years earlier, had given public mania new meaning and, it seemed, put the old values out of style forever. He slaughtered the Liberals, both in seats and in popular votes, everywhere across the country. The only exception was in Quebec, the Liberals' historic bastion, where their margin of victory was substantial enough to give them a tiny edge, on both counts, in the overall results. Significantly, Stanfield's Tories made dramatic gains across the prairies, the homeland of Diefenbaker loyalists who had plotted against the new leader, in parliamentary shenanigans and on policy, at every turn. Even more satisfying for the PC leader were his party's huge gains in the cities and among the young and the educated, the very demographic groups his progressive and pro-intellectual policies were designed to attract. Yet again, the Nova Scotian—so unlikely a political star—had far exceeded almost everyone's expectations. But, as always, he did not exceed his own. Stanfield: "The Man with the Winning Way." Six words. Great bumper sticker.

It was a good night for the PC Party, a good night for Robert Stanfield, and a good night for Tom Symons. At the end of a long day of meetings in Toronto, in his hotel room at the Park Plaza Hotel, Symons welcomed the results with a puff of his pipe, a sip of aged scotch, and a phone call of thanks from Stanfield. Two warriors joined in battle and now in triumph. Sometimes life *is* fair.

# Chapter 10

# THE SAUSAGE FACTORY

All along, under Robert Stanfield's leadership, the PC Party's process for preparing policy materials was analogous to the way liberal democracies generate legislation or bills. The latter process is classically likened to something not at all classy: the making of sausages, a metaphor coined by Otto von Bismarck. The way laws are processed—the wheeling and dealing, in particular—is no more appealing than how a sausage is made, even if, in the end, laws might not always be as appetizing. *New York Times* writer Gail Collins nails the point in her September 22, 2010, column: "The legislative process is almost never uplifting."[1] With laws, as with sausages, the final product is, typically, the remnants of the carcass—more sinews and scrapings than porterhouse and protein. The PC policy-development process was not *haute cuisine*, either. It, too, involved a lot of wheeling and dealing. Most of it was internal—for example, reconciling policy differences among Caucus members or between the Policy Coordinating Committee (PCC) and certain individual Tory MPs. By contrast, government has to balance competing pressures both within the system and outside, including public and special interest groups. (The PC Party in Opposition also had to do a certain amount of horse-trading with outside groups it was courting, just not as often and with lower stakes.)

Like a sausage, our policy in particular cases tended to be comprised of stuff from many different sources, not all of it premium cuts. At the beginning of the process, right after the 1968 election, a lot of the policy, for lack of prior work, was scrapings not from the carcass but from the abattoir floor. To meet a particular need, we sometimes had to freshen up whatever happened to be lying around. In the later period, from just after the 1972 election to the eve of the 1974 election campaign, the PC Party was not proceeding with a *tabula rasa*—a blank butcher's board, as it were. The party had a substantial amount of meat in the grinder; it was now a question of reviewing it to determine what needed to be discarded and what was still fresh but needed to be updated or supplemented.

When, on some issues, we had to begin policy papers from scratch, it was typically because the issue was new and political pressures had forced us to change priorities, or we simply had lacked the time or resources to focus on it before. In such circumstances, Tom Symons was more than the abattoir's general manager; he was also the principal sausage-maker. Even at the best of times, much later, when we had a substantial body of policy to work with, his role was central in the drafting of papers. His own methods are, therefore, germane.

Symons is nothing if not—besides a tea drinker—a reader. That is a little like saying the *Titanic* was a boat. He is a HUGE reader. The bookshelves at Marchbanks, his gracious mid-nineteenth-century home in Peterborough, Ontario, look like the

Parliamentary Library: wall-to-wall books, floor to ceiling, with other books and journals and documents stacked everywhere, including, in his case, on floors and windowsills. But more than books alone, he reads newspapers—from across Canada and also from other countries, especially the United Kingdom (he studied at Oxford). He reads magazines. He reads journals and reviews. He reads studies and reports. He reads everything but nutrition values on the backs of cereal boxes, and likely even those. Not content only to read the stuff, he underlines and notates everything that strikes him as particularly salient or just interesting. A newspaper article devoured and underlined by Tom Symons looks like the varicose veins on an advanced octogenarian with high blood pressure. But the article has a longer lifespan than the old man. An article would be cut out, photocopied, distributed widely, then discussed with staff and acted on, if necessary—and it almost always was. "Please, get that report. Please, follow up on those numbers. Please, call that department and see if it has more data. Please...Please...Please." The "please" in all this, for staff, is the "P" in the most dreaded combination of letters since the invention of the Morse Code: "*M.W.D.P.?*"...short for "*May We Discuss Please?*" This is what Symons wrote on each manila file folder stuffed with clippings to be discussed with staff and likely acted on. In this context, that staffer was me.

I did the initial rough drafts of almost all the PC policy papers. Symons would then review and substantially rework them, long before they proceeded to anyone else. We normally consulted experts at the early stages, about substance and for technical accuracy alike. By the time we gave the policy papers to the PCC, they invariably were advanced enough to withstand scrutiny by busy people. Their time, especially Stanfield's, was too valuable to waste with anything less polished. Particularly later in the life of the PCC, people knew the difference between a rough draft and an advanced one. Stanfield always did. It was not just that he was as sharp as a paring knife; as a former premier, he was far more experienced with a process of this sort than most other PCC members were. Our own process was similar to that followed in a major Cabinet policy committee. Indeed, the modus operandi and dynamics were much the same, as I was to learn first-hand a decade later when appointed to the Mulroney Cabinet. In many ways, Robert Stanfield the national PC Party leader never ceased to act like the Nova Scotia government leader he had been for eleven years. In contrast to John Diefenbaker (even when in government), he applied to the task not the mindset of Opposition but that of governing: methodical, step-by-step preparation towards specific policy goals, as though the man was still in office.

No matter who was involved in the process at a given time, PC policy papers would usually advance through as many as a dozen stages of line-by-line study and debate. In the process, the in-house expertise of the Research Office was invaluable.

# Diplomat and Wordsmith

Tom Symons is a skilled writer, with a great command of the mechanics and musicality and nuances of language. His father, Harry, and brother Scott were both award-winning writers. It is in the family DNA. Symons, however, has other distinguishing qualities at nuclear war with his writing gifts. My Queen's University graduate thesis advisor, political scientist Tony Lovink—son of an ambassador, Hans Lovink—described Symons as "the best academic diplomat in the country" when I informed him, in the summer of 1969, I was going to be working for the Trent University president on the Niagara Conference. As befits a diplomat, Symons had a preternatural aversion to controversy. This quality caused him to be, I think, unduly cautious, as an actual diplomat would be, in the revisions he himself made to the drafts before they went to the PCC to be scrutinized.

The papers—need I say?—left my own hands Shakespearean in their grandeur, Tennysonian in their poetry, Newtonian in their methodological rigour. Destined for immortality! By the time Tom Symons was finished with them, however, those self-same drafts no more resembled the originals than a deciduous tree in summer's brightest light mirrors itself in the darkest dog days of winter: a lot of greenery added, not many dead leaves pared. From my own drafting, many a "We will…" became, from Symons's pen, "We will consider…" or, even more grating on me, "We urge that…" The odd "We will…" became "We might…" or even "We possibly could…." Throughout, the new draftsman rendered sharp and unequivocal declarative statements on the most controversial subjects roadkill to tentative conditionals and timid subjunctives. Such was the official language of a diplomat. Obfuscation is the plasma of a diplomat's bloodstream. But it is a writing style that constituted a dead language to this St. Dunstan's University graduate. My prose and that of my classmates had often been drenched in red ink by our SDU English professors—Rev. Larry Landrigan, Rev. Frank Ledwell, and Dr. Brendon O'Grady—for employing this very mode.[2] Now, in the name of PC Party diplomacy, I had to reprogram myself all over again. (It was, however, good training for my later career as a diplomat in Boston, when communiqués from External Affairs headquarters in Ottawa were replete with the like and I was expected to respond in kind.)

No doubt, after these "improvements," the trees—pruned of my own magnificent handiwork but adorned with virtuosity by Symons—were fortified to survive the harsh winter: examination by Stanfield and the PCC. But it was at the expense of making the tree too leafy in many cases. That was the most common criticism by the media when they were not remarking on, and calling specific attention to, policy contradictions in the total package. The PCC was well aware of most contradictions throughout the drafting process. But, largely for political reasons, the contradictions were tolerated. It was often the only way to "reconcile" irreconcilable policy disagreements either within the committee itself or between it and, say, the parliamentary Caucus. Less often, the committee also had to adapt policy proposals to the views of a public or special-interest community whose support we were eager to attract. It was politics of the rawest sort. But this *was* politics, not academics.

It was often in this sort of circumstance that Tom Symons's dual skills as diplomat and wordsmith played most helpfully. A case in point was the party's call for an industrial strategy for the country. Like Stanfield's Guaranteed Minimum Income (GMI) plan, it was a novel idea then. The strategy would require the federal government to set its specific industrial goals for the country as a whole, then pursue them based on a cohesive set of detailed plans and policies. This more strategic approach would replace the ad hoc-ery that typically characterized how successive federal governments had fostered Canada's industrial growth over the decades under various prime ministers, regardless of party. For lack of a strategic approach, different measures, even within the same department, often worked at cross purposes with one another, undermining not only those individual measures themselves but also the overall effort. What Stanfield had in mind implied that the federal government, in concert with the provinces, would identify "winners" and "losers" in allocating tax incentives or direct subventions to help particular sectors to the exclusion of others. This, in turn, implied that individual industries would not be aided outside the overall strategy. Most people nowadays might view the concept as just commonsensical, even commonplace. Some others might think it anachronistic or, worse, simplistic and unworkable. It was, however, considered pioneering at the time. In this case, as in so many others, Stanfield was in the vanguard of modern public-policy thinking in his own era, if not well ahead of his time.

The PCC, prodded by Stanfield, embraced this new way of thinking about how best to stimulate and actively support industrial development in the private sector. Because the man came to the table with a lot of credibility based on his success in this area as Nova Scotia premier, it was not an especially hard slog for him—unlike his high climb in party circles with, for example, the GMI idea and, only slightly less difficult, official bilingualism. And yet, the PCC did not simply rubber-stamp Stanfield's industrial strategy proposal. There was vigorous debate. Most committee members recognized the political need to respond to particular cries for industrial help that would be difficult to provide other than on a case-by-case, ad hoc basis, outside a more strategic approach of the kind the leader favoured. For example, the continued existence of the Canadian magazine sector (especially *Maclean's*) was threatened at the time by foreign "dumping" practices, notably by *Time* and *Reader's Digest* (the largest paid circulation magazine in the world then). To attract advertising revenue in our country, American publishers were selling their magazines on Canadian newsstands for less than the cost of production. They could afford to do so because production costs would already have been met through high-volume sales elsewhere around the world, particularly in the United States. The retail prices of these US publications in our country were considerably lower than Canadian competitors had to charge for their magazines on the same newsstands for lack of that high-volume sales advantage. In the end, the PCC thought the government should support Canadian publishers, with either direct grants or tax benefits or both, to help level the playing field, even if publishing itself did not fit into a national industrial strategy. The fig leaf the committee decided to use to cover its naked effort to have it both ways in this instance—a strategic approach, *but*—was to say we would consider supporting certain industries separately, *but* "in the context of the industrial strategy." (The policy modification was more complex than that, but the reader will get the drift.) The compromise—considered a breakthrough—came, as it so often did, from Symons. Sometimes, the fig leaf was big enough to hide the bare-assed politics (more or less); other times, the leaf might as well have been cellophane for all the transparent duplicity. Diplomacy and wordsmith magic have their limits, even when practised by a magician like Symons.

The contradictions appeared, not only between different papers, but also within some of the papers themselves, specific examples of which some journalists were quick to note. The media's criticisms had much merit. Still, we were producing political documents, not trying to win a Governor General's Literary Award. The total process—of drafting and redrafting, massaging every word, burnishing every phrase, sanding away every splinter of possible controversy—caused what survived to be less than a classic sonnet by the Bard. The product was not so much the proverbial camel—a horse designed by committee; more like a rye-and-ginger highball that would have benefited from a little less Canada Dry and a bigger shot of Canadian Club. The amazing thing is that the verbal cocktail had as much kick to it as it did. For their breadth and depth and detail, the papers both surprised and impressed most media critics, despite specific criticisms. And the papers delighted party members, especially candidates. Re-reading some of the papers now, lo, all these many years later, I marvel, all things considered, at their quality and, in some cases, vision. They were not written for the distant future, but some pass the test of time.

# The Wrong Party?

As I studied the PC Party's policy papers from the era of Robert Stanfield for this book, not having seen them in the intervening four and a half decades, what struck me most about them, aside from their surprising thoughtfulness, was this: they constituted, collectively, a time capsule not just of the PC Party's positions on different issues of the day, but also, more fundamentally, the political values their principal authors held both as individuals and as a team. Those values appear on every page—unmistakably expressed, whether intentionally or unintentionally. Had I personally not known the papers' crafters, especially Robert Stanfield and Tom Symons, but others as well, I believe I would have been able to describe with some accuracy the nature of the persons likely responsible. A number of words come to mind. The first is "patriots." The authors, whoever they were, obviously cared deeply about their country, not just about their party's electoral chances, least of all their own personal fates. The second is "progressive." They did not fear—in fact, they warmly embraced—the state's acting boldly for the country and for its people. The third is "traditionalist"—or "conservative," if you will. Every word bespoke the drafters' eagerness to build something not entirely new but geared to improving upon the best of the existing order. And the last, but not least, word I would use to describe whoever wrote those policy papers is "compassionate." Even turgid analyses and policy positions about unemployment levels, cost-of-living indices, and economic and industrial growth were infused with a naked concern primarily for those most in need of public leadership and help: the unemployed and the working poor; people on fixed incomes ravaged by inflation, including the elderly; every person disadvantaged by an economy that soars without regard for such unintended consequences as urban congestion and pollution; and individual language and cultural communities in the crosshairs of economic and cultural change affecting the unity and integrity of the country itself.

Even had I never met the people most responsible long ago for producing what I read, I am certain of this much: I would have liked the individuals who produced the policies of the Progressive Conservative Party of Canada in that period. Could they possibly have belonged to the same Conservative Party that governed my country under Stephen Harper's leadership some four and a half decades later? Patriots? Progressives? Traditionalists? Compassionates? Or did the library archivist give me to read and study the wrong party's set of policies produced so many years ago? Worse to contemplate, is it possible that the two parties are one and the same, but something went desperately wrong with this institution in the intervening years? It is to wonder. It is to worry. It could be to cry.

# Chapter 11

# BRAINS TRUST

Canadian conservatism—as with any other political or ideological "ism"—reflects who the believer is at his or her core: how he sees himself, how he views his relationships with others, and, even more fundamentally, what he thinks his relationship should be to the collectivity in the form of government.

A job title in politics, as in most fields, can be very misleading. A regular viewer of public affairs programs on television might think that parties' "senior advisors" or "senior strategists" outnumber actual voters. For sure, none of the networks lacks a steady supply of such people to interview, engage in verbal combat with one another, and flood the airwaves with prefabricated talking points from each pundit's party. Rarely will the partisans' political credentials mentioned by the host or flashed across the TV screen reveal much beyond party identification or close association with one prominent politician or another. Values—except, possibly, identifying the political performing monkeys as from the ideological "right" or "left"—aren't mentioned, let alone stressed.

Everybody is shortchanged when defined—by anyone—by his or her job. It is our values that count in the end. They, not our job or salary, help define each of us as a unique human being. This principle applies no less to political advisors than to the politicians they advise. The practice of affixing "senior advisor" or the like to every bottle-blond or faux-macho political hack a network wants to present to viewers as important has had, over time, the opposite effect: Very few of these operatives any longer impress the politically literate with their high-sounding titles alone. In Robert Stanfield's era, however, Tom Symons's advisory role and title meant something. It certainly did to both men.

Because one's value system is so central to who he (or she) is, a major national political party leader does not rely on another individual to provide it. A politician at that high level is presumed to possess a value system of his own, and wishes to lead his followers in the same direction. Even his closest advisor cannot supply it. Nor should he try. Symons couldn't, and didn't. At most, the advisor helps the leader refine his values or sharpen them or bring them to the fore or express them or rethink them in certain, but not fundamental, ways. Most of all, the advisor helps the advised act on his values as leader.

This chapter is about *hows*: how Robert Stanfield's values were influenced by his senior advisor, Tom Symons, how other leaders' advisors operated, how Symons brought a conservative value system to bear on Stanfield's own, and how, to a very large extent, their roles were simultaneously reversed in the process. As so often happens in an advisor/advised relationship, Stanfield's search for his political moral compass centre was not conducted along a one-person path; for him, it was a path on which he linked arms with Tom Symons. I was fortunate that the path's shoulder was wide enough for me to tag along. As I did so, trying desperately with mixed success to keep pace with the two sprinters, I found my own conservative values coming steadily into sharper focus.

Ultimately, any person's search for values needs to be conducted on a path within himself. No other person, not even his or her closest confidant or counsellor, can get inside the searcher's head, still less soul. It's ultimately a lonely journey, one that does not end until the traveller dies. But the traveller can be guided by other people, either directly or indirectly.

# Tom, Charley, and Tom

"Senior Advisor to the Honourable Robert L. Stanfield" was Tom Symons's official title. It was almost as deceptive as "PC *Annual* Meeting," if not, like the other, an outright misnomer. This title evokes a Rasputin as he hovers about a czar so desperate to save his hemophiliac son that he puts the fate of his crown and kingdom in the hands of the mad and controlling monk. Stanfield was no captive Czar Nicholas II, Symons no controlling Rasputin. But neither was the Trent University president a policy advisor of the sort Charles McMillan would become to Brian Mulroney or Tom Axworthy to Pierre Trudeau. McMillan served as chief policy advisor to Prime Minister Mulroney from 1984 to 1987, and had played the same role when Mulroney was leader of the Official Opposition. McMillan was Mulroney's "intellectual bodyguard" and partisan alter ego. But neither man was captor or captive to the other, least of all in fundamental values. Axworthy, a Winnipeg native, joined Prime Minister Trudeau's staff in 1975 as understudy to Jim Coutts, Trudeau's principal secretary at the time, and then soared through the ranks to serve in the same capacity from 1981 to 1984.

I know Charley McMillan better than anyone else does, save his bright wife Kazuyo, a pharmacist born and raised in Japan. That's because, as readers will recall, Charley is my twin brother. My official narrative is that, when we Siamese twins were surgically divided at birth, I got the single brain we had shared. So, years later, he was reduced to working *for* a minister of the Crown—albeit the "First among Equals"—whereas I actually *was* one. The truth is we are fraternal twins. If no man is a hero to his valet, no brother is perfect in the eyes of his twin, either. True to form, Charley, a few minutes older than I, considers himself the First Edition, the Original, me a mere copy. For my part, I see myself as the Improved, Revised Edition: what God wrought, perfectly, after seeing His mistakes the first go. Certainly, Charley is even more congenitally incapable of punctuality than I. It is the characteristic we have most markedly in common, in kind if not degree. Sibling rivalry aside, Charley is—I have to admit grudgingly—a first-rate scholar and a brilliant man. It is to that brain I now turn to illustrate Tom Symons's very different relationship to Robert Stanfield compared to that between other policy advisors and their respective masters.

At the height of their advisor/advised relationship, one could almost have spoken of Charley McMillan's and Brian Mulroney's brains in the singular, for it was as though, like Siamese twins, they shared the one. My brother wrote the university textbook *The Japanese Industrial System*, translated into several languages, and has published other books and many scholarly articles.[1] An authority on Japanese management, he is professor of business policy and international business at York University. He is much in demand on the corporate and college lecture circuit and as a business consultant. Charley brought all this expertise to Mulroney's ambitions. But, as we shall see, he brought much more.

I, of course, know Tom Axworthy less well than I do Charley. Tom and I, however, were classmates at Queen's (graduate school in political studies), and we took some of the same courses. Like McMillan, he holds a PhD—Charley's is from the Bradford Management School, in England; Axworthy's is from Queen's. At different times, Axworthy has been a lecturer (Queen's, Harvard), community leader (Charles Bronfman Foundation, Historica, among others), author, public affairs commentator, and consultant, among many other things he does extraordinarily well. As he always has done, including while a student at Queen's, Axworthy dazzles with sheer brainpower and knowledge, not to mention uncommon charm and good humour. There is an interesting coincidence here. Charley McMillan and Tom Axworthy each had a brother in Cabinet while serving their respective prime minister as senior policy advisor: me for Mulroney (tourism, environment); Tom's older brother, Lloyd, for Trudeau (foreign affairs, transport, employment).

Both Charley McMillan and Tom Axworthy fit a certain model: the in-house expert, all-round intellectual guru, and brainy general factotum who has the ear of his boss, his eye on the ball, shoulder to the grindstone, and is not farther than a foot from the throne. Such people are strong on body parts, especially the cerebellum. For about the same time (about four years), each served as senior policy advisor to the prime minister of Canada. Each had a unique and august title: "Senior Policy Advisor" (Charley's); "Principal Secretary" (Tom's). But, when all is said and done, each was in the employ of his man. They were public sector *employees*. Mulroney and Trudeau themselves had big brains and virtually unlimited access to the brains and specialized knowledge of others, within the government and without. What the two leaders wanted, and got, from their respective senior policy advisors went well beyond brainpower and expertise: sharp instincts and mutual trust and unquestioned two-way loyalty on the *substance* and the *politics* of the issues, immediate and long term. Moreover, each man had a high level of compatibility with his boss on basic values, including religious beliefs in the case of McMillan and Mulroney—both are Roman Catholics; Trudeau, too, was Catholic, but Axworthy's family has deep United Church roots. Brains. Trust. That was what, for both Mulroney and Trudeau, "brains trust" meant.

As volunteers, Charley and Tom had been active, to one degree or another, in the affairs and proscenia of their respective parties: Charley, policy guard for Mulroney as the PC Party leadership aspirant struggled in the minor leagues before making MVP in the majors; Tom, a policy-oriented foot soldier in various electoral contests in Manitoba and nationally. Being a senior staffer in the Prime Minister's Office (PMO), however, was a completely different matter. For starters, one got a regular paycheque. Now, both boys were salaried professional partisan henchmen of the first rank. Young Turks. Sword-wielders. Political operatives. Part of the elite palace guard—the Praetorian Guard. For that, they were, each in his own way, ideally suited for the role—and for the palace occupant whose regal front door they guarded. Clearly, their respective bosses thought so.

I will use Charley as a "case study"—as they would say at York's business school—in contrasting the role he played for Mulroney with Tom Symons's role for Stanfield. Again, I know Charley's personal history better than I know Tom's. The essential points, though, apply to both advisors. If one wants to know how a Dr. C. J. McMillan or a Dr. T. S. Axworthy or a Dr. T. H. B. Symons did his job, it is essential to know who Charley or Tom or the other Tom, respectively, is as an individual.

# THE MCMILLAN MODEL: INTELLECTUAL BODYGUARD

Charles McMillan forged a bond with Brian Mulroney when they independently attended the PC Niagara Policy Conference in 1969. Charley was one of the few people, in Mulroney's tight-knit circle of most trusted friends and confidants, who worked for Mulroney in *both* of his bids for the PC leadership—in 1976, which failed; in 1983, which succeeded. Some of Mulroney's inner circle knew and supported him in 1976, but not 1983; conversely, some in 1983, but not 1976. Charley, rarest of birds, flew with Mulroney on both flights to the stars. His main role in the leadership races was as Mulroney's chief policy gatekeeper, a role he retained long after those leadership races ended. So he was a true charter member of the Mulroney team. It is an elite group whose membership is more select than that of the Sovereign Military Order of Malta. And, at that time, it was just as fiercely loyal and committed to a cause. For many in this group now, the shared cause is perpetuating the Mulroney legacy and protecting the reputation of the man himself.

Brian Mulroney's reputation took a big hit concerning shady dealings he was alleged to have had with a certain German businessman, Karlheinz Schreiber. It was in the context of Air Canada's purchase of a large number of Airbus jets while he was prime minister. Surely, that was as tawdry—and just plain icky—a relationship between a Canadian prime minister and a huckster as has ever been documented. A pan-partisan House of Commons Ethics Committee conducted hearings into allegations that Mulroney had received a $300,000 kickback. An independent public commission of inquiry appointed in 2009 by the Harper government and chaired by Jeffrey Oliphant, associate justice of the highest trial court for Manitoba, also investigated the charges. Both investigations found Mulroney culpable of only "inappropriate" judgment, not wrong-doing, least of all criminality. The damage to the former PM's reputation, however, could not be totally reversed. In any event, the man's entire decade-long record as prime minister should not be viewed exclusively through such a narrow and fuzzy lens. As University of Louisiana historian T. Harry Williams, Pulitzer-Prize–winning author of first-rate books about political giants such as Abraham Lincoln, has argued, "No politician should be judged by just one aspect of his character or career....Such a man has to be evaluated in the round, to be rated by what he did to and for society and to and for himself."[2] I agree. Mulroney's friends and supporters will need to convince Canadians to take this kind of broader view of him now that he is long out of politics. I know my former boss to be a person of high moral principles with extraordinary inner strength. Not just his family and friends and colleagues like me have benefited from these qualities; the country has, too.

Whether or not Charley remains a Mulroney disciple forever, one who definitely will is Bob Shea. He shared digs with Mulroney at St. Francis Xavier University, in Antigonish, Nova Scotia, and, like the former PM, is of Irish heritage. To this day, more than a half-century later, Shea is one of Mulroney's closest and most loyal friends. An American, he is a successful financier and lives with his vivacious wife, Trudy, in Boston's tony Back Bay. I got to know them well as Canadian consul general to New England based in their city. Shea is not an actual Knight of Malta, despite having been invited a dozen times to join this extremely exclusive Catholic lay charitable order founded in the Middle Ages. But he is the kind of True Believer whose membership in either the Knights of Malta or the Mulroney Loyalty Club would command the same fierce and undying devotion. Loyalty, especially to friends, is among Mulroney's most distinguishing human qualities and the one he most values in others, especially his followers. When a government leader holds loyalty dear, he or she tends to extend it well beyond family and friends and colleagues to his or her country. Faux scandals such as Airbus notwithstanding, Mulroney certainly did.

At the beginning, Charley's brain gave Brian Mulroney not only specialized knowledge, but also intellectual radar at a time when, as a mere candidate for leadership, the Quebecer felt he needed more help with both. With time, during the ascent up the political ladder, Mulroney depended less and less on Charley for specialized policy or issues support. The prime minister, with the snap of a middle finger and thumb, could get that within the public service or from any other source he wanted to tap. But, more and more, the PM needed Charley as his "intellectual bodyguard." Increasingly, people were shaking his ladder, as inevitably happens after the end of any new prime minister's political honeymoon, historically short in Mulroney's case. Lyndon Johnson once said, of his ecumenical approach to US presidential appointments, that he would prefer to have his enemies "inside the tent pissing out than outside the tent pissing in." Mulroney saw in Charley someone who would help guard him from those who would piss at him from both directions. Like Mulroney, Charley himself placed a high value on loyalty—to Mulroney as much as to anyone. If a senior advisor does not bring this quality to his boss, all other qualities he might have, no matter how strong, are irrelevant. Values matter in politics.

The role of a US president's bodyguard is to take a bullet for his boss—literally. Charley would have done that for Mulroney—at least figuratively. For Charley, politics is like a game of chess. How many other pieces remain on the board (queen, bishop, knight, rook, pawn) is inconsequential—if the king is knocked out, the game ends. So it was for him with Mulroney. The leader had to be protected at any cost; everyone else, including the senior advisor himself, was dispensable. My brother saw his role as one of guarding Mulroney in the policy sphere no matter what. He felt a particular need to protect the prime minister against insiders pushing self-serving secret agendas in the guise of candid disinterested policy advice. Offenders or suspects included everyone from political colleagues (even Cabinet ministers) to party bigwigs to lobbyists to senior officials. Such "advice" typically took the form of "options" skewed to restrict serious consideration of anything but the advisor's own preferred choice, if not vested interest.[3] Mulroney was well aware of the trap, and saw Charley as one of his strongest defences against it. Because the two men had long been in the political trenches together, the prime minister knew his senior policy advisor was one of the few he could trust implicitly not to have an agenda of his own—except to protect him. And Charley made no secret of that agenda. Loyalty was both his principal mandate and personal cause. It's lonely at the top. In the Mulroney-McMillan pairing, the combination of compatible intellects, shared political history, personal friendship, aligned partisan instincts, and mutual loyalty and trust helped keep the prime minister dry from the pissers and the political rains alike, especially since the personalities of the advisor and the advised were similar, though in some respects not at all the same. Charley's was a messy job, to be sure, but someone had to do it. For Mulroney, as for Trudeau with Tom Axworthy, who better to perform the task than a hard-nosed Young Turk who did not mind the odour and who could piss with the best of them? And, in Charley's case, he might even have taken a bullet for his man.

My brother, of course, supported the prime minister's major policies: free trade, the goods and services tax, fiscal restraint, the Meech Lake Accord, the Charlottetown Accord, acid rain, new national parks, and so on. He had a big hand in shaping, or at least in sharpening, Mulroney's thinking in most such areas. But, just as

Mulroney was not driven by ideology—recall the coffee pot, earlier—neither was his senior policy advisor. Undeniably, Charley, from both sides of our family, was congenitally an irredeemable Tory. Despite a rich political heritage, however, my twin was no more fanatically partisan than ideological—though more partisan, even if no more ideological, than Tom Symons. There was about as much chance of Charley's splitting with Mulroney over an issue as of either of them joining the Most Noble Order of the Garter. They were a team. They liked each other. They were both Roman Catholics, but not especially religious. They had similar outlooks on politics and issues. Their moral compasses pointed in roughly the same general direction. They were each Progressive Conservatives from a young age. Both men were fluently bilingual, so were able to exchange confidences, and curse common enemies, in either official language. The two men were in politics together, just as they had been from the beginning of the most active period. Not much more to it than that. The personal connection, not ideology or policies or issues, framed the relationship. Only to a limited extent were shared fundamental human values relevant. This dimension is what got Charley through Mulroney's front door at the Niagara Policy Conference back in 1969, but it did not get him beyond the foyer, much less into the private library. That intimate access came from a more personal connection, best summarized as *Personality*. Think of it as the *McMillan Model*. Now consider the *Axworthy Model*, which, though similar, is sufficiently different to merit separate attention.

## THE AXWORTHY MODEL: IDEOLOGUE

Tom Axworthy's role with Pierre Trudeau was primarily defined by *policy* in the context of personality; over time, Trudeau and Axworthy came to like each other a lot. Charles McMillan's role with Mulroney, by contrast, was defined by *personality* in the context of policy; the two political comrades' policies became almost identical over time. But, concerning fundamentals, McMillan's and Axworthy's respective situations as policy advisor were parallel. The geometry was the same—only the thickness of the two lines highlighted the difference.

Tom Axworthy is nothing if not an economic nationalist. His commitment to Canada's sovereignty and cultural identity defines his career and him personally, particularly his basic values mindset. Strip this man of his nationalism and one is left with a brainy linebacker who jokes and laughs a lot. Nationalistic values drive him with the urgency of a soccer mom running red lights to get her goalie son to his team's decisive game after it has already started. The same was true of Tom when we were classmates in graduate school at Queen's: he was a militant economic nationalist of the first rank. There was not enough room on his chest for all the war medals. Nor could enough mixed metaphors describe fully this complex human being and former political operative.

As I write, Tom Axworthy is president and CEO of the Walter and Duncan Gordon Foundation. In the early 1960s, he was a research assistant for the Task Force on the Structure of the Canadian Economy. This body was led by the late Walter Gordon, a Lester Pearson senior minister now the patron saint of Canadian economic nationalists. For Axworthy, Gordon was not just saintly, but godly.

Tom Axworthy began his surge up the Liberal political escalator when recruited by campaign manager Keith Davey for the 1974 election campaign. Axworthy was to write the Liberals' campaign plank on housing, a big issue at the time. His first major post was with Housing Minister Ron Basford, with whom he stayed when Basford was shuffled to the Department of National Revenue after the election; Tom likely saw the tax code as the best way to paper the US Embassy walls with red maple leaves and beaver pelts. He had already declined a job in the PMO—in fact, he had not been an early admirer of Pierre Trudeau, and did not support him for the Liberal Party leadership in 1968, when Lester Pearson retired. This fact contrasts sharply with Charles McMillan's support for Mulroney in the latter's leadership runs. As a militant nationalist, Axworthy changed his mind about joining Trudeau's inner circle only when Jim Coutts became Trudeau's principal secretary. Along with Davey, Coutts was another member of the Walter Gordon nationalist wing of the Liberal Party. In the PMO, Axworthy caught Trudeau's eye. With all those shiny military medals on his chest, how could anyone miss him? In 1979, after Joe Clark's Tories defeated the Liberals, Tom agreed to work for Trudeau, then leader of the Official Opposition, as "acting director and senior policy advisor."

Policy was Axworthy's thing, but that's a little like saying prayer is the pope's thing. Can anyone knowledgeable about recent Canadian history possibly think that Tom Axworthy did *not* have a big hand in Trudeau's ultra-nationalistic measures, particularly the Foreign Investment Review Agency and the National Energy Program in the early 1980s? Policy motivates Axworthy, period—just as it underpinned his relationship with Trudeau. Among other duties, Axworthy wrote speeches for his leader while on the public payroll. Charley McMillan (and others) played this role for Mulroney in the leadership races, but not officially when Mulroney became Opposition leader, and not at all in the PMO, where the job, primarily, was that of L. Ian MacDonald. For his part, Tom Symons never wrote a single speech for Robert Stanfield, a task mostly shared by Tom Sloan and Bill Grogan and performed by Joe Clark and others before he became an MP in 1972. Symons contributed many ideas and notes to Stanfield speeches. That, however, was the full extent. Tom Axworthy scrupulously separated his speech-writing and policy-advisor functions. For this book, Tom told me: "When I was writing for Trudeau, I forgot I was Axworthy. I tried to write as if I was PET. Therefore, before I started writing for him, I read all his writings in *Cité libre*, read the Catholic social activism literature he loved, and tried to understand how he thought about issues. I wrote as a surrogate Trudeau, not as Axworthy trying to influence Trudeau. I did try to influence him, of course. But that was through memos when I wrote to him, not for him."

Tom Axworthy's relationship with Trudeau was even closer than that between McMillan and Mulroney. For sure, Axworthy's with Trudeau endured longer after Tom exited politics (with Trudeau's own departure in 1984) than Charley's did with Mulroney after Charley left, in 1987, towards the end of Mulroney's first term (to return to academe, his first passion); Axworthy and Trudeau collaborated in 1990 on a book, *Towards a Just Society: The Trudeau Years*.[4] Of the two, Tom was more ideological, more issues-driven, more motivated by core values; Charley more personality/loyalty-driven. Over the course of the political wars fought side by side, partners in either kind of relationship (loyalty or ideology) inevitably develop a shared history. The bond between the two partners might have been forged originally by friendship and loyalty, as in Charley's case, or by issues and policies and values, as in Tom's. In politics, however, the two sets of factors tend to become inextricably linked. The loyalist (Charley) becomes ever more committed to the policies of the man he is loyal to (Mulroney); and, for his part, the ideologue (Tom), originally drawn to the object of his admiration (Trudeau) primarily because of his policies, develops a steadily growing loyalty to him on a personal level independent of policy. When Charley left Mulroney's office, he told me: "Brian and I did not differ on a major issue. In fact, I can't recall any that we disagreed on. Any dispute, and they were few, always concerned how to manage the issue, not over the issue itself. And, generally, we saw eye to eye on that, too." Tom informed me: "I did not start out as a Trudeau loyalist...I grew to love him, but it was not love at first sight." Sad to say, Pierre Trudeau is now deceased. Charley and Mulroney keep in touch, though not nearly as often as they once did even after each left government. Like former lovers, former political colleagues tend to misplace each other's phone number.

## THE SYMONS MODEL: MENTOR/PROCESS

Tom Symons's role as Stanfield's senior policy advisor could not have been more different both from Charley McMillan's with Mulroney and from Tom Axworthy's with Trudeau. Except that, as with McMillan and Axworthy, the human factor was crucial. McMillan and Axworthy were somewhat younger than Symons at the age each man began his advisory role. The two younger men were even younger than the Trent University president culturally. Quite apart from those personal differences, Symons's senior-policy-advisory role was not at all the same functionally as those of the other two men. The Symons Model was as different from that of the McMillan and Axworthy Models as aged scotch is from draft beer. Again, let's focus on Charley McMillan. (What's a twin brother for?)

Tom Symons had no personal history with Robert Stanfield, either intellectually or politically, before he became his senior advisor. Unlike Mulroney and McMillan when the former finally became leader, Stanfield and Symons had not really known each other at the time their relationship was forged; they knew only *of* each other by national reputation. Stanfield did not seek in Symons a political frat brother. He already had a good enough political fraternity of his own from his eleven years in government in Nova Scotia before becoming PC Leader. Mulroney, by contrast, had no government experience prior to his winning the Tory leadership. Stanfield had long cultivated a tight-knit group of smart and politically savvy people, mostly Maritimers, on whom he could rely for dispassionate and candid political advice and male friendship and with whom he shared core values—"Red Tory" values, primarily. These friends included fellow Nova Scotian Finlay MacDonald, who sold his house in Halifax and bought another in the exclusive Ottawa suburb of Rockcliffe to be near Stanfield as a special advisor on strategy and organization and help him become prime minister. He had been part of Stanfield's political career since the 1953 Nova Scotia provincial election. A prosperous broadcaster who headed a media group (CJCH Ltd.) that operated radio and television stations throughout the Halifax area, MacDonald became president of Industrial Estates Ltd., the provincial industrial promotion and development agency established by the Stanfield government. Meanwhile, he served as Nova Scotia PC Party president and three terms as national party vice-president. Finlay MacDonald was widely known to be Stanfield's most trusted friend and political confidant. Brian Mulroney once described MacDonald as "very intimate with Stanfield. He can tell [him] things nobody else can tell him."[5] After chairing Brian Mulroney's Opposition-to-government transition team in 1983, MacDonald was the first person Mulroney appointed to the Senate, in 1984.

Dalton Camp, Diefenbaker's nemesis from New Brunswick, was another member of Stanfield's close-knit fraternity. So was Flora MacDonald, from North Sydney, Nova Scotia. Flora was Stanfield's closest female political ally and friend—a virtual big sister, though younger. The many values shared by Robert Stanfield and Flora MacDonald were deeply rooted in Nova Scotian soil. Hers were decidedly of the Old World Scottish variety, with its fierce loyalty to kin and clan and country. If you had Flora on your side, you needed practically no other. Politically, she was a Joan of Arc, ready to do battle with all comers. If St. Joan was, as commonly characterized, "the maid of Orléans," St. Flora was "the maid of Cape Breton"—a lifelong spinster married only to politics. Flora was as militantly committed to her values as she was capable of fighting political wars to both advance and defend them. Most often, in the early years, the standard she bore into battle was in front of Robert Stanfield's army. The two Nova Scotians held basically the same political values, except Flora's Tory red was as flaming as her hair, his as muted as the clothes he wore.

Just as Robert Stanfield was not seeking from his senior advisor a political frat brother, so also he was not desperate for specialized advice, either. Stanfield himself frequently knew more about the issues than the experts or provincial Cabinet colleagues who briefed him. The most significant difference between the role played by McMillan and Axworthy, on the one hand, and by Symons, on the other, was this: Tom Symons, unlike Charley McMillan and Tom Axworthy, was not a paid public sector employee. Tom Symons was, in every sense, a *citizen servant*, not a *public servant* (in the bureaucratic sense). Nor was he a classic political operative, as Charley and Tom certainly were. And the final difference is truly paradoxical: of the three men, Tom Symons was the least partisan, yet he alone, not McMillan or Axworthy, had a mandate to help blaze a new policy trail, not just for his leader, but also for that leader's *party*. Partisans McMillan and Axworthy were asked to play a public role; citizen Tory Symons was asked to play a partisan role. If "freedom's just another word for nothing left to lose," in the words of the famous Janis Joplin song, politics is just another word for "nothing left but irony"—in this case, supreme irony.

Stanfield did not seek in Symons a politically astute brain, though Symons certainly was that. Nor did he seek a policy expert of the McMillan-Axworthy variety, though Symons was, in certain areas, that as well. Least of all did Stanfield feel the need for a close friend, though, to be sure, the two developed a warm relationship over time. Finally, Stanfield was not the sort to surround himself either with sycophants or people whose normative values were necessarily identical to his own. Clearly, he would never have recruited for the inner circle anyone hostile to his own core values—nor would Mulroney have recruited McMillan, or Trudeau Axworthy, had either of them failed to "get through the front door" by that standard. But Stanfield thrived on being challenged by individuals whose views he respected and from whom he could obtain not only sound advice, but also a good argument that might have practical "truth to power" value, or at least enlarge his intellectual or moral horizon. That said, the PC leader was not seeking in his chief policy advisor a mirror opposite in some effort to have a countervailing influence on his thinking. What Stanfield sought, instead, was a mature, academically well placed, and respected individual of the first rank who, by virtue of his personal standing, could help the leader advance his major priority: revolutionize the policy content of the PC Party and, thereby, transform the public face of a great national institution. He felt it urgent to do so because his predecessor, Diefenbaker, taking leave of not only the PC leadership but also his senses, had caused the public to perceive the grand old party of Sir John A. Macdonald to be no longer acceptable as an alternative to the governing Liberals.

As a brilliant but confused undergraduate at Dalhousie University, Stanfield had put virtually his entire academic welfare in the hands of Economics Department head W. Russell Maxwell, whom he always credited with turning his personal life around and who would become a lifelong mentor and trusted personal friend. Stanfield now sought his new Russell Maxwell to help him turn his political party's life around following the 1968 election debacle. And, in Tom Symons, he found that new mentor. At this stage, Stanfield needed a wise and mature progressive who would show him the way to where he wanted to go and help him get there. His predecessor had, for example, tied up Parliament for months maniacally opposing the country's noble effort to give itself something as basic as a distinctive flag. Similarly, the old man had recklessly campaigned and caballed and voted against bilingualism—a tenet of Canada's reality, a part of the very nature of the country, and at the heart of the Conservative Party's original English-French partnership with Macdonald/Cartier and the Conservative/Liberal coalition. The same spirit characterized Sir Robert Borden's efforts to avoid a national split along linguistic fault lines when forming a Union government in the First World War. In turning his back on this venerable Canadian Tory tradition, Diefenbaker was a "rogue," indeed.

Robert Stanfield was determined to follow a far different course from John Diefenbaker's. As we have seen, Stanfield's course would be carefully devised policy, in contrast to Diefenbaker's reliance on high-voltage rhetoric and sloganeering. To help him, the new leader was not looking for a political assistant with a postage-stamp-sized passport photo. He wanted an *éminence grise* whose gilt-framed portrait he could hang over the Tory mantle and blast with a mega-watt art gallery lamp. This was not to be a conventional political recruitment. Stanfield and Symons shared core values, were intellectually compatible, held similar views on the major issues of the day, and liked each other personally. Stanfield's choosing Symons as his senior policy advisor is easy to understand in hindsight, but it was not an obvious choice at the time, least of all to the party's old guard. After all, for more than a decade the PC Party had been led by someone who attached no importance to policy beyond his own political impulses. It had been even longer since the party had made any effort to develop policy systematically, however inadequately. Never before had the party's leader signalled that he intended to develop policy as his highest priority and in a long-term, broadly consultative, organic, and public way. Now, the new leader was recruiting a university president not just to advise him personally on issues, but, more important, to create and conduct a major policy-development process for the party right out in the open for all to see. What had the world come to? And who was this odd Haligonian, anyway?

---

Robert Stanfield did not enter the PC leadership convention in September 1967 as the front-runner. He shot to the top of an eleven-candidate pack from far behind with an elegantly crafted opening-day speech at the convention's *policy* session. Stanfield's first salvo rocked the convention, surprised the media, shocked the political pros, knocked his opponents off their feet, set the stage for his ultimate victory, and changed the history and the direction of the party for a generation. In the speech, with inspired literary help from Dalton Camp, this extraordinarily thoughtful and visionary politician, so unlike the man he was seeking to replace, told the delegates not what kind of leader *he* would be for the party, but, rather, the kind of *party* he wanted to lead. Stanfield said the party he envisioned "accepts there are no nice ideological solutions to economic problems, nor is there any Original Sin in economic planning." One can only imagine how badly that message was received by the greybeards at Toronto's port-and-cigars Tory bastion, the Albany Club.

To contemporary policy specialists, Robert Stanfield's pro-economic planning theme at the 1967 leadership convention might seem as quaint as a punch-key typewriter to a twenty-first-century college student. But at the time, that perspective was considered bold and futuristic, especially for a Tory leadership candidate. Whatever the merits of the concept itself, this was a way for the Nova Scotia premier to differentiate himself from not only the leader he was seeking to replace, but also the multitude of other candidates, whose themes were generally uniform, more conventional, and therefore utterly predictable. Most delegates were eagerly searching for fresh new leadership for their party, even if not necessarily this particular policy perspective. Stanfield's opening convention address resonated so powerfully with delegates because his alone captured their desire for change. Both what Stanfield said and the conviction and authenticity with which he said it demonstrated to an anxious party that, in him, and not in any of the other ten candidates, they had found their new standard-bearer.

On the third day of the convention, Stanfield said the party he wanted to lead was progressive, reformist, and modern, while faithful to the soul of its founding leader, Sir John A. Macdonald, the greatest Tory chief of them all. The leadership aspirant told delegates he was seeking to head a party "that will be recognized not merely for its affluence, for its comfort, for its power—but for its humanity, for its compassion, and for its decency." As leader, he would use many of the very same words and phrases to describe the direction he wanted to take the country. With Tom Symons at his side, Stanfield brought this overarching set of values to bear in shaping the party's policies on a broad range of issues of the day, both economic and social. This was timeless *Toryism* at its core.

No longer would John Diefenbaker's prairie populism be the way of the party, arousing passion though increasingly standing for little more than the survival of the embattled Chief himself as his growing mania alienated all but the cultist few. In its stead would be a new way for the party, rooted not in passion, but in thoughtful evidence- and fact-based policy aimed less at the committed few than at the uncommitted many whom the new Tory leader was determined to attract to his pew. Who better to help achieve that goal than Tom Symons—no rabid partisan, just a public-spirited and principled Citizen Tory; a man who saw in Robert Stanfield, just as this Trent University historian saw in Sir John A. Macdonald, both the progressive and the tried-and-true values that, if embraced by the party now through policy, *could* make him a rabid Tory?

Another difference between the policy-advisory role played by Charles McMillan and Tom Axworthy and that by Tom Symons was that, for most of the time, McMillan's and Axworthy's respective party leaders were in power, so they were tasked with helping literally to *make* public policy. By contrast, Symons's party leader was always in Opposition, never in government. Symons's task, therefore, was to help generate policy *proposals*. The Stanfield-Symons policy-development process sought to prepare an agenda for the PC Party should it win office. In theory, their proposals later could have become law in the event the party succeeded electorally. But, as Robert Burns lyricized, the best-laid schemes of men, as of mice, often get crushed by a plough in a farmer's field. Thus, although the distinction between making policy in government and simply proposing it in Opposition might be blurry theoretically, it is fundamental in the real world of politics. In understanding Symons's unique relationship with Stanfield, however, that distinction should not be overstated. Both Axworthy and McMillan had a relationship with their respective masters while those masters were also in Opposition—in Axworthy's case, in the period between Pierre Trudeau's electoral defeat by Joe Clark in May 1979 and his triumphant return to power in February 1980; in McMillan's case, between Brian Mulroney's election as PC leader in June 1983 and his becoming prime minister in September 1984. Neither the relationship between Axworthy and Trudeau nor that between McMillan and Mulroney changed significantly when the two leaders themselves crossed the House of Commons aisle to the other side.

I was the Official Opposition deputy House leader, responsible for the PC Party's strategy in the House of Commons daily Question Period during the entire time Mulroney was Opposition leader (more about that later). In this role, I worked closely with Charley McMillan and Mulroney (and others) to plot parliamentary strategy. Indeed, I met with Mulroney virtually every parliamentary day, early in the morning, unless he was on the road or otherwise engaged. I was able to see first-hand that Charley's role with Mulroney as "intellectual bodyguard" might have became even more central in the government period than while in Opposition. But his relationship with the man himself, both politically and personally, remained fundamentally the same on either side of the aisle—in fact, almost exactly as it had been in Mulroney's leadership campaigns. The same was true of the relationship between Axworthy and Trudeau; it did not matter whether they were in government or in Opposition. Witness the fact that, after the two men left government at the same time, they continued to collaborate much as they had always done before.

In summary, there are three basic models for a major political leader's senior policy advisor. They can best be thought of as the three "*P's*," representing, discretely, "*Personality*," "*Policy*," and "*Process*." Prototypically, Charles McMillan fit the "Personality" model, Tom Axworthy the "Policy" model, and Tom Symons the distinctly different "Process" model. The three models are not mutually exclusive, for each of the three advisors had many qualities and responsibilities the other two possessed. But these three models are at the core of the matter. Charles McMillan's relationship to Mulroney was based on *personality* (friendship, personal compatibility and comfort level, loyalty, mutual trust, shared political history and battles; common political and personal values; and, in execution, guarding the leader's policy flank, including from insider schemers). Axworthy's to Trudeau was based on *policy* (ideology, common policy interests, direct policy advice and speech-writing, intellectual stimulation, mutual academic respect, and, later, literary collaboration). What Stanfield sought, and found, in Tom Symons was an individual who could help him as much with *process* as with policy per se. In the context of shared positions on the issues and common values, the PC leader asked his senior policy advisor to mobilize the talent and resources required to develop policy, not necessarily to provide direct policy advice himself—though that, too, was part of his mandate, but only secondarily (the subject of the next chapter). It was this "*P*" that characterized, quintessentially and distinctly, the Symons Model: *process* rooted in a great cause: modernizing, and thereby saving the Tory Party, in the wake of the previous leader's years of neglect and, towards the end, mania.

# Chapter 12

# THE EAR OF
# THE LEADER

I have stressed the role of Tom Symons in helping Robert Stanfield transform the PC Party based on their shared commitment to making it more contemporary and progressive after a decade under John Diefenbaker's leadership. I have placed Symons at the centre of the narrative not only because he played a pivotal role in the history of the party in this period, but also because, to me, he, like Stanfield, embodied a genuine and admirable kind of conservatism that both reflected and contributed to the best traditions of this storied national institution. Symons the man, not just Symons the senior advisor to the leader, personifies and symbolizes what I am searching for in this book: conservatism at its core and in its finest expression, not as an abstract exercise, but as a beacon for the Conservative Party—and for the country, when the party holds power—to follow now and in the future.

The Conservative Party needs to reflect on the pattern of its positions on the issues over the generations, and how it developed those positions, as part of the process to correct its current course. But, just as valuably, the party also needs to remind itself of the kinds of individuals who led it for a very long time in its illustrious past. Tom Symons brought to Robert Stanfield's leadership and to the party superior management skills, deep knowledge of issues, and an uncommon ability to mobilize people and resources to help the party shift its course towards its truer light. But he brought substantially more: a profound sense of the party's tradition and heritage, of its fundamental historic values as expressed in its choice of leaders and policies over time, and, in particular, of the party's strong commitment to community, often at the expense of its own electoral advantage in the short term. Stanfield chose Symons to be both his *principal policy advisor* and, just as significant, *the public face* of the party's efforts, in partnership with the leader, to restore its best traditions through policy development. And he did so because, in his gut, the leader believed the man was a "true Tory" in the spirit of those traditions.

Tom Symons is knowledgeable about many different issues, expert in a number. His expertise is especially notable in education—Canadian Studies, in particular—Franco-Ontarian matters, cultural property and heritage, Aboriginal affairs, and human rights. But I would make two major points here. First, the areas where Symons is most knowledgeable—in a word: "social"—tend not to be the ones in which Robert Stanfield was most interested. The areas where Stanfield was expert, and most heavily involved, were primarily economic: federal-provincial fiscal arrangements; national monetary and fiscal policy, including by definition taxation; and income-support programs, particularly the Guaranteed Minimum Income (GMI) proposal he had long advanced; among others. These were not Symons's strongest suits.

One could view this asymmetry as an advantage, each man compensating for the other's policy "weakness." To an extent, that was true. Stanfield became more sensitive to, and informed about, certain social policy matters than he would have been had Symons not regularly briefed him on them, whether at policy meetings or in private discussions. It is revealing that, after leaving politics, Stanfield established the Robert and Mary Stanfield Foundation for Canadian Studies, with Tom Symons as a trustee. It is inconceivable that Stanfield would ever have earmarked his philanthropy in such a way absent Symons's influence over the preceding years. By the same token, in a reversal of roles, Stanfield influenced Symons's own thinking about, and deepened his understanding of, economics. He certainly did mine. A case in point is the GMI proposal, never far from the leader's mind, or lips. When I first met Tom Symons, during my "interview" in Brackley, PEI, I did not get the impression that he knew much about the GMI (but maybe it was the scotch). Before long, after I joined his staff, he could have given a lecture to Nobel laureates on the subject if required. That was partly Stanfield's doing.

Learning is not a quiet, one-way back alley; it is a multilane superhighway at rush hour. Symons's role was to put Stanfield on the 401 at suppertime. His primary function was to create a process within the party to develop an integrated body of well-researched and fact-based policy across a wide spectrum of issues in a systematic and methodical and timely way: policy that was practical, not theoretical or academic. His secondary role—and I stress "secondary"—was advising the leader on particular policy matters, a role he performed through both indirect and direct advice.

# Consulting the Experts

Canadian sovereignty, economic and cultural alike, was one area where Tom Symons influenced Robert Stanfield substantially. This fact was reflected in major speeches Stanfield gave in Parliament on the issue both in response to government legislation and in Opposition-sponsored debates—on foreign investment, in particular. One such was a December 9, 1971, speech on an NDP Allotted Day Motion, in the name of their leader David Lewis, on foreign ownership. Most of the speech—especially its call for screening foreign investment within a framework of an overall industrial strategy—came directly, some of it word for word, from the Sterling Lyon working group I detailed earlier. The leader began the speech by saying, "We in this party who are the direct political descendants of those who brought about Confederation will not take a back seat to anybody in our determination to preserve [the independence of] this country."[1] Georges-Étienne Cartier was every bit the Conservative Party forebear that Sir John A. was. Like Irish-Canadian nationalist Thomas D'Arcy McGee, he became a fierce champion of Confederation primarily out of fear of unfettered American expansion. Stanfield's own concern, tempered by sensitivity to the poorer regions' need for investment, followed this noble Tory tradition. The PC leader also wove some of the major points into media interviews, both formal and informal, including scrums outside the House of Commons. It is unlikely Stanfield would have given a speech at all on this sensitive and potentially divisive topic, let alone with such impressive confidence and substance, without Symons's influence and the resources the policy chairman marshalled, in concert with the PC Research Office and the leader's own staff.

Stanfield had an enormous capacity to read complex material, understand it at first reading, make it his own, synthesize it in a way that added a whole new layer to the original material, then, with the help of first-rate speech writers such as Tom Sloan and Bill Grogan, present it to diverse audiences in a readily understandable way. The leader placed a high value on research. And he typically required a lot of time to formulate his thoughts, edit drafts placed before him, and sign off on final texts. But he could rise to the occasion on short notice when required, especially if someone such as Pierre Trudeau—whom he did not greatly admire or like—got his back up. Beneath a pensive exterior was a street fighter when provoked, particularly if a matter of principle or his personal honour was at stake. The incongruity of an inherently even-tempered and reflective man acting calmly but with unremitting resolve was a sight to behold. Much more so than had his style been one of throwing tantrums of the sort for which Paul Martin and Stephen Harper later became notorious. Still waters might run deep, but in Stanfield's case they were also capable of considerable force, however placid the surface.

As if to compensate, perhaps, for his lack of expertise in economics, Symons ensured that, notwithstanding Stanfield's own expertise in this area, the leader had access to some of the best economists in the land. In late fall 1972, for example, Symons arranged for me to conduct a series of private, off-the-record meetings with top economists to pick their brains for Stanfield on the state of the economy and how best to manage looming dark clouds. I interviewed them, individually on their respective home turfs, right after the federal general election, when the extent of the economic mess the country was in became clearer. The Liberal government was able to downplay that mess only so long. Among the economic experts I consulted for the leader were: Arthur Smith (head of the Conference Board of Canada); H. E. English (Carleton University), an expert on international trade; David McQueen (Glendon College, York University), later principal of that college; John Crispo (University of Toronto), a MIT-educated economist, vocal champion of Canada–US free trade, and rising media star and darling; David Wilton (Queen's University), a labour, tourism, and macroeconomics specialist; and Stefan Dupré (University of Toronto), a Harvard-educated political economist. These were to be no idle chats. Stanfield had discussed with Symons exactly what he felt he needed to know. I had a carefully prepared script, though I asked follow-up questions, as well as others that I thought, on the spot, needed to be posed. I took copious and detailed notes, somewhat in the manner of a court stenographer. And later, I prepared draft reports, subsequently Symonized to the $n$th degree. Finally, and only then, we forwarded the product to Stanfield. Symons was nothing if not thorough, I myself nothing if not bone-tired. Reading the extensive notes more than four decades later, I was struck by how carefully they were prepared, how candid the economists had been, and how prescient most of their predictions turned out on such matters as the possibility of a worldwide energy-supply crisis; the likelihood of a major recession; the virtual certainty high unemployment would both persist and worsen; and the inevitability (no matter who won power) of the country's having to adopt wage-and-price controls at some point. Maybe David Slater, of Niagara Conference fame, had lured these economists to his clairvoyance sideline. And Thomas Carlyle said economics is the dismal science! Not when I was there. If I had had any doubt whether all this was worthwhile, it soon proved groundless. My own little private parlour game at Policy Coordinating Committee (PCC) meetings involved counting Stanfield's references to the briefing papers.

So much for Tom Symons's role as *indirect* advisor.

# The Advisor and the Advised

Tom Symons was as much a nationalist on culture as Tom Axworthy was on economic independence. But each would argue, as Symons did as a tenet of faith, that the two perspectives were only different facets of the same gem and, therefore, required the same high polish. And yet Symons was not a propagandist, even in the best sense. It was not in his nature to proselytize or preach to Stanfield. Nor was he inclined to do so to anyone else for that matter, but especially not to Stanfield. I say "especially" because it was not in Stanfield's own nature to be proselytized to or preached at. When the minister does not want to give a sermon and the congregation does not want to hear one, not much of a sermon is going to get heard. Symons's greatest strength as a communicator is an unerring sense of occasion and of audience, aside from felicity. He knew his "audience" in Stanfield. So, on no occasion, by either personal predilection or judgment, would he have lectured the PC leader. Had he done so, the student would have cut the lecture short, the lecturer off at the knees, and the course altogether. The two men, patricians that they both were, did not speak, in private or in public, the language of Nikita Khrushchev, pounding his shoe on the UN General Assembly dais, all fire and brimstone. Instead, they spoke the language of US Ambassador Adlai Stevenson on that occasion—"Could I have a translation of that, please?"—all disciplined composure and sweet reason and, particularly in Stanfield's case, rapid-fire wit.

Symons raised issues with Stanfield. He funnelled lots of ideas and proposals to him, in private as at policy meetings. He drew to the leader's attention learned articles and news items and opinion pieces alike that he thought worth reading. And he always made himself available to counsel the leader, either on a particular issue or range of issues, immediate or longer term, though rarely on technicalities—the job of the PC Research Office. In the countless conversations to which I was privy between these two men over the years, on the phone or in person, not once did I hear Symons try to foist an idea or proposal on a reluctant Stanfield. He would not; Socrates and Russell Maxwell would not have approved, and neither would Stanfield. If it had happened when I was not present to hear at least one side of a phone conversation (typically Symons's half), the policy chairman would have told me later. He always briefed me on his Stanfield conversations, as much to self-reflect out loud on what was said as to inform me.

The second major point to be made here—the first, earlier, being that their principal policy interests differed—is that Stanfield's choice of Symons as his chief policy advisor was not based *primarily* on his wish to have Symons advise him directly about issues—again, Stanfield was a virtual expert himself on a broad scope of issues and an actual expert on some others. Symons's main role was to establish and direct a complex and continuing *process* to develop policy ideas and proposals from others; to process the policy content through the relevant mechanisms—primarily the PCC, for which, with me, he served as the secretariat or steering committee; to recruit and cultivate the many experts required to ensure that policy was innovative (preferably), well researched and fact-based (always), and literate (more or less). Then, his principal mandate was to help deliver policy materials in the right finished format to its intended audience: the leader himself, Caucus, candidates, targeted public and special interest groups, the media, and, ultimately, the population at large. Full papers, summaries, background materials, pamphlets, resolutions, ballots, fact sheets or, depending on the particular circumstances, the whole nine yards, and then another bolt of cloth for good measure—that was the order of the day. Could the invasion of Normandy possibly have been planned with more attention to detail? In Symons's hands, nothing was done in half-measure, little left to chance.

With the passage of time, as Stanfield and Symons developed a higher comfort level with each other—particularly in private—they talked more often and longer, broadened the subjects discussed, picked more occasions just to chat about nothing or everything, and more and more enjoyed the other's company and the sound of his voice. When on the phone, just shooting the breeze as it were, the echoes of laughter and merriment sometimes exceeded the thoughtful pauses at both ends. And these were supposed to be reserved patricians! In that respect, Charles McMillan, Tom Axworthy, and Tom Symons had another thing in common, besides being brainy advisors to brainy leaders: each liked his leader and the leader liked him. Some scholars have asked me whether I thought Symons had nudged Stanfield, consciously or subconsciously, farther to the "left" than the leader might have gone of his own inertia without Symons's continuing progressive influence. This kind of question, though well intentioned, is fraught with gobbledygook. First, it assumes one knows for certain what "left" and "right" mean in the real world of politics as opposed to the Ivory Tower. Maurice Strong, a Canadian business tycoon in my time as Canada's environment minister, was one of the most committed and outspoken environmentalists, not just in Canada but throughout the world. Strong spearheaded the first UN Conference on the Human Environment, in Stockholm in 1972. He played the same role, with Norwegian prime minister Gro Harlem Brundtland, to launch the landmark UN-sponsored World Commission on Environment and Development. I participated with him in numerous national and international forums. And I consulted him often, including for an address I gave to the UN General Assembly in a major debate on the Brundtland Report. One would be hard pressed to define Maurice Strong's environmental passion in "left" or "right" terms. He just thought humanity was trashing the planet, and it was in the interests of everybody, including hard-nosed business leaders like him, to help stop the self-destruction. Environmentalism for most such practical people—among them, I include myself—is not a matter of theology or any other system of absolute values. From this perspective, it is no more appropriate to slap "left" or "right" on a particular public policy approach to the environment than it is to stamp "Catholic," "Protestant," "Muslim," or "Judaic" on it, either. To my mind, the same applies clear across the issues board. Such was, essentially, how both Tom Symons and Robert Stanfield saw things.

All this said, I believe a true "conservative" is, by definition, more oriented to environmental principles than is a true "liberal." That's because a conservative in the classic sense is primarily concerned about the "whole," and seeks to conserve and protect it. By contrast, the classic liberal is concerned about the individual, and wants to protect the person's freedom of action. Labels can capture such important distinctions, so they are sometimes helpful in distinguishing how people with different philosophical mindsets can attach different priorities to the same policy area. But couldn't a liberal be an environmentalist out of concern for the individual? After all, if the air the person breathes, the water he or she drinks, the soil that produces his or her food are trashed, isn't that individual's survival—set aside the entire community's for a moment—jeopardized? In my time as Canada's environment minister, an idea popular among many environmental activists was instituting an Environmental Bill of Rights, either legislatively, as with John Diefenbaker's Bill of Rights or, preferably, constitutionally, in the manner of Trudeau's Charter of Rights and Freedoms, possibly even as part of it. Either way, the approach is, quintessentially, classically liberal. It would greatly expand what lawyers call "standing." That means access to the courts to advance the claim of a particular individual, or that of a group of individuals with a shared interest, against an entity (individual, business, or government) that the claimant believes infringed upon his or her rights—in the case at hand, the right to a healthy and safe natural environment. Absent constitutional change, many of the measures environmentalists urged me to take as environment minister, and attacked me for not taking, would have been found illegal by the courts if I had actually tried to implement them. At a minimum, those measures would have invaded provincial jurisdiction—to Stanfield, the Original Sin. In their naiveté, many environmental non-governmental organizations believed the righteousness of their cause justified the wrong-headedness of their means.

Most political parties are populated with both conservatives and liberals and with people holding other value systems, as well as vastly different religious beliefs. Concern about the natural environment is not, and should not be viewed as, the domain of any political party—or, for that matter, any wing of a party, left, right, centre, or off the chart altogether. Otherwise, the kind of pan-partisan consensus required for action in this field will not be forged, and everybody—conservative, liberal, socialist, centrist, or however one wishes to construct the spectrum—will perish as the planet gets trashed. We're all in this together. As the saying goes, "we either hang together or hang separately." While dangling from the scaffold, our respective political or ideological labels, whatever particular ones they might be, are not going to save us.

Viewing politics through a narrow left-right lens is, except under certain limited circumstances, more American than Canadian. "Trying to make categories is very American, very stupid, and very dangerous," writer Gore Vidal stated. "The generalist, humanist point of view is that you start out with 'Everyone is a human being capable of good and bad'."[2] Robert Stanfield and Tom Symons reinforced my own view that the nature of our country and of our issues does not lend itself to herding people into rigid ideological corrals. Perhaps, in the United States, where everyone is expected to conform to a certain pan-national civic religion, or at least to assimilate into the majority culture, that simplistic perspective has explanatory power. But in Canada, with the high premium we place on cultural and linguistic and other forms of diversity, including political pluralism, we need to view ourselves through a lens more appropriate to our particular national circumstances. I cannot recall either Stanfield or Symons ever discussing policy, or even appearing to think, in left-right terms. I myself try to use the terms in their classic senses, not with their contemporary meanings. I do it because I believe the words are largely meaningless when loosely bandied about, as too often happens these days. Stanfield and Symons had a profound impact on my thinking in this respect, as in many others—much more so than my formal political science training.

It is pointless, in any case, to characterize as "left" or "right" any particular policy, or range of policies, Symons might have favoured himself or encouraged Robert Stanfield to consider in the policy process they devised together. Even if one could categorize policy in this way with any degree of methodological rigour, doing so would shortchange the pivotal role Symons played. The individual policies themselves were, of course, helpful to Stanfield and his partisan followers in parliamentary and electoral battles. But even more important was the process by which those policies were produced under Symons's direction. Stanfield and Symons were preparing the Progressive Conservative Party of Canada for power. And just as, in their vision, power was not sought for its own sake, neither was policy. Policy was the by-product of a process by which the party forced itself to think deeply about where it wanted to go, where it wanted to lead the country, and how it was going to get there. Policy was a road map. The routes could always be changed, the map replaced with a better one, but policy was not the destination. Nor was the process; it was the journey. The destination was winning power to achieve great things for the country. The process was a means to that end.

Robert Louis Stevenson said "[p]olitics is perhaps the only profession for which no preparation is thought necessary."[3] Stanfield and Symons defied Stevenson's truism. Both were committed to preparing themselves for government service and to ensuring their party was also well prepared. Modernizing the PC Party was, for them, a serious matter and of the highest priority. It was what their partnership concerned. John Diefenbaker viewed policy as merely a rhetorical weapon to slay political enemies. By contrast, Stanfield, with Symons at his side, saw policy as a way to attract public support by rebranding the PC Party as a progressive force. Even more important, however, Stanfield believed policy development was essential to readying the party and himself for office in the event of electoral success. Stanfield and Symons were, in biblical terms, "sowing the crop."

If Charles McMillan was Mulroney's "intellectual bodyguard," Tom Symons was Robert Stanfield's "intellectual caddy." The caddy not only passed his charge a nine iron to wallop the ball over the sand trap onto the green, but also advised him that it should be that particular club, not a pitching wedge, to land the ball there. The direction the ball took, left or right, to get to the hole was up to the man who made the shot. In the complex and important policy work Stanfield and Symons did for the party, and for the country, they were "golfing partners." But could they win a major tournament together? That's the subject of the next round.

# Chapter 13

# BEFORE
# THE FALL

Because of the razor-close results of the 1972 election, Robert Stanfield was uncertain about how to prepare for the end of Pierre Trudeau's minority government, expected by most political pros and media pundits sooner rather than later. On November 2, 1972, Tom Symons conversed with Stanfield by phone. This time it was to discuss strategy for proceeding primarily (but not exclusively) on the policy front. Symons was one of too few individuals who honoured yet another Divine Beatitude of politics: "Blessed are those who understand that a politician's most precious resource is time." Symons always carefully organized his thoughts when initiating a call to Stanfield or when expecting one (usually by prior arrangement) to avoid squandering the leader's valuable time. He typically organized the points he wanted to raise in the form of cryptic notes, written with a ballpoint pen in red ink on a small white pad. As he completed each point during the call, Symons would check it, one by one, either literally or in his mind's eye, depending on the complexity or total number.[1]

This time, immediately after the cliff-hanger 1972 election, Stanfield wanted to know what strategy his chief policy advisor thought he should follow in light of the closeness of the election results and the uncertainty they caused not just him but also the country. The Trent University academic advised caution, saying Trudeau's announcement that he intended to remain in office was not unreasonable, and that many people would view as arrogant any suggestion Stanfield might make to the contrary. The emphasis, instead, he advised, should be on a willingness to form a government if asked by the governor general, but the offer should not be made with "belligerence"—"sabre rattling" would be self-defeating. In a telling bit of advice, reflecting how he saw Stanfield himself, Symons told the leader: "You will be credible only if true to your character. Let Trudeau appear to be clinging to office, but do nothing yourself to foster that impression." He counselled Stanfield: "Use the time to organize for the run-off election and for the responsibilities thereafter, and work with the public in anticipation of the coming election. All the while, let [Trudeau] and his government [get] tied up trying to hold onto office and coping with the duties of office." Symons urged: "We should offer a clear statement of our policy alternatives...what we would do in office should Canadians honour us with the responsibilities of government."

A close examination of Stanfield's remarks to the media soon after he received this advice indicates two possibilities: either he had not been substantially influenced by the advice from Symons, since he was thinking along the same lines, in any event, or, before speaking with Symons, he had made up his mind to be aggressive, but modified his remarks in light of his senior policy advisor's cautions. I was in the room with Symons at the time of the call. I am convinced, from hearing his half of the discussion, that the second possibility is the more likely. In his written media statement, the PC leader *was* assertive in stating that voters had rejected the Trudeau government's record at the ballot box in the 1972 election and, therefore, the prime minister had lost the moral right to govern. But Stanfield's overall demeanour at the follow-up news conference could not have been closer to what Symons had advised: firm, but not belligerent; willing to serve, but not aggressively or unreasonably demanding to be allowed to serve; not resigned to Opposition, but eager to prepare the party to assume the reins of government should the people so wish; committed, in particular, to focusing on policy towards that end. It was as though, in content and tone alike, the senior policy advisor had written the script for Stanfield. To a large degree, he had.

When Stanfield became PC leader in September 1967, he had less than a year to prepare for the election that the new Liberal prime minister, Pierre Trudeau, called for June 25, 1968. In the short interim, Stanfield had time to do only so much: hire staff; try to unify the party behind him, especially the parliamentary Caucus and, more particularly, the Diefenbaker malcontents; whip the PC Party's national organization into shape; coordinate the national campaign with the federal party's provincial government and party organization allies, such as Ontario's "Big Blue Machine"; recruit candidates; raise funds; develop a media strategy; travel across the country to introduce himself to voters. And recover strength after an exhausting leadership contest. There was little time to prepare policy. As we have seen, it showed. In the 1968 election, on issues such as the Guaranteed Minimum Income (GMI), Stanfield was able to provide only general explanations, and then not well. By contrast, following the Tories' 1968 election defeat, he knew the new majority government headed by Trudeau would not likely go to the polls again for at least four years. That transpired. He had time. And he used it to great advantage. He applied himself methodically and diligently to policy development, among other things—but, to him, none more important than policy.

The political calendar was totally different following the 1972 election from that of four years earlier. Trudeau's minority government was not just weak, but perilously weak, its fate held in the balance by the grace and goodwill and political avarice of the New Democratic Party under its fiery leader, David Lewis. He and the NDP extracted every possible concession from a compliant prime minister and Cabinet eager to retain power at almost any cost, including, as it turned out, to the Canadian taxpayer. The government gave in to one demand after another for new programs on the NDP agenda, many of them fiscally extravagant. Among the costly measures the NDP pressed on the government was the creation of a publicly owned oil company, Petro-Canada. The legislation to establish the company was, in fact, introduced by the NDP, in 1973, and supported by the Liberal government—not the converse, the conventional parliamentary practice for government and Opposition parties. Eventually established as a Crown corporation in 1975, Petro-Canada received $1.5 billion in start-up money. This was a whopping amount given that the entire federal budget on the eve of Trudeau's election as Liberal leader had been $9.53 billion, as detailed by Finance Minister Edgar Benson in March 1968. Opposition Leader Stanfield and his PC parliamentary Caucus opposed the Petro-Canada measure, largely because of the enormous cost. The company would remain a target for Tories until the Mulroney government finally privatized it in 1991 while retaining a 19 percent minority stake. The state-owned oil company was long a favourite whipping boy of federal Tories. But Tories opposed to Petro-Canada—and not all were—saw it not as an ideological issue, but as the thirty pieces of silver the Liberals paid to the NDP to keep themselves in power while crucifying the Canadian taxpayer. When Trudeau retired from politics, his government had been consistently running annual *deficits* greater than the *total annual budget* at the time he became prime minister. Runaway spending, gigantic borrowings, and compounding interest payments on the accumulated public debt caused the national debt to soar during the Trudeau years. The trajectory towards national insolvency began during this minority government period. Prior to 1972, the national debt had been growing, on average, by 5 to 10 percent a year. In the decade after the 1972 election, the debt soared by an average of 20 percent a year, a rate almost unprecedented in the country's peacetime history.

In this uncertain environment, planning by Robert Stanfield and the PCs for the long term would have been folly, for there seemed no long term. In Ottawa, the Peace Tower clock was on amphetamines. Even at the best of times, and these were not those, in politics a time unit is calculated by a multiple relative to real time similar to that applied to dogs. Except, instead of one year equivalent to seven, as for canines, it can be more like one to a zillion in certain circumstances. Stanfield found himself in such circumstances now. It seemed he had only about two or three months, at most, to plan for the next election. A year or two—that would have been eternity to the square.

So the PC leader did not set his sights on a one-year or two-year framework to review existing policies, revise them as needed, and develop new ones on the same basis as he had proceeded before, through the Policy Coordinating Committee (PCC). Instead, the goal was more modest and, Stanfield thought, more manageable given the political realities. For policy, the leader had never depended only on the PCC. Nor did he have to rely on other party institutional sources, notably the PC Research Office. He had, for example, his own personal staff—initially, members such as Lowell Murray and Joe Clark; later, Tom Sloan, Graham Scott, Rod McQueen, Marjory LeBreton, Richard Le Lay, Françoise Morissette, John Rolf, and, from the beginning, as well, Murray Coolican, who became the leader's son-in-law (by marrying Stanfield's stunning daughter Mimi). Every staffer was well informed and some were, on at least one issue, expert. (Coolican specialized in several areas: Aboriginal issues, energy, and natural resources, principally.) Bill Grogan was in a class by himself as resident wit and humourist. As we have seen, he was a perfect match, as wordsmith and speech and comedy writer, for Stanfield's own native talent for droll humour and repartee. Most of these people were helpful on the policy front, a few especially so. They had more than enough policy competence and fluency to help the leader survive in a political tinderbox where the object was merely to avoid scratching a match and blowing up the place. Dazzling the voter with policy fireworks would have to be for another time. Maybe that time had passed. Without question, the political will to formulate new policy had passed for most people around the leader, even if not for the leader himself or for Tom Symons. Now retired from the Trent University presidency (as of May 1972), Symons was already preparing the groundwork for the next stage of policy development in light of the more limited time frame. He was well aware of the political realities. This was one academic whose mind was not locked in the Ivory Tower.

The focus ahead for the PC Party and the Symons operation would be, not on producing new policy materials, but on reworking ones that had already been produced over many months with an eye to the 1972 election campaign, now well behind them. New policy proposals would be generated, especially when, with time, it became increasingly clear that the Trudeau government might survive longer than originally had been thought possible. Meanwhile, however, an election was considered imminent with the drop of a dime—or of a writ. So the priority was the here and now, not the there and then. In this post-1972 election period, the party immediately began to place a lower priority than before on involving outside specialists, because we lacked the time and staff to consult them. We increasingly relied on the expertise and counsel of insiders. In addition to Research Office specialists, those included MPs and senators and, again, the leader's staff. Both Stanfield and Symons, however, were eager to maintain external contacts, particularly for urgent consultations on specific issues as they arose, often seemingly out of nowhere and at the most inopportune moments. The post-1972 period was like no previous one since Stanfield had become leader. There was even more to do, less time to do it, and greater pressure on all of us to get it done. For the first time in the Trudeau-Stanfield matchup, most Canadians—the media, the political class, the general public—felt the PC leader had a fighting chance of becoming prime minister soon. (The first Gallup poll after the 1972 election, conducted in January 1973, showed the Tories virtually tied with the Liberals: 36 percent versus 39 percent, respectively, with the NDP at 16 percent, substantially down from the democratic socialists' 21 percent support in the election.) Accordingly, participants in the PC Party's policy process viewed their work, consciously or unconsciously, as primarily laying the groundwork for possibly governing, rather than, as before, just preparing for an election—though that, too.

Tom Symons reapplied himself to the policy work with equal measures of commitment and diligence. Symons left many a younger participant, me included, panting and exhausted well before he lost first wind, let alone the second and third, which the man always appeared to have in reserve. A heavy agenda of diverse new public service assignments did not prevent him from devoting big chunks of his time to Stanfield's policy process. I had thought the "Bull" in his bus-route-sounding name— "This bus stops at Thomas, Henry, Bull, Symons, and downtown Peterborough"— bespoke the rich family heritage on his mother's side. Or "Bull" stood for the other half of the expletive I mouthed when he reduced my Shakespearian prose to "mere typing, not literature," the characterization Truman Capote once famously hurled at the runaway bestsellers of Jacqueline Susann. It did not take me long to discover the true meaning of "Bull" in Symons's multi-part name: it represented the fearlessness with which he attacked every challenge as though it were a matador and he a wild animal on the attack. In this battle of wills, I learned from Symons that one would be a fool to bet against the Bull.

As principal extraparliamentary policy director, Tom Symons forever acted the university president, even when, towards the end of the process, he no longer was one. He applied to the PC Party's policy-development process the same set of management and diplomatic skills essential to the smooth operation of a major academic institution, possibly the most difficult of all organizations to lead except for a political party. The "premier" and the "university president" at work, in partnership—a sight to behold! Sometimes the teamwork, one man bouncing his particular talents and insights off the other, was magical. The smiles and winks other committee members periodically directed both at me and at one another told me that I was not the only one who marvelled at the dynamic. Will there ever be the like again in the Conservative Party? I was never again to witness it, not even in the decade I was in Parliament.

A politician, especially one in Cabinet, is, above all, a professional meeting attendee. He or she spends (wastes?) more time in committee, of whatever size or type, than in any other activity. In all my time in public life, I met no one else with skill close to Tom Symons's as a committee chair: directing discussion, building team spirit, forging a consensus, converting it to action, getting the job done—in short, making the process work. With uncommon skill, he brought people together and created a shared sense of purpose. He navigated among individuals and groups from diverse backgrounds and with conflicting views, to say nothing of different and discordant personalities. His talent for this challenging role never ceased to amaze me. By this time, I had been with him half a decade. Years by his side did not blunt my admiration—quite the opposite, putting a lie to the old chestnut that "no man is a hero to his valet." The size of the gathering didn't matter. Whether in a policy committee or at a regional or national conference, the charm offensive and diplomatic dexterity and eloquent verbal gymnastics always worked their magic with participants. That was true even as the clock ticked fast and frantically in the lead-up to the 1974 election—as it turned out, his swan song with Robert Stanfield. Quite apart from the policy *product* itself, the policy-development *process* he devised and directed, in partnership with Stanfield, contributed mightily to party cohesion and inclusiveness. That was another way the two men were preparing the PC Party for power. This time, unlike when it all began back in April 1968, power did not seem elusive. No one, least of all the leader, was overconfident. But there was a sense in the air that, within a short time, instead of being at the board table at National Headquarters drafting policy for a campaign, we might find ourselves at the Cabinet table on Parliament Hill making laws for the country.

Again, however wrong the perception was for almost two years, the perceived imminence of the 1974 election changed the party's emphasis from generating new policy to remixing ones already in the sausage grinder. The party had to be ready to fight an election at any time. Everything had to be done either now or, preferably, yesterday. Mark Twain might urge, as he famously did, that one should never put off until tomorrow what he can do the day after tomorrow. But for Stanfield and the party, there was no tomorrow. Accordingly, with each passing week, Stanfield shifted his policy workshop farther and farther away from the PCC and closer and closer to the parliamentary Caucus.

What the party focused on now was not so much policy as a partisan platform based on policy. The distinction might seem obscure, but it was real. Policy constituted an officially approved set of integrated, research-based statements of principles and directions on a wide variety of issues that the party promised to follow should it win power. The platform, by contrast, was specific promises drawn from that set of policy materials that the party's candidates and activists could use on the hustings, emphasizing what was inelegantly termed "grabbers." This term, coined by PC Research Office policy specialist Les Horswill, meant specific promises and commitments that would "grab" the attention of voters. The term especially applied to parts of the platform devised to appeal to particular demographic groups and their priorities as revealed by internal party polling and other sources of political intelligence.

Typically, each PC Caucus policy chairperson assembled several parliamentary colleagues to serve with him or her on a committee struck to manage the relevant issue or bundling of related issues. One such policy chairman was Dr. James Gillies, MP for Toronto's Don Valley riding, elected in 1972 (and re-elected in 1974, before retiring prior to the 1979 vote). From York University's Faculty of Administrative Studies, Gillies was a world-renowned corporate governance expert. He drove much of the party's policy on a variety of economic and financial issues, both in Parliament and for the 1974 election (as he did for the 1979 election, as well). Those issues included wage-and-price controls, an issue that, as we shall see, would dominate the 1974 campaign and cause no end of grief for the leader and PC candidates.

At the very first meeting of the PCC, on November 26, 1969, Stanfield had defined what "policy" meant to him in the context of the committee's mandate. He said the PCC's role implied "more than mere development of basic principles," but was not one of "considering the adoption of a party platform without full consultation and discussion with all sectors of the party." This view was fully supported by Stanfield's chief policy advisor. Symons told The Canadian Press, in an interview he gave about the process on October 10, 1969, at the Niagara Policy Conference: "In a democracy, only elected representatives should make final decisions. Therefore, the party will only make recommendations for consideration by Mr. Stanfield and the federal Caucus." For Stanfield, as the 1974 election loomed, "all sectors of the party" effectively meant his parliamentary Caucus. Most of his one hundred-plus MPs would be seeking re-election. The leader believed that, if he was going to increase their numbers after the election with an eye to forming a government, he would need them both to help lead on policy and enthusiastically support the party's platform entering the campaign. For him, Caucus members' active involvement in the process and their support for the product were intertwined. In such ways, the PC leader was a cunning strategist, and read people well. Some of this astuteness came naturally. But by dint of hard knocks, he was also maturing as a national politician and party leader. It was a far more challenging job than being premier of Nova Scotia, a fact the man learned the very day he won the PC Party's leadership.

The PCC continued to meet about as regularly as before. Its focus, however, was on managing the body of policy materials the party had produced over the previous months as updated by the Caucus policy chairs in concert with the Research Office. On February 5, 1974, for example, the PCC worked on the following papers: "World of Work," "Cultural Opportunities," "Regional Development," "The Role of Women," "Parliamentary and Democratic Reform," and "Native Peoples." At this point, most papers had been processed through more stages than human life itself: from the genesis—in some cases, at the Niagara Conference (for example, "Parliamentary and Democratic Reform," under Flora MacDonald's direction)—to the working groups to the PCC's scrutiny to regional or local meetings back to the PCC to the Annual Meeting policy sessions to Caucus committees and back to the PCC, and on and on it went. In a few cases, if the policy statements had been white bread, and processed any further, a mosquito would have starved on the surviving nutrients. The policy materials were now well beyond the point where we needed to revise them further other than to keep the content current in light of, for example, new jobless and inflation data. One paper, on "Native Peoples," was sent back to the drawing board for major work on the grounds, Symons insisted, that it was just not good enough. All the papers continued to be modified in light of consultations with the membership of the party at large through such devices as questionnaires. At a meeting of the PCC on January 10, 1974, for instance, the party Headquarters director, John Laschinger, reported on the results of policy questions that had been mailed to 15,000 party members across Canada. Athenian democracy, indeed!

---

Many of the foot soldiers on the policy front who helped win the 1984 federal election for the PC Party had been conscripted by Tom Symons for Robert Stanfield a decade or so earlier. These policy activists included the general himself, Brian Mulroney. When I was appointed to Cabinet by Mulroney, following the 1984 election, what struck me most about the political face of the new government—from Cabinet members such as me to ministerial staffers to Privy Council appointees, and on and on— was the ubiquity of Symons's policy alumni. The House of Commons Speaker himself, John Fraser (after succeeding John Bosley), had been a major Symons recruit in the policy process when Stanfield was leader, from beginning to end. All such Symons recruits swarmed the place like bumblebees on a honeysuckle bush in spring.

During the Clark-Mulroney period, numerous successful candidates for the PC Party at the national level were themselves academics of high rank. The trend began towards the end of Stanfield's leadership with individuals such as the aforementioned James Gillies of York University's business school. Among others, later, was William Winegard, like Tom Symons, a university president (Guelph). Winegard served as minister of state for science and technology and then minister for science in the second half of Mulroney's period as PM. Winegard was one of several Tory Cabinet ministers with PhDs in this period—his in metallurgical engineering. Others were Tom Siddon of British Columbia (aero acoustics), Harvie Andre of Alberta (chemical engineering), Tom Hockin of Ontario (political science), and Suzanne Blais-Grenier of Quebec (sociology). Some, like Winegard and Osgoode law professor Ron Atkey— later Joe Clark's minister of immigration and employment—had been recruited to help the party develop policy prior to their electoral forays. Both Winegard and Atkey helped with the Niagara Conference and remained active in PC Party policy development long afterwards. Many other intellectuals who became Tory politicians under Clark's and Mulroney's leadership had worked with Tom Symons on party policy.

The size of this network rivalled that of the alumni Symons had grown at Trent University in not much more time, employing the same community-building skills. In hindsight, I am certain Stanfield knew the skill set he was getting from Symons when the PC leader conscripted him for the chief policy advisor role back in 1968. It's what Stanfield wanted, what he thought he needed, and precisely what he got. In this respect, as in so many others, the Nova Scotian showed extraordinarily sound judgment and vision. The extent of his leadership abilities became ever clearer to me with each passing year after he retired. When the PCs finally won a majority government in 1984, I was able to see at close range how much he had helped prepare us for office, even if he himself had not reaped the benefits as prime minister.

Stanfield's involvement in the PC Party's policy-drafting process, steady and active as it was, normally involved matters of fact or technicality, or minor substantive concerns. Anything major was, generally, of a political nature ("Will this upset Caucus member Ima Blowhard?"). He rarely threw the policy train off the rails, just encouraged the conductor to go more slowly or in a slightly different direction. The most substantive concern I can recall, or have a record of, concerned his recurring sensitivity towards provincial jurisdiction and, more particularly, Quebec's interests. On one such occasion, at a PCC meeting on January 24, 1974, he expressed alarm that, unlike the policy papers prepared for the 1971 Annual Meeting, ones being considered now (in the run-up to the 1974 election) had, in his judgment, a "centralist bias" and, therefore, were "not sufficiently sensitive to the views of French Canada and to other Canadians who favour a more decentralized federation." That objection might seem temperate. But it was analogous to a restaurant diner's telling the chef that he didn't need to change the meal order, but had to remove all the salt from every dish. For those of us who needed to revise the papers in light of Stanfield's concerns—altering the meal in the kitchen, as it were—the task would have been easier had the malcontent simply changed his mind and switched from the lobster casserole to lamb stew. Taking the salt out of the casserole was not as easy. Alas, the stew, too, was already made—with salt. But the casserole was redone and now salt free, it was delicious, and the customer was happy in the end.

Among other benefits Stanfield derived from the policy process, it helped focus and sharpen his own consideration of issues. The PCC, in particular, served as a valuable sounding board for his personal policy views before he risked expressing them publicly. With an election seemingly imminent, and the stakes as high as they had ever been, this factor assumed increased importance. Ever a cautious man, he often tested his thinking on particular questions with Symons prior to airing them even at the PCC stage. No doubt, he did the same with trusted staffers. But the man had once headed a government, in Nova Scotia. So he was well aware that too tight a circle of advisors risked creating the danger now commonly called "groupthink" (discussed later in the context of the Mulroney government). It was in his nature to seek the broadest-possible conduit of information and opinion. He was secure enough, both in his own command of the issues and in his intellectual powers, not to feel threatened by bright and well-informed people holding contrary views and challenging him directly. He revelled in the energy from a vigorous debate, provided it was focused and goal directed and not merely an academic exercise, however stimulating. Sitting as I always did with only Tom Symons between me and Stanfield at PCC meetings, by 1974 I had developed almost a sixth sense of when the leader felt a discussion had crossed the line between vigorous and wheel-spinning. It was almost always within seconds of Symons's registering the same sense. At which point, Symons typically steered the direction towards firmer territory, if Stanfield himself did not appear ready to do so himself, as he sometimes did. Although the leader was technically in the chair, the process, in effect, had two chairmen. This was no less true for being so subtle that even I, the principal functionary, was not always conscious of the fact at the time. It was as though, over time, the personalities of Robert Stanfield and Tom Symons had melded into one when they put their heads together and focused on the same policy challenge.

As secretary of the PCC, I continued to meet with individual experts on behalf of Stanfield and Symons and the PCC. I was asked to pick their brains either in a general policy area or on specific matters the party felt it did not have the resources to explore itself, say, through the PC Research Office. A case in point was a long session I had on January 7, 1973, with Reuben Baetz, then executive director of the Canadian Council on Social Development, one of the country's foremost authorities on poverty and welfare, and later a senior Cabinet minister in successive PC governments in Ontario.[2] I obtained his advice on possible further directions for the party on particular dimensions of two issues: the GMI, to which Stanfield continued to be committed, and unemployment insurance reform. The latter had loomed large in the 1972 campaign, and none of us expected it to disappear anytime soon as a concern of either Caucus or the country. I prepared detailed notes on my meeting with Baetz, which, after being Symonized every which way but loose, were forwarded directly to the leader.

Ever since the policy-development process had started, Symons met regularly with policy specialists from such groups as the Science Council of Canada, the Indian-Eskimo Association of Canada, and the Grocery Products Manufacturers, among many others. The purpose was to discuss matters covered by the party's draft policy papers. Meetings of this kind continued right up to the 1974 election. Most often, Symons and I went together. Other times, either he went alone or arranged for me to go by myself on his behalf. In all cases, we sought to ensure that the papers reflected, to the maximum extent politically advisable, the views of the relevant groups. The party was eager to court their support and mine their insights. The Science Council, for example, had done some pioneering thinking about the Canadian industrial strategy concept. This was an idea that Stanfield had embraced and made his own, often weaving it into addresses. For the leader, we were able to obtain insights into the concept that went well beyond what the council had published or otherwise publicly released. I presumed at the time that the council hadn't been able to reach in-house consensus on certain ideas, so they hadn't been included in its public documents. We were able to scoop those ideas from the cutting-room floor. Some were far better, and no less intellectually rigorous, than what the council considered publishable. For us, it was like finding a winning lottery ticket on the sidewalk. Stanfield built on information from such back-channel sources to develop his own, often surprisingly novel, thinking. Just as important, Symons—academic that he is, perfectionist almost to a fault that he is—wanted to make every detail of the papers as factually accurate as possible. Experts whom we consulted privately often saved Stanfield and the party embarrassment by catching errors of fact or interpretation that had escaped everyone else's attention either because we did not know any better or because of the sheer volume of materials that needed to be processed, or both.

For the 1974 Annual Meeting (March 17–19), the PC Party had advanced almost all its thirty-two policy papers—up from twenty-five for the 1972 election—to the point where, in the run-up to the meeting, we needed only to improve them editorially, modify them in light of changing objective circumstances (for example, unemployment and inflation rates), or fine-tune them based on developing political realities (say, voter opinion as reflected in internal party polling or, as often as not, Caucus angst). At this point, the party was using pollster Robert Teeter (who described himself as a "voter research consultant"), of Market Opinion Research. He was also the US Republican Party's principal pollster. Teeter's polling on issues, as on voter party preference trends, was astonishingly accurate and predictive. Indeed, Teeter's final numbers on the eve of the 1972 election could hardly have been more spot-on correct had God given him the election results beforehand. Teeter's consistently accurate private numbers gave Stanfield and his top strategists great confidence in their policy, advertising, and organization planning in the face of public polls that proved unreliable, and sometimes dead wrong, about the mood of the Canadian electorate.[3]

Unlike his immediate predecessor, Stanfield was comfortable with modern campaign tools such as polling. He was too smart and businesslike, too strategic and tactical, not to know their value when properly used with other mechanics, rather than in isolation. He considered them necessary weapons against the Liberals, who had long mastered these techniques. It was Stanfield the economist who took front and centre at the war room map; he wanted to know the numbers. In such respects, the Tory leader was a superb, clear-headed political operator, often ruthless when he thought he had to be. A case in point is his categorical refusal to sign nomination papers for Leonard Jones, the virulently antibilingual former mayor of Moncton, New Brunswick, nominated to run as a PC candidate there for the 1974 election. Not for him an almost total reliance on gut instincts, the way John Diefenbaker had operated.

In this particular respect, Robert Stanfield and Brian Mulroney, a decade later, had a lot in common as PC leaders. Both, however, also employed to great advantage gut instincts, which partly explains their historic electoral success: the former provincially, the latter nationally. Stanfield's dual modus operandi was shaped early on during his battles against Angus L. Macdonald's "Big Red Machine" in Nova Scotia, Mulroney's by the take-no-prisoners nature of politics in Quebec. In neither province did one survive, let alone win, without exploiting every advantage (datum and instinct alike) and bare knuckles when necessary.

Three months before the 1974 Annual Meeting, on December 5, 1973, Stanfield sent a "personal" letter to a massive list of thousands of party members in which (saliently, I think) he stressed the role the Caucus chairpersons had played in "modifying our basic policy position papers," in concert with the PCC. "The Caucus chairmen will have *their* respective papers updated and ready for discussion at the general meeting" [emphasis added]. The leader announced that he had called on Tom Symons "to assume overall planning responsibility for our policy discussions at the meeting." For this meeting, the party sent to delegates beforehand yet another thirteen thousand policy questionnaires, all the policy papers completed to that point, and a specific request from the leader himself for party members to forward their policy ideas to either his office or National Headquarters. True to the importance he had always personally attached to policy, Stanfield urged delegates to "do [your] homework on selected subjects." I have no doubt that this message, coming as it did from the leader himself, caused many party members to take the entire exercise more seriously than they otherwise might have done. That was what, for Stanfield, policy leadership was all about. A stern schoolmaster when it came to preparing himself for class, he was just as stern with his students. Each time the leader communicated directly to the membership in such a way, the number of policy ideas that both the leader's office and Headquarters received spiked. Tom Symons's Peterborough-based operation saw most of this correspondence. Many of the communications reflected a lot of thought and care, and they helped the leader take the pulse of the broad membership on sensitive issues. We incorporated some of the specific ideas into policy drafts. One of the most contentious issues was unemployment insurance reform, on which controversy raged as much within the party as in the general population. On issues of that kind, Stanfield never felt comfortable relying exclusively on instinct, let alone only on his personal views on issues, as his predecessor almost always did. The more he could quantify things, even if per force not precisely, the more secure he felt about the policy stands he took. He was invariably the social scientist—specifically, economist—rarely the performing artist. In few other ways could Stanfield have been more different from Diefenbaker than this one.

# Headed to the 1974 Election

The dynamics of the 1974 Annual Meeting were similar to those of the 1971 meeting. Just as delegates had felt they needed to be politically careful when debating policy in 1971, on the eve of the 1972 election, so also the delegates at the 1974 meeting approached their policy role keenly aware of the political implications of everything they argued about as the 1974 election loomed ever more ominously. A weak minority government hung in the balance. Most members felt their party faced excellent odds to win power this time. They sensed the stakes were the highest they had ever been since Stanfield was elected leader seven years earlier. Tory partisans, therefore, were prepared to cut their leader considerable policy slack in the lead-up to the election.

It was not that the issues themselves were any less controversial. If anything, they were even more so than in the 1972 campaign. Now both high unemployment and inflation, not just the former, were of major concern to the party and to voters. Canadians were being pummelled by these trends. Every facet of their daily lives was being affected—from interest charged on car and student loans to mortgage rates and bank fees, not to mention the added costs for manufacturers and service providers that needed to be passed on to consumers. The PC Party membership wanted to be seen as united behind the leader on economic and other policies he championed to address Canadians' mounting fears. Not since the earliest days of Diefenbaker's leadership, two decades earlier, had the party been this united and hell-bent on winning. For the party as a whole, even if not for their leader and his senior policy advisor, issues and policies were now secondary to electoral victory.

One of the 1974 Annual Meeting delegates was future prime minister Brian Mulroney. As the meeting advanced, he wrote to Tom Symons, on December 17, 1973, to tell him how impressed he was with the policy papers he himself was then reading and annotating to prepare for the meeting. "I have come to recognize," he said, "the indispensable contribution that you, in particular, as the moving force behind the committee, have made." For this book, I have read almost every scrap of paper in the files (my own and at the Trent University archives and elsewhere) concerning the Stanfield-Symons policy process, and am struck by how interested Mulroney was in that process, how actively he participated in it, typically in spurts, and how attentive he was to details, no latter how inconsequential the topics might strike most people today. It is clear to me now—from the correspondence, in particular—that the future party leader was motivated less by a passion for policy than by incipient plans to seek the leadership whenever it next became available. Whatever his motivation, the man did his homework. He always kept himself informed about the process, about the policies generated by it, and about the individuals involved. No doubt, the future leadership candidate saw these people as potential key allies and future voting delegates. One has to admire the apparent single-mindedness of his ambition and the professionalism he applied to it. Clearly, Mulroney's visionary and methodical ways were consistent over a very long time, which leads me to think that those ways are in his nature—not merely what he, as an older man, felt were necessary for victory when he became a political candidate, much less prime minister.

---

Robert Stanfield was a substantially more mature national party leader on the eve of the 1974 election than he had been only two years earlier when fighting the 1972 election, and indisputably light years ahead of where he had been in 1968. During that campaign, his inexperience in federal politics showed virtually at every stop, in every news conference, in every media scrum, in every effort to address policy questions. Always secure in his own skin, Stanfield, from the beginning of his leadership, worried much less, if at all, about his intrinsic aptitude to head the country than about the PC Party's preparedness both to do battle against formidable opponents and to govern well from the very first day should it win. In 1974, the Liberals would engineer their own defeat in Parliament to trigger an election, when they thought the winds at their back were strongest. By then, Stanfield felt he and the PC Party had done all they could to conduct a competent campaign and, if successful, to take office. Central to that preparedness, in Stanfield's mind, was the elaborate policy process he and Tom Symons had devised and the time and effort the leader had personally devoted to the process.

Whatever particular role the leader might have had in mind for Symons should the PCs win in 1974, Symons told me privately at the time that he would not have accepted a senior position either in the Prime Minister's Office or at the Privy Council Office or anywhere else in the bureaucracy. Symons said that he would have preferred to serve a Prime Minister Stanfield exactly as he had served Stanfield as Opposition leader: informally and without remuneration. From such conversations I had with him, I know Symons would not have sought or expected a Senate appointment, least of all as a payoff for policy services rendered. If a position in Stanfield's own office or the Privy Council Office were not an option for Symons, the leader would likely have chosen the upper house to ensure his trusted confidant remained close at hand as a personal advisor. From the Senate, Symons could have continued to serve Stanfield while still pursuing other interests, especially in Canadian Studies and human rights, without sacrificing too much of the personal independence he so highly valued. In any event, I doubt Symons would have been able to say no to a Senate seat and, therefore, to Stanfield, just as Symons had been unable to say no when Stanfield asked him to accept the policy leadership role in April 1968.

How Stanfield saw Symons's role—in Opposition and, potentially, in government—says as much about Stanfield the man as it does about the role itself. At the very least, it says that, in creating his inner circle, the Nova Scotian placed a high premium on brainpower, knowledge, life experience, a proven track record, wise judgment, and moral character. These were qualities both the leader himself and his chief policy advisor embodied. But, given how different Symons was from Stanfield in many other distinguishing respects, it was clear that the leader also valued diversity within his Praetorian Guard. With his elephantine tea thermos virtually a fifth limb, ever-present pipe virtually a facial feature, tortoiseshell eyeglasses lowered virtually to his chin, and stooped gate virtually a deformity, this courtly and gentlemanly scholar and academic statesman would have stood out among all the others in Stanfield's prime ministerial inner circle—like a Buckingham Palace Coldstream Guard among a bunch of uniformed Boy Scouts, but with bowler hat and walking stick, rather than busby and rifle. (In his younger and more ambulatory years, Symons could be seen toting the former set of accoutrements on long meandering walks in the residential back streets of Peterborough.)

———

The late Doug Fisher was a CCF/NDP Member of Parliament and briefly deputy leader of that party. He was elected first in 1957 in an upset victory over the legendary C. D. Howe ("Minister of Everything" in the St-Laurent government). After retiring from politics in 1965, Fisher became a journalist, espousing distinctly progressive (but not extremist) views. At the end of his career, at age eighty-six, in 2006, he was the dean of the Parliamentary Press Gallery and the most experienced political writer in Canada. In the middle of the PC Party's 1974 Annual Meeting, Fisher wrote, in his nationally syndicated column, "As a generalization, the Conservatives on coming to power would be rather like the Liberals back in 1963 [following the

Kingston Conference three years earlier]." Fisher added: "Then, Mr. Pearson had a satchel full of legislative initiatives."[4] This journalistic sage could have paid the Progressive Conservative Party no higher compliment. Nor could he have given a greater accolade to the two architects of the party's policy process that had produced these impressive results. Coming as they did from such a crusty, hard-nosed political pro and veteran reporter—and an NDP giant, to boot—Fisher's comments could not have carried more authority. To my mind, they captured the whole story, in a few sentences, better than any other pundit's commentary at the time did. Other journalists, though, commented in a similar vein, so Stanfield and Symons's policy achievements did not go unnoticed at the time. Except for Geoffrey Stevens's biography of Stanfield, however, the historic record has failed to do the two men and their policy achievements justice. Political party policy-making history had run the gamut—from the Liberals' 1960 Kingston Conference that helped transform the country's social programs under Lester Pearson in the mid-1960s, with NDP support, to the point where the Opposition PC Party was now, in 1974, better prepared for its legislative agenda, in government should it be elected, than it had ever been in its long and storied history. I would argue that the PCs were better prepared, with a longer and more diverse agenda, than even the Liberals were after their milestone Kingston Conference. This positioning was exactly as Stanfield and Symons—plotting strategy, step-by-step, in partnership and in shared vision—had all along not only intended, but also worked so hard to realize.

# Chapter 14

# OF MICE AND MEN
# AND MONOPOLY

Elections are a game of Monopoly. I know whereof I speak. I fought six elections as a federal PC candidate and worked tirelessly for countless other candidates, both federally and provincially, over many decades, beginning in my teens. Either for myself or for others, all my adult life I have written speeches, crafted political ads, drafted policy statements, manned phone banks, stuffed envelopes, knocked on doors, and much more. Well before getting into electoral politics, as a grassroots campaign worker in the midst of the 1971 Ontario provincial election, I wrote a speech on the highly charged abortion issue. It was for Peterborough PC provincial candidate John Turner—no, not *that* John Turner; the one who later became Speaker of the Ontario Legislative Assembly. Turner delivered the speech, at a Catholic high school in downtown Peterborough, word for word without reading one sentence beforehand. Turner defeated the great NDP incumbent Walter Pitman. Some Tory candidates can survive even my speeches.

I am also a former Atlantic Regional Monopoly Champion (1978–79), dared to enter the round-robin competition by overconfident Liberal activists for a charity cause. I cleaned their clocks then and in the following election, too. Many of those same Liberals cleaned mine in an election a decade later, in 1988. Meanwhile, I was a national Monopoly finalist and runner-up (in Winnipeg), following the regional victory, against mostly high-tech management types. They included a thirty-something mid-level McDonald's executive, the defending champion, whose strategy included recording each *Chance* and *Community Chest* card as it was drawn. He lost. So did I, eventually, having survived all earlier rounds, but not before amassing so much cash, at one point, that I owned almost every property on the board until the other players conceded. As in politics, you win some, you lose some. As an MP, I had not yet been asked a single time for my autograph. As an ersatz genius at Monopoly, kids at the tournament—and even a few adults—lined up for my John Henry.

Winning elections, like winning in Monopoly, combines luck and strategy. In both politics and Monopoly—and both *are* games—luck is sometimes more important. I taught my three daughters at a young age how to win at Monopoly. Now, hardly anyone can beat them. Unless bad luck strikes, and it inevitably does. Part of the trick in Monopoly is to go for broke: play aggressively, purchase everything in sight, mortgage to the hilt if money runs short, but buy, buy, buy. It works every time—except when it does not. If Lady Luck continually catapults your opponent onto premium properties such as *Boardwalk* and *Park Place* while sentencing you to *Jail*, no amount of strategy compensates. You lose. Your opponent wins. Former world heavyweight boxing champion Mike Tyson put it this way: "Everyone has a plan until they get punched in the face." The equivalent principle applies in politics, as Robert Stanfield learned in his toughest fight of all, the 1974 election.

For all his political experience and sound instincts, Stanfield discovered, more than he had in any previous federal or provincial campaign, that fate can be as unpredictable as she can be cruel. Before the 1974 election, the Liberals were defeated in the House of Commons on a non-confidence vote they themselves had stage-managed. They were eager to go to the polls and relieve themselves of the burden of managing a perilously weak minority government. The Trudeau government had also run out of tax dollars to bribe the NDP to support them in Commons votes. The election was called for July 8. Inflation would become the dominant issue—and the source of an electoral tsunami.

## "Zap, you're frozen"

In October 1972, when the previous federal general election was held, inflation was already emerging as an issue, and on election day the annual inflation rate was 5.2 percent. As voters headed to the polls again, on July 8, 1974, the rate had climbed to 11.5 percent; it would peak at the end of the year at 12.7 percent. The cost of living had become a major socio-economic issue across the country. This was a period of great economic turbulence, social change, and public uncertainty throughout the world economy. Canada was not immune.

The turmoil started in October 1973, when an oil embargo was proclaimed by the Organization of Arab Petroleum Exporting Countries (OAPEC), the thirteen Arab nations of the Organization of the Petroleum Exporting Countries (OPEC), plus Egypt, Syria, and Tunisia. Earlier that year, Egypt and Syria, supported by other Arab nations, had launched a surprise attack on Israel on the holiest day of the Jewish calendar, Yom Kippur. To help its strongest ally in the Middle East, the United States resupplied Israel with arms; OAPEC retaliated by disrupting oil supplies to the West. The oil embargo lasted until politics in the region could be stabilized in March 1974 with diplomatic initiatives led by US Secretary of State Henry Kissinger. Meanwhile, the disruption of oil supplies and the uncertainty it fostered caused the price of oil to skyrocket. In 1974, OPEC raised the price of a barrel of oil to $7, a whopping amount then, equivalent to $30 in today's dollars, from a lowly $2—more than a 300 percent spike virtually all at once. In Canada, as elsewhere, the price not only of home heating oil and gasoline, but also of every other petroleum-based product, rose steadily. Hardly a product or service was unaffected. The "oil price shock" was followed by several months of depressed stock market values and a worldwide recession deeper than any since the Great Depression of the 1930s. Between January 1973 and December 1974, the major stock markets in the world suffered one of the worst downturns in modern history.

With the price of almost everything escalating in Canada, organized workers were demanding, and getting, wage increases to keep up. In turn, rising pay packages were factored into every stage of pricing, causing prices to spike even more sharply. And up and up the spiral shot. The worst of it occurred in March 1974, at the very time the PC Party was holding its Annual Meeting, and only weeks before the federal election would be called. Heading into the election, Robert Stanfield thought the only way to break the vicious price spiral facing the country was something dramatic, even if it would impose, as he put it, "rough justice." Stanfield believed temporary wage-and-price controls were imperative to eliminate not so much the problem itself as the self-fulfilling inflation psychology that was causing or compounding it. Specifically, the PC leader proposed a ninety-day freeze on wages and prices both to break the inflation cycle and to give the government the breathing space needed to work with all "stakeholders" (industry, labour, the provinces, community leaders, and others) on a longer-term solution. His plan proved electorally disastrous for him and for the PC Party.

In a single-factor, tidal-wave election, a party's overall policy program—no matter how well thought out or carefully researched or fact-based—is a handmaiden to fate. This was certainly the case for Stanfield and his candidates in the 1974 federal election. If you were a Tory, it did not make a bit of difference what you said about any issue other than the one that dominated the campaign: wage-and-price controls. Your fate was sealed, for good or ill, as fast as Pierre Trudeau could say "Zap, you're frozen!" to denounce Stanfield's anti-inflation plan. Thanks largely to Tom Symons and his own efforts, Stanfield had a ton of policy with which to fight the election. What the PC leader did not have were the right words to defend himself and his party against the Trudeau assault. Denis Smith noted that the 1974 election "went badly for Stanfield from the beginning."[1] For sheer understatement, this comment was like describing the fall of Rome as a failure in urban planning. The Liberal onslaught against Stanfield expressed by Trudeau's zinger dominated the media airwaves, and drowned the Tory leader in political tidal waves of biblical dimensions. The PC leader tried his best to explain to voters what he meant— why Canada, facing runaway inflation, needed wage-and-price controls, and why, if he became prime minister, he would feel the urgent need to impose them. Stanfield was not the only Tory unable to explain and defend the party's inflation-control policy. My parliamentary predecessor and career-long political mentor, Heath Macquarrie, said of the 1974 election, his last: "The real problem was that we PCs were handicapped with a policy enormously difficult to explain and seemingly impossible to popularize."[2]

## Stanfield's Policy Mind

Robert Stanfield had graduated from Harvard Law School *magnum cum laude*. He had practised law briefly in Halifax before entering provincial politics. But, as a politician, he thought more like an economist than a lawyer. I always saw the former, rarely the latter, at PCC meetings. During the Second World War, having been rejected for active duty because of a congenital curvature of the spine, Stanfield served, in Halifax, with the Wartime Prices and Trade Board. This service taught him that, in a crisis, government can do a great deal of good for people, but its ability to achieve public goals is limited at either the best or the worst of times. Richard Clippingdale says that Stanfield told him in interviews for his book, *Robert Stanfield's Canada*: "I came away from the Wartime Prices and Trade Board with a strong feeling that regulations have quite a limited role to play *except in case of emergency*" [emphasis added]. On the whole, though, Stanfield believed that, in wartime circumstances, regulations "did less injustice than they prevented."[3] "Less injustice," "rough justice"—an irony, for it had been Pierre Trudeau who, in 1968, promised a "Just Society." But, in the spirit of justice, it was Stanfield, not Trudeau, who believed the country faced, in 1974, an economic emergency, if not a wartime one, and it needed to act swiftly, decisively, and, of equal importance, temporarily, towards *economic justice*. As Clippingdale noted, however, Trudeau had figured out the *politics of economics*—in this case, of inflation and, more specifically, of spiralling oil prices.[4] The Liberal Party leader was determined to exploit that knowledge against the PC leader and his party.

It was irrelevant that most economists believed that the basic approach Stanfield advocated was necessary to temper overheated economies throughout the industrial world in this period. In the United States, President Richard Nixon had already imposed wage-and-price controls in August 1971. His plan included the ninety-day freeze Stanfield was to call for in Canada, though Nixon's freeze actually lasted until well into 1973 for most goods and services covered by the program, and the cap on oil and natural gas prices persisted until long after the man was forced to resign the presidency in 1974 over the Watergate scandal.

Despite all the "Zap, you're frozen" rhetoric hurled at Stanfield and the PC Party, the Liberals themselves had in their back pocket an approach even closer to Stanfield's than to Nixon's to use if re-elected. But that fact was unknown to the voters. Instead, the Liberals were able to instill enough fear about the alleged dire impact of Stanfield's plan that the die was cast. As Trudeau himself said following his victorious campaign, "I kept up my attack on Mr. Stanfield, and I won the election."[5] The results on election night proved Trudeau's strategy devastatingly effective: 141 Liberals, only 95 Tories—ironically, 2 seats fewer than Diefenbaker had won in his last hurrah, in 1965, without any policy to speak of. Having won re-election on Stanfield's broken back, Trudeau and the Liberals then smashed him in the face eighteen months later by implementing, basically, the Stanfield inflation-control plan they had so ruthlessly ridiculed and won an election condemning. The Trudeau government's *Anti-Inflation Act* of 1975 contained wage-and-price controls on large parts of the economy, and remained in force until 1978. Only in early 1979, with another election pending, did the Liberals formally repeal the act and dissolve the Anti-Inflation Board established to administer it.

# The Power of Political Tides

All Robert Stanfield and Tom Symons's careful policy preparation, including on the inflation-control plan, was knocked off the Monopoly board with one throw of the dice. Just as Trudeaumania swept the country *for* the Liberals in 1968, and the patronage issue swept the country *against* the Liberals in 1984, so the Tories' anti-inflation program swept the country *against* Stanfield and his candidates in 1974. Canadian elections are often fought—and won or lost—on an overarching issue or theme. The candidate whose party is on the wrong side of a pivotal election issue—even if on the right side of history, but at the wrong time—despite personal plans and policies and prayers and pretty face, will be smacked down by Lady Luck. Stanfield judged that the 1974 election, like the photo-finish 1972 election, would not be dominated by a single issue, but by a range of them: jobs, inflation, unemployment insurance reform, bilingualism, perceived prime ministerial indifference to Canadians' plight, among others. A cautious man, Stanfield never relied on a single throw of the electoral dice, in any event. He preferred, instead, steady hard work and team-building and team play across a broad front. He calculated that this approach, rather than going for broke on one big bet as Trudeau would on the inflation-control issue, would pay off for him and his party in the end. He did not expect hurricane-force winds either at his back or in his face. His assumption was itself a big throw of the Monopoly dice. But he lost the throw—badly. Sometimes one player lands on *Boardwalk*, the other in *Jail*. It's the luck of the game, and of politics.

Unlike physics, politics lacks ironclad laws that render predictable the relationshuip between cause and effect—when X happens, Y will result; thus, Einstein's wisdom that politics is more difficult than physics. But certain political generalizations can be made with some degree of certitude. One of them is that fear is the most powerful emotion in politics, stronger than even anger (the second-strongest). And politics *is*, fundamentally, about emotion. A growing body of psychology and political science research has documented that fact. "The political brain is an emotional brain," famed clinical neuroscientist Dr. Drew Westen has written. "It is not a dispassionate calculating machine, objectively researching for the right facts, figures, and policies to make a reasoned decision."[6] Such might not constitute an iron law of politics with the methodological rigour of Einstein's Theory of Relativity in physics. But having fought in the political arena most of my adult life, I think it's as close to one as can be found in that complex domain. Unfortunately, in the 1974 election, Robert Stanfield found himself on the wrong side of the law—and of voters' emotions.

Russell Maxwell and Socrates notwithstanding, politics is not a deliberate and rational search for truth through process. It can be. At its best, it is. Even at its worst, it should be. But at its core, it is not. Elections are a competition among different sets of emotions represented by different carriers of those emotions in competition with one another. Ideally, policy should express alternative visions as to where the policy carriers intend to lead the followers. The voter then chooses. That is how Stanfield approached the game. In practice, "policy" is too often not policy at all, but rhetoric masquerading as policy. As we have seen, Diefenbaker's "policies" were exemplars. In all such cases, the purpose is not to lead followers, but to stampede them against the competing policy carriers by demonizing both what they are carrying and, by extension, the carriers themselves. Their emotions are wrong; ergo, they themselves are not only wrong, but also evil.

Pierre Trudeau learned the hard way that, to win an election, a politician is best advised not to advance a policy agenda of his (or her) own. Instead, he should demonize the policy of his opponent. And one should do so with the moral certitude and outrage of a Dante driving demons from Hell. It is not Maxwell and Socrates prodding their charges to Truth through process. Rather, it is Savonarola preaching hellfire and damnation against the Medicis and driving them out of Florence and, ultimately, the public square. In the 1972 election, Trudeau almost lost power by treating electioneering as an intellectual exercise in which the voter is engaged through a virtual Socratic "dialogue," the exact word he used to describe his campaign. His campaign's "The Land Is Strong" slogan, reflecting this approach, was the worst in Canadian history. He was not going to make the same "mistake" again—thus, the need to go with fear the next time. For that next time, 1974, Trudeau's Muse was not Socrates; instead, it was Machiavelli in the person of Senator Keith Davey—not an *éminence grise*, but an *éminence noire*.[7] Fear: get that in the wind at your back, you win; get it blowing in your face, you lose. One can take that law of politics to the Monopoly bank.

Fear among voters about a wage-and-price freeze trumped the sense of urgency most economists felt about the country's need to impose inflation controls. Trudeau intended to use that fear against Stanfield when he engineered his own parliamentary defeat and the consequent election. In virtually all the meetings I had with top economists on the leader's behalf before the 1974 election, they stressed the urgency to act boldly against runaway inflation. It was partly upon their advice that Stanfield campaigned on the issue in the campaign. However right Stanfield was—and he *was* right—the issue cost him the election and the opportunity, as prime minister, to do all the great things for the country he had planned so assiduously on the policy front. The issue drove him from the public square.

The public's hostility to the PC Party's wage-and-price controls plan blew out of the water all the party's other carefully prepared policies, rendering them virtually irrelevant to Conservative candidates' chances for success in the election. Ironically, for all the work Tom Symons's operation did for Stanfield and the party on a multitude of issues, the very policy around which the election pivoted was the one on which the PCC had exercised the least influence. As for the anti-inflation plan's real progenitors, after the election most not only denied parentage, but also acted as though the baby had not even been conceived, let alone born and raised to adulthood. "Success has many fathers, failure is an orphan," a Russian proverb says. A bumper sticker reads: "To err is human. To blame it on someone else is politics." How true those two sentiments are in the wake of an election defeat. The only thing faster than the speed of light is rats fleeing a sinking ship in politics. The disastrous wage-and-price-controls policy was the child of many parents, including PC Caucus economist James Gillies; other Caucus members; the PC Research Office, which had done admirable groundwork; the PCC, but only to a limited extent; and, not least, Stanfield himself. In such circumstances, someone has to fall on his sword. This time, it was the leader.

## Stanfield the Statesman

Stanfield told Richard Clippingdale, "I lost the election of 1974 because I made some mistakes after 1972."[8] He did not elaborate. Nor does Clippingdale interpret, or speculate about, what Stanfield meant. I myself am not certain what the Nova Scotian was thinking. But knowing the man as well as I came to, I believe what he meant was as follows. Put simply, Stanfield thought he should have, but had not, anticipated the ruthless and unprincipled campaign Trudeau would conduct against him on the PCs' inflation-control program. For this failure, he blamed only himself. Stanfield believed *he* should have seen it coming, and that he did not, or not soon enough— and, therefore, did not do enough to defend himself and his party and PC candidates against the onslaught—cost him the election.

One sometimes hears the political punditocracy use the term "winning ugly." By that is meant conducting a negative political campaign so ferociously aimed at winning at any cost that the highest cost of all is borne by the political culture. Typically, the embittered loser then refuses to join the jubilant victor in common cause for public purposes, no matter how urgent the common cause or how noble the public purposes. The entire community suffers when people of different political stripes can't rise above partisanship and bitterness from election campaigns to pull together to advance shared goals afterwards. Although capable of holding his own in tough political fights, Stanfield would not have tolerated even a discussion of such a take-no-prisoners approach, far less considered following it. For him, principle mattered. Respect for the democratic process mattered. Respect for his opponents as human beings mattered. Protecting the interests of the total community, not just his own or those of his political party, mattered. He hated the politics of artificially setting people against one another for narrow partisan gain, or for any self-interested reason. In this respect, as in many others, Stanfield's approach to elections and to politics generally followed the tradition of a long line of Canadian Tory leaders over the years—notably Sir Robert Borden, Arthur Meighen, and George Drew. As Hugh Segal has noted, "Stanfield would rather lose an election than abandon [his principles]."[9] Stanfield was not the sort of man who responded to defeat with rancour, let alone vindictiveness towards those who had defeated him, no matter how "ugly" the campaign might have been against him, as in 1974. In this, as in so many ways, he was distinctly different from his predecessor, John Diefenbaker. Particularly towards the end of Diefenbaker's career, he had become just a bitter old man: wizened but not wise, set on vengeance against almost everybody who had opposed him or who he thought had done so, both within his party and outside.

As early as February 1968, Stanfield had had an opportunity to force an election, and likely win it, when Lester Pearson's Liberal minority government lost a vote on Third (and final) Reading on a tax bill in the House of Commons. By tradition, a government is required to resign and call an election in such a parliamentary situation. The Liberals' parliamentary defeat was only weeks before they were scheduled to elect a new leader and probably enhance their electoral chances against the PCs under a new standard-bearer. Pearson conscripted Louis Rasminsky, the supposedly non-partisan governor of the Bank of Canada, to meet with the Tory leader and convince him that the country was gripped by a national monetary crisis so severe that an election then would devastate it in international money markets. Pearson then used the time Rasminsky's successful intervention bought him to go on national television and rally the country behind him to survive the political crisis. The prime minister orchestrated a new Commons vote that saved the government and his own political hide. However wrong-headed the Bank of Canada governor had been in allowing himself to be hoodwinked into playing such an unprecedented partisan role, Stanfield decided, in the national interest, not to press his certain political advantage. In the same spirit, six years later, putting principle above politics, the PC leader championed a politically risky inflation-control plan because he believed it was in the best interests of the country, even if demonstrably not in his own best partisan interests. Then, as in the 1968 election, he accepted his loss with grace and dignity. Courage and selflessness cost Stanfield the 1974 election. Losing "beautiful," however, is nobler than winning "ugly." This principled and decent man was too devoted to his country ever to want to win just *any* way.

Following the election debacle, Stanfield announced plans not only to resign the PC leadership but also, like the Medici family in Florence, to depart the public square altogether. I doubt, in light of three election defeats in a row, he would have given a moment's thought to doing otherwise. He was, however, taken aback by the vehemence with which even previously sympathetic editorial writers called on him to resign. Scolded the *Montreal Star*: "It is clear that the Conservative party will not regain a sense of direction until it finds a new leader...[There] is evident need to relieve Mr. Stanfield of a job he no longer has the taste for."[10] There was a time when a Mackenzie King or a Pearson—if he was patient enough, stayed long enough, and was lucky enough—could become prime minister after losing a number of national general elections as party leader. Pearson prevailed on his third try, in 1963, after losing in 1958 and 1962. Wilfrid Laurier, like Pearson, suffered defeat as national Liberal Party leader (1891 against Sir John A. Macdonald) until prevailing (against Sir Charles Tupper) in 1896. Laurier ended up winning more consecutive elections (four) than any PM in Canadian history (losing to Borden in 1911). Sometimes, it does not take either patience or time, just Monopoly luck and enough Keith Davey-style *noir,* to prevail in politics. Pierre Trudeau roared back with a majority government in February 1980, after Joe Clark and the PCs had defeated him only nine months earlier. Stanfield had been given three tries: 1968, 1972, and now 1974. The Tory leader thought his own time had come and gone in the face of three electoral failures. He knew all too well the toll taken on the reputations of politicians who stayed one election cycle beyond their "best before" shelf life. On the world stage, Winston Churchill, Konrad Adenauer, and Charles de Gaulle must have come to mind. In his own region at home, premiers Joey Smallwood (Newfoundland) and Walter Shaw (PEI) would also have weighed heavily in his calculations. In 1974, Stanfield was not interested in being a fading star who hung around too long.

On July 17, 1975, Robert Stanfield announced his resignation as PC leader in the West Block parliamentary office of my political patron, Heath Macquarrie. Stanfield's deep disappointment with the way the Liberals had defeated him and his party in the 1974 election did not prevent this great man from devoting his remaining years to noble public causes, often in concert with his former tormentors. Macquarrie had written his PhD thesis at McGill University on Borden—like Stanfield, a Nova Scotian. In his memoirs, Macquarrie observes: "Robert Stanfield in retirement has become our first elder statesman since Sir Robert Borden."[11] The former premier and national PC leader was to play that role, with great accomplishment and distinction, till the day he died. Among many other public services he rendered, Stanfield helped Prime Minister Joe Clark extricate himself and his government from the firestorm they caused across Canada and throughout the Middle East by promising to move Canada's embassy in Israel from Tel Aviv to Jerusalem. The former PC leader's one-man "study" commissioned by Clark helped to cool tempers, bought time for the government to smooth ruffled feathers both at home and abroad, and provided a dignified face-saving way for the rookie PM and fledgling government to reverse the policy itself. I have no doubt that, had the PC government survived longer than nine months, Joe Clark would have held Stanfield up his sleeve, as his ace of spades, for other such crisis-management tasks.

# The End of a Partnership

Tom Symons's policy work for Stanfield, begun in the spring of 1968, was now finished. So was mine. Just as he had done at the party's 1971 general meeting, Symons had orchestrated the policy sessions of the 1974 Annual Meeting with minimal damage to the leader's policy flank. Avoiding public controversy and party discord was always a measure of success at these gatherings. Immediately afterwards, the by-now former Trent University president drafted a resignation letter to the leader. The letter commented on Symons's own policy work over the previous six years and on the worth of all the policies that had been generated in that time under his direction: "I believe that a great deal of value has been accomplished and that some very useful service has been rendered to the Party and to Canada by this work." His assessment was understated to the point of being wrong. A more realistic assessment, in Symons's favour, was provided by PC Party president Donald J. Matthews, whose Executive Committee bore responsibility under the party's constitution for establishing the Policy Advisory Committee that Tom Symons had chaired and for the Policy Coordinating Committee for which Symons had provided the secretariat. Concerning all the work that had been done on policy over the previous several years, the party president wrote to Symons, on April 11, 1974, on the eve of the 1974 vote: "While there is no doubt that Mr. Stanfield has played a vital role by his active involvement and support, it is you who must be given credit for pulling all of the pieces together and making it happen."

The moment Prime Minister Trudeau called the election, Symons trashed his draft resignation letter. It was the only time I ever knew him to junk anything remotely archival. But I myself saved a copy for the history books. The last thing Symons wanted to do was abandon ship. The *first* thing he wanted to do was make himself available, at a moment's notice, to serve the man he had worked so hard to make prime minister and whom he was eager to help now: his protégé and friend. It merited one more try. The fact the effort failed to elect Robert Stanfield prime minister should not be the barometer of whether the attempt had been worthwhile. By engaging so many people in a process of thinking both deeply and broadly about how best to advance the public good, Stanfield, in partnership with Symons, elevated the political culture of the land as few other Canadians have ever done.

The Stanfield-Symons approach to developing a political party's policies could—and, I think, should—serve as a model for all parties. The model would be particularly helpful to Opposition parties, which, unlike the government party, can't rely on the public service to help them generate positions on the issues. The PC Party's approach under Stanfield's leadership was light years ahead of how even certain political parties in government still approach policy. The government of Stephen Harper was Exhibit A on that score. Its policies were far too often random and capricious, rather than systematic and orderly; formulated by a small core of insiders, rather than through broad consultation; emotion-driven, rather than evidence-based; ideologically inspired, rather than reached by independent judgment framed by the facts; motivated by partisanship, rather than aimed at the public interest; and inflexibly implemented, rather than adjusted, still less improved, as changing circumstances dictated. It is though Harper and his Cabinet had studied the Stanfield-Symons approach in detail, and then decided to do the exact opposite in every particular. As underscored here throughout, Robert Stanfield, with a university president's help, sought to replace rank amateurism in his party with professionalism of the highest order on all matters concerning both the policy-development process and the policies it produced. He succeeded spectacularly.

A cool-headed, rational man, Stanfield rejected the easy answer to every problem provided by ideology. He viewed as childish responding to issues based exclusively on feelings and popular prejudices, no matter how seductively expressed and proselytized with such political buzzwords or phrases as "conviction," "fundamental beliefs," "principle," "traditional standards," "family values," and "silent majority" or "moral majority." This is the Orwellian vocabulary of the American hard right and now, increasingly, of the Canadian Conservative Party ever since Stephen Harper cast his dark spell over it. Such terms are all too often dog whistles for what their users really stand for: racism, religious bigotry, misogyny, homophobia, and political intolerance. Robert Stanfield's values were the antithesis of such odious notions. But wasn't the grand old national political party that he once led also the antithesis of what passes for that same party today, following the 2003 Reform/Canadian Alliance/ Progressive Conservative merger? I have no doubt whatsoever that, if Stanfield were still alive, he would say with sadness that the answer is yes.

Stanfield had studied all the traditional ideologies—the "isms"—more profoundly than any Tory leader had ever done. Those included socialism, with which, as we have seen, he had flirted as a young man. But, as with all the other formulaic answers to complex problems, he found that "ism" a shoddy substitute for independent thinking based on solid evidence, objective facts, rational debate, consideration of all the options, consensus-building, decision-making through due process, and the application of collective wisdom that all those things enable. Without such ingredients, policy-making is mere guesswork at best, impulsiveness and irrationality at worst, a prescription for eventual failure in either case. Such is the domain of the gambler, not the rationalist.

With or without a chance to govern, the PC Party had a profound impact on how public policy debate was framed in Canada throughout the decade or so (1967–76) Stanfield led the party. Inflation control, income support for the working poor, unemployment insurance reform, industrial strategy, sovereignty protection, judicious deregulation, cost-of-living-indexed pensions and taxation, national unity—Quebec's place in Confederation (*deux nations*) and federal decentralization: in all such areas, Stanfield either placed the issue on the public agenda or elevated its priority; helped set, or, in some cases—as with the Guaranteed Minimum Income concept—alone set the terms of the debate; or paved the way for action, most notably on wage-and-price controls and indexation, and arguably on the capital gains tax, too.

On February 19, 1973, the Trudeau government announced in its Budget Speech, on the floor of the House of Commons, that it intended to amend the federal tax code to adjust fully for inflation each taxpayer's tax bracket and exemptions and deductions. It was exactly what Stanfield had advocated on the campaign trail in the 1972 election only four months before. With characteristic good humour, the PC leader rose from his Commons seat and took an exaggerated bow for his authorship. In acknowledgement, the packed chamber rocked to roars of laughter and applause and shouts of "hear, hear." The finance minister, John Turner, who delivered the budget address, joined in the good-natured pandemonium. It was by no means the only time Robert Stanfield could have taken an author's bow in Parliament. Stanfield's influence was reflected in many a law and public policy of the land. He continued to influence policy and decision-makers, particularly in the Progressive Conservative Party, long after he was no longer its leader, as "an elder statesman." Says Richard Clippingdale: "No other political leader [in Canada] in the twentieth century, with the possible exception of Mackenzie King, thought, wrote and spoke about our country, its needs and its troubles with such dedication and creativity for so protracted a period."[12]

One can only speculate how high Robert Stanfield and Tom Symons, together, might have lifted the country had things gone differently for them and their party electorally. It has often been said—including by Clippingdale in his book's subtitle—that Robert Stanfield was the "Best Prime Minister of Canada We Never Had." If so, and I believe it is the case, Symons was truly the best "Senior Policy Advisor *that* Prime Minister Never Had." The former Trent University president embodies the finest personal qualities and values of a classic Canadian Conservative. That is why Thomas Henry Bull Symons has loomed large in my narrative. If Symons is a "Stanfield Tory," as he describes himself to this day, I myself am proudly not only a "Stanfield Tory"—though I am certainly that—but also a "Symons Tory." And always will be.

Soon after the 1974 election, Tom Symons and Robert Stanfield spoke at length on the phone. Both men were despondent about the results. Unspoken was that this had been Stanfield's last hurrah in efforts to become prime minister—in fact, his swan song in public life. Symons did not need to be told. The two sages came to know each other so well that they could not only complete the other's sentences, but also divine what the other was thinking before he even began talking. So a painful truth was the last thing that needed to be said. What was said was "thank you" by a grateful leader to one of his most loyal followers—and, now, close friend.

Stanfield had always been a fortunate man, born as he was of privilege, wealth, high intellect, and family circumstance that often in life, though not always, lead to an elite education and valuable contacts and consequent professional success and yet more of life's advantages, as happened in Stanfield's own life. Stanfield was the kind of man, however, who likely would have succeeded even if nothing much had been handed him. Even in defeat, Robert Stanfield was still "The Man with the Winning Way."

At the end of his career, the *Right* Honourable Robert Lorne Stanfield—a rare designation bestowed on him by Queen Elizabeth—had been premier of a province for eleven years and leader of Her Majesty's Official Opposition for nearly a decade. To boot, he was scion of one of the country's most famous families and a man of considerable wealth. And yet he remained utterly devoid of pretense, a modest man without any reason to be. In a handwritten note to Brian Mulroney—following Mulroney's announcement, in February 1993, that he would be resigning as prime minister and PC leader—that's exactly how the Nova Scotian characterized himself: as "only a modest person."[13] In mid-July 2010, a glorious Handel concert was performed by the Theatre of Early Music in Ottawa. Former NDP leader Ed Broadbent introduced the performers. Acknowledging his own devotion to fine music, he noted that Robert Stanfield had shared his taste. Broadbent recalled meeting Stanfield on the street in Ottawa shortly after the latter had given up the PC Party leadership. When Broadbent congratulated him on his notable career, the former Tory leader paused, then replied: "Well it didn't amount to four bars by Mozart!" Many Canadians, I among them, would respectfully disagree.

Leadership has no specific ingredients, but is composed of certain raw materials either natural or born of experience, or both; either way, leadership cannot be taught, it cannot be learned, it resides within—in some unknowable and, therefore, unteachable way.[14] As I reflect today on Robert Stanfield as both a leader and a man, I cannot avoid comparing him with the half-dozen PC leaders who followed him: Joe Clark, Erik Nielsen (on an interim basis), Brian Mulroney, Kim Campbell, Jean Charest, Peter MacKay, and Stephen Harper. Each had or has many of the fine personal qualities and political talents Stanfield possessed, as well as some he lacked. One quality Stanfield lacked was "fabulosity"—that quality in a public person that causes people at first glance to exclaim, "Wow!" He more typically caused people to say, under their breath, "What a great man!" But to me, Brian Mulroney's comment about Sir John A. Macdonald, that "he was in a class of his own," applies also to Robert Stanfield. With or without "fabulosity," Stanfield *was* in a "class of his own." More than any other politician in modern Canadian history, Stanfield—provincial aristocracy that he exuded, noblesse oblige that he practised, high principle that he always acted on—had *class*. Historians tend to agree that leaders are both *born* and *made*, but not in a class and not because of class. The unique class Robert Lorne Stanfield occupied, both as a leader and as a man, he might or might not have been born into. But he *made* the best of it.

# Part II

# INSIDE LOOKING OUT: PROGRESSIVE CONSERVATISM IN ACTION

*Public life is regarded as the crown of a career, and to young men it is the worthiest ambition. Politics is still the greatest and the most honourable adventure.*

—Lord Tweedsmuir, Governor General of Canada, May 12, 1937.

# Chapter 15

# THE OPPOSITION YEARS: BAPTISM OF FIRE

By the time Robert Stanfield resigned in February 1976, he had led the Progressive Conservative Party for nearly a decade. Under his leadership, the party became a very different institution from the one he had inherited from John Diefenbaker. Stanfield had transformed the party by restoring the progressive tradition begun by its founders, honoured by successive Tory leaders throughout the generations, but largely abandoned by Diefenbaker, especially in Opposition after he lost power. Strategy is the alignment of means to ends. Although Stanfield did not succeed in his ultimate goal—winning power to do great things for the country—he did succeed in his main strategic goal: he made the party a modern, progressive force in Canadian politics with a fighting chance to replace the Liberals as the government of the land, if not as "the natural governing party."

When the PC Party chose Joe Clark as its new leader in 1976, he continued the course Stanfield had charted for the party throughout the previous decade. Indeed, the immediate transition from Stanfield to Clark was virtually seamless, even though Clark lacked Stanfield's government experience, maturity, extraordinary intellect, elite education, competence, sound judgment, political smarts, and overall gravitas. The fact Clark had served as a senior Stanfield staffer before becoming an Alberta MP in 1972 made the new leadership seem at first less like a changing of the guard than just a new drill by the existing one. For all their differences in style, Clark and his own successor, Brian Mulroney, were both progressives in the Stanfield mould. It was, consequently, easy for Joe Clark to accept Mulroney's invitation to serve as his external affairs minister after the PCs took power in 1984 with Mulroney as prime minister. On not a single major policy of the new government—from fiscal discipline to free trade to acid rain to constitutional reform to Canada's place in the world—did the two men differ significantly. Indeed, Clark proved himself one of the most effective advocates for Mulroney's agenda at home and abroad. For nearly two decades after Stanfield retired as leader, the party not only continued to be a force for progressive thinking and policies. It also made unacceptable within its ranks the anti-intellectualism that had characterized the party under Diefenbaker's stewardship.

# Taking the Plunge: Hillsborough

In April 1978, after finishing my full-time policy work with Robert Stanfield, I was nominated to run in the PEI riding of Hillsborough (now called Charlottetown) for the next federal general election, which was expected soon. But, faced with bad poll numbers, Prime Minister Pierre Trudeau postponed the election until the very end of his five-year term. The election was consequently not held until a full year after I was nominated, on May 22, 1979.

My predecessor in the riding was our old family friend Heath Macquarrie, who had decided not to run again. No doubt, it was Heath's sense of gratitude to my father for his own support back in 1957 that led him to support me in my successful bid for the Tory nomination. In a strange twist of fate, given Heath's initial problems with Roman Catholic voters in the riding, my main opponent for the nomination, a prosperous Charlottetown entrepreneur, Al MacRae, was supported partly by a group eager to block me because I was Catholic. With Heath's discreet but decisive help, I was able to beat them back. He endorsed me, just as my dad had endorsed him. And Heath did so publicly even though my second nomination opponent, University of Prince Edward Island biology professor Ian MacQuarrie (different spelling), was not only one of his best friends, but also—his cousin! Without question, this was Heath's way of repaying my late father. Over the years, when fuelled by the Appleton elixir, Heath would describe me as "my brilliant and most excellent young successor." That is, in fact, how he describes me in his memoir.[1] Had I known he was writing the memoir, I would have sent him a whole case of the demon rum at the time—why stop at such modesty? In the same spirit (in both senses), it was also Heath, the reader might recall, who first set me on the road to public life on a warm July evening back in 1969, with his phone call to my family's cottage in Keppoch about Tom Symons's wish to meet me. Like his supporting me for the Tory nomination in Hillsborough in 1978, the 1969 call probably would never have happened but for my father's pivotal role in Heath's electoral success, especially in his first election (1957), the most competitive one he would face among all his many federal election contests—eight in all, from 1957 to 1974. It is all of a piece. Although the MP felt eternally indebted to my father, Dad never thought the debt needed to be repaid. But it was, through me—twice over, and many times thereafter. Heath Macquarrie was to serve as my mentor throughout the political career he helped me launch—always wise, invariably unerring, and usually not far from the Appleton ambrosia.

In Heath's plans for my political career, no detail, however small, was unimportant to him. A few days after I won the nomination to succeed him as the PC Party's standard-bearer in Hillsborough, he—still the sitting MP for the riding—invited me to Ottawa. The purpose was to introduce me to a group of Press Gallery veterans—among them, the *Globe and Mail*'s chief political reporter, Jeffrey Simpson—whom he had gathered for drinks in his Parliament Hill office. Arriving early, I apparently sported a stubble beard darker than my mentor thought appropriate for either the occasion or his successor in any such circumstance. He suggested I grab a quick shave at the barbershop housed for MPs in the West Block, where his office was located. After the deed was done, my mentor examined my now clean-shaven visage, approvingly, as a first-time mother would count her newborn's toes and fingers to assure herself she had given birth to a healthy infant. Even long after I was well established in politics as a minister of the Crown and he was now a senator (appointed by Joe Clark), my mentor took a keen interest in my career. The senator would suggest I do this or that, or meet this person or that one—or, more often than not, stop doing something of which he disapproved. He was especially vigilant about my tendency, from time to time, to cite or directly quote in my speeches sources that he considered anathema to the Red Tory values to which he unfailingly subscribed and that he knew were true to my own political upbringing and ethos. The speed of neither sound nor light was faster than a phone call from my distressed mentor whenever I fell off the wagon of progressive Tory orthodoxy by referencing data—or, God forbid, perspectives—from either American Club for Growth or the US Chamber of Commerce. Heath gave new meaning to the expression "seeing red"—or, more accurately, not seeing it. I have to confess now to having periodically made such references in prepared speech texts for the sheer pleasure I derived from his verbal slap downs of "those awful American wing nuts," or much stronger language if the Appleton had been flowing particularly hard.

Robert Stanfield, my former boss, was the first party luminary to campaign for me in the riding following my nomination. His own strongest supporter on the Island had always been Macquarrie, including for the PC Party leadership in 1967. The powerful endorsement I got from the former national party leader boosted my campaign a great deal. Revered throughout the Maritimes by people of every political persuasion, not just Tories, ever since he came from nowhere to dominate Nova Scotia politics for a generation, Stanfield was then at the very pinnacle of his prestige both within the region and nationally. I could not have had a better advocate in the riding had my own principal opponent accidentally endorsed me. My late father's posthumous coattails accelerated the momentum Heath Macquarrie and Robert Stanfield helped me create. Heath told me that "the Dr. Joe factor" was worth a thousand votes to me in a small riding typically won by not many more—albeit with steadily diminishing effect after each election cycle as memories faded and his generation died off.

# Katherine Hambly of Charlottetown

Everything about the 1979 election in Hillsborough was hard to duplicate in subsequent elections. I was young, only thirty-four, and still single. The last entry would change a year later, with my marriage to Katherine Jean Hambly. We had been dating for several months to that point. Nine years younger than I, she had a confident bearing and an impressive professional and personal biography that, on our first date, led me to believe we were about the same age. When Kathy told me her real age, I felt like fleeing for fear of being arrested. Kathy's parents (Bill and Gladys) raised her and their three sons (Bill, Wayne, and Douglas) in a house considerably smaller than ours, sideways across the street. The Hamblys' great success in business—retail furniture, mobile homes and parks, recreational vehicles, and substantial real estate holdings and rentals—would come later, involving the father and Wayne and Douglas.[2]

When Kathy and I grew up in Charlottetown, everything about the city—in fact, about the Island as a whole—was organized along religious lines: schools, the two post-secondary colleges, hospitals, recreational centres, *ad infinitum.* I could practically see from my bedroom window the swanky new public high school in town, Queen Charlotte. And yet, it was unofficially but unmistakably Protestant. So my brothers and I had to trek over a mile twice a day, on either side of lunch at home, to another newly built "public" high school, Birchwood, which, true to form, was exclusively Catholic. Our two sisters, Eileen and Maura, attended convents, where they were star students. We McMillan children, therefore, did not have abundant opportunity to get to know the Protestant Hambly brood—least of all Kathy, given the marked age difference between us and her. Mother later told me that, when Kathy was barely old enough to skate, I kicked her off our family's backyard hockey rink because "She's a girl!" In any event, we Catholics, in that terribly dark hidebound era, were discouraged by the priests and nuns from fraternizing with heathen Protestants lest our own chances for everlasting salvation be jeopardized. Either I did not heed this religious counsel or, more likely, Kathy's striking looks simply trumped my eagerness for eternal redemption. We dated, fell in love, got married, and had three lovely girls: Kelly, Becky, and Emily. Kathy had completed an MBA at Dalhousie University in Halifax. She then worked for a period as a marketing specialist in Toronto with General Foods before returning to the Island to establish her own business while helping to care for her ailing mom. That business was *Katherine's Ltd.*, soon the province's most prestigious ladies' designer clothing store and among the most respected and successful of its kind in the Maritimes. Over time, many Island women, and quite a few off-Island ones as well, refused to buy even a pair of pantyhose without the style imprimatur of the proprietress of *Katherine's*.

Kathy's growing reputation for the best personal fashion sense in Charlottetown led to some pretty creative local gossip when both of us were being spotted together soon after each of us had returned to the province from living away for several years. Our first major public "coming out," at a black-tie ball at Government House, provided especially rich fodder for the rumour mill. Kathy stole the show wearing an elegant form-fitting floor-length black dress with a matching turban. The next day, word flashed on the street that my tall, slim, long-legged stylishly gowned date was a New York runway model whom I had flown in for the occasion. Well, as the Frank Sinatra song goes about the Big Apple, "If I can make it there, I can make it anywhere." Kathy—Protestant that she is, Liberal that she was, brutally candid as she insisted on being about my earliest efforts to market myself politically—chucked overboard two centuries of Island proscriptions against mixed marriages. And married me—a Catholic and a Tory! The earth shook in PEI on August 2, 1980. I had made it big time in "New York." But the planet stabilized. And now, with Kathy in it, so had my life.

# The 1979 Federal Election

By the late 1970s, the Trudeau Liberals were unpopular almost everywhere in the country and badly on the run. My principal opponent for the 1979 federal election in Hillsborough was Gordon Tweedy, a Liberal. In his mid-forties, Gordon, Hollywood handsome, was an excellent amateur hockey player in a local gentlemen's league, an established lawyer, and scion of a well-respected old Island family distantly related to my own on Dad's side. Gordon was also smart, much more so than some people believed "in the face of that face." But he did make the serious strategic mistake of impugning my Island bona fides by attacking the years I had spent out of province working for Robert Stanfield and Tom Symons. That was a pretty hard sell even when captured in the catchy campaign slogan he used to describe himself: "The Man from Hillsborough, the Man for Hillsborough." Like their Scottish and Irish forebears,

Islanders tend to view one another in terms of clans, not individuals. My family had been living in PEI since George III sat on the throne, in the mid-1770s. Trying to convince voters a McMillan was not an Islander was like claiming potatoes were not a local crop. Islanders didn't see "eye to eye" with Tweedy on that one—forgive the ocular pun.

As if all that wasn't enough going my way, the Liberal government in Ottawa was steadily consolidating and regionalizing federal offices and services in PEI as an efficiency and austerity measure. Many federal public servants were being transferred from the province to regional centres such as Halifax and Moncton. The policy was disrupting lives, and eliminating jobs, direct services, and spending power on the Island. I made this my major issue in the campaign. The local media were sympathetic to my efforts. Many were themselves affected through spouses or family, or they just felt loyalty to the homeland. I had a field day. Government spokespeople and Liberal candidates, including my own opponent, denied there was a grand plan to—in my words—"strip the Island of provincial status and render it an outpost of the mainland." Asked by CBC-TV in Charlottetown if the Liberals were lying when denying my charge, I said "lying" was too strong a word, but they were engaged in "rampant untruths." The first time I made this charge, in a different way, the *Guardian,* the Island's major daily newspaper, splashed the comments, with my official campaign photo, across the front page in big black banner headlines. My media team created a first-rate advertising campaign from start to finish. But nothing could equal the impact of the free media I was able to garner, day in and day out, just by exposing the facts about the government's regionalization policy and its dire impact on the province, especially the capital—my riding. As my campaign built steam, I could feel victory in the air. And under my headquarters door: in the dark of night, federal employees discreetly slipped brown envelopes containing yet more revelations of the government's secret regionalization plans. My fellow Tory candidate David MacDonald, still young but a political veteran, was seeking re-election in the western Island riding of Egmont. He told me a week before voting day: "Tom, you've run a terrific campaign. Your issue is helping the party everywhere across the Island. I know you're going to win, and so am I."

David was right. By PEI standards, I won in a landslide: 52.8 percent to Tweedy's 40.6 percent. I wasn't surprised—though, according to the grapevine, my opponent was shocked, particularly by the size of his loss. I was the first Catholic ever elected to the federal Parliament from Queen's County, the most populous one-third of the province geographically. No one outside my immediate family was happier with the outcome than Heath Macquarrie, one-time Orange Parade equestrian. After a drink or two of the Appleton rum, Heath would grandiloquently refer to me on many future occasions as his "duly anointed successor"—when not also "brilliant and most excellent." I was certainly the former, not indisputably the latter.

In the 1979 federal election, we Tories won all four seats in PEI by comfortable margins. The CBC, out of Charlottetown, did a television special the next day called "Four Seats, Four Tories." Interviewed in my den at home for it, I was seated in a large wingback armchair. In the middle of the interview, my enormous grey tabby cat, "Grit," suddenly jumped up on my lap, stretched out, settled in, stared at the camera for the whole interview—and completely upstaged me. My on-camera ad lib—"This is my cat, Grit. She's likely the only happy Grit on the Island today"—unleashed a ton of fan mail. To Grit! Ted and Elizabeth Reagh, a local husband-and-wife lawyer team (both cat lovers), sent me a sterling silver cat Monopoly token. Others mailed me photos of their cats. Still others wanted to know everything about Grit, including what I fed her. Politics, for me, would never again be better. I still have the Monopoly token from the Reaghs. Grit lived another eight years, dying at fourteen—still getting, to the very end, constituents' fan mail and compliments on her TV debut. Who said politics is boring?

Although Joe Clark had succeeded him as leader in February 1976, Robert Stanfield retained his own seat in Halifax until the new Parliament was elected three years later. I regret not being able to boast that Stanfield and I served together in Parliament. I missed that distinction by only weeks. Later, as federal environment minister, I spoke on the "Economics of the Environment" at a session organized for the G7 Summit in Toronto in June 1988. Robert Stanfield introduced me at the Summit session on behalf of the program committee. I have been introduced on a platform countless times in my public career, but among all the various introductions—some great, others not so great, still others simply dreadful—Stanfield's on this occasion means the most to me. No other comes a close second. Thereafter, Mr. Stanfield and I saw each other periodically, mostly at airports as each of us got on with a busy life.

Robert Lorne Stanfield did not ascend to the summit of Canadian public life as prime minister. But the office itself was elevated because he tried. In 1996, this great man suffered a debilitating stroke. On December 16, 2003, in his ninetieth year, he died. The former PC leader is buried with his first wife, Joyce, mother of his four children, and his second wife, Mary, in Camp Hill Cemetery, Halifax. A giant left us. I miss him still.

# The Clark Government, 1979–80

For a political junkie, there is no higher high than being elected to public office for the first time. Nor is there any lower low than losing office later. Electorally, I have been in both manic and depressive states. Losing is more extreme. My winning a seat in Parliament initially (in the 1979 election) was heady stuff. Of the six federal general elections I fought as a candidate, that one was the most fun. Actually, it was the only campaign of my own that I enjoyed. I always loved campaigning—meeting voters, sparring with opponents, jostling with the media, participating in the sport of the game. But the total experience—given the unremitting pressure, in particular—was much less than the sum of its parts. Once elected, everything is on the line, including one's livelihood. In each election, like a prisoner in solitary confinement, I counted the days when it would end. Anyone who has been a candidate for a fairly high office and says being one was fun is lying—and likely to himself or herself first. That's especially true if the stakes are high and the results uncertain. At a minimum, campaigning is backbreaking, exhausting, and all-consuming work.

If only the rest of my first term as an MP had been as much fun as my inaugural election. Joe Clark formed a minority government following the May 1979 election, with 136 seats, only 6 short of a majority (114 Liberals, 26 NDP, 6 Social Credit). Had we made any kind of meaningful alliance, formal or informal, with Social Credit, our party could have remained in office for close to the normal four-year period (constitutionally, five). Instead, Clark and his political advisors and staff combined hubris and incompetence and miscalculation and sheer bad judgment to squander it all.

I think the technical term in political science is "pissed it away." The paradox was that all these people, the prime minister included, were widely thought to be political pros of the first rank, having fought many elections over a long period. The "pros" included Lowell Murray, William Neville, and Duncan Edmonds, each one supposedly experienced and talented about such matters. But it was Amateur Hour at the OK Corral. In fairness to the political operatives in question, the PC Party had been out of power since 1963. As I detail later, their métier was Opposition, not government. And yet they faced pressures to be rodeo champions the first day they saddled up. As it turned out, there would not be time for them to learn the ropes, let alone break a bronco without landing on their asses.

Among the most politically inept, and self-destructive, steps Joe Clark took after being elected prime minister was his decision not to appoint parliamentary secretaries—in effect, assistant ministers. Then he reversed himself, but appointed none from Atlantic Canada except for freshman Halifax MP George Cooper over such veterans as Pat Nowlan, Bob Coates, and Mike Forrestall. My fellow Island MP David MacDonald was in Cabinet, and I represented Charlottetown, the provincial capital, so I reasonably expected to be appointed a parliamentary secretary myself. But I wasn't. Clark's serial ineptitude on the matter planted the seeds that would germinate, grow like crabgrass, and eventually help suffocate his leadership support (but not my own) within the PC Atlantic Caucus. Brian Mulroney, for all his vices, was incapable of such political malpractice. Clark, for all his virtues, seemed driven to it. Mulroney was a great military general, Clark hardly a corporal. That said, Joe Clark was one of the finest public servants in the history of Canada and, inarguably, among the nicest. One of the other downsides of Clark's mishandling of the parliamentary secretaries business—apart from alienating colleagues whose goodwill he would later need as he defended his leadership—was this: he missed an opportunity to expose the maximum number of Caucus members to hands-on ministerial experience as understudies. Even in the short time the Clark government was in office, that advantage would have been helpful when the party later regained power with Mulroney as prime minister. The day I became a minister, I had never before stepped into a minister's departmental office.

The new prime minister didn't call Parliament until October, five months after the election, one of the longest periods ever between an election and the opening of a new Parliament. Again, the PC Party had been out of office since 1963, so the Clark team thought it needed the extra time to prepare its legislative agenda. The time, however, was not wisely spent. Like other newly elected Tory MPs, I was nearly a casualty of the Greek tragedy that ensued. The Liberals marshalled their entire Caucus, save one, to support an NDP non-confidence motion—on which the Socreds abstained— to bring down the government. Lasting only sixty-six days from first sitting to dissolution, the thirty-first Parliament was the shortest in Canadian history. The Clark government lost the non-confidence vote by a 139–133 margin. The declared issue was the government's budget measure to impose a new 18-cent-a-gallon excise tax on gasoline as both a revenue and a conservation measure. But the tax was just a pretext. The real reason was naked partisan politics. The Clark government's popularity had plunged to 28 percent from 36 percent during the summer, nineteen points behind the emboldened Liberals. The new prime minister himself was generally perceived as likeable but out of his depth. Inflation was soaring and employment plummeting. And Finance Minister John Crosbie's "short-term pain for long-term gain" budget was selling across the country like beach balls and bikinis in the High Arctic.

Smarting over their earlier election loss to a Tory leader they did not respect, the Liberals were eager for a rematch. At a raucous Liberal Caucus Christmas party, where spirits soared as spirits flowed, the die was cast: they would crush the new government. More sober, but no less fired up, the NDP decided to do the same. Drunk or sober, the government was facing disaster. It would soon be history.

Pierre Trudeau rescinded his announced plans to vacate the Liberal leadership when the Clark government fell. And he roared back to power with a majority government in the subsequent election, held on February 18, 1980. Apparently, the voters didn't agree with the message, and slogan, of the Tory campaign: "Real Change Deserves a Fair Chance." The Clark government had lasted one day short of nine months; as John Crosbie famously quipped, "long enough to conceive, just not long enough to deliver." The results: 146 Liberals, 103 PCs, 32 NDPers; every one of the Social Credit MPs lost his seat. I retained my own seat in Hillsborough, but with a reduced margin—47.7 percent for me, 43.8 percent for my Liberal opponent, CBC broadcaster Gerry Birt. Gerry was a strong candidate and ran a good campaign; he would run against me again, unsuccessfully, in the 1984 election. Across the province, the PCs and Liberals each won two seats. Mostly, I tried to avoid the overarching national election issues, particularly the new gas tax. I focused instead on local issues, just as I had in 1979. This time my primary theme was not regionalization, but calling on the federal government to set up in Charlottetown a fourth veterinary college for the country. The veterinary college would remain a hobbyhorse of mine until it was established in 1986—largely because of my incessant lobbying. Meanwhile, I rode that hobbyhorse right into both the 1980 and 1984 campaigns.

Reflecting on the Joe Clark government debacle now, almost four decades later, I think the government's Commons defeat was virtually predestined. And yet, it was eminently avoidable. For all his intelligence and personal integrity and political experience, Joe *was* out of his depth. Perhaps it was his youth. He was barely out of his thirties when he became prime minister, the youngest in Canadian history. The man was only thirty-seven when he became PC leader. Or maybe, instead, he was just too nice for the cut and thrust of politics at the national level, though he proved himself an aggressive Opposition leader after the election. No doubt, the man had been toughened in battle. Whatever the dynamics, I do know this: on the night of December 13, 1979, when the government fell on the NDP non-confidence motion, we Tory backbenchers knew beforehand that our party lacked the votes to win. Several of our members, External Affairs Minister Flora MacDonald among them, were out of the country and wouldn't be able to return in time to vote. The government House leader, Walter Baker, controlled Parliament's agenda, so the vote that brought down the government could have been postponed for several days until those members returned. The powers that be, however, decided against exercising that right.

Did Clark and his advisors think the Liberals, despite the booze and bluster, would cave at the last minute? Did they think the Liberals would not want to fight an election with Trudeau retiring and a party leadership convention planned? Did the PC party pooh-bahs think the Socreds would not risk their own seats in a sudden election when they were just beginning to enjoy the fruits of office and were politically vulnerable? Did these same Tory strategists think a Commons defeat and a forced election would actually be good politics for the PCs? That the electorate would punish the Opposition parties for forcing an election so soon after the previous one? That, somehow, a sense of fair play would generate public sympathy for Clark and the new government because they had been given so little time to govern and prove themselves? That the PCs would stand a much better chance then against Trudeau than later against a fresh new leader? Or—the most painful of all possibilities to contemplate—that Joe Clark and his strategists just couldn't count parliamentary votes? Did Clark and company even know, for example, that the tiny Social Credit Caucus—which could have made the difference between winning and losing the vote—would abstain? I got to know my fellow parliamentary freshman David Kilgour, MP for Edmonton–Strathcona (brother-in-law of John Turner, later briefly prime minister). David's backbench seat was next to where the Créditiste contingent sat together in the Commons. Competent enough in French, he befriended these members. He told me and anyone else who would listen—which seemed not to have included our parliamentary strategists—that the Social Credit Caucus did not want an election, would much prefer to support the government, and needed only a face-saving way, with Clark government funding back in their ridings, for them to do so. The government refused to make it easy for this six-member parliamentary rump to side with Clark on the vote by accommodating at least part of their wish list. Worse, the PM had alienated the rump by refusing to accord it official party status in the Commons. His declaring he would govern as though heading a majority government made these members feel additionally marginalized. Had the Clark government followed a deliberate strategy to alienate the Créditistes, it could not have achieved that end more expeditiously than it did through sheer incompetence.

Early in the evening of the historic Commons vote, I was invited to dinner at the home of Joanne Handrahan (now Arbing). Also from PEI, she was a contemporary of my brother Colin at St. Dunstan's University, had worked with me at the Keppoch Beach Hotel the summer I entered SDU, and, as an Ottawa realtor, would soon sell me a three-bedroom townhouse in New Edinburgh, near Rockcliffe. We knew each other well. Outrageously outspoken by nature, Joanne said to me towards the end of our meal: "Tom, you are awfully boring tonight. You seem distracted, uninterested in being with me. What's up?" I said, "Joanne, I *am* distracted. The government is going to fall tonight. There's a non-confidence vote in the House of Commons, I have to be there soon, and we're going to lose the vote." She thought I was drunk. If only I had been! Alcohol would have dulled the unspeakable emotional pain I was enduring. Like other Tory backbenchers, I was all too aware that the pending defeat would likely mean that many of us would not return to Parliament. We felt like lambs being led to the slaughter. It was all so stupid, so unnecessary, and, we thought, so callous. I was made privy to recent correspondence between former senator Lowell Murray and my brothers Colin and Charley in a context unrelated to the subject at hand (their respective October 2015 federal general election predictions). I have always suspected that, as senior staff advisor to Joe Clark, my friend Lowell had the single biggest impact on the PC leader's calculations concerning the Commons vote that effectively ended his prime ministership. In that correspondence with my brothers, Lowell tossed a throwaway line: "I have endured a long reputational rehabilitative process following 1979 when I was unjustly accused of being unable to count [parliamentary votes]," he said. "My sin was far worse, actually. I knew exactly what the numbers were prior to the Commons vote; however, I was sure we could and would win the ensuing election!" I rest my case.

After the government's defeat, I travelled back to PEI with the Island's Cabinet minister, David MacDonald, Clark's secretary of state and communications minister (also responsible for the status of women). As John Crosbie's seatmate, he had seconded the finance minister's budget bill to which the NDP had attached its non-confidence "rider" that had crushed the government and forced the election. The shock we both felt was palpable while returning home to our ridings. We could hardly converse. Though not as defeatist as I about the coming election, David, youthful by nature, appeared to have aged a decade in only a week from all the stress caused by what had just transpired in Parliament. For my part, I felt a hundred years older from the uncertainty. Nowhere else in the country was the gasoline-tax issue more troublesome for Tories than in David's own Egmont riding. The Liberals' dishonest claim that the tax also applied to home heating oil—not exclusively transportation fuel, with significant mitigations aimed at helping those Canadians most severely affected and least able to cope—wreaked havoc for the party in his riding. It also did so, to one degree or another, elsewhere across the Island and the country at large. For us Tories, the middle of a bitterly cold Canadian winter was no time anywhere in the nation to have to defend increased taxes on gasoline or oil. As the public face of the government on the Island, seen locally as complicit in the unpopular budget, David was trounced by Liberal George Henderson. David would return to the Commons in 1988, but representing the Toronto riding of Rosedale; always the reddest of Red Tories, this finest of men would run unsuccessfully there for the NDP in 1997.

I do not—nor do I wish to—remember much else about this awful political period. I did, however, benefit from a strong support system. My brothers Colin and John, both living on the Island, actively campaigned for me in this and all later periods of my political career, just as they had done from the very beginning. So did their wives and many other extended family members, friends of mine, and a large network of Tory partisans from all walks of life and in every poll. My twin, Charley, was, as usual, well plugged into the party's national campaign from his home base in Toronto. He was a great source of political intelligence and wise counsel from on high, all the while helping on the policy and communications fronts on the ground within the riding during regular visits to the Island. My brother-in-law George Taylor Fulford III, sister Eileen's husband, was a diehard Liberal. In 1900, Sir Wilfred Laurier had appointed George's namesake grandfather to the Senate, where he represented Brockville, Ontario, until his death in 1905. George's father, George Taylor Fulford II, was a Liberal MP (for Leeds) from 1940 to 1945. And yet, my brother-in-law joined Eileen in generously donating money to all my campaigns. (My younger sister, Maura, was living and working out of province.) Whether George Fulford was ever able to bring himself to cast a Tory vote, even for me, is a secret he took to his grave. (I suspect that, as a strong "free trade" Grit, he did so at least once—in the 1988 election, fought on that issue.) My mother, a classy septuagenarian in this period, could charm from the trees birds of every beak and feather. As such, she was an invaluable campaigner, hosting, among other things, teas and receptions in the many senior citizens' residences operated by the provincial government in the Charlottetown area. In full Rose Kennedy mode, her presence in the campaign also helped perpetuate the mythic memory of my late father, always worth a ton of votes, even well after his death. Heath Macquarrie was also never far from the action—or my side.

All these kinds of dynamics were set in motion in my first campaign, in 1979. Pretty much the same ones played out in all four subsequent elections I fought on the Island. But in no other election were they more important to me than in the 1980 campaign, for that was the first one in which I had to campaign against a powerful national tide. In later such circumstances, in 1988 and 1993, I was a much stronger candidate from experience, and had a far better political organization from incumbency than the one Heath Macquarrie had bequeathed me, even if other factors denied me victory in those two elections. In the earlier campaigns, I needed all the help I could get from family members, grassroots workers, and local and national political heavyweights alike as I got my political feet wet. That help would continue to work its magic throughout my electoral career. What did not continue, except in the 1984 contest, was good luck in the form of favourable regional or national political tides.

I was blessed with one of the best constituency secretaries in the country. Shorter than a mushroom and wider than a cornfield, Jeannette Arsenault had the warmest smile, the sharpest mind, the keenest political instincts, the most competent managerial style, the greatest work ethic, and the most genuine devotion to constituents' needs that any Member of Parliament could possibly have hoped for as the public face of his or her riding operation and political organization. Think Helen Doyle, add nary a centimeter in height but a tonne of weight, mix in a toothy grin, and throw in, for good measure, a seemingly congenital incapacity to get past participles right—that was Jeannette. My constituents loved her. And I did, too. Jeannette always *done* good by me. She was so popular and widely respected that I featured her in political ads emblazoned with the tagline, "Every Great MP Has a Silent Partner." The text included the statement, "but Jeannette is never silent when a constituent is getting a raw deal."

After Kathy finally went home to sleep late into the night of the 1980 election, Heath Macquarrie and his divine wife, Isabel, and I continued to watch the last televised returns that confirmed that the Clark government had crashed to defeat at the hands of the Liberals. The Macquarries had rented a hotel room for the night at Charlottetown's Inn on the Hill, appropriately located on what to this day is called "Gallows Hill," where public executions used to be conducted. We Tories had now been publicly hanged, and Joe Clark's short career as prime minister was well and truly dead. Isabel retired for the night, and then Heath and I drowned our sorrows with the Appleton intoxicant until daylight broke and the bottle was at last empty. But, unlike the Clark government, our sorrows would not die. It remained to be seen whether or not the emerging sunshine, through the Macquarries' hotel windows, symbolized a brighter day for us Tories down the road.

# PC Leadership Battles

Joe Clark's star-crossed leadership merits reflection. Clark won the leadership to succeed Robert Stanfield in 1976 not because of his own qualities—though, in the eyes of delegates, he met the minimum requirement, even if only that. Rather, he won by default. All the other candidates proved unacceptable: Brian Mulroney because he was considered too glitzy and superficial at the time; Claude Wagner, a former Liberal minister of justice in Quebec, because he was not seen as a reliable Tory; Flora MacDonald because of gender—the "Flora Syndrome." I well remember standing adrift among a group of friends when, after the early ballots, it became clear that our respective candidates did not have the votes to win. My candidate was Brian Mulroney. The question loomed: who to support now? For us progressives, there were two choices. One was Joe Clark, whom I had thought much too callow a youth even to be a leadership candidate, much less leader. The other was Flora MacDonald, in whose hands I had literally placed a financial donation when she was campaigning for the leadership in Peterborough, Ontario. But, notwithstanding her many personal and political strengths, I very much doubted she could win a national campaign in an era when far too many Canadians—ironically, especially women—were hostile to having a prime minister who didn't shave in the morning and speak in baritone.

Lowell Murray had been a Stanfield staffer with Clark, was a close friend of his, roomed with him for a while when both were bachelors, and knew him as well as anybody. Flora had been Murray's comrade-in-arms in many different electoral wars over the years, especially in the Maritimes. And both were from Cape Breton. Clearly, Lowell was as conflicted as any of us about the leadership choice that needed to be made at this point. My future Cabinet colleague and I had known each other for many years. Indeed, Kathy and I would spend part of our honeymoon as guests of Lowell and Colleen, soon to be his wife, in Cape Breton four years after the convention. As the ringleader of a fairly large group of undecided friends and acquaintances at the convention confused about how to vote on the final ballot, I said to Lowell: "Who should we choose—Joe or Flora?" Lowell responded, with anxiety but confidence: "Joe. He stands the best chance of uniting the party behind him." If somebody had told me a day earlier that I would be voting for Joe Clark to be leader of the national Tory party, I would have fled the lunatic out of terror for my safety. Upon Lowell's advice, however, I held my nose and voted for Joe. So did virtually all my "followers." Clark won the leadership by a paltry sixty-five votes. There was at least half that number in our previously undecided coterie. "Joe Who?"—as the *Toronto Star* tagged for life the unknown victor—had placed only third on the first ballot, behind Wagner and Mulroney, in that order. He had been the first choice of only 277 out of 2,360 delegates. That was only 11.7 percent. By contrast, his predecessor, Robert Stanfield, had led an eleven-candidate field on the first ballot with 23 percent of all votes in 1967. In Clark's case, had this been a federal election for an individual parliamentary seat, instead of a national party leadership contest, the candidate, under the *Canada Elections Act*, would scarcely have qualified to be reimbursed by the government for 50 percent of his campaign expenses for lack of minimum-required popular support.

For all his good intentions and sterling qualities, especially of character, Joe Clark became prime minister just as he had won the PC leadership three years earlier—by default. The country wanted to rid itself of Trudeau. This fact was clear to me and most other PC candidates at the doorstep in the 1979 campaign. I knocked on every door in my riding in that election, beginning well before the writ was dropped. I can't recall a single voter telling me that he or she intended to vote Tory because of Clark. Most said they were voting against Trudeau. I won handily. Unfortunately, for the party and the country, Joe had neither the government experience nor the competence, least of all the political instincts, to avoid squandering his historic opportunity to solidify the Stanfield-Symons counter-revolution and, thereby, entrench the party as an acceptable alternative to the Liberals. Again, he was to prove a much more effective Opposition leader than prime minister following the 1980 election and Pierre Trudeau's return to power. But, deep down, most of Clark's parliamentary followers, including me, knew it was highly unlikely he would ever be prime minister again. We were in a holding pattern. Brian Mulroney was not the only one waiting in the weeds for Clark to fail in hopes of emerging as his natural successor.

# In Opposition, 1980–83

Soon after the February 1980 election, Joe Clark, now Official Opposition leader again, invited me to join his shadow cabinet as environment critic. I felt honoured by this demonstration of confidence in my abilities, for the environment was fast becoming a major issue everywhere in Canada, as elsewhere in the world. In theory, "shadow cabinet" means that group of individuals an Opposition leader selects from among his parliamentary supporters to develop policies and take public stands for the party in their designated areas. They must also hold accountable the government and the corresponding ministers in those areas. The shadow cabinet was, theoretically at least, a government-in-waiting in case an election or parliamentary defeat would require the government to resign and the Opposition "cabinet" to take power and govern the country. In more practical terms, a shadow cabinet is the primary way an Opposition leader delegates some of his own duties to Caucus colleagues, cultivates their skills and expertise with an eye eventually to governing, showcases the most appealing Caucus members (especially in Question Period), rewards individuals for loyalty or service to the leader himself or to the party, honours seniority, or advances some representative goal (for example, gender equality and geographic balance) within the Caucus and party as a whole.

In the previous Parliament, if my Commons seat had been any farther back, it would have been in the Ottawa River. In the new Parliament, my assigned seat was—to my pleasant surprise—in the second row, to the right of centre, and towards the Speaker. It was a prime piece of real estate for someone so young and re-elected for only the first time. Such a placement would not have been made lightly, let alone by anyone but the leader himself. Following the defeat of his government in the previous election, many Caucus members were bitter towards Clark. They held him personally responsible for the party's loss of power and for Trudeau's political resurrection. My first parliamentary secretary in the Mulroney government, years later, was Gary Gurbin, who represented the Ontario riding of Bruce–Grey. A medical doctor, he resigned from the Progressive Conservative Party and Caucus on December 17, 1981, citing concerns over Clark's leadership. He remained in the House of Commons as an independent until rejoining the party on January 28, 1982. Other Caucus members disgruntled about Clark's leadership did not take their concerns that far. Gurbin was, by nature, an especially serious-minded and principled individual. But he was by no means the only member of Caucus who felt strongly about Joe's leadership and was prepared to be publicly critical. Joe was, therefore, already sensing the need to defend his leadership and saw me, with good reason, as an ally. Plus, he had been quoted in the media as having been impressed with me in the previous Parliament and on the hustings. We also knew each other from his days as president of the national PC Youth Federation and mine as a campus Tory activist at St. Dunstan's University in Charlottetown. Moreover, we had many dealings with each other when he was a senior aide to Robert Stanfield and I a less senior one to Stanfield and Tom Symons on party policy. Almost as important in his eyes, I think, is that he considered me and the environment a good fit. This was a field of particular interest to young people and to intellectuals. I was, most certainly, young. And, if he didn't see me as an intellectual, he must have thought I could at least fake it.

I was determined to make the best of this opportunity, particularly because I had long been interested in the environment, although not formally involved in any specific cause or non-governmental organization (NGO). Politics is about impressing people

—one's leader, colleagues, adversaries, potential allies, the media, and, most important of all, the voters. That's how the politician gets ahead, advances issues or interests, survives in the political snake pit—and gets re-elected. I might not have been hell-bent on impressing, but I was on not failing.

As official spokesperson for the PC Caucus and Party on the environment, in the shadow cabinet, I had one primary job: to "shadow" Trudeau's environment minister, John Roberts. It was no mean feat, because Roberts, twelve years my senior, was a political veteran, having been first elected to Parliament in 1968 (for York–Simcoe, later St. Paul's) in Toronto. He had held such senior portfolios as secretary of state, and later would seek the Liberal leadership (unsuccessfully) following Trudeau's departure. While still trying to mentally process my new heavy burden, I was thrust into my first major challenge. Our PC Caucus leadership had decided to propose a motion of non-confidence in the Trudeau government for its alleged mishandling of the acid rain issue. With a majority government, the Liberals were in no danger of being defeated on the motion; it was just an occasion for the Official Opposition to score political points and put the minister on the defensive about his and the Liberal government's record—all part of the game. But it was no fun for me, because I needed to lead the gamesmanship and had no clue about how to play my hand. I had decided to make my lead-off speech high-minded and non-partisan, as befit, I thought, the environmental cause itself. Not having telegraphed my intention to anyone, I got a call from the leader. "Tom, you're leading the charge in the debate, so I want you to set the tone," Joe said. "You should rip the government's record to shreds. Go after Roberts with all you've got." So much for high-mindedness! There could be no stronger evidence than this that Joe Clark was ready to fight to become prime minister again. Not for him the kid gloves. Nor for me either, apparently.

Accordingly, in my twenty-minute address, right after Question Period, I did exactly what I was told. Mine was a nasty bit of rhetoric in which, at one point, I said the government's credibility on the environment had been "flushed down the toilet." Ugh! For his part, Roberts—speaking from a prepared text, likely written by his departmental officials—could not have been more non-partisan and magnanimous towards me personally. It was not a propitious beginning to my shadow cabinet career. I learned through back channels that Roberts was taken aback by my partisanship. He wondered if it portended how I would be "shadowing" him in future. He need not have worried. From then on, I decided to follow my own instincts, not somebody else's, not even Joe Clark's instructions. Certainly, there would be no more references to toilets. Thereafter, I was aggressive when I felt the occasion demanded, but not overly so and not often. Once, though, I appeared in a huge picture in the *Globe and Mail* attacking the minister in Question Period as though holding him personally responsible for destroying the planet. That aside, John Roberts and I got to like each other. We did our best to play the game with mutual respect and sensitivity to each other's political requirements. The two of us cooperated as much as we could in many different practical ways, both in Parliament and across the country, to advance our common environmental goals while also protecting our respective parties' interests. As I detail later, he and I served in the environment portfolio longer than anyone else, and for almost exactly the same length of time. Before leaving the portfolio—to become minister of state for science and technology and, later, minister of employment and immigration—he spotted me walking along the corridor outside his parliamentary office's Christmas party in the Centre Block. The revelry was already well-fuelled by the Screech his parliamentary secretary, Roger Simmons, had flown in from his native Newfoundland. The minister beckoned me to join the celebration. I did. Only Heath Macquarrie's Appleton rum, I discovered, was as strong as Screech. From what few things I was able to remember the next day and forever more, I had a great time.

Little did I know then that my years as the party's environment critic in Opposition would pave the way to Brian Mulroney's selecting me as his longest-serving environment minister and architect for most of his government's record in this area. Meanwhile, in Opposition, I spent much of my time travelling across the country. I was eager to build a network of environmentalists and NGOs for the party; immerse myself in the technicalities of what is, after all, a complex scientific domain; develop positions, as best I could, on the different issues of the day; respond to every possible media inquiry and interview request to enhance the party's, and my own, visibility and credibility on those issues; work with like-minded people and groups to address certain problems, in concert with government and private sector leaders whom I also cultivated; and, generally, stay out of political trouble.

By far the most politically contentious environmental issue of the day, and one of the most important on the Mulroney government's overall agenda later, was acid rain. It was an area in which I now think I contributed the most to public policy while in Opposition as PC environment critic. And it would have been as major a govern-ment priority in the United States as in Canada if the Reagan administration, bowing to powerful thermal power and coal industry lobbyists, had not pooh-poohed the problem. Clueless on the issue, the American president himself was widely quoted as proffering that acid rain was caused, not by industry, but in nature by ducks and trees. In Canada, by marked contrast, Tories and Liberals and New Democrats were united on the need to act and, generally, on how to do so.

I deal with the politics of acid rain in greater detail later. What I want to stress here is the pivotal role the House of Commons Sub-committee on Acid Rain played in what would become—along with the cleanup of the Great Lakes in an earlier era—the greatest success story in North American environmental history. The acid rain story would also be, after Reagan was succeeded by George H. W. Bush, one of the most constructive chapters in Canadian-US relations. The final outcome consti-tutes Brian Mulroney's most underappreciated accomplishment as prime minister and Tory leader. The parliamentary sub-committee's report, *Still Waters: The Chilling Reality of Acid Rain*, remains to this day one of the landmarks in North American environmental literature.[3] Its thirty-eight specific recommendations—particularly its call for a legally binding Canadian-US acid rain agreement, achieved by Brian Mulroney and Bush in 1991—formed the blueprint for the Mulroney government's, and my own, actions on the issue. Headed by its tenacious chairman, Sault Ste. Marie Liberal MP Ronald Irwin, the sub-committee comprised, among others, besides me, Conservative MPs John Fraser (Vancouver South) and Stan Darling (Parry Sound–Muskoka). At our public hearings across the country, Stan was the sub-committee's pitbull. He challenged industry polluters as though they had tried to poison his coffee. We travelled to acid rain–affected countries as far away as Sweden to collect ideas about how to tackle the problem based on their experi-ences. Rarely in Canadian parliamentary history has a pan-partisan group of MPs been as public-spirited, as committed to solving a major national problem, and as successful in influencing the solution as this group was. For me, the lead MP on the sub-committee for the Tories—despite Fraser's and Darling's parliamentary senior-ity—I could have had no better training for becoming the country's environment minister several years later. To be sure, the Clark interregnum itself, in 1979–80, did little to prepare me outside the work I performed as a parliamentarian in my own right. More's the pity.

# Pierre Trudeau

Pierre Trudeau was prime minister throughout my time in Opposition, save a couple of months. Trudeau prided himself on his lady-killer reputation. A personal experience, however, throws that reputation in doubt.

Trudeau and his wife, Margaret, thirty years younger than he, divorced after thirteen years of marriage. The marriage breakdown followed public scandals involving trysts she had conducted with members of the international jet set—among them (by her own admission) Ron Wood of The Rolling Stones, Ryan O'Neal of *Love Story* movie fame, US senator Teddy Kennedy, and other luminaries. The couple married in 1971, separated in 1977, but didn't divorce until 1984. When Pierre Trudeau was again a bachelor, Kathy and I were invited to a grand winter party by Governor General Jeanne Sauvé at Rideau Hall. Sauvé hosted the soirée for MPs and senators and members of the diplomatic corps. It was to be a dirty-world-of-politics-meets-clean-world-of-diplomacy social. The occasion was a mid-winter's night of mulled wine, skating, tobogganing, and horse-and-sleigh rides, followed by a fine multi-course meal and then dancing—all very informal and congenial. At least a couple of hundred guests were expected. This was to be the first of several such events Sauvé had planned. She intended to invite every MP and senator and Ottawa diplomat to one of these parties that winter or spring.

Alas, our winter party followed a ferocious Ottawa snowstorm. Though spent by then, the storm prevented all but the most motivated or mobile from attending. Meeting both criteria, Kathy and I were one of only about twenty-five couples present—for all that food! For the dancing afterwards, it was almost like having one's own private orchestra. Who should arrive fashionably late, doing a one-man, red-carpet strut as the orchestra played, but Pierre Elliott Trudeau! Amorously on his arm traipsed a lady young enough to be *my* daughter and *his* granddaughter. (He was about sixty-three at the time, though always fudged his actual age.) In what appeared a shameless bid for attention, Trudeau, on this bitterly cold winter's night, proceeded to dance up a gravity-defying storm of his own: leg splits and twirls and gyrations that would have challenged the Cirque du Soleil. The performance was all the more attention-grabbing since he and his nubile date were virtually alone on the dance floor by then. As the evening ended, I took leave of Kathy to retrieve our coats, returned to our table, and found Pierre Trudeau there—hitting on my spouse! Clearly, in Kathy's case at least, he was attracted to tall, slim, long-legged, and stylish brunettes with big brown eyes.

Kathy told me afterwards that Trudeau's romantic ineptness embarrassed her more than the come-on itself. "Haven't we met before?" was as original as he could manage. It was downhill all the way from there. Kathy is closely related to a long line of PEI Grit tribal chiefs on her mother's side (the Bevans). On the Island, our Tory-Grit nuptials constituted a real mixed marriage, more so than any Catholic-Protestant union would ever have been considered—though ours was that, too. Kathy had been swept up in late-1960s Trudeaumania as much as any other female—

young, old, or betwixt. Trudeau remained her idol—until that moment of adolescent clumsiness. The illusion had been shattered, the myth broken, the facts set right: Rudolph Valentino was really Forrest Gump!

If Trudeau was not the great Latin lover of personal mythmaking, neither was he the arrogant SOB his detractors characterized him to be or, indeed, even many of his supporters considered him. This fact I was also to discover personally.

Soon after my political party's return to the Opposition benches following the brief Joe Clark reign, I became, undeniably, the federal politician who fought the hardest for a fourth veterinary college for the country. As devoted as I was to my responsibilities as environment critic, my first priority was to fight for my constituents and province. An MP who doesn't achieve a proper balance between national responsibilities and attending to concerns back home soon finds himself without a seat. I made sure I maintained that balance, picking my local issues for maximum relevance, media interest, and voter impact. I raised the vet college issue continually in the House of Commons, but never before with the prime minister. It was usually with Agriculture Minister Eugene Whalen or some other relevant minister. In the latter category was, for example, Fisheries Minister Roméo LeBlanc—or, at a different time, Pierre De Bané—because of the marine dimension of modern veterinary medicine. During Question Period, a backbench MP can bob up and down, day in and day out, and never get recognized by the Speaker until, finally, either worn down or just convinced it's finally his (or her) turn, Her Honour does recognize the Member. That is, unless the backbencher is able to convince his colleagues to put him on the questioners' list for his party on a given day—not likely for a primarily constituency-related issue, as in this case.

As luck would have it, I did get myself on the Official Opposition questioners' list to raise my vet college issue. It was part of a regional development theme the party had decided to focus on in Question Period. The day was July 16, 1980, seared in my mind as if by a hot poker. Knowing the Speaker would recognize me, I notified the prime minister's legislative assistant, Joyce Fairbairn (later a senator), about the general nature of the question. Most Opposition MPs provide such notice about local matters because it's more important for them to get substantive replies for home consumption than to score partisan points by catching a minister or the PM unawares. The last thing the MP would want, for lack of notice, is an "I'll take the question under advisement" response. Ms. Fairbairn thanked me for the notice, promised she would brief the prime minister, and assured me he would be prepared.

When my moment in the limelight came, I posed my question with all the theatricality of which I was capable, sat down, and awaited the benefits from our carefully scripted drama. But the star refused to say his lines! Trudeau rose to his feet, glared at me as though I had just asked for the keys to the Royal Mint, and replied with the abruptness of a French Revolution executioner: "I am not on top of the problem of veterinary colleges." The prime minister then plunked himself back in his seat. I was shattered. My day on stage was a disaster. The show was shut down even before the curtain could be raised. It would be a month of Sundays before I would ever have such a starring role again, if ever. A let-them-eat-cake Trudeau shrug blew me off the stage and right out of the theatre.

The next day I returned to the Commons for Question Period. This time, I was part of the audience, not the cast. I looked across the chamber—the stage, as it were—and saw the prime minister glaring at me. And he continued to glare. "My God, is he going to have me guillotined?" I wondered. Seconds later, a House page handed me a note-size envelope. It contained the prime minister's official letterhead. Inside was a note with the salutation "Dear Mr. McMillan" struck and replaced, by the PM's own hand, with "Dear Tom." The note read: "Yesterday, in Question Period, I gave you an answer to your question that neither of us would consider adequate. I was distracted at the time, and did not give you the reply you deserved. Here is that reply now." The prime minister's reply stunned me as surely as any guillotine blade could have done. The response went far beyond my wildest prayers or imaginings— certainly well beyond what the prime minister would likely have said the previous day in the House, had he not been "distracted." The note, in effect, announced that the country's fourth college of veterinary medicine would be established and, by inference, located in my riding. I looked up and saw the prime minister awaiting my reaction. I smiled. And, with a discreet nod and wave, I acknowledged his thoughtfulness, and expressed my thanks and pleasure. He returned the smile, a smile as genuine as it was warm. Only then did the prime minister return to other "urgent" matters of state.

From my public release of the prime minister's letter, I received more media coverage across PEI and throughout Atlantic Canada than I had ever previously attained for anything I had done or said either within Parliament or without. Although I have spent nearly a lifetime in politics in one capacity or another, I am certain of few political generalizations. One of them is this: what Pierre Trudeau did for a then-obscure Opposition backbench MP from the boonies that day in the House of Commons demonstrated he possessed the rarest of qualities in a human being, let alone politician—real class. I might question, and do question, his actions or motives on particular issues. I think, for example, he did a disservice to the country by opposing the Meech Lake and Charlottetown Accords. He did so, it seems, not to reflect a principle, but to prevent Brian Mulroney from doing something he himself was unable to do: obtain Quebec's signature on the country's new constitution (more about that later). But seeing this complex man at close range, I will always think of Pierre Elliott Trudeau as one classy guy. Later, I was to learn the "distraction" that had prevented the PM from answering my question in the Commons was a vicious brawl he had had with his estranged wife, Margaret, only hours earlier. It concerned tabloid headlines she had made following a night on the town at Studio 54, New York's infamous celebrity Party Central. And yet, the PM still took time to right a wrong to this lowly backbencher the next day. Pierre Trudeau might not have been the suave Latin lover of reputation and self-image. He was, however, a class act—and, at his best, a gentleman. His two sons—one, Justin, now prime minister—and a third in the heavens have a right to be proud of him for that fact alone.

# Brian Mulroney's Ascendancy

Soon after the 1980 election, Joe Clark, now Official Opposition leader again, focused not on government or party policy, but on saving his own political hide. Most Caucus members—even those like me who supported the leader—thought Clark and his team lacked sound political judgment and were no match for Trudeau and the Liberals as strategists. The Grits had made a razor-thin minority last two years after the 1972 election. Our team couldn't make a near-majority government survive even a year. It was like comparing Batman to a bat—a baseball bat. The internecine political warfare over Clark's leadership would literally split families down the middle—to wit, my twin brother, Charley, and me. As at the 1976 leadership convention, Charley would serve as one of Brian Mulroney's closest confidants, this time to topple Clark. Leadership "review" had been a thorny issue for Tories ever since Dalton Camp—as a candidate against Arthur Maloney for PC president—had made it his main battle cry against John Diefenbaker at a national party gathering in Ottawa in November 1966. After the Clark government's electoral defeat, 31.5 percent of party stalwarts voted for leadership review at a 1981 national party Annual Meeting. At a January 1983 Annual Meeting of the party in Winnipeg, 33.1 percent supported a review, only a marginal improvement in the leader's standing in the intervening two years. Clark did not think 67 percent support was enough to sustain his leadership, and called for a leadership convention, to be held in Ottawa in June, at which he would be a candidate to succeed himself.

Why Joe Clark decided to call for a leadership race baffles me to this day. In any democracy, *50 percent plus one* defines an electoral majority. Besides, congenitally pugilistic with one another, Tories could hardly agree on the time of day or season of the year by a 67 percent margin. Political scientist George Perlin called the PC Party's characteristic lack of unity and internal discipline the "Tory Syndrome."[4] But, by refusing to signal at the outset of his leadership troubles what he considered an acceptable margin of support for his continuing to head the party—if not 67 percent, then what?—Clark allowed the media and his potential challengers, particularly Brian Mulroney, to define that margin high. I myself would have dared all comers with a simple-majority standard. This principled man, however, thought otherwise, at the expense of his survival. Yet again, the man's political judgment was flawed—to at least a third of the party, seriously so. As Kathy and I left the Winnipeg meeting hall following the leadership vote with, at our side, Clark loyalist Ray Hnatyshyn (later governor general), tears poured from all our eyes. The painful human drama unfolding then was almost unbearable. Despite her empathy for Joe Clark in his second-darkest political hour—the darkest being the defeat of his government and subsequent election loss three years earlier—Kathy was excited by the prospect that Mulroney might succeed Clark as leader. I shared her enthusiasm, but was deeply conflicted. I knew Joe Clark better than I did the Quebecer. I was always fond of Clark. He had been good to me as leader. I shared his fundamental values, and was uncertain about Mulroney's. And, Celtic to the core, I invariably respond viscerally to all such battles, as I was inclined to do this time, by supporting the beleaguered "clan chief," no matter how self-inflicted his wounds or uncertain I might be about his abilities. Again, Einstein was right about politics being a complex business.

Throughout the ensuing leadership campaign, I was plugged into both Clark's campaign, as a nominal Caucus supporter, and Mulroney's, through my brother, who was his chief policy guru and a major strategist. My heart was also partly with John Crosbie, as a fellow Atlantic Canadian whom I revered. He had stayed with Kathy and me at our heritage home, Duncan House, five miles from Charlottetown, while key-noting my PC Riding Association annual fundraising dinner one year. Kathy adored the man, charmed as she was by his in-person shyness and humility, despite the public bravado. (What a laugh I had seeing Kathy and the former finance minister of Canada unloading bags of groceries from the car for our dinner together that night! They looked like two college students piling up snacks and beer to watch the Grey Cup on TV.) Kathy and I subsequently would host a large reception for John at our home during the leadership campaign, in my case not as an official supporter but just as someone who, like Kathy, loved the guy and wanted him to do well, but not necessarily win. This led the media and Crosbie campaign strategists alike to speculate wildly about my intentions, which became the subject of a *Globe and Mail* feature. I didn't need, and certainly did not want, still less seek, that kind of public attention. Crosbie would later make incendiary remarks about his inability to speak French ("I don't speak Chinese, either"), implying less than full recognition of French as an official language of the country. His campaign afterwards sank faster than the ridiculous huge blimp part of his convention-floor demonstration, which—as always happens with such hot-air gimmicks—lost its moorings and floated aimlessly above delegates' heads.[5]

I was not the only Caucus member, let alone party supporter, deeply conflicted by the leadership race. The conflict was the subject of yet another *Globe and Mail* article. This time I shared billing with British Columbia MP Pat Carney. We were Exhibits A & B in a case the writer made about the delicate balancing act those such as we were facing: trying to reconcile personal loyalties, regional considerations, political ambitions, the good of the party, and pressures from one's own supporters and voters, to say nothing of personal preferences. My own constituency organization was split all over the place. Most supported Clark, some virulently.

My loyalty to the clan chief was never before stronger than when I started to see some of the people stampeding to back Mulroney. He did attract some of the best in the party, but he got more than his share of the worst, too. The latter were not just certified reactionaries, but self-seeking opportunists. To this day, I sometimes reflect on all the times Joe Clark had been kind and helpful to me. Once, for example, I had an especially heated exchange in the Commons with Charles Caccia, a long-time Liberal Toronto MP and environmental champion. Joe took me aside, as an older brother would his sibling, and said: "Tom, never show anger in the Commons based on personal animosity. I have learned the hard way not to take anything personally in politics. You shouldn't, either." Even on the tiniest detail, he was often a source of wise counsel. On one occasion in the House, I said, "Let me share with Members..." Afterwards, in the Members' lobby, behind the curtain, Joe said, "I'm always very suspicious of people who say they want to 'share' something. You'd be well advised not to express yourself that way." I never again used the word "share" with that particular meaning, inside or outside Parliament. Now, when I hear someone saying he or she wants to share something, I secure my wallet.

---

After my election defeat in 1988, I met with Joe Clark in his parliamentary office to seek counsel about my future. "Tom, I'd be glad to help," Joe said, "which is more than I can say for some of our Cabinet colleagues defeated in the election." He mentioned with particular contempt several who had been especially unhelpful to him in past leadership wars—Stewart McInnes, from Halifax, was one. Joe proved true to his word. Brian Mulroney would have been primarily responsible for my appointment as Canadian consul general in Boston. But, as external affairs minister, Joe would have needed to sign off on the matter. I learned he did so with alacrity. I will always be grateful to him for that. I respect and like this man a lot, so I am racked with guilt for not having a higher opinion of his political radar. It is his human qualities—so like Robert Stanfield's, but without the Nova Scotian's extraordinary intelligence and competence—that I most admire.

Although personally closer to Joe Clark than to any of the other leadership aspirants, I had voted privately for Brian Mulroney in his failed leadership bid at the 1976 convention, not having been free, as a PC Party employee, to take a public stand. Deep down, I thought Mulroney was right that, until the party had a fluently bilingual leader from Quebec—preferably a francophone—the Liberals would beat us nine times out of ten. "It's like running a hundred-yard dash and giving your opponent a twenty-yard advantage," he often told Tory audiences. Professionally engaged in retail fashion, Kathy was impressed by the glamour and youthfulness that Brian Mulroney and his stylish wife, Mila, brought to the party and to public life generally. This sense also weighed heavily on me. Like Pierre Trudeau, the Mulroney couple was that rarest of species in Canadian politics: English to the English, French to the French. Following a long line of quintessentially WASPish leaders—all of them, except for John Diefenbaker, seen as deadly dull—the PC Party now seemed to have lucked into a dazzling bicultural husband-wife "leadership" team.

Never before in politics had I been so torn. Faced with this conundrum, I ended up trying to do what classic Libras like me invariably do: balance opposite forces. I did support Joe publicly, but without much showiness. Needing to be out of the country for an extended period with the parliamentary acid rain sub-committee (thank God!), I loaned my principal Ottawa office assistant, Bill Chambers (son of noted journalist Greta Chambers), to Clark for his leadership campaign, virtually as a surrogate of mine. (Bill would later become Clark's chief of staff at external affairs in the Mulroney government.) All the while, I did what I could to help my brother's own policy work for Mulroney, as much for his sake as for the candidate's. As noted elsewhere here, for example, I saw Mulroney on TV giving a bizarre, and technically wrong, answer to a Quebec reporter's question on acid rain. I prepared simple bullet-form talking points on the subject, and handed them personally to the candidate, knowing as I did, from Charley, that this was the austere format the future prime minister favoured. When it came time for all of Joe's Caucus supporters to appear on stage together at the leadership convention to demonstrate his strength in PC parliamentary ranks, I was tempted to flee the city—and politics altogether. What a messy business! I paced up and down the parking lot outside the Ottawa convention centre in the sweltering heat, trying to decide whether to join the others on stage. What to do? Ottawa-area MP Paul Dick, an early Mulroney supporter, witnessed my obvious turmoil. He seemed sympathetic. Re-entering the convention hall, I linked hands with Kathy, walked up to Mulroney's right-hand man in Quebec, Michel Cogger (later appointed to the Senate), and all but paraphrased Christ at Calvary: "Forgive me, Father, for I know not what I do." I then walked on stage, but at the farthest extreme. I was likely noticed only by birdwatchers with binoculars who might have mistaken me for a kingfisher—the most cowardly of the species.

Brian Mulroney became my new boss, winning the leadership on the fourth ballot. Long afterwards, a number of people who had organized Clark's leadership campaign in 1983 told me that they, like Paul Dick, sympathized at the time with my personal conflicts on the leadership, especially with Charley a principal in the Mulroney campaign. Still, my memories of all this—especially conflicting emotions about the various candidates, Joe Clark and Brian Mulroney most of all—are largely negative.

---

I served under Joe Clark's party leadership both in government (briefly) and in Opposition (three years). I was a Cabinet colleague of his for more than four years in the Mulroney government, after he lost the leadership. In the introduction of his Pulitzer Prize–winning book, *Profiles in Courage,* John F. Kennedy adopted Ernest Hemingway's definition of political courage: "grace under pressure." I know of no one who demonstrated more of this quality than Joe Clark during his troubled political career. He is, and always has been, a brave and honourable man. That said, Clark squandered the power and opportunities Canadian voters handed him, albeit tentatively, in May 1979. This was a huge setback for the Progressive Conservative Party. It is said that one has only a single chance to make a first impression. So, also, this was the PC Party's unique opportunity to consolidate, in government, the progress Robert Stanfield had made in recasting the party as contemporary and reformist in the eyes of Canadian electors. By the same token, Clark was singularly positioned, as a former senior staffer to Stanfield, to present himself and his government to Canadians as standard-bearers for the ideals and progressive policies the public positively associated with the retired leader. But, with the suicidal instincts of a lemming, the maladroitness of a sloth, and the single-mindedness of a dog in heat, Joe blew it. In this era of ours, when almost everything that happens in the world is covered by the media as though it portends the apocalypse, a major national party leader is more than a politician; he or she is also a media star. As such, the individual needs to meet at least minimally the standards the public applies to the performance arts—television actors, in particular. Joe Clark was especially ill-equipped to meet those standards

Leadership is largely about inspiring. It is difficult for a leader to inspire when, as with Joe Clark, the public perceives him decent and likeable but klutzy and peculiar. Joe's image problems were not caused by the media. Before the 1979 election, the new PC leader travelled to Europe to meet world statesmen in an effort to enhance his international credentials in the eyes of Canadian voters. The visit was doomed from the start. When Clark's luggage was lost en route, the snafu symbolized the disaster-prone trip as a whole. Mike Duffy travelled with Clark throughout the trip as a CBC-TV reporter. Soon afterwards, Mike told me something revealing about the PC leader. At a news conference Joe Clark had held during the trip, a European journalist entered the venue late without any idea as to who Joe was. He looked at Clark at the podium, leaned over to Duffy, and asked: "Who's Howdy Doody?" Clearly, as this foreign journalist's reaction to seeing Joe Clark for the first time illustrates, the Canadian media could not be held accountable for the widespread impression that the man seemed odd. The response of the Canadian public to him—analogous to that of the foreign journalist in question—was visceral. In politics, it is not enough to be smart and knowledgeable and decent and well-intended, as Joe is all those things. Particularly at the highest level, a politician needs to radiate qualities that impress people at first glance. If he or she cannot pass that decisive test, then passing all the other tests, even with flying colours, is irrelevant.

# In Opposition: 1983–84

I was studying French on the campus of the Collège militaire royal in St-Jean, Quebec, when I got the call. It was on the heels of Brian Mulroney's triumph at the leadership convention just a few days earlier. Mulroney was phoning to say he wanted me to be his deputy House leader responsible for Question Period. I do remember using the wrong gender for "victoire" when congratulating him on winning the leadership in the half-dozen words in French I hazarded with this magnificently bilingual Quebecer. The rest is a total blur. That's because, if surprised by Clark's appointing me Caucus environment critic, I went into shock this time in the face of my new assignment. Was the man out of his cotton-pickin' mind? Question Period, whose TV ratings rival those for daytime soap operas (no coincidence), was the most important forum for Brian Mulroney and the PC Party to communicate with voters and impress and court them only a few months away from the next federal election. Mulroney was new to electoral politics, didn't yet have a Commons seat, and wouldn't for several months (in a by-election in Central Nova, which his long-time supporter, Elmer MacKay, vacated for him). I felt spectacularly ill-equipped, by temperament and experience, to serve as the MP responsible for orchestrating the party's most important concertos in the lead-up to the election. I was to discover from Charley, however, that the leader and his wife used to watch Question Period regularly on TV, were impressed with my performances and style in that forum, and he thought I could translate my own ways to the Caucus's total efforts on this most important of stages. Or it was some such delusion. Whatever the reason he appointed me, I guess I rose to the challenge. I remained in the position, without a complaint from Mulroney, throughout the year or so he was Opposition leader before becoming prime minister.

As PC deputy House leader, I was in charge each day of devising the party's list of Official Opposition performers for Question Period and choosing the topics each would raise. The forty-five-minute House of Commons drama is almost totally scripted beforehand. Contrary to public perception, the Speaker does not select which Opposition MPs pose questions to the PM or ministers. Each Opposition party decides for itself who its main questioners will be—and, of course, on what issues. It submits the list to the Speaker before Question Period, usually about a half-hour in advance. Only after the Speaker has recognized everyone on the formal list would she—in my time, Jeanne Sauvé—call on anyone else from the same party Caucus. At this later stage, the Speaker would have her own strategy. Typically, it combined: the first-come, first-served principle; rewarding individual backbenchers for their perseverance, from one day to another, if not yet called on; deference to veteran parliamentarians, especially those not often on the formal list; regional balance; or just personal favourites or pique (including personal scores to settle—yes, that, too).

Soon after Joe Clark lost the PC Party leadership race to Brian Mulroney in June 1983, Joe and I had lunch together in the Parliamentary Dining Room. It was right after I had been appointed deputy House leader. Despite the man's propensity for misfiring on the big political targets, I always found him surprisingly wise on the more personal level. On the occasion at hand, the former leader was, characteristically, a fountain of sound advice and insights, this time about my new role. He said something I will never forget. His remarks revealed a great deal both about how he saw me and, even more important, how he viewed himself and thought others viewed him. Jeanne Sauvé, a Quebec MP (for Ahuntsic), was first elected to Parliament in 1972, the same year Joe Clark became an MP. On the day Joe and I had lunch, she had been serving as Speaker of the House of Commons for many months, Trudeau's having appointed her right after his comeback in the 1980 federal election. As PC deputy House leader, I would soon be working closely with the Speaker every weekday. Sauvé, a former broadcast journalist, was educated in Ottawa and Paris. Although born in Saskatchewan, in a town so tiny that she once told me it no longer had people, the woman had a regal bearing—some would say *hauteur*. This trait might have been appropriate when she served as governor general (1984–90); meanwhile, however, it made some people, including Joe himself, feel she was looking down on them, and not just literally from the Speaker's throne. Over our lunch, Joe said to me: "Tom, you'll get along just fine with Sauvé. You're the kind of Tory she likes—classy and urbane." Joe added: "Jeanne Sauvé would see me as an uncouth hayseed, unworthy of her time or attention." This comment shocked me, coming as it did from a former prime minister, not to mention that I didn't necessarily see either him or me in such terms.

I had not previously known Jeanne Sauvé. But soon after my appointment, she invited me to her elegant House of Commons private Speaker's quarters, at the Centre Block, to discuss our pending working relationship for Question Period. I liked her instantly. She was charming, gracious, and good-humoured. The woman was not at all what I had expected from her public image. I found the Speaker especially endearing when she confided in me that her health was failing. Sauvé told me that she had just returned from a major trip—to the Soviet Union, I think it was—and had not been feeling well since. I got the impression from the concern on her face that the illness was serious. The new Speaker informed me that, because of her condition, she might have to be replaced periodically by the deputy speaker, Ottawa MP Lloyd Francis (Carleton–Ottawa West). It sounded like Sauvé would be dealing with some health problem well into the future. Francis would succeed Sauvé as full-time Speaker in January 1984, when she became governor general. I was never sure whether the illness to which she had vaguely referred during our first meeting was the beginning of the Hodgkin's lymphoma that killed her in January 1993. But whatever the malady, Madame Sauvé persevered heroically as Speaker—often, I know, when feeling weak and likely medicated.

As Joe had predicted, Jeanne Sauvé liked me personally. She invited me to a number of her elegant private dinner parties, and not just because we collaborated on Question Period. I rarely, if ever, saw any of my PC House leadership colleagues or counterparts in the other parties at these personal events. Sylvia Ostry was my dinner partner at one such private affair. An economist with a PhD, she headed the Organisation for Economic Co-operation and Development's economics and statistics department in Paris before returning to Ottawa, during the Mulroney government years, to become deputy minister of international trade. That department, along with environment, would play a central role in advancing the Mulroney government's national and international agenda. Sylvia Ostry was, unquestionably, one of the country's smartest women. For her part, the governor general was, by definition, at the the top of Canada's social register. And here I was, a small-town boy from PEI, in a corner gossiping over cocktails and caviar with two of the most fascinating women in the land. We traded gossipy stories about individuals and their goings-on that, had any of our comments become public, would have landed all three of us at the bottom of the social heap. How naughty we were! But what fun!

Contrary to Joe Clark's perception expressed to me over lunch, I learned at private parties that Jeanne Sauvé had the highest regard, and even affection, for him. And her respect had little to do with his exalted status as former prime minister and erstwhile leader of the Official Opposition. It was independent of his political status—much more personal. Had she not respected Joe, I would definitely have heard about it. Once I had gained her trust, she didn't hold back about anyone else after a sip or two of champagne—never unfair to anyone, always loyal to her office, unfailingly professional almost to a fault, and yet charming and surprisingly down to earth as a hostess and socialite. Concerning Joe's comments about me, about himself, and about Jeanne Sauvé over lunch, I now think: how sad it would have been had those comments been true; but how even sadder they were in fact, given that the man was dead wrong in thinking she disdained him.

In any case, we three individuals, despite our obvious differences (age, gender, seniority, looks, style), had much in common. We were all politicians—Clark and Sauvé also former journalists. Each of us had advanced university degrees. We were Catholics across the board. Clark, Sauvé, and I came from the "boonies"—he from Alberta, she from Saskatchewan, I from PEI. Not one of us was born in a big city: Clark in High River, Sauvé in Prud'homme, and Yours Truly in Charlottetown. We held, generally, the same progressive values. I doubt that, if given a truth serum, we would have disagreed on many issues of the day. Notwithstanding this shared personal territory, the three of us were basically strangers to one another. Even Joe and I—despite an association that went back to our university days—were not close friends. I was fortunate to become less and less a stranger to Jeanne Sauvé with each passing day as we collaborated on Question Period and socialized periodically. We were not exactly intimate friends—though she did call me by my first name, even if she was always "Madam Speaker" to me. But I once included in my quarterly constituency pamphlet a photo of her and me together, in formal evening wear, from a national heritage event in my riding for which she had been the special guest as governor general by that time. Her Excellency admonished me for having done so without authorization—apparently, any public use of such a non-official viceregal picture requires prior approval from the governor general's office, if not from the incumbent herself. And yet, I could tell our relationship had developed to the point where she was just going through the motions in raising the matter. It's hard to convey conviction with a smile across your face.

Joe Clark never became as paranoid as John Diefenbaker after losing the prime ministership and then the PC Party leadership. His mental stability was much stronger than Diefenbaker's to begin with. In many ways, though, political warfare is like real war; it is an intense human experience. In extreme cases, both forms of warfare take a heavy toll on combatants. Politics inflicts on some practitioners a form of post-traumatic stress disorder—one of the "invisible wounds of war"— analogous to that suffered by soldiers returning from real battle. The intense personal trauma to which Clark was subjected by the defeat of his government and later loss of the PC Party leadership transformed the man I once thought I knew, but hardly recognized in subsequent years. Jodi White, chief of staff of the Prime Minister's Office under Kim Campbell in 1993, was the first woman in Canadian history to lead a national election campaign: Jean Charest's in 1997. She was long one of Joe Clark's closest confidants and most senior staffers. In April 2006, I went to a dinner in Ottawa in honour of Brian Mulroney that almost everyone who had ever been anything in the Conservative Party over the years attended. Joe Clark was conspicuously absent. By this time, Joe was *persona non grata* in Tory circles, having publicly split with the party over its merger with the Reform/Canadian Alliance Party in 2003. I asked Jodi, whom I knew quite well but had not seen since 1988, how Joe was and why he had decided not to attend the dinner. She looked at me with sad eyes and said, "It's going to take a while longer..." She did not complete her thought. She did not need to. I knew.

Joe Clark deserves to be viewed as a wise elder statesman of the Conservative Party of Canada. The man will not be, however, until he has the equanimity to view himself that way. It is both his loss and the country's that the man has yet to attain such emeritus status. I am delighted Joe has now published a book in which he communicates keen insights into politics and government—concerning international affairs, in particular—based on over half a century of political experience. Perhaps, this is a step—if so, a major one—in his personal and public rehabilitation. I hope my colleague of old completes that journey successfully and soon. He has a great deal more to contribute to our nation.

# Question Period

As chief PC strategist for Question Period, I chaired the early-morning strategy meeting our Caucus held each day Parliament met. At the meeting, Tory MPs made their individual pitches either to have a particular issue raised or to get on the questioners' list (usually linked). Typically, about a third of Caucus attended, not always the same individuals from day to day. It depended on a lot of different factors, including the issues. But a core—mostly, the stars or the ambitious or both—did show up virtually all the time. The competition to get on the list was fierce. After all, Question Period grabs more media coverage and, therefore, public attention than anything else that happens in Parliament, least of all routine proceedings and debates. Consequently, this is the most direct route for an Opposition MP to earn or burnish a reputation and become or stay a star. Ultimately, I myself selected the party's performers in Question Period on a given day, after consulting (or at least informing) Brian Mulroney and the rest of our House leadership. I was, therefore, lobbied as though possessing the keys to the Kingdom of Heaven. In truth, the job was hell. I hated it! The only time I didn't was when we had an especially successful attack against the government and many Caucus members had not thought the strategy wise beforehand. I then felt a great sense of achievement and vindication. Being second-guessed went with the job. So was post-facto criticism. Everyone was an expert. But, as Winston Churchill said, "Expert knowledge is limited knowledge." What wasn't limited was the pressure. Even on the best of days, it was enormous. It never eased until the last questioner finished. Then, it was immediately on to the next cycle and a new round of pressure—and lobbying. Hell!

The biggest challenge I faced was the need to balance two different heavy weights: assembling the strongest-possible team to handle the issue or issues of the day, and satisfying the enormous political egos at play. The two weights often responded to different gravitational pulls. Even when in balance, the weights risked crushing me to death. There was hardly a minute I did not have the matter on my mind. I felt like a criminal on the lam, forever trying to avoid someone, often everybody. As Sir John A. Macdonald said of appointing senators, the chosen were ungrateful, the passed-over bitter. Only one other Caucus member gave me greater grief than Flora MacDonald in battles to land on the coveted Question Period list: fiery St. John's MP Jim McGrath. The source of the problem in this case was that unemployment was frequently the main issue. Flora's and Jim's respective positions in the shadow cabinet—hers, social affairs; his, employment—overlapped. When jobs were the focus of the attack, as was often the case given the high jobless rate at the time, each thought he or she had prior claim to be the lead-off questioner, by far the most coveted spot.

The bad blood between MacDonald and McGrath was exceeded only by that between McGrath and fellow St. John's MP John Crosbie, arch-rivals for the Newfoundland Cabinet seat if we later formed a government (John got the nod from Prime Minister Mulroney). Fortunately for me, Flora and Jim were among our best parliamentary performers. Both knew the issues, were passionate about them, had great presence in the Commons, projected well on TV, and could pack a punch—natural performers. So, I often was eager to put both on the Question Period list at the same time, just as I frequently did Crosbie for the same reason. (Crosbie, though, was much better as a speechmaker than questioner. The strict time constraints in the latter domain clipped his oratorical wings when pithiness there was of the essence.) But even when Flora and Jim both made the list, they still battled over who would go first. My job required the directorial skills of a Stephen Spielberg, the diplomatic gifts of a Lester Pearson, and the ruthlessness of a Jack the Ripper. And yet, I saw myself as only a near-neophyte backbench MP from Canada's smallest province. When either Flora MacDonald or Jim McGrath was put on the list but not both, the "loser" rendered my life miserable. I think the technical term for my particular psychological condition was Homicidal Syndrome: I sometimes wanted to kill them. Unfortunately for me, these two were not the only stage-struck MPs I had to manage. The Caucus was full of them. By comparison, the New York Actors Studio was a garden of shrinking violets. All the while, the limited enthusiasm I had for the job at the beginning was diminishing to the point where now it would have to be detected with an arthroscope.

Still, the consensus in political circles at the time, including among the media, was that this was one of our party's golden eras in Question Period. Our incessant assault, for example, against National Revenue Minister Pierre Bussières, for his department's callous and heavy-handed treatment of taxpayers, dominated the news cycle for months on end. Bussières was the Devil's plague on taxpayers—but God's gift to us. Perrin Beatty was especially impressive on the issue. He combined great empathy for the little guy and a steady source of whistle-blowing insider information that revealed the extent to which law-abiding citizens were being strong-armed by the government. I usually teamed Perrin with backbench Cambridge, Ontario, MP Chris Speyer, a young criminal lawyer, for a double whammy: Boyish Beatty and Slayer Speyer, both equally devastating, each in a different way. Perrin had the precise lethal bite of a rattlesnake, Chris the killer jaws of a great white shark (he swallowed whole). Terror in the Commons!

When Parliament is in session, Question Period is held every weekday at 2:00 P.M., except for Friday, when it's at 11:00 A.M. to give members time to depart Ottawa to spend the weekend in their ridings. Typically, Friday's Question Period lacks fireworks, for it is mostly devoted to Opposition members' local issues, setting the stage for their being with constituents once home. Ironically, one of the most successful assaults the PC Caucus launched against the Trudeau government during my time as deputy House leader was on a Friday. We led on the Revenue Canada issue that day, but intended no follow-ups. Suddenly, on the spot, sensing blood in the water, I got every one of our backbench MPs to forgo his or her planned constituency question and, instead, simply ask the beleaguered minister if he would resign for incompetence—one questioner after the other in a steady bombardment. By the end of it, even I felt sorry for the hemorrhaging Bussières. But the lapse was fleeting, because I, too, was a taxpayer. I had never before, nor have I since, seen a more bloodied minister than this minister on that day. We completely eclipsed the other Opposition parties, over many months, while the Revenue Canada issue was white-hot. We frequently did it on several other fronts, including Jim and Flora's jobs issue. I give all the credit to our performers, not least the new leader. I simply set the stage—and took the odd curtain call when things went exceptionally well.

Brian Mulroney was a terrific Question Period performer himself once he got the hang of it, which was almost immediately. But he had a few false starts. One of them was the low point for me as the party's impresario in this theatre. In September 1983, for one of the new leader's first questions to the government as both an MP and Opposition leader, Mulroney set his sights on Transport Minister Lloyd Axworthy. The Manitoba-based minister had just been appointed to the portfolio a month earlier. The leader demanded the minister assure Parliament that Atlantic freight subsidies would be maintained—seemingly a safe subject on which to put Axworthy on the defensive. What we should have known, but did not until too late, was that the minister had announced that very decision earlier in the day in New Brunswick. Generally a strong Question Period performer even at his worst, Axworthy was at his best that day. While flooring the PC leader with his reply, Axworthy flashed a grin that would have made a Cheshire cat look clinically depressed. As Brian Mulroney says in his memoir, "I looked foolish."[6] Few people knew at the time something that Mulroney himself does not likely remember now and certainly did not mention in his memoirs: We had been told about the minister's freight-rates announcement before Mulroney rose in the Commons to pose his question. Bob Corbett, our MP from Fundy Royal, alerted me when he arrived in the Commons for Question Period only seconds before the Speaker recognized Mulroney to lead our attack. By that time, however, it was too late to change strategy. I could only hold my breath, say a prayer, and hope for the best. Had the leader been more experienced in Parliament, we might have been able to improvise right then and there. But he wasn't, and we couldn't. Lloyd Axworthy wiped the floor with us. I felt especially humiliated. To my surprise, no one, except characteristically Erik Nielsen, held me responsible for the debacle, even if I felt I was. Mulroney says in his memoir, "I could only blame myself. I resolved that an episode like this would never happen again."[7] I was even more determined than he that it never would. And it did not.

The lion's share of credit for PC Caucus success in Question Period leading up to the 1984 election period belongs to Brian Mulroney. Supreme military strategist that he was, Mulroney knew instinctively that, despite my inexperience, it took a balance-scale Libra like me to navigate among the Caucus sharks. As much as I hated the job, I at least avoided getting eaten alive. That in itself was a measure of success and, therefore, vindicated his choice. In retrospect, I also believe that the leader saw potential in me and decided that the "man's reach should exceed his grasp" approach was best to harden me for even bigger and tougher responsibilities down the road. In the process, I learned a great deal about Mulroney's political judgment and management style, especially the premium he placed on forging a cohesive team from among talented but strong-willed individuals. Possessing a big ego himself, the man understood viscerally both the advantages and the dangers intrinsic to being surrounded by people whose hubris was as strong as their abilities were outsized. I learned, as well, the boundaries of my own political talents and comfort zone. I had never before been given responsibilities of this magnitude. Only after the job ended, with the calling of the 1984 election, was I glad that I had not told Mulroney that I considered myself unsuited for the role and must, therefore, respectfully decline.

Question Period is, fundamentally, the Opposition's forum, not the government's. The best the government can hope to do is survive unbloodied. Contusions are taken for granted. Time constraints, partisanship, the media culture, the public's appetite for conflict, and other factors dictate that, notwithstanding the nomenclature, it is all about jousting, not the Opposition's seeking information or the government's providing it: about half a minute for each question and a little longer for the answer. In theory, the function of the Opposition in this forum is to hold the government accountable. The main effect, if not express purpose, is to serve as an extraordinary echo chamber of the country. The questions that Opposition MPs typically raise reflect their constituents' concerns or issues, whether local or national, mostly the latter. Too often, though, the Question Period agenda is dictated by the day's headlines, not necessarily what affects average people's daily lives. The media's principal goal, here as elsewhere, is to maximize TV ratings or newsstand sales. The different Opposition parties feed on the stories the media consider newsworthy—attention-grabbing and, therefore, revenue-generating—in order to best both the government and one another. The media then feed on the politicians' responses to their stories, in a vicious cycle and self-perpetuating and self-serving symbiosis. Among the politicians and political parties, the winners and losers in this game are determined by the amount of favourable airtime or column inches they command as combatants. For their part, the media win any which way, provided the pot is stirred, the public gets riled, and the ratings or readers are spiked. The Revenue Canada scandal was a rare case where the issue originated not with the media but with politicians—our Caucus. That's why I stress it here—as a case study, so to speak. This was Parliament, not just Question Period, at it best and most democratic. The issue also provided the Canadian Fourth Estate with some of its finest moments as "bulwarks of democracy."

Some media, however, were slow to cover the tax issue at first—in fact, for a long time. But constituents were telling our MPs one horror story after another about being harassed and bullied by overzealous government tax collectors. From inside sources, we learned that Revenue Canada had installed an aggressive new tax-collection regime tantamount to imposing quotas on individual employees responsible for particular delinquent accounts. This, in turn, pressured departmental officers to employ police-state-type tactics: incessant calls to taxpayers' homes and workplaces, steadily more threatening payment demands, undue resort to wage and pension garnishees, even phone calls to neighbours to hunt down alleged delinquents, and worse.

It was Perrin Beatty and Chris Speyer who first convinced me that the issue had legs. When we did not get immediate traction in the media, some Caucus members implored me to abandon the issue, or at least downplay it. But I felt in my gut that Perrin and Chris were onto something. I myself had been harassed by a Charlottetown-based Revenue Canada official concerning a thousand-dollar government error on my previous year's tax return. So I was of a mind to unload on someone; the minister would do just fine, thanks kindly. Politics is sometimes reduced to such raw and basic human elements. In any event, I was prepared to take the heat in the hope the issue would, in time, click—or, at minimum, I would get my own pound of flesh. When the issue did finally click, *CTV National News* and the *Globe and Mail,* in particular, started running with the story as though we had just discovered a cure for the common cold. The more they covered the story, the more brown envelopes we got from Revenue Canada employees just as upset as we were about the injustices, to say nothing of the pressure those injustices put on their professional and personal lives. In turn, yet more constituents came forward to their MPs with horror stories of their own in an ever-building narrative of government heavy-handedness and abuse. The wild horses had escaped the corral, but we had no idea the direction the stampede would take. Many of the very Caucus members who had vilified me for devoting so much attention to the issue wanted to participate themselves in the assault against Revenue Minister Boussières, the scandal's *bête noire*. Central Casting could not have delivered a better actor than he for the part: a mean-looking little man with a permanent scowl—every citizen's worst image of the tax collector.

Strangely, only the CBC refused to cover the Revenue Canada story, even long after it was leading the newscasts of its main competitor, CTV, and getting blazing front-page coverage in the *Globe and Mail* and most other daily newspapers, day in and day out. Alan Holman was one of the CBC's senior parliamentary reporters at the time. Like fellow broadcaster Mike Duffy, he had grown up in the same upscale Charlottetown neighbourhood as I, and his parents and mine knew one another well. "Tom, everyone always hates the tax collector," Alan said to me. "There is no issue here. What is newsworthy about taxpayers being pissed off with Revenue Canada? You guys are barking up the wrong tree." Weeks later, after the issue had long become the major story in the entire country, Alan told me sheepishly that the corporation's top management had hauled him and his fellow Ottawa-based CBC correspondents on the carpet for ignoring an issue that demonstrably concerned Canadians right across the country. Bang! The CBC suddenly pounced on the story like flies on jam— all over it—and produced, albeit belatedly, some of the best investigative reporting of all on the issue, including by Alan Holman himself, a superb investigative journalist. (As publisher/editor of the *Country Line Courier*—a PEI news and sports and entertainment weekly—Holman publicly shamed Island premier Alex Campbell into voluntarily fessing up to, and then paying a fine for, one of his infamous high-speed car commutes between the politician's home in Summerside and his government office in Charlottetown. So Revenue Canada would not have been able to intimidate this reporter.)

Question Period is rightly attacked these days for being just a big verbal brawl, not a serious forum in which anything important is said or revealed. Critics attacked the Stephen Harper government for demonstrating noisy disrespect for the Speaker and stonewalling the Opposition at every turn. Nevertheless, the Revenue Canada example demonstrates the capacity of Question Period to hold Cabinet accountable, to identify and air problems of concern to Canadians, and to provide individual MPs with a unique forum to represent their voters and constituents. Thanks to our Opposition assault, the Reign of Terror at Revenue Canada ended. When John Turner succeeded Pierre Trudeau as Liberal leader and prime minister, in June 1984, the offending minister was fired. It's called "Parliamentary Democracy."

Robert Stanfield viewed progressive policy as the surest way to modernize the PC Party's public image and thereby broaden its appeal. Brian Mulroney advanced policies of the sort Stanfield championed, partly for the same reason, but also because he *is* a progressive. Mulroney considered Question Period one of the best ways to demonstrate to voters that he and the party were on their side. Much more than either Stanfield or Clark, he understood the power of the television lens. And he was more comfortable in front of a camera than either of his predecessors, even as he often squandered this advantage by rhetorical excess, especially as prime minister. The PC Party in Opposition in the 1983–84 period championed the little guy against the callous tax collector. It was a David-versus-Goliath combat, day in and day out in Question Period. Under Mulroney's early leadership, the party's performance in Parliament did more to project the party as progressive and modern and relevant than any particular policy or set of policies could ever have done in the short run-up to the 1984 election. Furthermore, Question Period showcased many individual Caucus members as potential Cabinet ministers. In a sense, though, the strong stand we took on taxpayers' rights *was* policy. It was no less so for having been developed in the heat of parliamentary battle, rather than in a formal structure such as Stanfield's Policy Coordinating Committee. In both cases, the party was forcing itself to think strategically about what it believed and valued and how specifically it would lead the country if elected to power. Our Question Period record in Opposition would have failed to advance that end had we not decided early on, under Brian Mulroney's military-style leadership, to pursue an overall strategy to hold the Liberal government in check. Too often, Opposition parties fly by the seat of their pants in a parliament or legislature—flitting from one issue to another, from one day to another—in response to and in pursuit of news headlines, which are fleeting almost by definition (maybe that's how Fleet Street got its name!). The PC Party's stand on taxpayers' rights in Question Period was developed and communicated by a team of committed individuals—many of them veteran parliamentary pros—in a thoughtful and coordinated way over several months. As such, it was in the best traditions of the Conservative Party, to wit: Leslie Frost's Human Rights Code, John Diefenbaker's Bill of Rights, and Brian Mulroney's demand for an official apology and compensation for the internment of Japanese Canadians in the Second World War. On all these counts, our campaign on behalf of taxpayers was cause for pride. It certainly was for me, as chief Tory strategist on that stage. Sometimes, Hell can prove Heavenly.

# Lead-up to the 1984 Election

Soon after Brian Mulroney won the Tory leadership, in June 1983, the Trudeau Liberals schemed to divide the PC Caucus along ideological fault lines in the lead-up to the 1984 election. One scheme—launched on the PC leader's second day in the Commons as a new MP—concerned a contentious language issue in Manitoba. The issue echoed a major language- and religion-related school question that had tormented the national Conservative government from 1870 right into the 1890s. The issue that Mulroney faced involved legislative amendments proposed by Howard Pawley, Manitoba's NDP premier, in the late summer of 1983, to provide certain provincial public services in French. (Roughly 47,100 Manitobans reported French as their mother tongue in a subsequent census.) Pierre Trudeau manoeuvred to federalize the contentious issue by introducing a Commons resolution that called on members on both sides of the aisle to support the Manitoba measure. The House resolution lacked any hook on which the Trudeau government legitimately could hang its rationale for this mischief-making. It was just as Trudeau had done with Robert Stanfield when tabling, in 1973, a resolution to affirm the principles of the *Official Languages Act*. As Rod McQueen has noted, "[t]he measure was totally unnecessary; official bilingualism had been approved in 1969 with Stanfield's full support." In both cases, what motivated the government—Trudeau, in particular—was as transparent as it was reprehensible.[8]

In the instance at hand, the Liberals believed the resolution would sow dissension in PC ranks, pit Mulroney against a vocal faction of his Caucus, force him on the defensive, and generally undermine his leadership. But, rather than oppose the resolution, as the Liberals thought he might and hoped he would, the new Tory leader supported it in an eloquent and soaring Commons address that flowed from his deep baritone voice right into the pages of history. In doing so, Mulroney not only circumvented the trap set for him; he also helped put to rest, once and for all, the Conservative Party's ghost of Louis Riel. A Manitoba Métis fighter for his people's French language and culture rights, Riel was hanged for treason in 1885, an execution that Sir John A. Macdonald controversially refused to commute. Macdonald's perceived complicity in Riel's execution damaged the party's image and reputation in French Canada, and plagued the party's own conscience, for an entire century. Now, with a single great oration—one of Mulroney's most exalted moments in public life—the new national Tory leader helped exorcise that menacing demon. Though aimed at producing the opposite result, Trudeau's mischief elevated Mulroney's standing in the country, unified the Tory Caucus, strengthened Mulroney's personal hold on that body, forced underground (at least until after the election) the hard-right elements of the party, and boosted Conservative support in French Canada for the coming election. Most important of all, the PC leader's adroit handling of the issue salved a wound that had been festering in English-French relations for almost as long as the country had existed. The wily Quebec Irishman was off to a strong start as new Tory leader. Had Georges-Étienne Cartier drafted Mulroney's address with Sir John A. holding his hand on the quill? In the moment, none of us cheering Mulroney on from our quarter in the Commons chamber would have fantasized otherwise.

People can admire Pierre Trudeau without being blinded to the fact that he was capable of placing partisan politics and personal ambition and ego above the interests of the country. Trudeau's mischief-making on the Manitoba language issue risked more than splitting the PC Caucus: it could have ruptured national unity. By contrast, as he reports in his memoirs, Brian Mulroney was prepared to expel from his Caucus any and all MPs who would not support him on this highly inflammatory matter.[9] His eagerness to ensure that the PC Party took the high moral ground, rather than pander to the anti-French, anti-Quebec elements in both the party and the country at large, was statesmanship of a high order. Trudeau always characterized himself as *rational*. Indeed, his estranged wife, Margaret, purposely titled her memoir *Beyond Reason* to contrast herself with him in that respect.[10] But *rational* compared to whom? Other Liberal prime ministers? Wilfrid Laurier? Louis St-Laurent? Lester Pearson? Hardly. Trudeau was ballsy and arrogant and truculent, but not more rational than those Liberal icons—at his worst, much less so. Trudeau was endowed with uncommon intellectual and verbal ability to use bogus arguments to deceive and mislead about his true intentions. He was, to his core, a sophist whose intentions were too often anything but noble. In the House of Commons, I perceived him sometimes more interested in winning arguments than in the arguments themselves. The intellectual dishonesty he demonstrated in the 1968 election about *deux nations* and later, in the 1974 election, about wage-and-price controls ("Zap, you're frozen") evidenced his sophistry. As an academic and polemicist before entering politics, the man frequently demonstrated such a penchant in his prolific writings—on language and constitutional questions, in particular.

As soon as it became clear to Trudeau that his strategy on the Manitoba language issue was backfiring, he retreated with his tail between his legs. Meanwhile, he stoked the embers of national discord without apparent qualms. As noted earlier, one of the biggest breaks I got early in my political career was the classy way Trudeau eventually handled my Atlantic veterinary college question in the House of Commons. To me, this was the man at his best. The Manitoba language issue exposed him at his worst.

Can any fair-minded person imagine Robert Stanfield ever having behaved in such a reckless way with national unity hanging in the balance? I know he would not have. As for Mulroney, his address on the Manitoba language issue made all of us in Caucus— even the few who had to be whipped into line to support him in the relevant parliamentary vote—extremely proud. Our collective confidence in his political instincts soared as the election fast approached. I sensed the outcome of this parliamentary saga—a clear victory for the PC Party and him personally, not to mention for the country—had the same impact on Mulroney's own self-confidence at a critical time in his leadership. Moreover, it strengthened his hand to tamp down dissension in Caucus over such hot-button social issues as abortion, gay rights, gun control, and metric conversion on which members, like the country at large, were deeply divided. He was thereby better able to get us to focus, instead, on the battery of policies he intended to use to bludgeon the governing Liberals in the coming election. Those policies were aimed at boosting employment, narrowing regional disparities, improving relations with the provinces (Quebec and the West, in particular), restoring the Canadian-US partnership, shoring up defence (specifically, the country's contribution to NATO), and expanding international trade, all encapsulated in his mantra, "Jobs, Jobs, Jobs." Such were the weapons with which the PC Party's military general intended to charge into battle against the Liberals and the NDP in the campaign, not the Manitoba language question. The latter, however, enabled him to sit tall in the saddle as he rallied his troops to charge the hill—Parliament Hill.

The second trap set by Trudeau and the Liberals for Mulroney— his most difficult challenge yet as PC leader—concerned reforms to the *Canada Health Act* introduced by Health Minister Monique Bégin. The reforms detailed the strict conditions and standards that the provincial and territorial governments would have to meet to qualify for federal transfer payments under the so-called Canada Health Transfer. The most contentious provision would ban extra-billing by doctors. The Liberals were convinced the PC Caucus would either side with doctors on the issue or split badly. Either way, they would weaken our party for the 1984 election. As in the country at large, opinion was strongly divided on the legislation within Caucus. Many doctors across the country, especially in Ontario and the West, opposed the bill. Indeed, the Canadian Medical Association (CMA) launched a seven-year legal challenge against the law on jurisdictional and Charter grounds. The association ultimately withdrew its case in 1991. According to my brother Colin, who then headed the association's Political Action Committee, the profession was resigned to defeat in the court of public opinion no matter how the issue was resolved in the actual courts. For us Tories, the issue was even thornier than the Manitoba language question because the former risked enflaming passions in more parts of the country than the latter. And this time, unlike before, the issue also entailed substantial federal funding.

At a weekend retreat for our Caucus and nominated candidates held at a resort a two-hour drive north of Ottawa, the health care issue loomed large. I wanted our party to support the government on the issue and circumvent the trap. I told Caucus I was the son of a doctor, the nephew of a doctor, the brother of a doctor, and the brother-in-law of a doctor, but "there are no votes in defending 'merchants of health' against the interests of ordinary Canadians." I was one of the youngest Caucus members or candidates in the packed resort conference room and, despite the grey-tipped hair, looked even younger. I sensed most attendees were more amused than convinced, if not bemused, by the argument made by this Oedipus-sounding *parvenu*. Then, Pat Carney—elected an MP in 1980 in Vancouver Centre—rose and said:

"Why are we all complicating the issue? We should simply do what McMillan has just urged: announce our support for the *Canada Health Act*, vote for the changes, show Trudeau we can't be messed with, get the issue behind us, and move on." Towards the end of the debate, Brian Mulroney made clear his own support for the act. He stressed that our party had pioneered public health insurance when John Diefenbaker was prime minister. (Diefenbaker had appointed the Hall Commission that recommended what later became the five pillars of medicare.) But it was not at all a foregone conclusion that the leader would carry his Caucus and nominated candidates on the issue at hand. Doctors had always been among the party's strongest supporters across the country. To boot, the Caucus contained several MDs—for example, veteran MP Bruce Halliday, from Oxford riding, in Ontario, and relative parliamentary newbie Gary Gurbin, from Bruce–Grey, also in Ontario. Still more doctors were among our nominated candidates for the coming election. Many at the retreat—not just medicos—were eager, this close to the campaign, that the party avoid alienating the medical profession and its broad network of sympathizers.

A respected economist considered no flaming socialist, Pat Carney, in one terse statement, helped turn the tide towards Brian Mulroney's (and my own) position. In April 1984, those in Caucus inclined to oppose Mulroney on the issue held their noses and voted for the *Canada Health Act* amendments, tossing a huge victory to the new PC leader. Not a single member broke ranks. Even Bruce Halliday, a highly principled physician who had publicly expressed deep concerns about the government's legislation, voted with us. Prior to entering politics, Mulroney had been president of Iron Ore Company of Canada, a large US multinational subsidiary operating in northern Quebec. I had wondered whether the man's background as a business titan would render him a corporatist, and not sufficiently a progressive, as PC leader when push came to shove on issues such as health care. My concern proved groundless. The impressive way he marshalled his Caucus behind him on the *Canada Health Act*, not just for tactical reasons but also on principle and substance, put my mind to rest: the Stanfield legacy was in good hands—his and those of rising stars such as Pat Carney.

---

My job as deputy House leader was no bed of roses at the best of times, a crown of thorns even when everything went as planned. I consoled myself that "this, too, will pass." I would have to settle for Crosbie's "short-term pain for long-term gain" until the gods had something more pleasant in store for me. The pending election was not so much the light at the end of the tunnel as the tunnel itself: an escape route to what I hoped would make public life more fun than I was having. Little did I realize how far the route would take me. And how much fun the journey would be.

# Chapter 16

# UNLIKELY ATLANTIC CANADIAN CHAMPION

For any Tory, the 1984 election campaign was exhilarating. For a Tory candidate, it was a cakewalk. In my case, in Hillsborough, it didn't hurt that I had the best campaign manager a candidate could have hoped for: Ron MacMillan, a Charlottetown lawyer not directly related to me, but married to my first cousin, Mary McQuaid. (He would run well but unsuccessfully in the riding for the Conservatives in the October 2015 federal election.) Our new leader, Brian Mulroney, sometimes spoke privately, including in Caucus, about his courtesy phone call from Liberal PM John Turner informing him of his decision to have the governor general dissolve Parliament, setting the stage for the September 4 election. Mulroney said that, during the call, Turner's overconfidence about trouncing him in the election was blatant with every condescending syllable. The overconfidence was mistaken, the condescension misplaced. Both sentiments merely served to fire up the Irish in the Tory leader, determined more than ever to prove wrong not only Turner but also his many detractors everywhere, including in some quarters of his own party. There are two things one never tells an Irishman: the pub is closed and he is a loser. By then a non-drinker, Mulroney focused on the personal insult. But his target was much more ambitious than proving he was not a loser: he wanted to win big—real big. And he was supremely confident he could, and would.

The new Tory leader's own confidence was not mistaken. Brian Mulroney won for his party the largest landslide majority government in Canadian history. The PC leader handed Turner, to that point, the worst-ever trouncing of a governing party at the federal level. The 1984 election decimated, perhaps forever, the Liberal Party's stranglehold on federal politics in Quebec. Out of 282 House of Commons seats, the PCs won a whopping 211, the Liberals a mere 40, the NDP 31. It was more a victory for Mulroney personally than for the party. From the very beginning of his leadership, he drove everything: the organization, the fundraising, the strategy and tactics, the policies, and the overall message of the campaign, that the Canadian people deserved better, a new way of politics was on its way to Ottawa, a different kind of leadership was in store for every citizen. Mulroney's electrifying performance in the party leaders' English- language debate ignited a groundswell of support for him and the party across the land. His blistering attack against Turner on patronage—

"You chose to say 'yes' to the old attitudes and the old stories of the Liberal Party. That, sir…is not good enough for Canadians"—clinched the deal with voters. It was downhill for Turner from then on, and to Parliament Hill for a record number of Tory candidates, including me.

My brother Charley, who travelled with Mulroney during the campaign, told me that, after his debate triumph, Mulroney—sometimes given to dark moods—was reborn. There was a glint in his eye, a bounce to his step, and a lilt in his voice that Charley had not witnessed before. During the debate, Turner said that he had been given "no option" but to confirm the heavy round of patronage appointments (some seventy in all) that Pierre Trudeau had made as he departed office. On the hustings, Mulroney became steadily more playful in mocking Turner's "no option" comment. In the Tory leader's eventual characterization, the punchline became "the Devil made me do it." The steadily burgeoning crowds turning out to cheer him on howled with laughter, which fired up the leader to yet higher levels of powerful campaign oratory not heard in the country since the heydays of John Diefenbaker. In my own riding, Mulroney attracted so many at a public rally late in the campaign, at the cavernous Charlottetown Royalty Centre auditorium, that organizers feared for people's safety. Nobody got trampled, only my opponent: I won by a landslide against Liberal Gerry Birt (53.2 percent to 39.3 percent). Ever a worrywart about election outcomes, even when everything pointed to victory, I phoned Charley at his Toronto home to vent my concerns about Hillsborough the day before the vote. He told me the results of the party's fresh-off-the-wire, in-house national poll and, based on it, predicted we would win more than two hundred seats in all. I thought he had gone stark raving mad. When he told me that I would win my own seat by "strong double digits," I knew for sure I was right about his insanity. Local reporter Len Russo of the *Eastern Graphic* was predicting "too close to call" in my riding. He dropped by my campaign headquarters early morning the day after my call to Charley. I said to him: "Len, not only am I going to win but I'll do so by *strong double digits*." He thought *I* had gone stark raving mad. Charley had been confident about Hillsborough. And, finally, after reflecting on the polling data he had shared with me, so was I.

Soon after the 1984 election, I was contacted by a high-level political operative and confidant of Brian Mulroney (not my twin brother). He told me that I would be sworn in, on September 17, as the country's minister of state for tourism. My mental response was unlike that to my appointment by Joe Clark to his shadow cabinet or to Mulroney's asking me to be his deputy House leader back in the day. This news did not surprise me. With David MacDonald long off the political stage, I was generally thought to be the most logical choice for PEI's Cabinet post in an era when every province typically was given one. The new Cabinet, at forty members, would be the largest ever—a lot of room, but no more than needed, for the prime minister to balance all the different factors that had to be calculated into its composition: not only regional and provincial balance, but also seniority, sex, language, ideology, experience, skill and ability, age, party unity, and, important to Mulroney, past loyalty and service to him, among other considerations. The election of such a large Caucus presented Mulroney with a Cabinet-making challenge of concomitant size. It was less an embarrassment of riches—though that, too—than a conundrum: how to produce a quality team to govern the country while keeping the maximum number of people happy, or at least not unhappy. And he wanted to set the stage for the next election. Brian Mulroney always took the long view.

In my own case, provincial representation aside, I did not have a strong claim to a Cabinet post by conventional criteria, least of all government or parliamentary experience and national standing. What's more, as part of the PC Party's preparation for its expected transition from Opposition to government, Yukon parliamentary and government veteran Erik Nielsen had prepared a highly confidential memo for Mulroney well before the election campaign had even begun that presented names of possible Cabinet choices with their respective strengths and weaknesses. The memo was astonishingly biased in retrospect, reflecting Nielsen's closeness to Diefenbaker, himself the ultimate holder of grudges. In any event, the "analysis" didn't exactly state I had more skills than a centipede has legs—though, given Nielsen's distaste for progressives like myself, particularly of the young and up-and-coming variety, he likely viewed me with the same disdain as he would such a creepy crawly creature.

Anyway, I was one of the Chosen. I had been cautioned to treat the fact with a level of secrecy associated with the US president's code for unleashing a nuclear attack against an imminent existential threat. Accordingly, I told no one, not even my wife, Kathy. A couple of days before the swearing-in ceremony at Rideau Hall, however, I ran into Tory MP John Bosley on Ottawa's Sparks Street Mall. He and I had engaged in rowdy, beer-soaked all-nighters playing Monopoly with others at my seaside home outside Charlottetown on his periodic visits to the Island as a friend. John had a much stronger claim than I to a Cabinet post, not least because he was fluently bilingual and from vote-rich Toronto. But he signalled to me that he had not been invited to join the Cabinet and that he was disappointed. Unbeknownst to John, Mulroney had him slated to be House of Commons Speaker, an announcement the PM would make only after releasing the names of his new Cabinet. No doubt viewing me as a potential rival—both of us fast-rising Young Turks—he assumed I had been already selected for the Cabinet and asked me discreetly whether I had been. Understandably, he seemed more interested in keeping his hopes alive if I hadn't yet been asked than curious about my actual fate. Feeling empathy for the obvious unease of a friend, I looked at John and, with my eyes only, telegraphed in the affirmative. I did verbalize that the post was "no big deal" and, therefore, he had no reason to feel one-upped. I swore him to this absolute confidence. I knew John, as a man of honour, could be trusted. He honoured my confidence. It was the only time in my entire Cabinet career that I did not hold 100 percent to my oath of secrecy, although I hadn't yet officially taken that oath.

## Taking the Reins

The Ministry of Tourism was, in 1984, a subsidiary of the Department of Regional Industrial Expansion (DRIE) under new minister Sinclair Stevens. The Office of Minister of DRIE had been created by statute in December 1983. Until then, it had been the Office of Minister of Regional Economic Expansion (DREE), created in March 1969. More than any other federal department, DREE/DRIE was widely considered Atlantic Canada's protector. No question, Atlantic Canadians themselves viewed it that way. Tourism Canada was the lowest rung on the now greatly elongated Cabinet ladder. It had previously been—within both DREE and DRIE—the back half of the Small Business and Tourism subministry, in nomenclature and priority alike. (Today, the two are linked again under the Industry Canada portfolio.)

I always suspected that Mulroney hived off Tourism from Small Business, as a separate ministry of state, more to meet a political need (Cabinet status for PEI) than to reflect any importance he attached to this public policy field, still less any competence he saw in me. But I didn't feel slighted. I was in the Cabinet. Most in Caucus weren't, and would have killed to be where I was. Shortly before the swearing-in, I was summoned to meet with the soon-to-be prime minister at an undisclosed location (in a suite at Ottawa's Carleton Towers Hotel). Like all the different secret locations for meetings with other Cabinet appointees, the venue had been carefully selected to prevent the media from tracking Mulroney's Cabinet choices. A chatty man when not down to business, Mulroney was just the opposite when focused, as in this case with me. The prime minister–designate got quickly to the point, all of it personal and political. He likely thought I saw Tourism, as no doubt he himself did, as a nothing portfolio. He said: "Tommy, you have the same title ['minister'], the same salary and perks, including a car and driver—exactly like the other ministers have. And you have a seat at the Cabinet table." That was about it, except for one puzzling comment at the beginning of our conversation that I have never quite fathomed. After inquiring about the results in my own Hillsborough riding in the election, which I knew he would have known anyway as part of his briefing, he responded, "Impressive!" And then this: "You've passed all the background checks." Pausing for effect and looking directly at me, he added, "Pretty much, anyway." Pretty much? Anyway? What could he possibly have been referring to?

My life had been boringly conventional, a paragon of probity and rectitude. Still, politics in PEI is played as a blood sport. Eugene Rossiter was a Charlottetown lawyer (now federal Tax Court judge). Rossiter was one of the hardest-punching Tory political thugs on the Island. He came from Morell, itself a hotbed of bare-knuckle politics in the province. This man once bragged to me that he could flash a nasty rumour about a political opponent across the Island in five minutes. It was no idle boast. No fan of mine, the flasher had sometimes spread untrue rumours about me. And Rossiter was supposedly a Tory heavyweight in PEI. In my riding and across PEI, the Liberals had said I was every evil thing short of the Boston Strangler. It did not matter that, from whatever source, such rumours were invariably contradictory: "He's broke and has millions in Swiss bank accounts"—that sort of thing. Some individuals are inherently capable of telling the worst lies about others and then believing the very things they themselves fabricate. Politics seems to give the offenders licence to engage in this practice to an extent they wouldn't consider acceptable in the normal course of life. Was that what the prime minister's oblique reference concerned—a rumour? When, clearly, I appeared unaware of anything disqualifying in my past, Mulroney moved on. Evidently, he was satisfied that I could not be blackmailed or otherwise rendered a ticking time bomb capable of blowing up the government.

---

Sinclair Stevens was not only my senior minister at DRIE, but also chair of Cabinet's powerful Economic and Regional Development Committee, a consolation prize for his not getting the Finance portfolio. Stevens had run for the PC Party leadership in 1976, finishing seventh in an eleven-candidate race and then throwing his support behind Joe Clark, the eventual winner, in the final balloting. Stevens's early support of Mulroney over Clark in the party's 1983 leadership contest positioned him well for Finance when the Tories took power the following year. But that was not to be, for Mulroney was under enormous pressure not to make the appointment. Many people both within and outside the party wrongly saw Stevens as a ruthless and unprincipled corporate tycoon. A lawyer by training (Osgoode Hall), Stevens had been a high-stakes wheeler-dealer in banking and trusts, once controlling twenty-three companies with assets of more that $130 million. His messy failed attempt to establish the first new bank in western Canada since the Great Depression (Westbank) made him especially suspect in the eyes of Tories loyal to the memory of John Diefenbaker, who, like them, was hostile to "the Bay Street barons." These Tories viewed Stevens as yet another in a long line of eastern con artists trying to rip off the West. Alberta premier Peter Lougheed was known to share this hostily towards the eastern money changers based on how the banks, headquartered in central Canada, had forced the liquidation of his own family's assets to pay debts after it lost its wealth during the Depression.[1] Had Lougheed blackballed Stevens for the finance portfolio? I don't know for sure, but suspected so at the time. In any event, Stevens's competence was surpassed by no other Mulroney ministers. This is not just my opinion; it was widely shared. In his memoirs, Mulroney himself refers to Sinc Stevens as "one of my best ministers."[2]

Though from the Toronto area (York–Simcoe), Sinclair Stevens became, in the DRIE portfolio, one of the best friends Atlantic Canada has ever had at the federal level. Many of the Mulroney government's achievements related to the region had Stevens's fingerprints all over them. One such achievement was the Atlantic Canada Opportunities Agency, established by the Mulroney government in 1987 to help build economic self-sufficiency in the region by working closely with its people, right in their communities, through their own institutions, and with their provincial and local governments and businesses. The goal was to create jobs, expand earned incomes, and lessen dependence on unemployment insurance and other government support cheques. Stevens's imprint was also on the 1985 Atlantic Accord, which governed revenue-sharing between Ottawa and Newfoundland and Labrador from offshore oil and gas production. This instrument was very much to the province's advantage. That was especially the case after the agreement was modified in 2005 to give the province 100 percent protection from equalization clawbacks arising from offshore revenues. Most economists credit the accord with converting Newfoundland and Labrador from a "have-not" to a "have" province three years after that modification.[3]

Sinclair Stevens deserves at least some of the credit—and, in some cases, all of it—in these and in many other areas where the economic and cultural life of Atlantic Canada was substantially elevated during the Mulroney years. Progress was particularly fast early on in the government's mandate, when Stevens was still in charge of DRIE. His chairmanship of the Economic and Regional Development Committee of Cabinet during the same period gave the minister a unique opportunity to advance the agenda of his own department and, therefore, the interests of Atlantic Canada. It was a serendipitous set of circumstances—a benevolent conflict of interest, so to speak—that continues to pay big dividends to my region to this very day. As stressed earlier, Mulroney strongly identified with Atlantic Canada, having graduated from St. Francis Xavier University in Antigonish, Nova Scotia. The appointment of such a party heavyweight to the DRIE portfolio, and as chairman of the Economic and Regional Development Committee of Cabinet to boot, telegraphed the importance the new prime minister attached to lifting a region of the country to which he felt deeply connected. As an Atlantic Canadian, I couldn't help but think that Mulroney's appointing me to head a junior ministry associated with DRIE—and with Sinc Stevens, in particular—was motivated, at least in part, by this consideration.

Put another way, Mulroney likely saw me as a natural fit with both DRIE and Stevens. That Mulroney was later to promote me within Cabinet from that perch, and that meanwhile Stevens and I were to work together so well, proved the prime minister's instincts right. At a minimum, though I did not realize it at first, I had lucked into obtaining a mentor in Sinc Stevens, who would prove as influential in my Cabinet career as Heath Macquarrie always was in my maturation as a politician.

# Visionary Leadership

An example of Sinclair Stevens's bold thinking concerned the Turks and Caicos Islands, a British Overseas Territory in the Caribbean, formerly governed from the Bahamas, but virtual international orphans since 1973, when the Bahamas became independent. The islands are a favourite vacation destination for many Canadians, including from Atlantic Canada, attracted by the idyllic climate, reliable sunshine, sandy beaches, beautiful landscape, and pristine natural environment. What the islands and their 31,500 residents lacked in the 1980s was the development required to make tourism a major industry, in order to raise the local population's living standards. Poverty there was a much bigger problem than it should have been, given the islands' natural assets and the resourcefulness of the islanders themselves. For generations, Canadians had been held in high standing by the islanders, many of whom saw Canada as the prime candidate to replace the United Kingdom as mother country now that they were on their own and struggling. Could Canada and the Turks and Caicos help each other through a formal partnership, even a territorial tie? Wasn't that possibility at least worth pursuing? The DRIE minister thought the answer was emphatically yes—or, at the very minimum, maybe—and was eager to try. Stevens saw it as a tremendous opportunity for Canada to get in on the ground floor of tourism and travel-related infrastructure development in a part of the world panting for it. At the same time, he thought, it would help address the serious travel-dollar deficit Canada faced from so many Canadians vacationing in southern climes in winter. Why couldn't the "snowbirds" be spending Canadian dollars in a territory of their own country? For their part, the Turks and Caicos Islands themselves would benefit from Canadian investments and a wide range of diplomatic and defence protections—not to mention a secure and reliable currency—provided by a country unburdened by the kind of imperialistic traditions that would have made most other major industrial countries untrustworthy for these purposes. "Win-win" appeared stamped all over this idea.

Alas, the princelings at the Department of External Affairs roadblocked Stevens's efforts at every turn. Their argument was that Canada's credibility as "an honest broker" around the globe—for example, for peacekeeping—stemmed largely from its not having had an imperialistic past. So, the argument went, annexing a group of islands far from our shores—albeit at their own request—would undermine Canada's capacity to play a benevolent role throughout the world as a middle power. This rationale was pure nonsense; "manure" is not too strong a word for it. Besides, given the plight and express desire of the impoverished residents of the tiny islands, an abundance of altruism on Canada's part—foreign aid, as it were—was involved. Wasn't this at the very heart of our traditional international role? Beginning with Robert Borden in 1917, Canadian Tories had a long tradition of seeking the very kind of territorial relationship between Canada and the Turks and Caicos that Sinclair Stevens championed. The Turks and Caicos idea even had substantial support within the NDP—hardly a bastion of imperialism and national military adventurism. Indeed, in 1974, NDP MP Max Saltsman had tried to use a Private Member's Bill to annex the islands to Canada. But Saltsman was stymied by the governing Liberals, captives of the same kind of hidebound thinking at External Affairs that was later to block Stevens's efforts. I totally agreed with those efforts. But one would not have needed to be onside to abhor a bureaucratic system that would extinguish the flame of an idea before the candle holder had a chance to demonstrate whether the flickering light could withstand the winds of open debate both within that system and in the country at large. Comfort—the comfort of absolute certainty—is not a democratic value. And yet, such a stultifying system, one populated with officials hostile to innovative thinking, too often operated without challenge or change during the Mulroney government's first few months in office until we discovered how to find our way in the dark.

What my senior minister learned from all this—a lesson I myself took to heart—was that a minister of the Crown sometimes needs to impose his or her own will on officialdom, not rely on winning them over when groupthink is manifestly too entrenched ever to be dislodged. Sinclair Stevens's subsequent major successes in Cabinet, particularly in advancing the interests of Atlantic Canada, came from his eventually making clear to everyone in the system that he knew exactly what he wanted to achieve, and that anyone who stood in his way, other than the prime minister, would pay a heavy price. And his adversaries usually did. It wasn't so much that the man was ruthless as that he never doffed his tycoon's hat once he left the corporate boardroom and entered the Cabinet chamber. It was similar to how, as national Tory leader, Robert Stanfield hadn't ceased to think and act like a provincial premier, particularly on policy matters, long after he ceased to be one. It is not just leopards whose spots never change. Sinclair McKnight Stevens—one of Brian Mulroney's best ministers, indeed—remained a formidable tycoon as a powerful government "executive." Until everything went terribly wrong.


# The Forced Resignation

If he trusted you, as he did me, Sinclair Stevens was, except for Tom Symons, the best delegator of authority with whom I have ever worked—and, public image to the contrary, one of the most charming. In 1986, only two years after the Mulroney government took office, Stevens would be forced to resign over a trumped-up conflict-of-interest scandal for which he was exonerated nineteen years later by the Federal Court of Canada. He courageously fought to restore his name all that time. It is a name well worth restoring. His public image notwithstanding, Stevens is a gentleman of the Old School. As a colleague and Maritimer, I adored the man. So his disgrace and Cabinet resignation over the phony conflict-of-interest scandal hit me hard. My brother Charley, a close friend of Sinc, was the Cassandra whom Brian Mulroney mandated to deliver the news that, as PC leader, the prime minister would not sign the now-former minister's nomination papers to run again as a Tory candidate in his York–Simcoe riding in the 1988 election. That the death warrant would be administered by a Maritimer for the political corpse of a man who had done so much to breathe life into the economy of the region was irony of the blackest sort. It's worth reflecting on this point because it reveals one important facet of Mulroney's personality and management style.

In his memoirs, Brian Mulroney says, "I had to call [Stevens] in 1988 and tell him that I would not sign his nomination forms. It cut my heart out, but politically I had little choice."[4] I do not question the truthfulness of this statement. But I do remember Charley telling me at the time that it was he who first informed Stevens, for the prime minister, that Sinc would not be allowed to run as a PC candidate in the 1988 election. It's fair to assume that, as a close friend of the disgraced former minister, Charley would have been asked to explain the rationale and technicalities surrounding the decision. The prime minister would then have followed up Charley's overture with a more personal message of regret. This is typically how Brian Mulroney handled such matters. He rarely, if ever, delegated his dirty work, and he always placed a high premium on the personal touch. That was especially the case with colleagues—or, as in this case, a former colleague—in distress. Even a one-thousand-page memoir like Mulroney's cannot possibly cover every nuance of every historical fact or interpretation therein. This is one among many examples I observed in the Mulroney memoir where the missing nuance is almost as important to the historical record as the basic facts presented. In this case, the facts are truthfully and accurately stated, but somewhat incomplete and possibly misleading, though doubtless without the author's intent. In the case at hand, Charley was not asked to do the prime minister's "dirty work," but, rather, to help make Stevens's exit from politics as clean as possible for the sake of the political exile himself. And, thanks to the prime minister's humane way of handling the matter, it was. The messiness derived from the bogus nature of the Opposition-ignited and media-stoked scandal from beginning to end. The forced resignation and consequent public humiliation of an outstanding public servant were as gratuitous as they were morally wrong.

Unlike my twin, I was not an actual personal friend of Sinclair Stevens. But, as a Maritimer, I considered him a friend no less, and still do. Every Atlantic Canadian should. To be sure, I learned from Stevens a great deal about both government operations and managing issues. And he helped build my confidence on the job. My ministerial overlord held virtually daily meetings with senior departmental officials, including from Tourism Canada, in our shared office complex in downtown Ottawa, not far from Parliament Hill. Stevens placed a high value not only on being briefed by officials, but also on keeping them fully informed of his own priorities, ideas, and plans, and picking their brains about them. A collegial spirit, sharing information and ideas, joint action, and mutual respect characterized the way he believed politicians and their officials should operate. From his example, this became my own model as a Cabinet minister. With him in the chair at ministerial two-way briefings with officials, I felt like I was participating in the deliberations of a giant private-sector corporation, rather than part of a government bureaucracy, albeit a huge one. No doubt, our "CEO" was bringing to bear on his Cabinet responsibilities the same management style he had applied to building and operating his multi-million-dollar business empire. A minister's work or professional background prior to his or her appointment to Cabinet really does matter. During our department-wide high-level meetings at DRIE, Sinc Stevens sometimes turned the floor over to me, not merely about tourism but about other matters as well. That was especially the case concerning measures directly affecting my region about which he thought I, as an Atlantic Canadian, was better informed than he or, at least, as well informed. The practice occurred steadily more often as his confidence in my judgment rose. Not once did he second-guess a decision I made or action I took as tourism minister. Nor did he ever undermine me in any other way. On the contrary, I was increasingly made to feel not so much a junior minister as a virtual understudy to the master.

In retrospect, I know Sinclair Stevens's treating me in this manner was not primarily altruistic, though it had that effect. Rather, it reflected the importance he attached to surrounding himself with and cultivating the strongest-possible policy and management team. There's a reason such people rise to the top in business, and in his case now in government: they know how to assemble and use talent, employing every available tool, not least psychology, to make a team the best it can be. According to legend—possibly apocryphal—novelist F. Scott Fitzgerald once said to Ernest Hemingway: "The rich are different from you and me." To which Hemingway responded, "Yes, they have more money." I learned that, at least in Sinclair Stevens's case, there's much more to it than that. His wealth was as much in human qualities as in dollars. While prime minister, Joe Clark passed up the opportunity to cultivate a farm team of future Cabinet ministers, either for his own short-lived government or for some future Tory government. I'm referring, in particular, to his having badly mismanaged the appointment of parliamentary secretaries, which he came close to forgoing altogether. By contrast, as his junior minister, I witnessed Sinclair Stevens in full bore as a first-rate manager of people and events, day in and day out, in the intimate conclaves of government—Cabinet as a whole, the Economic and Regional Development Committee he chaired, and the war room of DRIE. This intense learning experience helped qualify and prepare me for a major Cabinet promotion within less than a year, from Tourism to Environment. When faced with an especially difficult policy or managerial challenge in that new post, I frequently asked myself, "How would Sinc have handled this?" Any appointee to Cabinet—whether for the first time or to a different portfolio, particularly involving a promotion—would benefit enormously from the kind of mentoring I received from such an impressive man. It would help ensure the country was governed better, and by better governors.

## Chapter 17

# MOOSE, MOUNTAINS, AND MOUNTIES

How does a junior minister who reports to a powerful senior minister make his mark in a tiny piece of government bureaucracy that the prime minister had implied to him was not politically important? For starters, he stays out of trouble. Not just Sinclair Stevens, but five Cabinet ministers in all were forced to resign in the first two years of the new government over one scandal or another, real or (as with Stevens) fabricated by the Opposition or media. My first government-side Commons seatmate, André Bissonnette, was minister of state for small business. We had, in Stevens, the same senior minister, at DRIE. Bissonnette, about whom Mulroney had concerns at the best of times, would be forced to resign in January 1987 as part of another round of scandals that forced yet more ministers out of Cabinet. The Bissonnette case involved an alleged conflict of interest about a land deal in his hometown, St-Jean-sur-Richelieu. (He would later be acquitted by a local jury.) The "last-man-standing" principle can apply as much to politics as to boxing to determine a winner. With scandal-plagued Cabinet colleagues dropping as fast as the Ottawa temperature in mid-November, there seemed steadily fewer of us left to compete in the ring for the Silver Belt.

But I could not rely only on default to win rounds as tourism minister, still less a Cabinet promotion down the road. I had to deliver a punch. But how? I decided to move fast with a tourism strategy drafted by my officials. I didn't agree with some of the content, and found the writing bureaucratic and boring. But the idea itself to have a national tourism strategy, which the country clearly lacked, appealed to my natural predisposition to think strategically. And my years working for Robert Stanfield and Tom Symons had turned me into a policy wonk. Eureka! I had found my agenda. As if the draft strategy weren't enough to get me going, a throwaway comment by my brother Charley—the real policy expert in the family—unleashed a torrent of thoughts I had always held but never before articulated, let alone had an opportunity to implement. Unlike me, my twin had travelled, lived, studied, and researched in a larger number of countries than Canada has lakes. Based on this experience, he believed our main tourism marketing challenge was a lack of "brand-name recognition" for the industry's main products and services. There, I had it. Off to the boxing match!

I tested this theme, virtually off the cuff, at a speech in Hull, Quebec, to a large gathering of that province's tourism leaders. The response was mind-blowing: I got a prolonged standing ovation. Unbeknownst to me beforehand, Tourism Canada officials had planted one of their own at the back of the hotel ballroom to listen to the speech and take notes—in effect, to spy on their new minister and size him up. How much would the minister need their advice? Was he a pushover? Or was he, as suspected from the rumour mill, a self-starter? The corridors back at DRIE were abuzz with reports of the standing ovation. News travels fast—faster still at government water coolers. But what was important to me was not the enthusiastic audience response per se, but what it told me about the tourism industry: I was onto something, and the industry hungered for leadership. I was determined to provide it.

Fortunately, I got along extremely well with the top officials at Tourism Canada. The assistant deputy minister for tourism (the highest-ranking DRIE official within our own subministry) was Tim Reid. As befit a former Rhodes Scholar, he had a strategic mind and was the brains behind the draft tourism strategy I inherited. In a sense, we were both policy wonks. But, for my part, I intended to ensure that any policy from our shop was rooted in the real world—the world I was eager to attract to our country's shores. Tim was delighted that I had embraced the draft, and he was not at all bothered when I told him that I intended to reshape it. "Minister," he said, "we officials are going to have a hard time keeping up with you. But we're eager to try." I don't think either of us appreciated at the beginning how exhilarating or how successful our "time in the ring" together would be.

The first thing I had to do was rewrite the strategy. Years of working summer jobs at hotels, including my family's two small ones in Charlottetown, had given me some background in tourism as a college student. Admittedly, not a lot, and that had been quite a while earlier. But I hadn't slaved for Stanfield and Symons without learning how to navigate unfamiliar policy waters—and, if necessary, to fake it. A full column on the subject written by journalist L. Ian MacDonald (later Mulroney's speech writer) in the *Montreal Gazette* captured the essence of the challenge I faced. He noted that the draft strategy had said that Prince Edward Island—*my* province!—had little potential for growth in foreign tourism. Apart from being dead wrong, that statement with my signature on it would have been my own death warrant back home—politically and almost literally—given that tourism is PEI's second-largest industry, behind only agriculture. Now, an official federal government policy document draft was dismissing a major component of this industry outright. It was like saying that mining was unimportant to northern Ontario—or husbands to Zsa Zsa Gabor and Elizabeth Taylor. And some people wonder why regional alienation plagues the country! So, the relevant statement, quoted by MacDonald, became from my pen: "Given Prince Edward Island's geographic characteristics (deep red soil, magnificent beaches) and world-famous food such as Malpeque oysters, not to mention the fame of its heroine, Anne of Green Gables, especially in countries like Japan and England, the Island could enjoy much greater success as an international drawing card."[1] This was not priceless prose, for sure. But it was a heck of a lot better than writing off a PEI industry, including its fast-growing Japanese market, so vital not only to Islanders' economic future, but also to their traditional cultural identity and sense of self. Today, many Island restaurant menus are written in Japanese—not just English and French—reflecting the huge growth in the numbers of Japanesse tourists in the province over the years since the spirit of the strategy was followed, albeit not necessarily based only on it. And so it went with the rest of the draft—rewrite, rewrite, rewrite. Then it was finally done. "Hmm, not bad. Not bad at all," I thought. "I can run with this." And I did.

To fine-tune the strategy, I travelled the length and breadth of Canada, including the northern territories. I consulted everyone in the industry interested in participating in this consultative process. Many hundreds did. It wasn't as though I would have been missed as a target in the Commons. At one point, though, the so-called Liberal Rat Pack attacked me for including my headshot in newspaper and magazine advertisements for public meetings. Just wasteful and costly "self-aggrandizement," they charged. But I was able to respond truthfully that the photo idea had not been mine, but the advertising agency's; my mug shot had tested well in focus groups. Besides, I said, the department had won a Clio Award for advertising excellence in this connection. I heard no more about the "scandal," which dried up faster than a negative in a photographer's darkroom.

When Cabinet approved our tourism strategy, with no opposition and little debate, we released it to the media and public under the title *Tourism Tomorrow*.[2] The document garnered a surprisingly large amount of attention. It received, for example, front-page coverage and a glowing editorial in the *Globe and Mail*. My photo—no controversy or phony scandal this time—appeared on the cover of many industry trade publications, among them the January 1985 issue of French-language *Marketing Voyages*. Its cover featured not only my smiling face, but also a big bold caption in red letters against a black background: "Tom McMillan—*un ministre prêt à collaborer*." That was exactly the message I was eager to communicate. Clearly, the message was penetrating in both official languages.

The attention the tourism strategy gained initially, both within government and without, was partly due to a pre-release mini-scandal—this time, a real one of sorts. The stylized drawing of skiers on the cover had appeared to show male skiers in a state of—how to put this delicately?—"sexual readiness." The Tourism Canada point man for the document's distribution was Doug Fyfe, a rakish newcomer who, whatever his age (probably early thirties), exuded the mischievous demeanour of a mature but insouciant teenager. Doug was not a garden-variety civil servant. I especially respected and liked him. Sheepishly, he phoned me at my home on the Island at 7:00 A.M. from Ottawa to reveal the unintended graphic misfire. "Well, the snafu will certainly boost sales!" I responded. I found the whole thing funny, and was not at all annoyed. I learned later that my sanguine response was widely appreciated within the department. Before long, the story went national, mostly for its humour quotient. Tracked down in Ottawa by the CBC's Wayne Collins, I was asked, in an interview on his daily early-morning public affairs radio show from Charlottetown, where the offending graphic designer was now. I said, with my best *Laugh-In* inflection, implying he had either committed suicide or fled the country—"We *donnnnnnn't* know!" All copies of the "porno" cover were destroyed (though I myself still have an original), and replaced with a family-rated version. "Sales" of the document were brisk. All the while, the controversy spawned an industry of potty humour whenever and wherever two or more people congregated throughout the government, especially at DRIE, which was technically the publisher. "Will that be hard cover or soft cover?" got my vote for the funniest. At least, nobody was ignoring what we had produced. Soon, people began to notice what was inside, as well.

Public awareness of the strategy was helped by the fact I was learning how to communicate its main message in ways that captured media attention. The *Globe and Mail*, for example, featured on its front page an article quoting me as saying, "The problem with Canada's tourism industry is that our country is perceived around the world as a land of magnificent outdoors but with no place to boogie." My officials presented me with a montage of editorial cartoons the *bon mot* had unleashed. One of the most hilarious, in Saskatoon's *StarPhoenix*, featured maple leaf–donned beavers on a mountainside wailing with exaggerated teardrops, "We ain't got no place to boogie."

# Brand-Name Marketing

The more serious thrust of *Tourism Tomorrow*—building on the idea Charley had fed me—was that tourists are drawn to a foreign destination because of its brand-name attractions, not necessarily the destination itself. People feel their lives would be incomplete if they didn't experience those attractions for themselves at least once. Travellers are drawn to world-famous and easily recognized attractions whose images they can proudly send on "Wish you were here" postcards to friends and family back home. The basic problem with our tourism marketing, I said, was that it was "too democratic."

When I was minister, the federal government spent about $30 million a year to promote Canadian tourism abroad, equivalent to about twice that in today's dollars. Since 1995, Tourism Canada, in effect, has operated as a Crown corporation—it's called the Canadian Tourism Commission—which reports to the minister of industry. Meanwhile, in 1985, my shop had the largest advertising account in the country; by contrast, the US government's account to promote American tourism abroad was only the seventeenth-largest in that country. Our national government, however, did not want to offend any part of the country or any person or group whose tourism product was not featured by name in our advertising. Tourism Canada, therefore, promoted no names at all. Everything was generic, and treated equally and, consequently, boringly: a beautiful lake, but not *Lake Louise* by name; a great hotel, but not the *Château Frontenac* by name; a world-class ski resort, but not *Whistler* by name. There were no stars. Everyone was in the chorus line—and in the back row, to boot. That had to change, I insisted. I thought we needed to rethink many other ways we marketed Canada to the rest of the world. It infuriated me, for example, that Finance Department officials would not allow Tourism Canada to mention in tourism marketing targeted to the United States the substantial advantage our closest neighbours would enjoy by spending their premium dollar in Canada. The officials said it would undermine confidence in our then already-weak currency. But this kind of closed thinking was part of the reason our currency was weak in the first place. I was not in the portfolio long enough to win that battle. The calcified thinking among some officials at Finance paralleled the status quo–locked mindset at External Affairs that Sinc Stevens faced concerning the Turks and Caicos Islands. For us new Mulroney Cabinet ministers, it was like trying to quickly turn around an ocean liner in a narrow strait to avoid colliding with an oncoming vessel: the will far exceeded the way. Such is what happens when a country is run too long by one political party, as Canada, to that point, had been since 1935 with only brief interruptions by Diefenbaker and Clark. Current thinking becomes conventional wisdom, which becomes orthodoxy, which becomes almost holy writ—dangerous to challenge, difficult to change, and impossible to replace.

"We should not rest until everyone in the world wants to visit Toronto's CN Tower," I said. "Toronto is a beautiful city, but there are lots of those around the globe. We have to create a world demand to see, not just our largest beautiful city, but the tallest free-standing structure on the planet." I drove home that kind of message across the country. I argued that, if we could attract Japanese to Green Gables in Cavendish, PEI, we would increase the chances of getting them to visit a generic attraction while in the neighbourhood. "We can't, however, start and end with generics." I stressed: "We have to draw foreigners to our shores in the first place. And sexy brand names are the way to do it. Generic advertising doesn't cut it in a world that demands

Calvin Klein jeans, not overalls. What's more, we can't be, in the eyes of the world, only a country of moose, mountains, and Mounties." That last choice of words generated yet more headlines. And more cartoons! "Let's sing to the world the praises of our world-class cities—by name," I urged. When I said Canada should shamelessly exploit its French character, the *Globe and Mail* saluted me for it, but said we should do so not shamelessly but "with enormous pride." They were dead right to set me straight. At the news conference releasing *Tourism Tomorrow*, I held up a generic Tourism Canada poster of a beautiful Canadian beach, and challenged reporters to name it. Not one could, not even Alan Holman and Mike Duffy, two first-rate CBC broadcasters. The beach was Cavendish—in PEI. Their own home province! Point made.

As helpful as Charley was with the original "brand-name" concept, he did unwittingly help set a trap for me early in my proselytizing on the subject. Soon after I was appointed tourism minister, my main messages started to gain media traction. One of my points was that Canadians should better appreciate their own country's tourism destinations and attractions, not just those of other countries. My twin told some media contacts of his that he found this point mighty precious coming from me. "Tommy is the biggest beach whore in the country!" he said with characteristic bluntness. "Flash under his nose an airline ticket to a hot beach in winter and he's on an Air Canada flight before you can say 'Fort Lauderdale'." Hmm, maybe true, even if exaggerated. But, to say the least, the revelation was not helpful. In a live on-air studio interview I gave to a local Ottawa radio station, the reporter said: "Minister, your twin brother says you're a beach bum [he cleaned up the language] and you travel to Florida all the time for sun and surf. And your boss, Mr. Mulroney, and his wife spend their vacations in Palm Springs." Then the coup de grâce: "Sir, aren't you a hypocrite to insist that Canadians spend their tourism dollars in their own country rather than abroad?" But I had an answer. I said the point isn't that Canadians should refrain from travelling outside the country. "Canada has a cold climate and Canadian winters are long," I conceded. "It is only natural for us to want to enjoy a break in midwinter in warmer climes." Rather, the point, I stressed, is that "We need to attract more people from around the world to our shores, not try to prevent our own people from visiting theirs. Two-way commerce is what international trade is all about. And tourism *is* trade." As I left the studio, the interviewer caught my eye, waved, and said, "Good point, Tom. I agree with you." I soon found a lot of other Canadians did, too.

A strategy can be only as effective as the people who execute it. Just as soon as my appointment as tourism minister was made public, friendly voices in various provincial capitals told me how much they detested the Tourism Canada official nominally in charge of our marketing. They thought him a "pompous ass," as one put it. The official under fire was a real dandy whose high opinion of himself was exceeded only by how far off the mark he was in his self-assessment. This official was, to say the minimum, ineffectual. He was, however, charming and witty in an Oscar Wilde–flamboyant sort of way. The trouble was, I didn't need a "nothing succeeds like excess" personality to coordinate our marketing efforts with those of our provincial and industry partners. Required, instead, was a "screw it, let's do it," gung-ho type. I, therefore, asked the assistant deputy minister at DRIE to transfer "Dorian Gray" to a position outside Tourism Canada better suited to whatever he was better suited for. I also asked that official to help me recruit someone better qualified for the marketing job and, equally important to me, more acceptable to our collaborators. I had in mind a marketing specialist whom provincial officials and industry leaders would not only respect as a professional, but also want to help as a colleague.

This "deputy to the deputy" who I hoped would execute the plan listened to my plea, but he looked less enthusiastic than a patient undergoing a root canal without an anesthetic. In the face of his apparent resistance, I said, in my most non-threatening voice, "If this can't be done within the department, I will have no choice but to discuss it with the prime minister." In full feline-under-attack mode, my interlocutor all but arched his back, hissed at me, and bared his claws. And then, with the inflated sense of self-importance characteristic of the Tourism Canada official I was trying to replace for that very reason, he shot back: "This would not be the first time I have said no to a prime minister of Canada." For one brief moment, I felt like I had on my shoulders the full weight of the PC Party's having been out of office, in the face of Liberal hegemony, for all but a few months of the previous two decades. The two tomcats having deposited their scents to establish territoriality, the real "Tom" got his way with nary a loss of fur or flesh. The marketing official was removed, a competent one installed, and the cat house made happy all around. Thereafter, the senior DRIE official in question and I worked congenially and constructively together, albeit with appropriate feline caution in light of the back-alley fight. Years after I departed politics, that official and I encountered each other in a gas-station convenience store in a remote part of New Brunswick. We locked eyes briefly, registered mutual recognition, exchanged hardly a smile or nod, uttered no sound to each other—not even a hiss, much less a meow—and went our separate ways. Cats, not just elephants, have long memories.

Norman Atkins and Hugh Segal, principals of Camp Associates, which held the Tourism Canada advertising account, agreed with the new marketing approach I was touting. They did a lot of creative work to sharpen its execution. The prime minister called me at home only once when I was tourism minister. I was on the Island at the time, right after my appointment. Mulroney phoned to tell me that Camp Associates, which had done the main advertising for the PC Party's historic 1984 election landslide, would have to get the rich Tourism Canada marketing contract. When in government, the Liberals had always awarded the same account to their party's advertising consortium, "Red Leaf," without competitive bidding. So, there was no political hay for them to harvest against us. For their part, the media generally accepted the practice as standard. I told the prime minister that I had always admired Camp's political advertising over the years in the Maritimes, that I thought the agency had done superb work for us in the recent national campaign, and that I had already decided to give the account to Camp. For the record, I said, "This conversation has not happened." No one ever raised the matter.

Together, Camp Associates and my own team at Tourism transformed Canada's salesmanship to the world. A large part of its success hinged on our government's investing, through DRIE, tens of millions of dollars to upgrade the product—for example, ski-lift facilities, après-ski services, and on-site accommodations at ski resorts. Our ski hills are among the best in the world, but, in the big leagues, our on-site facilities and services were among the worst. In Quebec alone—through federal-provincial cost-sharing, paralleled with all other provinces—we earmarked $50 million, matched equally by the province, to enhance the tourism product. Much of it was for recreation, especially skiing. Towards the same end, as environment minister later, I obtained the funds to completely redevelop Green Gables at the Cavendish National Park on PEI's North Shore. I was to learn that tourism and the environment are as inextricably linked as a beach is to its ocean. An advertising adage says, "The worst thing one can do with a bad product is advertise it well." Our product *was* good.

And yet, it had to be made far better to compete with the rest of the world. The country faced a $2.2-billion-a-year deficit in world travel receipts. Our country's share of world travel had plummeted by half in the previous decade. Canadian tourism was then an $18-billion-a-year industry, employing 600,000 people directly and thousands more indirectly in some 61,000 enterprises. The stakes were enormous. I was determined to do all I could, and for as long as I could, to increase those stakes—in the best of all ways. With each passing day, I was converting ever more people, both within and without the government, to how I saw it could be done. The prime minister had originally seen Tourism Canada as a vehicle for achieving a political objective: PEI's representation in Cabinet. Now, he started to see the portfolio as both an instrument to fortify the government's economic record in an important industry and as a political asset for the party he led.

And yet, for me, the stench of scandal was hitting dangerously close to home. Among the three original Mulroney government ministers at DRIE—Sinc Stevens, the overall boss; and his two junior ministers, André Bissonnete and me—I was now the only one left standing in the ring. I was determined to remain squarely on my feet.

# Staying Out of Trouble

Any Cabinet minister can easily get himself or herself into political hot water from either flawed judgment or simple bad luck. As often as not, perception, rather than reality, shapes the contours. Rarely is moral turpitude the principal, let alone only, reason for political scandal. If he or she does something stupid or ill-advised—set aside, criminal; that's taken for granted—the results can hurt the prime minister and his government, potentially irreparably. Typically, it is the symbolic things, and not the substantive ones, that trip one up.

As my reputation and profile rose in the Tourism portfolio, increasing numbers of hotel owners or managers wanted me to stay in their biggest and most luxurious suites while an overnight guest on government business. All I really wanted, however, was a comfortable bed and a shower with a strong water stream. I didn't need a Jacuzzi tented with flowing drapery and hooded with a crystal chandelier seemingly absconded from Versailles. Much less did I require enough bedrooms for a harem and more clothes racks than a department store warehouse. Besides, in the maze of drawers and closets, I was forever leaving behind personal belongings upon checkout. Most of all, I was worried about the possible headline: "Tourism minister sticks government with $2,000-a-night hotel tab." It didn't matter that the hotel rate charged was typically nominal—sometimes below that for a standard room, if the suite wasn't altogether complementary—just as the fine print always gets lost among the headlines. Accordingly, I issued a ministerial order to both political staff and departmental officials for all my future travels: no more grand hotel suites with posted daily rates higher than most of my constituents would pay monthly on their mortgages. I said I wouldn't check in if the room were bigger than a studio suite, except when a larger one was needed for meetings and news conferences and media interviews. When a snafu occurred on one particular occasion, I switched my deluxe suite with a senior official's more modest accommodations. And then, I ensured any trace between me and the original reservation was erased. What some people would do for love, I did to keep out of trouble.

The last time I allowed anyone to check me into a luxury hotel suite as tourism minister was early in my time in the portfolio. It was for my remarks in Nashville, Tennessee, at an enormous convention of the North American Bus Association, a mega-trade association for US and Canadian motor coach operators and tour companies. It is one of the world's biggest annual conventions. I was booked into the Opryland Resort and Spa, minutes on foot from the Grand Ole Opry. The hotel, with 2,281 rooms and suites, was more than ten times the size of the largest hotel in PEI. And the suite assigned to me was the biggest and most luxurious in the entire hotel. The posted nightly rate was $2,300 in 1985 dollars (add at least another grand to that now). I recall my department was charged $145 a night. Still....

Media headlines about a politician's or a department's spending habits can markedly misrepresent the true facts. A Cabinet minister does not live exclusively in the world of reality, but also in that of public perception. A minister who acts otherwise can soon find himself or herself outside Cabinet and even outside public life. My own vulnerability in Nashville got steadily more menacing, to wit: The Bus Association invited me to be the honoured guest at its convention's official opening ceremonies, a musical gala more spectacular than anything I could ever have imagined. The climax was Lee Greenwood's performing his "God Bless The U.S.A." With the audience's jingo juices pumped to overflowing, a giant American flag—with stars as big as disco globes and stripes as big as fashion runways—descended from a stratospherically high catwalk, completely backdropping the mammoth stage. Americans sure do know how to put on a show—and to show the flag! Literally. As if not to be outdone, at this very moment, Canadian delegates en masse marched in, Olympic–parade style, with the flag of each Canadian province and territory held proudly aloft by a standard-bearer no doubt carefully chosen for the honour. As PEI's flag passed by, I thought: Not bad for little PEI—one of the most beautiful flags of all, and an Islander the guest of honour! All this happened almost two thousand miles from Charlottetown at a convention with more delegates than that hometown of mine had residents.

While returning to Canada on a government jet, no less, I reflected on the grandiosity of it all. And I asked myself, How would any of this read if reported, with me almost literally at centre stage, on the front page of the *Globe and Mail* or—worse for me at home—in the Charlottetown *Guardian*? It was then that I made my "no more grand hotel suites" pledge. I also decided not to use any more government jets unless absolutely necessary. And I would go easy on the "honoured guest" status at mega-events featuring pagan pageantry. The only exception I made to the no-suite rule was at the Banff Springs Hotel. It was part of a national park, and the general manager became a personal friend whose feelings would have been shattered had I not occupied his hotel's finest space. I did not see myself as "holier than thou," but, had more Mulroney Cabinet ministers asked themselves the basic question, "How would this look if...?" the government would have had a lot fewer scandals—real or just apparent. The dangers that lurk in politics are not exclusively in what you do, but also in what adversaries or critics can credibly say you are doing or have done when, despite appearances, the truth might be utterly otherwise. Politics is all about public perception. Both of my DRIE colleagues, Sinclair Stevens and André Bissonnette, were exonerated by an independent, non-partisan judiciary. In Stevens's case, the findings of a judicial board of inquiry into the minister's alleged conflicts of interest (the Parker Commission) had compelled him to resign from Cabinet. But, upon appeal, the Federal Court found that the Parker Commission had not only far exceeded its authority; it had also seriously erred on key points of the law. Following my trip to Nashville,

I decided not to take my own chances with eventual due process regarding any potential scandal that might ensnare me. Erring on the side of caution became part of my business model. I was determined that no spending scandal would flush my own career and reputation down the latrine. I would forgo both the reality *and* the appearance of ostentatious self-indulgence.

————

Most Canadians do not appreciate how much sheer knowledge their elected officials accumulate while in office, particularly at the highest levels. If a minister takes his or her job seriously, being in the federal Cabinet is an intense learning experience. The office holder works punishingly long hours, travels nearly all the time across the country and sometimes abroad, meets a huge array of interesting and well-informed people, continually studies detailed briefs on issues or problems, and is regularly briefed in person by officials or staff about every imaginable situation, even if sometimes only about schedules and agendas and concerns of locals for the next trip or meeting. The incumbent works with professionals, whether bureaucrats or staff or colleagues, who are, in most cases, bright and well educated and trained and specialized in one field or another, sometimes several. From the time I was a boy growing up in PEI, I was fascinated by tourism and tourists. Introduced to the industry early in life at my family's Dundee "Motels" and through summer employment at the Keppoch Beach Hotel, now, as Canada's tourism minister, I was finding my education soaring from kindergarten to post-doctoral fellowship virtually overnight. The following two experiences—the first from Banff, the second from my hometown, Charlottetown— say, as well as any other vignette could, "Welcome to my world." Every new day as minister brought me fresh insights into the fascinating world of tourism, and rendered me steadily more competent to navigate through the industry's challenging waters. Sometimes, what I learned were the nuts and bolts of the vessel that did the plying. I soon discovered this was the best way to understand what that hardware was holding together and, therefore, how to steer the ship most safely to shore.

Ivor Petrak was one of the most colourful and interesting men I have ever met.

He was general manager of the Banff Springs Hotel and vice-president of Canadian Pacific Hotels, Mountain Region. An eastern European with an elegant Slovak accent, Mr. Petrak was the quintessential hotelier of the Old School. Born in Czechoslovakia in 1922, the young Petrak became a lawyer in Prague, but he left law to train at the famed Swiss Hotel School, in Lucerne, to enter the accommodations business. This resourceful Slovak was an imposing, distinguished-looking, broad-shouldered man who, over the years, became one of the most famous and respected hoteliers in the world. He managed hotels and resorts from France to Switzerland to Monte Carlo to the Netherlands to the Bahamas to the United States. And, as of 1971, he was now managing the *grande dame* of the Canadian Pacific Railways hotel chain, the Banff Springs Hotel. That splendid edifice is a five-storey, two-winged, 600-room castle disguised as a hotel at the confluence of the Bow and Spray Rivers on the majestic side of Mount Rundle. Built in 1888, the hotel was greatly expanded between 1910 and 1928 and made a year-round operation in 1969.

For Ivor Petrak, no hospitality detail was too small to demand perfection, no guest too ordinary to merit his personal charm and attention. And, as it turned out, no visit of mine was too short for him to throw his hotel into highest gear. For whatever reason, Mr. Petrak liked me from the start, even more than he did anyone else who ever passed through his front door. That was his magic: he made everybody feel such a way. But not everyone got to stay in the hotel's "Queen's Suite" every visit—again, the exception to my no-suite rule—as I did, both when I was tourism minister and after I moved to Environment. In the latter, I headed national parks, of which the Banff Spring Hotel was a part—and the crown jewel. Needless to say, my stay was at the standard government rate for an ordinary room; $2,000 a night might have caused problems. The regal suite was a sprawling, multiroom opulence. It included: a private elevator; a large kitchen; a butler's pantry; a fully stocked bar; a library, books and all; a number of bedrooms, among them the huge master; a couple of bathrooms, one with a Jacuzzi; a Steinway grand piano; and enough crystal chandelier lighting to illuminate Paris. Most important of all, the Queen's Suite had its own tower and outside promenade with a breathtaking view of Mount Rundle above and the Bow River below. I say "most important of all" because it was not always thus. That fact was to shake the world of this proud hotelier of the Old School—and of considerable sensitivity as well.

During one of Queen Elizabeth II's several stays at the Banff Spring's Hotel, Ivor Petrak escorted Her Majesty and His Royal Highness Prince Philip, Duke of Edinburgh, to their suite. The suite was not the one just described, but it was the hotel's grandest at the time. Even at the best of times, the prince is given to a type of insouciant humour that borders on rudeness. As minister, I myself experienced that same trait first-hand on the many occasions I would subsequently deal directly with him, as I discuss later. People who know Prince Philip well, including Tom Symons, have told me that his particular brand of grating and unsettling humour is rooted in the wardroom culture to which the prince was exposed over his many years in the Royal Navy. At the Banff Springs Hotel, Mr. Petrak had a rude awakening, quite literally. When he escorted Her Royal Majesty and His Royal Highness to their suite, Prince Philip said to him: "Oh, you're not going to put us up again in this same old tired suite, are you? It doesn't even have a view of the river." As, indeed, it did not. Ivor Petrak was humiliated. This proud man, and even prouder hotelier, had been reduced to dust. Perfectionist that he was, failure that he thought he had been, this Slovak of the Old School decided on the spot never again to fall short as a professional, as a host, and as a man. He was especially eager never to do so a second time in the presence of two of the most famous hotel guests on the planet. Accordingly, Ivor Petrak contacted the president of CP Hotels, and demanded, and got, a million and a half dollars, a large sum then. With the money, he gutted and rebuilt the hotel's highest and largest and most majestic turret. And he transformed that turret into one of the most opulent hotel suites in the world—one fit for a queen, and even for the Duke of Edinburgh. More to the point, the new Queen's Suite boasted the best view of Mount Rundle and the Bow River money could buy. In the trade, we call it "making the guest happy." As minister, I myself was always happy to stay in the new Queen's Suite. Maybe, it was the view.

One night, when environment minister and no longer at Tourism, I arrived at the hotel well past midnight, hours after my intended and expected arrival. Mr. Petrak had ceremoniously lined up, and kept waiting to greet me, every single hotel employee from Prince Edward Island—all fourteen of them! I felt like a five-star general—if not a member of royalty—being asked to inspect the troops. In 1988, on the Banff Springs Hotel's hundredth anniversary, the Historic Sites and Monuments Board of Canada, which reported to me as environment minister, decided that, after much deliberation and with great regret, it could not designate and plaque the hotel as a heritage building: the original structure had been expanded and altered too much over the years to qualify. My periodic host and now dear friend, Ivor, was shattered—humiliated yet again, this time not by a prince, but by a precedent. I could not, and would not, overturn the independent board's decision. What to do? What I did do was discreetly consult Tom Symons, the board's wise chairman. And then, with his blessing, I struck my own ministerial plaque, hopped on a government jet, and flew to Banff, taking the bronze plaque with me. And I personally placed the handsome artifact on the Banff Springs Hotel on behalf of the Government of Canada and all Canadians. With the full authority of the Crown—the self-same Queen Elizabeth II, spouse of His Royal Highness Prince Philip, Duke of Edinburgh—I celebrated the hotel's magnificent architecture and exemplary hundred-year service to Canadians and the world in the presence of a beaming general manager and his entire staff. Among the staff celebrants were my fellow Prince Edward Islanders at the hotel. Sometimes, as I learned at the Keppoch Beach Hotel as a teenager, beyond a gratuity, a guest just wants to leave "a little something extra."

Following the installation of the plaque, Ivor Petrak hosted in my honour an intimate black-tie candlelit dinner in an elegant private dining room at the hotel. Seated to my right was the president of CP Hotels, to my left Mr. Petrak. Throughout the dinner, the hotel general manager regaled me with one story after another about colourful and scandalous or notorious individuals who had stayed at the various hotels and resorts he had managed in different countries over a long career. One such story involved a wealthy heir to a patent-medicine empire who had conducted an extramarital affair with a nineteen-year-old German upstairs maid at his palatial ten-acre estate on the St. Lawrence River in Ontario. The man, well into middle age, left his wife, married the maid, and was honeymooning at the Bahamian resort that Ivor was managing at the time. According to my *raconteur*, the maid, now a freshly minted bride, spent the entire honeymoon cavorting with handsome, randy young men much younger than her groom, whom she left unrequited both in love and physical attention. Mr. Petrak assured me that he was not fabricating this seemingly too-wild-to-be true tale. I assured my host that I believed his story—because I recognized the cuckold as my sister Eileen's father-in-law. Talk about six degrees of separation!

While on a cross-Canada tour consulting the industry about my ministry's proposed national tourism strategy, I met the CEO and president of Canadian Hilton Hotels, who was participating in a small private meeting of industry leaders I had convened. The man told me that his hotel chain had investigated buying the Prince Edward Hotel in Charlottetown (now the Delta Prince Edward), a 211-room, four-star hotel built by a local entrepreneur, Bernard Dale, a Czech immigrant. Dale had purportedly amassed a $50-million (net) real estate portfolio by acquiring office and residential buildings and then flipping them one after another in a hot market. Dale began with only a small apartment building in Charlottetown and, by the end, owned office towers in Montreal and Toronto and farther afield. As so often happens with ambitious and newly successful entrepreneurs, this real estate builder, developer, and speculator got in over his head by investing in something—in this case, the Prince Edward Hotel—outside his traditional comfort zone and expertise. Major League Baseball utility infielder Rocky Bridges said, "There are three things the average man thinks he can do better than anyone else: manage a baseball team, build a fire, and run a hotel." Bernard Dale was one such delusional man. When the real estate market chilled, Dale's hotel, already in trouble from having been overbuilt, caused his entire empire to crash, impoverishing him personally. His son Peter earned a

PhD in politics at Queen's University and was my closest friend while I did graduate work there at the same time as he. My friend became a partner with his father at a later stage in the latter's real estate career. The Hilton head told me that, with a view to buying the Prince Edward Hotel—then enmeshed in foreclosure-type proceedings with the Bank of Montreal—his engineers and architects had thoroughly audited the building. But the chain took a pass on the purchase because, he explained, the structure had been wildly overbuilt: the thickness of floors and walls were excessively beyond code, the public spaces and amenities were disproportionately large (not to mention unduly extravagant) relative to the number of hotel rooms required, and available, to support them, and too much money had otherwise been spent on "show," not enough on "revenue generation" (his exact words). The Hilton honcho told me that retooling the complex would have been prohibitively costly. Accordingly, Hilton Hotels, he said, could not foresee making a profit with the building "even if we were to purchase it for a dollar." It was yet another chapter in my tourism education.

The Halifax-based Keddy family once owned and operated the largest chain of hotels and roadside motor lodges in the Maritimes. Over the years, they had acquired certain formerly prestigious properties—for example, the Lord Beaverbrook Hotel in Fredericton, bought by the family in 1971, but sold in 1999. From time to time, the company upgraded some of its operations. But the Keddy name was synonymous throughout the region with budget—some would say "substandard"—accommodations. In 1999, after operating for thirty years, the hotel chain went bankrupt. As Bernard Dale's Prince Edward Hotel slid steadily closer to the same fate, threatening to topple his entire real estate empire, he and son Peter met with me in my Charlottetown riding office. Their purpose was to plead to have the federal government bail them out. Peter had contributed generously to my Hillsborough PC Riding Association and to my various election campaigns. And, again, he was a long-time friend. But the government was not in the business of rescuing owners of failed hotels, least of all from their own misjudgments. Sinclair Stevens, still DRIE minister at the time, would not have welcomed from me, or anyone else for that matter, an overture towards that end in the Dales' case. It broke my heart to have to say no to the father and son. The federal, PEI, and Charlottetown governments had all provided inducements to have the Prince Edward Hotel built. There was just no appetite among any of these governments to get more deeply entangled. Business scholars such as my brother Charley would say they were eager to "cut their losses."

After the Dales lost control of their hotel, the provincial government, along with the Bank of Montreal, controlled its destiny. Sensing blood in the water, the patriarch of the Keddy family, Donald Percy Keddy, phoned PEI premier Jim Lee to offer to buy the hotel for pennies on the dollar. If Keddy had been a lawyer, he would have been called an "ambulance chaser." The premier shot down the hotelier's proposal faster than Bobby Orr used to slam a puck. The rejected suitor immediately phoned me in great distress at my Charlottetown riding office. He said that Premier Lee had told him, "We don't want your kind in the province." (In government, Jim Lee was capable of that kind of decisiveness—to say nothing of guts. The more profane, like my twin, would say "balls.") Keddy asked me to intervene with the premier on behalf of his company. "If Keddy hotels are not good enough for Premier Lee, then they're not good enough for me either, and that's the end of it," I responded. The phone conversation was not nearly as long as the odds that the premier and I would ever change our minds. Subsequently, Delta Hotels acquired the Prince Edward Hotel—for a bargain price, but not quite "pennies on the dollar." (The details were always obscured.

But I recall being told that Delta paid $5 million for a property that cost $35 million to build.) With such a prestigious and reputable international chain in charge, the hotel's future was now secure. Ever since the sale, despite Hilton Hotel's negative prognosis, the former white elephant has been a resounding business and community success. Unfortunately, the friendship between Peter Dale and me was a casualty of this sad saga. I likely would have felt as embittered as Peter, had our roles been reversed. I don't think Peter saw me as the villain, but I expect he thought I could have helped thwart whomever he did see as the villain, possibly the bank. I still consider Peter one of the finest friends I have ever had and his father one of the greatest contributors to community life in PEI.

I learned a vital lesson from Bernard Dale's sad business experience and from many other such exposures I had to the harsh realities of the hospitality industry while serving in the Tourism portfolio: ultimate success in this sector heavily depends on good timing and sheer luck. God-given talent and hard work, though essential, are not enough. It was a lesson that weighed heavily on my mind as I contemplated a future in Cabinet. Risk-taking is required in any business. But a maxim of sound investing is *never risk more than you can afford to lose.* Practising that principle demands the ultimate ingredient for success: sound judgment. As tourism minister, I also learned that the Dale case was not unique. Many a failure in the hospitality sector happen when someone like him starts or acquires some ancillary enterprise far removed from his or her core business or profession. This hard-knocks lesson is also relevant to politics. And that's where my own political insecurities in Cabinet clicked in at the time.

The well-known Peter Principle states that managers rise to the level of their incompetence.[3] There's ample evidence of that phenomenon among politicians, both the established and newcomers. Would any Cabinet promotion of mine prove the Peter Principle right? Over the years, countless Cabinet ministers who have excelled in one particular portfolio have failed miserably once transferred to another quite beyond their comfort level and ability. A classic case is Atlantic Canadian political titan and regional overlord Allan J. MacEachen. Pierre Trudeau was forced to move this long-time government stalwart back to his External Affairs portfolio in September 1982 after a two-year stint as finance minister. That's because the Cape Bretoner proved himself one of the worst overseers of the Canadian economy in the twentieth century. Almost from the day of MacEachen's swearing-in at Finance, his public image changed from being the government's wiliest old political warhorse to an utter incompetent. He was compelled to revoke his major budgetary and legislative measures, one after another, in the face of blistering attacks from the media, the parliamentary Opposition, powerful private sector interests, and the general public alike. MacEachen later became Opposition leader in the Senate, from which hole the perpetually conniving fox forced the Mulroney government to fight the 1988 election on the Canada-United States Free Trade Agreement. It was a colossal miscalculation outside Atlantic Canada. The Liberal sweep in that region was all that prevented Mulroney from virtually repeating his historic national landslide four years earlier—the Peter Principle, indeed. Back in the day, I asked myself: Were I to leave Tourism to head a major portfolio, would I, like MacEachen, prove this principle true?

I was enjoying the self-fulfillment, industry-wide support, and media attention I was getting as tourism minister. So I wasn't eager to be moved, even though, given how low I was on the totem pole, any change (except for a firing) would have had to involve a Cabinet promotion. I still hoped I eventually would have a chance to make an even greater contribution to Canadian public policy and community life through Cabinet based on everything I was learning in Tourism. How I could do this without my leaving that portfolio was less clear to me. In a sense, I didn't so much want to eat my cake and have it too as foolishly believe that no such choice needed to be made. With these conflicted feelings, I wondered if the prime minister—ever the political strategist—was taking note of my progress on his team, and would reward my efforts accordingly. I soon learned he was, and would. Two questions then loomed large in my mind: As a young man fairly new to government, did I have both the competence and maturity to leap to a much bigger Cabinet job so soon? Or would I pull a Bernie Dale or an Allan MacEachen, and find myself disastrously out of my depth in new waters—a Peter Principle victim?

# Chapter 18

# "PM, WE HAVE TO STOP MEETING LIKE THIS"

The Mulroney government was rocked by more than scandal, real or contrived. Incompetence and political stupidity also walloped us. No minister demonstrated more of both than Suzanne Blais-Grenier, Brian Mulroney's first environment minister. She was not an accident waiting to happen; she was an accident happening all the time. Could the Opposition have hoped for a better target? Could the gods have bestowed on the Canadian environment a worse trustee? For the prime minister, the answer to both questions was increasingly no.

Rarely does a Cabinet minister think the way to impress the prime minister is to undermine the power and budget and moral authority of the very department the PM appointed her to head and champion. But that is what Blais-Grenier not only did, but also sought to do. She succeeded marvellously. Within a year, the woman was fired from the Environment portfolio and demoted to the junior Ministry of State for Transport—appropriate, for she had pursued a superhighway straight to self-destruction. A minister should honour one rule above all others if she places a premium on survival: *never get yourself on the wrong side of your own portfolio.* A Minister of Forestry who projects he doesn't like trees is going to be felled darn quickly. For Blais-Grenier, she appeared to revel in not liking trees, or anything else that constituted the natural environment. Soon, the prime minister did not like anything Blais-Grenier was doing as environment minister; she was hurting the total image of the government, not just in the eyes of increasing numbers of environment-conscious Canadians, but also with the public at large. The government's standing in the polls had dropped by 20 percentage points (from 60 percent to 40 percent) soon after the election. The environment minister couldn't be blamed for all the government's loss of popularity, but, almost as bad, she symbolized the problem. Few ministers can make a government; it doesn't take many, however, to unmake it. The number in the latter category had been climbing steadily. Mulroney felt he had to reduce it.

Suzanne Blais-Grenier had infuriated environmentalists by slashing funding for key programs, such as wildlife. She said she might open the country's national parks and conservation reserves to mining and oil exploration and logging. She alienated every environmental group in the country, which traditionally depended on support from this quarter. She was not even on speaking terms with many of her top officials—except to shout at them. The minister and her deputy minister, Jacques Guerin, practically needed to be protected from each other by RCMP security. He hated what she was doing to the department and to the environment.

She hated him for trying to do his job. This poor beleaguered public servant soon sought to escape his agony in the arms of another department altogether. Meanwhile, Blais-Grenier had instructed her political staff to be wary of officials. The directive bred distrust between the two camps when such relative serenity was possible during rare truces from open warfare. Instead of taking advantage of the enormous brainpower and expertise and institutional memory within the bureaucracy to pursue a constructive agenda, the minister cut the legs from under these dedicated people at every turn. Morale was at its lowest level since the department had been established in the early 1970s. More so than any other federal department, Environment Canada attracted people, including public servants from other departments, because of their idealism. They were genuinely committed to making the planet a healthier place. They believed an individual working in concert with other like-minded people could make a difference. They thought public employees like themselves, not just non-governmental organizations (NGOs), should champion environmental principles and be custodians of Canada's natural heritage. They were proud to be part of a frontier department generally considered home to some of the best and brightest and most educated personnel in the entire government. They knew a lot, worked hard, achieved much, took pride in their cause—and got slapped down by their titular leader.

## From Tourism to Environment

The prime minister was distressed about Blais-Grenier. Everybody was. Who wouldn't be? The exception was the Opposition, which was licking its chops. The minister's maladroit ways—verbal, administrative, political—were the talk of Ottawa, both in the government and on the street. One had only to watch the PM cock his head in Blais-Grenier's direction whenever a question was directed her way in Question Period. It was a sure sign that, as with other ministers who worried the PM, he thought she might say something awful that would require him to step in. Brian Mulroney was not a micro-manager. He preferred to allow ministers to run their own shop. But he knew a minister capable of always making small mistakes could sometimes also make big ones. Blais-Grenier proved herself adept at making both. She had to go.

I was happy at Tourism Canada. I loved the portfolio. What's more, I thought I was gradually making a mark with the tourism industry. I had an especially strong working relationship with the principals of Camp Associates. Marketing was at the core of our ministry's mission, and certainly of our budget. So, getting right my partnership with them was vital. I appreciated their respect for my marketing ideas, even coming as they did from a non-professional. For their part, they valued the fact that I deferred to their technical and creative expertise, not to mention keen political noses, which had served my own boss so well in the previous election. I would have been content remaining exactly where I was for the rest of my Cabinet career. Let others fight one another for the next rung up the political ladder. I was self-fulfilled and having fun doing the job I had. Little controversy, lots of challenge, wonderful colleagues, an opportunity to help an industry in a fashion never before tried, a great arena to learn a vast amount of interesting things—who could ask for anything more?

Brian Mulroney, that's who.

My chief of staff, Les McIlroy, was a wise and cagey marketing veteran. Party titan Jean Pigott had directed me to him following my appointment to the Tourism portfolio.[1] In late August 1985, I knew wily Les was up to something. That something involved secreting me in a Carleton Towers Hotel room to await—and, as it turned out, await and await and await—a meeting somewhere with someone important. The "someone" turned out to be the prime minister, the "somewhere" his official residence at 24 Sussex Drive. There, Mulroney, when ready, was awaiting *me*. In the library, after short and perfunctory pleasantries, the prime minister sat in a mauve, high-back upholstered chair in a corner. I was directed to a much simpler padded chair pulled up for the occasion. The PM looked straight at me with an intensity I had never before seen and have not since. Then he said: "I want an environmentalist to head the Environment Department. Our government's environment record is unworthy of us. I need you to take over. Your job is to make it right. You have my full backing. Start immediately." I had learned from my short time in Cabinet (not quite a year now) at least this much: when Brian Mulroney set his mind on something, it was unwise to stand in his way. The only substantive issue we discussed was the concern I raised about Blais-Grenier's budget-slashing. I said I thought the cuts damaged Environment's capacity to operate and undermined employee morale. And I would want to restore most of the funding and all of the morale. He responded sympathetically, but curtly: "It is now your job to fight those battles in Cabinet." Translation: *Don't count on prime ministerial fiat; you own the department now.* He did tell me that Norm Atkins and Hugh Segal of Camp Associates had lobbied him hard to retain me in the Tourism portfolio. But Mulroney said that he told them that, while tourism was an important industry, it wasn't important to him politically. The prime minister quoted himself: "I need McMillan at Environment and that's the way it's going to be."

I was then out the door—and into the biggest challenge of my life. It all happened in twelve minutes. In one terse conversation, the prime minister's way became mine. After certain swearing-in and other formalities were completed elsewhere, I began "immediately."

I had been environment critic in Joe Clark's shadow cabinet throughout his time as Opposition leader—more than three years in total. I had gained credibility in the field, built a vast network of environmental activists, amassed a lot of technical knowledge, and become comfortable with the issues, near expert on some, especially acid rain. From the prime minister's residence, I went almost directly back to Tourism Canada headquarters in downtown Ottawa to say my goodbyes to officials and staff. There was sadness all around, much of it mine. I soon crossed the river to Environment Canada headquarters in Hull. Officials and other employees of every rank—from the deputy and assistant deputy ministers to members of the secretarial pool—packed its spacious Conference Room to greet me. Relief over Blais-Grenier's firing and my own appointment filled the air. I looked around the room at all the happy and smiling faces and thought, I can do this. No problem. Called upon to speak, I said that my first priority was to restore Environment Canada to its former glory. "The task has to begin with ensuring that the political actors respect and partner with the government's career professionals." The response was deafening. Any stereotype I might have harboured of boring and unfeeling civil servants acting like automatons was smashed with one sudden enormous explosion of collective emotion. It was as though, for my new partners, months of physical pain and pent-up anxiety had been expunged with a single dose of some recently invented miracle drug. I sensed that, to them, I was less the wizard who had produced the wonder drug than the drug itself. If Blais-Grenier had been the source of their pernicious condition, I was perceived—rightly or wrongly—as the antidote. As much as I regretted leaving Tourism, I reflected: This is a great place, too. I can do a decent job here. But it remained to be seen whether I could.

Among my first acts as the new minister of the environment was to call, from my riding office in Charlottetown, the head of every single major environmental NGO in the country. When I ran out of national organizations to contact, I went to my list of regional and provincial groups. Exhausted placing calls, but characteristically determined to soldier on, my trusty riding secretary Jeannette Arsenault at one point said to me: "Tom, if you place any more calls to environmental groups, you're going to get arrested for harassment." I harassed on. Soon, I learned that those few phone lines I had not burned up myself were being burned up by environmentalists I had phoned. Each was eager to boast to all the others, in shock, "Guess who *I* just had a call from! You won't believe it." They did, because, without fail, I had also called *them*. If there was any major environmental leader in the country—or any lesser one, either—I hadn't called, it was not for lack of trying. Either they had been abducted by aliens or had eloped with Martians and voluntarily run away to plan new lives on Mars. Jeannette was convinced that, had I been able to reach them there, I would have done so. She was not far off the mark.

## First Tests at Environment

My new journey began in earnest with efforts to establish my first national park.

Ellesmere Island is at the very rooftop of Canada. It's an immense oasis of spectacular tundra and Arctic flora and fauna and four-thousand-year-old archaeological sites. Though not threatened imminently from oil and gas exploration, the area was vulnerable. This enormous territory is now a full-fledged national park, the second-most northerly park in the world (after Greenland National Park) and our own country's second-largest (after Wood Buffalo). I would not have rested until the park happened sometime while I was minister. But I made it my top priority—not just at Parks Canada but in the entire department—the first week I became environment minister. Much progress had already been made on it by different governments and ministers over the years prior to my arrival. Thus, it seemed a manageable file with which to start.

Almost every major law or public program is typically credited to one specific government or to a particular minister perceived to have been responsible for sponsoring it, either in Parliament (if statutory) or in Cabinet (if by decree). This was true of the Mulroney government and me concerning Ellesmere Island. Rarely is one government alone, let alone a single minister, the architect of a major achievement. In our system, as in most liberal democracies, programs and policies evolve over time, step by step, in an organic process. Progress in a specific case usually begins humbly and only much later might produce a landmark. Along the way towards the final achievement, many different governments, of different political stripes, likely would have contributed to it, even if only the government in office at the end gets the kudos. A classic example is the *Medical Care Act* of 1966, Lester Pearson's signature legacy. He richly deserves the credit historians have given him for that milestone statutory program, but it had its genesis in John Diefenbaker's *Hospital Insurance and*

*Diagnostic Services Act* of 1957. Diefenbaker's pioneering health care law built the five main pillars that support Canada's medicare system to this day: public administration, comprehensiveness, universality, portability, and accessibility. But even in this case, the groundwork that culminated in the 1957 act had been laid by the previous government, headed by Louis St-Laurent. The law evolved. It didn't rebel. So it was with the Ellesmere Island National Park Reserve—renamed Quttinirpaaq National Park in 1999, when the territory of Nunavut was created. As minister of the environment, I was fortunate to play the leading role in creating five new national parks. Again, my experience is that, as in other policy areas, any new park has many parents, even if only one minister's name ends up on the birth certificate. In this case, the name happened to be mine.

Among "my" five new parks, I know of only one that would not have happened, either when it did or likely at all, had it not been for the dogged leadership of the government and prime minister and responsible minister of the day. That park is South Moresby, in British Columbia, the government was Progressive Conservative, and the prime minister was Brian Mulroney. I am fortunate to have been the responsible minister who, with the PM, fought tenaciously for this park till the very end. And I am very proud to have done so. These majestic islands, now part of what is called Gwaii Haanas National Park Reserve, were being so rapidly stripped of the natural features that qualified them for national park status and protection that, had we not acted when we did, it would soon have been too late. The same factor applies when most parks are created. The government often just does not have the luxury to complete a park through a slow-moving evolutionary process endemic to any huge bureaucracy, public or private. Such was the case with South Moresby/Gwaii Haanas, which was a different kettle of fish—and giant black bears and magnificent bald eagles and handsome ebony ravens and lush green moss and towering Sitka spruce and soul-soothing hot springs and….

Sometimes a minister just benefits from political serendipity. That was true for me, in spades—and in hearts, clubs, and diamonds—concerning Ellesmere Island. The government faced a crisis with the United States on a potentially explosive sovereignty issue (sketched in another chapter): the US icebreaker *Polar Sea*'s unauthorized excursion into Canadian Arctic waters. At a full Cabinet meeting, the prime minister, flanked by his most senior Privy Council officials, instructed every minister to explore urgent ways each could, through his or her portfolio, advance the government's full-court press to assert Canada's claims to ownership of the High Arctic territorial waters in dispute with the Americans (and later the Russians). I ruthlessly exploited the sense of urgency on the matter to smash a logjam in my efforts to get Cabinet to approve the establishment of the Ellesmere Island national park. Before the *Polar Sea* episode erupted, I was not able to get the time of day from Cabinet on the park issue. Now, I got not only the time of day, but also $5 million as an immediate down payment on the park. It had been almost impossible to get a plug nickel from Finance and Treasury Board in the austerity regime that ruled the day—and the week, and the month, and the year. In the new climate, all I had to do was say "sovereignty" in English, French, and Inuit, and I got my way. Now, I was able to get not just a plug nickel, but a hundred million real ones. I was on a roll—a money roll.

When I announced Cabinet approval and my follow-up plans to sign an agreement with the Inuit to make the park happen, I received huge media coverage: Canada literally planting the Canadian flag on an Arctic icefield. The *Globe and Mail*, for example, splashed the story, with a big black headline containing the word "sovereignty," across the top of page three. A teaser paragraph containing the same value-freighted word appeared on page one. I got even bigger sovereignty-related news coverage, including on both national and international TV, once I actually signed the deal with the Inuit on an ice shield in the High Arctic on the snowy afternoon of September 20, 1986, only a year after I had become environment minister. While up North, towards the same sovereignty goal, I designated the area's first National Wildlife Area, at Polar Bear Pass. I didn't so much kill two birds with one stone as save flocks of them with one Cabinet doc.

A successful end to the Ellesmere Island park issue would not have been reached nearly as soon, and certainly not with such massive attention, had the sovereignty issue—and, in particular, the park's place of national honour in it—been off the front pages at the time. I couldn't claim anything but good luck on that score. I did not cause the issue to land hard on the national agenda. I merely exploited an opportunity when it did, like an aimless wanderer finding a cash-stuffed wallet on the sidewalk. At the height of the sovereignty crisis, I received a number of windfalls through no special ingenuity of my own. The greatest was Ellesmere Island, but my department and I accelerated progress on several other conservation issues affecting the Far North. I was getting endlessly more credit for political leadership and perspicacity than I deserved on the sovereignty/environmental front: I was just going with the ice floe.

———————

Kenneth Colin ("K. C.") Irving established Irving Oil Limited in 1924, when only twenty-five. His company became a multi-billion-dollar empire of retail gas stations, oil tankers, refineries, and forestry and other operations around the world. It rivalled everywhere it operated the world-wide giant Esso/EXXON, on which K. C. had modelled his own resource company—right down to the competitor's red, white, and blue colours and logo. It all started with a tiny operation in Bouctouche, New Brunswick. Irving moved his operations from there to Saint John to expand across the Maritimes through the 1930s, to Quebec in 1940, to Newfoundland in 1949, and to Maine in 1972. By the time Irving opened a gas station and "Big Stop" all-purpose truck depot in Connecticut in 2011, the Irving company had a major presence throughout the northeastern US states to complement its ubiquitous eastern Canadian profile.

When old man K. C. Irving was in charge, Irving Oil earned its reputation as heartless, stingy, and environmentally insensitive, if not reckless. But even before K. C. died, when his three sons (Arthur, James, and Jack) began taking control, the company transformed both its corporate practices and public image. In many different ways over the years, it became, for the most part, a paragon of good corporate citizenship and citizenry. Indeed, Irving has now been for quite a long time more environmentally responsible than almost any other resource-based industrial giant in the world. In 1977, Irving became the first Canadian oil company to offer unleaded gasoline at its retail outlets, well before I announced the Mulroney government's policy to outlaw this deadly metal in that fuel. In the late 1990s, Irving became the first oil company in Canada, and one of the first in North America, to offer gasoline with very low sulphur content, well before the Mulroney government acted on this front as well. It is one of the few energy companies in Canada to support the Kyoto Protocol on climate change, a cause that was dear to me, as an individual and as environment minister, almost a decade before there actually was an accord. One of the three Irving brothers, Arthur, has long been a power behind Ducks Unlimited. I would encounter him on site in hip-rubber boots, investigating the organization's progress as flocks of snow geese flapped about.

While minister of the environment, however, I found myself steeped in a major pollution controversy with the Irving empire in my own Charlottetown-area riding. On the banks of the Hillsborough River, on the southeastern fringes of PEI's capital, reside gargantuan, pastel-tinted gasoline storage tanks owned by Irving Oil. From their innocuous appearance, if one didn't know better, one would think the tanks stored pink lemonade. Unbeknownst to anyone but Irving insiders, however, the tanks leaked a quantity of gasoline dangerously close to the river and to the water table from which the city draws its drinking water. Once word got out, the company downplayed the quantity of gasoline disgorged from the tanks, but my Environment Canada officials knew otherwise. When I confronted the company about the spill—more as the local MP than as environment minister—Irving increased its estimate. Meanwhile, my officials, following further tests of their own, revised departmental estimates still higher. I was furious. I felt the company had not been honest with me or the community. I also worried the situation might get even worse, possibly out of hand. If that happened, I feared we would all have a catastrophe to manage. I also worried that, as before, the Irving company might try to mislead everyone, including me, about the true extent of the burgeoning threat and, in doing so, hamper, and maybe prevent altogether, a timely solution.

At the height of the crisis, I was scheduled to address the Charlottetown Rotary Club on a completely different matter at one of its weekly Monday noon luncheons. I decided to scrap my intended speech and, instead, lambaste Irving, not so much for the leak itself as for the company's apparent dishonesty about the magnitude of the problem. "For decades, Prince Edward Islanders have been among Irving Oil's most loyal customers," I ad libbed. "We purchased vast quantities of both motor vehicle gasoline and home-heating oil from Irving long before most other jurisdictions, especially in the US, even knew the company existed." Then I hit my audience with this: "The Irving family fortune started in small communities like our own. And now their reprehensible corporate behaviour threatens our drinking water, our health, and, if the situation worsens, possibly human life. We, their host communities and patrons and customers, deserve far better treatment from the company." That afternoon I returned to Ottawa from my riding. Within hours, Arthur Irving and his entire executive team were parked outside my ministerial office door, having flown on a company jet from Saint John, to address the steadily escalating media and public relations disaster my attacks were causing the company.

Cancelling all other commitments—including a scheduled private meeting with the prime minister, no less—I ushered the Irving honchos into my office, sat them down, and unleashed on them days of personal pent-up frustration and anger. For his part, Arthur Irving, who clearly had not been involved in the issue much before this point, put everything on the table. He revealed all the facts known to the company about the leak (my officials had been right all along); he committed himself and the company to taking every step technically possible to "set things right" (his words); and he promised to keep me directly informed from then on. True to his word, the company publicly released all the relevant information, capped the leak, cleaned up the affected areas, and ensured the river and water table remained in their original conditions. Arthur Irving was one capable and ethical corporate tycoon! More than ducks benefited from his environmentalism and wise leadership.

What this corporate leader knew, probably instinctively, is what politicians have come to learn the hard way ever since Watergate: it is not the problem itself that causes the most trouble; it's the cover-up. Crisis management experts—paid big money to help large corporations like Irving Oil handle public relations disasters—advise clients in a mess to follow two fundamental principles: reveal everything you know; admit everything you don't. Whether or not Arthur Irving was being professionally advised in such a manner, I don't know. But he acted exactly, albeit belatedly, based on those two principles. The worst—for Irving, for the community, and for me as local MP and environment minister—was thereby averted. To this day, I credit Arthur Irving for this constructive outcome, and for demonstrating how to act in a crisis. He is a wise and good man.

Without knowing anything about crisis management, I decided—I suppose, like Arthur Irving, intuitively—to "tell all I knew, admit everything I didn't" when my first and, as it turned out, worst national pollution-related crisis struck only days after my appointment as environment minister. It concerned what the media called "the Blob." The environmental threat in question was as ominous as it sounds. The Blob was Canada's first-ever "Pollution as TV Star," a "thing" discovered in the St. Clair River, which forms the international boundary between Canada and the United States, along which millions of people live, and which supplies drinking water for most of them. The waterway is an integral part of the entire St. Lawrence River ecological system, so the stakes were enormous. What was at play was the discovery of rapidly expanding globules of dark, dense, highly toxic, and certifiably carcinogenic perchloroethylene ("perk"), a colourless liquid used to dry clean fabric. By its very nature, the chemical absorbs everything within its grasp, including, in this case, any other toxic chemical leaked in the riverbed. The Blob was getting bigger and bigger, and darker and darker, and steadily more menacing, because the parental chemical was doing its job—absorbing like hell. In the process, the Blob became steadily scarier with every passing news cycle and ever more ominous for the Mulroney government and me—not to mention progressively more telegenic. TV newscasts, both local and national—and, increasingly, international—flashed underwater-camera images of the "creature" across TV screens. It was horrifying.

The problem, both scientifically and politically, was that the public, especially residents along the expansive areas directly affected, were demanding answers. But the scientists, and therefore the poor beleaguered federal minister of the environment, had no answers. Two overarching questions baffled us: Where did the Blob come from? Did it have friends? To find the answers, I mobilized, in concert with my provincial and US state counterparts, top experts from across Canada and around the world. Two possibilities were thought possible. The first was that the perk was slowly leaking from deep underground caverns into which toxic waste had been stored decades, even generations, earlier when nobody knew better than to do something so stupid. The second possibility was that the toxic chemical was leaking from either a single point source or from several associated with one or more chemical companies located along the St. Clair River. Experts thought the culprit was likely a major chemical company operating somewhere along the sixty-kilometre river flow between Lake Huron in the north and Lake St. Clair in the south. But they were not at all certain. And that fact alone was cause for the panic that growing numbers of officials and members of the public at large alike were feeling. Of these two possibilities—the cavern versus the point-source theories—the first was not only more serious, but potentially catastrophic. The second, though serious, would have been manageable. It was anyone's guess about whether the worse-case situation could be managed. Likely not—at least not easily. The drinking water and the very lives of millions of people on both sides of the border were held in the balance.

It is hard to imagine now, a quarter-century after the fact, the extent of the fear at the time, including in scientific circles. The issue dominated parliamentary Question Period for days on end. The prime minister and I were peppered with questions and demands for urgent action. The government's own MPs used this forum—usually the Opposition's preserve—to grill us. I typically spent about an hour being briefed by top departmental officials and political staff every day, during lunch, prior to entering this gladiators' arena. I would stuff my brain with every relevant fact and figure and suitable answer on the individual issues either they or I expected the Opposition to hit me with. Given how hot environmental issues were in that era, few other ministers—including, of course, the prime minister—would be questioned as often as I. Hardly a day would pass when I did not receive at least one set (the original and a follow-up), and the PM almost always redirected his own Opposition questions in this field to me. The Opposition devoted most of its time to the crisis and, therefore, to me—uncharacteristically, more out of genuine concern than in an effort to score partisan points. In retrospect, I believe the crisis released the best in everyone. I did not mince words. I said we were, in fact, facing a worst-case possibility—and that the toxic chemicals being found were cancer-causing. I told the Commons I had mobilized a crack team of experts to help me solve the crisis. Indeed, this team involved an unprecedented degree of cooperation, both scientific and political, between the federal and Ontario governments at all levels and between our two jurisdictions together and affected American jurisdictions.

Thanks to our dedicated multidisciplinary SWAT team of scientists and other experts, working around the clock, the mystery was solved: the perchloroethlene had not been seeping from underground caverns, as feared, but, rather, from a single source. The culprit was a large Dow Chemical plant in Sarnia, Ontario. The pipe discharging the perk was identified, repaired, and plugged, the chemical surge stopped, the river vacuumed, and the company hit with a major fine. And I, as lead player, was dislodged from the enormous sharp hook from which I had been precariously dangling for two months. I would not always be as fortunate on major issues, either in the House of Commons or with the media and public. But one thing I learned from the crisis, even if I did not consistently act on the knowledge: "Tell them what you know, admit what you don't." Throughout the crisis, I tried hard to be forthright with the facts, never downplaying the extent of the crisis. As Arthur Irving demonstrated in his crisis, honesty in such circumstances is not only the best policy. In politics, as in industry, to survive a crisis, it is also the only one.

# Environment and the Media

My relationship with environmental reporters was mostly good, particularly during the short honeymoon. I found most reporters on the environmental beat both committed to the issues and knowledgeable about them. They were not so much partisan as ideological, but that zealotry sometimes caused me to doubt their objectivity and fairness.

I was especially alarmed about the tight and cozy—and, I thought, perilous—relationship some environmental reporters (most of them Toronto-based) had developed over time with a tiny but obstreperous minority of Environment Canada scientists based at our major operations in that city. So fraught with danger was this relationship that my top officials and I worried that, if left unchecked too long, the problem would destroy the department's greatest asset: the credibility it enjoyed for scientific and intellectual rigour in protecting the country's natural habitat and treasury and, therefore, Canadians' health and overall well-being. A few of the offending scientists enjoyed being pursued by the media to the point where achieving public stardom eclipsed their willingness to do what they were being paid to do—serve. Leaking confidential government information, typically to win points with reporters for future consideration, was endemic to the game. Part of the game, too, was providing eminently quotable statements about matters not just within their specialties, but also on almost anything else in the environmental field about which they had opinions that interested reporters. It did not always matter whether those opinions were well informed. And yet, the quoted were cited as experts with the full authority of the Government of Canada. For their part, the reporters had, in these few scientists, a ready source of insider information and "authorities" whom they could liberally cite and quote to flesh out articles with minimal effort required of them. Such symbiosis between scientists and reporters bordered on professional malpractice by the ethical standards of both professions.

I was baffled by all this because it belied the professionalism that characterized most employees at Environment Canada, scientists and non-scientists alike. I drew great satisfaction from the warm working relations I had developed with my officials at all levels and across the country. As a non-scientist myself, I took particular pride in having done so with scientists. As a group, they were unfailingly helpful and loyal. One older scientist of great repute, for example, worked with me and two of my political staff from 8:00 P.M. until 5:30 A.M., literally through the night, on my major address as Graves Lecturer and Hoyt Fellow at Yale University in the spring of 1988. Ninety percent of the address was mined from his golden brain.

Environment Canada's Toronto office was central to the federal government's management of some of the most serious environmental challenges facing the country at the time—Great Lakes water quality, for example. For some purposes, the Toronto operation *was* Environment Canada. There, a miniscule group of scientists close to certain individual environmental reporters were making it increasingly difficult for the entire department to act as a team and speak with one voice on major issues of vital concern to the public. We could not collaborate with one another and communicate with maximum authority and credibility to the public in such circumstances. Freelancing sometimes undercut what even I myself was saying publicly about major environmental issues and federal government measures of the day, including on the floor of the House of Commons, based on departmental briefings. It was becoming almost impossible for me and my senior officials to devise and execute a coherent public information strategy on such issues as toxic chemicals. The measures about which we were attempting to communicate were themselves being hurt amidst the chaos.

No one was more outraged about this unprofessionalism within the department than other scientists there; they felt undermined by it. To protect Environment Canada's reputation as a source of reliable scientific information, to say nothing of the dire need I felt to assert my leadership, I had to address the problem head-on. The problem climaxed when, without appropriate authorization, the Toronto office published a document called *Storm Warnings*, containing inflammatory information about certain alleged—but by no means scientifically verified—human health and other effects of toxic chemicals. The Trudeau government had instituted specific guidelines that, no matter the topic, every division of the Government of Canada was expected to follow concerning any publication it planned to release in the name of the government. A publication of a scientific or health nature, in particular, had to be subjected to uncompromising multi-stage peer assessment, for which committees were established. The purpose was to ensure that the content met the highest standards of methodological rigour and technical accuracy, while being consistent with official public policy or expert consensus opinion. The Mulroney government, which embraced science as an athlete would sports, adopted the identical policy because it simply codified common sense.

The publication of *Storm Warnings* violated virtually every dictate of that policy. The publication had not undergone thorough peer assessment. Nor had it been evaluated in other ways required by the guidelines. The document could accurately be described as "rogue," for it lacked a chain of custody. *Storm Warnings,* seemingly out of nowhere, contained statements no more scientific than personal speculation and musings. Sections conflated the physical and social sciences, hard research and pop culture, rigorous analysis and social commentary. Environment Canada experts questioned entire parts on specific scientific and technical grounds. Intended as food for thought, *Storm Warnings* was a dog's breakfast. And yet, *Toronto Star* environmental reporter David Israelson treated the document as divine scripture. When Environment Canada decided to pull the document from circulation to protect the department's reputation for scientific rigour and reliability, Israelson attacked the decision as a conspiracy and cover-up. To him, the department—its minister, in particular—was trying to hide from the public nefarious secrets about the dangers that toxic chemicals posed to Canadians. He accused us of trying to protect the powerful chemical industry—as if it needed protection! We never were able to disabuse Israelson of his deep-dark conspiracy theory. No explanation of government policy or procedure governing the public release of such a document would tame his high dudgeon. Over many months, like the proverbial dog with a bone, he kept gnawing. Soon, Opposition MPs began pushing this reporter's cause in Question Period. Some became almost as dogged on the issue as he. When they first raised the issue in Parliament, accusing me of "muzzling government scientists" (Liberal MP Charles Caccia's words), I said this was not about freedom of speech, let alone of scientific inquiry. Rather, I argued, it concerned the need to ensure that, when a government scientist spoke with the full authority and credibility of the Government of Canada, he or she did so within his or her speciality, not just on a whim or from vanity. In the heat of Question Period, this was the only time Prime Minister Mulroney ever handwrote me a note. He motioned to a page, and asked the youth to deliver it right on the spot:

"Great answer, Tommy," the message said. I was dumbfounded by all the controversy about *Storm Warnings*. Departmental scientists not connected with the document were even more befuddled.

The unauthorized release of *Storm Warnings* convinced my deputy minister, Geneviève Ste-Marie, that the Toronto office was out of control and needed to be reined in. With my blessing, she made major changes both in personnel and in reporting arrangements, disciplined the main offenders, and served notice that future freelancers would be severely punished. The worst offender left his job with Environment Canada of his own volition. He started a company to develop and market a new technology for destroying PCBs—polybrominated biphenyls, highly dangerous, cancer-causing chemicals produced by human activity and, at the time, found in plastics used in many consumer products. Now on his own, he was free to say anything he wanted, about anything he wanted, and to whomever he wanted—pretty much what he had been doing all along as a renegade in our employ.

# The Conservative Party and Science

Throughout the time Stephen Harper was leader, the Canadian Conservative Party (not just while in government) turned its back on science—indeed, on evidence and objective facts more generally. This anti-intellectualism was eerily similar to that which the party embraced under John Diefenbaker's leadership, including when he was prime minister. The party's periodic flirtation with such a mindset weighed heavily on my own mind as head of the federal government department more reliant on science and overall intellectualism than any other—even Health and Welfare Canada (as it was then known). It could be truly said of Environment Canada, "Without science, nothing. With science, everything is possible." Yet, from the prime minister right down the line, the Harper government placed little stock in science, and its efforts to undermine federal science-based programs and muzzle government scientists led to protests across the country by the scientific community.

This fairly recent transformation in how Ottawa power holders viewed science was devastating the country in practical ways. Cases in the environmental field were of particular concern to me—but they were typical, not exceptional. Our national parks system and reserves, for instance, depend heavily on the work of scientists. This is a point I made to the Erik Nielson task force on government waste when successfully pushing back his efforts to gut funding for everything from the conservation of Parks Canada's precious cultural and heritage property to scientific research and demonstration projects required to protect wildlife and preserve Canada's special natural features—the very reasons national parks and reserves are established in the first place. In the spring of 2012, however, the Harper government slashed 30 percent of Parks Canada's operating budget and eliminated more than six hundred positions, nearly three-quarters of them physical, natural, or social scientists. It is a measure of how stupendously misguided the Harper Conservative government was about such matters that even Erik Nielsen would not have tried to do that much harm in the name of austerity or any other fiscal cause.

The Harper government, having eviscerated Parks Canada's science base, proved an equal opportunity destroyer. How else to explain why the axe fell on the National Round Table on the Environment and the Economy, the First Nations

Statistical Institute, the National Council on Welfare, and the Canadian Foundation for Climate and Atmospheric Science, "saving" the government a paltry $7.5 million in all? That's not just peanuts, but peanut shells compared to the immense value of all the work gutted. A previous Conservative government (Mulroney's) could proudly take much of the credit for the greatest single environmental achievement in North America since the cleanup of the Great Lakes: the Canadian-US acid rain program. The Experimental Lakes Area, a research station, produced critical evidence that helped stop acid rain in its tracks three decades ago. This agency has been responsible for some of our most groundbreaking research on lake-water quality. What could be more important to our country's environmental interests and, in particular, to our historic leadership in two areas of monumental progress? And yet the Harper government shuttered this operation at a time when its work remained as important as ever both to protect the gains our country had made and to ensure future progress. The closure saved the government a measly $2 million, but at a huge cost to the country's future. The unit in charge of monitoring emissions from power plants, furnaces, boilers, and other sources, for example, was abolished to save $600,000. Talk about penny wise and pound foolish! This is penny wise and our natural treasury foolish.

Just as foolish was the government's decision—against the advice of 625 fisheries scientists and no fewer than four former federal fisheries ministers of varying political stripes—to eliminate all regulatory scientific oversight of fish stock not deemed of "human value." As if that criterion makes any sense at all—certainly not to an Atlantic Canadian like me. When I was a boy growing up in PEI, everyone viewed mussels underfoot as ugly black beasts, unfit for human consumption. Now, they're considered delicacies and marketed around the world, including to the finest restaurants in Boston, as "Island Blues." The mussels are proudly identified, by brand name, as harvested in Prince Edward Island. My province is now better known in Boston and throughout the United States for mussels than for potatoes. Who could have predicted that outcome? On the Island, decades ago, well before my time, lobsters were considered so inferior a species that they were crushed and spread across the potato fields as fertilizer! For the same reason, Maine had laws to protect indentured servants and other labourers from having to eat lobster more than a certain number of days a week. Lobster!—the crimson seafood that one now has to take out a mortgage to order at any fine Boston restaurant. Yet the Harper government thought it knew what "human value" was?

Equally worrisome is what a "human-value" approach to managing natural resources said about the Harper government's evident lack of awareness of, and concern for, the value of biodiversity, the essence of the natural ecological balance on planet Earth. The need to maintain it is independent of the value any one living organism might or might not be understood to have to humans—presumably, for the Harper government, economic value. Some species discounted today not only might become the next delicacy tomorrow; they also could contain a particular feature (perhaps a gene) that holds the secret to the next great breakthrough in the search for a cure for cancer, Alzheimer's, diabetes, or other disease or condition that affects tens of millions of people around the world. Was all this wrong-headedness by the Harper government a product of ignorance or of not caring or of stupidity? I am at a loss to know which is worst. That government wreaked havoc across the scientific landscape, filling many different departments and divisions of government with the dead and wounded.

The Harper government's slashing of funds for science was decidedly *un*Conservative. That party—or, at least, its nominal predecessor—created the National Research Council when Robert Borden was prime minister. This creation is part of the party's rich policy heritage. No doubt, Sir Robert wept in the heavens when all the aforementioned was happening.

---

Whatever success I had as Canada's longest-serving environment minister (tied with John Roberts) was due mostly to one factor: my ability to work well with departmental officials at all levels, most of them scientists. I found that, to be effective, a minister of the environment has to either possess naturally or develop on the job the ability both to process complex scientific information and to work with the scientists and other experts who advise him (or her) and help implement the agenda. Few other federal departments require of their ministers quite this level of comfort with science. The minister must serve as the trusted public spokesperson on the various issues that arise within his orbit, in Parliament and in the country at large. In doing so, the office holder must employ, essentially, political, rather than scientific, skills. Scientists march to a completely different drummer. They act on principles and employ methods that have evolved over centuries. Uncertainty, for example, does not upset them in a way it might a policy-maker. Indeed, it is what spurs scientific research and invention and discovery. The very nature of science requires practitioners to communicate in highly technical—and, to the layperson, unintelligible—language. One term or phrase, which might strike everyone outside the relevant discipline as irritating jargon, can represent pages and pages of information or data that are common knowledge within that discipline. The credibility of scientists is real and unique, provided they stick to their knitting. When scientists stray beyond their expertise, they risk undermining the source of that credibility. A chaotic approach of the sort that characterized Environment Canada's Toronto office for too long while I was minister risks creating widespread public misunderstanding, undue anxiety and, in the worst cases, even panic.

Bringing order and predictability to the process, however, must not be a subterfuge for cover-up. The Canadian public sometimes needs to hear from the scientist herself, if only so everyone can be certain of getting the truth, not just some politically spun version of it. On occasion, government needs to trade off between due process and full disclosure; in which case, it must always err on the side of the latter. The exceptions are for public security or national defence or personal privacy or other demonstrably honest reasons covered by both the *Access to Information Act* of 1985 and the *Privacy Act* of 1983. *Storm Warnings* is a classic case of how *not* to manage government-generated and publicly funded science while honouring the taxpayers' right to access it. Politicians and scientists need to view themselves as partners in a common cause. But before that principle can be made real, there must be mutual trust between the two sides. Only then can Canadians at large have maximum trust in both the political *and* the scientific domains as far as the public sector is concerned. The Stephen Harper government fell far short of this ideal. Worse, it did not even believe that such a partnership was worthwhile, let alone necessary.

When a minister cannot be trusted, as few of the Harper government ministers could be on science, then the public will prefer to trust the scientist over the politician ten times out of ten. Political writers Linda Bridges and William Rickenbacker have noted that "trust is not only the irreplaceable basis of all communication but is also one of the more profound channels of connection between human beings."[2] Lack of public trust in politicians concerning science and politicians' hostility to either science or scientists themselves, within government or more generally, serves no good end, least of all the scientist's own best interests. The scientist needs the politician as a trusted and credible ally—above all to fight within the system to obtain the funding for scientific work. Surely, if a true conservative holds any tenet as pre-eminent, reverence for the natural environment ought to be it. Without respect for science, reverence for life and for the natural habitat that sustains it is mere sanctimony, to say nothing of political hypocrisy. Among all its many contributions to society, science demonstrates the myriad ways all of us can do our part to ensure life survives in a fragile ecosphere. Public awareness and understanding of climate change is but one area—albeit the most threatening—where science's role in advancing planetary survival is as indispensable as it is consequential. If respect for science—the key to sustainable development—is stripped from conservatism, what, pray tell, remains? One could then truly ask, as a God-believing person might, *Is that all there is?* For certain, it would not be much. To me, it would be nothing. In the "curse words" of one who truly believed in God, Helen Doyle, it would be "past talking about." To my mind, people of all political persuasions or of none at all can comfortably embrace this perspective. But it behooves the classic conservative—by definition concerned about the "whole," not just the "parts"—to do so as tenaciously as anyone. The Harper government fled from science as a swimmer would an approaching shark. But it was sound public policy—and, ultimately, the Canadian public—that got gored.

# Acid Rain and South Moresby

Although every issue I confronted as environment minister presented its own challenges and caused headaches, two in particular—acid rain and South Moresby—tested my mettle as no others did. Unlike with the Ellesmere Island issue, however, luck played no part in their successful resolution. Success required perseverance, hard work, and political courage, not least by the prime minister. I stress these issues in the several chapters that immediately follow for five discrete, but parallel, reasons. First, their successful outcomes now constitute significant parts of Brian Mulroney's record and legacy as prime minister. Second, the way Mulroney addressed them demonstrates how he handled most issues, no matter the substance or political stakes. Third, Mulroney's visceral responses to the two issues, as opposed to his political or partisan strategic actions, reveal a lot about who he is as a man and, therefore, what he fundamentally values—specifically, the kind of challenge for which he was prepared to throw his government into highest gear, take big political risks, deplete his political capital, and put his pride and reputation on the line, all for palpably dubious personal gain, but, potentially, to the country's enormous benefit. Fourth, I take greater pride in my own role in these two issues than in anything else I did while in Cabinet, setting aside measures that primarily benefited my riding or province. And, fifth, how the Mulroney government responded to the two issues—in fact, that it responded at all—shows the distance the PC Party had travelled on the progressive and enlightened road Robert Stanfield, with Tom Symons's help, had chosen for it a decade earlier.

# Chapter 19

# GETTING AN EARFUL

History has yet to get right how acid rain, once the country's most critical environmental threat, was wrestled to the ground and eliminated as both a national and a Canadian-US issue, as a serious challenge to bilateral relations, and, in particular, as the biggest impediment since the Diefenbaker-Kennedy dispute over nuclear warheads in the early 1960s to the ability of Canada and the United States to address shared problems while accommodating each other's policy priorities and political realities.

Brian Mulroney's management style was far different from what one might expect given his public image. The dogged way he pursued a successful outcome on acid rain demonstrated this fact in spades. For all his trademark charm and gregariousness, he was the most focused, goal-centred, and single-minded operator I have ever seen in action. My brother Charley once told me that he never saw Brian Mulroney act or decide anything outside a plan, even if the plan was clear only to Mulroney himself. My own experience with the PM's management style confirms that assessment.

In his first term, the Mulroney government's agenda was topped by two issues: free trade and acid rain. The resolution of both issues—to say nothing of the prime minister's personal credibility—depended on a partnership between the Canadian and US governments. I deal with free trade later. Concerning acid rain, it might be difficult these days for most Canadians, especially youth, to appreciate the political salience of the issue back in the 1970s, 1980s, and early 1990s, now that the problem has not been discussed since it was largely resolved almost three decades ago. But acid rain was a dominant issue in the Mulroney era, just as it had been most of the time Pierre Trudeau was prime minister. The acid rain problem alarmed not just environmentalists, but also anyone who had a stake in a resource-based industry—from tourism to the sports and commercial fishery to forestry to maple sugaring to agriculture. Even architecture and the built heritage were under siege from this lethal pollutant. Acid rain was affecting Canadians in every part of the country. The effects from Manitoba eastward to Newfoundland, on the ecosystem in particular, were considered especially alarming. The serious, and possibly deadly, impact of sulphur dioxide and fine sulphate particulates on human health would be demonstrated by scientists only later.

Generally, neither politicians nor the public at large are easily convinced that government needs to act urgently, or spend a lot of money, on most environmental problems. That's because the sacrifices and costs are immediate and tangible. By contrast, the negative consequences of not acting are typically felt later, often far into the future. So, people can too readily postpone dealing with such problems, if they don't ignore them altogether. Meanwhile, the lethal impacts of pollution in real time concern primarily scientists and the minority of the total population passionate and informed about them. For too many others, it's the old story: "out of sight, out of mind." Unfortunately for the environment, it can also mean "out of luck." For corporate polluters, the choice between instant gratification and long-term pain is even easier. If they don't spend the money required to check their waste—and that, essentially, is what pollution is—costs to them are minimized, profits increased. The costs to society at large, however, are not minimized.

The knee-jerk reaction of many politicians is to kick an environmental problem down the road. They think they'll suffer minimal, if any, political damage by doing so. Politics is not the art of the possible. It's the science of procrastinating about every problem except the unavoidable. By the time the Mulroney government took office, acid rain headed the country's list of the unavoidable. There was hardly a Canadian not immediately affected directly or indirectly by the scourge. Canadians may be lethargic about certain environmental problems, especially ones whose consequences appear longer term, if they appear at all. We might also delay action until we can no longer do so. It's human nature. But, throughout Canada decades ago, the toll acid rain was taking on almost everyone was as chilling as it was calamitous. The crisis could not be ignored, nor action postponed, either by government or by the general public. We Canadians are rightly proud of our natural heritage. It partly defines who we are. The country's "moose, mountains, and Mounties" stereotype isn't just a challenge to our international tourism marketing. Like most stereotypes, there's an element of truth to it. After all, Canada possesses a whopping 10 percent of the world's forests, for example. Our "naturalist" stereotype bespeaks something fundamental about us as a people: nature is beneath our feet, above our heads, and in our soul. When we think our natural habitat is threatened in the here and now, we respond. It was by acid rain and, true to our nature, we did.

The day I became Canada's environment minister, acid rain had already killed fourteen thousand of our lakes. The dead lakes were incapable of supporting any aquatic life, not even scavengers. There is a reason the parliamentary report on acid rain was called *Still Waters*: nothing moved in those waters because there was nothing alive in them to move. More than three hundred thousand other lakes were threatened, many of them within an inch of their lives. Hundreds of tourist operators in major lake areas were forced to shut down their businesses because there were no longer any fish for customers to catch. In northern Ontario alone, losses approached $230 million annually (many times that in today's dollars). Acid rain wiped out whole fish populations, and was threatening yet more in most provinces. World-famous salmon rivers once the pride of local communities everywhere could no longer support the species. Acid rain destroyed nine major salmon rivers in Nova Scotia alone. Sugar maples formerly plump with syrup were as dry as a desert well, falling victim to acid rain "die-back." Acid rain was causing the Parliament Building exteriors in Ottawa to deteriorate more rapidly in a decade than they had over the previous half-century. Particularly alarming was growing evidence that acid rain precursors (sulphur dioxide, sulphates, and nitrogen oxide) were causing serious respiratory and other internal diseases in humans. A link to Parkinson's disease was feared. The public was alarmed and demanded action. Politicians got the message. They could not avoid it.

# Joint Canadian–US Action

Even if we Canadians and our governments did everything in our power to address the acid rain crisis within our own borders, we could have solved, at best, only half the problem. That's because half the industrial emissions devastating the Canadian environment and economy originated in the United States. The principal sources there were antiquated, coal-fired thermal power plants in the upper Ohio Valley, from which many Canadians were downwind. Canada was extremely vulnerable to the sulphur dioxide that spewed from these filthy plants, particularly older ones grandfathered from pollution-control laws passed in more recent years.

For our part, we Canadians accounted for about 15 to 25 percent of the acid rain falling on the hardest-hit areas of the United States, primarily New England. Our main culprits were not coal-fired power plants, though we did have some of those. Rather, our chief offenders were sulphur dioxide–spewing non-ferrous smelters, producers of nickel and copper. Together, sulphur dioxide and nitrogen oxide emissions propelled far into the atmosphere from industry and transportation were combining and chemically reacting with every form of precipitation—rain, snow, sleet, hail, and ice. The resultant toxic stew was then falling to earth, drenching everything within reach in diluted but lethal acid. In some regions—for example, the Adirondack Mountains of upstate New York—scientists were measuring rainfall as acidic as vinegar. Action could no more be avoided than the impact ignored. Remedial measures needed to be taken urgently on both sides of the border if the two countries were to be saved from the havoc each was inflicting on itself and on the other.

By the mid-1980s, the Mulroney government had completed a bold program, in concert with the provinces, to slash acid-rain-causing emissions from all major domestic sources on a targeted and scheduled basis. The targets were not just smelters and coal-fired plants, but also smog-generating motor vehicles, a major source of nitrogen oxide. All the while, the US government, under President Ronald Reagan, was resisting Canada's plaintive calls for bilateral action to abate this lethal pollutant. For direction, the septuagenarian president relied heavily on his so-called Kitchen Cabinet, a small group of ultra-conservative wealthy cronies and benefactors from California, among them Edwin Meese III, Alfred Bloomingdale, Walter Annenberg, and Caspar Weinberger. The words "acid rain," like the word "AIDS," did not pass their lips. So, for the president, acid rain did not pass muster as an issue, either. Any time the two countries seemed to be making progress towards joint action on acid rain—usually immediately following summit meetings between the US president and the Canadian prime minister—Canada would end up sorely disappointed. The Americans were as recalcitrant as ever. Always in it for the long haul, the Canadian PM soldiered on. Senior Maine senator George Mitchell was not exaggerating when he said—as quoted elsewhere here—that Brian Mulroney had been the only one anywhere able to get the Reagan administration even to think about acid rain. Unfortunately for Canadians, the thinking was too often shallow, brief, and inconsequential.

Particularly alarming to the Mulroney government was that White House politicos doctored findings of their country's own scientists to minimize and marginalize the problem. They, for example, greatly overstated the extent to which nuclear energy would replace the offending coal-burning plants in future years (not a single new nuclear plant was on the drawing board); they excluded from their calculations damage being inflicted on small lakes (in the data, they included only lakes of over ten acres in size); and they also cooked the books on estimates of existing US levels of sulphur dioxide in the atmosphere (they said the levels had remained constant since 1919, when, in fact, by any reasonable scientific measure, they had soared by a staggering 200 percent in the previous eighty-eight years). Canadians were apoplectic in the face of this "Flat Earth Society" thinking. It would presage similar tunnel vision on evolution, creationism, and global warming among too many American Republicans in current times.

# George H. W. Bush

At their first summit, in Quebec City, on March 17, 1985—the "Shamrock Summit"— Ronald Reagan and Brian Mulroney had agreed, with much fanfare, to appoint former Ontario premier William Davis and former US secretary of transportation Andrew Lewis as special envoys on acid rain. The purpose was to advance the agenda of the two countries towards a solution of the problem on a "consultative and cooperative" basis. In Reagan's first budget after the envoys' appointments, however, no new significant money was designated for acid rain abatement, only for research. In Mulroney's mind, this omission clearly betrayed the spirit of their agreement. The slap both offended and embarrassed him. We in the Canadian Cabinet—the PM, in particular—risked looking like damn fools. We would have *been* damn fools not to respond. And urgently. The prime minister thought so. And he acted. Swiftly.

When progress on both free trade and acid rain totally crashed in early January 1987, Brian Mulroney phoned his friend "Ron" to rescue the strategy. I had never before seen the prime minister more alarmed about the fate of his government's agenda and of his own standing in the country. The PM was aware that growing numbers of Canadians viewed him as an American patsy and, worse, a captive to Reagan, whom, like most Republican presidents over the years, Canadians neither liked nor admired. In crisis mode, Reagan rushed his vice-president, George H. W. Bush, to Ottawa, on January 21, accompanied by the president's highest-ranking government officials, including Treasury Secretary James Baker, later Bush's secretary of state when he became president. A tiny team of Canadian ministers—Joe Clark (Foreign Affairs), Michael Wilson (Finance), Pat Carney (International Trade), Perrin Beatty (National Defence), and I (Environment)—met privately with Bush and Mulroney and the American cabinet secretaries. The venue, for secrecy, was off campus: the governor general's private guest quarters at 7 Rideau Gate. The purpose was what diplomats would euphemistically term, "a full and frank discussion;" the less diplomatic would say "a pissing match." It *was* a pissing match. Bush himself said afterwards, in a media scrum, "I got an earful!" The earful on acid rain came mostly from me. The PM had mandated his environment minister to handle Bush and his colleagues in that first and most important part of the meeting.

I had intended to be forthright while, true to my diffident nature, deferential to the high office of my interlocutor. But I was not much beyond my first sentence before Mulroney ordered me to "get to the point." I realized only later I was being goaded. Clearly, the PM was loaded for bear. And my role was to shoot for him. At which juncture, I thought: What the hell! He asked for it!—in both senses. Whereupon, I unloaded on Bush and his people in a manner that surprised even me. I know my response showed a side of me that neither the prime minister nor any of my other Cabinet colleagues had ever seen before, or probably thought existed.

In the course of dressing down the vice-head of the Free World, I described as "criminally stupid" a public communiqué on acid rain released the previous day by US Ambassador Thomas Niles. It called for "more acid rain research" and more "clean-coal technology development"—obvious smoke and mirrors for further foot-dragging instead of concrete action. These were buzzwords everyone in Canada, including the prime minister, knew were ones the Reagan administration retreated to when it wanted to appear environmentally enlightened but had absolutely no intention of actually being so. Bold as brass, I told Bush that fact. The PM, until then unaware, was shocked to learn about the ambassador's communiqué. He snatched the statement from my hand, stopped the meeting cold, read the release right under the Americans' noses, flushed every shade of red but pale pink, and looked like he was about to punch out—not me, but anyone wearing a US lapel pin. When the PM regained his composure, he told the Americans: "This is totally unacceptable." Translation: *I am mighty pissed off!*

It's worth pausing here to reflect on Brian Mulroney's grasp of a technical (essentially scientific) issue like acid rain. The complexities shaped how he approached the issue politically and strategically. Mulroney had at least one thing in common with Robert Stanfield, apart from shared political label and the same party leadership, at different times: he never liked to make any decision without knowing all the facts and options. In Mulroney's case, he demanded the information in the sharpest and clearest and most discrete terms possible—"bullets," he called the written format. Nor did Mulroney like to rely on a single source of information or advice. He insisted on multiple sources. And the sources had to be directly connected to what he was being told. He hated it when the content got filtered, and therefore in his mind corrupted, through a third party. The expression "right from the horse's mouth" must have been coined for him, if not by him. Typically, he wanted the horse right under his nose, if at all possible.

When I was consul general in Boston, for example, Mulroney ordered his staff and officials to ask me personally to prepare briefing notes for his scheduled visit with Massachusetts governor Bill Weld in early December 1992. The PM wanted to know everything about the governor's background and about what Mulroney could expect concerning every facet of the governor himself, both as a man and as an office holder. Mulroney did not want to rely on even his senior staff or senior External Affairs officers or senior Privy Council officials for this purpose. To him, they were too far from the ground. "Get Tommy to prepare me a package," I was told he instructed External. I got the call directly from the highest ranks there. The PM then insisted on receiving the notes directly from me, not in a form massaged by staff or officials. "Have Tommy forward them to me himself through a diplomatic pouch." I knew, from my brother Charley's long experience with Mulroney, that the PM needed not just the objective facts, but also a lot of spice about the Bill Weld human element. For sure, he would not receive any such seasoning from government officials. From everything Charley had told me over the years about Mulroney's management style, I also knew how to format the information. The "package" took me two full days to complete, working almost around the clock while sequestered with the one consulate staff member I could trust implicitly to help me research and write it. The final six-page document had more bullets than Bonnie and Clyde, more headings and subheadings than a *New York Times* front page, and more facts about Governor Weld as a man than a *National Enquirer* exposé about Bill Clinton. I told the prime minister everything about Weld short of when he had last had sex.

So it was with the acid rain issue. I felt as comfortable discussing the technicalities with Brian Mulroney as I did with my departmental officials. I knew his briefings were at least as thorough as mine. And, like me, he would devour the information as voraciously as a starving man would wolf down a meal at a soup kitchen. The irony is that, in all the discussions we had with each other about acid rain prior to the summit, the prime minister and I had never discussed the politics of the issue, only substance or strategy—in the latter case, concerning negotiations with the provinces towards forging bilateral agreements. The raw political dimensions, let alone partisan goals—how will this win us votes?—never arose. Not once.

And yet, I decided on the spot to appeal to our American interlocutors as political actors, not administrators or policy-makers. After raising with Bush the Thomas Niles communiqué that had so incensed the prime minister, I looked straight at the US vice-president and said: "Sir, the acid rain issue for the Mulroney government is not about environmental theology. It's about raw politics. The issue is killing us politically on the streets, in the bars, at the water coolers." And then I explained what I called the "political arithmetic." I said: "In the US, the polluters are in one part of the country—principally, the Ohio Valley. But, because of prevailing winds, most of the damage, from both American and Canadian sources, is being inflicted on another part of your country altogether—New England." (I knew the Bush family had deep roots there. Bush's father, Prescott, had been a long-time Connecticut senator. The VP himself, though a Texan now, was born in Massachusetts and graduated from Yale, in his father's home state.) "The polluters and the polluted in your country are from different regions," I noted, underscoring the obvious. So, I said, there was no congruence of interests between those regions on the issue. "One region wants action against pollution, the other wants to continue polluting. They can't agree on the magnitude of the problem, much less on how, or even whether, action should be taken." By contrast, I stressed, 70 percent of all Canadians lived in only two provinces, Ontario and Quebec. Those two provinces together had, by far, the largest land mass and the biggest total population among all our regions. And they both produced most of the acid-rain-causing emissions within Canada *and* received most of the damage from those emissions. In other words, I pointed out, unlike in the United States, the polluters and the polluted resided in the same region: central Canada. "Consequently," I said, "it is much easier for us than for you Americans to forge a consensus on the need to act and how to do so. And, for that very reason, there is enormous public pressure on governments at all levels *to act*." Then the clincher: "But we cannot act without the US as a partner." And, I emoted: "Canadians view all that talk from your ambassador about the need for more research on clean-coal technology for what it is—just an excuse *not* to act. Because that is exactly what it is. Canadians have had enough such talk. They demand action on the issue, and want it now." In fewer than ten minutes, I had my say. And Vice-President George H. W. Bush had his "earful."

When I finished, I glanced at the prime minister, seated to my right. His eyes were still locked on mine. The PM had been riveted. It was as though I had directed my monologue exclusively at him. Clearly, he had never before heard the issue expressed in such stark "geopolitical" terms—not by me, not by anyone else, certainly not by officials. He had known viscerally that the acid rain issue was important to Canadians, as it had long been to him. But he apparently had not fully appreciated why the political pressure was so strong across Canada, aside from the seriousness of the problem itself. In this case, as in others, an issue needed to be more than just urgent for action to be taken. It had to be one on which a sufficient number of Canadians *straddling the regions* were agreed both on the *need* to act and *how* to act. Then, and only then, would it become a national issue that could not be ignored politically—"the unavoidable." When one region was pitted against another on a major issue, rendering a national consensus impossible, the national government could not act without risking tearing the country apart. A classic case was the energy revenue-sharing issue—Pierre Trudeau's National Energy Program, in particular— in the earlier part of the decade. That issue had pitted the East against the West, rocking the country to its very foundations. It was the geographic and regional congruence of interests and concerns on acid rain in Canada—not just within central Canada, but in all parts of Canada—that was forcing the Mulroney government to act. A lack of such congruence across the regions in the United States was militating against action on the same issue in Washington and in the country as a whole. The prime minister's resolve to complete an agreement with the United States on acid rain was both fortified and made irreversible at 7 Rideau Gate. I was not responsible for this epiphany on his part. So, I deserve no credit. I simply turned up even higher the dimmer switch for a light already beaming in his mind.

I had learned on the spot a valuable lesson: when Brian Mulroney means business, all the Irish charm he radiates takes a back burner to other Irish traits, not the least a hair-trigger temper, a fighting spirit, and zero tolerance for being crossed. The PM felt he *had* been crossed, not just by the Niles communiqué, but also by the policy stance it reflected and, therefore, by the Reagan administration itself. Bush returned to Washington with his "earful"—and his tail between his legs. Acid rain and free trade were put back on the rails. And Canada eventually got bilateral agreements on both issues. On acid rain, at 7 Rideau Gate, it was Brian Mulroney's day, not mine. I was merely a conductor for the grand orchestration he had masterminded. Mulroney knew exactly what he was doing by handing me the baton. He wanted the vice-president to get an "earful." Better to have it come from me than from him. When, later in the meeting, Mulroney addressed the issue, his "earful" was forceful but prime ministerial by comparison. The PM's strategy was brilliant. Charley was right: with Mulroney, there was always a plan, whether or not anyone else knew what it was. In the case at hand, not even the man he chose to help execute the PM's scheme— me!—had the particulars beforehand. This much I also learned from the Mulroney-Bush acid rain summit: I would not want to be on the opposite side of the negotiating table with Brian Mulroney, or on the wrong side of him for any reason. And, in tough political bargaining, I would prefer to have him, over anyone else, on *my* side. In the case here, I felt honoured to be on his team. He had won a giant victory on the issue: for the government, for himself, and, most important of all, for Canadians.

Before the US vice-president and his team left Ottawa, Brian Mulroney hosted a luncheon for everyone involved in the summit. It was held at the prime minister's residence, at 24 Sussex Drive. The tension among participants had eased. Mulroney and Bush relaxed it further by avoiding any substantive discussion in favour of exchanging comments about recent books each had read. It was the safest, and therefore most boring, subject under the sun, given the circumstances. Mulroney knew when, and how, to switch gears to high diplomatic throttle to get himself and others out of a contretemps. Ontario premier Bill Davis once famously said about his own personal political style, often lampooned: "Bland works." At the luncheon, the PM proved "boring" works just fine, too. I don't know whether it was the dry white wine or the even drier conversation. But the rest of us had to struggle to stay awake as Bush and

Mulroney chatted incessantly about their darn books. (The PM's most recent read had been the autobiography of a modern-era US secretary of state. I thought it was Dean Rusk's, but I checked for the narrative at hand and Rusk's came later. I was so bored with the discussion at the time that the author's name didn't leave a lasting memory.) Mulroney and Bush acted more like spinster librarians than two of the continent's most powerful men. At one point, I myself lost the battle to keep awake when, for a second or two, my eyes closed until my head jerked back, returning me to consciousness. Or, was it a nudge from my American luncheon partner whom I had rescued from the same fate moments earlier? Finally, we Canadians and our American guests were on the same page—or, at least, the same book.

---

Just across the Canadian–US border, in Detroit, a huge, high-stacked trash incinerator was polluting the air in Windsor, Ontario. The plant was a big issue for area environmental groups and media and, of course, residents. Hardly a week passed without someone hounding me about the matter. District MPs often raised it in Question Period. Howard McCurdy (Windsor–Walkerville) of the NDP and Liberal Herb Gray (Essex West) were especially aggressive. As important as the issue was locally, it hardly merited being included on the agenda of our summit earlier. And yet, I knew area politicians and reporters would roast me for not raising it with the US vice-president, however unreasonable the attack. As I was leaving the prime minister's residence following the Bush luncheon, to attend Question Period, I saw the vice-president. He was momentarily standing alone by the grand piano in the living room. Bush was obviously deep in thought (the "earful"?). We caught each other's eye. I walked over to him. And I said: "Mr. Vice-President, there is no reason you should know anything about this. But a giant trash-burning incinerator in Detroit is fouling the air across the border in Canada, particularly in the twin city of Windsor. It is a big issue in that part of our country. For the record, I have raised that issue with you." Political pro that he was, Bush knew exactly what I was doing: in political parlance, "covering my ass." The vice-president smiled, gave me a thumbs-up, and replied: "You did, indeed."

The New Democratic Party did pose the question to me in Question Period soon afterwards. No doubt, they expected me to squirm for having neglected my duty. In a scrum outside the House of Commons following the exchange, the Windsor-area media swarmed around me like wolves stalking an elk. With sanctimony that would have put the NDP to shame, I was able to say in both forums: "*Of course*, I raised the Detroit incinerator issue with the US vice-president. It is a major binational issue that the Canadian government takes extremely seriously. And so do I." Talk about the cat that swallowed the canary! I devoured the cage, too. I have liked George H. W. Bush ever since.

# Ronald Reagan

I was involved in some summitry between the prime minister and the US president himself, Ronald Reagan, not just his vice-president. In April 1987, Mulroney and Reagan had the third of their annual summits, this time in Ottawa. As before, acid rain topped their agenda, above even free trade. Accordingly, as environment minister,

I was included among a small number of Canadian Cabinet ministers in the one plenary. It took place in the Cabinet room at the Centre Block. The two government leaders sat at the tennis-court-sized board table across from each other, flanked by their respective cabinet colleagues and senior officials. This part of the summit was largely a formality. The two sides had already fought out most of the contentious issues, including acid rain, in hand-to-hand combat on a smaller field, using the highest-ranked officers equipped with the most lethal weapons. Unlike my central role in the Bush meeting, my part in this one was more that of a private recruit than a senior officer. On our side, at the officials' level, sat, principally, Derek Burney (chief of staff) and Allan Gotlieb (ambassador to Washington). In practice, some officials outrank Cabinet ministers in certain circumstances; this was one. On the American side were, notably, National Security Advisor Frank Carlucci, Secretary of State George Shultz, and Secretary of Defense Caspar Weinberger. (Lee Thomas, head of the Environmental Protection Agency, EPA, also attended, but, though the main issue was acid rain, he, like me, did not play a major role. Who said politics was rational?) Nothing important remained to be resolved after the inner group had done its job.

At the plenary, about a dozen individuals—approximately an equal number from both countries—sat at each side of the table. Support personnel rimmed the walls, most of them standing. The PM began with words of welcome and warmth and wit, turning on the charm as only an Irishman can. It was a performance as effective in advancing our national interests as it appeared spontaneous and effortless—albeit neither; just as no strong performance truly ever is, whether in politics or sports or the arts. For his part, in response, and throughout the session, Ronald Reagan, the so-called Great Communicator, did not say a single word—not even "It's great to be in this beautiful national capital of yours"—without scooping it from his deck of neatly assembled recipe-sized cards, each one tucked on the bottom after use. Even his Irish jokes, exchanged with the PM's own—but, in the latter's case, delivered *sans* notes—were cue-carded. For me, it was like learning that the Three Tenors lip-synched their performances. But, unlike Carreras and Domingo and Pavarotti, the Gipper, in effect, did. Was incipient Alzheimer's the reason?

It is inconceivable that Brian Mulroney would ever have felt required to be so scripted on such an occasion. Nor would any other healthy major politician feel the need, either. Bill Clinton gave a major address on health care to a Joint Session of Congress in September 1993. As he began, he discovered the wrong text had been fed into the teleprompter, rendering him temporarily without a speech, except someone else's. He delivered the right speech anyway, from memory, without missing a beat, until staff, in a royal panic, could locate the president's text and program it into the machine. No one in the media or Congress knew the difference until afterwards, so smooth was Clinton's handling of the snafu.[1] Conservative Arthur Meighen, briefly prime minister of Canada, on-again, off-again, in the 1920s, was Canada's most brilliant and literate leader, Trudeau myth to the contrary. An authority on Shakespeare, Meighen once gave a half-hour address on the Bard to the Canadian Club of Ottawa. When the media asked him for a copy following his *tour de force*, Meighen replied sheepishly that he had forgotten it at home, and had needed to give the address by heart. But Meighen said he would be glad to recite it again so the media could file their stories. He did, word for word—from memory. I cannot avoid comparing all that with Reagan at the Ottawa summit. He appeared unable to remember where he was.

The climax of the April 1987 Mulroney-Reagan summit in Ottawa was the president's address to a Joint Session of Parliament (House of Commons and Senate). Technicians accompanying the president had set up a teleprompter on each side of a podium specially placed in front of the Speaker's throne for Reagan's address. At the last minute, Reagan's text was modified to reflect a compromise that officials from both countries had negotiated concerning a contentious detail. Reagan delivered the oration flawlessly until he got confused by the handwritten change programmed into the machine. The president stumbled, and then froze. For the address, I was in my usual Commons seat, on the government side (right of the Speaker) in the second row. (The area is permanently reserved, with the corresponding area in the first row, for Cabinet.) I could practically touch Reagan as he delivered his speech. His wife, Nancy, directly in front of me, never once averted from him the frozen beatific gaze for which she was often satirized on *Saturday Night Live*. The president's freeze because of the text change, though lasting only seconds, struck everyone as interminable, as life's moments of highest drama always do. Some observers, quoted later, said they thought the seventy-six-year-old leader was having a heart attack. I myself wondered if he was having a fainting spell under the hot klieg lights. The US president regained his footing and finished the speech with characteristic aplomb. But people remembered the stumble long after they forgot what Reagan had said.

Robert Stanfield might not have been a natural orator like Arthur Meighen, John Diefenbaker, Pierre Trudeau, Bill Clinton, and Ronald Reagan (with a prepared text and teleprompter, if all went well). But Stanfield developed considerable rhetorical competence, and confidence, as his political leadership at the national level advanced and matured. Intellectually dexterous and quick and witty, Stanfield, if confronted with a circumstance akin to the one Ronald Reagan faced that day on the floor of Parliament, would have been more a Meighen than a Reagan: fast and agile on his feet and able to improvise. And, at a meeting—high level or not—he never had to rely on cue cards. At the time, such thoughts kept gnawing at me concerning the US president. Was something more fundamental at play than an aberrant stubbing of the oratorical toe?

Ronald Reagan deserved his reputation as a first-rate communicator. His voice was raw silk, his delivery pure honey, his body language—calculated tilt of the head, disarming smile, and disciplined hand gestures—that of the Hollywood actor he had been. Imagine my shock, therefore, when I actually spent time with him in person and discovered he depended on cue cards as much as a human does on oxygen, seemingly utterly unable to express even the most mundane thought without being "plugged to the tank." Mulroney expresses this same surprise in his memoirs: "Reagan," says Mulroney, "always followed a script, even in…conversations. I will never figure out why."[2] The memoirs were written well after Reagan himself publicly disclosed his Alzheimer's diagnosis in November 1995, seven years into his post-presidency. So, it surprises me that, in his memoirs, the former PM never considers the possibility that Reagan might have been demonstrating symptoms of this form of dementia when the two men were dealing with each other as heads of their respective governments. While participating in the 1987 Mulroney-Reagan summit in Ottawa, I, like most people then, knew nothing about Alzheimer's, much less that Reagan might be afflicted with it. But, looking at the US president on this occasion, I thought to myself: There's something wrong with the man. Could it be old age? Incipient dementia? Just extreme fatigue? I remember rasing the matter with my cardiologist brother, Colin, the following week while at home. Colin said he thought the symptoms

I described were more brain-related than cardiological. When I watched Reagan's videotaped deposition concerning the Iran-Contra scandal some months later, but still before his Alzheimer's was publicly announced, I was convinced more than ever that both my own original hunch and Colin's "diagnosis" were right. The by-then former president's "I can't remember" answer to almost every question seemed honest, not Nixonian. Reagan's son Ron, in his testimonial memoir of his dad, notes it is now known "that the physiological and neurological changes associated with Alzheimer's can be in evidence years, even decades, before identifiable symptoms arise."[3] And, a real shocker, coming as it does from the late president's own offspring: "The question, then, of whether my father suffered from the beginning stages of Alzheimer's while in office more or less answers itself."[4]

All this had profound implications for Canadian-US relations during the Mulroney era. Let me illustrate. One of the most important achievements of the Mulroney government globally was the Montreal Protocol on Substances that Deplete the Ozone Layer. The protocol was a landmark international treaty designed to protect the ozone layer by phasing out the production of numerous substances believed responsible for its depletion. I assembled and chaired the world gathering in Montreal that produced this environmental milestone. I was also the lead negotiator for Canada on the treaty, and I signed it on behalf of the Government of Canada. The treaty was "opened for signature" on September 16, 1987, and entered into force on January 1, 1989. Scientists around the world say that, if the agreement is adhered to, the ozone layer will recover by 2050. EPA head Lee Thomas was about to leave office when the protocol was completed. But, uncharacteristically, he played the central role in the US delegation in Montreal—his diplomatic swan song, as it were. Typically, the lead player would have been a cabinet secretary. (Unlike Canada, the United States does not have a federal "environment minister" as such. The duties are spread among various office holders, including the secretary of the interior for such matters as national parks and other federal lands and natural resources. The EPA head has cabinet ranking but is not officially a cabinet secretary.) In any event, we Canadians were convinced that the Reagan administration would scuttle progress on an ozone-layer deal, as it had so often done before on other issues, including acid rain. These arch-conservatives were hostile to anything that smacked of international government, seeing it as a threat to US sovereignty. Powerful US chemical companies such as DuPont, however, calculated that the Montreal Protocol would give them a market opportunity they knew competitors in other countries would not be able to exploit as fully. That opportunity would come from manufacturing new substances to replace the ones banned—for example, those used in aerosol sprays, certain foams, fire-extinguishing agents, refrigerants, and air-conditioning chemicals. Even still, ideological forces in the White House typically conspired against progress on such global environmental matters, particularly when treaties were involved.

And yet, Lee Thomas—God bless his big South Carolina heart!—helped us achieve the Montreal Protocol against heavy odds. In recent times, I have seen on American TV various commentators stating as fact that both Ronald Reagan and British prime minister Margaret Thatcher enthusiastically supported the Montreal Protocol based on the science of the issue. I have no doubt that, as a chemist in her pre-politics professional life, Thatcher would have understood the ozone-depletion phenomenon and the urgent need to act. The United Kingdom was onside with us in Montreal, and it is possible that Thatcher encouraged her close friend Reagan to be, too. But I was heavily involved, on the ground, in every facet of the relevant international negotiations. I saw no evidence that either of these arch-conservative ideologues was enlightened about any environmental issue of the day, much less this one, which required an enormous amount of vision and political will to conquer.

I have an alternative theory concerning Ronald Reagan's role—or, more accurately, "non-role"—not only on the issue at hand, but also on a number of other environmental issues, including acid rain, on which Canada was able to make progress with the Reagan administration despite the president's intransigence. By this point, I had gotten to know Lee Thomas well, having worked with him hand in glove on diverse bilateral issues over many months. We had travelled to each other's country numerous times for this purpose. Just before he departed Montreal to return to Washington, I asked him: "Lee, how did you ever get the Montreal Protocol agreement past Reagan?" He smiled ever so sweetly, as they might say in the Deep South, winked at me, and said, "Who said I told him? What he doesn't know won't hurt him." Was this the same way US negotiators got Reagan "to agree" to advancing the ball on acid rain? In the end, Brian Mulroney's doggedness on the issue, the warm personal relationship he had developed with both Reagan and Bush, and the extraordinary diplomatic skills of our top professional negotiators were among the decisive factors that explain the acid rain success story. Still, one can only wonder this: maybe on acid rain, as on ozone depletion, the American negotiators in Ottawa, as in Montreal, thought: What the president doesn't know won't hurt him. I have absolutely no doubt that, at this point, what Ronald Reagan didn't know was a lot. That includes steps being taken by officials of his own government that eventually led, under his successor, to a legally binding treaty with Canada to tackle head-on the acid rain crisis on both sides of the border.

# Chapter 20

# RAINDROPS KEEP FALLIN'

I t is October 2, 1991. I am out of politics and now Canada's consul general in Boston. I have been invited to speak at the National Conference on Governmental Relations in Ottawa. I am to help celebrate the role played by two of Canada's pre-eminent social activists in the most important environmental achievement in North America since the cleanup of the Great Lakes a generation earlier: the signing of a legally binding acid rain accord by Prime Minister Brian Mulroney and President George H. W. Bush in Ottawa earlier that year. The two environmentalists being lionized are Michael Perley and Adèle Hurley, principals in the Canadian Coalition on Acid Rain.

Perley and Hurley are presented on stage as paragons of successful environmental activism, models for other environmentalists and non-governmental organizations (NGOs), heroes in the acid rain accord achievement. Commons Speaker John Fraser, environment minister in the short-lived Joe Clark government and a long-time Coalition patron, is a special guest. He introduces the two environmentalists with great flourish and good humour. I have flown to Ottawa from Boston for the occasion. I sit at centre stage—with the Speaker and the two honourees—glad to help acknowledge Perley and Hurley's role in the historic bilateral environmental accomplishment. But, as I listen to what's being said, I am becoming increasingly concerned that something important is being missed: the fact the accomplishment was a victory for all Canadians, not just career environmentalists, let alone only the two on stage with me. Nor, I think, do I myself deserve to step forward from the total cast to bask in the audience's applause, as I risk being seen to do by participating in the performance at hand. Where, in particular, is any ovation for the role played in the issue by successive federal governments (PC and Liberal alike); by most of the provincial governments (of different political stripes), which took big political risks in some quarters by acting boldly; and by the countless individual Canadians and community groups (not just NGOs, but also tourist operators, foresters, farmers, fishers, and so many others), many of whom helped launch the acid rain political movement before most people even knew what the term meant?

I decide to discard most of my own prepared remarks. After paying rightful tribute to Michael and Adèle, whom I like and respect personally, I try to provide a broader perspective. What follows in this chapter is that broader perspective, the gist of what I told the Governmental Relations audience in truncated form.[1] I hope, with its emphasis on the role played by the total community in the acid rain success story, and how the Mulroney government tried to include everyone in the effort, the reader will hear the voice not only of an environmentalist, but also of a classic conservative. On few other issues more than this one did I feel like that kind of conservative—and part of that kind of government, a Tory one at its best.

# The Canadian Coalition on Acid Rain
# versus Brian Mulroney

The Canadian Coalition on Acid Rain, the self-styled largest single-issue citizens' coalition in the country, was launched formally in 1981 by environmentalists and concerned citizens in partnership with the Trudeau government. The initial impetus came from Ontario cottage owners. Their lakes and ponds were placid and immobile and clear, not because they were beautiful in summer's glow, but because they were dead from acid's grip. The partnership between the federal government and environmentalists through the Coalition enabled the government to lobby Washington on acid rain in ways that otherwise would have been viewed as inappropriate, possibly even illegal, if conducted directly by a foreign government in another country's national capital. A lot of the funding was federal. The Coalition started with twelve member groups that represented tourism, naturalists, and sportsmen's associations, and it maintained offices in Toronto and Washington, DC. It was registered as a charitable organization in Canada and as a lobby group in the United States, the first-ever Canadian group so registered in that country. By 1991, the Coalition claimed it had grown to fifty-eight member groups, representing over two million Canadians. The claim was true, but more on paper than in reality. The organization was, in effect, executive coordinators Michael Perley and Adèle Hurley. They drew good salaries on contract—for all practical purposes, as consultants—and dominated all facets of its operations. Those included the board and chairman (mostly a figurehead), whom the two operatives appeared to me and others to have selected to serve their own agenda and interests, not only environmental but professional as well.

Perley and Hurley were virtual clones of each other—young and good-looking and telegenic and articulate. As such, they were the standout environmentalists of the era. These two shrewd operators could, and did, hold their own with the sharpest of American environmentalists. The latter were generally far more professional than our own—certainly, far slicker. Perley and Hurley soon became media stars in their own right. In its early days, the group they led and personified did a great deal to create public awareness of the acid rain issue in Washington power centres and among the US public at large. It worked closely with other groups, in both Canada and the United States, on educational and other projects to elevate the issue's profile and increase the likelihood of action on it. But, ironically, as the cause gained momentum, partly because of the Coalition's own successful advocacy, Perley and Hurley became increasingly less constructive and more partisan in the eyes of the Mulroney government and, to only a slightly lesser extent, in fact. Over time, the two transformed themselves and the Coalition into political attack dogs. No matter how hard the prime minister and his government tried to follow the very course the Coalition championed, Perley and Hurley often barked and bit. Their attacks against Mulroney became steadily more savage with every press release, news conference, interview, and media scrum the two environmentalists orchestrated. In fairness to the Coalition (Perley and Hurley, in particular), Mulroney was sometimes unduly sensitive to criticism, especially that which he considered *ad hominem*. In fairness to him, many of the attacks *were* reprehensible, some bordering on the personal, if not altogether over the line. But that was environmental politics as practised by almost every activist of the era. One cannot fully appreciate the magnitude of what the Mulroney government achieved with the United States on acid rain without understanding the political pressures the prime minister faced to approach the issue in a way completely different from the one he chose and that, in the end, proved him right.

The Canadian Coalition on Acid Rain was not the only Canadian environmental organization of the period that embraced what I would call "the politics of passion." Virtually all the country's environmental groups did. Canada's organized environmentalism had grown out of the protest movement of the 1960s and 1970s in the United States. That movement, in turn, was born of the two Kennedy assassinations, widespread race-based civil rights abuses, the murder of Dr. Martin Luther King, hostility to the Vietnam War, the Watergate scandal, and increased public concern, especially among young people, about unrestrained political and corporate might and abuse. The penchant for violence as an integral part of US political culture was never more manifest than in this period.[2] Antiwar protests on campuses sometimes ended in violence—most famously at Kent State, where the National Guard killed four students and seriously injured eight others. Buildings were occupied, properties damaged, students hauled off to jail, whole communities traumatized, and young people left alienated from political and economic power and society in general. Canadian youth were swept up in this social revolution as much as their peers in such social hotbeds as San Francisco. "Don't trust anyone over thirty" became the mantra of the Vietnam/Watergate generation. Credit—except to themselves for their activism—was a dirty word. To act otherwise was deemed to betray principle, even if the principle itself might not always have been clear beyond the need to fight "the establishment." This ethos had staying power well into the 1980s and early 1990s, when the Mulroney government was in office. Indeed, it was against that backdrop that the government was judged by social activists and large parts of the media that shared their ethos. Environmentalists were especially critical—and, I would argue, unreasonable. If the standard by which one is being judged is unduly idealistic, the judgment itself is bound to be unfair.

Passion and idealism can be good when channelled constructively. But, if that route is chosen exclusively, the risk for society is that, faced with a dogmatic and uncompromising organized constituency such as environmentalists, government could throw up its hands, ask what's the point, and invest political capital in other issues where the electoral payoff would be higher. Prime Minister Mulroney faced heavy pressures from within his own ranks to do just that on acid rain and other environmental issues. Many a time I heard Progressive Conservative partisans saying, in effect, "Why bother? No matter how much we do, environmentalists will always consider it 'too little, too late,' attack us for falling short, and vote NDP or Liberal, anyway."

The other side of the argument is that a pressure group like the Canadian Coalition on Acid Rain in its time has to take extreme positions to create the leverage necessary to compete with other interests and agendas in the political marketplace. Only in that way, the argument goes, would decisions be made and resources allocated reasonably and fairly. Joe Clark made this very point in his book, *How We Lead*: "[To] effectively pursue their goals, NGOs often have to push their priorities to a point where they can be seen as not simply 'non-government' but 'anti-government' as well. That is often essential to the role; NGOs would be of no use if they built a compelling argument for change, and then politely and regularly allowed themselves to be rebuffed."[3] To me, as both a former politician and an environmentalist, the truth does not lie totally with either side of the idealism-versus-pragmatism debate. It is a question of striking—as Hugh Segal would say and Robert Stanfield always sought—

the right balance. Protagonists on both sides overstate the merits of their respective cases and the high moral ground they claim in making their arguments.

Only after Brian Mulroney left office did the organized environmental movement in Canada start attaining anything close to the maturity and attendant political savvy, to say nothing of sense of fairness, that had long characterized the much older and more established environmental NGOs in the United States. There, the Sierra Club, founded in 1892, had written the book on how to make friends and influence people in high places. Meanwhile, in Canada, the Coalition both reflected and contributed to a political culture in which relations between government and environmental NGOs were mostly hostile, rather than conducive to joint action in common cause. Fortunately, the prime minister's frustration with the Coalition was far outweighed by his profound belief that the government needed to act on acid rain, because ignoring the problem would have had dire consequences for both the government and the country, let alone the danger for the party he led. The PM knew he could not count on the Coalition to be in his corner as he tackled the problem at home and also sought to partner with the US government to deal with it bilaterally. Almost as soon as Mulroney's Cabinet was sworn in, in September 1984, the Coalition's high-profile spokespersons made it clear that, to them, the Mulroney government was as much the enemy as acid rain itself.

Typical of the vitriol Michael Perley and Adèle Hurley poured on the government and the prime minister are public statements they made in late April 1988. By then, Brian Mulroney had invested enormous political capital, and much of his own time and energy and reputation, in trying to convince the US government to join the battle against acid rain. Mulroney had travelled to Washington for a two-day visit for this very purpose, meeting with President Ronald Reagan and his cabinet secretaries and other top officials. The president continued to resist Mulroney's efforts to get him to sign a bilateral accord on the issue. The PM was being treated badly by the US government and even worse, he thought, by the Coalition. At a news conference before departing Washington, Mulroney announced he would ask US Secretary of State George Shultz to hold talks with External Affairs Minister Joe Clark to advance the acid rain agenda. While acknowledging that progress towards a treaty had been frustratingly slow, the PM said he was, nonetheless, "encouraged." The prime minister was trying heroically. Shouldn't the Coalition have acknowledged and praised at least his effort? He thought so. The Coalition thought otherwise. Perley and Hurley pronounced any meeting Shultz would have with Clark "meaningless," a mere political "sop" by the Americans to the Canadians. The two environmentalists attacked Mulroney, in particular, for being unable to convince the Reagan administration to agree to specific targets and timetables to reduce acid rain. Goaded by the media to respond, the PM said angrily: "What do you do—declare war or persuade Americans of the value of acting?" It seemed to him that Perley and Hurley preferred war—certainly, a war of words. Such verbal warfare by the two activists against the Mulroney government had become, essentially, the Coalition's primary agenda in the eyes of the government, if not entirely objectively. In a sense, these environmentalists were merely doing their jobs. But the PM—as head of not only a government, but also a political party wishing to get re-elected in a very few months—was just doing his, too. Politics is never simple, much less a matter of black-and-white morality. Upon reflection, many years after all this transpired, I think each side's contribution to the eventual resolution of the issue was unique, integral to the overall process, indispensable, and, therefore, praiseworthy.

By the time the landmark Canada-United States acid rain accord was signed in March 1991, Mulroney and his entire government had long taken for granted that the Canadian Coalition on Acid Rain would never acknowledge, much less praise, any amount of progress it made on the issue. To the Coalition, government measures on acid rain were insufficient, belated, and thus not meritorious. But, bizarrely, these environmentalists claimed credit for the very actions they had derided. Inarguably, Perley and Hurley were being unfair, though perhaps not as much as the PM and I myself thought in our worst moments. Still, the two environmental activists' duplicity was as blatant as it was brazen. The Coalition urged the prime minister to sharpen his attacks on the US administration for failing to act on acid rain. When he did so, in a major speech to the Americas Society in New York City, the Coalition criticized him, saying such an approach would alienate the US public. The Coalition called on the Canadian government to launch an acid rain publicity campaign aimed at American tourists in Canada. When it did, the Coalition lambasted the effort, calling it "puffery." The Coalition criticized the Mulroney government for failing to convince New Brunswick and Nova Scotia to sign federal-provincial acid rain accords of the sort I had already negotiated and signed with five other polluting provinces—most consequentially, Quebec and Ontario. When I finally did, the agreements were dismissed as legally meaningless and a waste of time—"not worth the paper they were printed on." And so on and so forth. To us, the Coalition was elevating the "damned if you do, damned if you don't" cheap shot to new heights and levels of velocity.

The cost of all this was increased tension between the government and the Coalition. The benefit was our stiffened resolve to solve the acid rain problem per se. Perhaps that was the Coalition's Machiavellian purpose all along. Maybe the role it was playing was exactly the one pressure groups must, by definition, play: keeping up the "pressure." If so, it worked in this case. As Canada's environment minister, I tried to reconcile my admiration of Perley and Hurley's operational skills and personal gifts with the growing frustration I experienced about their almost incessant attacks against the prime minister, against our government, and increasingly against me as well. To compound the challenge, I liked the two individuals personally. To boot, I felt an allegiance to a dual cause whose very binary nature caused me internal conflict: the environmental movement these two operatives were seeking to advance; and the Mulroney government and national PC Party, whose political and partisan agenda included building the strongest-possible record on environmental issues—acid rain foremost among them. And, now, these two values were knocking heads. Not only that, I myself had come of age as part of the 1960s and 1970s generation that continued to believe, at this time, that all things governmental and political were suspect. Although never a "flower child," I could understand and sympathize with the undercurrents that risked pulling me out to sea. Einstein must have had me in mind when he said "politics is more complex than physics." As I struggled to help the government withstand the attacks from the Coalition, I was finding my job as challenging as life itself.

The Coalition kept shifting the goalposts, so its scope for criticizing the Mulroney government was boundless. For their part, the media did not require such public interest groups to be consistent, still less to be intellectually honest or fair. Reporters and newsrooms could always rely on the Coalition's glib spokespersons to provide pithy and quotable attacks against the government. And that's mostly what counted—not penetrating analyses but plunging stilettos. The deep downside in environmental terms was that, after a while, the prime minister, relevant Cabinet ministers, senior officials, and our diplomats at home and in Washington started to dismiss the Coalition as a reliable source of counsel, let alone as the partner it had been established to be—and, at the outset, was—in the acid rain cause. Mention the Coalition, and Brian Mulroney would get agitated. Speak of Perley and Hurley, and he would become angry. Draw his attention to their criticisms of him personally, and every sharp letter opener in the Prime Minister's Office needed to be hidden. Murder might not have been literally on his mind. But peace—of mind least of all—was hardly the order of the day.

I did not share this degree of hostility towards the two environmentalists. Throughout my time as PC Opposition critic for the environment, I had worked closely with Perley and Hurley on acid rain, gotten to know them well personally, admired their commitment, and considered them co-conspirators in the acid rain cause. I sometimes bristled at their attacks against the PM, against the government, and against me for every manner of alleged sin of both commission and omission. But I was not by nature as sensitive to criticism as Mulroney. And besides, he had the entire weight of the government and country on his shoulders. I was just carrying a part of that load for him. And yet, I knew better than to raise the Coalition in the PM's presence. Everybody else close to him knew better, too. I was, therefore, not at all surprised—but amused—to see that nowhere in Mulroney's one-thousand-page memoir does he mention either the Canadian Coalition on Acid Rain or Michael Perley or Adèle Hurley by name. Clearly, he wanted to get himself neither agitated nor angry nor put in a mood to wield sharp objects. And yet, the author rightly thought the acid rain issue itself merited many pages of attention.

By saying nothing about the Coalition or its principals in his memoir, Mulroney shows how little he thought of them. By addressing here many facets of the Coalition—both positive and negative—I take a contrary view. Even when not at its best, this organization helped keep acid rain in the headlines and on people's minds well before the Mulroney government was elected. The Coalition sometimes did act perversely. But who's to say, in the end, that its behaviour did not contribute, along with many other factors, to a reasonable and balanced resolution of a major environmental problem? In any event, it's clear that, in the memoir, the former PM is more interested in the acid rain outcome than in the process that produced it. A former senior ministerial staffer of mine has an alternative theory. He told me for this book, "To me, Brian Mulroney didn't write about the Coalition because he wrote them off as jerks whose influence [on the acid rain solution] was minute compared with other factors, most notably diplomacy, especially the prime minister's strong personal relationship with Reagan and Bush." I can't dismiss the Coalition's role quite so cavalierly. The media treated this umbrella organization as though it represented millions of Canadians, whether or not it actually did. So, politicians from all political parties, including the Mulroney government, accorded the Coalition's principal functionaries a central place in the national debate. It is easy to discount the Coalition as a mere distraction in the acid rain saga now that most people don't know that organization even existed, and many of those who do know have long forgotten the big role it played in the acid rain cause when the issue itself was big. But, as the country's environment minister throughout the relevant period, I know differently. The media, politicians, other environmental groups, and Canadians at large who followed such matters treated every pronouncement from the Coalition as though the pope's insignia were stamped on it with a red wax seal.

One fact is undeniable. As with, for example, the Meech Lake and Charlottetown Accords, the link between the process for resolving a problem and the eventual outcome was as tight on acid rain as on any other issue in the Mulroney era—the political equivalent of the "form follows function" principle in architecture and industrial design. It is to that process I now turn.

## A Successful Strategy

The Canadian Coalition on Acid Rain's contribution to the resolution of the problem it was established to conquer deserves to be recognized. But the strategy the federal government followed to achieve success with the US government on acid rain was the very one the Coalition repeatedly attacked as fundamentally flawed and, consequently, certain to fail. This, too, should be acknowledged. In an op-ed piece in the *Globe and Mail*, Canada's ambassador in Washington, Allan Gotlieb, wrote: "For some time, Canadian environmental lobbyists [read: the Canadian Coalition on Acid Rain] have been critical of everyone's efforts except their own. It's a good time to ask ourselves if this criticism is fair or misplaced."[4] In the article, and even more caustically with everyone within earshot in private, Gotlieb made clear he thought the Coalition's criticism of the government on the acid rain issue *was* unfair, *was* misplaced. Gotlieb was no Tory hack or Mulroney sycophant. His credentials as a career diplomat, External Affairs veteran, and public service sage had long made him, both at home and around the world, one of the most respected officials in the entire federal government. Gotlieb was the closest thing Canada had to a Henry Kissinger—without that former US secretary of state's imperiousness. The prime minister had enormous respect for him, as did everyone else in Cabinet, not least me. From practically the beginning, the PM made Allan Gotlieb a partner in the acid rain cause. The two men shared both an alarm about the issue and a commitment to resolving it. They also shared zero tolerance for game-playing from any quarter that would obstruct progress. Increasingly, they both saw the Coalition as more interested in its own success than in that of the game itself. The Coalition's duplicity—pushing a course of action and then attacking that very course when the government followed it—infuriated the prime minister as much as anything I ever observed in his company. Gotlieb's frustration was more measured but no less real. And yet, the two men remained focused on the long haul, convinced as they were that all the political capital the PM was personally investing in the issue would pay off for his government and the country in the end. Gotlieb helped fortify and sustain Mulroney's resolve in the face of repeated setbacks. Having by his side such a wise and widely respected veteran of public policy trench warfare increased Mulroney's confidence he would ultimately succeed on the issue. This was particularly true with the Americans, after his predecessor, Pierre Trudeau, had failed—not having tried with much commitment anyway. Towards that end, the PM decided to follow his own course. It was far different from the one the Coalition publicly touted and viciously attacked him for ignoring.

The Coalition's basic premise was that, in the persons of Ronald Reagan and his successor, George H. W. Bush, the president of the United States would never act on acid rain. It was, essentially, a defeatist attitude. The Coalition argued that the Mulroney government's efforts had to focus, instead, on the US Congress, where genuine allies could be found and progress made. In the Coalition's view, pursuing the president not only wasted time; it also diverted attention from the sole hittable target. The Coalition had a vested interest in a congressional focus because their lobbyists had access to legislators and their staffs. They had no access whatsoever to the president and his senior staff and advisors, who viewed this group with contempt if they paid any attention to it at all. The collective wisdom at the federal level —from Prime Minister Brian Mulroney to External Affairs Minister Joe Clark to me as environment minister to Ambassador Gotlieb to diplomatic and other officials on the ground—saw the situation completely differently. We knew the president was pivotal in the US political system. No matter how well-disposed Congress might have been towards acid rain controls—and that was uncertain at best—progress would have been impossible as long as the president himself was opposed or indifferent. He had ways to shape the agenda of Congress and influence how its members, especially in his own party, voted. Ultimately, the president could also have vetoed Congress on acid rain controls. And his veto would have been sustained if, as seemed certain, Congress was substantially divided and, consequently, unable to muster the two-thirds majority constitutionally required to overturn it. Therefore, Mulroney, against the Coalition's urgings, made acid rain the centrepiece of his bilateral summits with both Reagan and Bush. Congressional attention would need to be left to the Executive Branch.

As noted earlier, throughout the process, Brian Mulroney became comfortable with the science and technicalities of the acid rain issue. He was a brute for briefings—no doubt, the labour lawyer in him always to the fore. That said, when we appeared together in media scrums, as we often did, he stuck mostly to the government's overall positions, leaving the details to me. At no time did we discuss this approach; we simply followed it. From the first time we performed together, it was just taken for granted such would be our two-man act. It worked fine, the media were content with it, and the division of responsibilities became second nature to both of us before long.

Towards the end of my last year as minister of the environment, I, like the prime minister, had all but given up on the Canadian Coalition on Acid Rain—particularly Michael Perley and Adèle Hurley. They were significantly more intemperate than Liberal MP Charles Caccia or NDP MP Jim Fulton, the official environmental spokesmen for their respective parties. When it counted, both men were able to rise above partisan politics to link arms with us on a host of common concerns, including acid rain. For me, the last stand with the Coalition was a meeting I had requested with Perley in my Confederation Building parliamentary office. I invited him and his organization to join me and my department to create a mass media marketing campaign on acid rain targeted at American visitors to Canada in the high tourism season. We were confident that, by focusing on heavy-traffic vacation and convention destinations such as Niagara Falls, Quebec City, and Banff (I included all of PEI in my plans!), the campaign could have a real impact without breaking the bank. I had convinced Cabinet and the Treasury Board to part with more than a million dollars (several million in today's dollars), a lot of money at a time of strict government-wide austerity. To get the money, I shamelessly exploited my credibility within the system as the country's former tourism minister. (A phone call to Tory heavyweight Norm Atkins of Camp Associates didn't hurt, either.)

Our acid rain marketing campaign was exactly what the Coalition had urged. When Pierre Trudeau was prime minister and John Roberts environment minister, the principals had gladly helped with theirs. This time, however, Perley informed me:

"The Coalition has decided not to participate in your marketing effort. I myself want to be free to criticize it publicly, and I would not be able to do so if I were part of the planning." Perley made clear to me, albeit unintentionally, that he was far more interested in making news attacking the government than in having his organization help us act against acid rain in ways that wouldn't need to be attacked in the first place. Again, to be fair here, he and Hurley were as much bound by the prevailing environmental NGO culture as guilty of contributing to it. It was how most environmental activists felt pressured to play the game, especially to earn street cred. By this time, I thought the tension between the government and these harshest of environmental critics had to be eased if there was to be any hope of our acting in common cause. My efforts had something of the feel of a blind shepherd trying to herd a flock of tremulous sheep on the side of a steep and rocky mountain. Little wonder, then, that those efforts proved naive and misguided. And it was the shepherd who got fleeced.

It particularly grated on me that the Coalition took my department's generous funding for granted, neither appreciating nor graciously acknowledging it either in public or in private. Perley and Hurley knew that many senior Environment Canada officials had little regard for them as professionals, believing the duo were all about self-aggrandizement, personal ambition, and love of the limelight. In turn, before long, the Coalition principals plotted to dethrone the departmental official most responsible for the acid rain file at the administrative level. They wanted him replaced with someone who could act, in effect, as their stooge within the bureaucracy. The target of the plot was Dr. Robert Slater, the senior assistant deputy minister. Slater directed many of our most important programs, not just on acid rain. Except for Deputy Minister Geneviève Ste-Marie herself, he was Environment Canada's principal public service player on overall policy, on pollution control, and on all matters relating specifically to Ontario. The person Perley and Hurley wanted in his stead was a ladder-climbing self-promoter of no great distinction employed by the department in a mid-range position. The two plotters knew the man personally and, over several months, had been secretly grooming him for the intended role. When the time seemed right to them, they began a full-court press to both undermine Slater and promote their chosen one for the acid rain point-man job.

All this would baffle anyone familiar with how the public service actually functions. A minister, in fact, plays no direct role in the hiring or firing of career public employees, as distinct from his or her own political or contract staff. Outsiders have no role whatsoever. Hurley and Perley were deluding themselves about their ability to execute the coup and about the willingness of certain others, including me, to be complicit. The deputy minister's connivance would certainly have been required. But she was even less inclined than I to engage, let alone play a leading part. The shenanigans were as weird as they were underhanded. Once the deputy and I learned about the scheme, we killed it. Our doing so earned me and the government additional enmity from the Coalition. And now Dr. Slater had an even bigger target on his back. How time-consuming and emotionally draining all this was. It would have been far better had every one of us devoted the time and energy to solving the acid rain crisis itself instead of engaging in such backstairs parlour games. I felt like a football running back constantly being intercepted or thrown to the ground by players from his own team. Perley and Hurley weren't, and shouldn't have been considered, actual members of the government's team. Like the role of any NGO, theirs was partly to help keep us honest. It could be played only if there were a degree of distance between them and us. But did they continually have to be dishonest themselves not only by holding us to impossible and ever-changing standards, but also by undermining our efforts in this and so many other ways?

I continued to hope against hope that the Coalition would partner with us, just as it had with the Trudeau government and, ever so briefly, with our own government at the outset. I decided to request a meeting with its board to see whether, against heavy odds, I could still make common cause with the organization. I hoped I could convince the principals at least to stop subverting our efforts at every juncture. To set the stage, I informed the Coalition, through back channels, that it should no longer take its federal funding for granted. I would first need to review how the Coalition's relationship with the government could be made more constructive. As it turned out, my good intentions were exceeded only by my gullibility. I found myself dealing with operators far more Machiavellian than I. Unbeknownst to me at the time, they included someone on my own political staff.

Dr. Slater and I slaved on a multipage letter in which, over my signature, all the concerns the government had about the Coalition were detailed, one by one— more in the form of a brief than an epistle. As the basis for discussion, I planned to deliver a copy to each member of the Coalition board personally. I then intended to announce not that the funding would be reduced, let alone eliminated, but that it would be increased, albeit marginally. It was, for me, a token of good faith in efforts to place the government's relations with the Coalition on a stronger and less warlike footing. I also wanted to signal to the broader environmental network across Canada my own and the government's renewed eagerness to work with them on all issues, not just acid rain. When I met with the Coalition board, I distributed the letter, raised my concerns, and announced the increase. (The increase had been a closely guarded secret, shared only with senior departmental officials and select political staff.) With great theatricality, Michael Perley rose from his chair, walked across the room, and announced, in light of my announcement, that he was "calling off the media" he had lined up in anticipation of the Coalition's loss of federal government support. In retrospect, I believe his stunt was a ruse; no such calls were actually made.

I later learned from a Coalition insider that, a few days before the meeting, someone on my own staff had tipped off the organization about the content of the letter and the funding increase. So my announcement was news to no one. The quisling was Elizabeth May, long-time environmental activist and currently leader of the Green Party of Canada and MP from British Columbia. This fifth columnist had undermined our entire strategy—the element of surprise, in particular. My staffer had made clear to every official she could buttonhole at Environment Canada her opposition to the strategy, especially the letter. But this was my call, with which Dr. Slater and the deputy concurred—not hers. That said, my meeting with the board did not improve relations between the Mulroney government and the Coalition. All the time I had spent on mending fences proved a waste. May was vindicated, though she had improved her odds by surreptitiously undercutting the strategy from within our walls.

Elizabeth May frequently used such duplicity to make herself look prescient and wise in my eyes and to strengthen her hand throughout the department. The woman's cunning was extraordinary. And yet, how can any workplace function properly if an employee places self-interest above that of her employer, ignores the chain of command, and violates the oath of office (explicit or implied)? May is brainy, insightful, and shrewd well beyond the norm, and was experienced, knowledgeable, and strongly connected well beyond her years. So the skullduggery was utterly unnecessary. She easily could have achieved the same ends by applying her formidable talents above board. But, it seemed, the straight and narrow wasn't in her nature. Close to the ground, Environment Canada was filled with bright and observant people who soon saw through the young woman's guile. For my part, from on high, I was too busy running the place and uninterested in sophomoric antics to learn about most of her wheeling and dealing until long after the fact. In any event, following my meeting with the Coalition board, Michael Perley and Adèle Hurley continued to operate exactly as before. They just had more federal money—from my department!—with which to do so. Fleeced, indeed, was I.

I have to share the blame for the bad blood between the Mulroney government and the Coalition—Perley and Herley, in particular. Too often I let my frustration with these two individuals trump my eagerness to partner with their organization on the urgent acid rain cause. A player can't win if he thinks he has lost the game before it even begins. With the Coalition, I might not have been resigned to defeat that early, but lots of playing time remained when I largely gave up. I now realize this was a mistake. The environmental cause is too important for pique. The politician has to be the adult in the room. My experience, however, is that politicians typically don't, and can't, admit it when they're wrong, let alone try to understand why they are and mend their ways accordingly. For all their hostility towards "the Establishment"—less automatic now than a generation ago—most career environmentalists are deeply committed to making the planet a safer and healthier habitat for all humanity. No politician should ever dismiss these essentially good people as potential allies. I now wish I had possessed the equanimity to embrace that perspective more firmly when in Cabinet. As it was, I felt myself and the government continually under siege. It would have better served the public interest, not to mention our own partisan interests, had we possessed less of a siege mentality. That mindset can be self-fulfilling: conflict and distrust beget more of the same on either side of a divide. If ministers were formally trained and I their instructor, this lesson would top my syllabus for Cabinet 101.

That the hostility between the government and the Coalition didn't blow up the acid rain cause reflected its enduring strength. When it counted, the prime minister rose above it all, just as every strong leader does by nature. In this case, Brian Mulroney didn't so much cool down as decide to be cool: stop fretting about the Coalition's incessant attacks and ground-shifting and, instead, channel time and energy into solving the problem itself. And that is what he did. Success is the ultimate cool.

## A Historic Bilateral Action Plan

Brian Mulroney is nothing if not a stubborn man. When he sets a goal for himself, he pursues it relentlessly. Perhaps not even Mulroney himself knows when he first wanted to be prime minister of Canada. Likely, the decision evolved over time, starting with stardust in his eyes the first time, as a boy, he heard a Canadian PM speak.

Mulroney did not let the failure of his first serious attempt at politics kill the ambition. Following his humiliating defeat at the 1976 PC leadership convention, he regrouped for the next time. And in 1983, he achieved his goal of leading the PC Party. As noted earlier, party-related archives, including private ones such as mine, are spotted with the Hansel-and-Gretel bread crumbs the man left behind on his long path to the leadership, beginning well before he formally sought it. So it was with *Prime Minister* Brian Mulroney's seeking, against all the odds, to achieve an acid rain accord with the United States. The path was neither short nor certain. Nor, as with the famed Brothers Grimm bedtime story, without many obstacles. As John Diefenbaker frequently said on the campaign stump about obstacles he had overcome, "They said it couldn't be done." Diefenbaker liked nothing better than to tell audiences of the time his mother told him that a kid from Saskatchewan could never become prime minister, so he shouldn't be dreaming he would. But he willed it to happen. Many people, pre-eminently the Canadian Coalition on Acid Rain, were certain Mulroney's goal of achieving a Canada-United States acid rain accord was a fantasy tale or pipedream, too. But, as Mulroney did with his PC Party leadership ambitions, he persisted. Though "they said it couldn't be done," he did it. If individuals such as Diefenbaker and Mulroney easily took no for an answer, the country would have no prime minister. And Canada would not have attained a bilateral agreement with the United States to rid our country of the acid rain that was threatening to destroy it.

The groundwork the government laid with Ronald Reagan, however modest, finally paid off in windfall proportions when George. H. W. Bush became president. On June 12, 1989, Bush sponsored amendments to the *Clean Air Act of 1970* that would constitute, in his words, "a comprehensive program to provide clean air for all Americans." He proposed to reduce sulphur dioxide emissions by 10 million tonnes from 1980 levels. Within a year, the House of Representatives passed the legislation by a wide margin. On October 20, 1990, the Senate, which had amended the House bill, passed the legislation 89 to 10. On October 26, the House passed the Senate's revised version 401 to 25. On November 15, 1990, President Bush signed into law the final amendments to the *Clean Air Act* that established that country's acid rain program. The act would now cut emissions by nearly 10 million tonnes by 2000. Then, on March 13, 1991, in the Reading Room of the Centre Block of the Parliament Buildings in Ottawa, President Bush and Prime Minister Brian Mulroney signed the Canada-United States Air Quality Agreement on Acid Rain—long courted, and now wed. The bilateral accord was based on both the US *Clean Air Act of 1990* and the Canadian Acid Rain Program of 1985. The goal of a 50 percent reduction of sulphur dioxide emissions below 1980 levels in Canada had been set for 1994. (The Canada–US regime to control acid rain throughout the two countries contained parallel targeted and scheduled restrictions on all major sources of nitrogen oxide.) Historic as it was as a bilateral acid-rain-control master plan, the accord was substantially more than that. In a 1998 analysis, the Parliamentary Research Bureau stated: "The significance of the Agreement is much broader than acid rain in that it establishes a framework for dealing with other trans-boundary air pollution problems."[5] On March 13, 2012, Brian Mulroney, by then retired from politics, gave a major address at the Lester B. Pearson External Affairs Building in Ottawa to mark the twenty-first anniversary of the accord. He told the gathering of mostly former and current External Affairs and Environment Canada officials: "[The accord] could well serve as a template for a bilateral accord on climate change, as it has on other cross-border air issues."

To its credit, the Canadian Coalition on Acid Rain, along with US environmentalists, helped forge the consensus in Congress on the landmark acid rain amendments to the *Clean Air Act of 1990*. The contacts and goodwill that the Coalition's operatives had cultivated on Capitol Hill for almost a decade proved invaluable. Perley and Hurley's own first-rate lobbying skills, in particular, came to the fore.

But it was the president of the United States, George H. W. Bush, who sent the *Clean Air* bill to Congress in the first place. And he put the full authority and political weight and prestige of the Oval Office behind the lobby to get the bill passed in both houses of Congress. "When the president engages, the White Houses engages," Brian Mulroney has written, "and when the White house engages, the entire administration engages."[6] Mulroney should know: that was the essence of his entire successful acid rain strategy towards the US government. The prime minister and others in his government, including committed diplomats in Washington, deserve enormous credit for their relentless and skilful advocacy at the presidential level. As mentioned elsewhere here, George Mitchell, Senate majority leader at the time Congress acted on acid rain, told me, when I visited him in Washington as environment minister, that Brian Mulroney was the only person able to get the US administration even to think about the issue during the Reagan years. I encouraged the majority leader to repeat his statement publicly. He said he would be glad to do so. And, true to his word, he did. Mitchell's remarks, widely reported by the media at the time, are now part of the historic record—and, therefore, of Mulroney's.

The Mulroney government had been wise to ignore the Coalition's advice that it should not seek, at the heads-of-government level, a Canada-United States acid rain accord to enshrine each country's obligations to the other in this area. As Allan Gotlieb underscored in his *Globe and Mail* op-ed piece, "The views of some of our lobbyists notwithstanding, Canada does not derive its rights from the US Congress. It derives them from treaties duly entered into between sovereign governments."[7] In his memoirs, Mulroney describes the signing of the acid rain agreement with Bush as "one of the greatest days of my primeministership."[8] Inarguably, the agreement was one of his greatest accomplishments in office. The acid rain accords I negotiated and signed with the seven relevant provinces laid the foundation for the bilateral agreement. Together, those provincial accords constitute one of the biggest domestic achievements of the entire government during my time as environment minister. In this area, as in most others, the PM had been no mere chairman of the board, delegating everything to others. Rather, he had been more an orchestra leader for whom every note from every instrument had to harmonize with every other to achieve a masterful concerto. With the Canada–United States Air Quality Agreement on Acid Rain, Brian Mulroney had masterminded a magnificent orchestration whose melodious notes continue to echo across the continent—indeed, the planet—to this day. Since the agreement was signed, both peoples have not only honoured their commitments but also exceeded them.

Brian Mulroney had invested a great deal of his own and his government's political capital in the acid rain issue. And he had done so knowing full well that, given US intransigence over a very long time, the odds for success were heavily stacked against him. But the prime minister's perseverance paid off. One would be hard-pressed to cite another case in which either a federal or a provincial government leader risked, in personal credibility and public standing, as much as this prime minister did on a single issue with so little prospect of success in the end. It's called political courage. That Mulroney succeeded testifies to how visionary and wise he was to chart his own course, not the one that would have silenced his critics on the issue, both in Parliament and across the land, but done nothing to solve the acid rain problem itself. On the twenty-first anniversary of the agreement, Mulroney summarized what Canadians and Americans had achieved in partnership: "In ten years, we went from yelling at one another, to talking to one another, to negotiating with one another, to making an important agreement with one another. Now…acid rain is no longer a public policy issue. Not only has the dispute been resolved, the problem has been solved."[9] I myself would add only this: Would that every major issue facing the two countries could be resolved that successfully—and with such vision and courage.

Following the signing of the acid rain accord, Michael Perley and Adèle Hurley were out of jobs. I was still consul general in Boston. John Fraser remained Commons Speaker and patron of the Canadian Coalition on Acid Rain, or what was left of it after the issue had been eliminated from the public agenda—or, at least, put much farther down—by the historic bilateral agreement. Passionate critics of the Mulroney government, Perley and Hurley nevertheless lobbied hard, with Fraser's help, to get Environment Minister Jean Charest to award the two environmentalists a rich contract in the name of the Coalition. The contract would mandate them to "monitor" and publicly report progress by the two countries in implementing the agreement. I held no lasting animus towards Michael and Adèle. But, in principle, I thought it inappropriate for them to be paid to judge the success of a major international pollution-abatement regime produced by negotiations they themselves had opposed from the beginning. It would have been less a conflict of interest than a script with a predetermined ending before the plot had been devised. Though no longer directly responsible for any part of the Canada-United States acid rain control effort, I was eager that it succeed to the very end. I worried that Hurley and Perley would use the contract they were seeking to snipe at the two national governments responsible for implementing the agreement. I thought their machinations would risk undermining the resolve of those governments to persevere in the face of setbacks that invariably occur when an ambitious new program passes through the teething period. One call from me in Boston, doubtless made in the heat of the moment, to Charest's chief of staff in Ottawa was all it took to derail Perley and Hurley's lobbying for the contract. I was appalled by the prospect of their being able to continue to harp and carp against the Mulroney government for self-interested purposes while cashing cheques for doing so from the very object of their contempt. The Irish in me! But, more fundamentally, I just thought the acid rain control program was too important for both countries, and for the planet, to risk having Perley and Hurley muck around with it, possibly with partisan intent.

Although I played no direct role in forging the acid rain agreement at the end, I had helped lay the groundwork on Canada's side by negotiating, and then signing for the Canadian government, the federal-provincial acid rain accords. These agreements demonstrated the bona fides Canada needed to bring to the negotiating table to press the US government to take a bilateral approach to the issue on a targeted and scheduled basis. So I considered myself, if not the godfather of the agreement, then at least an honorary uncle. All my fellow MPs who had worked so hard on the parliamentary acid rain sub-committee back in the early 1980s—from the government and Opposition sides alike—also deserved this designation, as did many others, for their pioneering contribution to making the agreement happen. The sub-committee's landmark report, *Still Waters,* had provided the road map for the course ultimately followed to address the scourge. For my part, I was now determined to do all I could—limited as it might be—to ensure the agreement succeeded and, in the face of Perley and Hurley's new ambitions, pre-empt anything that might cast public doubt on the magnitude of what had just been accomplished by the two countries. Given the size of the acid rain challenge that both Canada and the United States once faced, and the spectacular success we achieved in meeting it in the spirit of common cause and hands-across-the-border friendship, this story makes one thing clear: no environmental problem—perhaps no bilateral problem of any kind—should be considered too big, too complex, or too politically difficult for our two countries to solve. What is required is the will to act.

# Environmentalism and Partisanship

Spokespeople for environmental groups were typically young, lacked maturity, earned little, and got easily caught up in the media attention they invariably received for attacking the Mulroney government on their groups' respective pet issues. Most activists were also bright, educated, knowledgeable, and well-meaning. But they had to compete with one another for outside funding and the media attention that helped them raise it. This competition caused an arms race among the groups to see who could launch the most lethal verbal missiles against the government. Denouncing Brian Mulroney in the harshest language permissible on the public airwaves or in print was how one was able to garner the most coverage. The government was deemed fair game for any attack by any group on any matter. The disproportionality between the rhetoric and the alleged offences was not considered relevant. NGO spokespersons were especially eager to get themselves on television. Newscasts and TV public affairs programs were, therefore, where one could find the most intemperate rhetoric against the Mulroney government from environmental foot soldiers, particularly of the "executive director" type. Within their ranks, it was not fashionable to be thought a Tory, much less actually be one. God forbid! NDP and Liberal were the street-cred labels *du jour*, in that order of cachet.

Widespread NGO partisan bias was ignored by the media, certainly not punished. Indeed, many reporters on the environmental beat were complicit in the partisanship, or at least the ideology, and made little effort to disguise the fact. Close ties between NGO spokespeople and particular political parties and politicians were as rampant as they were shameless, to say nothing of professionally unethical—and possibly illegal. These groups were funded directly by taxpayers through government grants and contracts and indirectly by donation-deductibility provisions in the tax code. And yet, there was—and still is in many cases—virtually no external (or even internal) oversight to ensure they operated in ways that qualified them for generous state-sanctioned privileges and benefits as not-for-profit, non-partisan entities. Staff of the typical environmental NGO routinely attacked the Mulroney government in the name of supposedly thousands of members. In fact, most of these groups lacked any kind of governing body wholly independent of paid staff to formulate policy, ensure the membership broadly supported it, instruct official spokespersons on what that policy was, and rein them in when they strayed. Virtually every staffer freelanced, shot from the lip, and did so with impunity.

I once asked to meet with a particular group's board to discuss an especially egregious case of this behaviour only to be told by the chairperson that the offending staffer had vetoed the request! Raising the problem with anybody, especially in the media, was a surefire way to get oneself branded an anti-environmentalist. I would draw an analogy with how some people are quick to play the race card when it demonstrably does not apply but serves their immediate self-interested purpose. They know the ploy is certain to bring an unwanted discussion to a sudden halt—nullifying a losing hand, as it were. To merit the label "McCarthyism," a practice does not need to be nearly as extreme as that practised by the US senator who gave the syndrome its name. In a democracy, no individual or group should be given an "unfairness pass," permitting them to say publicly, without fear of accountability or comeuppance, whatever they want regardless of the facts. It would have been safer for me as minister of the environment to criticize Mother Teresa and her Missionaries of Charity than an environmental NGO front man or woman. Certain Mulroney government critics in the environmental movement placed themselves on an even higher celestial plain than Mother Teresa's exclusively by association with their benevolent cause. Being perceived on the side of the angels insulated these people from scrutiny and criticism. Indeed, a whole activist community was allowed to operate largely without checks and balances to ensure it met at least minimal levels of competence, accomplishment, and professional behaviour by standards generally applied to entities substantially dependent on public funding.

For me, none of this is about bitter memories, sour grapes, or settling scores. It's about how I believe a specific type of public interest group ought to act if it is to help promote a healthy civic culture, an engaged citizenry, constructive social activism, strong community-based institutions, and government-citizen relations conducive to making our substantial corner of the planet a better place for Canadians from coast to coast to coast. After all, that is the implicit "participatory democracy" mandate of every interest group that receives public funding. Environmentalism is not just a theology to be preached or an invocation to be chanted in either a private temple or the public square. It's a commitment to community and human values to be honoured in one's heart and practised in the real world. Environmentalism is an empty and meaningless value system if its evangelists refuse to seek common ground among people with whom they might disagree politically. As an environmentalist myself, I profoundly regret that our noble cause is accorded the status of quasi-religion while some of its most visible faces too often fail to manifest the respect and comity towards others— set aside piety, humility, and charity—that would justify such reverence. The fact that their viciousness and warlike rhetoric are invariably aimed at public office-holders does not render it more acceptable. In a democracy, no one should be considered fair game for McCarthyism. Nor should it ever be open season on public officials merely because they're easy targets. The "all's-fair-in-love-and-war" principle is indefensible even in matters of the heart and military combat. In some circumstances, it can be illegal; one can't lawfully kill a spouse or commit war atrocities. Just as that principle flouts natural law, as articulated or interpreted by such intellectual giants as Plato and Aristotle and St. Thomas Aquinas, it is also utterly incompatible with generally understood tenets of environmentalism. Nor does it make sense as a practical matter for preserving the planet. Everyone's goodwill and involvement are required to preserve our shared natural heritage and secure humanity's health and survival. Corny as the nostrum might sound today, the 1960s and early 1970s generation had it right: "Make love, not war." That includes a war of words. The children's rhyme "sticks and stones may break my bones, but words will never hurt me" might play well on the playground. But this credo won't advance anyone's humanitarian interests in an advanced society. It's best that both verbal and physical violence be expunged from the political culture. Bullying is no more acceptable from the mouth than from the fist.

NGOs and politicians have something fundamental in common: their respective mandates are to serve the community, not themselves. Both sides are agents of the same master: the public. In that sense, they should consider themselves on the same side, just with different roles. A public interest group can play its discrete and necessary role—articulating a cause, fighting hard for it, and criticizing and opposing those, including governments, who stand in the way—without violating generally held principles of civility. The environmentalist and the politician can fulfill their fundamentally different responsibilities, disagree about issues, and find fault with each other's views and actions and still operate as natural allies, not mortal enemies. Protecting and saving the planet is too urgent a cause for either the environmentalist or the politician to exclude the other from his or her domain on ideological, political, partisan, or any other grounds.

When I left the Environment portfolio after serving for almost four years, environmental NGOs said that nothing—nothing!—had been achieved in the environmental area by the Mulroney government in all that time. Some of the NGOs not involved in national parks issues did acknowledge—how could they deny an objective, quantifiable fact?—that we had established five new national parks. But, since that area was not a priority for them, it didn't count in their scoring. Our failing grade must have surprised the likes of UN Secretary-General Kofi Annan and Norwegian prime minister Gro Harlem Brundtland, chair of the World Commission on Environment and Development, both of whom lauded the Mulroney government's leadership on the environment in diverse areas, including ozone depletion.

The problem for us wasn't just that each separate environmental group tended to judge our record *exclusively* on whether we had dealt with *all* the problems on its particular agenda while giving us little or no credit for anything we might have accomplished, however major, on another group's list. Most such groups believed it was in their interests not to give us credit for *any* achievement, no matter whose agenda it was on. The more we could be portrayed as the "bad guys," the easier it was for them to gain air time or column inches and, consequently, raise money as "the good guys." Shortly after I left the portfolio, Elizabeth May said that some environmentalists would prefer to have someone like Suzanne Blais-Grenier as environment minister, rather than a Tom McMillan, "so the issues could be black and white and so that everyone would know that the Tories are bad."[10] To this day, no other fundraising strategy has proved more successful for certain types of not-for-profit organizations than convincing prospective donors that their interests are directly threatened by a dragon the group itself has created in those donors' minds. And, of course, the group claims that only it can slay that dragon. For many environmental NGOs, the Mulroney government was the fire-breathing dragon and they were St. George to the rescue.

How much sooner would Canada have been able to achieve its historic agreement with the United States on acid rain had everybody—specifically, the Canadian Coalition on Acid Rain and the Mulroney government—pulled in the same direction from beginning to end? The answer is evident: a lot sooner than the seven long years it took. Meanwhile, an enormous amount of irreversible but avoidable environmental damage was inflicted on our country and the continent as a whole for lack of better teamwork. That is the main lesson from the Acid Rain Story.

In 1995, the Chrétien government appointed Adèle Hurley to co-chair the International Joint Commission (IJC), an important and coveted high-paying patronage position. The IJC oversees Canada-United States boundary water issues pursuant to the bilateral Boundary Waters Treaty of 1909. The Canadian chair—the Americans also appoint a chair—is invariably a partisan of the governing party of the day. Thus, no eyebrows were raised when the Chrétien Liberals chose Hurley. Her appointment was considered in some quarters an IOU marked "paid" for quasi-partisan service for the Liberals against the Mulroney government in the guise of environmentalism at the Canadian Coalition on Acid Rain. Hurley was extremely close to Charles Caccia, long-time Liberal MP for the Toronto riding of Davenport and his party's environmental spokesman; he served, briefly, as environment minister under Pierre Trudeau. Both Michael Perley and Adèle Hurley were also close to Ontario environment minister Jim Bradley, who enjoyed undermining Mulroney government efforts on a broad front. Indeed, they hosted a major public dinner in his honour—while he was still minister! Ontario Liberal premier David Peterson sent a private high-level emissary to discuss with me the premier's own concern about the bad blood Jim Bradley was causing not just between the Ontario government and me, but also, by extension, between it and the Mulroney government as a whole. Ontario's new deputy minister of the environment at the time told me privately—in the presence of my own deputy minister—that his first order and highest priority, on orders from Peterson, was "reining in" his minister to prevent relations between the Ontario and Mulroney governments from deteriorating any further because of Bradley's shrill partisan behaviour.

If political payoff was not the original intent behind Hurley's IJC appointment, it arguably was the effect. The appointment was generally viewed as such, certainly in Mulroney circles, including me. Whether this view is accurate—and I concede it is speculative—that the perception was widespread among Tories is a measure of how little importance Perley and Hurley had attached to appearing non-partisan while with the Coalition. Hurley is now director of the Program on Water Issues at the Munk School of Global Affairs, at the University of Toronto. In December 2014, she was made a member of the Order of Canada for her "commitment to the conservation and the protection of Canada's natural resources." I applaud her for receiving this distinction, one of the country's highest civilian honours. I do, however, doubt her political fairness and that of her environmental partner Michael Perley, at a much younger age when we in the Mulroney government had only limited success in making common cause with them on acid rain. Like those of us who lived through the turbulent 1960s, which gave rise to their kind of take-no-prisoners social activism, the Canadian environmental movement—at least most of it—eventually grew up. The movement and the country are the better for it.

## Environmentalism and Conservatives

History ought to give Brian Mulroney credit for the vision and courage and political wisdom he applied to reaching a historic agreement between Canada and the United States on acid rain. I have yet to see that history written, except partially by Mulroney himself in his memoirs. That said, no doubt the choice of Mulroney as "the greenest prime minister in Canadian history" was based largely on his government's historic record on acid rain. In public interviews, he has expressed the opinion that this is the case. But the historical record here remains incomplete. How does such a dearth give any subsequent government—a Conservative one least of all—an incentive to demonstrate environmental leadership the way Mulroney's government did? It has exactly the opposite effect. Any effort by environmental NGOs to deny credit to a government that acts effectively on an environmental issue does a disservice not only to that government, but also to the environmental cause itself. The political label of the government is irrelevant. Politicians of every partisan stripe should be criticized when they do not act wisely and praised when they do. Giving credit where credit is due should be as much a part of the environmentalist's role as helping to hold accountable anyone—government, politician, industry, or individual—whose actions or neglect hurts the environment. Aside from fairness, the duality of the environmentalist's role is important because, like anyone else, a politician responds to carrots *and* sticks, not just the latter. Human nature being what it is, both are required to advance the environmental cause. This was a point I made in many speeches and media interviews and in private comments throughout my time as the country's environment minister and long afterwards, including as consul general in Boston.

As environment minister, I urged PC Party audiences to make environmental issues a high priority on the grounds it was both the moral thing to do and in their own political self-interest. I argued that Tories should not abdicate the environmental field to Liberals and the NDP as we too often had done at our own electoral peril. I said other parties had successfully made the field their domain in the public's and media's minds while we allowed ourselves to be typecast as captives of big business and indifferent to environmental issues if not altogether hostile to them. I stressed that the Progressive *Conservative* Party should be the party of the environment for, by definition, *conservation* not only is a core value of *conservatism*, but also constitutes, in a variation of the word, half our dual name. I made this very argument in a major policy session at the Progressive Conservative Party's Annual Meeting in Montreal shortly after my appointment to the Environment portfolio in late summer of 1985. My theme received more news coverage—all of it positive—than anything else discussed during any of the policy sessions, irrespective of field. More to the point, the delegates themselves agreed. Delegate after delegate came to the microphone and addressed the matter passionately in a policy session that, up to that point, lacked spark. Where are those kinds of Conservatives today? I still hold the view that the party should attach supreme importance to the environment, if for no other reason than its own electoral self-interest. Indeed, the Canadian Conservative Party should be *Canada's environmental party*. But I very much regret that, under Stephen Harper's leadership, the party demonstrably was not that and, as I write, doesn't look as though it will be any time soon. It was fast becoming so by the end of Brian Mulroney's time as prime minister. In partisan terms, though not environmental, what a waste of progress!

The elimination of acid rain as both a major Canadian-US environmental threat and a serious bone of contention between the two countries is one of the Progressive Conservative Party's most important and historic achievements. It is right up there with, for example, the opening of the West and the construction of a transcontinental railway to make it possible. The party today should be proud of this landmark environmental accomplishment. And Conservatives should be inspired by it to once again grab onto environmental issues and run with them harder and faster and farther than any other political party. By doing so, they will win for themselves more than additional credit in the history books. They will win votes; just as, unquestionably, the Progressive Conservative Party did across Canada on a host of environmental issues while in government under Mulroney's leadership—notably, the bushel of new national parks it established. At the time, internal party polls, and many public ones too, confirmed the salience of environmental issues for Canadians who self-identified as supporters of one or other of all the major parties, including the PC Party. I have no doubt whatsoever that, in the face of widespread alarm about climate change in particular, environmental issues today are even more politically salient—not to mention urgent—than they were in my time in active politics a generation ago. The Harper government's downplaying them was both morally outrageous and politically stupid. The Conservative Party deserved to be kicked from office for that reason alone. Elective stupidity should always be considered a disqualifier for public office.

Until Conservatives themselves demand, and receive, the credit they deserve for past successes in the environmental area, including acid rain, the historic record will be worse than woefully incomplete. It will be dead wrong in a vital domain of public policy and our national cultural life. More important for the health of the planet, a major player, the Canadian Conservative Party, if the government of the country, will have that much less incentive to replicate on other environmental issues its historic success on this particular one. May Brian Mulroney stand as the conscience of the Conservative Party on the environment. His record as prime minister surely qualifies him for the role. I have neither a torch nor a can to carry for Mulroney as an individual. Unlike my twin brother's personal history with the man, mine is not all that intimate. Indeed, it has been mostly official. But I believe passionately that Mulroney's transformative leadership on acid rain could serve throughout our country as a template of vision and courage and acumen on the environment for all governments and political parties, federal and provincial alike, regardless of partisan stripe or philosophical orientation. May that kind of leadership inspire the Conservative Party of Canada anew now and long into its future.

# Chapter 21

# SOUTH MORESBY: A TORY VISION

O ne late afternoon, my brother Charley sat at a computer in his second-floor office at the Langevin Block, across from the Peace Tower on Parliament Hill. He was working on ideas and notes for a speech that Prime Minister Brian Mulroney was to deliver in the House of Commons later in the week. The PM popped in with his suit jacket doffed, his tie unknotted, his collar unbuttoned, and his demeanour relaxed and jovial. Mulroney spotted from the corner of his eye a large poster that his senior policy advisor had just festooned across the opposite wall in the boardroom adjacent to Charley's office. The coloured poster contained a marine engineer's conceptual graphic of the PEI-New Brunswick bridge. The design had been produced by one of the consortia interested in eventually bidding on the project. This was well before the project was scarcely more than a proposal that Charley and I almost alone were promoting in political circles in Ottawa and that I was tooting back on the Island virtually as a one-man band. The prime minister exited Charley's office through the usually open door, sauntered into the boardroom, walked over to the poster, paused, stared at the image, peered more closely, turned towards Charley, pointed at the bridge, looked straight at my brother, and exclaimed: "That is exactly what our party stands for—big ideas, building the country, national vision. Our government needs to be doing more of that kind of thing."

My twin was taken aback by his boss's exuberance. He had rarely heard Mulroney express himself about the government's mission with such spontaneity—or intensity. But Charley knew from many other discussions the two men had conducted with each other that the PM's comments on this occasion encapsulated how he viewed the PC Party, his own role as party and government leader, and the country more generally. My twin was as fanatic a supporter of the PEI-NB Fixed Link idea as I. "In Mulroney's PMO from 1984 to 1987, Charley McMillan drove colleagues to distraction with his persistence about a fixed link," penned L. Ian MacDonald, in a 2010 *Montreal Gazette* article.[1] MacDonald should know, for he was one of those very colleagues whom Charley had pestered. Right after the poster incident occurred, Charley told me about it. He made no effort to contain his excitement. I myself was thunderstruck. I had never discussed the Fixed Link with the PM. So, I didn't know what he thought about the project as I prepared to ask Cabinet to approve it in principle to trigger the necessary cost-benefit and environmental investigations and public consultative processes. Moreover, I was unsure where he placed such big-ticket infrastructure projects on the government's overall agenda, aside from the obvious employment and other economic benefits. Now, however, according to Charley, the prime minister was talking just as I had heard Tom Symons speak so passionately about the country and the Progressive Conservative Party, in particular—Sir John A. Macdonald's vision, the National Dream, nation building, expanding the country's horizons, knitting it together from coast to coast to coast, and all that. (Brian Mulroney discusses the now-named Confederation Bridge in this exact manner in his memoirs.)

Buoyed as I was about the prospect of having the PM as a potential ally in the Fixed Link cause, I was even happier for another reason: if this was indeed how he saw things, I could sell him on another big cause even dearer to my heart as an environmentalist. That cause was establishing South Moresby—a constellation of magnificent islands off the coast of British Columbia rich in natural and cultural treasures—as a national park reserve. The islands risked being stripped bare of their ancient first-growth towering trees and untold mineral wealth and exotic wildlife by voracious logging and mining and fish-processing companies and big-game hunters coddled by a provincial government eager to exploit the archipelago's uncountable bounty. The pressures on the federal government to save the islands from pillage and plunder as a park reserve were enormous and mounting, not just from across Canada, but also from around the world. As if to jam a rod up the spine of us Canadians to steel our resolve, the United Nations Educational, Scientific and Cultural Organization (UNESCO) had declared the islands a World Heritage Site on both natural *and* built heritage grounds. It was a dual distinction as rare as much of the wildlife that populated this Pacific paradise. Adding spinal steel of its own the same year, the Historic Sites and Monuments Board of Canada designated the area of unique national heritage importance. I thought our government's responding to such pressures to rescue the islands by turning them into a national park would be the quintessence of nation building—and of the Progressive Conservative Party's historic vision and pivotal role in making it happen. Rarely does any government get an opportunity to do something gigantic. It can sometimes reach for the skies, hardly ever beyond the stratosphere. This was a walk on the moon.

It's when a political leader rises to meet great opportunity that he or she achieves greatness in the eyes of history. The PM's comments to Charley convinced me that we Tories had an opportunity in our own time to do something truly great. It would stamp PROGRESSIVE CONSERVATIVE GOVERNMENT large enough on a page of Canadian history that a blind man without Braille would know it was there. We could share in the National Dream of the country's founding father, Sir John A. Macdonald. After all, Macdonald had created Canada's magnificent national park system. And this would be the most challenging—not to mention the most expensive—of all national parks to complete. It was a file that, as the country's environment minister, I was to put down only after South Moresby finally became not just an entry in my voluminous ministerial briefing books, but, in the world conservation community's judgment, the most precious addition to the country's national park system in its century-old history. I became almost obsessed with being part of making that happen. I had no idea then how right I would end up being about the prime minister's becoming a potential ally in this national and international cause. The spirit of Sir John A. was to prove alive and well and tangible among a bunch of exotic Pacific islands as far west as it was possible for us Canadians to travel and still be home.

Now, a quarter-century later, South Moresby is an integral part of our country as a secure and protected land and marine preserve that places it among the highest-rated officially designated national wilderness areas on the planet. Our total Canadian home is that much closer to being completed because the national government of the day acted to save South Moresby. Except for acid raid, this was the environmental issue in which the PM played his most active and effective and visionary role while I was minister—virtually the entire first half of his primeministership—and likely throughout the whole period he was in office. The Green Plan, launched in the second half, is the only other environmental measure that came close to taking as much of the PM's commitment and time and thinking as either acid rain or South Moresby did. Both for this reason and in South Moresby's own right, the story merits being told. Here is that story, the impossible-to-miss entry on the pages of Canadian history.

## The Misty Isles

I love islands. No doubt, it's because I was born and raised on one. Throw in an archipelago, and I swoon. That's how my Parks Canada officials said I responded when, on October 9, 1985, I first travelled with them to South Moresby, in the Queen Charlotte Islands (now Haida Gwaii), 130 kilometres off the west coast of British Columbia. I went to see for myself what all the fuss was about in a classic confrontation between loggers and miners against Aboriginal peoples and environmentalists over Canada's most exotic wilderness area. I fell under South Moresby's spell the moment my feet hit its stony shores. I was to return many times as environment minister, never passing up an excuse to soak up the magnificence of the "misty isles," and to luxuriate in the therapeutic magic of its bubbling and gurgling hot springs. In his superb book, *Silent Earth*, environmental journalist and writer David Israelson put it this way: "[S]hortly after he became Environment Minister in 1985, Tom McMillan went to South Moresby and fell in love with the region. When he got out of the helicopter that took him there, the Environment Minister of Canada sank into the moss and rolled around, laughing with delight." Said someone who accompanied him, the author reported, "He was like a little kid. I knew then that he was committed to protecting the area."[2] I *was* like a little kid! Every adult should be fortunate enough to have that sense at least once in life. I had it every time I travelled to these extraordinary islands. And they belonged to Canada. My country!

"South Moresby" was shorthand for a 1,500-square-kilometre, 138-island archipelago—including the largest island, Moresby Island, south of the Tangil Peninsula—that now constitutes Gwaii Haanas National Park Reserve and Haida Heritage Site. There, ancient forests of cedar and Sitka spruce harbour rare lush mosses and high-hanging ferns and unusual subspecies. All this, and much more, survived the glaciations that scraped those species from the planet's surface everywhere else during the Ice Age. *Canada's Galapagos*, the islands are called, and for good reason. They host luxuriant forest greenery, gigantic grey and hunchback whales, spectacular clusters of other ocean life, Technicolor seabird colonies, and outer-worldly sea lion populations. The islands are also home to the world's largest salmon, the world's largest black bears, the world's largest and densest population of American bald eagles, and among the world's biggest peregrine falcons. To me, the most striking feast to the eyes are trees seeded half a millennium before Michelangelo was born. As if all that were not enough to overwhelm mere mortals, the gods did something else to assert their dominance: they chose this paradise to house the Haida Nation. Over the centuries, the Haida have created giant outdoor works of art as spectacular as the natural features of the islands that provide the raw materials and inspire the spiritual values and artistry for these cultural wonders of the world. They include totem poles as towering as church spires and hand-carved seafaring canoes each big enough to transport a bevy of samurai wrestlers. The seven-thousand-year-old Haida civilization was already ancient when the pharaohs ruled Egypt. Nothing about these islands is small, least of all their history.

Not content to stack the genetic deck with all that bounty for one paradise, the divinities further bestowed on South Moresby, as it did on Banff, glorious hot springs—a huge weakness of mine. Whenever the media caught me frolicking in the hot springs, microphone jocks and their redneck callers mocked me on phone-in talk radio shows across British Columbia. Jack Webster, the infamous curmudgeon whose talk show was the best known in the country at the time, had a field day at my expense when I appeared in his studio as a feature guest. But I actually enjoyed the battle of wits with him and his callers. I had an ace up my sleeve: my mother, though born in PEI, was raised in British Columbia. So this, I said, made me half British Columbian. How could my detractors argue against that? Besides, I considered the ribbing a small price to pay for a short time in paradise. Like Sir John A. Macdonald with Banff, I would have fought to save South Moresby for the hot springs alone. If the bald eagles and ravens that flapped above got saved in the bargain, so much the better.

On May 14, 1987, the House of Commons debated a motion sponsored by the NDP on one of their cherished Opposition Days. The motion called on the country to establish the South Moresby national park. Even well before the debate ended, the Commons did something possibly unprecedented: it effectively approved the Opposition motion. I expressed officially the government's support. While only symbolic, this action had profound political implications, for it signalled beyond dispute that support for the park crossed partisan lines. I saw Parliament's action as the moral point of no return. Full speed ahead! Leading the debate for the government, I said this about my first visit to the Queen Charlotte Islands only twelve weeks after I became Canada's environment minister: "Despite advance descriptions from people who had visited before me...I was singularly unprepared for the magnificence...the awe-inspiring forest canopies, the bubbling hot springs, the teeming wildlife, the wide-open spaces, the pristine stillness, the sheer beauty of an unspoiled world....I feel a special kinship to those remote misty isles."

The many times I visited the islands were no mean feat; they resided as far from my PEI home as it was possible to travel and still be in Canada. But the islands kept drawing me back like a salmon swimming upstream to its gravel bed at spawning time. More than just seduced by the islands, I was driven to save them from what appeared certain ruin unless someone did something big and bold and breakaway to stop it. Why not the Mulroney government? I asked myself. Why not me? The battle to save all this natural and built heritage against massive clear-cut logging, open-pit mining, commercial fishing, and trophy shooting thrust the Mulroney government into one of its most politically tumultuous controversies, with me always in the eye of the storm. So contentious was the issue, and so high the economic and moral stakes, that, at one point, the RCMP had to provide bodyguards to prevent loggers from hanging this humble servant from the tallest Sitka tree—or anything else with a branch or a bough.

In the end, everything tallied, the South Moresby national park cost the federal and British Columbia governments, combined, close to $200 million in the late 1980s and early 1990s—equivalent to about a third of a billion dollars today. Innumerable people, both in government and from the public at large, helped make this expensive park a reality. A number of environmental activists deserve credit for their various valiant roles—among them, John Broadhead, Thom Henley, Vicky Husband, Colleen McCrory, Kevin McNamee, Gregg Sheehy, and many more. They put the lie to the argument that environmentalists are all about shouting from the rooftops, not acting on the ground. House of Commons Speaker John Fraser, NDP MP Jim Fulton, and Liberal MP Charles Caccia are among the office holders outside the federal and BC Cabinets who contributed heroically to the cause. Miles Richardson, head of the Haida Nation, contributed so much that mere words cannot do his role justice. He stands in a class by himself among the heroes of the saga.

Among the famous Canadians who helped lead the cause outside government were scientist and *Nature of Things* broadcaster David Suzuki, author and TV personality Pierre Berton, writers Farley Mowat and Margaret Atwood, singer Bruce Cockburn, and painter Toni Onley. Like other celebrities at home and around the world, they were never too busy or too self-important to devote their prestige and fame and creative products and money to the effort. These people and countless other Canadians—most of them neither famous nor supremely gifted nor rich— deserve laurel wreaths for what they did to secure a glorious victory for nature.

The fact is, however, South Moresby National Park Reserve (now Gwaii Haanas) was created by government, not by outside activists of the sort mentioned above. Only politicians and their officials and staff at the highest levels could have created something that cost the taxpayer that much money. Environmental activists and non-governmental organizations (NGOs) helped exert the public pressure without which the park would not have happened. But, vital as their roles were, environmentalists and NGOs made none of the difficult policy and funding decisions, at all the different stages, that led to the national park's completion—from the time the park was first proposed till the day the federal and British Columbia governments publicly signed the legal documents. My own political staff, in particular, merits a curtain call.

Ron Woznow, the chief of staff, worked tirelessly with me to help make the park a reality. Towards that end, he also partnered with each of his counterparts in the offices of all the various relevant ministers—principally Finance, Treasury Board, Indian and Northern Affairs, Fisheries and Oceans, and Energy, Mines and Resources. Among other staff members actively involved were my longest-serving assistant, Rob Burnett of Charlottetown, a young Dalhousie University–trained lawyer; Marc Grenier, a Franco-Ontarian who had been a parliamentary intern in my Opposition office before joining me in government; and senior policy advisor Sheila Kieran. Sheila is not only a wise woman but also a gifted writer. She served as executive director of the Book and Periodical Development Council of Canada when I was its board chairman in the mid-1970s, before my election to Parliament. Some of the woman's wisdom is derived from her having been abandoned by a husband and left with seven children, all of them born within eight years of one another, to raise on her own. Every minister should be fortunate enough to have on staff a smart and skilled Jewish grandmother such as Sheila. If, like Sheila, she could convert a laundry list to poetry with a flick of a finger on a keyboard, all the better. I must also mention my Parliamentary Secretary, Pauline Browes (MP for Scarborough Centre, 1984–93). Pauline served as a virtual *sous-ministre* most of the time I was environment minister, engaged as she was in every major decision I made. She became minister of state for the environment, a newly created subministry, in 1991.

# Closing the South Moresby Deal

One staff member who played a pivotal role in the creation of the South Moresdy national park was Terry Collins. A committed environmentalist in his own right, just as many others on staff were, Terry, my press secretary, stood front and centre in a dramatic sequence of events that rescued South Moresby from what appeared to be certain defeat. Those events occurred at the heart-stopping climax of the saga, in mid-June 1987, two weeks before the park deal was sealed.

Terry, a former *Toronto Sun* reporter, was home in Ottawa late one night when he got devastating news from Tom Van Dusen, communications point man in the office of Deputy Prime Minister Don Mazankowski. Hours earlier, the BC government had rejected Ottawa's $106-million offer (then top secret) for the archipelago we were trying to save by creating the national park. But so much was at stake, both environmentally and politically, that I could not accept no for an answer. I was hell-bent on achieving success at virtually any cost—including, as it turned out, to the public treasury. The BC government's opposition was not going to stop me from continuing to try.

Van Dusen infomed Terry that the deputy prime minister intended to announce the next day both the BC government's news—which, in effect, would have killed the national park option—and the end of negotiations. Terry pleaded with the deputy PM's staffer that our media line should be, instead, that "the offer is still on the table." It was a desperate gamble to keep the park option afloat. Van Dusen reluctantly acquiesced, but added he was sure the deal was doomed no matter what we did. Terry immediately called me at home well after I had gone to bed. We then decided on our own (a conspiracy of two) to leak to the media the federal government's detailed secret offer to pay British Columbia $106 million to make the park happen. In football, this is called a "Hail Mary Pass" But we were throwing the ball from the bleachers, if not from outside the stadium altogether. My press secretary hurriedly dressed, drove to our Environment Canada offices in Hull, fetched the official document containing the offer, photocopied it, and placed the contraband in a plain, unmarked brown envelope. He then furtively hand-delivered the envelope at the witching hour to the overnight newswire editor at The Canadian Press Ottawa bureau, at the corner of Metcalfe and Wellington Streets. All very cloak and dagger! Our only condition to CP was that it could not reveal Terry and me as the sources. Confidentiality was imperative. My own Cabinet position rested on it, as did Terry's government career, then and any time in the future. At best, we were stretching the limits of our oaths of office. At worst, we might have been breaking the law. But neither of us had time to worry about any of that now. Time was fast running out for the park. Details of the multi-million-dollar offer were on the CP wire by the time I woke up that morning. I had set my alarm for 4:30 A.M., two hours earlier than usual, to access the story. And there it was, burning up the lines from one end of the country to the other. Terry and I had thrown the football high in the air, and it was now speeding downfield. But would anyone catch it?

In Question Period later the same day, the key South Moresby question was posed by the Opposition. Indeed, we had planted it with NDP MP Jim Fulton of British Columbia, a militant supporter of the park and crypto co-conspirator. Liberal environment critic Charles Caccia of Toronto, equally militant and conspiratorial, was held in reserve if anything went awry. On this issue, dear to his heart, Speaker John Fraser could be counted on not only to cut us some slack, but also give us practically the whole Question Period if we needed it. It was not necessary. The Speaker recognized Fulton, the NDP MP rose from his seat, looked right at me, and fired away: "Can the Honourable Minister of the Environment confirm that the federal government has offered British Columbia $106 million to create South Moresby National Park?" The clip on every national newscast that night showed me, aggressive and uncharacteristically emotional, wagging a finger at an invisible BC government, and telling the Commons angrily: "Yes, I can confirm this most generous offer, and the $106 million deal is still on the table." Cleaning up New York Yankee Yogi Berra's English, I added, "It isn't over 'til it's over."

The media coverage, particularly in British Columbia, was massive—and massively hostile to the BC government. Most of it quoted British Columbians' outrage that their province's government would reject such a generous federal proposal, unprecedented in federal-provincial negotiations for any environmental purpose. The public soon rallied behind our offer. The extraordinary response was spontaneous and genuine. But local and national environmental leaders such as Vicky Husband employed their formidable organizational and media relations skills and vast network of contacts in diverse fields to maximize both the force and the impact of the public response. The next day, I handwrote a note to the prime minister detailing specific ways I thought he should become personally involved to rescue the national park proposal. It was the only time I ever communicated to him with such fire-alarm urgency. A few days earlier, I had phoned the prime minister at home to urge him to raise the issue with BC premier Bill Vander Zalm in his private meeting with him in Ottawa early the next morning, prior to their participation in a federal-provincial conference on unrelated matters. I told the PM that I attached enormous importance to the issue. I said I had been receiving more mail and other communications on it than on any other issue in my time in the portfolio. And I stressed how vital I thought it was for our government to act boldly on the cause. Never before had I called the prime minister at home about any question in my entire time in Cabinet. Nor would I ever again feel it necessary to do so. My nervousness about intruding on his personal privacy in such a way proved unwarranted. He welcomed the call, said he shared my sense of urgency about the issue, and assured me he would not only raise it with the premier, but would do so at the top of his bilateral agenda.

The PM had asked his Cabinet colleagues to take turns rounding out the delegation of federal officials seated behind him and any Cabinet member directly involved in the discussions at the horseshoe-shaped table during the aforementioned federal-provincial conference in Ottawa. (The stock public archival film footage and photograph of the conference show me seated behind, and slightly to the left, of the PM.) I used this opportunity, in my own case, to buttonhole the BC premier and lobby him on South Moresby. We had never previously met or even talked by phone, though we had exchanged correspondence and proposals. He greeted me warmly, said the PM had earlier "twisted my arm pretty strongly" on the proposed park, and expressed the hope that some kind of deal could be reached between the two governments. Whatever confidence the premier's assurances gave me crashed with the news from Van Dusen about the BC government's rejection of our king's-ransom–sized offer. I knew that only the prime minister's direct involvement in the issue at this stage could restore that confidence.

A crisis on another front prevented me from seeing the prime minister in the Commons to hand-deliver the urgent note suggesting how he should become involved to rescue the park. Terry Collins volunteered to serve as messenger, instead.

(Terry had access to the MPs' lounge just outside the Commons chamber, and the PM would recognize him as a former parliamentary reporter not hostile to either the government or him.) As the PM exited the Commons, Terry caught his attention, handed him the note, and quickly summarized its content. He mentioned, in particular, the public outcry, especially in British Columbia, about the province's rejection of our offer. Concerning Vander Zalm, Mulroney told Terry: "We'll let him sweat a little. Thank Tommy for me." Less than a week later, the BC premier announced he had undergone a change of heart and that $106 million was an acceptable offer after all. Public pressure is a marvellous force. And a potent one, too. In response, the federal government and British Columbia struck a deal. Canada was thereby able to add to its national park system not just another park, but one the international environmental and conservation community considered our country's most ecologically precious wilderness area. The football had been caught. Touchdown!

# The Denver Prayer

*National Geographic* thought the South Moresby archipelago so majestic that it did a cover story on it in July 1987. The timing could not have been better. I doubt it was a coincidence. The international lobby was huge, organized, well funded, ingenious, politically shrewd, and creative. It involved some of the most famous individuals on the planet. I got a three-page letter from Prince Philip—typed personally, with typos hand-corrected. Brian Mulroney notes in his memoirs that the Duke of Edinburgh had lobbied him directly to establish Grasslands National Park in Saskatchewan, which we completed later.[3] I made sure the PM also knew about Buckingham Palace's keen interest in South Moresby. He was already aware. The prince must have done a double whammy. As detailed later, the royal family of the Netherlands lived in Ottawa during the Second World War. From the Soestdijk royal palace, Prince Bernhard, Queen Beatrix's husband, lobbied BC premier Bill Vander Zalm, a fellow Dutchman, shamelessly exploiting their cultural kinship. *ABC News* anchor Peter Jennings, a Canadian, discreetly helped, including on the US network's national newscasts. He was no doubt encouraged by his sister Sara, a fanatic South Moresby champion. Jacques Cousteau lobbied hard from around the world—once calling me from a submersible on the high seas! Major stories appeared in newspapers in an array of countries, on every continent, notably the United Kingdom, India, West Germany, and the Netherlands. In Canada, Margaret Atwood signed a personal cheque for $1,000 for the cause. Other famous writers and entertainers and media personalities, at home and abroad, matched or exceeded her generous gift or otherwise lent their celebrity and tangible support to the effort. Artists donated valuable paintings and sculptures to raise funds for lobbying and publicity. I got calls of support right out of the blue from celebrities I had known only from movies or television or radio, but had never met. I spoke personally on the phone with singing sensations Bryan Adams (who had moved to British Columbia with his mother at age fourteen) and Corey Hart, among many others. The petitions and offers of help that mattered most to me, though, were from ordinary people. The rich and famous take the extraordinary as part of the natural order. That everyday people also viewed South Moresby as their cause was, for me, extraordinary.

In September 1987, I gave the closing address, immediately following a speech by Prime Minister Gro Brundtland of Norway, at the Fourth World Wilderness Congress, in Denver, Colorado. The congress, held in a different part of the world about every four years, is one of the world's largest and most prestigious international environmental forums. In Denver, over two thousand delegates from sixty-four countries attended. For anyone given a prime speaking time, this was Carnegie Hall. Prime Minister Brundtland was then at the height of her international fame and prestige as head of the landmark UN sustainable development commission that bore her name. Accordingly, she was given the honour of speaking for thirty minutes as the penultimate performer. I had the same amount as the follow-up and closing speaker. To my mind, unlike at the wedding feast at Cana, the best wine was not being held back to the end. It had just been served. The prime minister delivered an outstanding address, extremely well received. After hearing the raucous audience response to her spellbinding talk, I thought her act would be worse than hard to follow—it would be impossible. The wedding guests would now have to settle, if not for gut-rot, then, at best, *vin ordinaire*. Still, I was determined to do my best not to let down my country before the world community and international media.

To my pleasant surprise, the delegates responded well. They applauded at the right places, laughed at the right times, and looked rightly pensive when I attempted to be profound. And then, towards the end, something magical happened. At the climax of my speech, I said the words "South Moresby." The audience was suddenly transfixed. I reported that the majestic islands were under siege. I summarized the circumstances. I stressed my own and the Canadian government's alarm. I said I would not rest until the natural and cultural treasures at risk were saved as a national park. I had put this part in my speech purely as a self-indulgence, minutes before arriving in Denver. I had travelled the long distance from Ottawa late at night to deliver my mid-morning address. Staffers Terry Collins and Elizabeth May helped me create the speech from scratch in mid-flight against this fast-looming deadline. After we completed the task, I collapsed from mental and physical exhaustion on a long couch that only a private plane such as ours would have. I imagined this was how a mother must feel after delivering a baby—in my case, the text for one of the most important speeches I had ever been asked to give to that point. I arrived in Denver at 2:30 A.M., depleted, but happy to have finished my "labour." May, to her great credit, stayed up the rest of the night—what little was left of it—to type my hen-peckings. The text appeared under my hotel door when I awoke.

When pencilling in the addition about South Moresby, I did not know if anyone in the audience would even understand what I was talking about. Silly me. These were wilderness specialists and champions, after all. I added to the text:

*I was born and raised on another island on Canada's Atlantic coast. Prince Edward Island is as far from South Moresby and the other Queen Charlotte Islands, on the Pacific coast, as it is possible for my island to be and still reside in the same country—indeed, on the same continent. But I feel those other islands, thousands of miles from my own island, are as much a part of me, and as much a part of who I am as a Canadian, as they would be had I been born and raised there instead of where I was. Those Pacific islands are mine, just as they belong to every other Canadian…in fact, every citizen of the world. These unique natural treasures are everyone's because they need to be.*

Pandemonium erupted. It was as though Oprah Winfrey had just announced, "Volvos for everyone!" When the words "South Moresby" first flew from my mouth, the sound system momentarily caused the recorded voices of a children's choir to blare through the cavernous conference hall. I thought at that moment there must have been a mechanical failure. I learned later that the music and young voices were the conference organizers' signal to me that five minutes remained in the thirty minutes I had been allotted to speak. But nobody had told me beforehand that I would be given such a warning. Upon hearing the sweet children's voices filling the conference hall, without missing a beat I said to my enraptured audience: "You know, every time I mention South Moresby, angels sing." The packed convention hall went wild, according me a standing ovation and two curtain calls once I was able to complete the speech and exit the stage. Dr. Robin Winks, the distinguished master of one of the premier colleges at Yale University and former chairman of the US National Park System Advisory Board, had been in the audience. "Minister, you meant your 'angel' comment as a joke," he said to me afterwards. "But everybody virtually took it literally—and refused to doubt that what you said was true."

Even though the South Moresby entry was but a tiny part of my address, and at the end to boot, the speech will always be remembered by those who do recall it as "the South Moresby Speech." I had failed to realize fully until then that we who had been fighting so hard in Canada to save the islands were not alone. The world was watching, and supporting us. The Norwegian prime minister was the marquee name at this world wilderness conference—certainly not me. As geography professor Philip Dearden of the University of Victoria noted in his review of my speech in *Parks News*: "Frankly, the vast majority of delegates from the scattered corners of the globe had never heard of our man before he spoke, and were wondering what he was doing on the program."[4] They knew now. As the standing ovation and roars of approval continued long after my address, Prime Minister Brundtland, who had been watching it partly on a TV monitor near the stage, walked over, shook my hand, and said seemingly a bit puzzled by the continuing commotion: "Well, Minister, you and I certainly have different styles." Maybe. But what my speech contained that hers lacked was an archipelago paradise whose poetry found voice in the words of a small-town boy who grew up on another island a continent's width away from its majestic shores.

American environmental author, writer, and activist Bill Devall wrote afterwards: "The speaker who received the most enthusiastic response from delegates was Tom McMillan, Canadian Minister of the Environment."[5] Yes, no doubt. But I knew the delegates were not cheering for me. They were cheering for Canada's most precious wilderness area. Deardon wrote, again in *Parks News*: "[A]fter numerous interruptions by applause of [McMillan's speech] followed by a standing ovation, delegates from other countries came away with the idea that such environmental insight pervades the governance of Canada).["6] It once did—when Sir John A. Macdonald, founder of Canada's national park system, governed the country. I felt it did again now that Brian Mulroney was prime minister. For sure, the park would have gone nowhere without the courage and vision and leadership he linked with his environment minister's efforts. In Denver, I sensed the cheers were not for what I had said, nor necessarily for the way I had said it, least of all for me personally. Instead, the cheers were a loud collective prayer from the world community, as represented by the wilderness champions from around the globe at the congress. They had prayed that we Canadians would demonstrate to ourselves and to the global community that we possessed the courage and character and conviction to save a world treasure from certain ruin. As I left Denver, I did not know if we had it in us to answer that prayer. I would soon have the answer.

# South Moresby Rescued

On July 9, 1987, the Mulroney Cabinet made the final decision to save South Moresby as a national park reserve. The Cabinet authorized the largest amount of federal money ever showered on a national park. On July 11, 1987, Prime Minister Mulroney, BC premier Bill Vander Zalm, BC parks minister Bruce Strachan, and I signed the South Moresby National Park Reserve Agreement at a public ceremony in Victoria. Under the agreement, the Government of Canada was committed to spending $106 million on an accelerated timetable, over eight years; and the BC government some $31 million additionally, most of the total for forest compensation and replacement. The price would be even larger in the end, especially when a substantial marine component was added to the original plan. Only the price tag for Gros Morne National Park, in Newfoundland, came close to South Moresby's in the history of Canada's national park system. No other national park was more politically difficult to form, nor was any more important for Canada to achieve for both natural and built-heritage values. Finally, all these treasures would be preserved forever.

Minutes before the public ceremony in Victoria, a group of government officials, environmentalists, media sympathizers, conservation-cause philanthropists, and workaday South Moresby activists assembled in an elegant, chandeliered private room near the ceremony venue. Pat Carney, a long-time supporter of the park, both in Cabinet and without, addressed our gathering: "What is to be signed and made official today is what you will be remembered for. Announcements about ice breakers and bridges and dams are a one-day wonder. But this national park matters. It is important. It is an achievement that will last. And it is something for which future generations will thank you." As she finished her remarks, Pat—my erstwhile Commons seatmate, *Globe and Mail* morning newspaper sharer, health-care-position defender, and Ottawa hotel arm-in-arm promenader—looked in my direction. And smiled warmly.

On July 12, 1988, one year after the formal federal-provincial agreement was signed, an official signing of the relevant legal documents sealed the deal, making the agreement irreversible. Now, 138 magnificent and exotic islands and inlets 130 kilometres from the BC coast—called Haida Gwaii, "Land of the People" in the Haida language—would be made perpetually safe from the logger's chainsaw, the miner's explosives, the hunter's bullets, the fisher's traps, and the poacher's greed. Forever and a day, these splendours would be protected by the full might and treasure of the people of Canada through their national government. In 2010, the Gwaii Haanas Marine Conservation Area Reserve was added to the park, building on the groundwork laid when I was minister. Today, the park as a whole is the only area on the planet managed from mountaintop to sea floor to protect its natural features—and, in this case, built features as well. *National Geographic Traveler* today rates Gwaii Haanas National Park Reserve the number one park destination on the entire continent—above the Grand Canyon, Yosemite, Yellowstone, or any other US or Mexican national park. This was a mammoth achievement by Canadians—for ourselves, for the world community, for the planet. The Denver prayer was answered.

The happy outcome of the South Moresby issue did as much as any other single factor to advance the Mulroney government's public reputation and image as modern and progressive. Even our aggressive domestic and bilateral programs to combat acid rain did not have a greater impact. Our fight to save this natural paradise from being desecrated was especially popular in the big cities—vote-rich Vancouver and Toronto, in particular. I will always remain grateful to Brian Mulroney for supporting me on the issue. He faced enormous pressures to do otherwise, particularly from within his parliamentary Caucus. Understandably, BC members with big forestry and mining interests in their ridings were especially opposed. I was struck at the time by how viscerally Mulroney understood not merely the political advantages to our party and government from acting boldly, but also the importance to the country of our doing so. South Moresby constitutes one of the most glittering parts of Brian Martin Mulroney's public legacy. It is no less so for being eclipsed, but only in public consciousness, by his government's economic accomplishments—about which more later. South Moresby, though, is in an altogether different category—one elegantly inscribed with the words, "This is what we Canadians hold dear."

Today, as I reflect on my period as the country's environment minister, I can hardly believe I once had such a privileged opportunity to help build the country. The moment a minister of the Crown loses power, the cold air of reality hits him squarely in the face. The bounties of office are gone, and nobody any longer much cares what he says or does. I never attached importance to the perks and privileges of public life—the private car and driver, the grand offices, the generous hospitality accounts, and so on. I probably underused or underspent my government provisions or allowances by a wider margin than any other Mulroney government Cabinet minister. But I did value the power to make good things happen in concert with others. I considered myself especially blessed to have been environment minister. To me, it is the most important—though, obviously, not the most senior—portfolio in the federal government. Surely, a classic conservative should view the portfolio that way.

David Israelson, a dedicated environmentalist in his own right and chief environmental reporter for the *Toronto Star* when I was environment minister, was my harshest media critic, never content with anything I did or said. But his negativity appeared to reflect more an impatience with progress overall in this field, in Canada and around the world, than dissatisfaction with my own record per se. I never sensed he was overtly partisan, even though in 2011–12 he would become senior writer for Liberal premier Dalton McGuinty of Ontario. Towards the end of my time as minister, Israelson wrote an opinion piece in which he conceded that I had used the environment portfolio to set the agenda for the country on environmental and parks issues. He said I had eclipsed all my political adversaries in this public policy area: "[The] reality is that the Tories are setting Canada's environmental agenda now, not their opponents," he wrote.[7] Coming as it did from the pen of such an unforgiving critic, the column was, to me, a tremendous accolade—albeit reluctantly extended—to the Mulroney government's environmental leadership and to whatever role I played on the team that provided it. I received a number of national and international honours for my leadership in the environment portfolio, including the US Sierra Club's prestigious Dr. Edgar Wayburn Award and the Governor General's Conservation Award. *Outdoor* magazine, in its 1991 winter issue, named me one of three people in Canada who had done "their best and the most for Canada's outdoors" in the previous decade. To me, these recognitions were as much for the entire Mulroney government's efforts as for my own. Like many of the other things we did, the government's South Moresby achievement demonstrates that, to do great things for the country, the Conservative Party—or *any* political party—faces no limits other than those it imposes on itself. I felt honoured and proud that, on South Moresby, the government party of which I was a key member had decided there *were* no limits. We had walked on the moon.

# Chapter 22

# ELIZABETH MAY: MY MIXED BLESSING

There's another story here, beyond how the Mulroney government won the battle for South Moresby against powerful vested interests, turning this wilderness paradise into the country's most expensive-ever national park. The parallel story is one of deceit and betrayal. It concerns how a staff member of mine, deeply involved with us in the South Moresby issue, double-crossed me and the government for which she worked. Her name is Elizabeth May, currently leader of the Green Party of Canada and Member of Parliament for British Columbia's Saanich–Gulf Islands.

Born in the United States, Elizabeth Evans May moved as a young girl from Connecticut in 1973 with her parents and a younger brother, Geoffrey, to Margaree Harbour, Cape Breton, Nova Scotia. Her mother, Stephanie, had been a prominent anti-nuclear activist; her father, John, assistant to the vice-president of Aetna Life and Casualty; her godfather was Oscar-winning actor Cliff Robertson. On the Cabot Trail, the Mays operated a restaurant and gift shop from a land-locked schooner they had purchased and restored. Elizabeth graduated from Dalhousie University law school in 1983. All the time, she, like her mother, engaged in environmental activism in one cause or another. Most notable was a grassroots effort to stop aerial insecticide spraying (approved by the Nova Scotia government) over the forests of Cape Breton, about which she published *Budworm Battle*, the first of her several books—most, like this one, more like extended magazine articles than tomes, but provocative nevertheless.[1]

After Dalhousie, Elizabeth launched a career in law as a professional environmentalist, starting seriously as associate counsel with the Public Interest Advocacy Centre, based in Ottawa. That is the job she held when I recruited her to join my ministerial staff as, in effect, an ambassador between me and environmental groups across the country, into which she was well plugged. I felt the dire need for such a staffer because my honeymoon with organized environmentalists, always short for an environment minister at the best of times, had ended almost as soon as the marriage was consummated. Environmental non-governmental organizations (NGOs) were especially upset with me over plans I had announced to inaugurate Environment Week for June 1986. It was to be a seven-day period in which I had hoped each year Canada would mark environmentalism in the way Americans did on and around Earth Day. Unfortunately, there just had not been time to involve NGOs in the kind of extensive planning and execution of the first Environment Week that would characterize the program in subsequent years while I was minister. I soon discovered the hard way that, no matter how lofty the goal, unless funding for an effort such as this were funnelled through their purses, the activists would be hostile to the idea from the get-go. And they were. What's more, they mobilized themselves to kill my effort and to undermine me.

I had known of Elizabeth from media stories in the Maritimes about her environmental activism over the years. Moreover, my constituency assistant, Rob Burnett, had gone to law school at Dalhousie at the same time as she. He had introduced me to her in the Halifax airport terminal on one occasion. Elizabeth's path would cross my own periodically thereafter. But it was during the environmentalists' revolt over Environment Week that she caught my attention—and, as I was to learn, came to my defence—in a big way. Marshalling her formidable skills as a networker, she phoned and pleaded with everyone she could reach to give the minister a chance and not scuttle his plans until he could involve environmentalists more fully for subsequent annual celebrations of the environment. Her lobbying partly succeeded. The first Environment Week was not the disaster it was shaping up to be, and I lived to fight another day. Meanwhile, I decided Elizabeth was exactly the kind of person I needed on staff to help me not only extinguish such fires in future, but also to prevent them from igniting in the first place. She started her new job with me on August 1, 1986, only about six weeks after helping to prevent the Environment Week launch from becoming a fiasco.

No sooner had I brought Elizabeth May on staff than I was engulfed in a conflagration about hiring her endlessly bigger than I had ever contemplated she would help prevent. I had asked Elizabeth not to reveal her appointment to anyone until I could announce it in my own time and in my own way. But she jumped the gun, releasing the information in excited schoolgirl tones to the *Cape Breton Post*. The interview unleashed a firestorm in Tory political circles in Nova Scotia and soon right across the country, especially in Ottawa. The heat, for me, became unbearable. How could I have gotten myself—and, it seemed, the government—into such a colossal mess? The federal government switchboard lit up like Times Square as calls poured in from across the country to attack the May appointment. The calls included an urgent one to the prime minister from Nova Scotia premier John Buchanan. He felt his province had been badly burned, and mischaracterized, in the controversy concerning budworm spraying in Cape Breton in which Elizabeth had played so incendiary a role months earlier. Forestry executives and labour union leaders and ordinary workers alike, scorched by Elizabeth's perceived insensitivity to their profits or jobs in Nova Scotia in that controversy, called to protest. They demanded my head on a platter, preferably pulverized, still better drenched in sulphuric acid. The government received calls even from high-placed non-Tories who, at this early stage in our mandate, just wished us well and felt Elizabeth would bring nothing but harm to our fledgling administration. Nova Scotia's two ministers in the Mulroney government, Solicitor General Elmer MacKay and Supply and Services Minister Stewart McInnes, eviscerated me at Cabinet. It was my worst-ever moment in that or any other political forum. Was there any depth to which I would not plunge? Evidently not.

The prime minister opposed Elizabeth's joining my staff as soon as he heard about it, phoning me at my Ottawa home at 6:45 A.M. to chew me out. At home! At 6:45! The prime minister ordered me to rescind the appointment. "Get rid of her! She's bad news!" Those were his exact words. With unerring political judgment and instinct and prescience, exceeded only by his ire, he added the following words that pound in my head like a sledgehammer to this day: "I will not have a staff member of one of my ministers leaking Privy Council secrets to the NDP!" It was neither the first nor the last time I saw this political leader demonstrate the vision of a military strategist—

and the anger of a tormented bull. To her legion of detractors, Elizabeth May was a cross between Bernadette Devlin and the Wicked Witch of the North, with Jane Fonda thrown in for bad measure. Most of the backlash was over the top, for sure. But feelings ran high, a lot higher than my standing with anyone in Ottawa, it appeared. In the end, the future Green Party of Canada leader did betray me and the trust I placed in her. All those people, including the prime minister, would be proven right, I tragically wrong. How could I have been so misguided, and so naive?

By the height of the firestorm, I could honour only the spirit of the prime minister's order, not the letter. Elizabeth May had, in effect, a contract. Moreover, the negative response from the environmental movement had I fired her would have ended any chance of mine to succeed in the portfolio. I decided to try to ride out the storm by changing the new recruit's status from ministerial staffer to departmental contract employee. Mulroney himself had suggested my doing so when I told him the legal and political conundrum I faced. Government-wide rules in place well before the Mulroney government took office required a limited-term contract employee of a department to become permanent by the end of a specified period in order to stay. At the end of the relevant period in May's case, her status at Environment Canada would automatically revert to that of ministerial staffer to honour those rules. In deference to the prime minister's express concern about Elizabeth's untrustworthiness, every effort was made to keep her profile as low as possible, especially as far as he was concerned: out of sight, out of mind, out of firing range, as it were. (For simplicity, I refer to Elizabeth May throughout this book as a ministerial staffer, though, as a departmental contract employee, she was not strictly that most of the time.)

At the very beginning of her time with the government, I explained to Elizabeth the need to switch her employment status from that which we had originally discussed. I mentioned only the technicalities, not the rationale, least of all the prime minister's hand in all this. I stressed her responsibilities would remain essentially the same; it was entirely an internal administrative matter, and thus no big deal or cause for her concern. I sensed my new recruit felt there was a lot more to it than that and she had me over a barrel, whatever the particular circumstances. (She reads people and situations extremely well.) At which point, the new recruit demanded an immediate substantial salary raise based on the change—in effect, her first day on the job! And yet, this response was a total *non sequitur*. Remuneration was irrelevant to what was transpiring. At the time, I was shocked. I believed Elizabeth was using her status change as an excuse to nullify our prior salary agreement. Clearly, Elizabeth thought she had not demanded as much as I would probably have agreed to and now she had a chance for a do-over. Against my better judgment, I acquiesced to her salary demand, unreasonable as I thought it was. I just wanted to get the whole terrible mess behind me. The mess, however, was to get substantially worse.

Little did I realize that the Elizabeth May imbroglio would continue to follow me everywhere. It was like that perpetually moving rain cloud stuck permanently above the head of Joe Btfsplk, the world's worst jinx, in Al Capp's classic cartoon strip, *Li'l Abner*. As with Joe's cloud, mine brought bad luck not just to me, but to everyone in the vicinity. In this case, the "everyone" was the Mulroney government, from the prime minister to the office pool. My contretemps with Elizabeth over salary was the first inkling I had of her Machiavellian ways. I suddenly realized how extremely careful I would have to be about that ominous cloud she constituted above my skull. Now the cloud was as much a part of my political life as the green leather armchair and walnut desk assigned to me in the House of Commons.

Although the change in Elizabeth May's government-employment status got me through the initial crisis, much worse was in store. The cloud would soon get steadily darker and my political life correspondingly a lot stormier.

# The Betrayal

As federal environment minister, I considered the most important part of my schedule the major weekly briefing I received from officials, starting early in the morning and lasting at least a couple of hours. The meetings were sometimes held more regularly—in key periods, daily; in a crisis, almost hourly; in the most dire circumstances, non-stop. About a dozen people would sit around a long and wide oval-shaped board table, with me at the head as chair, in the department's Conference Room at our headquarters in Hull. The deputy minister and one or more assistant deputy ministers would conduct the briefings. Other officials might also be invited to address particular matters in their specialized areas. If an issue were especially important or controversial, departmental staff would be brought in from outside Ottawa to help. I placed a high premium on consulting the individuals most knowledgeable about a particular matter, not necessarily those highest in the chain of command. I routinely acted on this principle, whether in formal briefings or anytime I felt the need to place a call to, say, an Atmospheric Service or Parks Canada or Pollution Control officer or scientists out in the field. My chief of staff would attend the briefings, as would other staff members on a need-to-know basis. In this forum, we exchanged information and devised strategies. It was here that, for example, decisions were made concerning what to tell Parliament or the media or the general public about a burning question at a given time. Both candour and confidentiality were of utmost importance, as I repeatedly stressed to all present, officials and political staff alike. Otherwise, I knew participants would not have felt comfortable speaking "truth to power"—to me and the deputy minister, in particular. Unless all participants honoured those rules, I myself would not have felt at ease expressing unguarded thoughts on which I considered it important for officials to challenge me, if necessary, before a certain course was charted. This forum was my War Room, these people my council of generals, the candid and confidential exchange of information and ideas our collective military planning. I was to learn too late there was a spy among us.

While in my department's employ, Elizabeth May—unbeknownst to me at the time—freely shared with a large network of outsiders whatever she felt like confiding about our internal deliberations. The breaches of security included the contents of confidential Privy Council documents and communications, both within the department and between it and other parts of the government—among them, the Prime Minister's Office. It was precisely as the PM had warned me she would do. The extent to which Elizabeth had been violating the trust I had placed in her she revealed in an interview in the 1989 spring issue of *Borealis* magazine, a national parks NGO publication, shortly after leaving my employ.[2] In the interview, she not only admitted to, but also bragged about, having provided a direct pipeline from our inner sanctum to a large web of contacts: friends and acquaintances, environmental NGOs, both the Liberal and NDP Opposition parliamentary Caucuses, and even the Speaker of the House of Commons, John Fraser, with whom she was close, among others in the loop. In retrospect, I assume the recipients of these confidences included The Canadian Press reporter she was cohabitating with at the time (against my objections, given the obvious security risk). Some of this CP reporter's scoops demonstrably reflected access to insider information of the sort she could have provided.

The nature and reach of Elizabeth May's betrayal staggered me. Prior to reading the *Borealis* interview, hot off the press, I had no idea how shamelessly she had violated my trust and the government's security. Not once while she was sabotaging us had I considered her anything but a high-minded environmentalist—and a principled lawyer, to boot—incapable of such unprofessional and unethical behaviour. I was now discovering for the first time, from the interview in question, the full extent of the woman's conniving and underhanded ways, her sheer talent for deception, and her eagerness to use any means to achieve a personal or policy or ideological agenda. I had always taken pride in my judgment of people's character and abilities, particularly when recruiting staff. Not one staffer had ever before proven me wrong. Most had exceeded my expectations, some by a wide margin—especially Jeannette Arsenault and Rob Burnett in my riding office and Terry Collins and Sheila Kieran in my Ottawa operation. How could I have been so wrong in this case? It was as though the gods had sent Elizabeth May my way to teach me a lesson: I wasn't as good a judge of people as I thought. "Pride goeth before destruction, and a haughty spirit before a fall" (Proverbs 16:18). And how I was about to fall!

In the *Borealis* interview, Elizabeth May stated: "[At] our weekly meeting, McMillan would say, 'This information is to stay in this room, Elizabeth. You're not to tell [environmentalists] John Broadhead, Colleen McCrory or anybody else; it's a secret.'" Then she added: "So, when I called them to tell them what the latest development was, I'd tell them right off, 'This is a secret, I am not supposed to tell you this, but....'" The *Borealis* interviewer himself adds: "Unbeknownst to McMillan, May then went to the Liberal and NDP environmental critics to keep them informed on the latest developments." Concerning communications with the Speaker of the House, May is quoted as saying: "I hadn't told Tom that I was going to see [John] Frazier [*sic*]...Why tell him if he was just going to say no?"[3] And on and on the revelations of betrayal unfolded throughout the interview. When reading it first, I had to stop several times to catch my breath and compose myself. It was like reading my obituary. And all of it dwelled on my alleged worst traits and most dastardly deeds, each new to me. I *wished* I was dead. Almost literally.

Was Elizabeth May motivated to betray me and the government just by the sheer pleasure she derived from boasting about her access to some of the government's most sensitive secrets? Or was it to enhance her standing with fellow environmentalists? Or, more particularly, to ingratiate herself with movement activists who had ostracized her for "going over to the other side"? Or was the betrayal part of some ill-considered effort by an immature and unscrupulous zealot to advance issues and causes important to her personally—in particular, South Moresby. Or did the betrayal reflect the environmental NGO anti-establishment youth culture and mindset of the era? Or—as seems most likely, in retrospect—did the betrayal flow from all the above? To my mind, the motivation is irrelevant. May was being paid a handsome government salary. It was more than double her pay with the non-profit organization she had been working for prior to joining my staff. Her job was to be loyal to me, to the department, and to the government—her collective employers—in the service of the Canadian public. The young woman had no right to decide on her own when the rules that applied to everyone in government service could be broken, however noble she might have thought the purpose in her case. The "end justifies the means" principle is antithetical to a healthy democracy. It is a prescription for a total break-down in the trust factor among politicians, public servants, and political staff without which the system cannot function. Specific rules can govern human behaviour only so far. In the end, it all comes down to character and trust—in government as in any team endeavour. For sure, it is impossible for a minister to run a department compe-tently and responsibly if staff members are allowed to decide for themselves the rules by which they work or how righteous their own rules are or the proper boundaries for self-indulgence. A minister, no less than a trapeze artist, needs to be able to trust the person on the other "swing." When the trust factor is missing in the relationship between a minister and a subordinate at the centre of power, the former can crash to the ground mighty dangerously. As it turned out, trustworthiness was woefully absent in the character of my betrayer. Accordingly, I did crash—and without a safety net.

# The Resignation

All the high political drama surrounding Elizabeth May and me came to its fateful denouement when, having sucked every personal and professional advantage from "serving" in a minister's employ for two years, Elizabeth ceremoniously resigned on the eve of the 1988 federal election. She did so based on a bogus principle.

The issue concerned federal permits I had signed, at the recommendation of all my senior Environment Canada officials and advisors, for the construction of two dams in Saskatchewan: the Rafferty and Alameda, on the Souris River. Every relevant complex legal and scientific question had been resolved to the satisfaction of the vari-ous jurisdictions directly involved and potentially affected—both the Canadian and US governments, the provinces of Saskatchewan and Manitoba, and the border state of North Dakota. Negotiations had been conducted at every level, including in some cases among government heads, over many months. To make official and legally binding any complex multijurisdictional agreement of this kind, somebody's hand needs to hold the pen that signs on the dotted line for each party. In this case, for the Government of Canada, that hand was mine. But no one person's finger could so easily have been placed on the Rafferty-Alameda scale as Elizabeth charged me with having done. My signature was a mere formality and, accordingly, I deferred to my officials on the substance. This was how all such highly technical questions—in the case at hand, hydrological—were handled and always had been by my predecessors, regardless of party label. My senior officials had insisted there was no environmental or legal ground on which I could have refused to sign the permits in question. It was clear that, had I done otherwise, I would have stood rightly accused of imposing par-tisan politics on the outcome.

Elizabeth May had invited herself to the relevant decisive meeting between me and my officials, including Deputy Minister Geneviève Ste-Marie. Elizabeth told the deputy that I had invited her, and told me that the deputy had. Only afterwards did the two of us discover that each of us had been played against the other. I learned all too late that Elizabeth routinely used either my name and authority or Dr. Ste-Marie's in this fashion to worm herself into discussions or to access privileged information. As she said of me in the context of her betraying my trust with Commons Speaker John Fraser, "Why tell him if he was just going to say no?" At the meeting to decide the Rafferty and Alameda question, Elizabeth herself did not oppose the permits, only their timing. She urged I delay signing them until after the election to avoid controversy. This is a fact of history. Other meeting participants—all of them still alive and active today—could confirm it. For whatever reason, however, the media have hardly ever pursued the truth. Nor have most instant historians. Such people have generally taken Elizabeth's self-interested narrative as fact. They should not, because it is not. The way the pertinent circumstances typically have been commented upon by the media—and, thus, almost automatically recorded by historians—hardly reflects what fabled investigative journalist Carl Bernstein has said is the most fundamental responsibility of every reporter: "discovering the best obtainable version of the truth."[4] In this case, some might deem me insufficiently objective to be considered the best obtainable source of the truth. If so, then many others thoroughly knowledgeable about the facts and beyond reproach can attest to the veracity of my narrative. A few have done so anonymously. In a major excerpt of a book by investigative reporter Bill Redekop, *Dams of Contention: The Rafferty–Alameda Story and the Birth of Canadian Environmental Law,* the *Winnipeg Free Press* highlights the fact that federal and provincial officials insisted "there wasn't a shred of truth to May's story." Says Redekop: "Critics picked apart her story and found discrepancies. There were demands she produce physical evidence."[5] The article clearly implies she could not.

Subsequent judicial review undermined the Rafferty–Alameda project on narrow technical grounds. But that is irrelevant to the point at hand. It is also irrelevant whether the judicial review and court decision might have been politically motivated, as some charged at the time and believe to this day. What remains true is that all those involved in the permit-signing decision, including me, acted in good faith based on what we knew or were told at the time. When May's views did not prevail concerning when I should sign the permits, as opposed to whether I should sign them at all, she was off to the races—and I to my doom. From then on, the woman presented herself as an environmental martyr and me as a desecrator of all things great and pure. She had found what she considered the ideal pretext on which to resign on the highest-possible moral ground. From that ground, she intended to start slinging mud. And she soon did.

Elizabeth May told me she wanted to leave my employ during the World Climate Change Conference I was hosting in Toronto in late June 1988. At no time during our discussion did she mention the permits for the Rafferty and Alameda dams, let alone that this was the reason, on high principle, she intended to resign. (My ex-staffer would later add her opposition to the PEI-NB Fixed Link on environmental grounds as her rationale for quitting. We had, however, scarcely ever exchanged views on that subject, certainly not on the occasion at hand.) In fact, far from stating that she wanted to bolt my staff for environmental reasons, the young woman said she would remain with me if I made her chief of staff.

This conversation in Toronto shocked me. I was content with my existing chief of staff, Ron Woznow. He had a doctorate in chemistry, and had been a high-ranking environmental manager with Exxon when I recruited him upon the recommendation of people whose views I respected. So he was knowledgeable about the type of issues I routinely faced in the portfolio. Plus, he was hard-working and enjoyed the confidence of my political staff and departmental officials alike. Equally important to me, Ron had bona fides with the main actors throughout the political network in Ottawa, including people close to the prime minister. Indeed, his name was first drawn to my attention by Norm Atkins, the architect of the PC Party's 1984 election landslide. Ron had headed the Tory political organization in his own Toronto riding of Etobicoke Centre. He, therefore, had especially high standing with my Cabinet colleague, Finance Minister Michael Wilson, whose riding it was and whose goodwill I needed on a broad front. I also found disqualifying Elizabeth's backstabbing of Ron, her immediate boss. I thought, if she would stab him, who wouldn't she stab? Maybe the next victim will be me. How prescient I was on that score!

Not that I would ever have considered Elizabeth for chief of staff, anyway. This was a senior, high-paying political position in the government. The prime minister himself had restructured the position as such. He wanted every minister in his administration to be advised and supported by a political operative of the first rank whose impact would balance that of his or her deputy minister, operating within the professional public service. Reflecting the seniority the PM attached to the position, the salary range was made the same as, or very close to, that of a deputy minister. The top of the range, which Ron was earning by this time, was $85,000 (about $148,000 in today's dollars). This salary was substantially higher than Elizabeth's own salary ($56,000), generous as it was at the time in inflation-adjusted terms. (When I had recruited her for my staff, she misled me, far on the high side, about what she was being paid in her existing position. I discovered that disconcerting fact, by happenstance, only much later.)

Given the prime minister's expressed low opinion of Elizabeth May from the start, it would have been inconceivable for me to appoint her my chief of staff. She had no background in partisan politics, much less in the Progressive Conservative Party. I had hired her as an environmentalist, not as a political operative. When I explained all this to her, she still thought I should make her chief of staff. "But, Elizabeth," I said, "you're not even a Conservative." She replied: "No, but I could become one." I thought the discussion was fast descending from the fanciful to the outrageous to the utterly insane. Even had I myself been insane enough to fire Ron Woznow and replace him with Elizabeth May, the PM would have vetoed her appointment in a heartbeat, just as he would have done with any deputy minister of whom he disapproved. Brian Mulroney made a point of knowing about all such personnel matters. He saw a political appointee of this high-ranking sort as part of his own senior team in government. Having experienced the man's ire once before regarding Elizabeth—that 6:45 A.M. phone call at home!—I would have had to be not only insane, but also suicidal to want to risk it again. Whatever my deficiencies, I was neither. I needed Ron to stay and, now, Elizabeth to depart. As Abraham Lincoln said, "A house divided against itself cannot stand." But mine was to collapse regardless.

What backdropped Elizabeth May's ambitions and plotting, I was to discover, was the internal warfare between her and Ron Woznow. Her animus towards Ron, and her determination to eliminate him both as a boss and from the scene, is reflected in an interview she gave later to freelance writer Lisa Blackburn. Typical of the many interviews she conducted after leaving my employ, this one appeared in the September 1990 issue of the youth-oriented (and now defunct) journal *CM Archive*, published by the Canadian Library Association. In the interview, my former staffer used her characteristic charm and guile to kill two birds—me and Woznow—with one tongue: "I felt betrayed [about the Rafferty-Alameda dam permits]. I didn't blame Tom then, and I still don't blame him as much as the person who became the chief of staff [Ron Woznow]....I knew Tom had been manipulated [by him]."[6] If I had been manipulated, many politicians and officials at the highest levels and on both sides of the Canada–United States border would have had to be involved in the conspiracy. Not likely—or even possible, given how multijurisdictional agreements of this sort are negotiated over a long time and usually by successive governments, not just the ones that complete them. Again, journalists and instant historians can easily confirm Elizabeth May's chicanery by simply asking any of the many people intimately familiar with the events in question. As then-Saskatchewan-premier Grant Devine said, "[Elizabeth May] drew a long bow and took a cheap shot while betraying the federal minister in an election year. What the heck would she know [about the inter-jurisdictional Rafferty-Alameda negotiations], or if she knew [about what transpired], why didn't she raise it earlier? Why?"[7] I cannot understand to this day how my former staffer has been so wildly successful in hoodwinking virtually everybody into embracing the myth she has created for herself: that she left a well-paying and prestigious job as self-styled "Senior Policy Advisor" to a minister of the Crown on the grounds of noble principle. I say "virtually everybody" because of something my real former senior policy advisor, Sheila Kieran, told me. She herself had just left the position in high standing with me. By then, the Elizabeth May controversy had exploded into the public arena. Sheila informed me that senior officials at Environment Canada had privately described Elizabeth to her as "an ambitious careerist, not a true environmentalist." Elizabeth was proving it is easier to create a myth about oneself than to earn a reputation.

I hated such backstairs intrigue and drama among staff. I tended to deal with it by not dealing with it at all. In this case, my failing to see and hear the danger signals and respond pre-emptively proved politically fatal. In retrospect, however, I do not think I would have been able to match Elizabeth's sheer talent for palace politics. It is not my style. And, as Elizabeth demonstrated in spades, by outsmarting me to this day on the phony issue of principle, it is not my skill set, either. Indeed, I am totally out of my depth in matters of this kind. She is a master at misinformation warfare. I never had an interest in even playing the game, much less winning it. As the staffer departed my company on that late afternoon in June in Toronto, she set out to torpedo Ron Woznow, even if it meant sinking my ship. She was to succeed spectacularly on both fronts.

Elizabeth May demanded, and bargained with Ron Woznow, an obscenely generous severance package from Environment Canada (the lawyer in her, no doubt). My chief of staff would have paid almost any price—including this, it seemed—to eliminate the person he considered a double agent on the ministerial and political team it was his job to manage. When learning about the severance package by happenstance—my main way of learning about all things Elizabeth, apparently—I took matters out of Ron's hands and placed them squarely in my own. I insisted on dealing directly with the department's chief financial officer. A man of great competence and sound judgment, this official told me that he had objected to the original severance package, believing the specific terms to be well outside the norm for such a junior, short-term government employee. But Ron had overruled him in my name without either informing or consulting me. I felt compelled to trim this most golden of parachutes to avoid scandal should the details ever become public, as they surely would have sooner or later. Still, the parachute remained elaborately decorated in brilliant threads of gold—now more like eighteen carats than twenty-four, as before. My action compounded Elizabeth's rage against Ron, to say nothing of me. She felt he had reneged not only on a personal commitment, but also on a legal contract, albeit not yet promulgated.

For the first time, I began to question whether my chief of staff's first loyalty was to me or to the Privy Council Office and the Prime Minister's Office. Had they, all along, been conducting a watching brief on May at the PM's instructions?

In which case, were senior officials outside our own shop pulling Ron's strings and keeping me in the dark about their actions—protecting me against myself, as it were? I doubt the prime minister would have either forgotten or tempered his original concerns about Elizabeth, much less been unaware of her continued presence in my operation after expressing them to me. The PM forgot nothing important and noticed the smallest detail in everything he surveyed. More to the point, like a mother bear guarding her cub, the man monitored every threat either to him or his government, both from within and from without. He appeared especially vigilant about potential double-dealers in our ranks, whether they be officials or, as in this case, a staffer. Any qualm he might have harboured about stealthily invading a minister's territory would have been outweighed by his concern for the government's overall welfare. The mother bear would not have worried about rules of the jungle in the face of mortal danger. My chief of staff's blindsiding me now did not fit a pattern. He was too much the go-by-the-book scientist to play the renegade. So the involvement of a higher authority than he in these machinations seems the only explanation for why Ron might have betrayed my interests in this instance. In any event, when I instructed Environment Canada's chief financial officer to trim May's severance package, his relief was palpable. I sensed he was doing a happy dance at the other end of the phone. But my own sad troubles were just beginning.

Only after Elizabeth's reduced severance package was legally and administratively irreversible, several weeks later, did she begin her high-profile media interviews. In fact, her attacks against me and my chief of staff began literally that very day—no coincidence! The woman's Machiavellian ways were breathtaking. She conducted even more numerous and more vicious interviews off the record. In some, she attacked us in the most personal terms. In an interview with an Ottawa-based Canadian Press reporter, for example, Elizabeth impugned our very intelligence. The reporter then raised the obvious question: if Ron Woznow and I were so intellectually deficient, how were we able to complete post-graduate degrees, including Ron's PhD in chemistry, at first-rate universities? By this time, Elizabeth and the reporter in question, previously apartment mates and possibly more, had had a falling out. So, perhaps the bad blood between them explains why he felt free to express his scepticism in print. On the whole, though, the media were glad to lap up and report everything negative Elizabeth said about Ron and me as though it were self-evidently true merely because the source was an insider and this particular one, to boot.

Another knock my former staffer levelled against me—also in the *Borealis* interview—was that I was "weak-willed." This was by way of whining that I had too infrequently followed her advice while she was in my employ. But often the advice, if acted on, would have broken all the rules and protocols and conventions about how ministers of the Crown must operate, both officially and personally. My flouting them possibly would have landed me in legal jeopardy, and certainly in boiling water, particularly with the prime minister. After all, a Cabinet oath is a lot more than a promise of good intentions; it's a form of legal contract. That aside, isn't a staffer's publicly commenting on a former employer's negative qualities, whether true or not, contemptible? In the case at hand, one person's "weak will" is another person's sense of due process. For all her intelligence and shrewdness, I was often struck by how naive Elizabeth May could be about fundamentals, including a minister's need to navigate proper channels to advance an agenda in Cabinet government.

Elizabeth often acted as though her boss could make things happen simply by ministerial fiat. If I had operated as I later discovered she had done—"This is a secret. I'm not supposed to tell you this, but…"—I would have found myself fired from Cabinet. And I would have deserved to be.

In any event, Elizabeth's charge that I was weak-willed would surprise my family and closest friends and others who know me best. They would say I inherited more than my share of the "stubborn gene" from the McQuaid side of the family. And not necessarily as a compliment! The charge must have surprised Environment Canada officials at the time. Whatever they might have thought of me overall, I know they considered my resolve on such issues as acid rain and South Moresby among the department's greatest advantages while I was their minister and, together, we pursued an activist agenda. On the eve of retiring, the principal Parks Service negotiator with the provinces at the officials' level said this very thing while addressing me and his peers—including the deputy minister, Geneviève Ste-Marie—at the last weekly ministerial briefing he attended before stepping down. We had just sealed the deal with Ontario to establish the Bruce Peninsula National Park (in 1987). "No minister in my long career in government fought harder for a park than you did for the Bruce," this senior official said. "I want to thank you personally for helping me end my career on such a high note." And yet, to Elizabeth, as the *Borealis* interview revealed, we were all empty vessels into which she had poured her vintage wine. Concerning me, she said, "I was amazed by my own influence over him."[8] Clearly, from the *vino* did not come *veritas*. I still have a bad hangover from both the betrayal and my gullibility.

# Paradise Misrepresented

My betrayer then published a book, *Paradise Won: The Struggle for South Moresby*.[9] If Elizabeth May's worst critics are to be believed, she has an unbridled ego. True to this perception (right or wrong), in the book Elizabeth presents herself as though the marquee name in a theatrical production. Everyone else, including government officials—among them, even the prime minister and me—is reduced to mere extras, supporting her starring role. In politics, as in most fields, no staffer ever comes off as second-best in a post-employment memoir. That's true no matter the post held, the office holder, or the reality. In Elizabeth's memoir, she is far from second-best; she is the only one at centre stage, bringing the audience to its feet in wild applause with the sheer power of her thespian virtuosity.

*Paradise Won* is, I must admit, a good read. The book has a breezy, breathless voice and steady pace very much like the author herself. Elizabeth's memoir, however, should not be read as the Gospel Truth; more as some people believe the real gospels are themselves: not literally true, only allegorically so. Some of the events and direct or indirect quotes associated with me (mostly positive)—for example, from Cabinet discussions—just did not happen the way Elizabeth described them. Nor would she have known those events occurred the way she said they did. She wasn't present, and I didn't tell her or did so only to the limited extent necessary for her to follow up on specifics for me. Saving South Moresby was crucial for the country and constitutes a major part of the legacy of the Mulroney government—and of the prime minister, in particular. I think, therefore, it is vital that the relevant historical record be accurate.

Individual factoids of the narrative are not, in themselves, important, but accumulatively they present a picture that substantially misrepresents the true story when not getting it dead wrong.

Elizabeth May's book is sloppy, even reckless, with objective facts, not just interpretations. For illustrative purposes only, I note the following, among many other factual errors I could cite. The official South Moresby park signing by the federal and BC governments was in mid-July 1988. This signing should not be confused with the agreement signing a year earlier (by the PM, the BC premier, me, and my BC counterpart). Elizabeth says the official signing was not made a public event because my staff had double-booked me in PEI.[10] This is rubbish, a literary fiction at best. The real reason was that Elizabeth had connived to include in her golden-parachute severance package a requirement that the federal government pay all travel, accommodation, and out-of-pocket expenses for her to attend that event no matter where she resided anywhere in Canada or elsewhere in the world at the time. Environment Canada auditors informed me that the provision could cost taxpayers many thousands of dollars if, as likely, the event were held in South Moresby and, say, the government had to fly her there (and return) from Nova Scotia. To avoid the auditor general's ire and extricate ourselves from potential political scandal, given that Elizabeth was no longer a government employee, my officials and I cancelled the major ceremonial event planned in favour of a low-key legal signing. (Fisheries and Oceans Minister Tom Siddon, from British Columbia, represented me to sign the contracts for the federal side.)

May says that, for the first Environment Week, $650,000 was spent "to produce a rock video on an environmental theme, featuring Tom McMillan singing with the Edmonton Oilers."[11] This charge would be hilarious if it were not nearly libellous. I can't hold a musical note, and I didn't (and still don't) know the words to a single pop song. I find singing "Happy Birthday" a challenge, and even humming in the shower a threat to my throat and lungs. Nor have I ever met a single player with the Edmonton Oilers. The video featured, instead, top-name Canadian singers and songwriters and musicians. They volunteered their talents and time to create it in the spirit of the "We Are The World" video produced by Michael Jackson, with Lionel Richie and Quincy Jones, the previous year. Jackson's video raised millions of dollars around the world for African famine relief. The incidental technical costs for our video, covered by the Environment Week budget, were nominal. The $650,000 figure the book cites was approximately the total budget for Environment Week the first year, not just for the video. Though NGOs attacked the environmental video idea, just as Elizabeth does in her book, several groups (for example, Greenpeace) used the video itself for diverse purposes, including fundraising—the original intent.

The South Moresby agreement signing ceremony, in Victoria, was on July 11, 1987, not July 1, as Elizabeth records.[12] *The National Geographic*'s "direct circulation" was not fourteen million. It was, and still is, large—but much less than half what Elizabeth claims in a passage dealing with the impact of a South Moresby cover story.[13] Dalton Camp had not "ousted a prime minister of his own party nearly thirty years before [that is, 1957]."[14] Rather, Camp, as PC Party president, established leadership review as part of the party's constitution in 1966. John Diefenbaker, long since out of office by then, was not "ousted" as PM by Camp, but by party delegates a year later as party leader at a national convention. I did not "officially declare Last Lake a National Wildlife Area."[15] It had been done a century earlier. I marked its official designation as a heritage site by the National Historic Sites and Monuments Board, an independent body that reported to me. Elizabeth claims she had "discovered that Tom McMillan had agreed to sign permits for the construction of two dams on the Souris River [Rafferty and Alameda]"—again, the pretext for her resigning from my staff on high principle.[16] As noted above, her statement is simply not true. Elizabeth discovered nothing. She was kept fully informed. And, through the connivance described above, she actively participated in the meeting at which I made the decision, upon the unanimous recommendation of my departmental officials.

Elizabeth says: "McMillan's entire staff was composed of four special assistants, a speech writer, and the chief of staff. None of them was interested in environmental issues."[17] Questionable arithmetic aside, every one of my staff was a committed environmentalist. My press secretary, Terry Collins, was almost fanatically so, and over the past quarter-century he has devoted himself professionally to the environmental cause. Dr. Ron Woznow, my chief of staff, was, as noted above, a senior environmental manager with EXXON and an expert in certain areas of that field. I recruited him largely because he was an environmental specialist. Rob Burnett, a lawyer from Charlottetown, managed my constituency and PEI affairs from Ottawa, just as Jeannette Arsenault did on the spot in the riding. Rob also had special responsibilities for environmental issues related to the Island and Atlantic Canada more generally. Those included the Fixed Link. Elizabeth dismisses Rob Burnett as "an aide on and off."[18] He was, in fact, along with Jeannette, my longest-serving full-time staff member. The young man began working with me in 1978, fresh out of Acadia University, before I was even elected to Parliament—almost a decade before I met Elizabeth May. During that extended period, this staffer completed studies for a law degree at Dalhousie. But he continued to serve me more informally in the interval, especially in the riding and across the Island. He returned to Ottawa on a paid, full-time basis—the same as before—after completing his last law course. All that time, without interruption, Rob remained one of my closest and most trusted advisors, including on environmental matters—not "off and on." Even factoring in the legal studies at Dalhousie, he was with me *full time* for some eight years out of his eleven years of service in total—again, longer than any other staffer save Jeannette, irrespective of how one calculates it and Elizabeth's literary hocus-pocus notwithstanding. My political team as a whole is similarly mischaracterized and given short shrift when not, as in Ron's case, denigrated outright. Clearly, by disparaging and diminishing the team in this way, she hoped to elevate her own relative importance to me and the government in the South Moresby narrative and, therefore, in the reader's mind. How else could she have justified writing her book? And how would it have had any credibility or been taken seriously had she not claimed such an exalted status in the government? (Set aside her use of this false credential in pursuit of a political career.)

The book is replete with such factual errors and the author's self-serving rhetorical inventions. My experience as a voracious reader is that an author who is fast and loose with details, whether large or small, is typically unconcerned about getting the main narrative right, either. It's all about telling a good story at best, self-promotion at worst—or, as in this case, both. The heck with the truth! The South Moresby story is too important to the country to be lowered to that level of historical chronicling. It's why I consider it vital to set the record straight here. The record counts, history matters, but the truth—unless unearthed and told—does not necessarily will out. The facts presented here *are* the truth.

# Professional, Political Ethics

Innumerable factual errors aside, I think it is dead wrong for any staffer to rush into print, so soon after leaving a minister's employ, a kiss-and-tell book that reveals her former boss's most private thoughts and confidential communications in the way Elizabeth May's memoir claims to do. If committed to paper, such things, certainly in the case of Cabinet documents, are typically embargoed by law for a specified period. There are a number of reasons for that convention. To me, the most important is that, if a Cabinet minister fears his or her most private thoughts might be exposed to the world and possibly ridiculed in a book of this type, the minister will not engage in the kind of candour required for a constructive boss–staff relationship. The entire work environment would be poisoned. The wisdom of Winston Churchill's private secretary, Sir David Hunt, is instructive. He spoke in the context of medical ethics. His remarks, however, apply equally to any relationship a Cabinet minister—not only a prime minister—has with a subordinate in whom trust has been placed. Lord Moran was the wartime prime minister's lifelong doctor. Immediately after Churchill's death in 1965, Moran published a book that detailed and discussed his legendary patient's entire medical history. Sir Winston's private secretary said as follows about that unprecedented breach of professional ethics: "Lord Moran put literary fame and fortune before medical etiquette."[19] I was no Churchill, Elizabeth May no Lord Moran, and her breach not nearly as serious as his. Nevertheless, I believe that, in writing her book, Elizabeth both violated my trust and flouted professional "etiquette"—or, as I would put it, "professional ethics." Her follow-up media interviews in which she revealed, as before, everything that occurred while she was in my employ and confidence compounded the betrayal.

I saw, surreptitiously, a copy of an early draft of Elizabeth's book prior to its being substantially revised and then published. The draft demonstrated that the author originally intended to reveal many more confidential government documents and other communications than she ended up doing in the book. Some were of the most personal kind concerning me. What stopped her? The publisher's lawyers? Friends or advisors who had seen the draft and cautioned her about the legal or ethical or personal implications? Commons Speaker John Fraser? The book was dedicated to him. He is the soul of good judgment and discretion. A lawyer and close friend of the author, might he have brought her at least partly to her senses? It could not have been Elizabeth's own literary conscience. Had she had one at all, she would not have attempted a tell-all book of this kind in the first place.

The impact of Elizabeth May's machinations while she was a member of my political team in Ottawa extended far beyond me personally. When assembling that team, I believed it was important not to select too many individuals with identical or even similar backgrounds. Otherwise, I feared I would fall victim to "groupthink." Cabinet ministers—or decision-makers of any kind, for that matter—are vulnerable to groupthink when they surround themselves with staff and advisors who are virtual clones of one another. If a ministerial inner sanctum is insulated from outside opinions and perspectives, the minister himself or herself is likely to be cut off from influences that can make the difference between successful and disastrous decisions and actions. Most of my so-called exempt staff did have strong credentials in the PC Party, in addition to excellent qualifications by more conventional measure. So, party loyalty—indeed, loyalty to me personally—was well covered on staff by the time I recruited Elizabeth May. I sensed Elizabeth would add a missing element:

close ties with environmentalists across the country and broad personal experience in the environmental movement itself. At the very least, her addition to my political staff would help provide variety, guard against herd thinking, and ensure I was not captive to stale information and advice from too incestuous an advisory group.

In the 1980 federal election, when only age twenty-five, Elizabeth ran as an environmentalist against the former deputy prime minister, Allan MacEachen, in Cape Breton Highlands–Canso, placing fourth in a field of four candidates. That she had not run for the NDP or any other established party convinced me of her political independence, a fact confirmed by everything else I had heard about the young woman's social activism. But I learned from sources close to the Mulroney Cabinet that, at its very first meeting after I was no longer a member, following my defeat in the 1988 election, the prime minister cited my disastrous experience with Elizabeth May as Exhibit A for for a major point he felt compelled to make: how important he thought it was for all his ministers to exercise extreme caution in recruiting staff. I was told that the clear implication was, "Don't hire political infidels." Both in Caucus and in Cabinet, as well as in private conversations, I heard Brian Mulroney say many times: "God save us from our friends." Typically, he said it in the context of one mess or another a supposed member of the team had created for the government or the PC Party by an ill-chosen public statement or, worse, by mismanagement or scandal or, in the worst of all cases, alleged criminality. In general, Mulroney thought our own people damaged us more than did the other political parties or the media or any other adversary. Put simply, his guiding principle was: *In politics, your friends are always more dangerous than your enemies.* For the most part, the PC leader saw the media as enemies, particularly towards the end of his political career, when he made no effort to hide how he felt. The man thought this even of some reporters he considered friendly to the government or, at least, consistently fair to it. Clearly, my ill-fated experience with Elizabeth May reinforced his main concerns: how dangerous insiders of the wrong kind could be, and how complicit he thought the media generally were in advancing their interests at the expense of the government and his own interests.

To my mind, there must be a happy balance between avoiding groupthink and allowing a Trojan Horse to enter the city gates. I myself had not found that balance in recruiting Elizabeth May to my staff, so I can appreciate Mulroney's concern about Elizabeth at the time. I wonder, though, whether the prime minister's response might have later created a chill factor that caused at least some of his ministers to err in the other direction: having on staff *only* certified Conservative partisans, not even individuals utterly unaligned. If true, it was a prescription for herd thinking. Such would be especially unfortunate for an environment minister. The field demands an ecumenical approach aimed at mobilizing individuals and groups of every partisan sort and with no partisan stripe at all to protect, together, our fragile and vulnerable planet in common cause. A newly elected federal government has to start the process with its environment minister's recruitment of political staff. Everything flows from that, like the ever-widening circles formed on the surface of a placid lake from throwing a pebble into it. For sure, there wasn't a surfeit of Conservatives with proven bona fides in the environmental movement whom I could have hired as staffers. The best of them—for example, historian Robert Page at Trent University and Murray Coolican, formerly on Robert Stanfield's staff—were already heavily committed professionally. Not to mention how unlikely it was that, in order to join a minister's staff, they would have been able or willing to deep-freeze distinguished careers and diverse extracurricular activities in which they were already making big impacts on community life, including public policy. And that was in an era when the Conservative Party was endlessly more interested in environmental causes than it was under Stephen Harper's leadership. This is the broader context—beyond the problem-plagued launch of the first Environment Week discussed earlier—in which I thought it important to bring Elizabeth May onboard. I, of course, had no idea at the time that she would help sink my vessel. Brian Mulroney, a better captain than I—indeed, a first-rate admiral—could see much farther towards the horizon on those rocky seas.

My disastrous experience with Elizabeth May fortified the bias of many federal politicians (Cabinet ministers and backbenchers alike)—certainly of the Tory variety—to hire only individuals of their own partisan stripe. For the rest of the Mulroney era, no Cabinet minister or backbencher of whom I am aware hired a single political staffer who was not a certified Tory. Indeed, Elizabeth's *Borealis* interviewer himself noted, in April 1989, that, "[in light of Tom McMillan's negative experience with May]...no one like her in the environmental movement is likely to be appointed to such a powerful position again."[20] To my knowledge, he has been proven right to this very day. The PM himself became ever more vigilant about possible transgressors. For a long time afterwards, "Elizabeth May" became code in Tory circles for "Beware of Greeks bearing gifts."

Elizabeth May's mischief and machinations received endlessly more attention from the media—and, therefore, the public—than they ever would have garnered had she remained a garden-variety NGO environmentalist instead of presenting herself, as she did in the 1988 election campaign, as my former "senior policy advisor." This was the title she usurped, and used without authority, when Sheila Kieran departed my staff to do freelance speech-writing for Governor General Ray Hnatyshyn and other high-level public figures and officials. But I had not transferred the title to Elizabeth, and only I was authorized to do so. I would hardly have bestowed such an august moniker on this junior staffer given the prime minister's hostility to her. Indeed, until the election, I did not even know she had been using it. I had negotiated the title with, and tailored it exclusively for, Sheila Kieran in light of her mature age and personal reputation and illustrious former career as an author and journalist and freelance writer.

In retrospect, from the very beginning, Elizabeth appears to have had a hidden agenda while in my employ—self-aggrandizement and a political career of her own down the road. As long as being part of the government advanced that agenda, she exploited every benefit for herself from "serving." When it no longer did, my assistant departed. She did so not with a whimper, but with a bang, for the manner of her leaving itself advanced the same selfish purpose better than a more discreet and conventional departure would ever have done.

For all the damage Elizabeth May inflicted on us, I know she helped me and the government achieve great things for the environment. Without her, we might not have achieved certain measures at all or executed them nearly as well or completed them remotely as soon as we actually did. I credit Elizabeth with, for example, helping to mobilize certain pockets of the federal government—well beyond Environment Canada, let alone the Parks Service—to get the Ellesmere Island park negotiations back on track. Talks with the affected parties (the Inuit, in particular) had stalled within the system. Our being able to breathe new life into the cause early in my time as environment minister did much more than make it possible to complete that park. It also created momentum to achieve many more departmental successes later, not only on the parks front but on several others as well. We all felt galvanized by the accomplishment; it proved that bureaucratic and political inertia could be overcome with commitment and ingenuity.

As so often happens with high achievers, the qualities that Elizabeth May employed so effortlessly to promote her own interests at the expense of the government and me were the very ones she also effectively used to help advance our environmental agenda. For her, the highest priority on that agenda was making South Moresby a national park reserve. Elizabeth's strengths include native shrewdness, keen political instincts, frenetic energy, and disarming charm. The last she has used as a weapon to vanquish adversaries and surmount obstacles, rather than to necessarily endear herself to others. Though untrustworthy and disloyal, my staffer proved herself a formidable force in pursuit of an agenda important to her. Elizabeth May is also capable of considerable kindness and generosity and self-sacrifice, to say nothing of a great sense of humour and a flair for fun. She is a complex person, for sure—not a reliable soldier to have with you in a trench, but no better companion with whom to quaff a beer in the mess hall after battle.

A minister of the Crown is rarely truly off duty. But one of my fondest memories from my time in Cabinet concerned a goofy "off-duty" evening at the Ottawa Press Club. With Elizabeth May's mother, Stephanie, at the piano keyboard, I joined both Elizabeth and some of the rest of my political staff in a singsong, my own vocals doubtless causing the harmony quotient to plunge to utter discordance. Possibly the most touching and memorable moment I experienced with any staff member personally was on the promenade of that grand Banff Springs Hotel suite described earlier. There, during one of my last official visits to Banff as minister (and "mayor"), Elizabeth presented me with an album containing photos of me and my two very young daughters that, over time, she had assembled and hand-decorated with skilful and imaginative drawings and inscriptions. The gift meant a lot to me at the time. And I value it even more highly almost three decades later, now that the two girls are fully grown (Emily was not yet born). Such is the sunny side of Elizabeth May. It's what so often radiates both in private and in public, engendering fierce loyalty to her as an individual and as a politician among countless admirers. It is challenging to reconcile this dimension with the side of Elizabeth that ended up costing me and the government dearly—including my seat in Parliament and Cabinet. When I viewed online Elizabeth's haunting public meltdown in a lava flow of profanities at the Annual National Parliamentary Press Gallery Dinner on May 9, 2015—an affair at which, as we have seen, Robert Stanfield had always outshone all the other national political party leaders as a fellow guest speaker—I was both saddened and surprised. Saddened because no empathetic person enjoys seeing a well-known figure make a spectacle of herself in such a public way, especially when, as with me, that figure was once a colleague. Surprised because, until this happened, I never thought Elizabeth would ever be so undisciplined as to allow the public to see the Edward Hyde side of her "Dr. Jekyll and Mr. Hyde" dual personality.

Of this I am certain about Elizabeth Evans May: she now has few equals in Canadian public life as a *bonne vivante*, environmental gadfly, political and social activist, and government parliamentary critic. The woman is one of the most natural politicians I have ever known personally. In one seductive package, Elizabeth combines high intelligence, a powerful work ethic, a strong commitment to populist causes, expertise and credibility on a broad range of issues, a mellifluous tongue, and a non-threatening and approachable persona. When she applies her natural gifts in ruthless pursuit of social causes or personal ambition, the woman can be unstoppable. Her popular appeal, both real and potential, extends well beyond the minority of electors who are passionate about environmental issues, let alone supportive of the Green Party of Canada. She is steadily becoming, and likely will soon be, what she has always desperately longed to be: a superstar. A former ministerial staffer of mine reminded me, for the book at hand, that I had predicted all this for Elizabeth way back when she first worked for me. "For all her faults and sins," he said, "Elizabeth has become something of a Mother Earth figure in Canada and beyond — which you correctly predicted back in the day." He added: "My recollection of your comment: 'That woman will become the *grande dame* of the environmental movement one day.' And you, Tom, contributed in a big way to that."

If I discovered Elizabeth May in the manner a film director might have launched the career of a talented actress by casting her in the first significant role she played, I doubt Elizabeth would have gone unnoticed for long, with or without my help.

# Political Epilogue

Brian Mulroney has, in recent years, come to admire Elizabeth in certain respects, just as I continue to do, despite my star-crossed history with her. I assume that the role Elizabeth played with many others in honouring Mulroney as the country's "greenest-ever Canadian prime minister" influences his current view. The "time heals everything" factor also probably has something to do with it. In his memoirs, Mulroney cites Elizabeth twice, in two different sections. He quotes her, not as a former staff member of mine, but as former executive director of the Sierra Club and as current leader of the Green Party of Canada. In both quotes, she lauded Mulroney's leadership as prime minister on environmental issues: achieving the March 1991 Canada-United States Air Quality Agreement on Acid Rain[21] and saving from failure the June 1992 Earth Summit on biodiversity.[22] Praise is the pixie dust of politics—a sprinkle can turn a mortal enemy into an eternal friend. Elizabeth May never loomed large enough in Brian Mulroney's mind to rank as a "mortal enemy." Nor would he to this day trust Elizabeth enough for her to earn his friendship, much less status as "an eternal friend." There are limits to flattery. But most of us mellow with age, typically for the better. Without question, Mulroney has done so. What have not changed about this man over the years are his fundamental values, among which loyalty is, I think, the former PM's most cherished political one. It is a value he unfailingly demonstrates to colleagues, former colleagues, and friends alike. I am but one of countless individuals who can attest to that fact from direct personal experience. In any event, it is unfortunate I did not act more fully on the PM's order, and on his wisdom and foresight, that summer morning when he called me very early at home to demand I fire my new staff recruit—now, it seems, so long ago. He just did not think she would be loyal to me or to his government. And he was proven right. *C'est la vie. Ça c'est la politique.*

# Chapter 23

# ROYAL VISITS, ROYAL DUTIES

From a young age, I have been a monarchist—or, as I prefer, "royalist." I think that, like everything else, it must be in the DNA. I descended from United Empire Loyalists. The first of my PEI McMillan forbears (Captain Alexander McMillan) settled on the Island after King George III had given him a large tract of land for his loyalty and military service to the Crown in the American Revolutionary War. It's not that I get caught up in all the pomp and ceremony and celebrity surrounding the royals. But there's also a little of that at play, I must admit. Governance is by nature pedestrian, so a bit of royal sparkle makes being governed a lot more fun. More important, it's a good and proper thing that the person who symbolizes one's country (head of state) be different from the individual who heads the mundane affairs of governing. Do we Canadians really want a mere politician, involved in the grubby and sometimes corrupt affairs of politics, to embody who we are? I don't.

To me, a constitutional monarchy makes sense on symbolic and substantive grounds alike. One of the greatest values the monarchy advances in our political culture is continuity, a core classic conservative principle. Another significant role the monarchy plays in our system is especially dear to classic liberals: defending liberty. But this cause is important to Tories, too, just as continuity isn't an exclusively Tory value, either. Such values are at the heart of who we are, collectively, as a people. That the monarchy helps protect and perpetuate a range of values salient to many different types of Canadians defines the unifying role of this institution in our constitutional system. It can be assumed that most Canadian Tories (almost by definition) support the monarchy, but Liberals and New Democrats have tended to lean that way, as well. Throughout the fifteen years Pierre Trudeau was our country's prime minister, for example, he never once publicly advocated abolishing the monarchy. Nor is there reason to believe he did so privately.

In Canada's constitutional tradition, the Crown retains significant powers, even if "the royal prerogative" is mostly exercised through the government of the day. Principally, the queen may refuse a government's request to dissolve Parliament and call an election if she believes an alternative government could legitimately be formed. She also has the right to select the prime minister, particularly following an inconclusive general election. What's most important is not the constitutional theory surrounding the monarchy's role and privileges but the national values that underpin the theory. In our country's case, those values include—but are not limited to—the ones detailed in the Charter of Rights and Freedoms, enshrined in the Constitution by a Liberal prime minister (Trudeau). The Charter, in turn, reflects values expressed in a Bill of Rights legislated by a Tory one (Diefenbaker). The NDP and its predecessor, the Co-operative Commonwealth Federation, heartily supported both measures.

Certain values unite us. Indeed, they make our nationhood possible. The Crown is our ultimate civic value because it embodies and symbolizes all the rest. For us Canadians, the Crown is not just a headdress of precious metals and dazzling jewellery, but a constitutional idea. In fact, the institution represents the very *idea of Canada*. There's a reason the Fathers of Confederation originally wanted to call their creation "the Kingdom of Canada" and would have formalized the name had they not been blocked by the Colonial Office in London. The Crown symbolizes who we are as a community, what we collectively believe, and the future to which we together aspire. This perspective has been shared unfailingly by every Conservative Party leader from Sir John A. Macdonald to the present. It is likely the Tory principle on which John Diefenbaker and Robert Stanfield most strongly agreed. Even Stephen Harper, with his reckless disregard for Canadian traditional values, is not at heart an anti-monarchist; as prime minister he just undermined the institution insidiously. A true value is neither old nor new. It is timeless. So, to my mind, being a royalist is as contemporary as the weather. And, as with the weather, anybody would be misguided to try to change it.

Maybe the Americans had it right for themselves when they combined in one office both the symbolic and political functions of state. After all, for their new country, they deposed one king, George III, while shooting and killing their way to independence from him and the British Empire. It would not have made sense, nor been politically acceptable, for them to then establish a monarchy of their own, but that is what, in effect, they did. Constitutionally, the Americans fused three offices in the person of the president: head of state, head of government, and head of the military. In the process, over the years, our neighbours have created "the Imperial Presidency." In what other liberal democratic country do the media hordes stand when the head of government enters a room? They generally do not in Canada. And it's a good thing they don't. The media are supposed to help keep our political leaders honest—not bow and scrape to them. Let us reserve such practices for the governor general in the absence of the queen herself, who symbolizes us as a community. In doing so, we honour at once Her Royal Majesty and ourselves.

Having given their highest public office holder no more regal a title than "Mr. President," Americans compensate by calling him that for life, even long after he has left the presidency. They do so no matter how briefly he might have served. Gerald Ford held the office only twenty-nine months, from August 1974 to January 1977. To boot, he was not elected either vice-president or president; he was appointed to both positions. The ignominious fall of Richard Nixon demonstrates how inherently dangerous it is to have a politician symbolize one's country. By marked contrast, in Thomas Jefferson, the United States produced one of the finest men and most gifted statesmen who ever lived. Both men, however, symbolized the American republic as head of state. What does that say about the United States? If head of state, head of government, and commander-in-chief were separate, as in Canada, instead of fused, as in the US system—it would say, thankfully, a lot less.

# Prince Philip, Duke of Edinburgh

Given my royalist sympathies, it was fitting that my first act as a freshly reminted minister of the Crown and member of Her Majesty's Privy Council should be to host a member of the royal family. Minutes after I was promoted from minister of state for tourism to minister of the environment, in late August 1985, the Prime Minister's Office (PMO) phoned me urgently. The purpose was to tell me that a government jet was waiting with its engines running on the Ottawa Airport tarmac to whisk me to Banff National Park. My predecessor, Suzanne Blais-Grenier, had been committed to hosting His Royal Highness Prince Philip, Duke of Edinburgh, at a grand luncheon at Chateau Lake Louise to celebrate the centennial of Banff and the Canadian national parks system. With Blais-Grenier gone, the commitment was now mine to honour. The government jet, its throttle in high gear, delivered me to the ceremony just in time to greet the prince.

At the luncheon—my first occasion to meet His Royal Highness officially—Prince Philip sat to my right at an eight-person, round head table. Government officials had prepared me for my first formal act as environment minister: I was to toast Her Majesty on behalf of her loyal Canadian subjects. I had been handed the formula only minutes before. After I survived this first test of both ministerial competence and official duty to the Crown, the prince leaned over to me and whispered: "It isn't only darkies who have their tribal rituals." His remark gave me newfound sympathy for Ivor Petrak and his own encounter with the prince's serpentine tongue. And it thickened my skin a tad to withstand the venom His Highness would sting me with on many future occasions.

My initial bad impression, however, proved terribly wrong. Now, many years later, perhaps with the maturity that comes only with age, I appreciate endlessly more than I did then how truly mistaken I was about the prince as part of an institution, the Crown—a "symbol of a symbol," in a manner of speaking. My respect for the prince *as a man* was to rise even higher. Put simply, he is the single most effective environmentalist and conservationist in the world. His Royal Highness did not make it easy for me to reach that conclusion, but this one man, as much as the queen herself, fortified my belief as a classic conservative in the fundamental soundness of our monarch-based constitutional system. I am convinced that Canadian anti-monarchists—especially those who champion a US-type presidential and congressional system for Canada—would feel far differently if exposed as directly as I was to the Crown "in action."

I first met the prince, not in Banff, but at Rideau Hall, the official residence of the governor general of Canada. It was in mid-September 1984, when the newly elected Mulroney government was formally sworn in. On that occasion, each minister was introduced, separately and privately, to Queen Elizabeth, with the prince and Prime Minister Brian Mulroney standing on either side. When my turn came, I felt it was like an official receiving line for one—me. The PMO later gave me a framed coloured picture of the queen (with her two august escorts) extending a white-gloved hand towards me, beaming as though welcoming me personally to the Throne Room at Buckingham Palace. Beat that, US Cabinet Secretary of Whatever! The queen and the prince were in Ottawa as part of an official visit to her dominion to help celebrate the bicentennials of New Brunswick and Ontario. My spending time with the prince in Banff, however, was a new experience for me as official royal host. I was to squire Prince Philip, and spend a lot of time with him, on many future occasions. Indeed, I had more dealings with the Duke of Edinburgh than any other minister at the time—possibly even the prime minister himself—because His Royal Highness was deeply involved in environmental causes. The prince has been especially active with the World Wildlife Fund (WWF), including serving as its widely respected international president from 1981 to 1996. In my time as Canada's environment minister,

I knew no other group, international or national, more effective than the WWF at drawing public and media attention to its work and issues in this field. In Prince Philip, they have had the best in the game as a co-conspirator. It is no wonder that the WWF has held onto him for more than half a century.

I found the royal man as well-informed and passionate about environmental issues as he was outspoken and, on occasion, verbally injudicious. Indeed, the WWF's own website describes their president emeritus as "often controversial and always a man of conviction." Translation: *He sticks his foot in it all the time.* To his great credit, Prince Philip has often been proven well ahead of his time when candidly expressing insights into specific environmental issues and lamenting the declining state of nature more generally. As early as the 1960s, he warned about the environmental harm from wildlife poaching, the indiscriminate building of mega-dams, and the uncontrolled use of toxic chemicals by industry and consumers alike. But policy-makers largely ignored such problems. As far as I am concerned now, he can express himself on all issues of this kind in four-letter words in every language of the globe if he wants. It's the cause, not the choice of words, that counts. And he has always counted big time on the environment, expressing himself with rare vision and courage.

In my encounters with Prince Philip, though, without exception, I was stung by one remark or another from the prince's sharp tongue. I never knew what would next shoot from his mouth—a verbal insight or a lethal sting. One such experience occurred at Last Mountain Lake Sanctuary, forty kilometres northwest of Regina. The Sanctuary, created in 1887, was the first officially designated wildlife area in North America. It's yet another example of Sir John A. Macdonald's visionary leadership and part of the Conservative Party's solid environmental record when at its best. It's also further evidence that the party's co-founder was—long before Teddy Roosevelt served as US president similarly—the continent's first "green" leader of a national government. Stephen Harper's successor as Tory leader—whoever he or she will be as I write—needs to be reminded that both Roosevelt and Macdonald headed *conservative* parties. So environmentalism and conservatism are not mutually exclusive "isms"—not even different sides of the same coin, but equally shiny reflections of the same side of a single coin. Canadian Conservatives debase their political currency by not knowing their own party's history and failing to be true to it.

The Last Mountain Lake Sanctuary's centennial was a big deal in conservation circles around the world. Accordingly, the Duke of Edinburgh, for the WWF, flew into Saskatchewan in April 1987 to help celebrate this historic milestone. The National Historic Sites and Monuments Board, under Tom Symons's chairmanship, had designated the area as a heritage site of country-wide importance. Though independent, its board reported to me, and, as a built-heritage champion in my own right, particularly in PEI, I was especially committed to this body's mission and work. In that role and spirit, I officiated at the designation ceremony at Last Mountain Lake. I spent two and a half hours touring the area by helicopter with the prince—just he and I and the pilot, intimate confines, for sure.

I don't wish to disparage a man I greatly admire, particularly for his dedication to the environmental cause. It's just that, at the time, I could not understand why a person so sensitive to the interests of humanity could seem so insensitive to the feelings of particular human beings. On the occasion at hand, Prince Philip was the honoured guest at a reception I co-hosted with the Saskatchewan government. We had invited a long list of locals active in the conservation and heritage causes. One middle-aged activist could not contain her excitement when introduced to

His Royal Highness: "This is the most exciting moment in my entire life," she gushed to the prince. With what I considered a hauteur that would have made the eighteenth-century French royal court take notice, the regal object of her admiration said: "My dear woman, what would ever compel you to say something so foolish?" I sensed that the lady felt guillotined, but I failed to appreciate what I now know to be a much more likely possibility: the prince was simply expressing great personal modesty. I am certain now that the lady in question took the remark in that spirit, rather than as an insult, and, as I so often did with the prince, I just got it all wrong. Only later, when I got to know the prince better and could place such incidents in a broader context, did I see the light. This incident, as with so many others like it I was to experience, was part of my learning process about the man.

On another occasion, also in Saskatchewan, the prince and I officiated at an outdoor wildlife habitat ceremony when powerful winds suddenly struck. The gusts threatened to blow the two of us, and all the other platform guests, right off the highly elevated stage. Some of my speaking notes did blow off the podium into the crowd just as I was addressing it. Without my notes, I was forced to improvise—and, worse, struggle to remember the name of the provincial PC government's minister of parks and renewable resources whose conservation record I was in the act of extolling. The tribute was well deserved because the minister was an unrelenting champion of wild-life habitat, and finished his time in the portfolio with a remarkable record. In 1986, I negotiated and signed for Canada the North American Waterfowl Management Plan with US Secetrary of the Interior Donald Hodel. The Saskatchewan minister whose name I temporarily forgot was responsible for making his province and the Grant Devine Tory government the first to participate in this historic continental conservation program and commit funding to it. He also oversaw the designation of about 1.7 million acres of Saskatchewan Crown land under the provincial *Critical Wildlife Habitat Protection Act*, among many other landmark achievements he racked up as minister. This was the Tory Party writ provincial at its best. And yet, momen-tarily, while I was lauding the responsible minister's record, neither the man's first name (Colin) nor his last name (Maxwell) leaped to mind—a politician's worst night-mare. The mental paralysis had never happened to me before on a public platform, nor has it since. (I can forget my own name, but not others'.) Maybe I was exhausted. More likely, I was distracted by the ferocious winds and by the nakedness I felt in royalty's presence without my speaking notes. In any event, I was making a royal ass of myself and knew it. I was experiencing a "senior moment" two decades before actu-ally becoming a senior.

Though at this point Colin Maxwell had been living in Canada for about twenty years, he was born and raised in Tillicoultry, Scotland, and spoke with a strong Scottish brogue. In full oratorical flight, doing the best I could in the cir-cumstances, having forgotten the minister's name, and now without my notes to prod me, I said: "And this fine son of Saskatchewan has done as much as anyone in the country to…" Son of Saskatchewan! That was the best I could do? It was. When I sat down, the prince leaned towards me, exuding the air of a nineteenth-century schoolmaster about to whip the daylights out of a delinquent student. Then he said: "You foolish man, 'Son of Saskatchewan!'—the man is no more a son of Saskatchewan than I am."

On another occasion, I chaired a small roundtable with the prince in Regina for heads of environmental groups throughout western Canada. I began by welcom-ing the royal guest and thanking him for his time and interest. I had intended to introduce each participant and the organization he or she represented—as much to pay tribute to them as to inform the duke. But he interrupted me in mid-sentence, only seconds into my remarks, and said: "Cut the crap. Let's not lollygag."

But just when I was about to become an official member of the Anti-Monarchist League, His Royal Highness, Prince Philip, Duke of Edinburgh, totally redeemed himself in my eyes. This was the real prince, the real man—not the object distorted by my foggy lens. In Regina, in June 1987, during Environment Week (our second annual one), a gala $500-a-plate fundraising dinner was held, jointly sponsored by Ducks Unlimited and the WWF. Premier Grant Devine and numerous corporate CEOs and other luminaries attended. Among the attendees were Adam Zimmerman (president of Noranda Inc.) and media tycoon Douglas Basset (Baton Broadcasting, CTV, among others). Yet again, the prince was the guest of honour. The highlight of the evening was a silent auction to which many of Canada's foremost wildlife artists had donated extraordinary works of art, mostly paintings, but statuary and other creative objects as well. The prince showed intense interest in these works. I learned later he had discreetly purchased a number of paintings himself through a third party complicit in the stealth. One of the works, which, like the others, the prince bought *with his own funds*, was a $35,000 painting by BC artist Robert Bateman. As I recall, the subject was a magnificent white pelican.

Prince Philip deserves much of the credit for making the event the colossal success it was, both environmentally and financially. His mere presence at events of this sort ensured that they would be well attended, heavily covered by the media, and, in the case of fundraisers, hugely profitable for the relevant environmental cause or organization. The prince has a singular talent for shifting the attention his own celebrity attracts away from himself to the cause he chooses to promote. This modesty, no doubt, reflects the same dimension of the man I had mistaken for arrogance in the incident involving the gushing woman at the earlier reception. On the rare occasion when that talent failed him, the prince would berate both the fawning crowds and the media for losing sight of why he was present and why he thought *they* should be there: not to see him, but to support the cause at hand. And he would lecture them all about their misplaced priorities.

At the right moment, the prince has a great, if droll, sense of humour—a real one, not the kind that humiliated Ivor Petrak and unnerved me so often. In *Paradise Won*, Elizabeth May tells a story that I remember well—and that she does not embellish, unlike so many other vignettes in the book. One late-June evening in 1987, I was scheduled to speak at the Annual Meeting of the Canadian Nature Federation in Saskatoon. (I did officiate in other provinces!) In the afternoon, I helped launch a WWF project to restore the endangered burrowing owl population. The event took place at the farm of Grant Fahlman, who had agreed to leave a tract of land out of production and to limit the use of chemical insecticides on his entire property to help save the bird. In the scorching heat, behind strong ropes, was a cordon of several thousand conservationists, royalists, and country-fair enthusiasts. To begin the official program, Prince Philip and I were introduced to the endangered burrowing owls. Lorne Scott, head of the Saskatchewan Wildlife Federation, had rigged one of the owls' nests to reveal the tiny, naked, ugly, and squawking infant birds in the blinding sun. As the baby birds were handed around to His Royal Highness and me and local VIPs, the prince showed his baby owl to the crowd. Meanwhile, my own little beast in hand decided this would be an ideal time to have a watery bowl movement—all over my right palm and wrist! Elizabeth May always seemed equipped for every emergency, whether a needle and thread to repair the minister's popped suit button as he was about to address an audience or, in this particular case, a serviette at the ready for a major cleanup. True to character, she discreetly handed me the item. I wiped myself clean of the smelly yellow slime and then handed the now badly soiled tissue back to her. Nothing lost, nothing noticed. Or, so I thought. Moments later, I introduced Elizabeth to the prince. About to extol my staffer's credentials as an environmentalist in her own right, His Royal Highness, as usual, interrupted me in full rhetorical flight. "Yes," he said, "I know who she is. She provides you with Kleenexes." So much for my going unnoticed—and for Elizabeth's credentials in the eyes of the prince. As Elizabeth notes in her book, "If Prince Philip were a bird, he would definitely be a raptor. He has sharp enough eyes."[1] I learned from my Colin Maxwell snafu that the prince has sharp ears, as well.

But even more important, I discovered—albeit belatedly—the man has one of the sharpest minds in the entire environmental movement. Throughout the time we spent together on the environment front, the prince demonstrated high intelligence, vast knowledge about the environment, a genuine passion for his particular environmental or conservation causes, and a powerful dedication to advancing them in concert with activists. He also brought great energy and enthusiasm to every task or event, often of the most unglamorous and unregal sort.

On a number of occasions after returning to Britain from Canada, the prince wrote me long and thoughtful letters detailing personal observations and insights and recommendations inspired by his Canadian travels. In every case, he had not only carefully composed the letters himself, but also had meticulously typed them personally—typos always fastidiously hand-corrected. All said, Her Majesty Queen Elizabeth II, Queen of Canada and head of the Commonwealth, married well. The prince's sheer humanity, with all its strengths and weakness, is what helps make him one of the world's greatest living environmentalists and conservationists, an outstanding servant of his fellow man. *Royalty as servant*—that is what shrouds the monarchy in paradox and irony, steeps it in mystery, and layers it with sheer wonderment, making it the most illustrious dimension of our great Canadian democracy. It is the reason we should forever retain it at the centre of our system of responsible government. Americans can only pretend to have what we have in reality as our birthright. Just as all the shine and sparkle that emanate from the royals sometimes blind us to their humanity, so also their humanity—with all the failings intrinsic to being humans—can make us miss the majestic qualities that render the monarchy the most special feature of our constitutional form of government.

# Prince Edward, Earl of Wessex

I had the distinction of hosting, for the Government of Canada, the first official solo visit anywhere by Queen Elizabeth and Prince Philip's youngest son, Prince Edward. The visit happened on June 24–25, 1987, in Charlottetown. He was then only twenty-three. Although already beginning to get a bit "thin on top," as the saying goes, he looked every bit the boy/man he was: youthful, ruddy of cheek, trim, well turned out, and, appropriately, as dashing as a prince. The highlight of the visit was a gala black-tie state dinner I hosted in his honour with more than 350 invitees. I had some discretion, but not a lot, about the invitation list, of which I controlled about a quarter.

Most guests were *ex officio*: individuals (and their spouses or partners) who could reasonably expect to be invited by virtue of the office or position they held in the community.

Premier Joe Ghiz asked to see me several weeks before the dinner. Because the visit was under federal government auspices, not provincial, protocol dictated that the premier would have no formal role in the visit other than that extended to him as a courtesy, including an invitation as a special guest to the dinner itself. But, for Ghiz, no opportunity, least of all a royal visit, should be missed to pursue a partisan advantage. In this case, he suggested a deal: if I gave him thirty-five invitations to the state dinner, he would give me an equivalent number to the gala performance of the stage musical *Anne of Green Gables*, hosted by the province in Prince Edward's honour the next evening at the Confederation Centre of the Arts. It was hardly a symmetrical *quid quo pro*: he had over a thousand invitations, I (at most) a hundred outside the "must invites." The premier was, in effect, asking me for about a third of my entire discretionary invitations. In turn, I would be receiving fewer than 4 percent of his. I viewed the state dinner as a community event, not an occasion to reward or court partisan support. But I thought that haggling over the affair would sully it while making me look small. I, therefore, let the premier have his invitations. Of course, almost all went to Liberal fundraisers and donors and campaign workers, including in his own electoral district.

Prince Edward was dapper and handsome in his white dinner jacket for the state dinner. I was determined that our province's namesake prince would see the best of "his" community and its people. Upon arrival, I was stunned: I had never before seen so many Islanders under one roof looking so elegant. Obviously, they felt as I did: this was an historic occasion—for the Island and for its prince. The Prince Edward Room at the Prince Edward Hotel looked grander than I had ever seen it before. Was there a flower petal left anywhere in the world, or had the hotel bought the entire supply? My money was on the latter. The meal was marvellous, the PEI Symphony Orchestra heavenly, everything else perfect in every detail. For my twelve-minute after-dinner welcoming remarks, prior to giving the official toasts to the guest of honour and the queen, I had decided to go light. I wanted to stress the humour in Prince Edward Island's welcoming its namesake prince on his first official solo visit anywhere. "Your Royal Highness," I began, "no matter where you may travel elsewhere in the world, it is only here that you, Prince Edward, can dine in the Prince Edward Room, of the Prince Edward Hotel, on Prince Edward Island." Prince Edward's laughter was as loud as anyone's.

Prince Edward Island was named after The Prince Edward, Duke of Kent and Strathearn (1767–1820), the father of Queen Victoria—the contemporary Prince Edward's great-great-great grandfather. The forebear Prince Edward was the first member of the royal family to stay in North America for more than a short visit. His father, George III, had appointed him military commander-in-chief for North America. For much of his career, he served and lived in Halifax. During this period, he visited Prince Edward Island, his namesake colony. I informed the young Prince Edward, at the state dinner in his honour, that, on his ancestor's own visit to PEI, he had watched a cricket match in Charlottetown's Victoria Park. During the game, the royal personage had been knocked senseless by a wildly thrown ball. "And that incident on our little island," I told Prince Edward, "almost changed the course of history and, in the process, the succession of the British throne." There was more laughter all around. "I assure you, Your Royal Highness, you yourself have nothing to worry about: we no longer play cricket in Prince Edward Island—at least not when a member of the royal family is in town." There was yet more laughter, most of all his.

Some years earlier, Premier Richard Hatfield had welcomed the newly married Prince and Princess of Wales (Charles and Diana) to New Brunswick on their first official visit to the province since being married, in July 1981. Known to take the odd puff of something stronger than a cigarette, Hatfield was inclined towards the maudlin and the melodramatic at the best of times. He chose the state dinner during this royal visit to make it the worst of times for the young royal couple. Hatfield waxed poetically, and none too briefly, about the wonders and virtues and splendours of young true love in the persons of the recently betrothed royals. The couple was, as Queen Victoria would have said, "not amused." Nor was Buckingham Palace. Henceforth, all such remarks by local welcoming hosts had to be cleared with London prior to delivery. Or, at least, the request was made. It was in my case and I obliged.

Obviously briefed about my own intended levity at the dinner, the prince himself came prepared in kind. He was masterful. "I am delighted to be in my namesake province," he began, "the land of Anne of Green Gables. Everyone likes to see his or her name up in lights. But I must confess that it has taken a while for me to get used to seeing my own name everywhere I travel in Prince Edward Island." Much laughter. "Especially when I see it on the side of a bus!" The audience roared. He hit the cricket ball right out of the park.

For the rest of the two-day visit, I showed the young prince what I could of Prince Edward Island: Province House, where Canada was born; Cavendish, site of Green Gables, the legendary heritage farmhouse associated with Lucy Maude Montgomery and her literary heroine, Anne Shirley; the rest of the North Shore national park, with its miles of peach-pink sandy beaches and red-cliffed coastline; and many other natural and heritage sites. By happy coincidence, all the most illustrious sites on the carefully planned tour were under my jurisdiction as environment minister, so I was able to pull rank to ensure maximum impact. I said in my state dinner remarks: "As minister also responsible for the country's Weather Service, I am no less proud to have arranged for the clouds to part and the sun to shine for the arrival of our namesake prince in the province earlier today." I cautioned him, though, "If the weather should turn inclement for the rest of your visit, I will count on the premier to perform the next miracle." Everyone but Joe Ghiz laughed. Prince Edward's first official solo visit anywhere could not have been more successful, including weather-wise, had I, in fact, possessed such divine powers.

There was, however, one small downside from my perspective. For the informal part of the tour—for example, viewing the North Shore beaches—I took along, hand in hand, my three-year-old daughter Kelly. I did so because I wanted to humanize this part of the program. I was right: the media visuals were terrific. The prince came off looking like a typical tourist, exactly what I had in mind. Parks Canada staff took some splendid pictures of the prince and Kelly and me together and developed them almost on the spot. At the end of his official visit to PEI, I asked the prince to sign or initial one of the photos for Kelly to cherish when old enough to appreciate it. He refused. In my hubris, I thought: Why not? I'm a minister of the Crown, to say nothing of all the time and effort and care I have devoted to making his official debut a rousing success. But, of course, the royals do not give out autographs. The prince is not some second-tier Hollywood actor or TV reality-show celebrity. Placing him on that plain, as I was in effect attempting to do, would have been antithetical to the dignity and grace that characterize the Crown he represents and that help make it magical.

As environment minister, I was to host Prince Edward again a year later. This time it was in Newfoundland, for several days in early June 1988. The main event was to dedicate Gros Morne National Park as a World Heritage Site. The park is a breathtaking 1,800-square-kilometre wonderland of mountain peaks and rocky fjords and ocean vistas on the province's west coast. "Breathtaking" does not do the area justice. During this state visit, Prince Edward and I practically lived out of each other's suitcase. Like the baggage, our joint schedule was packed—with events and travelling. Most memorable for me was a two-hour stop at what was billed as "a typical Newfoundland homestead" for a "modest lunch." It was all that, but only if "typical" means a spacious modern suburban home scoured to within an inch of its life. Its sprawling manicured lawn would have made the greens at Augusta National look like Kansas cornfields. The walkways and driveway had been edged and clipped and accented with brilliant white pebbles—as though the red carpet for a royal entrance. The lunch itself was "modest," if that word can be applied to lobsters as big as Maine Coon cats, to scallops and oysters and crabmeat more succulent than Bacchus ever devoured, and enough wine and beer to sink a full-masted sailing ship. It was a feast fit for a prince—literally. The young married couple who hosted the luncheon must have slaved for weeks, and blown their retirement fund, to prepare the royal spread.

At the home, the prince was suitably charming, regally correct, and expressly thankful. But I am not certain he noticed as keenly as I did the enormous amount of time and effort and expense the two delightful Newfoundland hosts had devoted to making his visit perfect in every way. After all, unlike him, neither they nor I were raised from birth in palaces and castles, where, one presumes, all such attention to detail must be both routine and taken for granted by occupants. But I would bet my own castle, if I had one, that this couple will remember to the day they die the dazzling smile he flashed them when, while departing their welcoming home, he expressed his appreciation for the hospitality they had extended to him.

With the visit over, both the prince and I were exhausted—overbooked, over-travelled, and now overjoyed to have it all behind us. Seated together in the back seat of a parked limousine, I said to my royal tour partner of several days and, now, of two separate royal visits—more as one young man to another, joined in onerous official duties: "Well, we got through that one just fine, don't you think?" He smiled and nodded agreement. Indeed, we had done just fine—he without question, me thanks to a royal assist. This young royal proved himself to be a real prince in both senses of the word.

# Prince Andrew and the Duchess of York

In July 1989, a year after Prince Edward came to PEI, the Duke and Duchess of York (Prince Andrew and Sarah Ferguson) paid an official visit to the Island to attend the Canadian Scout Jamboree, held there for the first time. It was a provincial visit, not a federal one. So this time Premier Ghiz hosted the state dinner for the royal couple, on behalf of the province. Ghiz, therefore, controlled the invitation list. He did not need to horse-trade with the province's federal minister for a piece of the action, as he had done with me for the Prince Edward dinner. In fact, with me gone from office, following the 1988 election, there was no longer a federal minister for the Island. Now recently appointed consul general in Boston, I, as a privy councillor was automatically invited to the state dinner ("business suit," not "black tie," this time). At the dinner, I saw not a single Tory other than those whom, like me, Joe Ghiz was compelled to invite, typically because of the office they held—in which cases, protocol trumped politics even for so hyper-partisan a man as the premier. Otherwise, the place was so packed with Liberal hacks I felt like I was attending a Grit fundraiser. That's Island politics. The occasion risked dragging the Crown dangerously close to partisanship.

As taken aback as I was at the time, I now have a different perspective about this "Liberal" event. Even partisans of different political stripes, no matter how divided they might be on issues, are united in appreciating the sheer magic of the Crown and of the royals themselves. Besides, the royals have been in the "family business" for centuries. With unerring vision, they can spot the potholes in front of the royal carriage and know exactly how to circumvent them. The Duke and Duchess of York did so this time. Their technique—no doubt the family formula—was mostly to comport themselves with regal dignity while not allowing anyone to place them in situations (including photographs) that could embarrass the Crown then or later. Instead of serving as props for someone's "Guess who I was with last night" photo shoot, the two royals carefully focused their time and attention on the premier and his wife, honoured guests, and official community representatives, rather than on political hucksters whose intentions at such events are invariably as transparent as their boorishness is insufferable. I learned from my own experience as royal host that Palace espionage and on-the-ground advance work for public events of this kind are thorough but subtle, protective but undetectable, and flexible but unerring. Nothing is left to chance—not even an official host's welcoming remarks. There's a reason this institution has endured for well over a thousand years.

The state dinner was enjoyed by everyone. Regardless of political labels, we Islanders like a good party—and know how to throw one. In this period, we all gained a lot of experience hosting and entertaining young Windsor royals. It is no wonder, then, that William and Kate (the Duke and Duchess of Cambridge) chose Prince Edward Island for the Atlantic Canada part of their first official visit to Canada as a married couple, in the summer of 2011, only two months after their nuptials. I have no doubt that royal-visit Palace veterans recommended the land of Green Gables to the royal pair. As with the monarchy itself, why not go with what works?

## Queen Beatrix of the Netherlands

It did not take me long to think that my job as environment minister was, essentially, to escort royalty. Every time I looked at my schedule, there appeared yet another royal visitor whom External Affairs and my own departmental officials were expecting me to meet and greet. This time, it was Her Royal Majesty Beatrix Wilhelmina Armgard of the Netherlands and her husband, His Royal Highness Claus von Amsberg (a former German diplomat). The newest royal visit was in August 1988. I liked both of these royals from the time I set eyes on them. They were delightful—and, like their British/Canadian royal counterparts, real pros.

Queen Beatrix, who shared with her subjects a passionate interest in the natural environment, would end up being the longest-serving monarch in the history of the Netherlands, before abdicating in favour of her son in April 2013, at age seventy-five.

Meanwhile, her country was plagued by an array of pollution problems, most of them affecting the quality of its precious water supply. Of special concern to the queen was the heavy runoff into her country's rivers and streams from farm-animal waste used to fertilize crop fields. Her Majesty spoke with vast technical knowledge of the issue and with great personal alarm.

Queen Beatrix followed events in Canada with uncommon vigilance for a foreigner. But that's because, after the Germans occupied their country in 1940, the Dutch royal family had spent most of the war years in Ottawa. Indeed, Beatrix's sister, Margriet, was born there in 1943.

As part of that interest in things Canadian, Beatrix had been following the federal government's international leadership on such environmental issues as climate change, ozone depletion, endangered species, and negotiations with the United States on acid rain. What's more, Canada was the indisputable trailblazer in research and remediation techniques for freshwater quality and protection. This was the very area of most interest to Her Royal Majesty. What better country to visit for environmental purposes, she thought, than the world leader that happened to be her wartime home? The queen was determined to exploit every scintilla of information she could extract from our country's experts and from touring our environmental facilities and research centres. Her Royal Majesty asked the Dutch ambassador to Canada to meet with me to explore any interest I might have in her visiting Canada for this purpose and in chaperoning the royal couple during their stay. Does a Prince Edward Islander eat potatoes? I donned my royal slippers before the ambassador was out the door. Soon, the queen and Prince Claus were on a royal plane to Ottawa. And, as an environmentalist, I began what turned out to be my most enjoyable and rewarding royal visit of all.

The Dutch royals had long ago shed fussy formality and remoteness from the common folk to forge a new "business model" for the modern monarchy everywhere that stressed not only personal ties to the people, but also the promotion of, in this case, the Netherlands' practical interests both at home and abroad. Like their British counterparts, the Dutch royals increasingly had become as much economic and trade and cultural ambassadors as national symbols. It was in that spirit that the Dutch royal household had engaged me, as Canada's environment minister, to serve as escort and tour guide.

Towards this professionalizing and popularizing of her country's monarchy over time, Queen Beatrix presented herself in many ways as a homemaker not much different from most of her compatriots—except with a major equity stake in Royal Dutch Shell, an estimated personal fortune of $300 million, and nice frocks. For his part, Prince Claus was a trim, greying, distinguished-looking, dapper man who, to me, resembled Charles Boyer in his later years. I had been told privately that the prince suffered bouts of depression, never having quite adjusted from being a professional diplomat to having to play a royal on the public stage. I myself found him pleasant, charming, and likeable, even if quiet and reserved. By marked contrast, the queen was gregarious, had great presence, and smiled easily and often. Whether by nature or upbringing, she exuded regality without appearing at all imperial, much less imperious. Her impeccable but understated grooming and attire and manners were much more those of a successful businesswoman in full professional bore than of a pampered woman of leisure with too much time on her hands.

Meetings, consultations, tours, private briefings, scientific demonstrations, discussions, and information exchanges filled the royal visitors'—and, therefore, my own—backbreaking schedule for their week-long stay in Canada. The queen threw herself into the schedule like a heavyweight prizefighter training to defend a world title. She did not intend to lose a single round. For her, the highlight of the visit—which she had personally requested—was the tour of Environment Canada's world-renowned National Water Research Institute (NWRI) in Burlington, Ontario. Ironically, this was one of the department's major assets that my predecessor, Suzanne Blais-Grenier, had placed on her chopping block. I didn't just bury the meat cleaver; I destroyed it. The NWRI is the largest freshwater research entity in Canada and, by any standard, the best of its kind in the world. Its Water Science and Technology Directorate generates the scientific knowledge and models needed to sustain Canada's water resources and freshwater ecosystems. Without it, many Canadians would be drinking from drain spouts and boiling water to bathe. The queen and prince were enthralled. The scientists and support staff pulled out all the stops for the royals, doing wonders for the Institute's reputation in royal circles, and with me: I increased its budget not long after returning to Ottawa. As media cameras flashed, film rolled, and pencils were put to pads, the research centre's public visibility and prestige soared well beyond our shores. The Government of Canada could hardly have bought that kind of favourable public attention for the work of one of its most important facilities had it emptied the Royal Mint for the purpose. Like Prince Philip, the Dutch visitors were well aware of the power of their celebrity, and wielded it with the precision of an Olympic archer—and, in the case of the Dutch royals, the diplomatic dexterity of an *apostolic nuncio*. The impact of the visit on all concerned, including me, lasted a long time.

Unlike Prince Edward's visit to Newfoundland, Queen Beatrix and Prince Claus's trip to Canada did not end with me and royalty in the back seat of a limousine. This time, standing at the Ottawa International Airport tarmac, where their royal plane awaited, the queen and prince gave me a warm embrace—and lovely gifts that I will always cherish. Having given so many gifts to royals on behalf of the people of Canada—to Prince Philip in particular—I found it refreshing to be on the receiving end. The gifts to me from Beatrix and Claus included a paperback-sized cut crystal ornament box with the royal crest etched on the lid. And, even nicer to my mind, was a majestic coloured photograph of the couple, beautifully framed in rich, dark-green leather accented with the Dutch crown—in gold. The photograph, though not autographed, was personally monogrammed. A Dutch-born and -raised acquaintance of mine in Boston once spotted the elegantly framed and personalized photograph in my apartment and almost fainted. "Oh, Beatrix and Claus, they're long-time friends of mine," I said offhandedly, as though commenting on next-door neighbours. I was being only half-facetious. Having spent only a week with the royal couple, I was indeed made to feel like their friend.

# The Governor General and Lieutenant Governors

If the royal visit of Queen Beatrix and Prince Claus taught me anything, it was that "Dutch" is a five-letter word for class. The visit also reminded me, yet again, of the force for good a first-rate constitutional monarchy can be and how fortunate we Canadians are, and should consider ourselves to be, to have such an institution ourselves.

For all the glitz and glamour associated with the institution, I believe the monarchy makes eminent practical sense—yet another irony about it all. To me, the greatest tangible benefit we Canadians derive from that institution is through the monarch's official representatives in our country: the governor general and the lieutenant governors of the provinces.

Jeanne Sauvé became minister of the environment upon her first re-election, in 1974, and served in that portfolio until Pierre Trudeau appointed her minister of communications a year later. Sauvé loved presiding over Environment Canada and, like me and Jean Chrétien, had an especially soft spot for national parks. Later, after she became governor general in 1984, I decided to take advantage of this serendipitous fact by prevailing on the woman—although there was seldom any resistance—to lend the prestige of her office to foster diverse parks-related causes. The GG accepted my invitation, for example, to participate in week-long activities in Charlottetown to mark the restoration of Province House, where the Fathers of Confederation met in 1864 to give birth to Canada.

I was determined that the activities to celebrate the restoration should be at least as grand as the many socials Island politicians had held in Charlottetown in 1864 to fete the Fathers during their visit. The events back then included an elaborate ball at Government House. (The visit itself went mostly unnoticed by ordinary Islanders because a circus was in town at that very time. Why bother with the birth of a nation when one can see baby elephants?) For the restoration celebrations, Governor General Sauvé threw herself into my plans with gusto. They soon became *our* plans. Among many other social affairs, we planned a gala black-tie ball at Fanningbank, the official residence of the Island's lieutenant governor, replicating the theme of the 1864 ball held there. In Her Excellency's name, we invited to this once-every-century event everyone associated with the restoration, scores of community leaders and officials throughout the province, and lots of everyday folks to represent the population at large. Sauvé, always elegant anyway, looked like a queen that night in a shimmering silver floor-length gown and sweeping cape with diamond jewellery aglow. Stunning! Only a member of the royal family itself could have pulled off the kind of regal entrance she did with such effortless aplomb. The governor general had a terrific time. Consistent with protocol, I was, at one point, approached by the GG's aide-de-camp to waltz with her. As with our joint execution of the program for the week, we moved marvellously together.

With the exception of Georges Vanier (1959–67), no other governor general in recent decades has brought to the office quite as much star power, regal panache, and chutzpah as Jeanne Sauvé did. Perhaps, women just do the job better in these terms than most men can. Likely it's partly the diamonds. The entire week's festivities, especially the ball at Government House, would not have been nearly the smashing success they were without the lustre that—again, short of one of the royals themselves—only the GG could have lent to them. National symbols are crucial to a people's sense of collective self. They create visual, verbal, or iconic representations of the national spirit and shared values, goals, and history, and help us see ourselves as one people with a multifaceted and yet cohesive cultural identity and singular destiny. The Crown is our country's ultimate national symbol. The monarch embodies our national soul, our history and traditions, our held truths, and our foundational aspirations. All this is not just romantic poppycock. It has practical value in making the nation possible, in making it work, and in making the "people" a word that means more than the plural of "person."

Until around the early 1970s, the lieutenant governor of PEI lacked a significant government-supplied hospitality budget for the official residence, Fanningbank. Moreover, there was a dearth of volunteers, and no formal structure or process, to help furnish the place and ensure it continued to meet strict heritage standards while serving as a quotidian home for the lieutenant governor and his family. The incumbent himself was expected to pay to maintain the residence and grounds and gardens. (There would not be a woman lieutenant governor until Marion Reid was appointed to a five-year term in 1990.) Consequently, the "governor"—as Islanders have always called the office holder—needed to be wealthy in his own right, for the financial burden of holding the post was substantial. Only after 1973, with more generous public funding and the formation of volunteer committees, were plebeians able to put their names forward for the position without fear of becoming broke in it. Meanwhile, the lieutenant governorship was virtually the exclusive domain of "Island Brahmins" such as Benjamin Rogers (1910–15), Frank Richard Heartz (1924–30), George DeBlois (1933–39), T. W. L. Prowse (1950–58), and Walter Hyndman (1958–63)—a veritable tableau of the Island's bluest of bluebloods.

The first Acadian governor, Joseph Alphonsus Bernard—from Tignish, Helen Doyle's home village—was distinctly not an Island Brahmin. He was both Roman Catholic and "new money," having prospered as a merchant "Up West," as Islanders are given to saying. My father was private secretary to Bernard while the latter served as governor from 1945 to 1950. I assume "Dr. Joe" was conscripted for the task, as he was for many others, because of his flawless French—to say nothing, in this case, of his flawless bona fides as a Tory. Dad told me that Governor Bernard almost went bankrupt trying to "keep up appearances" while in the viceregal post. No doubt, having to support thirteen children also drained his pocketbook. Almost every Islander capable of doing so, for example, attends the governor's New Year's Day levée, at which people from across the province pay respects to the Crown. Attendees then expect the governor to offer hospitality after they have endured the endless receiving line. In Bernard's time, as now, that did not mean orange or cranberry juice. A teetotaler, John George MacKay, served as lieutenant governor from 1969 to 1974. He refused to serve the expected fortified libations at his various socials, including on New Year's Day. When this abstemious practice soon became known, the Island had a virtual constitutional crisis on its hands. But, being a resourceful people, Islanders improvised, especially at major functions such as balls: the Government House parking lot became a sea of open car trunks from which portable bars not only quenched the thirst of rapacious revellers, but also rescued the monarchy from certain disrepute. Nowadays, the public purse provides adequate, if not extravagant, funding for such purposes. This provision helps stabilize the Crown on the Island, even if not always the legs of partiers at Government House functions.

An expert volunteer committee ensures the décor of Fanningbank no longer depends on the whims and taste of the lieutenant governor or his or her spouse. In the absence of heritage advisors, over the decades this historic building was too often furnished with La-Z-Boys from Eaton's and velvet paintings from Woolworth's. Now, thanks to the heritage committee's oversight and aggressive outreach to the community, it's Mark Butcher highboys from the Confederation era, original Robert Harris portraits and other paintings from the Island's past, fine early Persian rugs (including a donation from me), and additional period furnishings, both large and small, from benefactors such as my late brother-in-law, George Taylor Fulford III. Formerly an unapproachable stately mansion behind high gates on a hill, the lieutenant governor's residence is now very much the people's house. All the while, it also serves as literally the queen's home away from home during her periodic visits to the province. This architectural gem is also a visitor-friendly museum lovingly furnished and cared for by discerning and knowledgeable locals from all walks of life. The transformation of PEI's own viceregal residence in these ways reflects how the monarchy itself is retaining its relevance and a place in people's hearts.

# Prince Charles and Lady Diana

Allow me to emphasize another royal family member's dedication to public service—that of the heir to the throne, Prince Charles. Public duty is the real "family business" of all the royals. "Like father, like son" is probably truer of Prince Philip and Prince Charles than of any other famous father-and-son pair in contemporary times. In the manner of his royal father, Charles palpably exudes community service, as I was to see for myself at the closest range. Before meeting the man personally, I was not especially enamoured of him. I had thought the prince a tad stuffy and stiff and rather awkward-looking—sort of a royal Joe Clark. As with my original misperception of the royal father, I could not have been more wrong about the royal son. Prince Charles proved to be as charming and fun-loving as he was knowledgeable and insightful. I ended up being very impressed with the prince and captivated by him personally.

As if to prepare me for my future role as royal escort, I spent time with the Prince and Princess of Wales during their official visit to Prince Edward Island in early June 1983. By then, I had been a Member of Parliament for four years, but was not yet a minister of the Crown (that would come a year later). The prince and princess had been married for only two years when they visited PEI. Their visit to the Island included a large lawn party for provincial community leaders and social activists held at Fanningbank. For the royal couple, I was not an official host or even escort. But the visit was mostly to Charlottetown, virtually congruent with my federal riding, so I was included in all the events, among them some private ones to which only a handful of people were invited.

By the time Prince Charles arrived in PEI as a newly married man, he had made the built heritage his principal personal cause. The prince was fast earning a worldwide reputation for both his specialized knowledge and his candour in this area. Many people in the United Kingdom and, indeed, around the world respected him for attacking what he considered the bad design of many modern buildings and the desecration of superior traditional ones by demolition, ill-advised remodelling, or inappropriate nearby development. His overarching theme has been that England, in particular, risks turning into a soulless, impersonal place in the name of progress. He has been especially outspoken about trends in downtown London. Prince Charles lamented, for example, the £500-million office and shopping complex designed by the French modernist architect Jean Nouvel for an area close to St. Paul's Cathedral, Sir Christopher Wren's iconic masterpiece. It has been a long time since a member of the immediate royal family was willing to take a public position on a controversial issue with the kind of passion Charles brought to this one. Not even Prince Philip in his heyday dared to do what his son now does routinely: risk the wrath of the country's rich and powerful and influential stratum—in his case, from elite architects to major developers to business tycoons to big-project contractors to real estate wheelers and dealers to large-portfolio landowners to wealthy investors, not to mention the dominant building trades and the politically active labour unions that represent them. At one point, the Royal Institute of British Architects tried to organize a boycott against him. And yet, the prince's courage has paid off in both social impact and public esteem, even if the latter has been grudgingly accorded him by those whose feathers he has ruffled. Aristotle said, "Courage is the first of human qualities because it is the quality which guarantees the others." How true of Prince Charles. The man has demonstrated a natural talent for the royal bully pulpit. He knows, perhaps instinctively, when and how to use it for maximum advantage to his various causes.

The built-heritage cause has always been close to my own heart. I am proud to have been honoured by the PEI Museum and Heritage Foundation for my work in this field with my brother Charley. At the garden party, the prince and I wandered the spacious grounds of Government House, with its meticulously kept rose gardens. Those splendid gardens are planted and cultivated by a volunteer committee of local amateur, but talented and experienced, horticulturists. As His Royal Highness smelled the fragrant posies during our joint promenade, he pointed toward Fanningbank and said to me: "In my view, this is one of the finest official residences in the entire Commonwealth"—high praise from an occupant of Buckingham Palace and Windsor and Balmoral Castles. The prince was especially keen about what local heritage enthusiasts had done with Fanningbank's interior and grounds.[2] The latter comprises a large chunk of Victoria Park, which overlooks the Hillsborough River, one of the most beautiful waterways in the country. On this day, I saw not so much a royal prince and heir to the throne as an antiquarian, a history buff, an architectural historian, a built-heritage preservationist, and a cultural-property crusader.

As I reflect now on Prince Charles's passion for the *built* environment, I cannot but liken it to the passion for the *natural* environment his father would later demonstrate during the many hours he and I spent together after my appointment as Canada's environment minister. For years now, Prince Charles has also been interested in his father's cause. Indeed, he has linked his own with his father's by urging architects to work with the Prince of Wales's Charitable Foundation—one of the largest independent philanthropic operations in the United Kingdom—to devise ways to develop sustainable buildings that could reduce carbon emissions linked to climate change. A few years after his Fanningbank visit in Charlottetown, the future king produced a book titled *A Vision of Britain: A Personal View of Architecture* that echoes some of the themes he discussed with me at Fanningbank.[3] Surely, the interest Prince Charles shares with his father in the total habitat of humanity—both built and natural—cannot be a coincidence. Each man is contributing enormously to improving public awareness of the importance of the cohesively linked architectural and natural environments to humanity's survival and quality of life. They are performing this role in a manner that, given their exceptional status as royals, few other individuals on the planet could. In light of the high stakes, the Crown that Prince Philip and Prince Charles represent, and that the latter will inherit, is playing a more important role in world affairs now than ever before in its long and storied history.

The Royal Yacht *Britannia* is now a ship museum permanently berthed in Edinburgh. At the time of the visit of Prince Charles and Princess Diana to Charlottetown in June 1983, however, this marine castle was still operating as the royal family's principal mode of oceanic transport. As the ship was about to enter the Hillsborough River, it passed right by (in the Hillsborough Bay) the waterview heritage home Kathy and I lived in with our children, five miles from the provincial capital.

A few hours after the aforementioned afternoon Government House garden party, Kathy and I attended a reception for the royal couple at the Charlottetown waterfront on a docked Canadian Navy frigate. It was an intimate affair, with scarcely more than a dozen guests, mostly public office holders and their spouses, including Premier Jim Lee and his wife, Patsy, and Charlottetown mayor Frank Moran and his wife, Shirley. We were all older than Princess Diana, some by decades. Even her royal husband was a dozen years older than she. The one and only exception was my wife, Kathy. Nine years my junior, she was still in her twenties at the time. Princess Diana, then twenty-two and new both to her marriage and to her royal status and duties, had not yet developed the personal confidence and social poise, let alone the extraordinary fashion sense, that later became her signature qualities. She was desperately shy in this period of her life. That fact was obvious to me, if not necessarily to everyone else, at the reception. The famous lowering of the head with raised eyes that so palpably and famously betrayed her shyness and lack of confidence were much in evidence. Kathy was not only roughly the same age as Princess Diana, but also almost equally tall. Kathy is a take-charge person, as befits the successful businesswoman she has long been. But at that young age, she, like the princess, had not herself developed the self-confidence and social grace among strangers and near-strangers that, with age and maturity, are among Kathy's own most distinguishing qualities now.

With unerring instinct, Princess Diana seemed to sense in Kathy the same shyness that she herself then possessed. And seeing, as well, someone of the same sex and approximate age, she made a beeline to Kathy like a ship rushing to the nearest port in a storm. For the same reason that Princess Diana gravitated towards her, Kathy welcomed her contemporary's overture as though the princess was for her a safe harbour, too. The two saved each other. For much of the rest of the reception, the two were inseparable, gossiping and giddying and gaggling like two schoolgirls, which, given their youth, they more closely resembled than they did seasoned socialites. In Kathy's company, head up and eyes forward, Princess Diana came alive—and commanded the room.

# The Monarchy and the Citizen

We Canadians sometimes don't realize how much space the monarchy occupies in our total value system and in our hearts. Outside sports and partisan politics, can anyone imagine our getting worked up about any other facet of the country's culture as much as we do when a member of the royal family, especially the queen, visits the country? Perhaps it is a measure of how important this civic value is to us, and how deeply embedded it is in our political culture, that we do not feel the need to shout about our loyalty to the Crown or wear this dimension of patriotism on our sleeves— except in PEI when the governor's spigot stops spouting Dogpatch joy juice!

No doubt, some Canadians have a weaker attachment than others to the Canadian monarchy and the particular democratic values it symbolizes. With every passing year, the country is becoming more and more culturally diverse through immigration. The monarchy is not part of the cultural history of a fast-growing number of newcomers to Canada, and they know little about the practical and symbolic importance of the institution to the nation. This dimension of being Canadian will need to become a bigger part of the curriculum at all levels of the educational system if the monarchy is to remain relevant, particularly to the younger generation. The fact that our entire governmental and political system pivots around the Crown's constitutional status and role has to be stressed. It would be a question of teaching straightforward civics—not of rah-rah proselytizing, hardly the role of education in any event. If Canadian Conservatives don't take the lead in defending, explaining, and celebrating our own national symbols and institutions and customs, all embodied in the Crown—not as ends in themselves but as representations of who we are as a distinct people—who will? What's needed is not more passion, but more education and basic information about the Crown. The passion will ensue as inexorably as greener grass follows bright sunshine and fresh rains in spring.

Alas, the government of Stephen Harper did not always share this perspective. The government's creation in 2011 of national honours separate from those of the governor general—and, thus, of the Crown—suggests that Harper himself valued the monarchy less than previous Canadian Tory leaders did. Can anyone imagine John Diefenbaker ever having gone down that road? As a proposal, the "Harper Awards" would not have survived a policy paper's first draft with Robert Stanfield in the chair at a PC Policy Coordinating Committee meeting. That's assuming Tom Symons would not have killed the idea much earlier. The decision to establish the so-called Prime Minister's Awards reflected a steady presidentialization of the office of prime minister and of our political culture more generally by the Harperites. Where is true Canadian conservatism in that? The presidentializing trend predated the Harper government by several decades, but it accelerated in that period. Had Stephen Harper stayed in office longer, what would have come next for the PM—a "Hail to the Chief" marching band, a primeministerial seal, an official directive that everyone stand for his entrance, and making him "commander in chief"? Back in the 1960s and 1970s in many different forums, including the conclaves of the PC Party, political scientist Denis Smith continually warned about the dangers of this trend in the context of the Trudeau government's proclivities. The alarm he sounded still needs to be heard and heeded a half-century later.

Why would we Canadians—least of all Conservatives—ever want to weaken, much less discard, the central feature of our governmental system and political culture that we chose for ourselves among all the democratic models available to us at the time of Confederation: responsible government symbolized by the Crown. It is a governance model that the Americans purposefully rejected in favour of a system of "checks and balances." And how is that system working for them nowadays? "Three co-equal branches of government" sounds lofty in constitutional literary rhetoric. But gridlock characterizes how it operates—or, more accurately, fails to do so—in practice, especially in the hyperpartisan atmosphere that has become the norm in Washington and across the land. Making our Senate an elected body—Stephen Harper's original preferred option—is not just a pathway but a superhighway in that direction. Our constitutional monarchy not only works, but also is uniquely magical. Would we really want to replace it or allow it to be changed incrementally beyond recognition over time? In the name of what? Nationalism? Patriotism? Constitutional patriation? Populism? Democracy? Modernity? But at what price? And what might be the unintended consequences?

Although, no question, attachment to the Crown is much stronger in some parts of the country than others, among anglophones than francophones, among older Canadians than younger ones, among the native-born than recent immigrants, this is a durable institution in a world of questionable change and attendant uncertainty. The special relationship Aboriginal peoples have always had with the Crown underscores this fact. The bond was forged in the eighteenth century by the Royal Proclamation of 1763. Aboriginal peoples have long viewed that document as their Bill of Rights in our part of North America. In the document, George III proclaimed that they had rights to the lands they occupied, and he promised to protect and not "molest them." The king's commitment survives to this very day in Article 35 of the *Constitution Act, 1982*. And the set of rights based on this commitment has been reaffirmed in a plethora of separate Supreme Court of Canada rulings. The monarchy is woven into the fabric of our total governmental-political-values system in countless such ways. Anyone who believes that this institution could be replaced without fundamentally changing the nature of the country should seriously consider taking a crash course in basic Canadian civics. A course in dendrology (the study of wood plants) would be a good idea, too, for it is surely required by anyone unable to see the forest for the trees. Psychiatric counselling would also help. If all else fails, the iconoclast should move to a country that would provide a better outlet for his or her hostility to national history, tradition, heritage, intergenerational collective wisdom, and the value that encompasses all the above—*continuity*.

Like other peoples around the globe, Canadians need more constants (and protections) of the sort the Crown fundamentally provides not just Aboriginals, but all Canadians. In 1948, as the whole world seemed to him in revolt, King Farouk of Egypt said: "Soon there will be only five kings left—the King of Spades, the King of Clubs, the King of Hearts, the King of Diamonds, and the King of England." We Canadians should continually remind ourselves that the "King of England" is also our own. Our process of succession or transition—from one monarch to another, from one government to another, from one prime minister to another—is as seamless as the Kohinoor diamond in the royal crown. And that diamond is considered the biggest and most perfect in the world. How appropriate! Symbols matter. Our system makes great sense in sheer practical terms, not just magic. The beauty is that it is right for us on both counts. Why would we want to dismantle any part of the royal scaffolding our Founding Fathers built for the magnificent national edifice they created for the distinct people we are?

# Chapter 24

# THE MULRONEY GOVERNMENT

The Progressive Conservative landslide in the September 1984 federal general election, under Brian Mulroney's leadership, was an aberration in the post–Second World War electoral pattern. Indeed, in Canada's entire history, only John Diefenbaker's historic victory in 1958 had ever come close (by a hair) to Mulroney's triumph. Even in ideal circumstances, a political party's odds of winning federal power with the kind of massive majority each of these two Tory leaders amassed are extremely long. Mulroney was not eager to test those odds his own next time around. He was determined to govern as though every vote counted. Because it did.

The Prime Minister's Office (PMO), located in the Langevin Block, across from the Peace Tower on Parliament Hill, is the political nerve centre of the Canadian government. It is comprised of the prime minister and his staff, who are not members of the public service, but partisan supporters of the PM who advise him on all decisions he has to make. They also help implement his decisions. Brian Mulroney became prime minister at a time when cellphones, the Internet, and social media were infants. By today's standards, the national government he headed was primitive in how it operated internally, related to other governments at home and abroad, interacted with the private sector, responded to the media, and tried to serve the public. Then, there were only about a half-dozen personal computers throughout the entire rabbit warren of offices and cubicles in the Langevin Block. The ways Mulroney and his otherwise technologically savvy team—most of them young— operated were characteristic of a much simpler time than today. The whole group's values remained communitarian, not libertarian, a distinction and trend I elaborate upon later.

Brian Mulroney and the PC Party took power with a heavy policy agenda. Some of it reflected promises made in the election campaign. A lot of it, though, just landed at the government's door—from demanding and, in some cases, obstreperous provincial governments, from a struggling domestic economy, and from fast-moving world events. It was a period of considerable uncertainty at home and historic upheaval abroad. Two federal budgets would need to be brought down in the Mulroney government's first eight months. The unexpected death of Soviet leader Yuri Andropov and meteoric rise of his successor, Mikhail Gorbachev, would turn the whole world upside down. Suddenly, the new government was faced with a boatload of domestic and international issues that its principals, including the prime minister himself, had not needed to master, let alone develop detailed policies on, while in Opposition or on the campaign trail. Many fast-emerging challenges—for example, Arctic sovereignty, resource exploration and environmental protection in the North, Hibernia, the oil sands, and federal-provincial energy revenue-sharing—were interrelated and, therefore, impossible to manage expeditiously. All the while, the new prime minister felt too many people, both within the government and without, were demanding his time and attention. He was overwhelmed with problems and inundated by paperwork. It was a far cry from what he'd ever had to bear before, either in his private sector career or during his short time as Opposition leader.

Alberta premier Peter Lougheed had confidentially counselled Mulroney that half his time as prime minister should be devoted to thinking, listening, and consulting people, as distinct from attending to day-to-day exigencies. The PM discovered this judicious balance was hard to achieve. Hardly any of Mulroney's political staff had ever served in government before. The prime minister himself had not. Nor had his chief of staff, Bernard Roy. As inevitably happens in such circumstances, "We pretty well allowed the system to run us with little push back," as Geoff Norquay, a senior PMO colleague of my brother Charley, remarked privately years later in correspondence with him. On the plus side, Brian Mulroney's inner group had all worked for him and the PC Party ever since he won the leadership in June 1983, some much longer than that. So, creating a sense of team was not a challenge. But even this positive became a negative before long.

On the policy front, the principals included—in addition to Charley—Norquay, Ian Shugart, Jocelyne Côté-O'Hara, and Fred Doucet. Geoff Norquay had served as director of research for the PC Party in Opposition from 1981 to 1984. (As we have seen, Dr. E. R. Black and then Geoffrey Molyneux had played that role for Robert Stanfield when he was PC leader.) Norquay brought most of his Opposition research staff with him to the PMO. They had helped prepare the 1984 Tory election platform; now they were entrusted with helping to make it the law of the land and to run the country. At the end of the first year, the prime minister and his chief of staff reviewed the state of the government to that point. The review led to some major changes in how decisions were made, especially concerning use of the PM's precious but overtaxed time.

The Privy Council Office (PCO)—like the PMO, located in the Langevin Block—is the secretariat of the federal Cabinet. It provides non-partisan advice and administrative support to the prime minister and his political team. The PCO also coordinates and supports all the various departments and agencies of the government. Mulroney would arrive home every night weighed down by briefing books and memoranda from the PCO. Though a fast and attentive reader, the PM found that he just could not keep up with the sheer volume of what he had to study and consider. A new system was installed to better screen everything put before him from the PCO, the PMO, and every other source, including a heavy volume of public mail. The purpose was to identify more effectively what Mulroney needed to see, what could be handled by others, and what priority should be attached to every item in both categories. The new system reduced demands not only on the PM's tight schedule, but on his physical and intellectual energy as well. It also gave him more opportunity to think and reflect, just as Lougheed had recommended. Equally important to him, he then had more time to devote to personal matters and to his wife and children. And to recharge his batteries. The measure of a strong leader is not whether he or she finds the job challenging. It's whether the person rises to the challenge. Brian Mulroney proved he could.

The new system devised by the prime minister and his chief of staff operated without much change until Derek Burney succeeded Bernard Roy as Mulroney's power behind the throne two years later. Around this time, a consensus was fast forming on Parliament Hill, including in Cabinet and the PC Caucus, that some individuals whom Brian Mulroney had brought with him to the PMO from leadership battles and the Opposition period were becoming unduly comfortable both with one another and with the prime minister, just as he was with them. Mulroney plucked Burney from External Affairs' senior ranks to replace Bernard Roy as chief of staff to run a much tighter ship. The man's long service in the diplomatic corps embraced stints in Japan and South Korea, the latter as ambassador. Derek Burney strengthened chains of command, clarified the responsibilities of and expectations for each staffer, and brought more discipline to how everybody operated. Certain staffers had been acting as though they thought their long-time ties to the PM placed them higher in the pecking order than members of Caucus and even Cabinet. Indeed, some senior PMO staffers stood accused of bossing ministers of the Crown and, in the worst cases, summoning them to their Langevin Block offices for that purpose. Peter White, one such staffer—a long-time Mulroney confidant and former *confrère* of Conrad Black at Hollinger Inc.—called me to his office to discuss a major environmental crisis that had erupted in Montreal's East End. I told him I would be glad to meet with him any time, but that he knew where my ministerial office was. "Yes, of course. I'll be there in twenty minutes," White replied. Not every senior staffer had White's grace and class. Burney terminated all such imperious practices—forthwith. He also made major personnel changes in the PMO both to advance the same end and to prepare the government party for the 1988 election, by this time steadily approaching. Burney promoted Geoff Norquay, for example, to an important new position. Under Bernard Roy, Norquay had served as principal gatekeeper for everything placed before the prime minister to read or discharge. It had also been his job to manage routine correspondence and help write the PM's speeches (primarily the responsibility of former Montreal journalist L. Ian MacDonald). Now he was reassigned to direct policy and help prepare a platform for the next election.

It was around this time that my brother Charley left the PMO to return to teaching at York University. He also wanted to recapture a semblance of family life after so many months at Brian Mulroney's side in party leadership campaigns, in the federal election, and now in government. Ian Anderson, Mulroney's director of communications, also departed the PMO, in his case to reclaim a successful journalism career. Time nor tide might wait for no man, but neither, forever, do careers and family. Fred Doucet, Pat MacAdam, and Derek Burney himself assumed different facets of Charley McMillan's role as "senior policy advisor." Hard-nosed broadcast journalist Bruce Phillips succeeded Anderson as Mulroney's communications overlord. Bill Fox, another no-nonsense media professional, was elevated from assistant press secretary to "special advisor"—in this instance, Ottawa-speak for "media strategist and propagandist." Marc Lortie, a kindred spirit of Burney at External Affairs, replaced Michel Gratton as press secretary. Lortie would become one of Mulroney's most trusted confidants both while he was prime minister and after he retired. If the PMO had been more an officers' mess than a war room before Derek Burney took charge, he and Mulroney transformed it into a well-prepared trench in which they readied to do battle. The general and his aide-de-camp did not intend to lose the war.

The support system that Derek Burney established for the PM remained in place, in much the same form, throughout the rest of Brian Mulroney's time in office, certainly well into the second term. Burney would serve Mulroney until shortly after the 1988 election, when the PM appointed him ambassador to Washington, where he served until 1993. His replacement as chief of staff, in 1989, was Montreal corporate lawyer and former deputy minister of finance Stanley Hartt. He found Burney a difficult act to follow. Recruiting Derek Burney as his Man Friday was the single most important (and best) management decision Mulroney made after forming his Cabinet. Burney brought to the prime minister's central operation equal measures of toughness, managerial competence, mastery of the bureaucratic system, policy expertise, keen political instincts, a warm rapport with the PM, and amiability (if not exactly charm) with everyone else. As consul general in Boston when he was our ambassador to Washington—and, in effect, my immediate superior—I was to discover that the man brought these same qualities to running the country's affairs in the US capital. As chief of staff, Burney had a hand on the helm for every major Mulroney government direction and decision. Those included many relating to my Environment portfolio, particularly Canada's acid rain negotiations with the United States. With Burney at his side, Mulroney had righted the ship.

# Policy Sources

Every government that functions well has a consensus enforcer. Sometimes a tragedy, a crisis, or a threatening deadline compels politicians to act on an issue, rather than follow their more natural inclination to just discuss it to death, postpone a final decision, or avoid dealing with the matter altogether. Under normal conditions, consensus is typically forged from the cut-and-thrust of verbal battle in the conclaves of power. When all else fails, and consensus is either imperative or just desirable, the leader imposes his own will. If Prime Minister Brian Mulroney did not rule with an iron fist, he inarguably did do so with a fist of high-grade copper. Mulroney was a strong-willed, not to say stubborn, operator who knew his own mind and was not easily dissuaded from a path he wanted the country and his government to follow. When a course was agreed upon at the end of whatever process, the PM had zero tolerance for freelancing. Meanwhile, diverse views were welcomed, policy differences aired, disputes among ministers and Caucus members resolved, and remaining wrinkles ironed smooth either formally or informally. But, as noted elsewhere here, the prime minister was a man of action and decisiveness. He had little patience for debate for debate's sake, still less for undisciplined dissension, and none at all for grandstanding. Definitely little appetite for the kind of time-consuming deliberative process that Robert Stanfield favoured and for which he had much patience. At the end of the day, for Mulroney, a course set was one he expected all his ministers to embrace, publicly support, help implement, explain, defend, take pride in—and never apologize for. To the man's admirers, this was the essence of leadership; to detractors, bull-headedness. I was decisively in the former camp.

To the extent I myself was able to build a record while in Cabinet, particularly in the environmental field, I did so largely because the PM backed me to the hilt on issues about which he also felt strongly. In not a few cases, it was he who pushed my measures through the inner sanctums of Cabinet of which I was not a member but to which I was given privileged entry as the need arose. In which cases, it was more to hold his vestments than to be the lead celebrant, except concerning whatever knowledge of dogma and moral authority he felt I brought to the altar. I learned that, with Mulroney, the "first among equals" definition of a prime minister leaned much more heavily on "first" than on "equals." But, since we were usually both on the same side as far as environmental issues were concerned, that imbalance was fine with me.

The government's agenda came from diverse sources. The PC Party was in Opposition for only about a year under Mulroney's leadership: June 1983 to September 1984. Unlike the time frame Stanfield had faced between the 1968 and 1972 elections, Mulroney's Opposition period before the 1984 vote was too short for him to do much more than organize for the campaign (recruit candidates, raise funds, plan logistics, hire personnel, devise media strategy, coordinate with Tory provincial governments and their electoral machines, and on and on). During that short period, the new PC leader also had to campaign in a federal by-election to win for himself a House of Commons seat from which to lead his parliamentary troops prior to the general election. The political pressures and time constraints that Mulroney faced in the lead-up to the 1984 summer election, after winning the party leadership, were akin to ones Stanfield experienced between the 1972 cliff-hanger election and the 1974 vote. In both cases, there was no time for, let alone priority attached to, a deliberative policy process, though more in Stanfield's case because of the nature of the man than in Mulroney's because of his. Even if there had been time, Mulroney, as we have seen, did not attach much importance to extraparliamentary policy development—far more than Diefenbaker, but far less than Stanfield.

And yet, as noted above, the new Mulroney government took power with a heavy agenda. Again, much of it was circumstantial. The weightiest burden was fiscal. The federal government bank account inherited from the Trudeau/Turner regime was empty—indeed, in deep overdraft. Finance Minister Michael Wilson briefed the full Cabinet early on—flanked by projection charts with revenue arrows that ominously pointed to Hell and deficit and public debt arrows that aggressively aimed at the stars, but definitely not Heaven. For me, it was like attending a funeral without an Irish wake: depressing. Wilson himself was a frugal frat boy of Bay Street, determined to whip the country's finances into shape. This eagerness, which the PM shared, set our course for the entire first term in office—in fact, for the rest of the party's time in power under Mulroney. All decisions of Cabinet were made, and largely dictated, in that context—some disastrously so. Suzanne Blais-Grenier's bludgeoning wildlife and other foundational programs at Environment Canada was the worst case.

The march to fiscal responsibility continued after Mike Wilson moved from Finance to Trade in 1991. Don Mazankowski, the new finance minister, pursued the same agenda as his predecessor. It was partly because the prime minister was still calling the shots. But it was also because Mazankowsli was himself of this mind, reflecting no doubt the premium westerners generally attach to living within one's means. Reforming the tax system, broadening the tax base, lowering tax rates to stimulate growth and thereby revenues, eliminating many tax loopholes, not to mention the Canada–United States Free Trade Agreement to strengthen the country's and government's overall economic and financial health—all such measures stemmed, directly or indirectly, from the fiscal imperatives of the times. Blais-Grenier aside, that sense of urgency was generally acted on with the care and planning and sober calculation of military generals. This was especially true of Mulroney, Wilson, and Mazankowski, who formed a virtual triumvirate within the government for the purpose at hand. Mulroney provided the imprimatur, Wilson (and later Maz) printed the book—in the form of successive budget statements, literally. Later, in 1990, the 7 percent goods and services tax (GST) was introduced. (It was slashed by the Harper government to 5 percent on January 1, 2008.) The GST is widely credited with leading the federal government budget to surplus after many years of mounting public debt under Trudeau. But the tax was not even in the government's hangar, much less flying high, until late in Mulroney's first term. (It was not a major issue in the 1988 election, only in 1993, when Jean Chrétien flew with it in a rocket to Mars, though the astronaut never landed there after take-off.) But this later-controversial tax, too, was grounded in anxieties about the fiscal mess in which the new government found itself from the first day the keys of power were handed to its trembling hands.

The other major concern was that the manufacturers' sales tax that the GST replaced—built into the cost of domestically produced products but not imported ones—was killing Canadians' jobs by making imports comparatively cheaper and, therefore, more competitive than our own products. But this consideration, as well, had a distinct deficit-control dimension, from the perspective of lost or forgone tax revenues. It was as though, in the person of Brian Mulroney, the late-stage more benevolent Ebenezer Scrooge had leaped from the pages of *A Christmas Carol* and hijacked the Canadian government. No wonder the misguided Blais-Grenier misread the signals. What she missed was the prime minister's eagerness to do all the above as sensibly as possible while building a personal and government legacy beyond fiscal responsibility. The environment minister had no common sense of her own, least of all an instinct for Brian Mulroney's policy mind. Nobody knew better than I the extent of the horrors she created, for I had to restore Environment Canada after she all but destroyed the place. Most Cabinet ministers had a much better sense than she of where the prime minister wanted to take the country—certainly not down the road to rack and ruin. Mike Wilson and Don Mazankowski knew best of all the PM's policy cartography. Mazankowski's enduring contribution to the PC Party and the Mulroney government in this period was less as finance minister than as the prime minister's overall Mr. Fix-It. Maz kept an eagle eye on all goings-on in Caucus and Parliament, he shrewdly anticipated and did his best to solve potential problems well before they became critical, and he competently managed those that reached crisis status. The man did all this while heading a succession of portfolios with a level of success that earned him a reputation as one of Mulroney's most able ministers by that standard alone. Brian Mulroney could not have found a stronger pair of hands than those of Donald Frank Mazankowski in which to entrust the job of deputy PM.


# The Prime Minister's Agenda

The new government's agenda was not driven solely by the fiscal circumstances it inherited. Brian Mulroney took power with his own agenda, some of it congruent with the policy imperatives just described, but other parts entirely different. He had campaigned for the PC Party's leadership twice (in 1976, when he lost; and in 1983, when he won). In both campaigns, especially the latter, he articulated positions on a wide range of issues. In the second leadership bid, Mulroney published his detailed positions in a book, *Where I Stand*.[1] That he had, in my brother Charley, a virtually full-time policy advisor always by his side for long periods leading up to his election as prime minister attests to the premium the Quebecer placed on being well-informed and able to credibly address the issues of the day in public forums and with the media. On a few subjects—notably federalism, national unity, language, and culture—Mulroney did so with uncommon insight and prescience. When read now, his statements have something of the clairvoyant quality that characterized David Slater's brilliant analysis of likely trends in the 1970s Canadian economy as that decade approached. (The reader will recall that Slater presented his *tour de force* at the 1969 PC Niagara Policy Conference engineered by Tom Symons for Robert Stanfield.) Mulroney's own clairvoyance was especially visionary on Quebec-related issues. It's as though he, like Slater, had been peering into a crystal ball.

In retrospect, one can divine in Mulroney's speeches and interviews before he became prime minister in 1984 the premium he would place throughout his time as PM on getting Quebec to sign the new Constitution. No one could reasonably deny that, prior to becoming PM, Mulroney was knowledgeable, if not expert, on a wide range of Quebec-specific constitutional issues, on other facets of federal-provincial relations, and on labour and industry questions—relating to *la belle province*, in particular. He had established a near-legendary reputation in Quebec as a lawyer, negotiator, and dispute arbitrator. That reputation soared following his high-profile role in the 1974 Royal Commission that investigated corruption in the Quebec construction industry. The Cliche Commission made headlines across Canada for its unflinching exposure of organized crime in the province. As an aggressive and high-profile member, Mulroney became as much the public face of the commission as the man who headed it, well-known lawyer and NDP-leaning political activist Robert Cliche. Mulroney's involvement in the Cliche Commission, like the keen interest he took in PC policy development during the Stanfield period, presaged his approach to public policy after he became prime minister: a passion for information and knowledge; intensive preparation; almost obsessive attention to detail; intolerance for untested conventional wisdom or insupportable pat answers; an aversion to ideology-dictated conclusions; a reverence for research and expertise and first-hand experience ("the horse's mouth"), but no automatic deference to experts merely because they are considered wise; and strong confidence in his own views once formulated after careful preparation and reflection. Although much of the above could also have been said of Stanfield's policy mind, the difference between his and Mulroney's was this: Mulroney relied more heavily on his own instincts about issues, Stanfield on synthesizing the knowledge and insights of others whose judgment he trusted. Little wonder, then, that the latter constructed an elaborate extraparliamentary *party process* for policy development while the former depended, for information and advice, on a wide network of *personal contacts* he had carefully created across the country, beginning well before he became PC leader. After being in Cabinet for a while, I once told my brother Charley that I thought the prime minister was failing to take full advantage of the broad membership of the PC Party as a source of policy ideas and expertise in the manner Stanfield had done. He dismissed my concern as a consumer might the fine print on a product warrantee. "Why does Brian need to consult the party?" he asked. "The man's got his own network." For Stanfield, the two were the same; for Mulroney, much less so.

By nature, Brian Mulroney was nothing if not a plotter and a planner and, in the case of the Cliche Commission in particular, a public performer. If "preparedness" was not his motto, it certainly was his modus operandi. He was *always* prepared, if not sometimes for the unexpected, as happens in politics and government. I have characterized the man as a superb military general for this reason. His preparedness on policy and issues was no exception, even as it took a less intellectually deliberative or Socratic route than the one more natural to Stanfield. These were two different kinds of men and, therefore, in some respects opposite types of leaders.

In addition to Charley, Mulroney surrounded himself, from his earliest days, with friends and confidants who themselves were interested in government and politics, knowledgeable about issues, and passionate about certain ones, not always the same across the ranks. Boston financier Bob Shea was among the earliest of these. So also were Fred Doucet, Sam Wakim, Pat MacAdam, and Lowell Murray from Mulroney's years at St. Francis Xavier University. Doucet served for a time as Mulroney's chief of staff. Wakim was briefly (in 1979) a Toronto MP, and always remained close to Mulroney. MacAdam became a senior assistant to Mulroney in the PM's office with special responsibility for Caucus relations, badly neglected by the Clark government. (MacAdam had been editor of the *Xaverian Weekly*, the St. F. X. student paper; Elizabeth McMillan, eldest daughter of my brother John and now an award-wining CBC reporter currently based in Halifax, became its editor years later.) Lowell Murray would be appointed by Joe Clark to the Senate and by Mulroney as both government leader in that body and his minister of federal-provincial relations. A bit later, after the "X" years, Lucien Bouchard joined this fraternity from the Université Laval connection. So did Bernard Roy. Individuals such as Michael Meighen and Jean Bazin (both appointed by Mulroney to the Senate) were perhaps not personally as close to Mulroney as the aforementioned; they belonged, nevertheless, to the same intimate group of Mulroney *confrères*. The man consequently had a ready source of policy ideas, and well-informed people to discuss them with, over a long period leading up to his election as prime minister. It was not unlike the political and personal fraternity Robert Stanfield had formed in the Maritimes with the likes of Finlay MacDonald, Dalton Camp, and Flora MacDonald. This is no coincidence.

Most people do not realize how substantially Brian Mulroney self-identified as a quasi-Maritimer after his years of study in Antigonish while at "X." One should never discount the power of geography in shaping a person's world view and, in the case of politicians, their public policies. In Mulroney's case, the Maritimes would prove as big an influence on the kind of prime minister he would become as his native Quebec. For evidence Mulroney strongly identified with the Maritimes, and many Maritimers with him, I would cite five examples. First, the core of his support outside Quebec for the party leadership in 1983 was from this region. It involved, notably, Nova Scotia premier John Buchanan as his principal public cheerleader. The main team also included veteran Nova Scotia MPs such as Mike Forrestall, Bob Coates, and Elmer MacKay—indeed, almost all that province's parliamentarians, in the Commons and Senate alike. Not to mention the fact Mulroney chose to run for a seat in Parliament in Nova Scotia after winning the party leadership. Second, among the new government's earliest measures was one of its most important: the creation of the Atlantic Canada Opportunities Agency. ACOA revolutionized how the federal government approached regional development across the board, not just in the eastern provinces. This was one of the prime minister's highest personal priorities. So, also, was the cleanup of Halifax Harbour, my third example. Mulroney announced the plan himself, at the city waterfront, with Premier Buchanan and me at his side in supporting roles. Fourth, in the environmental field as well, nobody, including me, had to brief Mulroney about the environmental disaster of the Sydney Tar Ponds, the major cleanup of which our government also launched, reflecting the priority the PM personally attached to it. During his "X" years, in Antigonish, Mulroney lived less than 200 kilometres from the huge pool of black toxic stew from the Sydney Steel coke ovens. Like me, he thought this, too, needed to be addressed as a blight on our nation's environmental record and literally on its landscape. Fifth, and most important of all, as mentioned earlier, Mulroney details in his memoirs how powerfully he was influenced by St. F. X.—Dr. Moses Coady's Antigonish Movement, in particular—both as a man and as prime minister throughout the nine years he was in office.

An entire book could be written on this dimension of the man. It could be credibly titled, *Brian Mulroney: Maritime Prime Minister.* Mulroney was not technically Canada's first Maritime prime minister—that distinction belongs to Nova Scotian Sir John Thompson, Canada's fourth PM (1892–94). But no prime minister except for Thompson, Charles Tupper, and Robert Borden knew the Maritimes better from both direct personal experience and from the depths of his soul than Mulroney did. And Thompson, Tupper, and Borden, unlike Mulroney, were all actual Maritimers. The distinction, however, is mere accident of birth. In the man's very bloodstream, there is as much saltwater as maple syrup. This idiosyncratic but crucial fact about his personal biography was reflected in a plethora of major Atlantic Canada–related policy measures on which the new government was geared to act on Day One. Mulroney's rich Maritime record in government includes the Confederation Bridge connecting New Brunswick and Prince Edward Island, and the development of the Hibernia oceanic oil field. The record of the Mulroney government in all areas of Atlantic Canada is the most underappreciated, most inadequately chronicled, and least commented upon part of this prime minister's total legacy. Where are Canadian Studies when the foghorn blows? Why must its blast be drowned out by the screeching wheels of the commuter trains of the Golden Horseshoe? A Canadian invented the former, not the latter.

Both Stanfield's and Mulroney's respective sets of informal advisors and confidants were akin to Ronald Reagan's "Kitchen Cabinet" in California. The two Canadian groups, however, were much younger, less ideological, and more politically hard-nosed than their US counterpart. In 1984, the new prime minister did not enter his Parliament Hill office suite without knowing how to turn on the light switch. He had laid his own welcome mat there long before the previous occupant's lease expired. The man was well prepared to become prime minister—and to lead the country in a distinctly new direction. And that is exactly what he ended up doing.

# Political Allies

Once in government, Brian Mulroney had at his beck and call the public service. This rich resource was no longer part of the Liberals' "permanent policy machine," as Hugh Segal put it. Instead, the government's bureaucracy was Mulroney's to draw on for both policy expertise and implementation and administrative support. The new PM also had another valuable resource. No fewer than seven of the ten provincial governments were headed by Progressive Conservative premiers throughout the earliest part of the Mulroney government's first term: Bill Davis in Ontario, Peter Lougheed in Alberta, Grant Devine in Saskatchewan, Richard Hatfield in New Brunswick, John Buchanan in Nova Scotia, Brian Peckford in Newfoundland, and Jim Lee in PEI. Davis would soon retire as Ontario PC leader and premier, to be replaced by Frank Miller, whom Liberal David Peterson would beat electorally within a year (in June 1985).

This last historic fact is crucial in the context of the Mulroney government's long-term planning. Miller's Tories began the 1985 Ontario provincial election with a significant lead over the Opposition parties in all the major public opinion polls. Peterson's Liberals, however, steadily increased their support as the campaign progressed. In a stunning upset for many—certainly, the Tories themselves—

Peterson won a narrow plurality of the popular vote. At the time, rural areas, the Tory stronghold, were still marginally overrepresented in the Legislative Assembly. The Liberals, consequently, won only forty-eight seats to the PCs' fifty-two, despite having prevailed in the popular vote count. Normally, the Tories would have been able to form a minority government with their plurality of legislative seats. But, under Bob Rae, the Ontario NDP, with twenty-five seats, held the balance of power. They allowed the Liberals to govern for a two-year period while refusing to join them in a formal coalition. Frank Miller should not have lost the election—after all, Ontario had been rock-ribbed Tory for nearly half a century. And, when the election was called, Ontarians told pollsters they weren't eager to change government any time soon. George Drew and then Leslie Frost had crafted for the Ontario Conservative Party the greatest provincial political dynasty in Canadian history, winning every single election since 1943, typically with large majorities. They had held onto power with progressive, people-centred policies and programs. That Tory dynasty crashed in 1985 largely because, for the first time in over forty years, the party, under Frank Miller's leadership, bolted to the hard right. It was not where a substantial number of Ontarians wanted to be. They voted accordingly. Ontario had not been, before the election, nor would it be for quite a while afterwards, that kind of conservative polity, even if it did become so a decade after the Mulroney government took office, with Mike Harris's "Common Sense Revolution"—which was called a "revolution" for a reason.

Brian Mulroney was determined that the federal Progressive Conservative Party would not suffer the same fate as that of the Miller Tories and for the same reason. The new prime minister was alarmed about runaway annual federal deficits and the country's fast-mounting total public debt. He was particularly conscious of compound interest charges on the credit card the Trudeau government had maxed out during its decade and a half in power. So, even if discretionary spending were pared to the bone, as actually happened in Mulroney's first term, the numbers still piled up furiously, like a major win on a Las Vegas slot machine—except that the payout was being borne not by the casino, but by Canadian taxpayers. And the "house" was dead broke. Mulroney was committed to reversing the trend. He was equally eager, however, that this be done with maximum care to ensure that the burden did not fall disproportionately on the poor and the unfortunate—and, more to the point, on the average voter. His would be a government with a heart, not just an abacus. Working closely with provincial and territorial partners was a central part of the strategy. The large number of PC governments in provincial capitals presented a huge opportunity for the new national government to advance its progressive but fiscally responsible agenda. Those provincial governments, with or without Tories now in control at Queen's Park, could be counted on to help. And they did. But shared party label alone did not account for this harmony any more than having the same DNA guarantees good relations among siblings. The prime minister worked hard to produce the desired outcome. And he expected his ministers to do so as well. Most obliged. Those who did not soon found themselves ushered out the door like an uninvited and unwelcome guest at a wedding reception.

I experienced first-hand—initially as tourism minister—provincial governments' benevolent impact on the Mulroney government. Thanks mostly to Norm Atkins and Hugh Segal (the common link through Camp Associates), Tourism Canada and its Ontario government counterpart jointly created the Mulroney government's highly innovative new tourism marketing strategy for Canada, stressing brand names, not generic advertising. When I addressed the annual meeting of the

Ontario Resorts Association in Toronto, soon after becoming tourism minister, what I noticed first was the sea of faces in all the front rows—from the Ontario government! They led the standing ovation afterwards. It was much less a tribute to any performance art of mine than a reflection of their own role in formulating the major policy I announced on this occasion. Other ministers felt similarly supported by provincial Tory governments across the country in their respective policy fields. As a so-called regional minister, I worked closely with Jim Lee's PC government in PEI before Joe Ghiz's Liberals defeated it in May 1986. The same was true of other federal regional ministers with their respective provincial governments—again, all but three Tory in this early period.

No federal government in Canadian history worked more harmoniously on policy and planning with provincial governments of the same partisan stripe, at both the political and public service levels, than did Mulroney's during his early years in office. Diefenbaker's government was far different when first elected in 1957. By then, the PC Party had been out of office nearly a quarter-century. It faced an unfamiliar—and, in Diefenbaker's view, hostile—public service. It also had to work with generally unfriendly provincial governments. Leslie Frost's in Ontario was a big exception, but only before such issues as the dumping of the Avro Arrow project and slumping national and provincial economies ruined relations between the two governments. (Correspondence between Frost and Diefenbaker at Library and Archives Canada in Ottawa are sulphuric.) For its part, the Union Nationale government of Maurice Duplessis in Quebec opposed almost all of Diefenbaker's major measures on constitutional grounds (as we shall see). It was, for example, only through the innovative transfer of tax points from Ottawa to the province that the Diefenbaker government was able to circumvent Duplessis's rejection of federal funding (initiated by the St-Laurent government) for Quebec universities. (True to character, Diefenbaker denounced this very practice when the Pearson government later resorted to it.) Robert Stanfield's government in Nova Scotia—elected in 1956, a year before Diefenbaker's—consistently supported the new prime minister. The premier himself remained one of Diefenbaker's most loyal defenders throughout the latter's time in government and long afterwards, although that loyalty was not reciprocated when Stanfield replaced Diefenbaker as national party head. Nova Scotia, however, was an exceptional case. Walter Shaw's government in PEI (elected in 1959) was another. (New Brunswick premier Hugh John Flemming was also a great Diefenbaker champion, but he lost power in 1960 and then became Diefenbaker's minister of forestry.) All other provincial governments either were never on side to begin with or deserted Diefenbaker before long—mostly the former. Mulroney's honeymoon, at least as far as the provincial governments were concerned, was truly one of conjugal bliss; Diefenbaker's more like a rancorous and litigious divorce.

# Relations with Public Servants

My twin brother, Charley, always scrupulously maintained boundaries between his role as one of Brian Mulroney's most senior PMO advisors and his personal relationship to me. My brother knew his first loyalty had to be to his boss. After both of us were long out of government, however, he told me that Mulroney had kept careful tabs on each of his ministers without ever coming close to micromanaging their respective departments, let alone restricting his ministers' freedom to run things as they saw fit. Scrutiny was conducted largely through the clerk of the Privy Council (Paul Tellier in my time). The clerk, in turn, worked for this purpose through the deputy ministers, who reported directly to him on the flowchart. Charley told me that the PM placed a particularly high premium on both the ability and the eagerness of a minister to collaborate with his or her public service officials, mining their expertise and experience and institutional memory. (Clearly, Suzanne Blais-Grenier's failure by that standard at Environment Canada was one of the reasons Mulroney transferred her from such an important and politically sensitive portfolio.) After I was no longer a minister, Charley hinted that I had scored extremely high on this count, but not nearly as well in forging bonds with Caucus, on which the PM also placed a premium.

This dimension of Mulroney's leadership style as prime minister could not contrast more starkly with that of Diefenbaker. Basil Robinson, a veteran federal public servant, became undersecretary of state for External Affairs in 1974. From 1958 to 1962, he was the department's liaison to Diefenbaker, helping to navigate External Affairs officials through the rocky shoals between themselves and him. Diefenbaker was suspicious of anyone in that department because of its illustrious connection to Liberal Party leader Lester Pearson, who had served as undersecretary before entering electoral politics (Dief called those officials "*Pearson*alities"). Robinson, who died in December 2012 at age ninety-three, had been a Rhodes Scholar a generation before my brother Colin was. But both had selected Oriel College as their residential and academic home base at Oxford. In Robinson's obituary, the Oriel College *Record* quoted Robinson as having told confidants that Diefenbaker was "stubborn, parochial, nationalistic, unbeguiled by the glamour of international politics and no favourite in either Washington or London, despite Canada's close connections to both the United States and Great Britain."[2] In his memoirs, *Diefenbaker's World: A Populist in Foreign Affairs*,[3] the former federal *éminence grise* developed this theme. Mulroney's government, by contrast, could not have had better relations with External Affairs officers at all levels and with the public service as a whole. Nor could Mulroney's relations with Washington and London, in the persons of Ronald Reagan and Margaret Thatcher, have been closer, even when negotiations on acid rain and free trade careened off the rails, in Reagan's case. Those excellent relations with Washington would continue when George H. W. Bush succeeded Reagan, albeit with nothing like the same warm friendship that "the boy from Baie-Comeau" had with "the Gipper." Bush, more a cool New Englander (by birth and rearing) than a warm-blooded Texan (by relocation), lacked his predecessor's Irish bond with the Canadian PM. Just as Mulroney was eager that his government work well with the public service and Canada's allies around the world, so he also wanted constructive relations with each of the provincial and territorial governments, irrespective of political stripe. In this respect, he differed fundamentally from Pierre Trudeau—and, for that matter, from not only Diefenbaker, but, counterintuitively, also Joe Clark. Political science has a hard time factoring, let alone quantifying, such human dimensions of politics. That's when the memoirist takes a front seat to the political scientist—unless, as in my case, he is both!

# Provincial Government Relations

Prime Minister Joe Clark's relations with some Tory provincial governments bordered on murderous. He had especially bad blood with Ontario's Bill Davis—on energy-pricing and revenue-sharing, in particular. Clark and Davis fought almost from the first day the former took power. The Davis government actively opposed Clark's 1979 austerity budget, which included an 18-cent-a-gallon gasoline tax hike that toppled the government only seven months after it was elected. In the 1980 federal election, the Liberals used Davis's criticism of Clark's budget in campaign pamphlets and ads, and the discord between the two governments played a significant role in the Tories' big loss of seats in Ontario (from 57 to 38), a swing in support that almost alone enabled the Liberals to regain power (146 Liberals; 103 PCs).

Joe Clark's relations with Peter Lougheed, the premier of Clark's own province, Alberta, were never better than civil at the best of times, though not nearly as bad as with Queen's Park. The two men's personalities and backgrounds were markedly unalike. Lougheed came from money, played football for the Edmonton Eskimos, graduated from Harvard, and retained his youthful macho image well into later life. For all his own strengths, Clark's life story was far less impressive, at least in Lougheed's eyes. Clark had helped him in his first run for the Alberta premiership in 1967 and served as chief assistant to the future premier as opposition leader. Lougheed viewed Clark as too callow and fey for the team of rugged candidates he sought to assemble that year. Eager for a political career of his own, Clark had to run as a provincial candidate in the lost-cause riding of Calgary South, where virtually no other Tory wanted to offer. (The surprise was that he came as close to winning as he did, losing by only about four hundred votes.) In his memoirs, Brian Mulroney quotes Lougheed as having told Lee Richardson, a close confidant of the future Alberta premier, that, had Clark won in Calgary South, "[he] would [not] have wound up in my cabinet."[4] Lougheed himself won handily in Calgary West to launch a Tory dynasty in the province after thirty-five years of Social Credit hegemony. According to David Humphreys, Clark's biographer, from the start the future prime minister and eventual Mulroney Cabinet minister "regarded Lougheed with some suspicion as a wealthy Calgarian."[5] The first impression each man forged of the other early in their political careers hardened when both men attained power in their respective jurisdictions. Mulroney was much more Lougheed's kind of "man's man" than Clark was, so they got along famously. Their personal compatibility expedited progress on shared policy priorities. This was particularly true when Mulroney dismantled Trudeau's National Energy Program (NEP) early in his mandate. To the premier and most Albertans—indeed, to westerners as a whole—the NEP was the seed of the Devil. Mulroney was just as eager as they were to see the NEP exorcised.

I dealt directly with Peter Lougheed on a number of matters, particularly national parks, which have always loomed large in Alberta's economic and cultural life. As environment minister, I had to respond to the unbridled fury of year-round park residents and business owners over what they considered usurious tax hikes—technically, Crown lease rent increases—that Parks Canada had planned to levy on their properties. The proposed regime was part of an effort by the federal government to maximize economic value from national park assets based on the "highest and best use" principle then in vogue. The effect, if not the publicly stated purpose, was to force from the local real estate market occupants of small-scale properties deemed capable of being replaced with ones that would produce higher revenues for the Crown through either expansion or modernization or both. A Lougheed second home in Banff—owned by successive generations of the family—got snagged in the net. Most such proposed "rent" increases were as shamefully unfair as they were sloppily conceived. The whole business had been handled by the federal government—politicians and officials alike—in a ham-fisted and insensitive manner. Locals were being treated like feudal serfs. The Banff park superintendant resided within the park in a grand stone house owned and maintained by the government. Not surprisingly, the man was seen more as a lord of the manor than as a servant of the public. Given this kind of thing, no wonder so many westerners were hostile to Ottawa in the 1970s and early 1980s. The reality was bad enough, the symbolism often worse, the harm done to the federal government's standing among westerners worst of all.

For days on end, my bedtime reading was a pile of Banff property leases, many of them dating back to Alberta's becoming a province in 1905. Attached to each was a departmental memo detailing the relevant proposed increase in the levy. I was appalled by the magnitude of the changes being considered. Ironically, one of the most egregious was on the Lougheed property. Tempers in Banff bordered on hysteria. By this time, Don Mazankowski was deputy prime minister and Tory political baron for the entire West. In response to pressure from the Alberta PC Caucus, Maz arranged an emergency meeting of that group and placed me squarely on the firing line. (He would not have done so had he thought I would fail to survive. The man knew each minister's strengths and weaknesses better than they did themselves.) I told the irate MPs not only that I was in command of the problem, but also that I had read all the disputed leases, something none of them had done. What's more, I informed them, I had already instructed my officials to reverse direction. Before long, I cancelled or slashed virtually every increase, including on the Lougheed cottage. I did all this as, in effect, mayor of Banff under the *National Parks Act*. Premier Lougheed phoned me in Ottawa from Edmonton to thank me personally for acting on his family's property. He made clear that, for him, the issue was not about his own pocketbook, but about a principle: the federal government's treating the West as a cash cow, rather than as a partner in Confederation. I had felt exactly the same. I heard through the grapevine that, whenever the premier crossed paths with an Alberta MP, every one of them Tory at this point, he praised the swift action I had taken on the leases, not just his family's. My stock with the Alberta Caucus soared from a depression-level low to a boom-time high in just a few trading days. Every time I subsequently visited Banff, townsfolk treated me as though I were a native son returning from war. The only thing missing was the bunting and brass band. That came when Banff had a "Tom McMillan Day" after my defeat in the 1988 federal election to celebrate my time as their "mayor." The previous summer, the same people had funded a $1,900 full-page advertisement in my hometown newspaper, the *Guardian*, to thank me for all the work I had done for their community. Perhaps it takes a Canadian from one extremity of the country to understand the concerns of Canadians in the other. It was much the same as the instinctual feel Brian Mulroney, a born and reared Quebecer, had for the Maritimes and—I would argue—we for him. What a magnificent country!

I was likely not substantially more Lougheed's kind of "man's man" than Clark was. But my twin brother knew Lougheed well from dabbling in provincial politics while doing an MBA at the University of Alberta in the late 1960s. This was the very time of Lougheed's political ascendancy in that province. I have always assumed that Charley's good standing with him partly explains why the Alberta premier and I were able to work so well together even before my action on the Lougheed Banff property helped forge a bond. In 2012, the Institute for Research on Public Policy named Peter Lougheed the best Canadian premier of any province or from any political party in the previous forty years, and Ontario's Bill Davis the second-best. I agree with both rankings. Among all the Tory provincial governments throughout the relevant period, the Lougheed and Davis administrations were least like the government of Stephen Harper in political philosophy and governing style. Is this why these two men are generally considered the most competent and accomplished and caring of all premiers in their era? It's why, I suspect, historians will rank Harper as among the worst Canadian prime ministers. I do. The Lougheed and Davis governments were also most like the Mulroney government, and the two premiers most like Mulroney himself, in recent memory. That said, Lougheed and Davis were totally different personalities. Friction between the two men could have set ablaze a rain forest in the middle of a monsoon. Indeed, the animus caused Davis not to run for the national Tory leadership in 1983; he knew Lougheed would have headed an "anyone but Davis" movement. The hostility between the two premiers stemmed mostly from the Davis government's position on energy, which was much closer to Trudeau's than to Clark's. The Lougheed/Davis/Mulroney common denominator, however, was a belief in activist government tempered by fiscal discipline—*progressive* and *conservative* government. The Harper government did not pass muster even by the second criterion in the contemporary meaning of the word. Many of its policies, particularly in the environmental area, were not so much penny wise and pound foolish as pound foolish plain and simple. False economy is no more economic than a fine mess is fine. What a departure from the Mulroney and Lougheed and Davis paths.

The close working relationship between the Mulroney government and provincial PC governments across the country on a broad array of overlapping concerns helped the national PC Party transition fairly painlessly from Opposition to government following our landslide 1984 election victory. Federal-provincial cooperation partly compensated for the fact so few of us in the new federal Cabinet, including the prime minister himself, had any prior government executive experience—municipal, provincial, or federal. Our new government's ability to complete, for example, complex and politically delicate agreements on acid rain with all seven of the relevant provincial governments is largely attributable to the harmonious federal-provincial relations described here. Around the time we completed the last two of these agreements—with Nova Scotia and New Brunswick, in that order—there were three or four fewer Tory provincial governments than when we took office. But early in its mandate, the Mulroney government had communicated that, in marked contrast to the Trudeau government's hostility towards the provinces, partnering with the other jurisdictions was the route we intended to follow. The importance the prime minister and his government attached to healthy federal-provincial-territorial relations paid big dividends to us and to the country throughout the entire time Mulroney was prime minister. For sure, it made our pathway to building a strong legacy, in the environmental field as in others, a lot shorter and smoother.

Brian Mulroney did not share the obvious delight Pierre Trudeau took in provoking fights with premiers and their governments seemingly just for the pleasure of it. Mulroney telegraphed throughout the federal system his commitment to what Lester Pearson had characterized as "cooperative federalism." With ministers, the Tory PM policed the implementation of this principle as a Toronto cop would direct motorists and pedestrians following a car crash at midday at Yonge and Bloor.

Many a time, Mulroney blew the whistle to keep traffic flowing. I found myself whistled at from time to time either by the man himself or by a senior staffer at his behest. The experience was not pleasant. The public service felt the same pressure from on high. My deputy, Geneviève Ste-Marie, discussed it with me a number of times to ensure our own shop toed the line. Both of us were conscious that the constabulary was ready to toot at the first sign of a transgression. At an especially delicate point in negotiations with the provinces on the Meech Lake Accord, for example, the PM ordered the entire Cabinet to avoid doing anything to offend provincial sensibilities. For this reason, I had to postpone a major counter-proposal to British Columbia's official offer on establishing the South Moresby national park reserve. I knew that that my new offer would cause controversy in the province, not least in Premier Bill Vander Zalm's office. (My staffer Elizabeth May was furious with me for, in her words, "buckling under pressure from the prime minister." Weak-willed was I, she charged.)

The extent to which the prime minster knew the overall direction he wanted his government to take was extraordinary. So was the clarity with which he communicated his intentions throughout the government at the beginning of his mandate. Such was possibly unprecedented for a newly elected prime minister ever since the national government had become a bureaucratic leviathan after the Second World War. Lester Pearson might have done it equally well. But Pearson headed a minority government when coming to power in 1963, so had nothing close to Mulroney's freedom—even if better prior knowledge of the system—to exert his will. In any event, as John Diefenbaker proved by leaping from one unforced error to another, it is one thing for a PM to have a massive mandate but quite another to use it well. Mulroney was determined to avoid Diefenbaker's mistakes. And Joe Clark's, too. With notable exceptions—sometimes with disastrous consequences—he succeeded. The following examples, from my own experience, are typical of federal-provincial dynamics in this period.

New Brunswick premier Richard Hatfield once flew from Ottawa to Montreal en route to Fredericton to meet with me—in the middle of his last election, no less—while I was in Quebec on other government business. His purpose was to haggle over certain final details in the Mulroney government's agreement with his on a joint acid rain abatement program. Hatfield was the last of the seven premiers to agree to sign a federal-provincial acid rain accord. He was concerned about the effects on NB Power, a provincial Crown corporation whose atrocious environmental record at the time would have provoked St. Francis of Assisi to strangle a wild pheasant with his bare hands. Pressured by fellow Maritimer Dalton Camp—a senior advisor in the PMO from 1986 to 1989—the New Brunswick premier finally came on board. It's possible that Hatfield also foresaw his pending defeat and said to himself, What the hell! Might as well take one for the team. The politics were not easy for the premier on the home front, and we feds didn't think the agreement possible. But it did happen. I credit Maritime solidarity—Hatfield/Camp/Mulroney/McMillan—for the victory. It was the environment, however, that really won.

I had the dubious distinction of appearing with Hatfield to announce our acid rain agreement at what proved to be his last news conference as New Brunswick premier, just days before the 1987 provincial election in which his government was routed. It was also a week before my forty-second birthday. The agreement was the best advance birthday gift I could have received. But defeat for the premier and his party was so thick in the air that it could have been touched by a blind man with no hands. My most lasting (and saddest) memory of the news conference was the final question:

"Mr. Premier, how does it feel to attend your last media event as premier before losing on Tuesday." Richard was stunned, and sadness filled his eyes. The premier flushed, forced a smile, said nothing, got up, and left as though sleep-walking to his grave. The Liberal Party would proceed to win the election, for the first time since 1967, in a land-slide of historic proportions, capturing every single seat in the legislature. I felt like the man's undertaker.

Often attacked for spending so much time out of province in hot spots such as New York City, the premier was once quoted as saying, "Just because I'm premier of New Brunswick doesn't mean I have to live there." Now no longer premier, he was free to live wherever he wished. Hatfield was as devoted to his province and country as he was certifiably eccentric—one of a dying breed that included British Columbia's "Wacky" Bennett and Newfoundland's Joey Smallwood. After Hatfield was defeated in the 1987 election, Mulroney appointed him to the Senate. He died on April 26, 1991, of brain cancer at age sixty. This great Atlantic Canadian was bur-ied in Fredericton, not far from his home. Richard Bennett Hatfield was one of the outstanding Tories of his generation. He was so unlike those who called themselves "Conservative" in the Stephen Harper Cabinet, who doubtless would have denigrated the man if he had been a premier in their time in office. But they could have learned much from Hatfield about what it means to be a classic Tory—in his case, a Red Tory of the most wonderful hue.

My relations with Hatfield's successor, Frank McKenna, proved excellent. Even younger than I (by three years), McKenna was the ideal Liberal leader to demolish the Hatfield government, which most New Brunswickers perceived as too grey, too long in office, too entrenched, too entitled, and too tired to merit their continued support. Following his government's swearing-in, McKenna met with Prime Minister Mulroney and then paid individual courtesy calls to select federal ministers, includ-ing me. In my case, the premier wanted to communicate that he—unlike his PEI counterpart, Joe Ghiz—supported the building of the PEI-NB Fixed Link. McKenna told me that he thought the project would benefit New Brunswick even more than the Island but would be a boon to the entire region. The premier offered to help sell the idea to his own people and to all other Maritimers. "I'm totally on side," he said. McKenna did and was.

As consul general in Boston later, I paid courtesy calls of my own on all three Maritime premiers. Only one assembled his full Cabinet to be briefed on how their province might better use the consulate to advance trade and other opportunities in New England, their closest and most important international market. That pre-mier was Frank McKenna. As much as I liked and admired Richard Hatfield, New Brunswickers elected a first-rate man to replace him. Although the two governments had different political labels, McKenna's administration and ours became strong allies on many major measures, not just the Fixed Link. Among them was the free trade agreement with the United States. But McKenna reversed the Hatfield govern-ment's approval of the Meech Lake Accord. This action caused the federal-provincial consensus to start unravelling, opening the door for Newfoundland and Manitoba to withhold their support. The death of a potentially historic achievement began with the New Brunswick premier's opposition. His subsequent introduction of a parallel accord—a set of companion resolutions—failed to hold the Grim Reaper at bay. The other two principals in the deathwatch—Newfoundland premier Clyde Wells and Manitoba legislator Elijah Harper—merely provided the death rattle and accelerated rigor mortis. I would be surprised if, today, Frank McKenna does not regret his action.

It was a small-minded thing to do. And he is a big man. On the Fixed Link, as on free trade and many other issues of common import to the Mulroney and McKenna governments, the premier acted big. And big things happened as a result—in both jurisdictions. Down the road, though, will Frank McKenna's place in history be limited to his helping to kill Meech Lake? If so, more's the pity.

I pursued a particular environmental course that riled Quebec's Robert Bourassa, who believed it egregiously violated provincial jurisdiction. The matter concerned specific provisions of my *Canadian Environmental Protection Act* (CEPA), then moving rapidly through the federal legislative pipeline. The Quebec premier expressed his concern to Brian Mulroney privately during a federal-provincial conference on unrelated issues. The PM discussed the premier's comments with me immediately afterwards. He considered them important, and now so did I. This was one Mulroney minister not eager to hear the "cop's whistle." The offending provisions were changed in light of the contretemps not only with Quebec, but also with other provinces that had communicated varying degrees of opposition on the same jurisdictional grounds. The PM hadn't exactly instructed the change. But he did not need to. It was one of those "Will no one rid me of this troublesome priest?" situations. Everyone concerned knew "Henry II's" will without his having to issue a decree. So, the deed got done. And yet, I was determined that "Thomas Becket" have an afterlife. The resultant CEPA compromise was crafted following delicate negotiations between the two levels of government. In a nutshell, the federal government set tough new national standards for regulating in the marketplace the most environmentally damaging toxic chemicals. The provinces would enforce the standards and, if their actions met those high standards, the law would be deemed honoured. If not, the federal government would exercise its own authority. As I told the House of Commons—using a phrase much parodied by the media afterwards—"We will *swoop in* and act if a particular province refuses to do so itself." One media wag quipped that I was no longer the minister but "the swooper." Meanwhile, all kinds of monitoring and reporting mechanisms were built into the new law. The revised CEPA passed the test of time—and muster with all governments long after the legislation received Royal Assent. This account typifies how the national government practised "cooperative federalism" throughout Brian Mulroney's period as prime minister. In numerous public statements he made or wrote as a private citizen, Mulroney had tipped his hand about the kind of federal-provincial relations he would conduct if ever he were in a position to do so. Now the script was being played on the biggest stage of all: the Government of Canada.

# National Tensions

Sometimes I believed our government, under the prime minister's influence, was unduly sensitive to provincial concerns and too quick to factor them into our measures. I vented my frustration in Cabinet Committee on one occasion, provoked as I was by Senator Lowell Murray's hectoring on the subject in the context of CEPA. Murray had been appointed to the Senate by Joe Clark in 1979, one of the few major appointments Clark made in the nine months he was PM, much to the ire of party supporters. But Murray's connection with Brian Mulroney was just as strong as it was with Clark, and it went back even further, for Murray and Mulroney attended

St. F. X. at the same time. And they kept in touch through the years when not actively collaborating in politics. Mulroney appointed Murray as his government leader in the Senate and minister of state for federal-provincial relations. "Lowell, it's all well and good for a senator to be concerned about provincial government sensibilities," I said in my Cabinet Committee outburst. "But the rest of us in Cabinet have to get re-elected in our own ridings, and most premiers aren't going to help us much with that." Old political warhorse that he was, the senator smiled broadly and nodded agreement, at least on the political reality, if not the implied philosophy of governance. In 2003, Murray joined Clark to oppose the merger of the Progressive Conservative Party with the Canadian Alliance to form a new Conservative Party. After the new party was created, the senator refused to join its parliamentary Caucus, which comprised both senators and MPs.

Until leaving the Senate in 2011 at the mandatory retirement age of seventy-five, Lowell Murray remained one of two senators to sit as "Progressive Conservatives," even though the federal PC Party no longer existed either in name or—to both senators—in spirit.[6] As much as any other minister, Murray reflected Brian Mulroney's view of federalism. I presume that is why his long-time friend and political comrade put him in the Cabinet as minister of federal-provincial relations to begin with. This was an excellent choice, one I doubt Mulroney ever regretted making. Notwithstanding my outburst, I thought the PM, Lowell, and our government as a whole mostly had the right approach to the provinces. I was prepared to meet my own provincial counterparts at least halfway on matters of joint concern. I discovered that walking in the middle of the road was sometimes the surest way to risk joining the porcupines and skunks as roadkill.

Environmentalists attacked me mercilessly for caving into the provinces on the *Canadian Environmental Protection Act.* For their part, some provinces—but by no means all—attacked me for invading their jurisdiction with the legislation. Clifford Lincoln, Quebec's environment minister, was an elegant and courtly gentleman. Born in Mauritius, Lincoln later became a federal MP and briefly a national Liberal Party leadership candidate. I respected and liked him a great deal and we got along well. At a federal-provincial meeting of the country's environment ministers in Ottawa, however, the man felt the need to put on the record his premier's concerns about CEPA on jurisdictional grounds. The Quebec government was also upset about certain actions I had taken in Montreal involving PCBs. This dispute also revolved around jurisdiction. Lincoln spoke with equal measures of firmness and—in deference to me—rhetorical restraint.

Jim Bradley, Ontario's environment minister, was always firm but rarely restrained. Sensing blood in the water—mine!—he went on the attack, and piled on…and on and on and on. Earlier that day, the media reported that Bradley had appointed as a senior advisor Colin Isaacs, executive director of Toronto-based Pollution Probe, one of the country's best-known environmental advocacy groups. Isaacs, a former NDP member of the Ontario legislature, had savaged me for allegedly kowtowing to the provinces on CEPA. With Bradley in full throttle, I turned to federal officials sitting behind me. (They included the current governor general, David Johnston, then principal of McGill University. He had just been appointed chair of our National Round Table on the Environment and the Economy.) My Irish dander fast rising, I said to Assistant Deputy Minister Bob Slater: "Give me the damn news clipping about Isaac's appointment." I then quoted all the terrible things Bradley's new senior advisor had said about how I had become "just a valet to the provincial governments on environmental issues." I said, "Provincial governments attack me for invading their jurisdictions. Environmental organizations attack me for bowing at the waist to the provinces, instead of asserting federal power." Then, for the coup de grâce: "I must have it pretty much right when I'm being attacked from both directions." That stopped my attackers in their tracks. Next agenda item, please.

The federal government *did* take a middle-of-the-road approach to CEPA, reflecting Brian Mulroney's concept of federalism: a balance between asserting federal authority and respecting provincial jurisdiction and rights. The Mulroney government took this approach on all issues where it felt the need, either constitutionally or politically, to act in concert with the provinces—virtually our entire agenda. Had there been even a modicum of balance in such government measures as the NEP and the Federal Investment Review Agency (FIRA), tensions throughout the country would have been substantially ameliorated from the late 1960s to the early 1980s, when Pierre Trudeau practised a significantly more unilateral form of federalism. Mulroney considered the NEP so unacceptable to the West, not to mention inherently wrong-headed, that it was unsalvageable. He, therefore, scrapped it outright. His government did not abolish FIRA, but clipped its wings while retaining its basic mandate and functions. The kind of agency FIRA ended up being was reflected in its new name, *Investment Canada*: vigilant about the national interest but open to foreign investment per se. This was exactly as Stanfield had proposed while PC leader almost a decade before the Trudeau government created the agency in a burst of well-intentioned but misguided nationalistic fervour. Anyone wishing to connect the dots between all such measures—from CEPA to the NEP scrapping to the FIRA reform to Meech Lake to the Charlottetown Accord, and on and on—would have to possess very poor eyesight, or else an extremely shaky drawing hand, not to see the straight line from one of these stances to another. They were all of a piece.

I was speaking mostly in French at a large ceremonial indoor event in Montreal, held in early evening. The occasion involved officials from the federal government, the province, and Quebec municipalities of every size. I had never before met Robert Bourassa. Normally, at an informal event of this sort, the premier would have discreetly departed after completing his own perfunctory duties. In this case, it would have been easy for him to exit, for there was no head table. We were all packed into a cavernous atrium, standing and mixing as guests would at a huge cocktail party. Instead of leaving immediately, however, Premier Bourassa stayed to listen to my own equally pro forma remarks. It soon became clear to me that he was not merely being courteous to a federal colleague. The premier waited until I finished, caught my eye, hurried over, and then congratulated me on my French—more for the effort than the execution, no doubt. "I know you're aware I criticized you to your boss," he said. "I did what I had to do, just as you were doing what you thought you had to do as a federal minister. No hard feelings." I might not be quoting the premier exactly right; some of his words were in French. But the message could not have been clearer had he also illustrated it on a flipchart with crayons. I was deeply moved by his sincerity and thoughtfulness, not to mention the masterful diplomacy he employed to avoid discomfiting either of us. I was struck even more by the implied but unmistakeable subtext: he wanted relations between his government and ours to be harmonious and productive, not rancorous or partisan. On all such occasions, no seasoned government head ever considers himself or herself off duty once the formalities have ended. Nor does he or she miss an opportunity, however minor, to advance an agenda. Small talk is never small. That is exactly what the premier was up to in my company on this occasion. And, of course, enjoying my PEI French!

A very similar thing happened to me with Ontario's David Peterson, another classy politician of the first rank. He and I shared a head table at a large conference on Great Lakes water quality in the popular resort of Mackinac Island, Michigan. The conference was attended by a variety of Canadian and US politicians, including several US governors, and their officials throughout the Great Lakes region, in addition to environmentalists and media from both countries. The elaborate affair was held at a big white colonial inn backdropped by a stunning natural setting. Jim Bradley, Peterson's environment minister, and I had just had one of our disagreeable public spats. It related to what I considered Bradley's partisan efforts to undermine the Mulroney government's growing success and reputation on the environmental front. He could be petty, I trigger-happy to respond in kind—two hot-tempered Irishmen at their worst. Jim and I were equally guilty. Nothing was gained from it on either side—and opportunities for joint action, to the benefit of both jurisdictions, were sacrificed along the way. We should have been ashamed of ourselves. I am now, long after the fact, especially since we liked each other personally.

The Ontario premier shared the prime minister's eagerness to avoid this very kind of tension between our two governments and in federal-provincial relations more generally. It was at the Mackinac Island conference that I met David Peterson for the first time. The premier used the occasion—from the head table in his own welcoming remarks to conference participants—to pay tribute to me. His remarks were totally out of context, so they caught me utterly by surprise. But I no less appreciated their obvious intent: to signal to me, more or less, "Tom, all this bad blood between you and Jim is not how I myself feel towards you and your prime minister and new government. Let's just all get along." The message was more subtle than that, just as Bourassa's had been before, but the code was easy to break. Like Bourassa, Peterson never passed up a chance to make even the most mundane act do double duty. In this case, most of the premier's remarks before hundreds of people were aimed at an audience of one: me. What class acts these two men were. And how badly I needed to hear the Ontario premier's gentle scolding in the guise of public praise.

David Peterson's prominent role in creating and promoting the Meech Lake Accord contributed to his government's electoral defeat in October 1990. This was at least as big a factor as the slumping provincial economy or the so-called Patti Starr scandal, which involved alleged illegal fundraising for the provincial Liberal Party. Like Canadians elsewhere across the country, many Ontario voters believed the Meech Lake Accord ceded too much constitutional ground to Quebec. Others thought the proposed reforms undermined the federal government's authority more generally. Peterson's continued support for the accord in the face of steadily growing opposition from his own electors was one of the great acts of Canadian statesmanship in this era. His vigorous opposition to the Canada-United States Free Trade Agreement hurt the Mulroney government and PC candidates such as me in the subsequent federal election. But, in contrast to Joe Ghiz—the only other premier to campaign against the agreement during the election—Peterson acted without demagoguery or ill will or hyperpartisanship. In politics, it is often not what is done but how it's done that separates the heavyweight from the bantam. Peterson practised politics like a world champion, Ghiz like a Little Leaguer. The difference is not attributable to the size of the province each man represented, but, rather, to the depth of his understanding of the meaning of statesman.

# The Prime Minister's Zeitgeist

Personal relations are the calcium that makes federal-provincial bones strong. Under Brian Mulroney, the calcium count was higher than it had been at any time since Pierre Trudeau declared federal-provincial relations "dead" early in his time as prime minister. This fact had profound practical implications for public policy across a broad front during the entire time Mulroney was prime minister. Like the bones of even a healthy person, federal-provincial relations sometimes fractured over such issues as Meech Lake and free trade, despite Mulroney's best efforts. But no matter the personality or party label concerned, the PM carefully nurtured relations with each of the provincial premiers, both personally and officially. His approach greatly improved the health of all the governments, not just his, and fortified the country's skeletal structure as a whole.

Among all their policy differences, Diefenbaker's and Stanfield's sharply contrasting positions on Canada's French Fact separated them the farthest as national Conservative Party leaders. Diefenbaker's mindset was negative and mean-spirited, Stanfield's generous and constructive. It was this fundamental difference that defined the Maritimer as a classic conservative and the westerner as a rogue in the tableau of PC Party leaders over the generations. In a similar fashion, Trudeau's and Mulroney's opposite perspectives on federalism constituted the most marked difference between them as prime ministers. Trudeau saw the parts—provinces, territories, even populous municipalities—as potential threats to Canadian unity. Like Stanfield, Mulroney saw them as integral to the country's fabric. He was eager that the weave be as tightly knit as possible. Trudeau was, basically, a centralist; just as were many of his disciplines—Newfoundland's Clyde Wells was an extreme example. Mulroney, by contrast, viewed the parts as working harmoniously together—both the federal government with the other jurisdictions and the other jurisdictions with one another—as the essence of Canada and, therefore, of making the country work. Mulroney was a "modified decentralist." By that I mean the man understood that, by definition, Canada's federal system requires the national government to respect the powers the Constitution grants the provinces (and, through them, the municipalities) and must act accordingly. But he still saw a major role for the federal government in the country's economic and social affairs. He thought that role could best be played through partnerships between the federal authority and the other jurisdictions in areas of shared or overlapping jurisdiction or just common concern. In no sense did Mulroney see himself as head waiter to the provinces in the manner Trudeau so often characterized any federal politician he deemed too respectful of provincial government sensibilities. To Trudeau, Mulroney was not just head waiter but also busboy and dishwasher. The fifteenth prime minister of Canada hated what the eighteenth prime minister of Canada stood for on fundamentals. No love was lost in the other direction, either.

Brian Mulroney's vision of Canada was that of a classic conservative in the Canadian tradition. He viewed the country as a highly differentiated but smoothly integrated organic system. I do not believe that, myth to the contrary, Pierre Trudeau's antithetical view of Canada always reflected some lofty overarching vision of his—one that rendered him, say, a classic liberal. The man was indisputably committed to a form of federalism in which the central government was powerful and the provinces were virtual creatures of the federal authority almost in the way municipalities are creatures of the provinces under our Constitution. Maybe he thought that only a strong central state could protect individual freedoms and liberties, to which he was passionately committed. This interpretation would explain both the man's centralist bias and the tenacity with which he fought—ultimately with success—to entrench the individual citizen's rights and freedoms in a constitutionally enshrined federal charter. By its very nature, federalism seeks to accommodate sociological and political diversity within the constitutional framework of a single polity. The classic liberal would be inclined to view such an accommodation as incompatible with the principle of human equality and the advancement of individual rights and freedoms based on that principle. But were Pierre Trudeau's constitutional views always that cerebral? That high-minded? That benevolent? Or were they often a way of gunning down political foes? In this respect, weren't Pierre Trudeau and John Diefenbaker more like "brothers from another mother" than "strangers in the night"?

Gordon Robertson beamed light on the subject. For more than three decades, Robertson was at the centre of government power in Canada. He served as clerk of the Privy Council and secretary to the Cabinet, the top position in the Canadian public service. He was also senior advisor to Pierre Trudeau on constitutional matters. "Trudeau defined individual rights in a way that was unduly antagonistic to the spirit of federalism," Robertson writes in his memoirs. "He insists that in a liberal society the freedom and equality of individuals must prevail over the rights of communities."[7] Trudeau's views on federalism were substantially more in the American classic liberal tradition than in the British/Canadian Tory tradition. The latter has had a greater concern for the totality, rather than the individual parts; the interests of the entire nation, as opposed to those of the private citizen; but a respect for the individuals and subgroups that are an integral part of the whole. This was the tradition to which Robert Stanfield and Brian Mulroney proudly belonged.

I would like to think high principle alone motivated Trudeau to oppose Mulroney's efforts to enlarge the new Constitution to include Quebec. But I cannot. I believe the man's motives were sometimes darker, more sinister. Trudeau just did not want his successor to put his big muddy meathooks on the lily-white constitutional altar cloth the former had woven. If a man views his handiwork as sacred, he's not likely to want a pagan anywhere near the sacristy, let alone the tabernacle. Having described that handiwork as something that would "last a thousand years," Trudeau believed that Mulroney's time in office was at least a millennium too early for one tiny thread of it to be altered. Trudeau's earliest and most complete public statement on the Meech Lake Accord was published simultaneously in *La Presse* and the *Toronto Star* on May 27, 1987. In that statement, "[h]e provided no legal analysis whatever," Robertson says. "[It] was a purely political and highly emotional attack skillfully designed to excite all the suspicions that could so easily be aroused about the most inflammatory subject in Canada."[8] Doesn't that also describe Diefenbaker's earlier ranting and raving against *deux nations* and Canadian bilingualism? In what must rank as one of the strongest indictments ever penned by a former senior Canadian federal public servant concerning the actions of a prime minister he had once advised, Robertson says Trudeau's "irresponsible interventions after retirement to block [the Meech Lake and Charlottetown] agreements Mulroney had achieved may well be more determining of our future than [Trudeau's] positive contributions during all his time in office."[9] Expressed in plain English, *Pierre Trudeau hurt the country more than he helped it.* That assessment strikes me as unduly harsh. But the credibility of the source renders it difficult to dismiss the analysis outright.

Not for a moment would Brian Mulroney question Robertson's assessment. Nor would Robert Stanfield have done so, either. Among all of the twenty-two prime ministers who preceded Justin Trudeau, only Pierre Trudeau and John Diefenbaker enshrined citizens' rights and freedoms in law—Trudeau in the Constitution, Diefenbaker in legislation. But doesn't the kinship between the two men extend well beyond this latticework of history? Didn't they both exploit tender linguistic and cultural sensitivities for personal and partisan purposes? And didn't they do it at the risk of the very national unity they purported to have devoted their public careers to advancing? In the late 1960s, the two men used *deux nations* as a sledgehammer to bludgeon Stanfield. Two decades later, Trudeau did the same with the Meech Lake and Charlottetown Accords to slay Mulroney. It's one thing for politicians to disagree with one another on an issue. It's quite another when one side tries to demonize the other in the process. That's exactly what Trudeau and Diefenbaker did, not just on language and culture but—as we saw with Trudeau on Stanfield's wage-and-price-controls policy—on other issues as well. Like siblings, demagogues can be found in different forms—from the brooding intellectual, as in Trudeau's case, to the fire-brand stump orator, as in Diefenbaker's. Language and culture in Canada are no more noble than race in the American Deep South or religion in Northern Ireland or ancient tribal and sectarian loyalties in the Middle East when employed as political weapons to incite the citizenry, achieve or retain power, mobilize supporters, dispirit opponents, exploit vulnerabilities, divide and conquer, refight lost battles, settle old scores, defend a legacy, prejudice history, or just indulge in mischief. When self-aggrandizement is also the motivator, as it was for Canada's foremost political demagogues, John George Diefenbaker and Pierre Elliott Trudeau towards the end of their lives, such are the firebombs of political pyromaniacs, not the tools of statesmen. It's all destructive. Nothing good can come of it.

While tourism and then environment minister, I took my lead from the prime minister on how to approach the provinces on federal issues in which they had a stake—to wit: getting rid of that senior Tourism Canada marketing official with whom the provinces could not work, mentioned earlier; negotiating legally binding agreements with the provinces to tackle acid rain across the country as a *national*, not exclusively *federal*, cause; meshing the federal and provincial government enforcement regimes through CEPA; and on and on. Most other ministers also followed Mulroney's lead. It was clear what was expected of us. We might have placed the image on the canvass, choosing this subject and not that, this composition rather than another, this combination of colours in preference to alternatives. But Brian Mulroney set up the easel and taught us artists how to paint. He ran the studio, and every one of us did his bidding. Those who did not or could not soon found themselves painting at another studio or—as with Suzanne Blais-Grenier—not painting at all before long. For such offenders, it was the political equivalent of being tossed out with the trash.

# A Tale of Two Cities

As we have seen, the government of Brian Mulroney was not bereft of policy when it took power. Nor, unlike Diefenbaker's, did it fail to exploit every policy resource available to it, both inside and from without, as it proceeded to become one of the most reformist national governments in Canadian history on diverse fronts. Mulroney felt passionately that one of the biggest failings of the Trudeau government was not helping to foster among Canadians a deeper sense of community. He thought Pierre Trudeau had picked fights with the provinces to get his way on issues, setting a negative tone and example for not only the entire federal government but also the country.

Mulroney's governing model could not have been more different from Trudeau's had they led completely different countries. As his overarching priority, Mulroney sought to achieve what he called "national reconciliation" after years of federal-provincial turf warfare and interregional tension. He had often used that phrase on the campaign trail across the country in the 1984 election. As a candidate at the time, I considered the phrase clunky, unduly abstract, hard to explain at the doorstep, and unsexy. In Cabinet, however, I soon realized that "national reconciliation" captured better than any other catchphrase could have done the man's philosophy of governing and, indeed, his vision for the country. "One of the main goals of my government since assuming office [was] to establish a climate of national reconciliation," Mulroney says in his memoirs.[10] It would prove to be, not *one* of his main goals, but his *principal* goal.

The new prime minister saw Canada as, in effect, a family in which he was the benevolent *pater familias*. This was how his political and policy mind worked. Nowhere was that clearer than in his relations with the PC Caucus. "As far as I was concerned, my caucus was to be treated as family—a group to be trusted...a place where all MPs—from the prime minister on down—would receive support and understanding."[11] This way of viewing the PC Party and the country was rooted in his classical education. But the perspective was adapted to contemporary circumstances to embrace the more modern idea of consultation and involvement among all "family members." Just as most Canadian fathers today would not be a "my way or the highway" family figure, as in Roman times, so also this prime minister saw himself as a more sympathetic and inclusive "head of the household." To Mulroney, the *pater* did not so much dictate what everyone ate for dinner as ensure that whatever meal was served made for a happy family. As he said of his massive Caucus following the 1984 election, which he viewed as a microcosm of the country, "Our meetings were to be a place of frankness, and for honest and open debate without fear of recrimination."[12] Brian Mulroney's view of Canada as a united community—a nation from sea to sea to sea with him as the "national reconciler"—was to frame virtually everything he did as prime minister. One cannot understand why Mulroney invested so much of his political capital in certain areas and at such high risk of failure—most remarkably, the Meech Lake and Charlottetown Accords—without appreciating this fundamental dimension of the man. In the two examples at hand, the absence of Quebec's signature on the 1982 constitution frustrated Mulroney as prime minister, challenged him as a Canadian federalist, and offended him as a Quebecer. To listen to him address the subject in Caucus and Cabinet was to hear a pained and driven man. He believed that Trudeau's heavy-handed and insensitive treatment of Quebec had caused the province to exclude itself from a transformational family compact. Mulroney's anguish was analogous to that of a father whose favourite daughter had chosen to skip Christmas dinner because she felt the other members of the family no longer liked her.

Mulroney would have done almost any reasonable thing within his power to get Quebec to return to the "table." In fact, with the Meech Lake and Charlottetown Accords, he *did* do almost everything. That he failed was undeniably his greatest regret as prime minister. That he tried should be viewed as his most noble act. That Pierre Trudeau actively undermined the efforts of his successor on such a central part of his national agenda was Trudeau's most ignoble act in a long and otherwise distinguished public career. That Jean Chrétien opposed the Meech Lake Accord (and later the Charlottetown Accord), so obviously to follow Trudeau, was Chrétien's most ignoble act in his own accomplished public career. Chrétien allowed himself to become Trudeau's headwaiter. On one side or the other of the moral divide, for these men, as Charles Dickens would have said, "It was the best of times, it was the worst of times, it was the age of wisdom, it was the age of foolishness, it was the epoch of belief, it was the epoch of incredulity." Let the reader have no doubt on which side of the moral divide I plunk each man in this context. For Canada, the failure of Meech Lake was "the worst of times." In light of that accord's failure, the Charlottetown Accord—named after my hometown, where the essentials had been agreed upon— was doomed from the start and, thus, a product of "the age of foolishness." By contributing to the Charlottetown Accord's doom, just as they had to Meech Lake's, Pierre Trudeau and Jean Chrétien were complicit in that foolishness. While noble in principle, the Charlottetown Accord sought too hard to accommodate all the groups and constituencies that had opposed the Meech Lake Accord on diverse grounds. The many compromises to reach consensus caused the Charlottetown Accord to create—in the words of political scientist Ron Watts—"more enemies than friends."[13] On October 26, 1992, it was killed in a national referendum by a 55.4 to 42.4 percent margin. Four months later, Brian Mulroney announced he would retire as prime minister. No coincidence. Time had run out on the constitutional front—for Mulroney, forever; for the country, for at least a couple of generations.

Brian Mulroney's community-oriented zeitgeist, as a man and as a political leader, also motivated his actions on the world stage. He viewed the human population as "a family of nations," a term he used. The phrase is too often trotted out by statesmen and despots alike as a rhetorical flourish on grand international occasions. But Mulroney both believed passionately in this concept and acted on it as prime minister, and not just while in the world spotlight—to wit: his government's strong public stand against apartheid in South Africa, in defiance of both Washington and London; his government's willing acceptance of refugees and immigrants from countries with murderous regimes or troubled economies; and the government's leadership in the building of multilateral opposition to tyranny and invasion, most notably to stymie Saddam Hussein's incursion into Kuwait to annex its territory and grab its oil. At the United Nations in the first year he was prime minister, Mulroney shocked many observers by the vehemence with which he attacked apartheid in South Africa and by threatening "total [Canadian] sanctions" against the country if it did not fundamentally reform it racist and regressive regime. The PM used the term "reconciliation" when calling for harmony "within South Africa and between South Africa and its neighbours." That word echoed his "national reconciliation" mantra at home. This was a prime minister, and this a man, true to the communitarian ideals that St. Francis Xavier University had instilled in him as an undergraduate. It was as though he were placing St. Augustine and St. Thomas Aquinas front and centre at both the federal-provincial conference table and the United Nations dais.

# Stanfield/Symons and Mulroney

Only a few specific policies developed by the Stanfield/Symons policy process a decade or more earlier survived in the exact same form with the Mulroney government. But some did in their "pith and substance," as lawyers are wont to say. A major one directly under my ministerial roof was a commitment to reform the federal environmental review and assessment process (EARP). This idea was championed as early as when Joe Clark was PC parliamentary spokesman for the environment, well before becoming party leader. John Fraser, Clark's environment minister, relentlessly advocated the idea both then and long afterwards. As environment minister myself, I picked up the theme, once reminding the NDP in the Commons of its rich Tory pedigree when that party was gunning for me in Question Period on a related issue. (I can well remember Mulroney's listening to my Commons statement with keen interest and obvious approval, as if to telegraph to the corner of my eye, "Yes!") The Mulroney government did reform EARP, making the process mandatory—not just discretionary as before—for all major projects under federal authority. The PEI-NB Confederation Bridge, for example, was subjected to this process in the same spirit.

Other core policy principles on which the party had worked hard under Stanfield's leadership girded major measures of the Mulroney government. Who would deny that the *deux nations* concept—so controversial in the late 1960s—underpinned the Meech Lake and Charlottetown Accords? The special recognition these agreements sought to give Quebec as a distinct society was true to that concept. Throughout their political careers, neither Stanfield nor Mulroney budged an inch from a shared belief that the Constitution needed to reflect the sociological reality that Quebec *is* distinct as the only province—the only society, the only *nation*—with a majority French language and culture within Canada. And, to boot, it has a civil law tradition, unlike the rest of Canada, where the common law prevails. (Both men were lawyers.) The two men embraced passionately a central political reality: only by receiving distinct-society recognition in the Constitution would Quebec feel fully part of the Canadian family. After the federal-provincial pact that produced the 1982 Constitution excluded Quebec—in what Trudeau himself characterized as a "*coup de force*"—Stanfield and Mulroney also shared the belief that the Meech Lake Accord (and, later, the Charlottetown Accord) provided the best, and perhaps only, way to obtain the province's willing acceptance of the country's new Constitution. Jack Pickersgill was a Liberal heavyweight from Newfoundland in the Cabinets of Louis St-Laurent and Lester Pearson. Like Pickersgill, Stanfield feared that Meech Lake's defeat would hurt not just Quebec, but also Atlantic Canada. There, the French-speaking population loomed large, particularly in New Brunswick, Canada's only officially bilingual province.

As on the constitutional front, a host of taxation reforms by the Mulroney government paralleled policies Robert Stanfield had advocated, especially in the 1972 campaign. As stressed in earlier chapters, Stanfield was the first major politician in Canada to champion the concept of a Guaranteed Minimum Income (GMI), the brainchild of economist Milton Friedman, who detailed it in his 1962 book, *Capitalism and Freedom*.[14] Called by Friedman the "negative income tax," the program was not legislated by the Mulroney government as such. But Friedman's central rationale for that program—the need to address the plight of the working poor while rationalizing the public social safety net—was embraced by Michael Wilson throughout his seven years as Mulroney's finance minister (1984–91). Wilson's biggest step in this direction was removing tens of thousands of additional lower-paid income earners from the tax rolls. That measure gave the working poor more take-home (or net) pay with which to meet basic needs for themselves and their families. This had been the primary goal—more so than bureaucratic streamlining—of Stanfield's GMI proposal.

The Mulroney government's position on federal-provincial energy revenue-sharing was a page ripped directly from Stanfield's policy playbook. Several westerners who later became Mulroney Cabinet ministers participated actively in the Stanfield/Symons policy process either from the Opposition benches, in the case of MPs, or as private citizens. Don Mazankowski had played a particularly large role while a front-bench Opposition MP. He was generally considered the party's foremost authority on transportation—railways, in particular; Maz would become minister of transport in both the Clark and Mulroney governments. These westerners helped shape Mulroney's views on the energy-revenue-sharing issue. But, philosophically, Mulroney would no more have embraced the contrary principles that underpinned Trudeau's NEP than renounce his citizenship or change his religion. For his part, as noted earlier, Stanfield continued to think like a premier on all such issues long after he ceased to be one. More fundamentally, like Mulroney, he believed the energy-producing provinces were entitled to the resource revenue they needed to meet the requirements of their people and thereby be full partners, not dependents, in the Canadian family.

The NEP increased the federal share of energy revenues at the expense of the producing provinces. The NEP's Petroleum Gas Revenue Tax (PGRT) instituted a double-taxation mechanism for natural resources. Oil and gas were treated one way; gold, silver, copper, nickel, and others were handled differently. That tax change must rank as one of the most regionally discriminatory and unfair fiscal programs ever launched by the federal government. To western Canadians, especially Albertans, the change made the Banff property-lease-levy hikes look like gifts from God. The PGRT's express purpose was to insulate the Canadian economy from the shock of fast-rising global oil prices. It did that by requiring Alberta and the other oil-producing provinces (mostly also in western Canada) to subsidize Canadian fuel consumption in non-producing provinces (mostly Ontario and Quebec). The NEP cost the Alberta government treasury alone over $100 billion in lost or forgone revenues. Partisan politics heavily overlaid the program. The governing Liberals lacked a single seat west of Manitoba, where the NEP's pain was primarily inflicted, while their parliamentary majority was overwhelmingly based in central Canada, where the program's benefits primarily accrued. But partisan politics don't come close to explaining either Stanfield's or Mulroney's opposition to the NEP. The program was fundamentally inimical to the two men's shared federalist (as opposed to centralist) vision of the country. For symbolic and substantive reasons alike, scrapping the NEP was one of Mulroney's most urgent priorities as PM upon taking office. Accordingly, it was one of the first measures his government took. To him, a boil on the body politic needed to be lanced. And it was.

Public hostility in many parts of the country—not just the West, but especially there—forced the Trudeau government to dismantle some of its most nationalistic programs, including parts of the NEP. To save face, it did so one budgetary measure at a time over several months, rather than reveal all the changes at once in a single package. John Crosbie quipped that Allan MacEachen, the finance minister, was engaged in "a dance of the seven veils," evoking the image of a striptease artist coquettishly removing one garment after another as randy male patrons shouted for more.

But some "veils" remained to be discarded when the Mulroney government took office. In 1985, the new government launched the Western Accord. It deregulated domestic oil prices while abolishing import subsidies. It also eliminated the export tax on crude and oil products and the petroleum compensation charge. The PGRT was phased out, and controls on oil exports were lifted. All these measures concerned *land-based* oil and gas development—again, primarily in the West.

The Mulroney government took the identical approach to managing *offshore* energy production and revenues, principally in Newfoundland through the Atlantic Accord. Yet again, connecting the dots would reveal a straight line. And that line could be traced all the way back to Brian Mulroney's earliest statements, in the 1970s and early 1980s, on federalism and how he viewed the country more generally. The same line could also be traced back to many of the causes for which Joe Clark fought while Opposition leader. Indeed, one of his most successful gambits in Parliament concerned efforts to block the NEP legislation. I'm referring to the famous 1982 bell-ringing episode, in which the entire PC Caucus paralyzed Commons business by boycotting proceedings. It was the single most dramatic parliamentary event in which I participated in my entire time in the Commons, on either side of the House. Everyone's adrenalin—that of Opposition and government members alike— flowed like a slashed aorta. This extraordinary parliamentary ploy, engineered by Erik Nielsen, was not just a matter of political one-upmanship, though it succeeded spectacularly by that standard. The whole PC Caucus—not merely western MPs—felt passionately that the West was being lynched on the scaffold of the Trudeau government's energy-revenue-sharing measures. We PC Atlantic Canadian MPs didn't feel at the time that our region had a direct stake in the outcome. But, as the House of Commons sounded more like a big-city fire station at five-alarm alert than a deliberative parliamentary body in full session, our passions were as charged as powerfully as anyone's. On the Tories' quarter of the Commons, the West and Atlantic Canada were as one.

That same sense of interregional unity came into play when the Mulroney government forged the Atlantic Accord. It was supported as enthusiastically by House leader Erik Neilsen (Yukon) and future deputy prime minister Don Mazankowski (Alberta) as by its principal Atlantic Canadian champions in Cabinet, John Crosbie (Newfoundland) and Elmer MacKay (Nova Scotia). (The name Atlantic Accord was also used, much later, to describe a cash-transfer agreement between the federal government and the governments of Nova Scotia and Newfoundland and Labrador.) Weren't analogous forces in play when I, a Prince Edward Islander, went to bat for the people of Banff on the usurious levy increases on national park property leases discussed earlier? The voice and conscience of Robert Stanfield concerning federal-provincial relations often reverberated in my head as I wrestled with one such issue after another both at Tourism and at Environment. Stanfield's political values had a similar impact on the thinking and actions of other Mulroney ministers, not least ones from Atlantic Canada. Whether or not we saw it literally this way at the time, a Stanfield Doctrine existed in effect: *Canada is only as strong as its most vulnerable region and poorest citizen.* The Nova Scotian's entire public career was devoted to making the country stronger based on that principle. Stanfield's major stands as national PC party leader cannot be understood outside the dual values they imply: (a) the need to narrow regional economic disparities and ameliorate language and cultural tensions between different parts of the country; and (b) the importance of placing a social safety net under the disadvantaged, especially the working poor.

Embracing Canada's French Fact—specifically, *deux nations* and the Meech Lake and Charlottetown Accords—and championing the Guaranteed Minimum Income concept were among the concrete ways he acted on this doctrine.

Most Mulroney Cabinet ministers, including me, shared Stanfield's preference for a decentralized form of federalism. More than any other minister, Joe Clark embraced that "community of communities" vision of Canada. But Stanfield's basic constitutional and federal-provincial values were Brian Mulroney's, too. Both while Opposition leader and while prime minister, Mulroney regularly consulted Stanfield. He particularly respected his views on—not to mention support for—the Meech Lake and Charlottetown Accords. "I admired Bob Stanfield from the start and was greatly taken by the political know-how he demonstrated," Mulroney says in his memoirs.[15]

The pathway between the policies Robert Stanfield embraced as national PC Party leader and the measures Brian Mulroney took as prime minister constitutes fertile ground for scholarship. Having walked both ends, I know that pathway might have twisted and turned. But the overall direction was the same for the two leaders—progressive, not reactionary. This can hardly be said of any route between either of these men's legacy and the record of what passed for the Conservative Party under the leadership of Stephen Harper. It is as though Stanfield and Mulroney headed a different party altogether from the one Harper led. Only the party label seemed the same, and half that had been trashed, too—to Stanfield and Mulroney equally, an illustrious half: *Progressive*, made doubly rich, and given exponentially additional force, when combined with *Conservative*. Nowhere in the panoply of issues that the Progressive Conservative Party addressed in the Stanfield/Clark/Mulroney period were classic Tory values more visibly displayed than on all matters concerning the relationship between the federal government and the provinces and territories. All three men were committed to advancing the interests of the "whole" by respecting and seeking to nourish those of the "parts" as integral to that whole.

# Policy Structures

Cabinet is central to Canada's system of responsible government and political culture as a whole. Everything revolves around it, as symbolized by the Crown. (The government is Her Majesty's, serving at her pleasure as guided by her ministers as chosen by her subjects.) Technically, Cabinet *is* the government. The public service helps develop and implement its policy program. Parliament passes and helps to legitimize that program and acts to hold its crafters responsible. To the public, a Cabinet minister, especially the prime minister, is the face of the government. The populace looks to these people for leadership, passing ultimate judgment on their performance at the subsequent election. How a particular government operates is dictated in no small measure by such entrenched institutional frameworks, traditions or customs, and values. Each government has some room to create its own structures and processes. But not nearly as much as most people might think. The sheer size of the PC Party's election victory in 1984 helped determine the Mulroney government's modus operandi. To the extent its ways were similar to those of previous governments, the aforementioned institutional and cultural boundaries help explain why.

From my perspective inside, the Mulroney Cabinet structure was like a set of Russian nesting dolls. The largest "doll" was the full Cabinet. At forty members (twenty-nine "full" ministers and eleven ministers of state), including the PM, it was not so much a Cabinet in the conventional understanding as a smaller doll itself, nestled inside the government party's parliamentary Caucus—a mini-Caucus, so to speak. As such, it was a forum in which the PM could brief all ministers on progress or problems. It also served as a sounding board for his own thoughts and proposals. It helped ensure all ministers were in the same deep-water channel as the ship of state set sail. It approved—typically as a mere formality—decisions made in other Cabinet conclaves. And it provided ministers with a vehicle to exchange views, share information, and vent emotion on matters of broad interest or concern. The substantive policy debates and decision-making were most often conducted in Cabinet committees, of which there were five major ones in this period. The most important two were *Economic and Regional Development*, and *Social Affairs*. The others were *External Affairs and Defence*, *Communications*, and *Regulations*. A Cabinet member was assigned to a particular committee primarily based on his or her portfolio. (As discussed earlier, Environment was considered "social," so I was automatically placed on the Social Affairs Committee.) For reasons I could not understand, the PM thought I had a flair for communications—the main reason he appointed me Tory Question Period strategist in Opposition, the reader will recall. He liked, for example, my constituency "householder," a quarterly pamphlet-style newsletter custom-designed by each MP or his or her staff and mailed postage-free to every constituent in the riding. I was for that reason also put on the Communications Committee. Like each of my colleagues, I attended a given meeting either because I was a regular committee member or because a committee of which I was not officially a member was considering a subject that related to my portfolio or interested me personally. In theory, every Cabinet member was free to attend any policy committee, except for Priorities and Planning ("P & P") and Operations (discussed below). But, due to time constraints, ministers tended to be very selective about going to meetings of committees to which they had not been formally assigned.

The real battles within Cabinet were most often fought—and won or lost—in major Cabinet committees. In effect, it was in these forums that policies were approved, programs launched, funds allocated, communication strategies devised—and the fate of individual ministers and their agendas sealed, for good or ill. In all such committees, housekeeping or routine matters were invariably dispensed with summarily. Uncontroversial, but still-substantive, items were handled as one might expect: methodically and yet with minimal discussion and rancour. (My *Tourism Tomorrow* strategy paper was discussed by the Economics and Regional Development Committee, where it was given a courteous hearing and approved without dissent and, it seemed to me, with only enough questions or comments to demonstrate that everybody had actually read it.) Sometimes, committee debate could become protracted and heated. This was almost always true when the dollars at stake were big. It was also the case when the issue was controversial—either in Cabinet or in the country at large or both—but funding was *not* central. I recall a particularly contentious debate on a proposal concerning the legal age of consent for sex. The matter involved, in particular, a defendant's allowable grounds for defending himself or herself in court against charges of having engaged in sex with someone underage. In all such tricky cases, Cabinet ministers possessing a direct stake in the issue, or just keenly interested in it, could find themselves lined up on one side or the other with other members strongly opposed. In the worst case, though never in mine, the sponsoring or opposing member might find himself or herself fighting as a battalion of one.

The business of these committees mattered. They were not just ways to keep Cabinet members busy and out of trouble; we were endlessly capable of busily getting into trouble with or without institutional help.

Then there were two smaller "nesting dolls," each with power and importance inversely proportionate to its size. The larger of the two, Priorities and Planning, was, in effect, a steering committee of the full Cabinet and a conduit for the work of the aforementioned major policy committees. About fifteen members, carefully selected by the prime minister, attended. These were his most senior and important Cabinet colleagues, either by portfolio or in his eyes. As noted in the next chapter, Mulroney immediately elevated Lucien Bouchard to P & P following the latter's election to Parliament in a Quebec by-election. But neither of his portfolios (first secretary of state, then environment) would automatically have placed him there without the long-time close personal connection the two men enjoyed before it ruptured over Meech Lake. P & P acted as a clearing house and Checkpoint Charlie for all the policy decisions made and funding approved by the larger policy committees. Most matters would then go directly to the full Cabinet, where they would be only briefly discussed (if at all), hardly ever opposed, and then practically rubber-stamped. By this juncture, the ministers most interested in a given issue would have participated, and won or lost the day, in a smaller "doll." In cases of major irreconcilable differences between or among ministers in committee, the individuals were expected to settle disputes on their own through so-called bilaterals. My contretemps with Energy Minister Marcel Masse over CEPA was a case in point.

Before going to full Cabinet to be finally disposed of, if necessary, an especially important or challenging issue would be handled in the smallest—and most powerful—"doll" of all. Its name was Operations, consisting of about six to eight members, depending on Cabinet turnover and the like. If P & P was the inner Cabinet, as it was commonly viewed and sometimes called, Operations was the inner, inner Cabinet, rendering the doll analogy especially apt. As with P & P, Operations was always chaired by the prime minister or, in his rare absence, by the deputy prime minister. The main policy committees were chaired by senior ministers chosen by the PM—for example, early on, Sinclair Stevens, Economic and Regional Development; Jake Epp, Social Affairs; Joe Clark, External Affairs and Defence. All these chairpersons sat on both P & P and Operations. It was in Operations that the most important or most politically delicate or "most expensive" issues of all were considered and resolved. I cannot recall—and have no record of—having ever attended P & P. I did, however, attend Operations several times, usually to seek authorization for legislation but, most memorably for me, to obtain $10 million to fund my Rouge National Urban Park wilderness plan for Scarborough, Ontario. I was surprised by the Rouge outcome; whereas, on previous occasions concerning other matters, the result was more certain beforehand. I almost swallowed my tongue when Mike Wilson, whose Toronto constituency was not far from the proposed park, called me in PEI to say he would support me at Operations on the Rouge. (After this funding was made public, Ontario Liberal environment minister Jim Bradley publicly denounced me for invading his jurisdiction.) The idea that the environment is the preserve of leftists is absolute bunk. Wilson's supporting the Rouge typified how almost all Mulroney Cabinet ministers felt about environmental issues. When joining a meeting of Operations to seek approval for one major environmental measure or another—provided I had done my homework, had a solid case, and had made the rounds beforehand—I found not so much a den of lions as a clowder of domestic cats. "This is a shop with which I am well pleased," the prime minister said of my department after our Rouge funding was stamped approved. I could have walked on air as I left the room to share the good news with my officials and staff.

As one might expect, on all issues the PM had an outsized impact on Cabinet discussions and outcomes—"first among equals" and all that. This was particularly true at P & P and Operations. (He never attended the large policy committees.) I knew that, if the PM supported me on a particular matter near the finish line, I would likely cross it without crashing. Otherwise, I might as well have stayed home and cried in my beer. A Canadian prime minister's veto is much more powerful than an American president's pen; the former's can't be overturned by Parliament, the latter's can by a two-thirds vote in Congress. All ministers were aware of this political reality and factored it into their strategizing. Catching Mulroney off guard was the surest way of ensuring trouble for oneself, not to mention his ire. But staff and officials throughout the system always kept him well briefed on everything important even if a slacking minister might have failed to do so. Every time I went to Operations, it was like how I would imagine entering the College of Cardinals as it chooses a new Pope: power palpably filled the air. It would have taken almost a revolt within full Cabinet to overturn, or even modify, a decision made in Operations. By contrast, pitchforks and shovels would not have been required to reverse a P & P decision, but a dissenter would have had to bear at least a hand-weeding folk and trowel. I can't recall an uprising ever happening in full Cabinet against a decision by either Operations or P & P. Certainly, none of my measures suffered that fate. No matter the minister or department, PMO knights would have forestalled any rumblings of discontent against the king well before the castle's drawbridge needed to be raised and its towers and turrets manned against a rebellion by the hoi polloi.

Just as Brian Mulroney had little patience with debate for debate's sake, so also he disliked personal confrontations between or among ministers. He deliberately structured the "nesting doll" committee process—from the full Cabinet through to Operations—to maximize consensus-building within the government while minimizing rancour and unproductive dissent. That said, he actively encouraged lively and sometimes protracted arguments on important issues, not only in Cabinet but also in Caucus, even as he sometimes tended to dominate more than I thought helpful to fostering a genuine consensus. On issues such as free trade, Meech Lake, and abortion—to name but three among many—he believed a vigorous debate in these forums hardened him and the party for the verbal battles they would face in Parliament and the country as a whole. He knew that opposition from outside the "family" would be substantially more hostile and less manageable than from within. The appearance at Cabinet or its committees of individuals such as chief free trade negotiator Simon Reisman and his second-in-command Gordon Ritchie was often the best show in town. Reisman, in particular, could be counted on to provoke a donnybrook with John Wise (Agriculture), Flora MacDonald (Communications), and Pat Carney (International Trade), among others. Though less vituperative than Reisman, Ritchie was as aggressive as he was opinionated. The man could rile up ministers in both official languages. This intramural league helped prepare not only ministers but also the prime minister himself to win skirmishes out in the country, especially on the election campaign trail. The PM believed that a policy or program that a sponsoring minister could not easily explain and defend before colleagues was not likely to be understood, let alone supported, by the voter in front of his or her TV. The Cabinet policy process was designed in part to ensure that the government's measures could be both sold and bought. Mulroney had learned hard lessons from his party's disastrous experiences with Stanfield's wage-and-price controls policy in 1974 and with Clark's 18-cent-a-gallon gasoline tax in 1980.

One of the most contentious Cabinet debates in my time concerned abortion, on which Senator Lowell Murray chaired a Cabinet sub-committee. The debate followed the Supreme Court's landmark *R v Morgentaler* decision of January 1988, in effect eliminating abortion restrictions on Charter grounds. "The discussions [on abortion] were detailed and sometimes intense and emotional among colleagues," Murray remarked to me recently. How well I remember! Could a single member of Cabinet or Caucus besides the prime minister influence the outcome of such a debate? Yes, without question. I saw it happen often in both forums. I had some success of my own from time to time. And I was, by nature, more taciturn than most colleagues. I was a mute compared to, say, Jim McGrath in Caucus and John Crosbie in Cabinet—both, not coincidentally, Newfoundlanders. Another "Newfie" was Ross Reid. He succeeded McGrath as MP for St. John's East (1988–93) and was minister of fisheries and oceans in the short-lived Kim Campbell government. To this day, more than two decades after the fact, Tory MPs at the time remember Reid's low-key but powerful intervention in a heated Caucus debate on sexual orientation. Fredericton MP Bud Bird (1988–93) had an equally powerful impact on a separate Caucus debate on AIDS. Bird's moving account of his son's losing struggle with AIDS convinced many a Caucus member that more federal research funding was urgently needed for that then-fatal disease. That Bird was Caucus chairman rendered his remarks all the more poignant—and swaying. Both Reid's and Bird's interventions postdated my time in Parliament. But my now hearing about those interventions from so many who heard them such a long time ago confirms my own parliamentary and political experience: a single voice reflecting the best in humanity can unleash the best in others.

Again, the Mulroney government's "nesting doll" Cabinet committee structure was required by the XXL size of the Cabinet itself. The Cabinet's size, in turn, reflected the fact the government had been elected in 1984 with the biggest parliamentary majority in the country's history. Under Mulroney's immediate successor, Kim Campbell, the Cabinet's size was slashed from well over thirty-five ministers and ministers of state (forty at the outset) to only twenty-three. The number of Cabinet committees was also correspondingly reduced. Her own successors, beginning with Jean Chrétien, have kept the Cabinet's membership to approximately thirty. Stephen Harper's original Cabinet had twenty-seven members and the number didn't vary appreciably thereafter. Justin Trudeau appointed thirty to his Cabinet (besides himself), seemingly the post-Mulroney norm. For a long time now, the "nesting dolls" have been both smaller and fewer than they were in the Mulroney years. Whether the dolls have been better behaved is a separate question.

# Policy Orientation and Ideology

Underpinning the narrative of much of this book is how difficult it is to draw boundaries accurately around any politician's ideology—if he or she has one at all. It is challenging enough merely to establish criteria by which to determine whether an individual is liberal or conservative or socialist or something else altogether. But, if pushed to the wall and threatened with death—or, almost as bad, having to defend the Harper government's environmental record—I would say the following. Some Mulroney Cabinet ministers were distinctly on the left of the political spectrum, others just as surely on the right, and still others in the "in-betweeners" category. That said, almost all of us were sufficiently open-minded that deep-seated philosophical orientations, if they did exist, never obstructed our best judgment on issues that rarely, if ever, lent themselves to being resolved ideologically. Most informed observers would consider several ministers Red Tories or left-wingers in this parlour game where the rules are designed to advance the fun but not necessarily produce any winners; for, as I have stressed, in the Canadian context, though not the American, ideology is more a circle than a straight line. Labelling individuals or their positions in left-right terms can be worse than a futile enterprise. In extreme cases, it can also be dangerous. Rolling the dice if I must, however, I would put, indisputably, Flora MacDonald, Marcel Masse, David Crombie, Joe Clark, Jean Charest, and Lowell Murray, along with me—not to forget Brian Mulroney himself—among others, on the Red Tory square. Erik Nielsen, Harvie Andre, Robert Coates, Barb McDougall (but only on economic issues, not social), perhaps Don Mazankowski, Michael Wilson (but exclusively on budgetary matters), John Crosbie (except on all things Newfoundland), Bill McKnight, Otto Jelinek, and Gerry St. Germain, among others, could be found on the farther-right square. Many others—prototypically, Jake Epp and Perrin Beatty and (perhaps surprisingly to some) Sinclair Stevens—would straddle the squares: a bit on this one, a bit on that. It depended on the issue and, more often than not, on whether the minister had a direct political stake, especially back in the riding. But you could never be sure in what direction the wind might blow in any particular case—a classic one being Gerry St. Germain.

In 1983, St. Germain won a federal by-election in British Columbia on the same day Brian Mulroney won his in Nova Scotia. As a backbencher, St. Germain took arch-conservative positions on almost every issue that crossed his path. (The man later became the first Reform/Canadian Alliance Party senator.) He aggressively fought, for example, my efforts to establish the South Moresby national park in his province. Let the log chainsaws and mine explosives and fish dragnets go at it—that was his stance. Eight months before the 1988 election, my nemesis joined the Mulroney Cabinet as minister of transport (later forestry), the first Métis federal minister in history. On the day he was sworn in, my new Cabinet colleague took me aside. "Tom, I have fought you tooth and nail on South Moresby," he said. "Now that I'm in Cabinet, we're on the same side. You can expect my full support." I could not have been more surprised had he shown me Karl Marx's image tattooed on his back. As Yogi Berra said, "It's tough to make predictions, especially about the future."

Whatever any minister might do or believe or say, the prime minister sets the direction of his government. And he calls the shots on questions important to him. My brother Charley was right when he said that Brian Mulroney was no more ideological than a coffee pot. In his memoirs, Gordon Robertson supports former NDP Ontario premier Bob Rae's assessment that Pierre Trudeau's greatest weakness was that "he became the prisoner of his own rhetoric, an ideologue despite himself, and curiously rigid as he tore strips off anyone who chose to disagree."[16] Like Robert Stanfield, Brian Mulroney was completely different from Trudeau in this respect. Mulroney was neither ideological nor rigid. And the man "tore strips off" someone, if ever he did, only when he felt personally wounded—for example, on Clyde Wells's backstabbing him on Meech Lake. It rarely, if ever, happened over an issue per se—in Wells's case, the accord itself. Still, the PM did have strong values, not least a determination to be the best prime minister he could. For him, that meant eschewing simple solutions to complex problems based on template thinking, whether of an ideological or a partisan sort. Most politicians play it safe on contentious subjects to avoid alienating voters who might disagree. They're as vacuous as a fortune cookie. Brian Mulroney did not fit that mould. But neither was he an absolutist.

Like Robert Stanfield, Mulroney was a principled communitarian pragmatist. Less intellectual—but, in many ways, no less smart—than Stanfield, he sought to solve problems, not prove himself virtuous, an ideology righteous, or his party best. Arguably, Mulroney forged a closer personal friendship with both Ronald Reagan and Margaret Thatcher than any other Canadian prime minister has ever done— before or since—with any other US president or UK prime minister. (Reagan's widow, Nancy, invited Mulroney to deliver a eulogy at his funeral.) But these trinational transatlantic friendships obscured a fundamental fact about Mulroney: Myth to the contrary, he was no ideological kindred spirit of Reagan or Thatcher, though these two conservative zealots were demonstrably that to each other. Mulroney neither preached nor practised the free market, trickle-down economics dogma, the socially conservative ethos, or the jingoistic militarism on which Reagan and Thatcher based their careers, earned their reputations, and created their political identities. For his part, Pierre Trudeau appeared genetically programmed to engage in argument for argument's sake—always to *appear* right, but not necessarily *be* right; always to win, but not necessarily *deserve* to win. He was no Reagan or Thatcher, either. And yet, certain of his distinguishing character traits were more like those of Reagan and Thatcher than of Mulroney, especially the dogmatic mind, the rigid policies, and the sense of moral certitude that oozed from every pore in all three cases. Trudeau had an extraordinary intellect, a quick and facile tongue, and a keen instinct for the jugular. Why let all that God-given talent go to waste? "Give a boy a hammer and everything he meets has to be pounded," said philosophy professor Abraham Kaplan.[17] The gods gave Trudeau a hammer, and he pounded to his heart's content on a range of issues concerning which, throughout his life, he never released his grip—particularly Quebec's constitutional and political relationship with the rest of Canada.

For all his pragmatism, Brian Mulroney was, at heart, a Red Tory in the sense that term is generally understood: a person who embraces progressive, reformist policies, and is comfortable with government activism for the public good. That does not necessarily make him an ideologue, merely a thoughtful person with a certain political predisposition. *New York Times* columnist David Brooks has posited that a classic conservative appreciates the limits of human ingenuity, believes in steady but incremental change, prefers reform over revolution, has a healthy respect for hierarchy, values precedence as a moral and policy compass, seeks balance and order, favours public and private discourse that is prudent and measured and responsible, and sees the nation as one organic whole.[18] By that standard, Brian Mulroney did fit the "classic conservative" bill as prime minister of Canada, even if not entirely. (Measured discourse?—hardly a Mulroney hallmark!) However Mulroney might be categorized politically or philosophically, who could reasonably deny he loves his country? Imbued with a strong social conscience, the man believes passionately in the capacity of the public sector to improve the lives of all Canadians in the spirit of community. And he does so from a deep well of caring. All that Catholic social teaching was not for naught. This much Brian Mulroney did have in common with Pierre Trudeau: he could be unhealthily self-focused, recklessly vain, rhetorically heavy-handed, and woefully misguided. But, with Robert Stanfield an obvious exception, the same could be said of most who attain high elective office—from Winston Spencer Churchill to William Jefferson Clinton to Stephen Joseph Harper, to cite examples from three different liberal democracies. Notwithstanding his flaws, Martin Brian Mulroney is a good and decent man who, from the beginning to the end of an accomplished public career, did his best for Canada and for Canadians. Surely, in the board game of politics, such is the best of all squares to occupy.

# Brian Mulroney and the Media

I have never known or followed or studied the career of any major politician in Canada or elsewhere who loved the media. The job of the media—electronic, print, or online—is intrinsically to make a nuisance of themselves: identify the story, investigate the circumstances, select the relevant facts, hound their prey, assemble the information, package it, and then disseminate it to the public. The media are in the news and truth business. Fact-finding is their stock-in-trade, communicating what they have discovered their mission. The politician's job is to make decisions for the public and generally represent and serve it. His or her first priority, however, has to be getting elected and then re-elected in the event of success. Otherwise, he or she can't serve in the first place or loses the opportunity if booted from office. This entails the politician's always putting his or her best foot forward even if the other foot is a mangled wreck. It's the task of the media to ensure that the public gets to see the mangled foot. By nature, the media aren't interested in showcasing the good one. The politician is deemed capable of doing that without their help.

Thomas Carlyle attributed the origin of the term "Fourth Estate" to Edmund Burke, who used it in a parliamentary debate in 1787 when the press were first allowed to cover the British House of Commons.[19] The term refers to the three Estates of the Realm—the clergy, the nobility, and commoners—in medieval times. Nowadays, the media are viewed, not least by themselves, as democracy's bulwark against the abuse of power by the other Estates, principally our contemporary equivalent of nobility: politicians. Thus, there's a built-in tension between politicians and the Fourth Estate. The better the media do their job, the less the politicos like them. So it was with the highest of our "nobles" in my time in government: Brian Mulroney. Often the man's response to his "bulwark" was not very noble. A peek at the clash of swords and shields in which he was engaged while master of the court reveals much about him as an individual and as a political operator.

Brian Mulroney's hostility towards the media began almost the day he entered politics as a candidate for the leadership of the Progressive Conservative Party in 1976. It was after Robert Stanfield announced his intention, in the parliamentary office of my Hillsborough predecessor, Heath Macquarrie, in July 1975, to retire. Mulroney felt badly burned by how the media covered his unsuccessful run for the PC leadership then. Journalists typically characterized his campaign as extravagantly expensive and ostentatious. As, indeed, it was. "Cadillac" was the word most often used to describe his style. In light of the harsh media criticism of his earlier run, Mulroney deliberately ran a lower-key—or, at least, less obviously costly and showy—campaign in 1983, when he finally won the party leadership. From 1976 on, however, Mulroney distrusted the media, often describing them in private as mean-spirited, self-important, ill-informed, lazy, and (in the worst cases) stupid. That was when he was in a good mood! Every politician is an actor, good or bad. Most political leaders claim not to read their reviews. Pierre Trudeau generally didn't. Mulroney followed virtually everything important the media said about him.

Between the time I left Cabinet and Mulroney offered me the post of consul general in Boston in July 1989, I gave an interview on the environment to Maclean's magazine. I said that, on environmental issues, Mulroney did not let himself get bogged down in scientific detail or policy technicalities, but "what is important is that his heart is always in the right place" (I echoed Tom Symons's choice of words to describe a "Stanfield Man"). The magazine paraphrased me as having said something very different: that, while the PM might not have known the science and technicalities of environmental issues, his heart is always in the right place. It was not so much a quote out of context as a misunderstanding of what I had said, perhaps not clearly enough. The magazine reported me as saying that the PM didn't know the complexities but it didn't matter. What I meant was that he did know them, but the details were less important to him than the big picture—a substantial difference. At this time, my brother Charley was back teaching at York University but remained close to Mulroney though no longer in his employ. Charley phoned me in PEI to say that Mulroney had "not appreciated your comment one bit." We both knew that the prime minister was in the throes of appointing me to an important position. In that light, Charley cautioned me: "Don't piss off Brian if you know what's good for you." I decided not to piss off Brian. I gave no more such interviews till after l was appointed. Afterwards, I took great care with the media never to offend my benefactor again. I returned to the man's good graces. Or, at a minimum, didn't piss him off.

Mulroney often warned Caucus that no politician ever lost a single vote by avoiding a reporter's notebook, only from talking into one. He did not always heed his own advice. Many observers believe that this prime minister blew what could have been his greatest legacy, the Meech Lake Accord, had it not been for a now-infamous interview he gave to the *Globe and Mail* on June 9, 1990. In the interview, the PM created the impression that he had been ready to "roll the dice" like a casino gambler with the fate of the country to achieve a deal with the provinces. In his memoirs, Mulroney argues that he had frequently used the "roll of the dice" metaphor before without implying anything sinister. And this time, he claimed, those words merely meant, "I had to try everything humanly possible in that limited time frame to achieve success."[20] Close to the referendum on the Charlottetown Accord (October 26, 1992), I was at the Canadian Embassy in Washington on business as consul general in Boston. L. Ian MacDonald, who had been a Montreal journalist before becoming Mulroney's speech writer and biographer of sorts, headed the Embassy's public affairs office between 1992 and 1994. In a chat with me at the Embassy, Ian said he thought the accord's chances in the pending referendum were good "provided Brian doesn't blow it out of the water by bragging about how skilful a negotiator he is." This remark obviously referred to Mulroney's disastrous *Globe and Mail* interview on Meech Lake. Because the accord involved constitutional change, it required the consent of all provincial legislatures within three years to become law. Evidently, even someone as supportive of Mulroney as MacDonald believed that the interview had shaken, if not sabotaged, the provinces' unanimous support for the accord. The massive hostility to Mulroney's comments across the country, particularly in certain provincial capitals, triggered a set of events that didn't so much murder Meech Lake as cause it to die a natural but ignominious death.

I have no doubt that, given the opportunity to withdraw any one thing he ever said in public, Brian Mulroney would choose his "roll of the dice" remark. The media's saturation coverage of the prime minister's misstep extinguished any flame of hope he might have kept burning that he could thaw his frigid relations with the Fourth Estate before leaving office. Immediately upon seeing his words in print, the PM knew he had employed appalling judgment. The man also knew that he would have to press himself into full damage-control mode to deal with the predictable fallout. That was particularly the case in Newfoundland and Manitoba, where support for Meech Lake was fragile and the premiers or legislatures were unreliable. Mulroney blamed himself for the colossal mess the *Globe and Mail* interview had created for the accord. But the self-flagellation did not obviate the anger he felt about the media's contribution to that mess and the obvious delight he thought some journalists took in seeing the accord unravel largely because of his own maladroit words. A cowboy does not think more highly of a rattlesnake that has bit him merely because he faults himself for having trod where the predator was lying in wait to pounce and poison.

In December 1992, only two months before publicly announcing his retirement as prime minister, Mulroney visited Boston primarily to meet with Massachusetts governor William Weld. The PM was also to speak that evening at a public forum at Harvard University, where his only daughter, Caroline, was studying. The *Boston Globe*, founded in 1873, was for generations owned and operated by the Taylor family. They still controlled the paper when Mulroney visited Boston—though it had "gone public," as stockbrokers say, a couple of decades earlier. Under different owners, the *Globe* has long been by far the pre-eminent newspaper in all New England. A meeting with the *Globe's* editorial board is, therefore, de rigueur for a major foreign government leader while he or she is in the area. This newspaper's politics are unmistakably progressive, its journalistic standards high, and its interests much broader than is typically the case with the US media, which tend to be parochial and ethnocentric when not altogether xenophobic. Although not plentiful, articles about Canada or Canadian events in this classy and storied newspaper are generally well-researched, thoughtful, literate, and fair. (Some local politicians, especially of the conservative variety, do not share my high regard.)

During Brian Mulroney's time in Boston, he met off the record with the *Globe's* editorial board. I was present throughout the meeting, having helped organize it. The PM's command of the various issues (most of them international) bedazzled his hosts. That was no mean feat, for these were hardened newspaper veterans. After departing the Cabinet exactly four years earlier, I had seen Mulroney only once before in person—in Ottawa in March 1991, when he and George H. W. Bush signed the Canada–United States Air Quality Agreement on Acid Rain. Until now in Boston, I had not noticed the marked change in the man in those four years. Physically, he had aged much more than I would have expected—a lot greyer, noticeably heavier (especially of face), and much less boyish in that Irish glint-in-the-eye way so characteristic of him. But he had also matured in a different, more positive way: as a public figure, as a politician, and as a human being. Brian Mulroney possessed a certain gravitas he lacked before, even towards the end of my time in Cabinet—a self-confidence, a comfort and fluency with the issues, an air of authority both in what he said and how he said it. The man had grown into the role of statesman, not just the job of prime minister. It was as though I were meeting for the first time a smarter and more accomplished older Mulroney brother.

I knew several of the *Globe* board members fairly well, not so much personally as professionally, through my relations with the paper as consul general. When I met privately with the board myself, early in my time in the position, one of the most senior members told me that most of his forebears on one side of the family had been from Prince Edward Island. I now sensed that he and the other *Globe* editorialists were surprised by how well-informed Mulroney was about the thorny issues they raised with him—most of them involving then-hot foreign affairs matters. These old pros appeared especially struck by how insightful, not to mention candid, the PM was concerning the war then raging in Bosnia and the social and political turmoil in the former Yugoslavia and in eastern Europe more generally. (Mulroney's wife, Mila, is the daughter of a Serbian doctor, Dimitrije Mita Pivni ki, from Sarajevo.) Almost all the other subjects the board raised with Mulroney were of similar life-and-death import—for example, famine and war and refugee homelessness in sub-Saharan Africa. The PM's answers to all such serious and complex questions were detailed, fact-laced, tight, heartfelt, and forthright. I was extremely impressed—and surprised. So obviously were the *Globe's* editorial writers. I felt proud for our country. To me, and no doubt them, Mulroney sounded less like a politician than a foreign affairs expert. Having now been prime minister for almost a decade, he had, in fact, become one. As stressed elsewhere here, government service at a high level can be an intense learning experience. Mulroney had learned a great deal on the job. It showed. And yet, he never showed off. The whole performance appeared as unaffected as it was effective.

Immediately after Mulroney's meeting with the *Boston Globe* board, in a heavily attended scrum—primarily involving the travelling Canadian media corps—the only thing reporters were interested in asking him about was a controversy surrounding extravagant luxury hotel charges he was alleged to have placed on the Canadian government's tab while attending, a few days earlier, a meeting in Paris of government heads from around the world. (It was later revealed that the host country, not the Canadian government, let alone Mulroney himself, was responsible for the arrangements and paid most of the costs.) Our going from the thoughtful and disciplined meeting with the *Globe* editorial board to this rude and unruly media mob encounter was like leaving the Bolshoi Ballet to watch a women's mud-wrestling match on cable TV. Mulroney was in no mood for the culture shock. His spirits and intellectual juices, spiked by the earlier session, soured as fast as reporters could shove microphones into his face, blind him with flash cameras, and shout deafening questions into his ears. When a reporter did finally get around to asking the PM what the *Globe* editorial board had raised with him, he shot back with anger and sarcasm: "They asked me why the Canadian media were so damned small-minded that reporters were interested only in my travel expenses." (In fact, the subject had not come up.)

I had planned to host the Canadian media travelling with the prime minister at an informal late-evening social at my official residence. Nothing fancy, just a few steps up from beer and pretzels. I knew many of the reporters personally from my days in Cabinet. It would have been nice to renew acquaintances. The party would not have involved the PM or his immediate entourage. Moreover, it was to occur after all official events had ended and the media filed their stories. So, I hadn't felt the need to inform him. When Mulroney learned about my plans by happenstance at the eleventh hour, he ordered me to cancel them: "No God-damned way we're going to give those bastards another opportunity to write about government expenses—your grand residence and lavish hospitality!" he bellowed. I cancelled the simple event I had organized.

I would make two general observations about Brian Mulroney's visit to Boston, coming as it did at the end of his time in office—the prime minister's swan song abroad, at least in the United States. First, the man had become jaded about politics and public life generally during his nearly ten years in power. His view of the Canadian media, in particular, had gone from bad to worse to godawful in that time, reflecting an overall cynicism about the political game. In the short time Brian and Mila and I spent privately together at their Boston hotel—albeit with a lot of personnel going about their business all around us—it was clear to me that Mila was just as fed up as he with it all, possibly more so. In retrospect, particularly in light of Mulroney's memoirs, I think that the sad outcome of the Meech Lake and Charlottetown Accords accounted for much of their shared funk. The latter had been defeated in a national referendum only a little over a month earlier. I was seeing the man at the nadir of his public career. At the time, these were not happy people. I sensed that, like prisoners about to be released from jail after serving lengthy sentences of hard labour, they were both looking forward to being set free. Seeing their daughter Caroline on her new home turf was a badly needed tonic for them. Spending time with Governor Bill Weld, with whom the prime minister had established a strong personal bond, served the same purpose. Despite the heavy official agenda, everything about the Boston visit smacked of therapy. Brian and Mila's spirits steadily lifted with each passing event, including the *Globe* editorial board meeting—which, again, was a smashing personal success. He treated that meeting more as a catharsis than a challenge. And the man performed all the more impressively for having done so—letting it rip, as it were. Undeniably, the respect and civility these veteran American journalists accorded him was a refreshing change from the brutal treatment he felt he was getting from the Canadian media, including those tracking his every word and action— and expense—on this trip.

No one can read the former PM's memoirs without sensing how especially embittered he is towards the CBC's Ottawa bureau for having led the media attack against Meech Lake and Charlottetown, for providing a vehicle for Pierre Trudeau's vicious personal assaults against him in that context, and for helping to undermine public support for these two attempts of his at historic constitutional reform. Mulroney charges that the bureau's one-sided, mean-spirited, shrill, and alarmist coverage of the issue violated the CBC's nation-building mandate as a publicly funded body. The bureau chief, Elly Aboim, vies with Trudeau and Clyde Wells for the distinction of being, in Mulroney's eyes, the worst culprit in the plot to kill his plans to "bring Quebec into willing acceptance of the [1982] constitution."[21] I doubt that either Brian's or Mila's bitterness towards all three men will ever disappear.

All this said, by the end of his time as prime minister, Mulroney had not lost either a capacity to wow an audience or his keen sense of humour. There was still plenty of kick in this aging stallion. The formal address at Harvard University, before a packed audience at the John F. Kennedy School of Government, was a personal triumph. Senator Ted Kennedy introduced the PM and Governor Weld formally thanked him. Neither Harvard nor the prime minister intended this to be anything but a major public event. The PM's sharp and sparkling and witty performance in the follow-up question-and-answer session especially impressed and entertained everyone, not least me. He was at the top of his game in a game that counted. After all, Harvard is no mere local university—it's where world leaders go to leave an impression. Brian Mulroney impressed. There had been much speculation about Mulroney's expected retirement from politics early in the New Year. One rumour making the rounds, including in Boston, was that the prime minister would head American Express. That company's famous TV ads at the time featured such international celebrity endorsers as comedy mega-star Jerry Seinfeld and renowned film director Martin Scorsese. Each endorser ended his or her sales pitch by holding up the company's iconic consumer card and saying into the camera its catchy signature slogan, *Don't Leave Home Without It*. At the end of the question-and-answer session, one Harvard student rose from his seat, hurried to the front, grabbed the mobile microphone, looked the prime minister straight in the eye, and asked him point-blank whether he was planning to resign as Canadian PM to become president and CEO of American Express. The audience laughed nervously. Then suddenly, it went silent. Shocked? Embarrassed? Or just impatient to hear Mulroney's response? Without missing a beat, the PM raised his right hand, pretended to hold an American Express card between his fingers, flashed the phantom card at the student, then at the audience, and quipped, "Don't Leave Home Without it." The place went wild. Boisterous laughter, wild applause, and piercing two-fingered whistling rocked the multitiered amphitheatre from floor to rafters. For a shining moment at the Crimson Campus on the Charles, Brian Mulroney was retiring Red Sox legend Ted Williams in his very last at-bat at Fenway—he hit a home run right out of the park. With a proud daughter in the audience and loving wife at his side, Mulroney—the government leader, the politician, the public performer, the man—was in his element. And in the best of form.

## The New Media and Greatness

For all his distaste for the Fourth Estate, Brian Mulroney is not himself a distasteful man. He is imbued with a love of life, rare charm, a terrific sense of humour, a wonderful playfulness, and a flair for making friends and colleagues feel glad to be in his company. And he laughs easily and often and boisterously—a sure sign of a good and joyous nature. I always enjoyed my personal and professional relationship with him. I know my brother Charley did, as well.

I do not argue that the Fourth Estate treated Brian Mulroney unfairly throughout his political career. I simply note that, for whatever reason, media coverage of him failed to communicate to Canadians anything close to the true nature of the man as a fully rounded human being—the man I came to know. Perhaps it is not the role of the Fourth Estate to show the public a political leader's best foot, only the mangled one. But I believe the media should at least inform the public that there are two feet.

In this iPhone era of non-stop Twitter chatter, everyone is a 140-character political critic. Around-the-clock all-news cable channels fill the airwaves and, therefore, people's heads with a never-ending supply of political commentary, much of it negative when not altogether calumnious. More than ever before in the history of broadcasting, especially in the United States, the airwaves are now controlled by powerful corporate interests. They advance blatantly self-serving partisan and ideological agendas, demonize contrary views, and seek to discredit people who hold them. They do all this with little, if any, sense of professional ethics (Fox News, on the far right, by far the worst offender). All the while, special interest groups and shady political fundraising entities are also helping to destroy individual politicians' reputations with fewer and fewer scruples as each election cycle passes. The era of the political superhero—Abraham Lincoln, Sir John A. Macdonald, Franklin Roosevelt,

Winston Churchill, John Kennedy, Golda Meir, Charles de Gaulle, Indira Ghandi, et al.—is as dead as an Egyptian mummy. In contemporary times, the reputations of even our most moral and principled politicians cannot survive the no-holds-barred scrutiny to which they are routinely subjected. A lot of the scrutiny is unfair and unbalanced or just plain wrong. By the time offenders are exposed and taken to task—if that happens at all—the public, with the attention span of a hummingbird, has already flitted to the next hyped "BREAKING NEWS" story, the next faux exposé, the next manufactured scandal, or whatever else is in line to feed the rapacious ratings beast. And the "news" cycle continues. Perpetually.

National political leaders in all modern democratic societies, including our own, should be given the slack they require to perform the job they were elected to do: lead. Why should we care with whom our leaders sleep as long as they govern well when awake? Would John Kennedy survive a single primary, let alone win his party's presidential nomination, in today's poisonous political culture and media climate? Far better that he slept with Marilyn Monroe than conspire with G. Gordon Liddy. It's not a matter of looking the other way; it's a question of looking the right way. But the chances of that happening in this nasty media age are worse than a team of limbless blind men winning a tug-of-war on rollerblades. Given the media's rapacious iconoclasm, will any current or future political leader be able to inspire the citizenry to follow him or her into the Dark Unknown? That's the essence of great leadership. It's what Lincoln did to save the American Republic, Roosevelt did to lift the Great Depression, Churchill did to vanquish the Nazi scourge. If the media and special interests are able to define every leader as having "two mangled feet"—even if, objectively, neither foot is actually disfigured, only imperfect, as every human part is—perhaps greatness is truly dead. The "perception is reality" shibboleth is true. The modern media culture drives perception and reality so far apart that they collide at the extremes with only perception surviving. Then, facts don't matter. Neither does the objective historical record, if it any longer exists. Meanwhile, the gulf between the governing class and the governed steadily widens. When the citizenry is conditioned to disrespect and disparage its leaders despite the reality, those leaders can no longer effectively lead. Nor, long afterwards, will they be seen to have led, still less with greatness.

Competent and caring leaders in a liberal democratic society deserve from their citizenry not fawning reverence or unquestioning deference or—God forbid—mindless idolatry. Rather, the citizenry owes its mere mortal leaders simple respect based on old-fashioned principles of human decency and fairness, provided such respect is reciprocated. Current trends in the other direction coarsen the political culture and debase both those who govern and the governed. The way Brian Mulroney was widely viewed when he left office would make a visitor from Mars think he was an axe murderer, rather than a man who had devoted the prime of his life to the service of his country. The man's public approval rating was down to 15 percent in June 1993. It had been even lower in mid-1991 (12 percent in an Environics poll). A Gallup poll conducted in August 2005 showed that a larger percentage of Canadians than that believed in witches. Given Mulroney's historically low numbers, who but the man's most hardened partisans remained in his corner? Did the public's view of him at the end reflect an objective assessment of his record? Or, over time, had his political adversaries and media detractors succeed in conditioning the public to see him in a certain way independent of who he actually is as an individual or what he actually did in office? This is not to deny the legitimate role of political criticism of the sort Mulroney relentlessly faced. Nor is it to suggest that the criticism itself was uniformly groundless.

Politics has always been carnivorous. Every Canadian prime minister should expect his critics to exact their pound of flesh. But, as Portia asked the usurious money-lender Shylock in *The Merchant of Venice*, should he also be compelled to spill blood? It's a question of proportionality.

Could Mulroney's final job approval ratings have been any lower had he, in fact, committed a heinous crime? A Pew Research Center poll revealed that Richard Nixon's approval rating was 24 percent when he was forced from office for demonstrably criminal and, consequently, impeachable behaviour. That's a lot higher than Mulroney's rating as he left office. Shouldn't the public's most extreme levels of disapprobation be reserved for leaders like Nixon who truly deserve them? For all his faults and failings, Mulroney surely did not. In the long list of scandals of which the Mulroney government stood accused virtually from the beginning—including the most serious one, involving Sinclair Stevens, setting aside the Airbus brouhaha—hardly any were shown to have had a scintilla of foundation when impartially investigated by the judiciary or a special commission or a pan-partisan parliamentary committee. Meanwhile, a small group of Liberal MPs, in particular, was able to whip up storms of scandal, one after another, that over time helped blow the House of Mulroney down. That group called itself "the Rat Pack."

The Rat Pack principally comprised Sheila Copps (Hamilton), Brian Tobin (Newfoundland), Don Boudria (eastern Ontario), John Nunziata (Toronto), Jean Lapierre (Shefford, Quebec) and, until his death in 1989, Jean-Claude Malépart (Montreal)—all of them then fairly new to Parliament. George Baker, from Newfoundland (now a senator), was also sometimes associated with this group. But humour, not invective, was his weapon of choice. Baker frequently sparred with fellow Newfoundlander John Crosbie in a continuing two-man parliamentary vaudeville act rumoured to have been largely pre-scripted by the principals for extra laughs. For the certified Rat Packers, however, no accusation or insult was too cheap, too outrageous, too unfounded, or too personal to hurl. More than the prime minister and government's reputation suffered. Parliament itself was diminished. They did not call themselves a pack of rats for nothing. Most of their charges turned out to be a pack of lies. Meanwhile, the Opposition truly got their pound of flesh—and plenty of blood as well. The very people who most loudly and tenaciously denounced the Mulroney government on high moral grounds demonstrated a cellar rat's lack of morality of their own.

Scandalmongers follow the same formula no matter the issue or facts or jurisdiction: make an outlandish charge; demand a public inquiry based on the appearance of wrong-doing that they themselves created; cite the very fact of the inquiry as proof there must be some truth to the charge; move onto the next "scandal" after the previous one has run its course; then claim that the pattern of scandals they manufactured proves that any one of those scandals must be true. This was the Rat Pack's way and Mulroney's fate. It was not so much self-fulfilling prophesy as circular argument—A is true because B is true; B is true because A is true. Such is the feeding ground of the illogical mind. More to the point, the circular argument is the muckraker's rhetorical weapon of personal destruction. With the Rat Pack, where was the fairness, the justice, the concern for human consequences? "Which office do I go to get my reputation back?" Raymond J. Donovan asked famously after being acquitted of larceny and fraud in a high-profile New York subway construction-contract case in the 1970s. Mulroney could have asked the same question after his government's many "scandals" were proven, one by one, to have been bogus.

Mulroney did not have to suffer "the slings and arrows of outrageous fortune" from either cyberspace or twenty-four-hour cable news channels. The iPhone was invented fourteen years after he left office, Twitter a year after that, all-news networks four years before he took power, but with nowhere near the impact cable news has today. Nevertheless, Mulroney was vulnerable to many other forms of media weaponry. Television coverage of the House of Commons began in the autumn of 1977, following years of study and debate. But it was only while Mulroney was in office, much later, that the Standing Committee on House Management recommended, and Parliament approved, relaxing the rules governing television camera angles for House proceedings. This innovation was a boon to the Opposition, especially during Question Period, which, as we have seen, is largely their forum, not the government's. More usable video footage available to the news media from this source expanded the role of television in both covering and shaping political events. That development narrowed the advantage government traditionally had enjoyed over the Opposition in communicating a message, controlling the public agenda, and influencing how people think. "Brian Mulroney was the first Canadian prime minister with open television exposure," I heard my brother Charley say. Unfortunately for Mulroney, much of that exposure was negative. The enlarged role played by television in politics was a gift not only to the Opposition parties, but also to special interest groups and their causes. Their howlers and hell-raisers now had a bigger megaphone than they had ever had before—and countless more people to hear it. Empowered by partisan or ideological media sympathizers, these groups found their political influence soaring to unprecedented heights in the Mulroney era. Outside the business community, few of them were on the prime minister's side. Most—from influential environmental non-governmental organizations to militant labour unions such as the postal workers—opposed him, often on blatantly partisan grounds.

All this happened too rapidly for anyone to fully notice its impact on the political culture, least of all the toll it was taking on political reputations, especially that of the prime minister. John Diefenbaker said that the job of the Opposition is to oppose. Following the 1984 election, the media felt they needed to offset the government's massive majority by doing the job the parliamentary Opposition was initially too numerically weak, unsettled, and dispirited to do themselves: oppose the Mulroney government. And they did so at every turn. Prominent journalists such as *Ottawa Citizen* editor Keith Spicer made no bones about either their militancy or motivation. (Spicer's admission was made on Radio-Canada's *Le Point*, as Brian Mulroney notes in his memoirs).[22] What was done in the name of balance soon took on a life of its own, creating an even worse form of imbalance: The Fourth Estate became powerful in its own right, not just a check on the other power holders. *They* were now dictating the national agenda, no longer merely reporting it. The wielding of power—some would say abuse of it—had come full circle. The "nobles" were now the oppressed, "the bulwark of democracy" the oppressors. The impact on the government's public standing, and that of the prime minister in particular, was far out of proportion to the facts on the ground. Everyone except the government itself—the media, the Opposition, the special interest groups, anyone within an inch of a megaphone—was just having too good a time. The contagion soon reached dimensions that rendered it incapable of being stopped or at best slowed, even if the instigators wanted to discipline themselves—and they did not. It is no wonder, then, that there is such a wide disconnect between the actual record of the Mulroney government and how it was perceived—and between the actual man Brian Mulroney is and how *he* was viewed.

If the town crier shouts it loudly and often enough, he can make townsfolk believe that the butcher, the baker, or the candlestick maker lacks a trade. Surveys conducted by Numeris, a Canadian organization that measures television audience size, revealed that, on average, Canadians watch a whopping thirty hours of TV a week. That's a lot of time to brainwash people into believing that their pork sirloin, their baguettes, and their candelabra tapers come not from a tradesman, but from someone else. In the land where television is king, perception, not reality, sits on the throne. This medium never lies because it creates its own truth.

Distanced from all the ground noise, which only now is beginning to abate for Mulroney, historians eventually will be able to judge dispassionately the extent of this prime minister's greatness in office. Then, when the record is allowed to speak for itself, it might finally be heard. One thing history teaches us is that time reshapes the narrative of most historical figures and events. It likely will in Mulroney's case. I believe that, in time, the man *will* be rated in the top tier of Canadian prime ministers. His record on the environment alone—the best of any Canadian PM in history—makes him at least a contender. Meanwhile, the obstacles any major politician faces in receiving history's laurel are much bigger now than ever before. The biggest of all is the untamed Wild West frontier that the Internet has opened. In that vast, unregulated media wasteland, everybody packs a .45 Colt but no one wears a sheriff's badge. So the public figure—not just the politician, but also the entertainer, the professional athlete, the bestselling author, the media personality, and every other type of celebrity—is forever on the firing line. This is not democracy but a new form of anarchy. It places no value on personal privacy or public reputation or the truth about people. What titillates and entertains, rather than what informs and elevates, drives the narrative—right over the cliff of objective facts.

The Internet—such a force for good in many other ways—has rendered politics a murderous killing field for people's reputations. That's because, as we have seen, politics, more than any other field, is all about individuals marketing themselves to others—what I call the three "W's": *who* they are, *what* they believe and know, and *why* the voter should support them. "Politicians are their own product," David Brooks has said.[23] Never before has that product been more vulnerable to indiscriminate attack. Nor have its defences ever been weaker. The belligerent nation-state is no longer the strongest threat to world order and civilization. Rather, it is ISIS-type borderless terrorist organizations. By the same token, "democratic" political combat has changed fundamentally since the dawn of the Internet. For a major politician, cyberspace, not any official political opponent or party on the other side, poses the greatest challenge to his or her reputation and electoral prospects. In such a war game, no soldier is safe, especially from anonymous assailants. Put another way, in this new world every emperor is shown to have no clothes—sometimes literally when hackers wreak their havoc. Consequently, all contemporary and recent national political leaders alike, among them Brian Mulroney, face long odds of being considered great—"clothed in ermine," as it were—while still alive, if ever. The bile heaped on Mulroney has not substantially abated, in toxicity even if in amount, in the almost quarter-century since he left office. With the passage of time, might history and Canadians treat Brian Mulroney the way history and Americans have come to view, say, Harry Truman? Like Mulroney, Truman left office under a cloud, if not in disgrace. Historians now rank this president in the top ten out of forty-four presidents in all. Despite the apparent long odds in this Internet Age, my bet is the same will happen for Mulroney. In the following section are my reasons.

# An Impressive Environmental Record

When Brian Mulroney left office in June 1993, he and his government were deeply unpopular. Any government tends to be disliked after an extended time in power—nearly a decade in Mulroney's case. This is especially true if, as with this government, the administration has been activist. The more one does, the more oxen get gored. Mulroney had bloodied many an ox by the time he departed 24 Sussex Drive. "Not surprisingly, a time came when Canadians wanted some relief from high-octane nation-building," Joe Clark has noted.[24] Years after retiring as prime minister, Mulroney defined transformative leadership as that which "makes a significant difference in the life of a nation—[and] recognizes that political capital is acquired to be spent in great causes for one's country."[25] The former prime minister made that statement in the context of Winston Churchill, but I believe he could have applied the term "transformative leadership" to his stewardship of Canada from 1984 to 1993. No question, the man had spent virtually all his own political capital—I believe overwhelmingly for the public good—by the time he officially closed the account and departed the institution. But the PM could leave office with his head held high, for he had created a rich legacy with that capital. I have identified many of his major accomplishments in different parts of this book, particularly in the environmental field because of my special interest and involvement there. Some of that environmental record bears mentioning—or repeating—here. The Mulroney government was, for example, the first in the world to ratify a landmark biodiversity convention. It had the same distinction on climate change. In the face of hostility from Atlantic Canada, where the federal Tories had several provincial governments and many federal MPs, the government nevertheless placed a moratorium on cod fishing to restore badly depleted stocks. That took guts—and an ethos greener than an Irish meadow. The Mulroney government's Green Plan, which contained a multiplicity of specific measures and pronouncements, was the first-ever effort by Ottawa to take a strategic approach to environmental planning.

On my watch as environment minister, the Mulroney government established or completed, besides the first stage of the Rouge National Urban Park, five other new national parks: Ellesmere Island, Pacific Rim, Bruce Peninsula, South Moresby, and Grasslands. In the same "green" spirit, our government overhauled the *National Parks Act* for the first time in half a century. Among other long-overdue reforms, we criminalized certain offences against endangered or threatened wildlife, jacked up fines (previously just licences to kill), and made serious jail time the penalty for worst offenders. The Mulroney government also reformed, strengthened, and consolidated federal pollution laws through CEPA. Targeting in particular the country's most lethal toxic chemicals, this landmark legislation replaced the antiquated *Environmental Contaminants Act* and *Clean Air* and *Water Acts*. The Mulroney government also signed legally binding acid-rain-control agreements with every one of the relevant seven provinces, most notably Quebec and Ontario. Though important in their own right domestically, the agreements gave Canadians clean hands to successfully press the United States to strike an acid rain treaty with our country.

The Mulroney government's worldwide leadership on climate change came a full generation before Al Gore helped make the issue a major international concern and received the Nobel Peace Prize for doing so. The Montreal Protocol on ozone depletion that the Mulroney government orchestrated was the first major global agreement on the environment since the Law of the Sea. It was also the most important, for the ozone layer is all that shields humans from the sun's most lethal cancer-causing rays. "Perhaps the single most successful international agreement to date has been the Montreal Protocol," UN Secretary-General Kofi Annan has said. In September 2014, Achim Steiner, executive director of the United Nations Environment Programme, announced that the ozone layer "is on track to recovery by the middle of this century." Scientists have documented that all but 2 percent of the ozone-depleting substances to be eliminated under the terms of the Montreal Protocol have now been phased out. Steiner echoed Kofi Annan's assessment, calling the achievement "one of the great success stories of international collective action in addressing a global environmental change phenomenon."[26] This milestone would never have happened, or at least not as early as it did, but for the leadership of a Canadian Tory government. Sir John A. Macdonald, take a bow. The Mulroney government also outlawed lead in gasoline throughout Canada. It slashed allowable motor vehicle nitrogen-oxide exhaust emissions, a precursor to acid rain and key component of smog (ground-level ozone). Indeed, overall it was the most activist federal government in history on the environment—and the most productive.[27]

Any assessment of Brian Mulroney's overall record as prime minister should award him points based not only on the political salience *today* of specific challenges he faced head-on, but also on how the public viewed those challenges *at the time*. Climate change, for example, is a huge issue now. But Brian Mulroney's government acted courageously on that issue when few outside the scientific community understood its potential gravity and most politicians didn't even know what it meant and weren't much interested in finding out. That does not make the government's achievement back then any less praiseworthy. It makes it more so. Vision counts. Conversely, it would be easy to discount, if not overlook, the government's strong record on acid rain. Hardly anyone mentions acid rain nowadays, but it was top of mind then, when the problem itself was critical. The issue was removed from the national agenda a generation ago because the Mulroney government acted to solve it. Leadership requires vision *and* action. Great leaders are credited with both. Historical context matters in rating political leaders long after the issues that shaped their legacies have dropped from the public agenda and disappeared from voters' minds. It will be the job of historians to chronicle the issues Brian Mulroney faced, the vision he showed, and the actions he took while they assess by those standards the legacy he left. May historians be more balanced and fairer than Mulroney's harshest media, parliamentary, and interest-group critics were in real time.

# Other Major Measures

Among other major accomplishments outside my own bailiwick, the Mulroney government actively supported the UN coalition to drive Iraq from Kuwait. It modernized Canada's military, including a range of equipment from trucks to small arms. The government privatized some twenty-three Crown corporations no longer deemed vital as government assets to the national interest. These included Air Canada and, as we have seen, Petro-Canada. The country accepted large numbers of refugees from El Salvador and Guatemala while leading the whole world in famine relief in Ethiopia. The government set annual immigration targets at a minimum 250,000 a year, no matter our country's economic conditions at any given time.

And in 1988 it passed the *Multiculturalism Act*, legally enshrining multiculturalism as official state policy. In the same spirit, under Mulroney the national government formally apologized to Canadians of Japanese ancestry for interring them or their forebears during the Second World War, as he had called on the Trudeau government to do while Opposition leader. Moreover, the government also paid $300 million to compensate about 22,000 Japanese-Canadian families whose property had been wrongfully confiscated as part of the internment. (The Reform/Alliance Party was born, in part, in opposition to such policies. Not all Canadian Conservatives are the same—or equally moral.)

Elsewhere here, I detail efforts Brian Mulroney made to appoint more women to important government positions and to promote those already in the system— for example, my own deputy minister, Geneviève Ste-Marie, at Environment Canada. The biggest step he took in that direction was placing strong women—among them, Flora MacDonald, Barbara McDougall, Pat Carney, and Kim Campbell—in major Cabinet posts and in the most powerful Cabinet committees, including P & P and Operations. I have no idea who he privately supported to succeed him as PC leader and, automatically, as prime minister. But, indisputably, he tipped the scales in Kim Campbell's favour by promoting her from Justice to Defence as the leadership campaign got under way. This action not only elevated her profile and standing, but also enriched her credentials and broadened her policy specialties.

Other Mulroney government measures already mentioned but worth repeating are: replacing the jobs-destroying manufacturers' sales tax with the goods and services tax; negotiating the Canada–United States Free Trade Agreement (later the North American Free Trade Agreement); making valiant efforts to recognize Quebec as a distinct society in the Constitution (Meech Lake, Charlottetown Accord); and helping to lead the fight against apartheid in South Africa, flouting the wishes of some of Canada's strongest allies, notably the United States and the United Kingdom. These and other initiatives one could list constitute a remarkable record of activist government. They sought to improve the lives of Canadians, build the country, strengthen its place in the world, give Canadians more confidence in themselves as a people, increase their collective pride in their homeland, and advance the interests of Canadians not yet born, particularly through aggressive actions on the environment. Many Canadians might have ended up not liking Martin Brian Mulroney by the time he left office. But no reasonable person could gainsay his commitment to the country and his legacy in important areas of our national life—not least, Canadians' natural heritage.

Let those who were disillusioned with the Stephen Harper government be reminded of this indisputable fact: there once was a Canadian Conservative Party that believed government should act with fiscal discipline but boldness and vision in the interests of the country and all its people. Despair should not be allowed to extinguish hope that such a Conservative Party could exist again. For all the water that has flowed under the Tory bridge since Mulroney's enlightened period in office, the structure still stands and the current below remains vigorous even if the former is tottering and the latter strayed far from its true path in the Harper era. The bridge was strong and the current right recently enough that the span could be rebuilt and the water's course rerouted. Some smart engineers and skilled carpenters are needed to make it happen. But the first requirement is a new foreman or forewoman able and willing to reach back in time for a reliable set of blueprints to get the job done.

Just as everyone committed to good governance should look to the way Robert Stanfield prepared himself and his party for office through well-developed, evidence-based policy, so also it would be well to reflect on Brian Mulroney's substantially different leadership model towards the same end. It is a model that relied much less on a protracted deliberative process, as in Stanfield's case, than on building a powerful network of personal relationships across the country and then employing them systematically and strategically to win and hold power. Stanfield's model is unlike any before or since. Though unique, it is eminently capable of being imitated and improved upon if only the political will could be summoned.

Brian Mulroney had less legislative or governmental executive experience prior to becoming prime minister than any other PM in Canadian history. But the Quebecer knew the political value of personal relations, of winning chips based on the human factor, hoarding them until the stakes were highest, and then cashing them in when the pot was richest. Is it any wonder, then, that the infamous "roll of the dice" metaphor would have flowed so naturally from the man's tongue concerning Meech Lake? This phrase reflected the wheeling and dealing—and, yes, gambling—nature of politics when conducted by a master of the game. That political game is in Mulroney's blood, just as Robert Stanfield's more painstaking, deliberative, and cautious approach was in his. The Stephen Harper government urgently needed, but never received, a transfusion of either Robert Stanfield's or Brian Mulroney's blood type, ideally a vial of both. The Canadian Conservative Party's tradition as a force for progressive policies and values—already badly weakened after these two men departed the Tory leadership—will perish altogether if, in the post-Harper era, the blood transfusion is not soon conducted.

Unlike Stanfield's and Mulroney's managerial styles—*process* and *personality*, respectively—Harper's modus operandi could be best characterized as the *cult model*. A leader in this tradition is his or her own senior advisor. He or she expects deference—not merely respect but submission—from everyone within the system. When followed, this model centralizes power in the leader's hands at the expense of democracy itself. "I have been involved with Canadian cabinets and ministers for more than fifty years going back to the Diefenbaker period," Joe Clark has penned, "and Stephen Harper [accumulated] more personal power, as prime minister, than anyone else in that half-century."[28] Clark argues that Harper achieved an unprecedented concentration of power by, among other things, limiting the amount and types of information made available to Parliament and the public; politicizing the Prime Minister's Office well beyond the acceptable norm; and using the traditionally non-partisan Privy Council Office as, in effect, an adjunct of the prime minister's partisan operation.

Tom Flanagan, a US-born academic based in Calgary (whom I profile later), helped shepherd Stephen Harper to power. He has written about Harper's "desire to exercise unhampered control over the [Conservative] party." Flanagan says this desire "was…congenital to Harper's basic personality, which is dominant and controlling in all matters in which he is personally involved."[29] This is the classic definition of the cult figure. His detractors notwithstanding, Brian Mulroney was of a far different sort as a politician and government head. Although Mulroney ran a tight ship as prime minister, he was no William Bligh, his government no HMS *Bounty*, his crew no band of disgruntled mutineers. Keeping shipmates happy so they could advance as a team through troubled waters was the very essence of his leadership style. John Diefenbaker's antithetical style, analogous to Harper's, did cause his ranks to mutiny.

If the Canadian electorate hadn't booted him from office, mightn't the same fate eventually have befallen Harper? History teaches us there's always a breaking point. Margaret Thatcher is a classic case abroad, Joey Smallwood at home. Their respective parliamentary caucuses—not their electorates—forced both politicians from office.

Integral to the *cult model* is a heavy dependence on zealotry and exclusiveness. The Harper government had a parliamentary majority at the end. But, as Joe Clark has observed, it always had a minority mindset, preoccupied as it was with consolidating its own political base, "rather than encourage or construct any serious national consensus." Clark says these people "[did] not believe in active government, and [thought] that previous governments had become active in fields they should not have been." He notes that the government devoted more time and energy to reversing measures taken by other governments than to taking legislative and other initiatives of its own. The prime minister and Cabinet had, he argues, "a substantially negative view of government, which contrasts sharply with Canada's historic and bipartisan creation of public institutions as essential partners and leaders in building a strong country, economy and society."[30] In a nutshell, this was a government with a blinkered vision of Canada's potential and of its place in the world. The Harper government's limited mindset caused the country to forgo opportunities to build a stronger future for its people at home and to seek common cause with other nations in such areas as the environment and human health, so important to human beings everywhere. Like beauty, leader-centred cults and ideological zealots are only skin deep—devoid of substance beyond the surface, of longevity beyond the now, of allure beyond the ephemeral glow. If the Canadian Conservative Party's historic role as a vehicle for progressive values is to be restored in the post-Harper era, those from that era still in charge will need a vision beyond the beauty only they can see in their own reflection.

However imperfect the Mulroney government might have been, and however flawed Mulroney himself doubtless was as prime minister, this was a government and he a leader that did much good for the country. It is a standard by which the Stephen Harper government fell far short. When the Mulroney haters and virulent attackers finish their say—which, to this point, has smothered the voices in praise of the man and his achievements—historians will speak. I have no doubt they will be more positive about this prime minister and his government than contemporary critics have been. Surely, there must be some categories in which dispassionate observers are prepared to accord him, if not "the best Canadian prime minister" accolade—as environmentalists belatedly have done in their field—then at least a gold star. Expanding foreign markets for Canada's goods and services and breaking down international barriers against what we produce and sell? Fiscal discipline? Tax reform? Narrowing income inequality? Restoring badly damaged relations with international allies, especially the United States? Fighting for and advancing human rights and gender equality at home and abroad? Strengthening national unity? Laying the groundwork for parts of Atlantic Canada (Newfoundland, in particular) to become "have," rather than "have-not," Confederation partners? Promoting understanding and harmony between English- and French-speaking Canadians? Championing federalism in Quebec? Striving to obtain that province's signature on the country's new Constitution? May a fairer assessment come of Martin Brian Mulroney's record in all such areas before the man himself is history.

# ROGUES GALLERY

Politics is not for those who crave friendship. "If you want a friend, get a dog," Harry Truman famously said of Washington, DC. The same applies to Ottawa—Cabinet life in particular. Friendships are especially hard to make among ministerial colleagues.

How strong a factor is shared political label or ideology or philosophy in cementing personal relationships among colleagues? Not very. Three factors explain why. First, Cabinet ministers rarely get to know one another well, let alone forge strong personal bonds. They work too hard and travel too often and are too exhausted to find time and stamina to connect with one another outside politics. Commuting between Ottawa and the riding—for some MPs, thousands of miles each way—is itself tiring, physically and emotionally stressful, and time-consuming. The system, for all its rewards by certain standards, is fatally punishing—in some cases, literally.

The second reason is institutional. In Canada, at the federal level, most Cabinet decisions—save the most "macro" and political—are made in major Cabinet committees. Lose the battle there, and all is lost. Win it, and all that remains is the laurel ceremony. The process pits one Cabinet minister, and one portfolio, against another in a fight to the death for the few bones in the yard. The process is adversarial and confrontational. The big, voluble, wisecracking panda bear that was John Crosbie in Question Period only minutes earlier is now a killing machine tearing into your pet project. Well, his is next! The norm involves many more ministers chasing many more dollars for many more programs or projects than there is funding to disperse. The competition and attendant rancour can get nasty and the consequent toll on personal relations high.

The third reason friendships don't typically blossom among Cabinet colleagues is that, apart from a shared party label and commitment to public service, few have much, if anything, in common with one another as individuals. Seldom is there enough shared personal experience, or even common demographics, to support anything but the most superficial personal link. I was, for example, a full generation younger than many of my Cabinet colleagues, Jean Charest *two* generations younger than some of his. Politics is the only profession or trade that does not require of practitioners common education or training or licensure or other common denominator, except for getting elected. In other fields, these requirements bind practitioners to one another at every stage, from enrolment to graduation to internship/articling/practicum to professional or vocational practice. The very process of becoming, say, a lawyer, transforms the individual in a way that automatically gives him or her kinship with others in the same profession, even total strangers. There's a reason one speaks of "a legal mind." All lawyers are presumed to have, generally speaking, the same kind from the process that made them lawyers in the first place. By contrast, politicians enter politics and get themselves elected in as many different ways as there are candidates and politicians. It's hardly the basis for communality. A disproportion-ate number of lawyers populates politics, though that is changing. But it is the fact they are lawyers—not politicians—that gives them whatever kinship they might feel towards one another professionally or personally once in the public arena. Politics, by its very nature, is adversarial. Just as that's true of Cabinet colleagues battling for both scarce tax dollars and career advancement, so it is also true of candidates doing battle on the hustings. The system drives players apart. It does not bring them together. Even within my province, I had no more in common personally with any one of the other three Island MPs (PC or Liberal) with whom I served in three Parliaments than I had with my barber, my dentist, or the kid who mowed my lawn. Fellow Tory Island MP David MacDonald, a United Church ordained minister, bap-tized my first child, Kelly, at our home in PEI. She should consider herself blessed in more ways than one, for there is no finer man than he. But geography and hectic schedules stood in the way of our becoming closer. Most of my colleagues across the country experienced the same lack of personal bonding with colleagues. The excep-tions were the few who, to economize, shared apartments in Ottawa while separated from their spouses and families back in the ridings. In those cases, more than space and rent were shared: companionship and mutual support were, too. But even then, how much quality time did such apartment mates actually spend with each other? Not a lot, in most instances—again, too busy, too ambulatory, too tired. At the politi-cal level, if not the bureaucratic, the nation's capital is a sea of strangers in different ships passing one another silently in the night—when not colliding in pursuit of the same deepwater channel.

That said, in my time in government, I formed either positive or negative impressions of all my Cabinet and Opposition colleagues. I sketch some of those col-leagues below as exemplars of the qualities I most admire in politicians or—in excep-tional cases—most detest. Within Cabinet, I begin with a fellow Atlantic Canadian, John Crosbie, quintessentially in the first category. My penultimate Tory case, Erik Nielsen, is quintessentially in the latter. As for Opposition portraits in this ancient Rogues Gallery (Jean Chrétien and John Turner), the view was both too close and too far—not to mention from too partisan an angle—for this Libran to know his own mind fully. So, based on "what mine eye doth catch," as Shakespeare would say, the reader must decide.

# The Good, the Bad, and the Ugly

## JOHN CROSBIE

No other minister in the Mulroney government in my time in Cabinet battled harder for his or her province than John Crosbie did for Newfoundland. He was tenacious, tireless, and almost always triumphant. For that, every Newfoundlander should feel grateful; without question, every Newfoundlander is the richer for it. By hook or by crook or by Crosbie, no other province, with the exception of Quebec, benefited more from discretionary federal spending, in particular, because of Cabinet clout than Newfoundland did during this period. That said, there was nothing so like déjà vu as John Crosbie in full Newfie bore trying to squeeze every last copper penny for his province from an overextended Treasury. This was especially true in the policy-structured Cabinet committees, where the stakes were highest and he was at his strongest competitive advantage. As we have seen, it was there that, typically, the pivotal spending decisions were made before being approved—virtually *pro forma*—by the full Cabinet. For certain major decisions, Priorities and Planning or Operations was where the real power was wielded. John Crosbie served on both committees. There was no escaping this man's grasping hooks.

John Crosbie was the most brilliant individual at the Cabinet table. He is part of a wealthy established family whose influence Peter Newman has said "[had] no equal in Newfoundland."[1] John is the grandson of Sir John Chalker Crosbie, founder of the Crosbie dynasty. Sir John's son Ches, the eldest of eleven children, turned an emerging conglomerate into a modern commercial behemoth of construction and other companies with annual revenues of tens of millions of dollars and nearly three thousand employees at its peak. There was no area of the Newfoundland economy in which the Crosbie family was without a major stake. Airways, merchant ships, hotels, trucking operations, newspapers, insurance agencies, and factories of diverse kinds were dominated by the family. John Crosbie had excelled academically: University Medal winner in political studies at Queen's; University Medalist in Law at Dalhousie; Viscount Bennett Scholarship winner at Dalhousie as the outstanding law student in his graduating year (1956). No one was going to challenge John Crosbie in Cabinet without being darn sure of the facts, prepared for a bloody fight, and resigned to probable defeat—even if all went the best it could for the challenger.

I had little in common with John Crosbie. Certainly not his extraordinary brainpower and academic record—hardly anyone around Ottawa could compete with him by that standard. Moreover, he was much older than I: he was born in 1931, I in 1945. Plus, he was more senior in Cabinet. But we did share three major factors. First, we were both islanders: he from Newfoundland, I from Prince Edward Island. Second, we were both from Atlantic Canada. Third, our provinces (and British Columbia) were the only jurisdictions that had negotiated terms under which they had joined Confederation. This last common denominator between John Crosbie and me was not just an interesting and uniquely shared historical footnote. It sometimes had massive federal spending implications, including for the two of us — not always on the same side. The tale of the two islands' circumstances demonstrates how the Mulroney government functioned both managerially and politically. More to the point, it shows John Carnell Crosbie's formidable impact on that government.

In 1864, the colony of Prince Edward Island hosted the Charlottetown Conference, the first meeting of the Fathers of Confederation on their journey (often literally) to forge a new country from disparate and distant pieces of real estate. Initially, these were the parts that now constitute the provinces of Ontario, Quebec, Nova Scotia, and New Brunswick. But even though we Islanders cradled the birth of Canada, we did not join the baptism in 1867—only the confirmation in 1873. By the latter date, the Island was broke and getting steadily broker. We had become destitute by defying Archimedes' tenet of physics: the shortest distance between two points is a straight line. Responding to the "gold rush" in real estate values occasioned by the building of the Island's railway, local politicians of the day wound the rails through as many different properties as they could. The practice lined the pockets of certain landowners close to the governing clique, but it emptied the colony's coffers. Worse, the railway wasn't completed. Put simply, PEI joined Canada to be bailed out. We had no alternative. The colony had to be literally railroaded into Confederation.

The Island used what little bargaining power it had to negotiate entry to extract—in a short and simple legal document—several significant Terms of Union. Among other things, the newly formed federal government was required to maintain and operate specific public services, the most important of which was "[e]fficient steam services for the conveyance of mails and passengers." In practical terms, this meant a commitment to complete the Island's creatively circuitous railway and to operate it permanently, and also to guarantee a continuous ferry service between the new province and the mainland. It was in the spirit of these particular terms of PEI's entry to Confederation that, more than a century later, the Confederation Bridge would be constructed and, in 1997, completed. The Island's railway, which at one point travelled by ferry, was eventually eliminated. As was the ferry service itself following construction of the bridge, except between the Island and Nova Scotia from early May to late December.

For its part, Newfoundland settled its Terms of Union with Canada on December 11, 1948. Then a protectorate of the United Kingdom, it became a province of Canada three months later, on March 31, 1949, by an act of the Imperial Parliament in London. Unlike PEI's, Newfoundland's terms were long, detailed, technical, and legalistic. Provisions covered everything from public debt to education to margarine. For the new province, the federal government agreed to operate rail transportation throughout Newfoundland and between it and the mainland (effectively through Canadian National Railway, a federal Crown corporation). If anything, the federal rail commitment was even more important to Newfoundland than to PEI because the former was much farther from the mainland: 154 kilometres versus 13. It still takes over five hours in the summer, and more than seven in the winter, to ferry one way between Newfoundland and the mainland. By contrast, the required time—aside from lineups, often long—was only about thirty-five minutes when the ferry service operated between PEI and New Brunswick.

All of which brings me to Exhibit A to demonstrate John Crosbie's powerful clout in Cabinet and the massive amount of money he was able to extract from the federal treasury for his province and—as a big dividend—for his own continuous re-elections, often in the face of strong tidal waves against the PC Party, nationally, regionally, or both. That's not just because, from earliest times, his riding (St. John's West) had a strong Tory core. It's also because Crosbie consistently brought home the bacon. Or, since it is John Crosbie being discussed here, prime Kansas rib-eye steak.

The Government of Canada hemorrhaged a fortune honouring its commitment, under Newfoundland's Terms of Union, to operate the province's railway. CN had been losing $23.5 million—equivalent to over $100 million today—every year as far back as the mid-1970s. A special federal-provincial investigation, the Sullivan Commission, established in 1977, urged that the Newfoundland railway be eliminated within ten years, beginning immediately. The recommendation was accepted by all parties concerned. By June 1988, the last phase was announced. In exchange, the federal government was to give Newfoundland a staggering $800 million for a "Roads for Rails" package. In effect, rail (including passenger service) would be moved to highways, for which the funds would be used to expand and upgrade service.

I participated in the Cabinet committee debate about the required funding. If John Crosbie could not get Cabinet approval at this stage, the proposed new transportation strategy would not proceed. If he succeeded, the funding would probably be approved by Cabinet as a whole and the plan set on track—or, rather, on the road. Crosbie had already conducted all the relevant "bilaterals" with the treasury and finance ministers. Like some other ministers, however, I believed Crosbie had gone to the federal well once too often for Newfoundland. And I thought he had done so unfairly at the expense of other provinces, my own included. But, in fairness to him, that was how the game was played: every minister for himself or herself, every province for itself. Collegiality stops at the water's edge, in this case the rocky shores of Newfoundland.

Originally appointed minister of justice when the Mulroney government took office in September 1984, John Crosbie became minister of transport in 1986. Following the completion of the Canada-United States Free Trade Agreement, after the 1988 election, he became minister for international trade. From these various high perches, Crosbie engineered the federal government's becoming a minority but vital stakeholder in the multi-billion-dollar Hibernia oil development in Newfoundland. The total public-private price tag was $16 billion over nineteen years. The federal government's commitment, for its 8.5 percent share, was $1 billion; federal loan guarantees would total $3.7 billion. In return, the government would receive 10 percent of the profits. Though the final Hibernia deal post-dated my time in Cabinet, the federal government's initial commitment to become involved was made while I was in Cabinet in the mid-eighties. Oil production would not begin until a decade later. The first barrel was, in fact, produced only in 1997. Whatever the merits of the project itself, the political and corporate *cognoscenti* believed at the time—and, certainly, Crosbie argued vociferously in Cabinet—that, without the federal government's equity involvement, the project could not, and would not, advance. As always, Crosbie got his way. The federal government's commitment to the mega-project was made. Hundreds of millions of federal dollars were earmarked for Newfoundland for this purpose, on top of an already-mountainous pile. The Hibernia project marched—on a field of federal cash.

The fact Hibernia proceeded, against all the political and financial odds, can be explained by two factors—and two only: *John Crosbie* and *Brian Mulroney*. They were the sole ministers in a forty-member Cabinet who wanted the federal government to rescue the project when it was at the point of total collapse after one of the major petroleum company partners (Gulf Canada Resources) withdrew its equity participation. All this came to a head at the very time Newfoundland premier Clyde Wells had sunk the Meech Lake Accord. Lowell Murray, the government Senate leader at the time, told me: "Some ministers/MPs from Quebec and elsewhere found our generosity [to Newfoundland] almost impossible to swallow; and others reflected a majority opinion among economic/financial commentators who believed [Hibernia] would turn out to be a losing investment, period." And yet, Crosbie's clout with the prime minster was sufficient to turn the tide. And now, in my time in Cabinet, the same minister was seeking from Cabinet an almost equal commitment of federal dollars for highways in his province. "If Cabinet refuses to approve this funding, our party will not elect a single goddamned MP in Newfoundland in the next election." That's what Crosbie said about the $800 million he was seeking for "Road for Rails." He made the same charge so often in Cabinet about so many other Newfoundland causes, both large and small, that it should have been tattooed on the man's tongue. It would have saved us all from having to listen to it incessantly.

I argued vehemently at Cabinet that $800 million was too much money for a single province, especially one that had received so much previously, and would be getting still more for Hibernia. I also argued that the province's premier, the hot-headed Brian Peckford, would not give us any credit if the money were approved. Elected premier in 1979, Peckford retired from office in January 1989. Meanwhile, the nominal Tory spent a decade attacking virtually everything the Mulroney government did. Nothing was ever good enough, big enough, or timely enough for his province to suit him. But then, he took credit for it all, anyway. The premier spared no venom against the Mulroney government, including John Crosbie himself, with whom he often publicly feuded. Crosbie conceded my point but pressed on, nevertheless. Yet again, he got his hundreds of millions. True to form, Peckford took the lion's share of the credit for the "Roads for Rail" program. Just as he was to claim total credit in Newfoundland for the Mulroney government's Atlantic Accord concerning management of revenues from the island's offshore oil and gas development (detailed earlier). The premier also took credit for the Atlantic Canada Opportunities Agency (ACOA), the creation of which was for the whole Atlantic region, not merely Newfoundland! Brian Peckford spent most of his re-election campaign in April 1985 stylizing himself as the "Great Negotiator" for having won all such wonderful federal prizes for the province. It was as though John Crosbie and Brian Mulroney had played no role whatsoever—or had even been born. Peckford's head had as many rocks as his province. But, again, that's the way the game was played at the time. Newfoundlanders played it as well as anyone. In the 1985 provincial election, the premier won a landslide—49 percent to the Liberals' 37 percent.

The first federal general election after John Crosbie had scooped up all those federal billions for Newfoundland over a four-year period, under threat of PC annihilation in the province if we didn't act, was in 1988. In that election, the national PC Party lost every seat in the province except Crosbie's and one other. Crosbie did not run in the subsequent national election, in 1993. In that election, when the highway and oil money that Crosbie had finagled for Newfoundland was pumping into the Newfoundland economy faster than water from a firehose, the national PC Party lost *every* seat in his province. The PCs lost even the seat Crosbie himself had held since 1976—almost two decades in all. So much for Newfoundland votes for federal money! The technical term in political science is, I think, "Newfie Joke." This time, the joke was on the Mulroney Cabinet. I had warned them!

My "I told you so" sentiments reflect, no doubt, sibling rivalry between a pair of Cabinet ministers who represented Canada's two poorest provinces at the time. Our islands shared not only poverty, but also parallel circumstances as Confederation partners—geographic, historic, and cultural. Both jurisdictions—one a high rock, the other a low sandbar—are insular fragments of the British Isles struggling to exist in hostile waters in the North Atlantic. In my time in Cabinet, as long as John Crosbie was around, Newfoundland was at a tremendous advantage over PEI and most other parts of Canada in the fiscal wars. The reason wasn't just Crosbie's political heavyweight status. It was his oversized persona and presence, too. The man was as much a giant physically as politically. His very height and weight, which nearly topped the charts in the latter case, gained still greater dimension merely by his being John Crosbie. In every way, this was an extraordinary politician, and he a unique man. The Newfie giant entered politics and government to do a job: fight for Newfoundland and Labrador's interests against all challengers and obstacles. David had not a slingshot's chance on Jupiter against this Goliath and his mighty one-man army—himself. No reasonable person can fault him for having won virtually every battle and all the ones that counted. I don't. I have nothing but admiration for the way he pressed his advantage and rolled over anyone who tried to block his passage. I tried to do the same for my province, albeit from lower ground and without all the Newfie titan's armour and weaponry.

But here's the thing. In my own time in politics, I was the most vocal public champion for the Confederation Bridge between Prince Edward Island and New Brunswick. That permanent connection between our province and the mainland we Islanders had dreamed about from the first day a spike was hammered into a rail. Although no longer in Cabinet when the so-named Confederation Bridge was finally built, I can say this in the name of the last laugh: We islanders on the Sandbar, not those islanders on the Rock, got the billion dollars for a permanent link to the rest of Canada. Our Confederation bargain was the more complete. Truly, the last laugh *is* the best laugh. Sometimes, David's slingshot—even against Jupiter-strength gravitation pull—*does* hit its mark.

John Crosbie blessed public life merely by being in it. He began as a Liberal in Newfoundland. Indeed, Crosbie ran for the provincial Liberal Party leadership against Joey Smallwood in 1969. Soon afterwards, he converted to Tory, helping to defeat Smallwood and elect Frank Moores premier in 1972, following a virtual tie between the PCs and Liberals in the provincial election the previous year. If, as the saying goes, "there is no zealot like a convert," that explains why John Carnell Crosbie became one of the most zealous Tories of his generation. And, to my mind, one of the finest.

## PAT CARNEY

One Cabinet colleague I especially liked and admired was Pat Carney, from British Columbia. First elected in 1980—a year after me—she and I were seatmates for a time in Opposition. We often shared the same House Duty—purgatory MPs had to endure, in the Commons on a rotation basis, a minimum number of hours each week to help ensure a quorum during routine proceedings. Like others, Pat and I would use the time to attend to the prosaic duties of an everyday MP: correspondence, reading, committee preparation, speech-writing, and so on. And chat. I learned, for instance, that the dazzling gold-set "ruby" she always wore (inherited from an aunt, as I recall) was not a ruby at all but a mere garnet. This fact she had discovered when getting the ring appraised for insurance. "But I love it just as much, anyway," she told me in the House with obvious sincerity. Everything about Pat Carney herself was genuine and sincere, including her infamous temper. If the gods had made Pat part of the natural landscape, instead of the larger-than-life person she actually is, it would have been a volcano—and always active, at that. Was there anyone in Ottawa she did not lather in lava? She lathered me a number of times (more later).

As international trade minister, Pat Carney carried the government's heavy free trade negotiations on her substantial frame. Pat's feuds with chief Canadian negotiator Simon Reisman—no quiet prairie wheatfield himself—were legendary. Brian Mulroney characterizes the Carney/Riesman relationship as "venomous" in his memoirs. Ten years my senior (born in Shanghai in 1935) and a single mom, this former economics consultant and journalist "had not had an easy life," Mulroney notes.[2] I did not know that then; but, maybe, I had sensed it intuitively and this was our bond. For whatever reason, I was one of Pat Carney's biggest fans. And still am. We usually sat next to each other at early-morning Question Period strategy meetings while in Opposition, before I became chairman as deputy House leader. Pat and I would exchange sections of the *Globe and Mail* ("Our *Globe*," she always called it). We would commiserate if either of us had taken a reporter's hit, which happened more often as our respective stars steadily rose. She headlined one of my annual Hillsborough PC Riding Association fundraising dinners, as did other colleagues; among them Perrin Beatty, Jean Charest, John Crosbie, Flora MacDonald, Mike Wilson, and even Mulroney. Most—but not Mulroney—stayed with Kathy and me at our home in Keppoch. So something like a friendship was possible in politics. But, alas, as with Pat and me, there was not much of a personal relationship after we entered Cabinet. Indeed, not once did I ever have coffee or tea—much less dinner and real drinks— just for the pleasure of it with a single fellow Cabinet colleague, including Pat. There was never time.

When Pat Carney was upset with you about something, she let you know—and the world, too. It was common for her to lash out at a colleague at Caucus or Cabinet. A dressing down by Pat was almost a badge of honour, for it placed you in good company with others she had lashed with her sharp tongue. The worst thrashing I received from Pat at Cabinet concerned Pacific Rim National Park Reserve. It is one of the five national parks I am generally credited with having completed while environment minister. The first agreement for the park had been signed in 1970 by the Trudeau government. It became a full-fledged park reserve, however, following difficult negotiations I conducted with the BC government a decade and a half later. Among many sticking points was a long-standing $25-million debt (plus interest) the province claimed the federal government owed it since 1970 regarding a contentious detail tied to the previous agreement. I decided it was not worth holding up a final agreement to complete the park over such a relatively manageable amount. My department's total annual budget was marching smartly towards a billion dollars and would, in fact, reach that level not long after I departed the portfolio. Meanwhile, it was usually possible to find loose change within existing budgetary reserves without resorting to time-consuming haggling with Treasury Board, with invariably unpredictable results, to get additional funding for this kind of thing. As a gesture of good faith, I calculated that we needed to come up with an immediate $8 million towards the total amount allegedly owed to British Columbia. I directed my officials to locate the money from the Parks Canada budget, cut a cheque, put it in my hands, and keep the matter a secret from BC officials and everyone else until I could make the grand gesture by presenting the moolah in person. This is how I knew Jean Chrétien would likely have done it when he was the parks minister.

My strategy was to arrive in British Columbia and by stealth present the cheque to Stephen Rogers, Minister of the Environment and Parks. That way, the province would be denied its excuse to hold up the Pacific Rim Park. Nor would it have time to concoct another bogus one. Secrecy was paramount. But I learned that nothing is more impossible in life than keeping secret an actual $8 million government cheque—as opposed to an electronic transfer, the typical government-to-government mode of payment. Rogers discovered my secret, from my own officials, of all people. Unbeknownst to me and my staff, they had put the information in a news release! I did, however, present the cheque (at a meeting in British Columbia on February 18, 1987). And soon afterwards, I got the park. When Pat Carney discovered I had given her province this money, she was furious. As the "regional minister," she thought she was entitled to be told beforehand and invited to present the cheque herself. Trying to explain to Pat Carney why the presentation had needed to be kept secret, as part of our poker-game negotiations on the park, was like justifying to a jilted bride her groom's sudden need to flee the altar. Pat was in no mood to forgive—or forget. In my memory's ear, I can still hear the tongue-lashing that Pat gave me at full Cabinet. I could tell, however, that everyone was on my side. Written all over their faces was the "Oh, no, here we go again!" look they always showed whenever Mount Vesuvius erupted and buried an unwary villager—in this case, me.

Soon afterwards, all *was* forgiven and forgotten. She and I were attending separate functions at the Carleton Towers Hotel. As I approached the lobby elevator to ascend to the mezzanine for my meeting, I encountered Pat face-to-face inside as the door sprang open following hers. She was totally immobile, incapable of moving a heel or a toe. My colleague had suddenly been hit with the chronic lower-back problem that had so often immobilized her before. "Tom, I can't move," she said plaintively. "Please help me out of this damn elevator." I became her St. Bernard. Hotel patrons and staff were treated to a choice sight: two ministers of the Crown walking arm-in-arm at a swanky hotel as though in the beginning stages of an illicit affair. The earlier cheque contretemps between us suddenly seemed small bore. Long after the fact, one realizes that, no matter how big it might seem at the time, almost everything in politics and government is small bore. But, as with John Crosbie, there is nothing small about Pat Carney—not her person, not her character, not my fond memories of her in Cabinet. Even when I was being entombed in black lava from her white-hot flames.

## PERRIN BEATTY

Another fast-rising Mulroney government star was Perrin Beatty. He famously drove himself to Rideau Hall for the first official Cabinet swearing-in, in September 1984, instead of having his chauffeur do the honours, as the rest of us did. On one occasion, some months afterwards, I was rushing on foot to attend an early-morning meeting about a dozen blocks from Parliament Hill. True to form, Perrin was driving himself somewhere farther afield, spotted me, pulled over, and suggested we have breakfast together some place. I would have loved to, for he was another of my Cabinet favourites. I had to take a rain-check—too busy, too rushed, now running behind too late. Too bad. The breakfast never happened in Ottawa. Not even coffee or tea. Only right after the 1988 election, when I was no longer in Cabinet, did Perrin and I have a private meal together in Ottawa: dinner at a downtown restaurant. That night and place, quite a few re-elected ministers individually hosted defeated Cabinet colleagues. Perrin hosted me. The occasion was congenial but the atmosphere more like that of a wake than a wedding. Are the affairs of state so urgent that almost every second of a Cabinet minister's routine schedule needs to be committed, from daybreak to day's end? Wouldn't everyone, including the public, gain if the system allowed its chief operators some time to smell the coffee, or at least have one? Preferably together.

Perrin and his delightful and mischievous wife, Julie, did stay with Kathy and me a number of times at our home on the Island when he was in the province on government or political business—again, once headlining a fundraiser for me in my Hillsborough riding, just as I did for him in his. First elected in 1972, Perrin became, seven years later, in the short-lived Joe Clark government, the youngest Cabinet minister in history to that point (minister of state for the treasury board). He understudied Treasury Board Minister Sinclair Stevens, just as I was to do with Stevens at the

Department of Regional Industrial Expansion in the Mulroney government before being promoted from Tourism to Environment. Perrin proceeded to hold an array of portfolios—Revenue (1984); Solicitor General (1985–86); Defence (1986–89); Health and Welfare (1989–91); Communications (1991–93); and Secretary of State (1993)—before losing his seat in the Kim Campbell wipeout in 1993. So well-liked and respected was Perrin Beatty across the political divide that Jean Chrétien appointed him to head the CBC following the Liberals' 1993 election win. (He is currently CEO of the Canadian Chamber of Commerce.) Seldom in politics does an individual combine in one package as compactly as Perrin did, throughout his political career, the ideal qualities for public office: intelligence, competence, broad knowledge, communication skills, devotion to duty, personal and political integrity, compassion for the underdog, personality, presence, and sheer likeability. The system, especially media reportage, has a way of erecting an opaque glass panel between steady but unflashy politicians like Perrin Beatty and the public. So their sterling qualities are not appreciated fully—if at all—until after they leave politics. As in Perrin's case, only when the former politician demonstrates in a different field altogether the exact same qualities that he or she had brought to politics do most people stand up and take notice. Meanwhile, the individual is judged by a completely different standard, usually how aggressive or theatrical he or she is in political combat.

When Perrin lost his Commons seat in 1993 and departed politics forever, I was struck that hardly any political pundit commented upon this big loss to public life. The same applies to many such people who leave politics either of their own volition or from electoral defeat. Many a time these people, having contributed the best years of their lives to public office, depart the political stage with nary an ovation or critic's notice for their solid performance. When I was first elected an MP in 1979, Perrin, though five years my junior, was already a veteran of two parliaments. Upon my election, he offered me this advice on how to proceed in my new career: "Always do what you think is right, even if it means offending colleagues. You can always apologize or explain afterwards." I tried to heed his admonition, particularly after being appointed to Cabinet. I never knew Henry Perrin Beatty to do anything but act on his own wise counsel.

After leaving politics, Perrin Beatty lost a young son in tragic circumstances. So, also, did my former Cabinet colleagues Mike Wilson and David Crombie. I had met only David's son, Jonathan Crombie. He was an accomplished actor who played Gilbert Blythe in the Kevin Sullivan-produced Anne of Green Gables films for Walt Disney, PBS, and the CBC, which, of course, were set in my home province. Perrin, Mike, and David now share not only uncommon talent and a powerful commitment to public service, but also the need to meet, with their spouses and families, the biggest challenge fate could have tossed them: the death of a child. These three extraordinary men elevated politics as a vocation by the way they conducted themselves day in and day out, both in private and in the public eye. The world is a lesser place because each of the three sons met an untimely death, well before realizing his full potential. The charmed life most people think politicians have is an illusion. The son of US vice-president Joe Biden, Boe, was cut short by brain cancer far short of living his biblical "three-score years and ten." At age forty-six, Boe was about to seek and likely win the governorship of Delaware. One's heart aches for all such parents.

*Every man who has given any attention to the condition of things and the neces-
sities involved by the entering of the Island into Confederation must admit that
such a tunnel must be constructed if the thing is reasonably practicable.*

—Wilfrid Laurier, letter to the Charlottetown *Guardian*, February
15, 1891

*The tunnel would receive favourable consideration, if cost is a reasonable
amount.*

—Sir John A. Macdonald, House of Commons, June 24, 1891

From 1986 to 1988, Stewart McInnes's Cabinet portfolio was Public Works (also responsible for Canada Mortgage and Housing Corporation). Like me, he was defeated in
the anti–free trade Liberal sweep across Atlantic Canada in the 1988 federal election.
(Liberal Mary Clancy trounced him in Halifax.) Meanwhile, McInnes's singularity in
Cabinet was not derived from any high public profile he achieved, for he had little;
nor from his being especially competent or accomplished, for he wasn't; certainly not
from his ability to dazzle with personal presence, oratory, or sheer personality, for
he couldn't. His most distinguishing quality as a politician was a capacity to be spectacularly maladroit. He would get virtually every Cabinet colleague's vote for the class
member most likely to provoke the response, "How could anyone that smart be that
inept?" McInnes *was* smart. But the man was capable of making the most "I can't
believe he really said that" dumb remark in Cabinet. Worse, he continually made decisions that, however right they might have been managerially, were sure to cause problems for one colleague or another at some point. That colleague most often was me.

On paper, the man's credentials were impressive. He was a senior partner in the
solidly reliable, long-established law firm of McInnes Cooper, which bears his family
name. At Dalhousie law school, he was a contemporary of PEI Tory bagman Alan Scales
of Charlottetown (discussed later). Both men excelled as lawyers. The two remained
friends through the years. And they actively supported Brian Mulroney in the Maritimes
for the national PC Party leadership in 1983. McInnes's close ties to Mulroney were his
strongest claim to a Cabinet post, apart from geography. He was, however, the worst
possible minister to hold the Public Works portfolio when he did. That's because by
far the largest item on his agenda was the proposed billion-dollar Fixed Link between
Prince Edward Island and New Brunswick. This controversial project was so fraught
with potential danger for any politician who touched it that Harry Houdini would have
been challenged to break free from its lock and chains. Even a politically astute and
agile minister of the sort McInnes certifiably was not would have found the issue daunt-
ing. That the accident-prone McInnes was responsible for the Fixed Link file guaranteed that the politics of the project would lead to disaster. And it did.

I discuss the Fixed Link at greater length elsewhere in this book. Suffice it to say
here that two core issues engulfed the project: first, whether replacing the Marine
Atlantic ferry service between PEI and NB with a permanent link made sense in economic cost-benefit terms; and, second, its possible negative environmental impact—
on the Northumberland Strait it would cross, on the fishery, even on the climate (so
opponents claimed), not to mention the Island's elusive "way of life" (mostly characterized by poverty, the project's champions argued).

By a long shot, the more politically explosive of the two core issues was the project's potential environmental impact, for it is impossible to prove a negative. Opponents could, and with intellectual dishonesty did, exploit that iron law of political logic. They made every possible outrageous claim that the project would bring environmental ruin to the Island. How does one prove, for example, that a bridge across the thirteen-kilometre Northumberland Strait would not turn the Island into a desert and thereby ruin potato crops, as charged? Or that lobsters would not stop breeding? Or that mackerel would not become genetically altered and start sporting two heads? As long as one of the three leading proposals for construction was a tunnel, such shrill demagogic arguments were difficult to make and unlikely to scare most Islanders. Because a tunnel would be built *under* the ocean floor, this option was perceived to threaten the Northumberland Strait—or the broader Gulf of St. Lawrence—and its aquatic life far less than a bridge. A bridge, by contrast, would require over sixty massive piles (essentially, concrete pillars) planted deep into the ocean floor to support the span. The construction itself was said to threaten the environment, in addition to the harm allegedly posed by the operation of the bridge once built. The bridge was considered, at a minimum, a potential aesthetic blight—some enormous engineering dragon monster that would overwhelm the Island's pastoral landscape while crushing to smithereens its pure and peaceable ways. For many bridge opponents, the romance of a ferry, compared to a stationary structure, held sway. To these Islanders, as for some others, the tunnel was less offensive than a bridge on "out of sight, out of mind" grounds. They at least would not have to witness the fire-breathing dragon flounce and flail, rampaging fertile farmlands and sylvan fiefs. The beast would be corralled in the darkness of the ocean's depths.

Such were the politics of the tunnel. The facts were substantially different. In truth, the tunnel option had been largely discredited, both in Ottawa and in PEI, among those who knew the practical implications. Vehicles could not have been driven under their own power through an undersea tunnel without posing enormous cost and engineering challenges concerning ventilation. To avoid the ventilation problem, a tunnel would have had to incorporate a rail system that loaded cars and trucks and their drivers and passengers onto an electrically propelled train that towed them all under and across the Northumberland Strait. The requisite technology, however, would have provided travellers little or no net benefit, in either time or convenience, compared to the existing ferry service, much less the competing bridge alternative. Informed critics believed that the tunnel option had been kept alive by influential contractors and investors who would have benefited from building the structure but weren't necessarily committed to the travelling public's welfare or to PEI's economic and social interests. A group of engineers in the federal Department of Public Works was also thought to have had a professional or career stake in the tunnel option. On the other side of the argument, tunnel critics warned that many motorists would resist taking this mode from claustrophobia or other fears, including not being allowed to smoke during the still time-consuming crossing (forty minutes, at a minimum, from loading to unloading). These critics were right—or, at least, not far wrong—on all counts. So, though the bridge proposal was problematic politically—albeit likely doable as a practical matter—the tunnel, by contrast, was already dead in the water long before Stewart McInnes formally spread its ashes farther at sea. But this fact did not prevent the anti–Fixed Link forces from decrying the tunnel option's demise as if a tragic death in the family.

Rational discourse was drowned in a torrent of crocodile tears. The Fixed Link's most militant opponents, especially their standard-bearer David Weale, would have remained opposed to anything but the ferries had God empowered everyone to walk on water across the strait. The elimination of the tunnel option just provided these people with an additional talking point to further demagogue the issue to death. Just as Fixed Link opponents used the tunnel to try to kill the bridge, they would have used the bridge to try to kill the tunnel if the former, rather than the latter, had been eliminated from competition. This deflection tactic was as intellectually dishonest as it was blatant. It was, however, effective with some Islanders, particularly ones viscerally opposed to the Fixed Link but needing a reason to be.

Stewart McInnes could not understand the far-reaching political implications of the bridge-versus-tunnel choice. Nor could he comprehend the need to avoid enflaming political passions as the 1988 election fast approached. He was worse than a bull in a china shop; he was a storming bull elephant in a glass menagerie. On September 30, just fifty-two days before election day, the minister announced the three finalists from among the seven serious project proposals—each advanced by a different mega-contractor—that his department had been considering for the construction of the Fixed Link. The only tunnel proposal among these seven had not made the cut. The PEI-NB crossing would, therefore, definitely be a bridge. The minister had dealt Fixed Link opponents the Ace of Spades—and the project's champions a potentially mortal blow. I tried to warn McInnes of this danger. But he would hear none of it. The minister was hell-bent on extracting maximum publicity from the announcement to enhance his personal profile within the region and nationally and, thereby, improve his uncertain re-election prospects in Halifax.

As environment minister, I had to pull off a treacherous balancing act: on the one hand, continue to lead the project's cause on the Island, in the federal Cabinet, and with the public at large; on the other, remain neutral on all substantive decisions. That neutrality was required because I was responsible for the exhaustive Environmental Review and Assessment Process to which the project would need to be subjected. To preserve the integrity of that process, and prevent any real or perceived conflict of interest, I had decided to recuse myself from the bridge-versus-tunnel choice and announcement. So I was at an enormous disadvantage in trying to prevent my Cabinet colleague from committing hara-kiri with the elimination of the tunnel option before the election.

When Stewart McInnes held a news conference in Charlottetown to announce the three project proposal finalists, all of them for a bridge, I did not attend. At this point, my answering media questions about the potential environmental impacts of a bridge, let alone of one particular bridge proposal compared to others, would have compromised the review process from the start. I refused to succumb to that temptation, however much I might have benefited in my own riding from all the publicity such a major federal government decision would have generated in the short term. Beyond the immediate headlines, I thought that holding the news conference so close to the election was colossally misguided. It would trigger controversy, motivate and mobilize Fixed Link opponents, fortify their arguments, render me an easy target as the public face of the project, and muddy the political waters at a time when I appeared about to sail to easy re-election. But it was just not in my nature to stand in a Cabinet colleague's way on a matter of such import to him. I also thought the choice of finalists could be explained as just part of a much bigger process that preserved the right of the federal government not to proceed with the project at all unless every economic, social, cultural, and environmental concern were satisfied. But I greatly overestimated Stewart McInnes's ability to provide this explanation or even to understand the need to make it. It was only his performance at the news conference that made me fully appreciate the bull elephant's propensity to smash every glass figurine in its path.

Unfortunately for me, my motives were impugned in certain crucial quarters, particularly the media. The stage was set by how CBC Charlottetown covered the McInnes news conference: it highlighted my absence. The CBC took great delight in sending a separate camera crew to film me, at the very time of the conference, attending a student/faculty arts event at Holland College in my riding. I had been invited by the arts department head, Henry Purdy, one of the province's most respected artisans. The ensuing CBC news story implied that, at best, I attached more importance to arts and crafts than to the Fixed Link; at worst, I was trying to distance myself from any political fallout that the Fixed Link announcement might cause. The visual of my being shown how to mould clay at a potter's wheel did not help. How Nero of him!—it implied—potting while the Island burns! What was burning was my political capital.

From all media reports, the minister handled himself poorly at his news conference. He appeared unable to answer even basic Fixed Link questions to anyone's satisfaction. I had asked a senior staffer of mine, Rob Burnett, to monitor the conference for me. I needed a complete and accurate account, and felt I could not get it through media coverage. Rob, born and raised in Charlottetown, is from an old Island family that once owned and operated the Charlottetown *Guardian*. He had been involved in the Fixed Link project for me from my very first days as minister and knew the issue better than anyone else in the province. My staffer did not totally share the prevailing media assessment that Stewart McInnes's news conference had been a disaster. Rob thought McInnes had survived the firing squad with only contusions, not succumbed to a mortal shot. But it soon became clear to me that this day marked the beginning of a very rocky road for the bridge with the PEI media. That road would not end until well after the election—indeed, until the bridge was built nearly a decade later. For some reporters, it has not ended even to this day. They remain opposed and wish the structure had never been constructed. All along, the Fixed Link had been a challenging but manageable issue for me and the Mulroney government. However, with one news conference that was at least clumsy and ill-advised, if not disastrous, Stewart McInnes transformed that issue into the hottest political potato on the Island in over a century. As public works minister, McInnes proved himself an incompetent road builder.

On October, 3, 2015, Stewart Donald McInnes died at age seventy-eight. His own life's journey had ended. I was saddened by Stewart's death. Largely because of him, the Confederation Bridge took a much rockier route politically than it needed to take. But the project did get launched on his watch as public works minister. I believe this great public works project stands as a memorial to him and to all others now deceased who helped make it happen—from politicians and senior officials who approved it to contractors and construction workers who helped build it. Their labours brought us Canadians that much closer to realizing our Founding Fathers' National Dream: "He shall have dominion also from sea to sea, and from the river unto the ends of the earth."

## FLORA MACDONALD AND BARBARA MCDOUGALL

Prime Minister Brian Mulroney was committed to ensuring women were well represented in Cabinet. There were six out of forty when I was there—not great, but a vast improvement over previous governments, including Pierre Trudeau's, in which there were only two after he was returned to power in 1980. Several of Mulroney's women Cabinet members were in the most senior posts and in the inner Cabinet, either originally or later. These included Flora MacDonald and Barbara McDougall, both of whom served as minister of employment and immigration at different times: the former from September 1984 to June 1986; the latter from March 1988 to April 1991. Women's place in Cabinet under Mulroney was greatly disproportionate to the total number of women in Caucus. Indeed, after the 1984 election, only twenty-seven women from all parties sat in the House of Commons: 9.6 percent of the 282 parliamentary seats. By the end, Mulroney boosted women's representation to 28 percent of Cabinet. It would plunge to 10 percent under Jean Chrétien immediately afterwards. (To Justin Trudeau's credit, half his thirty Cabinet appointees are women.) A measure of how far the PC Party had advanced on gender equality from Robert Stanfield to Brian Mulroney is that no one in Caucus even seemed aware of the long reach of Mulroney's "affirmative action," let alone wished to make an issue of it. To the extent Caucus was aware, everyone—man and woman alike—thought the prime minister was on the right track. As, indeed, he was.

I might have the distinction of being the only Cabinet minister in Canadian history heckled not just by one but by two prime ministers from different countries at the same time. The heckling occurred on the subject of women's representation in Cabinet. It happened in June 1988 in Toronto at the World Climate Change Conference I was hosting. Prime Minister Mulroney and Prime Minister Gro Brundtland of Norway and I appeared on stage together for the official opening ceremonies. Each of the two PMs was to give substantive remarks. I was to introduce both prime ministers. In my Brundtland introduction, I noted that the Norwegian PM's cabinet at the time—her second (from May 1986 to October 1989)—had eight women out of eighteen members in all. It was, to this point, the largest number of women in a government in the history of the world. Brian Mulroney, proud of his own women's-equality record, shouted from his seat: "And I appointed the largest number of women to a Cabinet in the history of Canada." He actually had—a fact I intended to make while introducing him next. It was bad enough to be heckled, worse by one's boss, worst of all in the act of being upstaged—but all in good fun. Riding the wave, I decided to ad lib that Gro Brundtland was the only environment minister in history ever to head a national government. I added: "My wife Kathy, who would be quite content to have me out of politics altogether, is not eager that I tie that record." It was lucky for me that this time the prime minister did not heckle, "You don't have to worry about that ever happening!" Brundtland, however, did shout, "You must aim for that." Now I was being heckled by *two* prime ministers, one a man and the other a woman—gender equality! It was a terrific equal-opportunity opening ceremony.

I always thought the lack of collegiality within Cabinet was "a guy thing." One would have thought that Barbara McDougall (External Affairs, at the end) and Flora MacDonald (by then, Communications) would be natural allies—and friends. After all, Flora had spent a lifetime chipping away at the glass ceiling that, to this day, blocks many women in politics, as in other fields. Barb had done the same in her private sector professional life as an economist in Toronto. To boot, she was minister of state for the status of women at one point. But the two women were far from being fast friends.

When Barbara McDougall was external affairs minister and I consul general to New England, she came to Boston on official business. At the visit's end, I assembled a few people to meet the minister over drinks—martinis extra dry for her. Apropos of nothing (the strong martinis?), the minister confided to our group that she had always been "totally intimidated" by Flora. Another double scotch, my own drug of choice on the occasion, could not have floored me with the force of that revelation. I thought I was the only one intimidated by Flora. And yet, among all my Cabinet colleagues, she was the one I knew best before either of us became an MP. Flora had been administrative secretary of the politics department at Queen's when I was a graduate student there. Before that, she had been a long-time senior functionary at PC Headquarters. John Diefenbaker foolishly fired this party favourite as part of efforts that paranoid man made to purge the ranks of anyone he perceived a threat to his continued leadership. The aging former prime minister viewed Flora as one of the worst of the "termites." I knew Flora MacDonald from those Headquarters days, too. Flora had always been helpful and kind to me at Queen's, the same to all other students. Certainly, I cannot fault her for a single thing during our time in Cabinet together. On the contrary, of all my colleagues, she was the quickest to congratulate and encourage me each time my political star rose (when I received the US Sierra Club's prestigious Edgar Wayburn Award, for example). But when I was deputy House leader in Opposition, the situation was totally different. This heavenly creature sometimes made my life hell (as discussed earlier).

I still feared Flora MacDonald's wrath throughout our Cabinet days together, even if by then—as in Barb McDougall's case, no doubt—there might have been no rational basis for my trepidation. That said, I always admired Flora. She did as much as any other of her generation to enhance the public image of the party as progressive and humanitarian and sensitive to the interests of everyday Canadians. She was courageous, and almost always right, on the issues. She paid higher dues to the PC cause (before and after becoming an MP) than almost anyone else. As Canada's first woman foreign affairs minister, in 1979–80, Flora helped free some of the fifty-two Americans held hostage in Tehran by Iranian student revolutionaries. This distinction alone assures her a place in history, Canadian and American alike. She continued her good works after leaving political office, particularly on long-term development in central Afghanistan through Future Generations Canada, a registered charity she founded in 2007. Flora visited the country more than a dozen times. When she was defeated in her Kingston-area riding in 1988, after sixteen years in Parliament, public life lost a giant, the party one of its most progressive voices, and women a trailblazer for their gender on the big political stage—a model for public servants of any gender. Few other people embodied better than Flora the virtues, the beliefs, the values, and the nobility that Robert Stanfield brought to public life, all too rare in government and politics nowadays. It can't be a coincidence that the two were from Nova Scotia. From Tupper to Borden to Stanfield to Mulroney (part Nova Scotian at heart), that province, for well over a century, has been breeding national Tory leaders in whose company Flora Isabel MacDonald would—and, in Stanfield's and Mulroney's cases, did—stand tall. I was deeply saddened when, in July 2015, at age eighty-nine, this beloved and esteemed Canadian political pioneer died.

And then there was Erik Nielsen. When I think of him at the same time as I do other former colleagues such as John Crosbie, Pat Carney, Perrin Beatty, Flora MacDonald, and Barbara McDougall, it's like my head is rejecting a brain transplant. His name linked with theirs is, for me, as incongruous as bile and butterflies. Erik Nielsen could not have been more different from them had all the gods assembled to demonstrate their collective capacity to confound mere mortals by placing him on Earth with them simultaneously. It's as though Nielsen and they were not of the same animal species. In William Blake's lyrical poem *The Tyger*, the gentle lamb symbolizes goodness, the terrifying tiger evil. Blake is baffled by the mystery of how, or even whether, the same God could have created a creature as innocent as the former and one as evil as the latter. The poet asks of the tiger, incredulously: "Did he who made the Lamb make thee?" He implies the lamb might have been the handiwork of the Divine, the tiger that of the Devil. This is how I felt about Erik Nielson relative to all my other Cabinet colleagues when I was a minister myself. Nielsen was the Devil, they divine by comparison.

I was not personally victimized by Erik Nielsen, at least not especially so; he was an equal-opportunity destroyer. In his vengeful memoir, *The House Is Not a Home*,[3] he takes an indirect crack at me. Nielsen reprints, in the Appendix, a transition-to-government "Potential-Cabinet" memo he had done for Brian Mulroney prior to his election as prime minister. The memo dismisses me as a Cabinet prospect for lack of skills. The PM obviously rejected this assessment and appointed me to Cabinet, anyway. But, compared to the acid that man poured on many of his other former Cabinet colleagues in the memoir, his comments about me were as bath powder on a baby's bum. Heath Macquarrie served with Nielsen for a long time in Opposition. Both were first elected to Parliament in 1957. Heath despised Nielsen, often telling me how mean and spiteful he considered him to be. As, in fact, he was most of the time.

The Yukon MP made his name in Opposition in the Diefenbaker era as a vicious attack dog against Pearson government ministers for every manner of scandal, real or manufactured, often the latter. He served as the PC parliamentary Opposition leader for a few months between Joe Clark's resignation as leader in early 1983 and Brian Mulroney's by-election win in Nova Scotia, following Mulroney's leadership victory in June of that year. And he was deputy prime minister under Mulroney from 1984 to 1986. In the last role, Nielsen acted as a veritable *enfant terrible*, terrorizing almost everyone. The prime minister eventually fired him to avert a Cabinet and Caucus revolt. In his memoirs, Brian Mulroney refers to his former deputy prime minister as "domineering."[4] These are not qualities a prime minister would want, or should have, in his alter ego.

As deputy prime minister, Nielsen was known as "Velcro Lips" for his secretive and stonewalling ways with the media and public. Behind his back, some of us referred to him as "the Tyrant." Private thoughts are unquotable. Nielsen humiliated even senior Cabinet colleagues in front of their officials. He tried to do the same to me when I appeared before the government waste task force he headed. After I had referred to "my department" in response to one of his questions, he bellowed: "*Your* department!" For added emphasis: "*Whose* department?" As if the point had not already been scored: "When did you get to *own* it?" A newly appointed minister has enough to acclimate to without his boss—at least Nielsen presented himself as that—undercutting him (or her) in front of his officials. I stared right into the man's soulless shark eyes and pursed crocodile smile and shot back, with all the sarcasm this freshman Treasury Board member could drip: "The department of which I am the head, the ministry for which I am responsible, that division of government on whose behalf I am appearing today!" The Irish in me! Everybody in the room, including *his* officials, was shocked. Apparently, I had done what everyone else there had long wanted to do, but was too afraid to do: retaliate for being humiliated by this cruel and imperious man. Strangely, my stock with Nielsen rose because of what I had done. Evidently, when in Rome one should do as the Romans do: lash and slash. But, even more to Nielsen's liking, when one is a Christian being slaughtered by a lion, he should do what the lion does: chew off the adversary's head. This was the man's operating principle in politics. It was not mine. I did not want it to be.

Erik Nielsen appeared to lack both common sense and due respect in the presence of Brian Mulroney. As deputy Opposition House leader, I spent a lot of time with the leader, and with senior Caucus officials such as Nielsen, plotting strategy for Question Period, for which I was ultimately responsible. If I were to apply one word to Nielsen's demeanour towards Brian Mulroney during this period, it would be "condescension." He reeked of it. Nielsen patronized Mulroney even when the latter became prime minister of Canada. Mulroney was not oblivious to the practice. He was particularly offended by Nielsen's patronizing putdown when, as outgoing interim PC Party leader, Nielsen introduced Mulroney as the new leader at the June 1983 leadership convention. The incident followed Mulroney's victory on the final ballot. In his memoirs, he says Nielsen's public reference to him on that occasion as "not my first choice as leader" was "inappropriate." This is likely the only time Brian Mulroney has ever understated anything, either on a podium or in print, in his entire public career. Mulroney says Nielsen "cast a pall over the convention."[5] That additional comment is much closer to the mark. But the future prime minister should not have been shocked by such disrespect: Nielsen felt superior to everyone. He was, in his own mind, king of the jungle. The rest of us, including the prime minister, were his subjects—and lambs for slaughter when he was in the mood, as he often was.

In Nielsen's eyes, Cabinet and Caucus colleagues came in two types: those he liked and those he was not too fond of or detested outright. In the first category were the "the real men," the big burly stereotypical "man's man." Women Cabinet colleagues were in neither category, for to him they were non-persons unless they were a Margaret Thatcher type—and we had precious few, if any, of them. Among the Chosen Few, for example, were XL-sized Bill McKnight. For a while in government, he was my Commons seatmate. A farmer/businessman from Saskatchewan, Bill, who held various portfolios over time, including Indian Affairs and Northern Development, was a wonderful colleague and kind man. Another Nielsen favourite was Harvie Andre, a husky chemical engineer from Calgary (who died in 2012 of cancer). Harvie served, successively, as minister of supply and services, associate minister of national defence, minister of consumer and corporate affairs, and minister of regional industrial expansion. But he made his name shaking up the post office and curbing its spendthrift ways. He was a sharp, competent, and hail-fellow-well-met personality. Yet another of Nielsen's favourites was Don Mazankowski, a former auto dealership manager from Alberta and of Polish descent. He became deputy prime minister when Mulroney fired Nielsen. "Maz," as everyone called him, was one of the best-liked and most respected ministers by all members of Parliament, not just on our side. Among Erik Neilsen's Chosen Few, too, was Sinc Stevens. To Nielsen, Sinc's killer instincts in the Commons during our Opposition days compensated for his lack of manly size.

All these men were worthy of respect, including by Erik Nielsen. But it was not their humanity he respected; it was their perceived über-masculinity. And yet, Nielsen defined "acceptable maleness" in a way that did justice neither to those to whom he applied it nor to colleagues who, in his eyes, fell short of the standard. Erik Nielsen's political machismo was so like that of George W. Bush and Dick Cheney as they strutted and strode and swaggered on the public stage in a later period. The only thing missing in Nielsen's case was the ten-gallon hat, the oversized belt buckle, and the tan leather cowboy boots. But he could make a Texas or Wyoming pseudo-swashbuckler look like a sissy. It was not at all in his favour.

In Nielsen's "not too fond of" category were most of the rest of us in Cabinet: colleagues whose style, for his taste, was too much that of gentlemen in the British Tory parliamentarian tradition. Again, ladies hardly existed as peers in Nielsen's world, unless they possessed personal and political characteristics that he believed qualified them as virtual men. Among those "lesser" colleagues were, for example, David Crombie (Indian Affairs and Northern Development, later Multiculturalism); Jake Epp (Health); Ray Hnatyshyn (Justice) and Jean Charest (originally Youth). And, of course, me in Environment—a field that, by definition, would make any holder of that portfolio suspect in his eyes (Blais-Grenier an exception). Nielsen viewed those of us in this "inferior" category as lambs, not tigers, in a reversal of Blake's moral order. We were not sufficiently warlike towards opponents. Was there an ideological pattern in the two lists? Nielsen would have viewed those on the first as right-wing and, therefore, kindred spirits; those on the second as left-wing and, thus, morally suspect, if not dangerous.

On one of my first days in Parliament, after the 1979 election, Erik Nielsen saw me speaking with NDP MP Pauline Jewett (New Westminster–Coquitlam). With a PhD from Harvard (1949), she had been director of the Institute of Canadian Studies at Carleton University. I knew her through my work, in the mid-1970s, as senior research associate of the Commission on Canadian Studies, sponsored by the Association of Universities and Colleges of Canada. Nielsen practically tore my head off after seeing Pauline and me together. He warned me that she was a dangerous socialist whom I needed to avoid at any cost—including, evidently, his respect. Nielsen had also just seen me introducing myself to a true socialist icon: Stanley Knowles (Winnipeg North). He was then dean of the House of Commons and a CCF/NDP veteran with whom Nielsen had often crossed swords in the Diefenbaker era. From the very beginning of my parliamentary career, Erik Nielsen pegged me as "one of them." Compared to him, I was. At least, I hoped so. I much preferred being in their company—both philosophically and literally—than his. They were nice people. He was not.

As a subtext of his elegant memoir, *Gentlemen, Players, and Politicians*,[6] Dalton Camp said that politics magnifies, out of all proportion to the truth, both a politician's strengths and his or her weaknesses. I think Camp was right. While reflecting on Erik Nielsen, I have to take care not to magnify his weaknesses beyond their real dimensions. It requires much less discipline for me to avoid magnifying his strengths, for to me he had few. I don't consider bullying a strength or a bully strong. The tiger is much bigger and more powerful than the lamb. But, as Revelations 22:3 tells us,

"No longer will there be anything accursed, but the throne of God and of the Lamb will be in it, and his servants will worship him." In the end, no one worshipped Erik Nielsen but himself. That was one too many.

## LUCIEN BOUCHARD

I was Lucien Bouchard's first House of Commons seatmate. It was after he won a Quebec by-election in the spring of 1988 and immediately entered Cabinet as secretary of state. We got along extremely well. I thought him a nice guy and liked and respected him. I was the first colleague—indeed, one of the first individuals—he told he was going to marry his American girlfriend, Audrey Best. He informed me of his marital plans even before telling the prime minister, his fellow Université Laval alumnus and long-time friend.

Lucien Bouchard succeeded me as environment minister after I was defeated in PEI in late 1988. After my defeat, the PM asked me to remain in Cabinet for several weeks, even without a seat in Parliament, to help Bouchard make the transition. When he actually took over, on December 7, the new environment minister asked me to join him at his Centre Block parliamentary office to discuss a range of matters. For about two hours, we candidly discussed the Environment portfolio, personnel, specific issues, and politics. When the meeting was ending, Lucien sat back on the couch we shared. He began to speak to me more as one friend to another—man to man—than as one colleague to another. And yet, we had not known each other long enough to be more than congenial colleagues. It was then he told me about his marriage plans. Lucien said he wanted much more out of life than the professional success he had enjoyed. He wanted a life partner and children and all the blessings that could come to a man only from love and friendship, preferably from the same person but also from others. I was deeply moved by the humanity he displayed: a warm and demonstrative man capable of opening himself up to others. I had not before experienced anything close to so touching a moment with any of my other colleagues. And I was not, at that stage, capable of baring my own soul in such a way—with a colleague, a friend, or anybody else for that matter, including my wife or family. "What a superior human being!" I left Lucien's office thinking.

I know Lucien Bouchard played a hand in my appointment as consul general in Boston seven months later. On several occasions subsequent to our December meeting, we had discussed the possibility of something like it. He was then one of the PM's closest confidants, so would likely have been consulted. I, therefore, have the most conflicted feelings about the man. Bouchard took every one of my major suggestions for the Environment portfolio. With or without my help, he was a big success in that portfolio before bolting the PC Party and the Mulroney government to join the Quebec separatist cause, eventually becoming Quebec premier. I am glad someone of his ability and commitment followed me as environment minister to continue the course I had set the government on in this area after the Suzanne Blais-Grenier train wreck. By selecting for the post one of his closest friends, and then immediately elevating him to the inner Cabinet (the Priorities and Planning Committee), Brian Mulroney underscored how seriously he was taking the environment both as an issue and as a government department.

And yet, I soon came to wonder whether, as with Elizabeth May, a "Dr. Jekyll and Mr. Hyde" personality hid behind all the apparent warmth and natural charm and personal openness that Bouchard had demonstrated towards me. Could there have been an even worse possibility? Brian Mulroney knew him (or thought he did) a lot better—and, certainly, a lot longer—than I did. The PM ended up admitting he got Bouchard all wrong. Had I done so as well? Maybe there *was* no dual personality. Appearances to the contrary, perhaps Bouchard was, as Mulroney came to believe, a con man from the very beginning. Mulroney had not only launched his supposed friend's political career; he had also given him other rich opportunities, most notably appointing him Canadian ambassador to France in 1985. Nevertheless, Bouchard betrayed him heartlessly in the end. In his memoirs, the former PM details, in many poignant passages, how Bouchard did so. Mulroney characterizes the trust he misplaced in Bouchard as one of the worst decisions of his life, one for which both he and (worse, he says) the country paid dearly. It's the reason, he says, "I will never forgive myself." Likely never before, in the entire history of Canada, has any prime minister written a more devastating indictment of a former close friend and Cabinet colleague than Brian Mulroney pens in his memoirs about Lucien Bouchard: "With the benefit of hindsight, I could clearly see for the first time how foolish I had been in placing such loyalty, trust and friendship *in a man incapable of reciprocating such feelings.*"[7]

In light of the knife Mulroney believes Bouchard plunged in his back, this is one Cabinet colleague I was probably fortunate not to have become any closer to than I did. In an interview reported in The Canadian Press on August 21, 2014, Bouchard said his ruptured relationship with Mulroney could never be repaired. "We run into each other occasionally in Montreal or elsewhere," Bouchard stated, "and I think we have an agreement to not embarrass each other." The farther I get from politics, the more saddened I become about the damage it can inflict on practitioners and on their relationships with one another, on both the same and opposite sides of the political fence. Indeed, as in the case of Mulroney and Bouchard, the enterprise can drive even close friends to opposite sides though they once helped build one of those sides together. Harry Truman might well have been right in recommending a dog over a politician for friendship.

Just as Robert Stanfield's *bêtes noires* throughout his leadership were the Diefenbaker insurgents, including the former leader himself, so also the Mulroney government's most dangerous enemies operated from within the fortress walls. The Mulroney regnum was the first extended opportunity the PC Party had, in government, to consolidate the gains Stanfield had made in rebranding the party as contemporary. Progress towards that end should not be measured only by what John Crosbie, Perrin Beatty, Pat Carney, Flora MacDonald, Barbara McDougall, Chris Speyer, et al. did to advance it; what Lucien Bouchard and Elizabeth May did to set it back is equally relevant. It was all of a piece.

Unfortunately for the Mulroney legacy and for the party's rebranding efforts in that era, the positives—which, by any objective standard, far outweighed the negatives—were often overshadowed by the negatives. The media invariably focused on the likes of Bouchard and May, too rarely on those trying to help the prime minister build the government's record and his own. "Any jackass can kick down a barn but it takes a good carpenter to build one," storied US congressional Speaker Sam Rayburn once said. Both Bouchard and May, knocking down the barn, had their personal agendas: in his case, Quebec sovereignty; in hers, redemption with the environmental movement and perhaps a political career farther down the road. These two self-seekers left pieces of the barn flying in every direction as they helped kick the building down, left the field, and walked into the sunset.

If Cabinet colleagues typically do not get to know one another well as individuals, it is even harder for ministers to befriend people across the Commons aisle. The highly combative nature of our parliamentary system works against it. Still, mutual respect between a Cabinet minister and an opponent—perhaps the next-best thing to a real relationship—is possible, even in the heat of battle. My time as a minister and Jean Chrétien's as an Opposition MP (before he became Liberal leader) overlapped for just a few months. But we did have direct dealings with each other and were on a first-name basis.

There are many things in life I cannot understand. One of them is electricity. Another is Chrétien's mammoth success in politics. After all, if Jean Chrétien were a vegetable, rather than a man, it would be a stumpy and knarred rutabaga, not a long and lean and elegant carrot. Anyone able to read a roadside billboard without a telescope could see that Chrétien possessed few attributes conventionally associated with political superstars, least of all polish and eloquence and good looks. Fathered by a papermill machinist; eighteenth of nineteen children; raised as much by extended family members as by his real parents; afflicted by Bell's palsy at birth; paralyzed for life on the left side of his face by that affliction; deaf in the ear on the same side and for the same reason; "unable to speak either of Canada's official languages," as Allan Fotheringham said famously; unable to speak English at all when first elected to Parliament in 1963—Jean Chrétien, nevertheless, achieved, both in his own federal riding and right across Canada, almost unprecedented electoral success. He defied all the laws of politics—and my own comprehension.

Never before Chrétien had any Canadian political party leader become prime minister without being able to speak either the Queen's English or the King's French. Nor had any French-speaking leader succeeded in English Canada without speaking English better than most native English speakers themselves. If true, it's an unfair standard. It would disqualify for our highest elective office people who might not pass muster by that standard but could by the standards that most count—what I would call the three "C's": Character, Competence, and Caring. Two of our francophone prime ministers (both from Quebec), Sir Wilfrid Laurier and Pierre Elliott Trudeau, spoke English as well as not only the monarch but also God—appropriate because people thought Laurier *was* God, and Trudeau thought *he* was. In oratory, Chrétien was a far cry from both men, in either official language—or any other known to man or beast. Robert Stanfield wasn't naturally eloquent, either. But his electoral appeal was understandable, particularly in Atlantic Canada. Nobody could gainsay his high intelligence, elite education, illustrious family background, strong moral values, and sheer classiness (however inelegant compared to Laurier's, unglamorous compared to Trudeau's). Through the generations, Canadians have voted for national party leaders who combined some or all of the qualities Stanfield embodied—to wit: William Lyon Mackenzie King (family pedigree, superior education, extraordinary intelligence, and otherworldly shrewdness) and Louis St-Laurent (personal integrity, public virtue, managerial competence)—Honest Bob, Rex, and Uncle Louis, as Stanfield, King, and St-Laurent were known, respectively, either by the public or (in the case of King) intimate friends.[8] But Jean Chrétien? And across English Canada? *Especially* in English Canada?

Jean Chrétien was the Muggsy Bogues of Canadian politics. Tyrone Curtis ("Muggsy") Bogues is a fifty-year-old retired professional basketball point guard, having played for fifteen seasons in the NBA. And yet Bogues is only 5 feet, 3 inches tall—

the shortest man ever to compete in the NBA. Both Jean Chrétien and Muggsy Bogues defied the conventional requirements of their respective professions. I failed to understand Chrétien's political success for one reason: I couldn't see beyond his "height." The fact he lacked the qualities and talents typically associated with conventionally gifted politicians blinded me to a certain essence of the man that enabled him to connect with voters and them with him on a deeply primal level. This quality I call the *Helen Factor*.

The *Helen Factor* is a concept I will return to a number of times. I mean by this term all the characteristics of certain types of individuals that cause the public to bond viscerally with them because, consciously or not, it sees in those people the best in human nature and, therefore, in itself. This set of qualities—whether charisma or just an abundance of decency—does not depend on the social or economic status of the person who possesses it. Nor does this special something depend on the status of the people who respond to it so powerfully. At one extreme of the social hierarchy, the *Helen Factor* can be found in a person as magnetic a plutocrat as Franklin Roosevelt in the United States or as low-key a one as Robert Stanfield in Canada. At the other social-hierarchy extreme, this special set of qualities can also be found in someone whose life is as humble and mundane as Helen Doyle's. The term covers both extremes. Exemplars of this rare human essence among the celebrated, like FDR and Stanfield, typically act as though they are uncelebrated—with humility. Exemplars among the uncelebrated, like Helen Doyle, possess a capacity to affect other people's lives in ways, however quotidian, that earn those exemplars a precious value typically associated with the celebrated: respect. In the second category, in literature as in life, my own favourite example comes from Margaret Mitchell's *Gone with the Wind*: Scarlett O'Hara's childhood nurse, behaviour scold, and moral compass, Mammy. Like Helen in my eyes, Mammy had few equals as a human being – a view the wealthy and worldly Rhett Butler had in common with Scarlett. "Mammy's a smart old soul. And one of the few people whose respect I'd like to have," he tells Scarlett. That is the essence of the *Helen Factor*, whether applied to kings and queens or to peasants and paupers.

My detailing in the first chapter who Helen Doyle was and what she meant to our family, and then attaching her mononym to the type of qualities I most admire in others, is my way of saying that I wish more politicians would demonstrate those she embodied. It would increase the public's respect for the governing class, nowadays rarer than a beard on a newborn baby girl. Who in the government of Stephen Harper, including the prime minister himself, elicited from Canadians the kind of respect every member of my family had for Helen? Franklin Roosevelt and Robert Stanfield—both of them aristocrats—earned that kind of respect from their respective countries, even among people who never voted for them. When I worked for Stanfield, I couldn't imagine anything more personally affirming than receiving his approbation for a particular task I had completed. The *Helen Factor* hardly characterizes either the Harperites' political ethos or their record in power. It does Chrétien's, which helps account for the man's massive electoral success. The "little guy from Shawinigan" dunked the ball almost every time.

For sure, like all of us, Jean Chrétien was an imperfect person. For example, he didn't always honour his election promises—least of all, scrapping the goods and services tax (GST). But Chrétien's essential character meets the standard in question: a certain set of exemplary human qualities that drew people to him like a feline to catnip. He generated their respect. "People get the government they deserve,"

Thomas Jefferson stated. The public does *not* get the politicians they deserve. They get the ones they *vote for*. Too often, politicians hoodwink the voter with bait-and-switch electioneering. Pierre Trudeau's duplicity on wage-and-price controls in the 1974 election is a classic case. (I believe Chrétien actually intended to honour such Liberal election promises as scrapping the GST but afterwards discovered he either couldn't or shouldn't.) On the other hand, voters have a civic duty not to allow their politicians to hoodwink them—thus, no doubt, Jefferson's reasoning. More of the *Helen Factor* in both the governing class and the governed would improve the odds that the citizenry will get, at one and the same time, the government they deserve *and* the one they think they're electing.

Jean Chrétien resigned his seat in the House of Commons in 1986, at about the time my own Cabinet career was beginning to climb. After John Turner defeated him for the Liberal leadership in 1984, following Pierre Trudeau's retirement, Chrétien returned to practising law. In retrospect, it's clear that the man was biding time until his next political opportunity struck. In 1965, he had been appointed Lester Pearson's parliamentary secretary, a coup for a young MP first elected only two years earlier. By then, he had been able to make himself functional in English—barely. Later, he would hold every post in the gift of the Crown but the queen's colonial secretary: Minister of State for Finance (1967); National Revenue (1968); Indian Affairs and Northern Development (1968–74); Treasury Board (1974); Industry, Trade and Commerce (1976); Finance (1977); Justice and Attorney General (1980); Energy, Mines and Resources (1982); External Affairs (1984); and Deputy Prime Minister (1984). Upon winning the Liberal leadership when Turner's failed interregnum ended, in 1990, Chrétien became leader of the Opposition. By 1993, he was prime minister, serving for a full decade. How did "*le petit gars*" from Shawinigan do all this without most of the attributes conventionally associated with phenomenally successful politicians? The same way Helen Doyle of Tignish, out of Rustico, accumulated her wealth without the attributes usually associated with successful entrepreneurs. They both possessed the *Helen Factor,* that "something special"—rare, elusive, consequential, partially explicable but ultimately indefinable.

My dealings with Jean Chrétien included an incident one Thursday afternoon in the Commons when I was doing House Duty. (Even Cabinet ministers were required to do it.) While sitting virtually alone in a quiet section of the Commons, I was signing constituency correspondence. Chrétien moseyed over from across the aisle to the empty seat to my left, plunked himself down, and began to petition me, ever so endearingly, about a parks issue in his Saint-Maurice riding. As environment minister, I was responsible for Parks Canada and the national parks system. This was not long after he had been beaten, and some thought humiliated, at the 1984 Liberal leadership convention. And yet, he was not too preoccupied with his shattered ambitions to petition for the real love of his political life, national parks; one of which, La Mauricie, he had established in his own constituency in 1970. Chrétien spoke to me about the park problem with the urgency one would apply to ailing infant sons—twins, perhaps. His passion for parks was less a constituency file to be closed than a window to his soul opened.

Close up, Jean Chrétien reminded me of Helen Doyle more than anyone else I had ever met: the same primitive simplicity, the same easy unaffected rustic charm, the same humility but rough-hewn confidence, the same essential goodness, the same eagerness to do good for and by others, the same effortless floating above the fray while others plunged head-first into the *Sturm und Drang* of life. Ever the street-smart fighter, capable of both taking a punch and returning it, he survived each battle as though never actually having been in it, his reputation as *le petit gars* from Shawinigan firmly intact—impenetrable, untouchable, irreproachable. A pay-for-play contract scandal rocked the Liberal government after he retired from politics, but a judicial inquiry laid the blame at his feet. The scandal, however, did not substantially diminish his standing in the country. Nor will it likely reduce his place in history, either. Most people loved Jean Chrétien. At their core, some people at the highest level have as much in common with people at the lowest as they do with people at their own level. This was the case with Chrétien. In Helen Doyle's case, the converse was true. She related well to all people, a doctor with four university degrees no less than her best friend, Rose Gallant—also, with little education, a family housekeeper to a prosperous Charlottetown family.

When Jean Chrétien was defeated by John Turner for the leadership, in what looked to most observers like a gang-bang by the party establishment against "the little guy" who had served their cause and Canada's for so long and well, he was dismissed and dissed as "Yesterday's Man." And yet, everybody's heart, not just that of a Liberal, went out to him. Liberal Party president Iona Campagnolo spoke for everyone when, following Chrétien's defeat at the hands of Turner and the Big Red Machine, she told him at the convention: "[You came] second on the ballot, but first in our hearts." Her words inspired the title of the fallen warrior's autobiography, *Straight from the Heart*.[9] It was an instant bestseller, earning its author a small fortune in royalties. And still more admirers and followers.

Most people, I among them, thought that, when he resigned his Commons seat in 1986, that would be the last anyone would ever hear from, and of, "Yesterday's Man." As a former House of Commons colleague, and especially as the minister responsible for national parks, I wrote Jean a personal letter to wish him well in the private sector. I told him that I was writing to the man who had established more new national parks than any other Cabinet minister in Canadian history. I said I was doing so as the minister who had established the next-most, but who was proud to settle for second place behind one of our country's finest-ever public servants.

Some weeks later, I was in Toronto at the Lester B. Pearson International Airport. The building was named after the man who had given Jean Chrétien his first leg up in a steady climb on the political ladder. Someone tapped on the window as I walked by the glass partition separating the restaurant and bar from the corridor that I was walking along to catch my flight. It was Jean Chrétien. He sat alone inside—eating a club sandwich and having a beer, as I recall. My former parliamentary colleague beckoned to me. I went in and said hello. "Tom, I really appreciated your letter. *Thanks a thousand times*," Chrétien said—Helen Doyle's mantra. I nearly fainted! Did I hear what I thought I heard—"*tanks a tousand times*"? Am I losing my mind? Jet lag? Exhaustion? "Sorry I have just had so many letters to answer," he said. "But yours is next, I promise."

True to his word, Jean Chrétien wrote his note, and it arrived two days later. The handwritten message could have been composed by Helen: the same primitive handwriting, the same phonetic spelling ("rite" instead of "write"; "herd" instead of "heard"; "sorry" with one "r," and so on). There was the same kind of fractured grammar, too. The man's effort was so like the notes Helen regularly wrote to each of us McMillan children attending grad school in far-flung places. For all their semi-illiteracy and phonetic spelling and mangled syntax, Helen's letters were always packed with the kind of detail and human element that neither Dad nor Mother, with their formal education and university degrees, seemed capable of expressing in their letters to each of us. Just as, despite our steadily growing education, we siblings never appeared capable of capturing anything like the humanity Helen so effortlessly conveyed in hers as we carbon-copied our missives and mailed them throughout the family in a free-flowing round robin of letter-writing and sharing. Jean's note to me was replete with a primitive but genuine humanity. It was this very humanity that caused Canadians to take him "straight into their hearts" through ten election victories in his own riding and three majority governments as Liberal Party leader in the country as a whole. Tom Symons always sought out and recruited individuals with the "it" factor and then did his best to retain their services. It was that indefinable essence that, like the greatness in a fine work of art, is impossible to quantify or even describe. But one knows it when he or she sees it. Canadians detected, and wished to reward electorally, the quality in Jean Chrétien that they might not have been able to quantify or describe. But they knew *it* when they saw it, too. And they saw in Chrétien an essence that I can only call, not the "it" factor, but the *Helen Factor*—his simple, unassuming, but competent and giving humanity.

Jean Chrétien's path crossed mine again in an unlikely place: at the Dulles Airport, near Washington, DC. I was in the American capital for meetings on acid rain with high-level US officials, including the secretary of energy. The Prime Minister's Office (PMO) had insisted I fly on one of the Canadian government's Challenger jets to ensure my speediest return to Ottawa. The Environment portfolio was continually in the eye of parliamentary storms. And government House leader Ray Hnatyshyn and Deputy PM Don Mazankowski didn't want to risk my not being in the Commons for long, especially for Question Period, should the Opposition decide to spring a surprise in my absence, as they had already done a number of times. The NDP, for example, had designated an Opposition Day to attack the government on it environmental record while I was addressing the North American Wildlife Federation in Baton Rouge, Louisiana, over two thousand kilometres from Ottawa. (The government flew me back on a Challenger to orchestrate, and then lead off our defence, in the Commons. They had packed the plane with officials and staff to help me prepare, in mid-flight, my own address and suggest lines of arguments for Tory parliamentary colleagues.) My trusty media secretary, Terry Collins, knew Chrétien from covering his leadership campaign in Terry's previous career as a *Toronto Sun* reporter. By then, Chrétien—in Washington on business—sat on the boards of several corporations, among them Power Corporation's Consolidated-Bathurst, the Toronto-Dominion Bank, and Brick Warehouse. During our stay in the US capital, Terry ran into Chrétien having breakfast alone at a hotel restaurant.

Without an opportunity to consult me, my press secretary took the liberty of inviting Chrétien to hitch a ride with us back to Ottawa on the government plane. The invitation was accepted. Throughout the ninety-minute return flight, Chrétien regaled us, with surprising candour, about his political ambitions in the face of growing speculation that he would make another run for the Liberal leadership (he did, of course; this time, winning). When I checked some facts with Terry, now a successful environmental consultant in Toronto, about the episode, Terry reminded me: "You considered putting a bag over your head when leaving the plane upon arrival in Ottawa to avoid any political gossip about keeping company with such a prominent Grit." Probably, at the time, that was true. But not because I lacked the highest regard for Jean Chrétien—even if real friendship, as with other colleagues on either side of the aisle, was not possible.

I did not know Liberal Opposition leader John Turner well personally. We had even less opportunity to get to know each other when, briefly, he was prime minister. But the two of us did cross swords numerous times in the Commons. Turner often led Question Period on environmental issues. In full throttle, he was tarring and feathering me one afternoon in that forum. The issue was the Mulroney government's alleged neglect of St. Lawrence River pollution—true at the time; not later, when we launched a major cleanup. I was often shocked by how badly the Liberal leader and his staff researched his Commons questions. In this case, he based his whole series on the assumption that pollution in the river was primarily municipal waste. And yet, for days on end, the Quebec media had reported or editorialized on a major policy speech I delivered in Montreal on the condition of the river. I had identified by name the three major industrial giants responsible for most of the pollution—not municipal waste but toxic chemicals. There was a huge difference between the two categories and, accordingly, they required completely different remedies. Quebec environment minister Clifford Lincoln was furious with me for entering his territory and attacking local industrial polluters in such a specific way. But I shot back that the St. Lawrence was both a national and an international waterway—not just a provincial river, however major. I said the St. Lawrence was part of a total ecosystem that extended well beyond the borders of Quebec and even of Canada. I argued that, if Canada's environment minister was not allowed to address pollution within the boundaries of a given province—in this case, Quebec—he could not do it in any other province or territory, either. So, I asked, how was he supposed to meet his responsibilities not only to the nation as a whole but also to the world community? Lincoln was stumped. John Turner, however, seemed unaware of this toxic-chemicals controversy when he based his Commons questions, instead, on municipal waste. He just got it all wrong. This was not the only time that Turner made a Mulroney minister's job easy in Question Period for lack of preparation. In the Commons, for all his high-voltage rhetoric, Turner did not intimidate anyone on the front bench, least of all the prime minister.

Many of the famous witticisms of history's greatest parliamentarians were not the spontaneous rejoinders they were made to seem and thought to be. Winston Churchill, for example, kept in reserve his best *bon mots* for exactly the right occasion. Such towering parliamentary performers left little to chance. The day Turner attacked me on St. Lawrence River pollution, Rat Packer Sheila Copps shouted "blow-dried minister" across the Commons. It was an obvious crack at my helmet of thick, greying hair that then, as now, wouldn't muss in a wind tunnel. Without missing a beat, Turner incorporated the "blow-dried" heckle into his bombastic assault. A more gifted Opposition leader would never have made such an elementary mistake. Any parliamentarian reasonably quick on his feet could have hit that strike-zone hardball right out of the park. As I rose to respond, Cabinet and Caucus colleagues— among them Jake Epp, Ray Hnatyshyn, and Stan Darling—shouted suggestions for a retort. Every one of those suggestions would have floored Turner. I went with my own, instead: "Mr. Speaker, I would rather be blow-dried than a blowhard." Inane as that response was, it destroyed the attacker's salvo. Speaker John Fraser was unable to contain his laughter. Still less could he control cheers or jeers or guffaws from every side of the chamber. The Commons, from the floor to the public galleries, was in chaos. All this was absolute nonsense—great fun, but puerile no less. By the end of it, no one could even remember the issue Turner had raised, so this minister's hide remained intact. My own starring role in the melodrama brought the country's democracy momentarily to a halt. It was one of the most raucous Question Periods in which I was ever embroiled.

Pierre Trudeau was not an effective Opposition leader, either. He served only briefly in that role, following his defeat in May 1979 to Joe Clark. Allan MacEachen was interim leader when Trudeau announced his retirement, which he subsequently reversed for the 1980 election. Nor was Jean Chrétien effective in this role when he succeeded John Turner after the latter lost the 1988 election to Brian Mulroney. Robert Stanfield, a former provincial premier, had a government orientation, not Opposition mentality. But John Diefenbaker, Joe Clark, and Brian Mulroney thrived in Opposition. By contrast, a succession of Liberal Party leaders in this period hated being in Opposition and serving as leader of the Official Opposition, in particular. It showed. Except for seven years, the Liberal Party had governed the country non-stop from 1935 to 1984, almost half a century. Truly, they were the "natural governing party." In that same period, we Tories were the "natural Official Opposition party," always campaigning but rarely winning. The governing and Opposition roles require completely different skill sets and—even more fundamental—mentalities. Opposition was our forte; governing, not Opposition, the Liberals'. Just as practice makes perfect, so also lack of practice makes imperfect. The Liberals simply lacked Opposition practice and, therefore, usually played the role terribly. By the same token, when we Tories finally won office the odd time, usually by accident or default, as with Joe Clark's victory in 1979, the teething period proved tortuous—for us and the country.

For the most part, then, the Liberal Opposition in the early period of the Mulroney government was comprised of rank amateurs as government critics. They, of course, gained more experience the longer the Mulroney government remained in power—almost a decade in total. It was in the early period, however, that the media and public formed their impressions of both sides of the Commons aisle. And, like most first impressions, these didn't change much with time. Such was not to the new government's advantage. Nor, ultimately, to the Opposition's, either. The reputation of Parliament as a whole suffered from the poisonous atmosphere created by the scattergun approach the Liberals took to attacking the government. Parliamentary veterans would have been both more strategic and more focused than this group of neophytes. "Big-game hunters don't go after gophers!" John Diefenbaker used to say. The so-called Rat Pack chased everything in sight, right down to the tiniest field mouse. The Monday-to-Friday Commons Question Period was the main hunting ground, and it soon became a killing field. John Turner was unwilling or unable to discipline the Rat Pack, force them to better target their prey, or coordinate their firepower with his own. The Liberals lacked any cohesive long-term plan. They aimed at anything that stirred in the weeds and hoped to hit a trophy animal. Much of the time, they just shot themselves in the foot.

The Mulroney Cabinet dreaded the Rat Pack's fire-at-anything tactics, for any one of us could be struck at any time. As the saying goes, even a broken clock is accurate twice a day. But we did not regret that the Official Opposition appeared to lack an overall war plan. How did winning a given day's skirmish—and, therefore, news cycle—advance V-Day? Many of the real war veterans in our parliamentary ranks would scratch their heads over the Liberals' obvious disarray. Edmonton West MP Marcel Lambert, for example, saw action in Dieppe in the Second World War, achieved the rank of lieutenant colonel, and served as parliamentary secretary to Diefenbaker's minister of defence. A former Speaker of the House of Commons, Lambert was generally considered the PC Caucus's foremost expert on parliamentary procedure—our Stanley Knowles. Marcel would rail in Caucus against the Rat Pack's shameless violation of parliamentary rules and procedures and traditions for naked partisan purposes—but to no good end, including their own. He was especially incensed by their behaviour in Question Period. And he attacked Commons Speaker John Bosley's inability, or unwillingness, to discipline the offenders. Some saw his criticisms as sour grapes for Mulroney's not having selected him as Speaker. But it contributed to the widespread belief that Bosley lacked the will, the competence, and the personal stature to control the Commons. He seemed to have given the Liberal Opposition a *carte blanche* to practise almost any form of McCarthyism they liked without an eye on the Question Period clock, broken or not. "Nothing was sacred as this campaign of denigration and smear…went on unabated for a decade," Brian Mulroney says in his memoirs.[10] Eventually, Bosley was replaced as Speaker by John Fraser, a far more experienced and authoritative parliamentarian, so Mulroney's comment had more merit about the earlier period than the latter. Meanwhile, for every pint of blood the Liberals extracted from our beaten body, they hemorrhaged at least that much from their own. The public's "plague on all your houses" view of the government and Official Opposition alike made it difficult for John Turner to sell himself as the Great White Hope for the Liberals—and, consequently, potentially for the country—that, some years earlier, he was broadly perceived to be. In that sense, in the end, Turner might have paid the highest price of all for the Liberals' undisciplined and trigger-happy parliamentary behaviour. If the Liberals shot themselves in the foot for lack of Opposition target practice, it was Turner's limb that got amputated.

The decade John Turner had been absent from politics showed. He was rusty both in Parliament and on the campaign trail. People remembered the man in his prime as the studly young Adonis who had waltzed with Princess Margaret. Toronto Cabinet minister David Crombie—the city's former "tiny perfect mayor" and Joe Clark PC candidate recruit—famously likened Turner's political reincarnation to the re-emergence of American billionaire Howard Hughes after many years as a recluse. Hughes appeared at his coming-out news conference with shoulder-length straggly and thinning white hair, rotting yellow teeth, and long dirty fingernails. The once-dashing and dark-haired member of the international jet set had been an aviation pioneer. Now the former storied playboy was an emaciated, addled, and irredeemable junkie—hardly a flattering Turner alter ego for the Canadian voter to contemplate.

Crombie's John Turner/Howard Hughes comparison was, of course, outrageous rhetorical hyperbole, but right up to the 1988 election, we Tories never felt threatened by Turner. The man seemed to have lost his political mojo while practising law in Toronto. He had also acquired some grating verbal tics—for example, clearing his throat in mid-thought with a stream of harrumphs. Worse, he had failed to keep up with what voters considered socially acceptable behaviour. A TV camera infamously caught him patting the derrière of Liberal Party president Iona Campagnolo (later appointed British Columbia's first woman lieutenant governor). This classy and striking-looking middle-aged lady with salt-and pepper hair said she didn't take offence. But the public, especially women, did. Even the man's political vocabulary had become dated (for example, "make-work" instead of "job-creation," "aircraft" instead of "planes"). Nor, from the very beginning of Turner's leadership, did the Liberal Party itself seem to have its act together. The Liberal leader once spoke at a major luncheon forum on women's issues in Toronto. His advance people failed to remove a huge fork graphic behind the podium, the sponsoring association's logo for the annual event. In TV and newspaper coverage of Turner's speech, the fork appeared to be sprouting from Turner's head, making him look like the Devil—literally, with horns atop. Brian Mulroney's political machine would never have made such an elementary blunder. Nor did they when Mulroney spoke separately at the same event. Health-care providers are taught that their first principle is *Primum non nocere*—"First, do no harm." In a similar fashion, a party leader's first obligation to himself is to avoid getting in his own way. With help from ineffectual Liberal Party strategists and organizers, Turner often blocked the very road he travelled. Calling a snap election as PM in 1984—requiring both the queen and the pope to cancel planned visits to Canada (always the gold standard for prime ministerial photo ops)—was his biggest mistake. Using the Liberals' Senate majority to force an election on free trade four years later was, as it turned out, a close second. Do no harm, indeed. Turned did great political harm to himself.

We Tories entered the 1988 federal election confident that Turner and his Liberal candidates would fail to win Canadians over to their side on the central issue of the campaign, the Canada–United States Free Trade Agreement. For many weeks in the Commons beforehand, John Turner had railed against the agreement without drawing much blood. The Rat Pack had been too busy with politics of personal destruction to make any impact of their own on the issue. After his first salvos, Turner's rants against free trade became stale, repetitious, predictable, and boring, including to his own supporters. With each passing week leading up to the election, he was getting steadily diminishing traction in the media and with the public at large. The once "Future Best Hope" of the Liberal Party, in the late 1960s and early 1970s, was now flailing in the Commons. He resembled an aging heavyweight boxer who had taken one too many haymakers to the head and was about to hit the canvass in his last major prizefight.

Even well into the election campaign, the free trade issue seemed to lack legs. At this time, John Turner suffered painful and debilitating lower-back spasms. The CBC reported that senior Liberal backroom strategists were considering replacing Turner with Jean Chrétien for the remainder of the election in a desperate effort to salvage the Liberals' campaign. And yet, Turner had passed a leadership review at a national Liberal convention only two years earlier. I remember overhearing this news report while canvassing from door to door one evening in my riding. I thought to myself, "Jeez, we Tories have this election in the bag. It can't get any worse for the Grits." It, therefore, shocked us Tories—certainly, Brian Mulroney—when, in the party leaders' English debate towards the end of the campaign, Turner fought the fight of his life. He knocked cold not only Mulroney, but also NDP leader Ed Broadband. John Turner—the man and the politician—appeared reborn. With a few well-rehearsed blows against the prime minister—"With one signature of a pen, Sir, you sold out Canada"—the Liberal leader flipped both the free trade issue and the campaign on their heads and set us Tories on our heels. The PM and PC Party soon recouped lost ground on the hustings, except in Atlantic Canada, and won re-election handily, though with a reduced majority (169 seats, with 43 percent of the vote; down from 211 with 50.03 percent four years earlier). Meanwhile, in the key leaders' debate, Turner had his finest hour in Opposition—and, arguably, in public life. He proved not only that he could still be an agile prizefighter, but that he had an accurate shot as a big-game hunter as well.

Although John Turner's political comeback ultimately failed and he personally faltered, this fine man was no Howard Hughes in the tragic final stages of the latter's drug-wasted life. The former track star and Rhodes Scholar was a true gentleman politician who had maintained his handsome looks, athletic form, and disarming charm as an older man. It was just that Turner's particular style of politics, and the man himself, had gone out of fashion by the time he tried his political comeback. Like the grand Chrysler Imperial that used to turn every head when rounding bends, John Turner—once so sleek, spiffy, and sparkling, and still no slouch—saw time pass him by. The Canadian electorate had moved on. And, now, Turner was forced to do so, too.

The irony is that, notwithstanding all the verbal blows we exchanged in the House of Commons, I never had an actual conversation with John Turner. The closest I came occurred when he sat directly across the aisle from me on a commuter flight between Ottawa and Toronto. Several hours earlier, we had engaged in one of our most heated Commons altercations. As I took off my suit jacket, placed it in the overhead bin, and was about to sit down, our eyes locked. Turner smiled at me, nodded and, with characteristic Old Boy formality, said: "Hello, Mr. McMillan. Have a nice flight." Returning the smile, I replied simply: "You, too, John." That was it. Nevertheless, I feel instinctively that, had the opportunity ever arisen, he and I would have felt comfortable trading political war stories over a beer—or, more likely in his case, scotch in a crystal highball glass. Although he was sixteen years older than I, and even longer in the tooth in life and political experience, both of us knew all too well that politics is largely a game. It is no less so for being played as though the sillier parliamentary and other goings-on of the sort described here really count. They don't. Despite the wide gap between us in age and maturity, John Turner and I— blow-dried or not—had the same type of hair.

## GENTLEMEN (AND LADY) POLITICIANS

Erik Nielsen was a completely different political archetype from most of the others I knew in my career in politics: He was ruthless, mean-spirited, and committed to winning at any cost, including human suffering. As an individual, he was rare, but, like all archetypes by definition, representative—in his case, of political predators. Tom Symons was not just a rare individual. He was unique. Each of us is, in our own way. Symons's uniqueness, however, defies description more than that of anyone else I have ever known. It's as though he was plucked from a period of history long before his own. He is not so much anachronistic as timeless, incapable of being defined or understood by standards rooted in a particular period, least of all today. How else to explain a man who never drove a car or used a typewriter or operated a computer? And yet, the former Trent University president has written reports on human rights and Canadian Studies and other subjects so visionary that his insights remain futuristic decades after publication. As a political player, however, Tom Symons was yet another archetype—completely different from the Nielsen and even Turner ones, though much closer to the latter than to the former. The Symons archetype is, in Dalton Camp's term, the "Gentleman Politician." I would broaden the concept to "Lady," for the relevant qualities apply to the likes of Jean Wadds, Flora MacDonald, Iona Campagnolo, Pauline Jewett, and, from my own province, Catherine Callbeck. Most of my Cabinet or PC Party colleagues over the years could be located somewhere along the continuum between these two extremes.

John Henry Cardinal Newman was the most famous English convert to Roman Catholicism of the nineteenth century. His definition of a gentleman (from *The Idea of a University*, 1852) stands as the classic: "one who never inflicts pain." It's a variation of the Golden Rule: "Do unto others as you would have them do unto you." That was Tom Symons as a political player in the Stanfield years. The man could be as tough as a ghetto street fighter when he had to be, kick near the groin if circumstances required, and throw the odd temple punch in the event all else failed—but never a sucker punch, even to retaliate. The same applies to Robert Stanfield. They were both Gentlemen Politicians, the latter literally. Like Symons, Stanfield was not faint of heart. Neither man, though, sought to inflict pain for pain's sake on an adversary. Notwithstanding Pierre Trudeau's arrogance and testiness in office and his truculence once out—on constitutional matters, in particular—I would also place him in this Gentleman Politician club. After my Atlantic veterinary college imbroglio with Trudeau in the Commons, I was never again able to view him as anything but a gentleman. I can only imagine how proud this loving father would be had he lived long enough to see his son Justin elected prime minister of Canada—and, to boot, with a larger majority than he himself attained at the height of Trudeaumania in 1968. Appearances to the contrary, considerable humanity resided in the elder man's heart.

For Erik Nielsen, in contrast, inflicting pain on foes was *the* goal and the standard by which he judged both political success and the individuals who sought it, including himself. Unlike Stanfield and Symons and Trudeau and Turner, he was no Gentleman Politician. Erik Nielsen's firing came too late— in June 1986, almost two years into the government's first mandate—to undo the damage. By then, the PM had allowed himself to be typecast as a thug scarcely more civilized than Nielsen. To some, he was even worse. The man's oratorical gifts were a big asset on the campaign trail and a powerful force in the Commons chamber, at least to the ears of his parliamentary supporters, who egged him on to their own detriment. But the man's intemperate political rhetoric proved a major liability when not calibrated to TV viewers' living rooms. Truly, the medium is the message. Towards the end of the government's first mandate, Canadians liked less and less both the message and the messenger. By the end of the second, voters didn't like either at all.

Can a lamb—Stanfield, Symons, (McMillan?)—survive in the political world of tigers? I do not know the answer. The self-styled king of tigers, Erik Nielsen, could not himself survive the wilds of the jungle. Nielsen left the government fired and disgraced. As he petulantly slammed the door behind him on the way out, he tried to finagle the richest-possible patronage post he could from the prime minster and others of his former colleagues. Nielsen succeeded spectacularly, for he was appointed chairman of the Canadian Transport Commission. With a hefty six-figure annual salary, it was among the richest sinecures in the gift of the Crown. He received this windfall courtesy of those whom he had roared at and savaged with such obvious relish while the country's second-most-powerful politician. These were the very colleagues Nielsen later attacked in a memoir for undermining his lonely efforts to cleanse the government of patronage. What hypocrisy! The political tigers versus the political lambs—in Blake's immortal words:

*Tyger! Tyger! Burning bright*
*In the forests of the night*
*What immortal hand or eye*
*Dare frame thy fearful symmetry?*

Looking back now, almost three decades after the fact, I do not hold a grudge against Erik Nielsen, just as I don't against any of the other political actors with whom I once crossed swords. Just as, deep down, there might well have been some goodness in Erik that I was never able to divine, so also some of my colleagues did not know me fully, either—likely because I was either unwilling or unable to allow them to see beyond the surface of my own portrait in the Rogues Gallery. Politics doesn't just grind; it also blinds. How much did even the prime minister know me as a person, or I him at the time? I did not know Brian Mulroney nearly as well, nor for as long, as my twin brother did. But I knew Mulroney a lot better than I would have, had Charley not been so close to him. Only my family and closest friends, especially ones who have known me since I was a boy, call me "Tommy" instead of "Tom." To me, it's like rings on a tree: I can tell how far back someone goes in my life by whether he or she calls me one or the other. But, because Charley has always called me Tommy (when not an expletive), and Brian would never have heard Charley refer to me otherwise, I was always "Tommy" to Brian Mulroney. He addressed me that way even at Cabinet meetings. For his part, he was "Brian" to me, except in the presence of officials and on formal occasions. All this said, Brian Mulroney's calling me "Tommy" and my calling him "Brian" suggested a friendship that existed only in the loosest sense.

In any event, Erik Hersholt Nielsen is now deceased. He died of a massive heart attack at his home in Kelowna, BC, in September 2008, at age eighty-four. No question, he had been a devoted son of Yukon, fighting tenaciously for its interests throughout a long career as its MP, thirty years in all (1957–87). No one could reasonably deny that he loved the North, Canada, and, in a perverse way, the Progressive Conservative Party. Appropriately, in his memory the Yukon government renamed the main airport at Whitehorse, the territory's capital, Erik Nielsen International Airport. Most people who knew Nielsen in Ottawa, however, do not need an airport to remember him. I do not. And my memory of him is generally not positive.

In February 2007, Prime Minister Stephen Harper officially renamed the Halifax airport Robert L. Stanfield International Airport to honour the late PC Party leader. The international airport in Toronto had been renamed to honour Lester B. Pearson, and Montreal's Dorval airport rechristened to honour Pierre Trudeau. Given that politicians spend so much time catching flights to or from one place or another, how appropriate that some of them should end up with their name on an airport. As a Maritimer and disciple of Robert Stanfield, I am delighted that the seventh-busiest airport in Canada, by passenger traffic, has been so named. When passengers soar into the clouds on a plane from Halifax, they can be sure they're that much closer to the soul of this great Canadian. Whether passengers soaring in a plane from Erik Nielsen International Airport are closer to, or farther from, the soul of the person after whom it is named—only God or the Devil knows for certain.

# Chapter 26

# FIGHTING THE HOME FIRES

Prince Edward Island is a great place to grow up, a beautiful place to live, a wonderful place to be from. But it's an almost impossible place to represent in the federal Cabinet. Only about 145,000 people live on the Island, equivalent to a city borough elsewhere. Most Islanders depend on Ottawa for their livelihoods, directly or indirectly—many both ways. In my time in Cabinet, 22 percent of Islanders were unemployed. Total unemployment insurance payments ($160 million) exceeded cash receipts from potatoes, our biggest crop. Government accounted for 85 percent of the economy. Widespread poverty, hidden behind a wall of federal cash, rendered the Island a ward of Ottawa and the provincial government a mere agency to dispense federal largesse in diverse guises. Of all government activity on the Island, 65 percent was federal, and about 45 percent of provincial government revenues came from Ottawa. So, there was a lot at stake when the federal government did virtually anything. And, typically, whatever the government did was bound to upset some people, with fast-acting rippling effects everywhere across the province. That's because "anywhere" in such an intimate place *is*, for all practical purposes, "everywhere." PEI is one big village. And the federal Cabinet minister is its *Bürgermeister*. He had best watch his back if he knows what's good for him. Every issue, every voter, is a potential assassin, not just in the minister's own riding but throughout the province. Everyone considers himself the minister's boss and, therefore, entitled to his time and services—and his hide if he missteps.

But how does the incumbent protect his back when, per force, he is not always present to see the assassins planning their attacks from grassy knolls? The minister's responsibilities are carried out as much in Ottawa and across the country and, indeed, abroad as they are at home. It's a dangerous balancing act. In a big metropolitan constituency, voters don't necessarily expect their Cabinet minister to be always accessible. In provinces with more than one minister—almost all the others—the ministerial load is shared. So is the blame. But that is not at all the case on the Island. There's only one game in town. And the minister is it. The game had better be good or the knives will fly. When the political stripe of the provincial government is different from that of the federal government, the premier is available full time on the spot to undermine the federal minister at every turn, if so inclined. Most often, he is able to do it in the minister's absence. On the Island, politics is treated like a zero-sum game: if one politician or political party gains, another loses and vice versa. When the premier is especially partisan, as he was most of my time as minister, political mischief replaces statecraft as the order of the day. And before long, in Lilliput, everyone is tying Gulliver down. Such were the circumstances in which I increasingly found myself as the clock ticked steadily faster towards the 1988 national election.

# Prescription for Success,
## Avoiding Failure

A Member of Parliament appointed for the first time to Cabinet is typically gung-ho about his or her new duties. If the individual were not strongly committed to public service, it's unlikely he or she would have entered politics in the first place. The opportunity to serve one's riding, province, and country in the inner sanctum of national power is heady stuff. For someone like me, long involved and interested in policy matters, it's especially satisfying. When a citizen has the burden of advancing his province's interests as the lone Cabinet minister from that province, the task can be—and, for me, was—both exhilarating and challenging. In retrospect, I believe I threw myself into the job with more energy and commitment than judicious discipline and caution. Eagerness to do good things is an admirable trait. The cause is ill-served, however, if it is at the expense of not being understood and supported by the people who elected you. "The loneliest feeling in the world is when you think you are leading the parade and turn to find that no one is following you," Franklin Roosevelt said. "No [politician] who badly misguesses public opinion will last very long."[1] Wisdom and pacing are equally essential to long-term political survival. Those who violate this principle pay a heavy price. I did.

The politician most likely to succeed is the individual who takes the long view, and one step at a time, towards achieving political goals. The elected official needs to keep a clear eye on the rearview mirror to ensure that, as he or she leads, there are followers. In the end, the cautious politician likely will achieve a smaller agenda, build a more modest legacy, earn himself less credit in the eyes of history, and do fewer things for his community than the bold and the brave. But the former lives to fight another day. The latter might not.

An archetype of the cautious politician during my time in federal politics was Elmer MacKay, first elected to Parliament in 1971 for the Nova Scotia riding of Central Nova. Father of later federal Cabinet minister Peter MacKay (Justice and Attorney General), the elder man served in various Cabinet portfolios over the years (Regional Economic Expansion, Solicitor General, National Revenue, Public Works, Canada Mortgage and Housing Corporation) without losing a single election before retiring in 1993. In a political career that spanned more than two decades, Elmer MacKay rarely made a splash nationally. But neither did he drown back home. The man will likely be best remembered, not in his own right, but as father to Peter, the final leader of the Progressive Conservative Party of Canada.

Though never losing an election in either his own riding or as national PC Party leader, Brian Mulroney was an archetype, writ large, of the other extreme, particularly in the man's second term as prime minister. He tried to do too much too fast—with disastrous results for his party in the 1993 election. As with all things, the trick is to find the proper balance between the two extremes—whether one considers caution another word for cowardice or courage a euphemism for carelessness. Either way, by the end of my time in Cabinet, I had not found the right balance. I tilted towards the "Mulroney," not the "MacKay," extreme. I have only myself to blame for the electoral consequences.

Two issues plagued me as the Island's representative in the federal Cabinet: free trade and the Fixed Link. A third issue, a Litton Industries plant to be built in Charlottetown, also threatened my political health. But Tory premier Jim Lee took most of the fever from it. Many of the Islanders opposed to Litton were against free trade and the Fixed Link, too. So, as my political life force withered, Litton was more heartburn than heart attack. But it added to my growing discomfort, nevertheless. Either free trade or the Fixed Link alone was life-threatening. The two issues striking at the same time created an exponential factor that cried out for a corpse. Liberal premier Joe Ghiz was eager to serve as undertaker, and he had me in his sights for burial.

## Canada–United States Free Trade

Brian Mulroney's pursuit of a free trade agreement with the United States is often cited as evidence that he is a continentalist, not a true Tory in the nationalist Macdonald/ Cartier tradition. This is yet another falsehood about Mulroney that floated in the political mythosphere, to coin a term. In fact, his instincts had always been to oppose such an arrangement with the United States: that was his official position when he campaigned for the PC leadership in both 1976 and 1983. But economies everywhere were rapidly becoming globalized. China and India, historically weak, were emerging as major world competitors. And international trade was increasingly being conducted between, and within, a steadily rising number of mutually exclusive trading blocks, from all of which Canada was excluded. At the same time, Canada's largest market by far, the United States, could no longer be taken for granted as it completed or pursued special trading relationships with other countries. It did so even as American protectionist voices became louder and gained more followers in Congress. A growing body of evidence convinced Mulroney that Canada had no choice but to seek membership in a free trade zone of its own. Otherwise, the PM thought, the country risked losing markets and jobs to countries adapting better to fast-changing conditions in the global marketplace. A free trade agreement (FTA) with the United States struck Mulroney as not only the best, but, indeed, the only option. The PM was especially won over to this view by the Royal Commission on the Economic Union and Development Prospects for Canada. The Macdonald Commission—named after its chair, former Liberal finance minister Donald Macdonald—had been established by Pierre Trudeau in 1982, but it reported to Mulroney in 1985. An FTA was one of that body's three major recommendations. Ever the hard-nosed businessman and pragmatist, Brian Mulroney placed the national interest above his party's—and his own—orthodoxy on the Canadian-US "reciprocity" issue. Borden morphed into Laurier; the Conservatives, not the Liberals, became the standard-bearers for free trade. The change, however, was not one of soul but of urgent circumstance.

One of the major assaults against the idea of an FTA was that an accord with the Americans would give them unfettered access to our fresh water. Opposition leader John Turner and my own province's Liberal premier, Joe Ghiz, made that argument, as did most other opponents of an FTA. I was, in effect, Canada's minister of water. As such, I crafted the country's first-ever National Water Policy, based on the report of the Pearse Commission, which, like the Macdonald Commission, had been created by the Trudeau government. The water policy I recommended categorically opposed large-scale freshwater exports, and the Mulroney Cabinet adopted it without dissent. Not a single colleague of mine supported large-scale water exports. Most opposed the idea virulently; the rest did so either with moderate passion or not much interest in the subject. At the behest of Cabinet, I also drafted a *Water Act* not only to demonstrate that concern on this score was unfounded, but also to outlaw the exports themselves and heavily penalize transgressors.[2] (The bill died on the Order Paper when the 1988 election was called and Parliament dissolved.)

Water in the context of a Canada–United States FTA was a phony issue, a weapon to attack the government and undermine support for free trade more generally. Not one of my department's senior officials gave any credence to the concern. Throughout the federal bureaucracy, top Environment Canada personnel were reputed to be "flaming reds," albeit among the best-educated and most authoritative on scientific and resource matters. So, one would have expected them to embrace the free-trade-will-plunder-our-water argument if there had been any validity to it. They didn't, and there wasn't.

Throughout the course of the negotiations with the United States, the Mulroney Cabinet was well aware of the powerful emotional "water" argument opponents could use, however falsely, to undermine support for an agreement. At the most pivotal point in the pre-1988 election debate about the trade deal, as final approval and implementation awaited, Governor James Thompson of Illinois threw a verbal Molotov cocktail into what was already an explosive issue. Certain parts of his country had been experiencing record drought, a phenomenon that had spiked an unexpectedly large turnout of major US news media at the milestone World Climate Change Conference I was hosting at this very time in Toronto (late June 1988). Suddenly, Americans were beginning to credit the warnings of scientists around the world, including their own, about the alarming heating of the planet and its impact on the environment. Not just drought, but also rising sea levels—especially the effects on low-lying coastal communities—started to shake our southern neighbours from their complacency. Governor Thompson was but one among many leading Americans calling on Canada to come to their rescue by diverting substantial amounts of our plentiful, but by no means unlimited, fresh water to hydrate Uncle Sam's palate.

What alarmed us in Cabinet was, in particular, the Illinois governor's call for the diversion of water from Lake Michigan, via the Chicago River, to the Mississippi. At the time, the Mississippi was suffering the lowest water levels since measurements were first taken in 1872. Thomson wanted to divert a staggering four billion gallons of water in total—enough to lower Lake Michigan by at least an inch. We in Cabinet were worried that this proposal, if acted on, would be the thin edge of a hefty cleaver that could chop a huge chunk out of our natural environment. Although "only" one lake was at stake in this case, the Great Lakes are a delicate and dynamic ecological system: drain one lake and all are affected—in this case, especially Lake Huron. Normally, Canada's interests would have been protected against such folly by the International Joint Commission, the bilateral body established in 1909 to manage the Great Lakes jointly. The kind of water-diversion scheme Thompson proposed typically would need to be approved by the commission. The Michigan case, however, was unique. Unlike the other giant lakes that make up the total system, Lake Michigan is wholly within the boundaries of the United States. The governor and other champions of his scheme argued, speciously, that neither the commission's nor Canada's approval was, therefore, required. But the Mulroney government was not willing to take any chances with the stakes so high.

I reminded my Cabinet colleagues that, while Canada is blessed with abundant water, 60 percent of its fresh water drains into the Arctic, thousands of miles from our big cities, where it is most needed. It would, consequently, be short-sighted to open the spigots to the Americans when we might well need every litre of Canadian water for our own purposes; if not soon, then sometime later. Besides, I told Cabinet, the diversion itself could have disastrous environmental consequences—many of them unpredictable and, thus, especially menacing. I was preaching not so much to the choir as to the College of Cardinals and, in the case of the prime minister, to the pope. They already had the religion. Not a single Cabinet member thought that the Lake Michigan diversion proposal idea was anything but "insane." I used that very word to describe it in the House of Commons. *Time* magazine gave my comment, and the debate in general, big play in a July 25, 1988, article that featured mug shots of Governor Thompson, Flora MacDonald (acting prime minister that week), and me looking as though we all badly needed water, if not cardiopulmonary resuscitation. Canada's ambassador to Washington, Allan Gotlieb, delivered a toughly worded formal statement of protest to the US State Department condemning the unilateral Michigan diversion plan. Thanks to the massive resistance from the Mulroney government, joined by saner voices in the United States itself, including the US Army Corps of Engineers, Governor Thompson's idea dropped dead on arrival. So was any other proposal of the kind. The governor's plan was the only one that would have had any chance to succeed, if any were to do so. It failed spectacularly. Both Canadian and Americans involved in the free trade talks considered the proposal killed and buried; not that, in retrospect, it ever had much life to begin with—except as a political cudgel.

The fact the water-export issue got the traction it did confounded me. The Mulroney government was going to do everything in its power to squash even the most harebrained scheme, such as Governor Thompson's. The issue in the context of free trade was completely bogus and not worth anyone's time, even though it got a lot of it. Nor should any time have been devoted to Joe Ghiz's claim that he was opposed to free trade partly on this basis. And yet, he also got a lot of attention for his opposition. Did he ever!

As consul general in Boston, I once hosted a dinner party well after the 1988 election at my official residence. The guests included Premier Joe Ghiz and other Prince Edward Islanders, as well as former Boston Bruins hockey legend Bobby Orr. At this dinner party, I overheard the most puzzling and surprising statement I have ever heard a politician make off the record. Ghiz was not a heavy drinker. But, after even one scotch, this normally loquacious man became a veritable chatterbox—and not a very circumspect one, at that. In such a circumstance, he loved to hold court, expressing himself with equal measures of magniloquence, grandiosity, and often unintended candour. Over after-dinner drinks in the residence living room, Joe told his courtiers that he thought Liberal leader John Turner should have opposed the Meech Lake Accord and supported Canada-US free trade, instead of the converse. It was clear this assessment reflected not what Joe Ghiz thought would have been better politics for Turner and the Liberals, but, rather, at heart, what Joe himself believed on substantive grounds. And yet, Joe had campaigned hard for the accord and against free trade, particularly in the 1988 election in the latter case. In opposing the Mulroney government's trade agreement with the United States, Joe stood alone among all the premiers except for Ontario's David Peterson.[3] Ghiz's opposition boosted the anti–free trade cause far out of proportion to PEI's geographic size or population or economic importance. As the expression goes, he was "fighting above his weight." The PEI premier gave cover to Peterson, who would never have fought the trade agreement without at least one other premier at his side. Otherwise, Ontario would have been viewed as the lone-wolf heavy against the other Confederation partners—an untenable position for Peterson to place the province in, and he knew it.

I could never understand Joe Ghiz's opposition to free trade other than as a way to undermine the Mulroney government and thereby help defeat Tory MPs from the Island, me especially. I found it particularly hard to fathom his express concern about freshwater exports to the United States, one of the main grounds for his opposition. After all, the Island had only one freshwater lake, and a tiny one to boot. To listen to Joe Ghiz's shrill rhetoric, however, one would think PEI was Finland. Ghiz had been president of the Liberal Party of PEI before becoming provincial Liberal leader. The man was one of the most partisan individuals I have ever known. He once told his Charlottetown law partners (at Scales, Ghiz, Jenkins and McQuaid), prior to entering electoral politics, that he would not rest "until every goddamned PEI Tory is driven into the ground." Once Liberal leader, he was eager to make good on that promise, even using provincial government offices and personnel and other resources to do so while premier.[4] For him, free trade was as good a weapon as any to slay his political opposition.

With a tiny local market for its bountiful produce—potatoes and fish, in particular—PEI, from the earliest times, had always fought tenaciously for free trade. It did so to maximize its access to external markets, especially in nearby New England. So committed to open markets was the Island colony before Confederation that "Free Trade" was stamped on its colonial coinage in the 1850s. Indeed, the Canadian-American Reciprocity Treaty of 1854 provided for free trade in raw materials and agricultural produce between PEI colony (and other British North American colonies, including the rest of the Maritimes) and the United States until 1865. The treaty was ended mostly because of opposition from the United States—not the colonies, least of all PEI, which long afterwards struggled to have Canadian-US reciprocity restored. Free trade is in our DNA and always has been.

In March 1987, the Ghiz government's own Trade Negotiations Secretariat released an official document—*Canada-United States Trade Negotiations: Principles and Objectives*— detailing the province's official support for free trade. In the final FTA, the Mulroney government accommodated every one of the few policy and technical reservations the Ghiz government identified in that document concerning PEI's distinct circumstances. In a CBC special broadcast in the spring of 1988 (several months before the federal election that year), Joe Ghiz and I publicly debated the issue. In the debate, I quoted from the aforementioned PEI government document to demonstrate Ghiz's hypocrisy on free trade. Apparently staggered by the salvo, he replied lamely: "Well, Tom can quote from some document, but let me assure you...." The premier dismissed the official published policy of his own government as just "some document." Politics does not get much weirder than that, even on the Island. The Joe Ghiz I overheard at the dinner with Bobby Orr confirmed what I knew almost from the beginning: the PEI premier's anti–free trade stance was partisan, insincere, intellectually dishonest, inconsistent with Islanders' historic ambitions, and against the interests of the province and people he was elected to serve. In this case, as in so many others, Ghiz placed partisanship above those Island interests. In doing so, he helped distort the course of the national debate on the issue by creating the impression there was far more official opposition to Canada-United States free trade than actually existed, particularly in Atlantic Canada.

# The Fixed Link

Joe Ghiz's opposition to the PEI-NB Fixed Link, until powerful Liberal backers forced him to reverse himself in the end, is another example of how he placed partisanship above all else, including the Island's own best interests. Ghiz later revealed that he had voted against the project in the Island-wide plebiscite his own government sponsored in January 1988.[5] This fact should have surprised no one—certainly, not me. UPEI's Institute of Island Studies was the hotbed of intellectual opposition to the project. Most of the arguments against it were manufactured and provided to other opponents by the Institute's principals. Their fodder was not so much research and reasoning as rhetoric and talking points. Ghiz had arranged for UPEI historian David Weale and the Institute's director, Harry Baglole, to organize the plebiscite.[6] It was like putting the town arsonists in charge of the fire station. Ghiz's choice of such a group to organize the vote prejudiced the outcome from the start. Virtually all local CBC reporters and producers also opposed the project and were hostile to the Mulroney government in general, particularly for its policy on free trade. That the organizers of the Fixed Link plebiscite were so tightly connected with this major media outlet compounded the stacking of the deck. The Fixed Link would be the biggest single federal government development project in the history of the Island (in partnership with the private developer). And it would be one of the largest in all Atlantic Canada outside oil and gas exploration. I was the province's federal Cabinet minister. And yet, the premier did not even inform me, let alone consult me, about his decision to hold a provincial plebiscite on this massive federal project. I learned about the vote on CFCY radio while driving to a meeting. Not a good omen!

I almost careered off the road from shock when I heard the premier's plebiscite announcement. It was not that I opposed the idea of a province-wide vote on the issue. It was the way the vote was so obviously being organized to undermine the project's chances of getting built, either then or at any time in the foreseeable future. The plebiscite was a ruse for the premier to eat his cake and have it, too: scuttling the project in the name of consulting Islanders while not appearing to be opposed outright. Indeed, Ghiz insisted he was giving the proposed project a "fair hearing" by holding the plebiscite and launching the attendant debate. But the plebiscite was never intended to be anything but an obstacle to the Fixed Link, rather than a genuine step to address the proposal on its merits, one way or the other. This fact was demonstrated by how Ghiz responded to the results of the plebiscite when, to his surprise, they did not go his way: Islanders supported the Fixed Link 59 percent to 41 percent. Having said he wanted to be guided by Islanders through the plebiscite, the premier immediately discounted majority opinion once it had been expressed. He dismissed the results out of hand. That night, Ghiz appeared on CBC-TV's national flagship news show *The Journal*. The premier told veteran host Barbara Frum that his primary concern was for the views of the *minority* of Islanders who had opposed the Fixed Link in the vote. He made it sound as though the anti–Fixed Link side had lost by a vote or two, instead of by a substantial margin by Island standards. When Frum expressed incredulity, Ghiz viciously attacked her as an arrogant Upper Canadian interfering in Maritimers' internal affairs. (Senior Ghiz advisor Rick Coles told me the next day that he had always urged Ghiz never to give a live interview later than 9:00 P.M. or after imbibing a single alcoholic drink. "Joe, you can't control either your temper or your tongue when you're tired or drinking," Coles said he had advised. How right the man was in this case.)

The organized opponents of the Fixed Link called themselves "Friends of the Island." (Supporters were "Islanders for a Better Tomorrow.") The overarching strategy of the Friends was to tie up, and ultimately bury, the project in environmental process, realizing that they would lose the substantive argument on its merits. Rex Murphy has written that "[the] Environmental Review Process is actually neither clinical nor neutral...it is just a political stage show, an act during which politicians can temporize and equivocate."[7] It was exactly that in this circumstance. Accordingly, after the plebiscite failed to achieve its purpose, Ghiz demanded a Federal Environmental Assessment and Review Process (EARP) panel be struck and public hearings started immediately. He did so knowing full well that, by legal protocol and precedent, such would normally be done only towards the end of an environmental impact assessment process—not, as Ghiz insisted in this instance, at the beginning. That subterfuge was less a second kick at the cat than dousing its Purina chow with arsenic.

I tried to explain the correct process sequence at an impromptu media availability session in my constituency office. My main point was that to conduct public hearings on the Fixed Link before all the scientific and engineering spade work had been completed would "subvert due process." Privately, I believed that, if public debate were based on objective information, rather than on pure emotion and misconception, fewer Islanders would be seduced by the Friends of the Island's demagogic opposition to the project or, for that matter, by exaggerated benefits ascribed to it by the Islanders for Better Tomorrow. My phrase "subvert due process" proved disastrous. I had handed the demagogues a weapon to bludgeon me while putting the Fixed Link cause itself on the defensive from the get-go. CFCY and CBC media personality Jack MacAndrew rushed to the airwaves and accused me of attacking all Islanders opposed to the project as "subversives." This was not at all what I had said, much less meant, still less would ever have wished to telegraph. But that was MacAndrew's knowingly false charge, which he regurgitated in his many media forums, not just CFCY and CBC. Other Island reporters made the charge their own. Soon it became central to the Fixed Link debate. It also further accelerated the already fast-developing political mythology that began to attach to me personally, and so dangerously, like potholes on a city street after winter's frost: I was obsessed with having the Fixed Link built, and the Island's best interests and Islanders' own views be damned. My road ahead was going to be bumpy, indeed.

Horace Carver was a Charlottetown lawyer closely tied to David Weale and to the Friends of the Island militants opposed to the Fixed Link. In *Maclean's* magazine, well-known local freelance journalist Kennedy Wells described Carver as a "prissy Protestant fundamentalist."[8] This self-important "fundamentalist" was a three-time Conservative member of the provincial legislature and PEI attorney general for two years. Though supposedly a Tory, he never missed an opportunity to publicly misrepresent and then denounce my Fixed Link stance and the Mulroney government's approach to the issue more generally. Early in the Fixed Link saga, I told the Island media that I was eager to have the federal Cabinet "fast-track" a decision to explore whether the idea of the project was or was not a good one in principle and, therefore, should or should not be considered based on all the factors, both positive and negative. At no time did I say that the project itself should be fast-tracked, a far different matter. This, however, was what Carver continually insisted was my position. Anti–Fixed Link zealots and their media sympathizers also repeatedly recycled that charge. It joined MacAndrew's "subversive" charge and, before long, the mythology that I was forcing the project down Islanders' throats spread like a pernicious virus for which nothing, least of all the facts, constituted an antidote. The Fixed Link debate was fast becoming a fact-free zone where emotion supplanted reasoning, rhetoric trumped information, and bias expelled truth.

The fact the project survived all this demagoguery, chicanery, and skullduggery by Joe Ghiz and the Friends of the Island testifies to the collective wisdom of Prince Edward Islanders. Over the generations, Islanders have been inclined to stubbornly resist change. Our forebears opposed, for example, allowing the railway and, later, automobiles into the province. Among other concerns, they feared that these new fandango inventions would scare the horses. Or set the farm fields on fire. Or collide with milk cows. That said, to paraphrase Israeli diplomat Abba Eban's remark about mankind generally (while visiting Japan in 1967), we Islanders invariably do the right thing in the end, even if only after exhausting all other possibilities. Unfortunately, in the late 1980s, the Island was in the grip of one of its periodic spells in which a certain part of the population idealized a much earlier era in the province. These Islanders could be easily convinced by the right demagogue that turning back the clock was absolutely the right and necessary thing to do. The reactionary views of that very kind of demagogue in this case, David Weale, were encapsulated in the title of his regular CBC radio commentaries: *Them Times*.[9] Weale all but preached that a hundred years ago or so had been the best of times, and now we should return to "them times." Our insularity was sanctified, every external influence condemned, and any link between the two demonized as the handiwork of the devil. This characterization is far less exaggerated than the evils that opponents of the Fixed Link ascribed to it. If, for example, weather patterns could be so easily changed by the mere construction of a bridge, as was charged, wouldn't mankind have long since used this device to bend climate to its advantage? Nonsense had no bounds, its perpetrators no conscience, and its market seemingly no satiation point.

John Maloney was a brilliant Charlottetown obstetrician and gynecologist. My father and his urologist brother, Frank, had recruited him as a partner in their Charlottetown Clinic. He was also a neighbour of both brothers and their families in the city's upscale Brighton area. A diehard Liberal, and briefly provincial minister of health, Maloney was best known for his pioneering work in the Industry and Development portfolio in the Alex Campbell government in the 1960s and 1970s. Many of Maloney's government measures were similar to—and possibly inspired by—the industry-promoting innovations of the Stanfield government in Nova Scotia. A reform-bent intellectual of mercurial temperament, John Maloney could not stomach the simple-mindedness of Island Luddites like David Weale. At one point, both Maloney and Weale participated in a small private informal group discussion of the Fixed Link and related issues. Another participant was John Eldon Green, a senior provincial government public servant and prominent Catholic layman and writer. Soon after the group met, Green told me, in the presence of a few others, that Maloney had lectured Weale: "You want PEI to relive the nineteenth century. Let me tell you about 'Them Times.' When people got seriously sick, they shit their pants and died. There were no vaccines, no antibiotics, no penicillin, no insulin, and precious little medical knowledge to save them. So, the ill could not be saved. Weale, you're living in a god-damned fantasy world that never existed and bloody well shouldn't be created today." The life expectancy of a PEI male in 1900 was only forty-seven. That was approximately David Weale's own age at the time John Maloney dressed him down. So, had the Fixed Link plebiscite been held at the end of the prior century that Weale so romanticized—instead of 1988, when it actually was—one fact is clear:

the odds are at least even that this man, as a nineteenth-century crusader in his forties, would not have been young or healthy enough—if even still alive—to lead the charge against the project then. Fantasy, indeed.

One can only imagine how violent Islanders would become if, in some fantasy world today, the federal government were to dismantle the Confederation Bridge and restore the ferry service extolled with such passion and high morality by the likes of David Weale in the name of "Them Times." It seems hard to believe now that 40 percent of Islanders were seduced by Weale's demagoguery and Joe Ghiz's duplicitous political manoeuvring. Demagoguery is no substitute for democracy, high emotion no substitute for rational debate—and, as events have proven, the ferries no substitute for a permanent transportation link between PEI and the mainland.

My own position on the Fixed Link was not to build it come hell or high water, as MacAndrew and Carver and others of their ilk charged. Rather, I believed that the Fixed Link would produce net benefits for the Island; that we Islanders ought to explore every facet of the idea (both good and bad); and that we should find out if the project could be constructed in a cost-effective and environmentally sound way. Machiavelli was right: the odds are rigged for those who support the status quo and against those who seek to change it. Innovative ideas, however, are the only things that have ever improved and extended people's lives. Prince Edward Island needed a big idea in this dark period of the province's history. The Fixed Link proved to be that big idea.

"Journalism is the first draft of history," legendary newsman Philip Graham, who co-owned the *Washington Post*, famously said. For the sake of PEI history, I hope Graham was wrong. But I fear he was right. It is an outrageous assault against the public record that the media have lionized Joe Ghiz's role in the building of the Fixed Link. The fact is, Ghiz did everything he could to scuttle the project. The Graham Principle is reason to believe that historians will launch the same assault against the truth. For sure, that will happen if they rely on biased or ill-informed media reports of the sort that have characterized coverage of the issue almost from the start. Indeed, it is already occurring. The Institute for Research on Public Policy invited a jury of thirty "experts" to rank the best Canadian premiers over the previous forty years. They were to base their judgments on a list of eighteen possible candidates given them. Ghiz was ranked ninth (tied with British Columbia's Gordon Campbell). "[The Confederation Bridge] simply wouldn't have been built without Premier Ghiz's kind of instinctive feel for taking Prince Edward Islanders where they wanted to go," wrote L. Ian MacDonald, then editor of *Policy Options*, the Institute's monthly publication. Absolute rubbish! Ian, whom I know and like and respect from our Mulroney days together, did not know what he was talking about. "Talking through his hat" is the expression that leaps to mind. What leaps to the tongue is unprintable. "Where Islanders wanted to go," and in fact ended up going, was in the exact opposite direction of where Ghiz wanted to lead them. He reversed direction on the Fixed Link, and only at the end, because powerful Liberals, and others, forced his hand on the steering wheel. A modicum of original research that sidesteps incipient mythologies would reveal this fact.

That 40 percent of Islanders voted against the Fixed Link in the plebiscite was due in no small measure to the fact Joe Ghiz himself opposed the project and actively supported individuals and groups also hostile to it. The pro–Fixed Link vote would have been even larger without the premier's underhanded efforts to bury the infant project before it had drawn its first breath. Every public and private poll showed that, for months on end before the premier tipped the balance with his plebiscite shenanigans, the spread was, on average, roughly 70–30 in favour of the project, with hardly anyone undecided. Just a few days before the vote, I delivered a pro–Fixed Link speech in front of a gathering of Charlottetown-area business leaders, community-minded activists, and service club members (Kiwanis, in particular). The speech—a virtual manifesto for the cause—was massively covered by the local media, especially the *Guardian*, which editorially supported the Fixed Link and, accordingly, reported my address at length and almost verbatim. Thanks to my House of Commons free-postage mailing privileges, I was then able to mail copies of the speech to thousands of Islanders from one end of the province to another, just as they were about to vote. Many informed observers at the time, including anti–Fixed Link militants themselves in anger, believe that, had it not been for my high-profile intervention in the campaign at this pivotal point, the split between those for and against the project on voting day might well have been still narrower than it ended up being.

Put simply, at the eleventh hour, my constituency staff and I pulled out all the stops, with the complicity of well-placed individuals and groups in the community, to save the Fixed Link cause against the possible consequences of the premier's underhandedness. Joe Ghiz came perilously close to robbing Islanders of the gigantic opportunity the Fixed Link afforded them to help secure their future. Stating the opposite, as MacDonald and other commentators have been doing over the years since, does not make that fact any less true. It only makes the truth less well known. Journalists have written a terrible draft of history on the Fixed Link. It is up to historians to rewrite the draft. They owe it to their profession and to the public record to get history right.

## Partisanship and Island Politics

The 1986 PEI provincial election led to a change of government from the PCs under Premier Jim Lee to the Liberals under Joe Ghiz. Towards the end of the campaign, at a crucial point, Lee stumbled on the issue of "equal pay for work of equal value" for women. The premier appeared insensitive to this growing cause within the province and elsewhere. Soon afterwards, Diane Porter, a strong local Liberal supporter, and a group of like-minded adversaries of mine positioned themselves to attack me in front of the Island media following a major speech I was about to give on this issue at the Charlottetown Hotel. Porter was chair of the PEI Advisory Council on the Status of Women at the time. Joe Ghiz, the new premier, frequently used such surrogates to do dirty political work for him so that he could kick his opponents without leaving behind a partisan footprint. In the case at hand, Porter and company expected me to align myself with Lee's untenable position on the pay-equity issue, but my would-be attackers were shocked when I did the opposite. I detailed, chapter and verse, both the many measures the Mulroney government had already taken and those it was planning to take towards pay equity under Status of Women Minister Barbara McDougall. When I stunned them with my views, they, instead of responding positively, said nothing whatsoever to the media. For their part, the media just left the hotel and scarcely reported the speech at all, having geared themselves to give it massive coverage in anticipation of Porter's bombardment. My most lasting memory of the event was seeing the CBC camera crew turn off their klieg lights just as soon as Porter indicated that she would not be commenting on my speech as planned. It was as though she and the CBC had scripted a Broadway show that closed seconds before the curtain went up. Their collaboration reflected an unhealthy alliance between the lead actor and the lead reviewer. Except that the actor in this case was not I but Porter. And she had decided on the spot that, contrary to theatrical tradition, the show must not go on. For her, in light of my support for pay equity, there was no partisan mileage to be gained. For the CBC, there was no news in good news, only in bad, especially when I was the intended target of the bad. All this was, for me, sadly reminiscent of the time a virulently anti-Tory *Ottawa Citizen* reporter called my press secretary, Terry Collins, about a story he was about to do. It was along the lines that, as environment minister, I talked a good story about the Americans needing to act against acid rain. But, so the argument went, I didn't take the time, make the effort, and have the courage to go to the United States to communicate that message directly. When Terry handed the reporter a multipage list detailing all my speeches and media appearances south of the border on that very subject, the *Citizen*, rather than report this information, killed the story outright. For the reporter who had intended to do the story, like many reporters and producers at CBC in Charlottetown, good news was no news, particularly if the news concerned a politician whose reputation some of them were eager to undercut.

Whether any politician is supported or opposed by certain interest groups or the media or anyone else on a given issue is not fundamental. What *is* basic is that, in a democracy, every issue be aired and everyone heard as fully and fairly as possible without unreasonable impediment. When political decision-makers act on this principle and the public perceives them to be doing so, their actions are likely to be more broadly supported—including by those on the losing side—than when that principle is flouted. A decision rendered for an entire community then becomes, ipso facto, everyone's position. Democracy means freedom to participate, not necessarily getting one's way. Majority rule is the engine of democracy, minority rights the engine's lubricant. This perspective should appeal equally to the classic conservative's commitment to collective community action and to the classic liberal's fear of tyranny, including of the minority. In holding a plebiscite on the Fixed Link and then supporting the minority result, Joe Ghiz got the mechanics of democracy assbackwards. Islanders who continue to oppose the Fixed Link to this very day would be well advised to study *Democratic Engineering 101*.

Throughout my public career, I was struck by the large number of people who pay loud lip service to democratic values, but who remain deathly silent in the face of abuses when not actively complicit in them. Social activists are sometimes the worst offenders, no doubt because they are among the most passionate about issues. A deep sense of moral superiority can cause such people to feel entitled to violate democratic principles and receive a get-out-of-jail-free card when caught doing so. The nobler the public perceives an organization's cause, the more probable the spokespeople for that cause will escape public scrutiny and disapprobation no matter how badly they misbehave. Environmentalism—for many, the unofficial state religion of the modern era—is virtually bulletproof against criticism. To oppose an environmentalist's stand on an issue or to criticize his or her professional ethics is tantamount to picking a fight with God. I have seen far too many activists in this field promote their particular cause in the name of democracy while violating that very value system to get their way or to try to nullify a duly-made decision when they couldn't.

Before the federal government decided to build the Fixed Link, it launched a thoroughly transparent public consultative process to give every interested individual and organization an opportunity to consider and discuss all arguments for and against the project. The process involved thousands of Islanders over many months. On both sides of this contentious issue, most participants conducted themselves with discipline, calm, and respect for others' opinions. That is typically how we Islanders conduct our affairs, whether public or private. It is not in our nature to be wild-eyed about anything—passionate and opinionated, yes; fanatic and uncontrollable, no. At public meetings, people shared with one another their deeply held principles, strong views, knowledge, and personal experiences. The intervention I remember best was that of Donna Murphy, whom I had regularly dated when we attended St. Dunstan's University two decades earlier. Donna, Sophomore Queen at SDU the first time we went out together, had been an active Tory on campus. At a massive public meeting at the Prince Edward Hotel in Charlottetown, she spoke with equal measures of conviction and eloquence against the Fixed Link on environmental grounds. And almost convinced me! Her opposition was based on the harm done to the North River (near Charlottetown) by a small causeway built across it some years earlier, not many miles from Cumberland, where her family lived and farmed. All such Islanders, whatever their perspective, brought to the consultative process not only insights of Donna Murphy's kind, but also, more fundamentally, a profound love of Prince Edward Island and a strong desire to secure its future. How the federal government proceeded on the Fixed Link was shaped by the express views of all Islanders. It was not based exclusively on the massive amount of scientific and engineering research the government amassed at each stage, on the advice of technical experts it sought from around the world, and on the mountain of facts of every other kind (both empirical and anecdotal) it gathered—economic, social, environmental, and cultural. So, the Mulroney government's decision to build the project, in partnership with the private sector, was not forced *on* the community. That decision was informed *by* the community. This is how democracy is supposed to work. In my time in politics, however, no group of social activists violated democratic principles more shamelessly than the most militant opponents of the PEI-NB Fixed Link. At every turn, they tried to hijack the consultative process surrounding the project and scuttle the project itself.

Much of the PEI labour movement, too, was opposed to the Fixed Link, but, ironically, labour's overplaying its hand advanced the cause to have it built. Islanders were generally wary of the role Marine Atlantic ferry workers—represented by different unions, mainly the Canadian Brotherhood of Railway Transport and General Workers—were playing in the opposition camp. In late August 1973, at the height of the tourism season, the ferry workers had gone on strike, crippling all vehicular and passenger traffic between the Island and New Brunswick for ten days. So harmful was the strike to the provincial economy that Liberal premier Alex Campbell mobilized a crack team of lawyers from both PEI and Ottawa to help him seek a legal remedy. They sued the federal government—Trudeau's, no less!—for failing to honour the province's term of Confederation that promised "continuous communication" with the rest of Canada. In 1977, the Federal Court of Canada found in the province's favour, declaring that the strike had breached the federal government's constitutional duty. Asked by the media after the Fixed Link plebiscite how he had voted, Campbell, by then a PEI Supreme Court justice, unequivocally and proudly declared: "FOR!"

The strike, and the threat of future strikes, made me eager, as PEI's federal Cabinet minister, to obtain federal government guarantees that the privately operated ferry service between PEI and Nova Scotia (Northumberland Ferries) would continue to operate if a Fixed Link were built, thus eliminating the Marine Atlantic ferries between PEI and New Brunswick. Put simply, following the construction of the Fixed Link, no circumstance—not inclement weather, not engineering failure, not labour strife, not any other act of either God or man—would be allowed to sever Prince Edward Island's constitutionally guaranteed connection to the rest of Canada. Not willing to leave anything to chance, my political staff and I sought to render the improbable the impossible. Towards that end, we worked with Northumberland Ferries—specifically, principal owner Colonel J. David Stewart and Captain John Aspin—to specify and then nail down the guarantees both politically and legally. Colonel Stewart, as blueblood a Tory as the queen is royalty, had been a senior Cabinet minister in Walter R. Shaw's government. So, having him in our quarter for the purpose at hand was like being counselled by Cardinal Richelieu. I also arranged a personal meeting between Finance Minister Michael Wilson and Stewart and Aspin, which my staffer Rob Burnett and I attended and then followed up on. This was one of the first in a long series of negotiations that led to the building of the MV *Confederation*, now plying the PEI-Nova Scotia route. Not since PEI's terms of entry to Canada were negotiated in 1873 had we Islanders left so little to chance concerning our physical connection to mainland Canada as we did throughout all these negotiations at every level of the federal government. "You guys obviously mean business," Wilson said to me at one stage.

Our guarantees to the Northumberland Ferry workers were kept. Also honoured were federal government assurances that the Marine Atlantic ferry workers displaced by the Fixed Link would be treated well, including being given priority for jobs operating the bridge once built. Fishers and lobster harvesters adversely affected by the Fixed Link, both during construction and afterwards, were similarly treated not just fairly but generously. And yet, one would never know any of this from listening to the charter opponents of the project who, to this day, two decades after the fact, continue to regret its having been built. On the tenth anniversary of the Confederation Bridge, anti–Fixed Link ringleader David Weale told the *Guardian*: "Today, I use the bridge quite often and I'm glad for the convenience, but I still wish it wasn't there." One of the Island's highest-profile labour leaders is Sandy MacKay, past president of both the PEI Union of Public Sector Employees and the Federation of Labour. Some years after the bridge was built, MacKay and I encountered each other at a Charlottetown gym. He told me seriously that he had not yet crossed the bridge and, on principle, did not intend to do so—ever. Dr. A. E. "Bud" Ings, a well-respected Kings County veterinarian, served as minister of agriculture and forestry and, at a different time, minister of health and social services in the Alex Campbell government in the late 1960s and early 1970s. He militantly opposed the Fixed Link during the plebiscite and for a long time afterwards. But before his death, at age eighty-nine, he told the *Guardian* that he now thought that the Confederation Bridge was a marvel of engineering and "the best thing that ever happened to the province." The overwhelming majority of Islanders agree with Ings, not with Weale or MacKay. Evidently, for the David Weales and Sandy MacKays of the world, the democratic process is perfectly fine provided it produces outcomes they like. Other times, not so much. Democracy's fairweather friends can be just as unfriendly to this value system as its sworn enemies.

Another Machiavellian stratagem of Joe Ghiz was to use government money to pay certain well-respected Islanders, preferably with a veneer of non-partisanship—or, better still, with ties to the PC Party—to do his dirty political work for him.

The first Mulroney budget after the 1988 election announced the closure of a bevy of military bases across the country. The list included PEI's air force base in Summerside, the province's second-largest community. Derek Key is a prominent Tory lawyer from that area, the son of former provincial PC party leader George Key (1968–73). Lo and behold, Derek Key suddenly emerged as a community-spirited crusader, on behalf of the local area and the Island, to try to embarrass the Mulroney government into reversing its decision to close the Summerside base. The base, he argued, was vitally important to the PEI economy, and Key presented himself as the facility's potential saviour. I appeared on a two-man panel with him hosted by a national association of daily newspaper journalists holding their annual meeting in Charlottetown. The visitors from across the country were tremendously impressed that Key would attack his own party so aggressively in this connection. Key seemed to be putting his commitment to community above partisan loyalty. They did not know, nor did I myself realize at the time, what only a tight circle around the premier then knew: that Premier Ghiz was using provincial tax dollars to pay Key many thousands of dollars, on a fee-for-services basis, as the government's "above-politics" hatchet man on the airbase-closure issue. In short, Derek Key was a hired gun. And his gun was aimed squarely at the Mulroney government.

Eddie Rice is an eccentric but amiable Charlottetown realtor with an on-again, off-again career in municipal politics. As I write, Eddie is currently a member of Charlottetown City Council for Ward One. Unofficial town gossip, he knows everybody's business; it's likely the main reason for his substantial success in real estate and local politics alike. Eddie, whom I like and admire and consider a friend, made a practice of haunting provincial government corridors when Joe Ghiz was premier, though he pretended to be non-partisan. Whatever his political allegiance—probably Liberal—the man was, for me and many others, a reliable source of information about all things Island close to the ground, both social and political. Eddie frequently told me whenever my anti–Fixed Link nemesis, David Weale, received payments from Premier Ghiz for "assignments." My informant led me to believe that the relevant contracts involved a lot more for this lay cleric and preacher than interpreting Holy Scripture. From Eddie Rice and sources more formally tied to Joe Ghiz, I learned early in his premiership that Ghiz intended to hire David Weale as a full-time speech writer and in-house policy advisor. Weale had played this staff role for Tory premier Angus MacLean. The fact Ghiz's intentions were communicated to me by high-level Liberal sources substantially higher than Rice led me to believe that the dynamic at play constituted a trial balloon. In the brief period when the premier was trying to appear politically ecumenical, he was seeking to discover how I would respond if he appointed Weale. Through back channels, I discreetly signalled that I would consider such an appointment to his senior staff an act of political warfare against me, if not also against the Mulroney government, to say nothing of what it would communicate about the provincial government's intended ideological direction. I thought that the Island had already paid far too high a price, both literally and culturally, for having had this reactionary so close to power during MacLean's premiership. David Weale had cast a spell over the premier, practically paralyzing any reformist instincts the man might have had. I said that the province could not afford another mistake of this kind, still less the identical mistake. The premier dropped the idea.

It was only after the 1988 federal election that Joe Ghiz supported major Mulroney government policies such as Meech Lake. By then, his priority had shifted from driving PEI Tories into the ground—mission accomplished federally—

to elevating his own national profile. Meanwhile, he viewed me as a rival for "brightest political star" status on the Island, instead of, as I had hoped, an ally to advance Island interests in the spirit of bipartisanship. That rivalry was captured in an *Atlantic Insight* cover story in August 1988, close to the calling of the federal election that year. Titled inside "A Classic Confrontation: Ghiz vs. McMillan," the article quoted Island reporter Len Russo as saying that "[Ghiz and McMillan] are head and shoulders above every other politician [on the Island]. There's Ghiz and McMillan in one category and then there's all the rest."[10] I didn't see it that way. I thought the premier and I were on the same team: the Island's. He thought there was a single team all right: his own. For him, there was no room for a rival. I had to go. And he was prepared to use all the resources of the Liberal Party *and* the provincial government, if need be, to achieve that partisan end.

Despite early and continuing efforts to seek a partnership with Joe Ghiz, I did not handle my relationship with him as effectively as I could and should have done. Russo, not always an admirer of mine, wrote a column in the *Eastern Graphic* whose headline captured the gist of his argument: "McMillan is better speaker than Ghiz." The Liberal premier always fancied himself a powerful orator. He delivered a major speech—written by David Weale, I was told at the time—at the "Birthplace Explored" built heritage conference in Charlottetown in the early nineties. I gave the closing address. Commenting on the Ghiz speech at a later session, UPEI president William Eliot generalized that Ghiz mistook shouting for eloquence. Many delegates, especially from off-Island, said they agreed. I foolishly reprinted the relevant Russo column in my quarterly constituency mass mailer in a burst of self-promotion and vanity. I have no doubt that Ghiz was offended by my hubris, just as I would have been had he done the same to me. With the advantage of hindsight—and, I hope, with age, a lot more maturity—I appreciate now how much responsibility I sometimes shared with Ghiz for our not having forged a better personal and political mutual bond to advance the Island's interests. Too often, two big egos obstructed our being both better co-trustees of the Island's welfare—and better men.

# PEI and Litton Industries

The most damaging blow Joe Ghiz's partisanship levelled at the Island directly concerned a decision made jointly by the Mulroney government and US defence contractor Litton Industries to establish a $20-million high-tech plant in Charlottetown. Ghiz's malevolence on the issue began while he was Opposition leader and not yet premier. The Litton plant was to build components for a new multi-million-dollar, low-level anti-missile radar defence system to help protect NATO installations and troops in Europe. I did everything but sell my soul—and, maybe, a bit of that, too—to land the plant for the Island in stiff competition from other communities right across Canada. I cashed in every chit I had with Cabinet colleagues—particularly Finance Minister Michael Wilson and Defence Minister Robert Coates—to win them over to our bid. Not only would the federal government provide the pertinent defence contract; it also agreed to subsidize about a quarter of the total cost of the plant. When our bid succeeded—the decision was announced on December 11, 1985— Tory premier Jim Lee had a big feather in his cap for the pending provincial election campaign. The plant would inject millions of dollars into the Island economy; it would employ some four hundred skilled workers, most of them Island youth trained at the local community college (Holland College); and it would create far-reaching industrial spinoffs, the most important of which promised to be the development of a mini-Silicon Valley in the province. Several other off-Island high-tech companies were seriously considering locating in Charlottetown to cross-fertilize with the Litton plant in research and development. One such company, in Montreal, had already decided to come to the Island for this very reason.

Tragically, Joe Ghiz, then Opposition leader, decided to undermine the political advantage the Lee government gained from the new plant by pandering to a tiny but militant group opposed to Litton's presence on the Island. Backed by the local CBC, the group was led by UPEI professors David Weale (the self-same future anti–Fixed Linker) and Gary Webster, a political scientist. Opponents charged that the measure would suck the Island into the arms race, thrust Islanders into the lap of "merchants of death," and make us complicit in nuclear proliferation—the biggest lie of all, for the system was purely for conventional defence. Webster, a Vietnam-era American draft dodger, presented himself as the province's pre-eminent pacifist. But he declared war against Litton Industries' coming to the province. All Islanders ended up casualties of battle.

One of the first official statements from the Joe Ghiz government after the Liberals defeated the provincial Tories on April 21, 1986, attacked the Lee government's contract with the Mulroney government and Litton Industries. It did so in Gary Webster–style rhetoric more appropriate to describing war criminals than a company about to pump millions of dollars into the Island economy. By the time Ghiz realized how massively his government had misfired, it was too late. Litton decided the new Cabinet was too hostile to the company for it to feel confident setting up shop in PEI. The defence contractor used technicalities to break its agreement with the Island government. It then unceremoniously withdrew from Charlottetown, not its preferred location for the plant in any event—just the federal government's and, course, mine.

Unbeknownst to almost everyone to this day, my brother Charley, for the Prime Minister's Office, and I arranged a top-secret meeting at the King Edward Hotel in downtown Toronto between Joe Ghiz and the president and other senior executives of Litton, who had flown in on a private jet from afar for our purpose. That purpose was to literally beg Litton to reverse its decision to abandon the Island. "If you require me to eat crow and get down on my knees, I'm here to do whatever it takes," Ghiz said to the Litton president. But the company dug in its heels and refused to budge. Litton built the plant, instead, at the Halifax County Aero Tech Industrial Park, in Nova Scotia, its first choice from the beginning. The wealthiest province in Atlantic Canada had snatched the winning lottery ticket from the hands of the second-poorest province in all Canada. More accurately, our premier presented the ticket to Nova Scotia on a tasselled silk cushion. By the time the premier tried to grab the ticket back, it had been redeemed. Ghiz had given Litton an excuse that the company could not have contrived on its own to locate in Nova Scotia instead of in PEI. In a flash, the Island premier cut adrift both his own province and the federal government. The American industrialists from Litton played Ghiz like a harpsichord. But it was he who chose the song sheet. Americans are not called "Yankee traders" for nothing—or as a compliment.

Kathy Large was the principal political reporter for CBC-TV in Charlottetown. A member of an old established Island media family, she was widely viewed as a Liberal partisan. Indeed, on this ground the weekly *Eastern Graphic* published a major editorial complaining about what the editors considered her professionally unethical access to the premier, including at-home interviews rarely, if ever, granted any other journalist. At the media's request, I held an availability session with them at the Charlottetown Hotel following the bombshell announcement by Litton that it was definitely cancelling plans to establish its plant in PEI. In light of all I and others had done to land the plant for the Island, I had a brief fit of anger after the news conference had formally ended but while some reporters continued to linger. Mostly to myself, I said something crude under my breath about the premier's role in the debacle. Only Kathy Large heard me. Within minutes, the premier phoned to implore me not to say the same thing publicly, presumably less profanely. Without a doubt, Large had tattled on me with the premier within seconds of my indiscretion. She had a direct pipeline to Ghiz and he to her. As often as not, as in this case, it was at my expense and that of the Mulroney government. It took me a long time to get over the disastrous end to the Litton saga. No words, profane or otherwise, do justice to my regret. The loss to the Island was incalculable and is felt to this day.

Establishing a specialized hi-tech plant in Charlottetown was right out of the PC Party's science and technology policy paper developed under Tom Symons's direction, through the Policy Coordinating Committee, when Robert Stanfield was our leader. The paper stressed a novel idea at the time. It proposed creating—and providing federal government incentives for—Centres of Excellence, including in more remote or smaller communities such as Charlottetown. That was exactly what the Litton plant concerned. The concept had been articulated by Mulroney science minister William Winegard as far back as the PC Niagara Policy Conference in 1969. He was then Guelph University's president and I a new recruit for Stanfield and Symons's policy process. Winegard argued that creativity is a collaborative process, not solitary; that the process might begin with a unique idea in one person's brain, but the idea thrives in a community of talented people—be it a private lab, a university, or a company; and that the idea comes to fruition when its progenitor, a collaborative team, a support system, and funding—from private investors or institutions or government or, as in the Litton case, all three—merge. All such factors conflated serendipitously for PEI with the Litton plant. We were creating not just a plant, but also an environment—in particular, a scientific R&D community—in which innovative ideas could be nourished and supported from the earliest stages right through to the production of new or different or better widgets and services for the marketplace to the province's massive advantage.

The Litton plant was just a seed, but a vital one. Since the Industrial Revolution, people have known the advantages of industrial clusters—in which producers, specialized suppliers, and workers nestle together to their common and mutual benefit. For personal gain, Joe Ghiz, despite his brilliance and advanced education, crushed the seed to smithereens. It was as though he were trying to return the Island to a pre-industrial age. His motives, however, were palpably much more sinister and partisan, but ultimately just as destructive. He squandered this golden—or, more accurately, "green"—opportunity to lift PEI into the modern industrial era. The Island lost an unprecedented chance to diversify its economy beyond potato and fish exports and Anne of Green Gables–focused tourism into environmentally clean, job-intensive, skills-based, hi-tech, and innovative small-scale industry.

After retiring from politics in 1993, Joe Ghiz was appointed dean of law at Dalhousie University. Ghiz soon became bored from having to do much more public outreach for the school, especially fundraising, than he had expected. In 1995, the former Island premier successfully lobbied the Chrétien government for a seat on the PEI Supreme Court, and left Dalhousie after only two years. Ghiz had long been in denial about the seriousness of his declining health, and within a year of his appointment to the Court was dead of cancer. Indeed, the man became far too sick to perform his duties on the Court much of the time in the few months he sat before dying. This is a pity, for Ghiz would have been a first-rate justice and might have become PEI chief justice down the road.

Unlike Joe Ghiz, Jim Lee was anything but an intellectual. In fact, trained as an architectural draftsman, he was not a university graduate. Lee had been a full-time professional organizer for the PC Party on the Island before getting himself elected to the provincial legislature. Like Ghiz, Lee, therefore, did not float above partisanship. In marked contrast to Ghiz, however, Lee had the vision to see the great opportunity the Litton Industries defence plant would have provided PEI. When Lee and I joined forces, during the two years our incumbencies overlapped, great things did happen. Not the least was the building of Canada's fourth veterinary college at UPEI, with the initial boost coming from the Trudeau government. Apart from meeting an urgent national and regional need for more animal and marine veterinarians, the Vet College put UPEI on the academic map nationally and, to some extent, internationally as well. The college has produced huge spinoffs throughout the university and the Island as a whole, especially in agriculture and the fishery.

The crucial common denominator between Jim Lee and me in advancing Island interests in such ways as the Vet College was not partisan label, much less friendship. The truth is, Jim and I did not always get along, either politically or personally. My relations with Jim were especially strained after he was no longer premier and the Mulroney government refused to appoint him to the Senate, a position he had coveted. Meanwhile, Premier Lee and his Cabinet tended to assume that, just because both their government and ours were of the same partisan stripe, we in the Mulroney government should automatically open our purse to them for particular PEI projects without their having to make much of a case for the funding. My having to tell them that this was not the way either the Mulroney government or I operated further strained relations between the premier and me. One PEI project we did help fund, early in our mandate through the Department of Regional Industrial Expansion, was Red Rock Brewery, established by local entrepreneur Billy Ricks. The brewery eventually went belly-up, bringing down Rick's entire business empire, including Charlottetown Metal Products, its long-established flagship operation—another case of an entrepreneur's losing it all by straying outside his business comfort zone. Ricks knew nothing about establishing a brewery or brewing beer. "We produced one lot of skunky beer," Ricks told me when the brewery started to stumble after some initial success. "And that made customers afraid of our product." No doubt. But poor management and judgment doomed the brewery from the start.

Jim Lee and I might not always have seen eye to eye on substantive questions. But I liked and admired Jim and his wife, Patsy, and their three wonderful children: Jason, Laurie Anne, and Patricia. Jim and I both believed that it was important to set aside differences between us, either politically or personally, for the good of the province and its people. And we did. Joe Ghiz believed, and acted, far differently. Prince Edward Island, not either of us, paid the price—Island youth the highest price of all. In an e-mail, my brother Charley told a number of scholars researching Island politics of the era: "I grew up [with Joe Ghiz]. He had immense charm but was perhaps one of the worst premiers [in PEI history]…[He] spent Ottawa money like a drunken sailor, all consumption, no investment—fought everything that would build the province, from the Fixed Link to free trade." Anyone familiar with that era, and the facts, would find it difficult to prove Charley wrong.

# Island Premiers

To my mind, *Joe Ghiz* (1986–93) was, at best, a disappointment as PEI premier. With his brains, education, charm, and political talent, he could have been one of the province's—and, perhaps, even the country's—greatest premiers. Had he been bilingual, or just functional in French, the man had the potential to become prime minister of Canada. But he fell far short of his political potential, and not just because he died young. The most courageous and visionary of all PEI premiers in modern times was Liberal *Alex Campbell* (1966–78).[11] A future PEI Supreme Court justice, he—unlike Joe Ghiz—was willing to risk political capital to invest in the Island's long-term future. He would get my vote for "best PEI premier" in my time. The most underrated, and among the most accomplished, was Tory *Jim Lee* (1981–86). After Joe Ghiz, the most overrated was arch-conservative Tory *Angus MacLean* (1979–81), whom I discuss at greater length later. MacLean had been a war hero and Diefenbaker fisheries minister. Until current Cardigan MP Lawrence MacAulay (now Justin Trudeau's agriculture minister) broke the record in March 2014, MacLean had been the longest-serving federal politician in Island history—exactly 9,250 days, more than twenty-five years—prior to entering provincial politics. With David Weale as his Rasputin, Premier MacLean sought to turn the Island back to an agrarian Dark Age, all with the lofty-sounding and seductive slogan "Rural Renaissance." Ghiz was less a reactionary—which MacLean certifiably was—than a politician unwilling to risk alienating a single swing voter. He always practised the art of "feel good" politics, not the politics of pursuing the best-possible outcome for the Island. Tory *Walter R. Shaw* (1959–66), who had been the province's deputy agriculture minister and became premier at age seventy-two, was, by far, the greatest orator among Island premiers in recent decades. Liberal *Alex Matheson* (1953–59), a prosperous Charlottetown lawyer (six feet, five inches tall!), was the second-most-gifted orator in this select group. Liberal *Catherine Callbeck* (1993–96), a business teacher in New Brunswick and Ontario before returning to the Island to enter the family retail hardware and building supplies enterprise based in Bedeque, became the first female premier to win a general election—though she was not the first female premier; British Columbia's Rita Johnston has that distinction. Tory community developer and sheep farmer *Pat Binns* (1996–2007) was, for me, the most likeable. Ironically, given that he was born and raised in Saskatchewan, Binns, along with MacLean (his mentor), also had the keenest feel for the Island and its people. These Island politicians are an impressive lot—every one of them, even those with whom I would have differed and, in some cases, actually did. (I have not included in this august company Liberal *Bennett Campbell*, a teacher, who was premier for only about a year, from 1978 to 1979. He ran on the slogan "Doing More with Less." Alas, Islanders compared this well-meaning but dull man with his charismatic and dashing predecessor, Alex Campbell, decided they were now getting "less" rather than "more," and defeated the new premier within a year.)

I began this chapter by drawing a distinction between politicians who play it politically safe and those willing to risk political capital for an activist agenda. Joe Ghiz fell in the former category. In late spring 1993, New Brunswick premier Frank McKenna asked me, as consul general in Boston, to set up a meeting with Boston mayor Ray Flynn (1984–93) so that McKenna could invite him to the annual Irish Festival on the Miramichi. I knew Flynn well and prevailed on him to oblige. Unfortunately, the day McKenna was in town was also Flynn's last day in office, not long before the mayor became Bill Clinton's ambassador to the Vatican. "Tom, I'll see the premier," Flynn told me, "but only if he'll meet me at an Irish pub in South Boston, because that's where I'll be all day." I drove McKenna to his "meeting" at Woody's L Street Tavern. Joe Ghiz had stepped down as PEI premier a few months earlier, in January. On the heels of a severe recession and sharply declining tax revenues, virtually all provincial governments had been slashing budgets. But the Island's business-minded finance minister, Gilbert Clements, had failed to convince Ghiz to tame their government's runaway spending, unprecedented in Island history. En route to seeing the Boston mayor, McKenna informed me that Ghiz had told him why he resigned as PEI premier: "Gilbert wants me to cut, cut, cut. But I just want to spend, spend, spend." So much for political leadership!

Joe Ghiz was an endearing and charismatic politician and individual. With a Harvard law degree, he was among the most intelligent and highly educated of all PEI premiers. When stricken with the colon cancer that killed him in November 1996, the man demonstrated a serenity and graciousness towards former political foes that eluded him while healthy. Towards me, I sensed a death-bed respect, especially for my leadership on the Fixed Link in the face of his opposition. I have an especially vivid memory of seeing him for the last time. We both were attending a large reception at Fanningbank, the PEI lieutenant governor's residence. Looking uncharacteristically rail-thin but otherwise quite himself, Joe, with obvious deliberation, crossed the entire expanse of the spacious front-hall reception area, sought me out, shook my hand, and greeted me more warmly than he had ever done before. Something indefinable both in his voice and in his eye contact told me that Joe was making peace not so much with me as with an important dimension of his life that I, to his eyes, symbolized: partisan politics. Near death, he asked to be driven across the largest completed part of the now-named Confederation Bridge well before the total structure was ready for public traffic. Why would a dying man make this request unless he recognized that the bridge connecting PEI to the mainland fulfilled a dream that Islanders had held from earliest times and he wanted to experience at least once the grandeur of what would soon finally be achieved?

My brother Charley devotes a full chapter of his book *Eminent Islanders* to Joe Ghiz.[12] Like Charley, I respected Joe's talents and always enjoyed his private company. I will long value certain gestures he made to reconcile with me before dying, including the above-mentioned one at Fanningbank. And I was saddened by his untimely death. My mother voted for Joe Ghiz the first time he ran for office, in 1982. Mother admired Joe and was fond of the family, especially his mother, Marguerite, who she was quite sure had voted for me. (I believe this, too.) Moreover, Joe's Tory opponent, Barry Clark, though Mother's neighbour, had not asked for her vote, whereas Joe and his running mate, Paul Connolly, from across town, had. Dorothy Eileen McQuaid was likely the first member of our extended family ever to cast a non-Tory ballot since the invention of paper—for Joseph Atallah Ghiz. This truly "eminent Islander" would have been proud that his son Robert would later serve in the position in which Joe, of Lebanese descent, made history by becoming the first person of non-European ancestry to be a premier. Robert himself repeated history by becoming the second PEI premier's son to lead the province (2007–15); the first was Alex Campbell, son of

Thane Campbell (premier, 1936–43).[13] I bear no grudge against Joe Ghiz. But I profoundly regret the opportunities the Island missed because, as premier, he too often placed partisanship above partnership. The Island continues to need more economics and far less politics.

I did not know well Joe Ghiz's wife, Rose Ellen—though, of course, we met many times officially when he was alive, particularly in our government years. Soon after Joe died, she mailed me a copy of the aforementioned *Atlantic Insight* magazine issue whose cover story featured Joe and me as PEI's two pre-eminent politicians at the time. The cover picture showed us facing each other, nose to nose and eye to eye, as though about to begin a duel. (I was amused that, no doubt for dramatic effect, we were shown to be the same height, whereas I was, in fact, considerably taller than he—talk about Photoshopping!) The personal handwritten note to me that Rose Ellen affixed to the magazine said that, while going through her husband's papers, she had found this item. She stated that the article had brought back many memories of her late husband's government and political dealings with me. I had no doubt at the time that she would have assumed I already had a copy of that well-known issue. So, I accepted her gesture in the spirit in which she had likely intended it: burying the hatchet between two Island political families. I was deeply moved by Rose Ellen's thoughtfulness. May Joe rest in peace.

# Chapter 27

# "IF IT MOVES, PENSION IT— IF NOT, PAVE IT"

Patronage is the bread and butter of Canadian politics. It motivates political party activists—from poll chairs and workers to fundraisers to campaign managers to the candidates themselves. Many defeated candidates expect to be "taken care of" should their party form a government either then or down the road. This is especially true in Atlantic Canada. "Atlantic Canadians continue to consider politicians as 'cash cows' and the pork barrel as the just reward of power," political scientist Nelson Wiseman has written.[1] I spent three years at Queen's University getting honours and post-graduate degrees in political studies at a time when that university had—as it likely has to this very day—the pre-eminent politics program in Canada. I was fortunate to study with some of the best teachers and scholars in my field. One professor of mine had not one but two PhDs. Some of my fellow grad students became senior prime ministerial advisors or respected political science scholars or politics textbook authors or public opinion pollsters. As high-achieving students, they themselves were a great source of knowledge and insights that served me well for decades after I shared classes and seminars with them. And yet, nothing of this sort prepared me for being Prince Edward Island's sole federal Cabinet minister and, therefore, dispenser (or perceived dispenser) of all things good and rich in the gift of the governing party in Ottawa. I was to learn the limits of knowledge.

For political partisans in my province, the most coveted patronage appointments were Ottawa senator and federally appointed PEI Supreme Court justice. Both were, for all practical purposes, lifetime jobs, with late mandatory retirement ages. By Island standards, the positions paid extremely well. Today, a senator makes a six-figure salary. He or she enjoys housing and travel allowances and other benefits and perks—many of them tax-free—that render the effective remuneration substantially higher than it appears on paper. A judge now is paid more than a quarter of a million dollars a year, with generous pension and health and other windfalls worth tens of thousands more. In constant dollars, a senator and Supreme Court justice got paid much the same in my time in Cabinet as now. On the Island, I knew few party workers who did not want to be appointed senator. Many of them actively sought the position. I knew even fewer lawyers who didn't covet a seat on the bench. Realistically or not, most planned their whole careers around the possibility that someday they might make a short list for a judgeship. Law practice, especially in a province like PEI, is typically a monotonously repetitive job after the novelty wears off. I can count faster than a fruit fly mates the number of lawyers I know who don't want an exit from routine practice. A judgeship is the most elegant exit of all. In PEI, a judge's total remuneration package is much beyond what any but a few lawyers in the province could possibly earn in their best year. And, with eight justices for only 145,000 people, the work load for each judge is lighter than that fruit fly.

On the Island, getting appointed to the Senate or the PEI Supreme Court is like winning the lottery. Lesser positions in the gift of the government are just as alluring for many partisans. One has to be a lawyer to become a judge. You just need to be alive for most of the rest. Pierre Trudeau called all such government appointments "goodies." In PEI, for the majority, a patronage nod is as good as it gets. Many more people seek patronage than there are positions to be dispensed. Still, the odds of landing one are substantially better than for a lottery jackpot. One need only be on the right side of the government party, especially its principal political operative— the province's federal Cabinet minister. At least, that is how everyone perceives the game. Unfortunately for me, the incumbent, that perception made life miserable. Very miserable.

The highwater mark of PEI patronage in modern times followed the provincial election of 1966. On election night, May 30, the governing Tories under seventy-nine-year-old premier Walter R. Shaw ended up in a dead heat with the Liberals led by thirty-three-year-old Alex Campbell: fifteen legislative seats each! After the writ had been dropped but before election day, the 1st Kings district Liberal candidate, William Acorn, died suddenly. His death forced a deferred election, on July 11, to choose two members of the legislature in that district. (The Island had sixteen two-member districts at the time.) Thus, which party would form the government, and which party leader would become premier, hinged on the outcome of this deferred election in the tiny 1st Kings district. Desperate to retain power, the Tories showered the district with largesse, prompting a local wag to characterize their slogan as, "If it moves, pension it; if it doesn't, pave it." Alas, for the Tories, the patronage orgy did not win them either of the two seats. The Liberals won both and, accordingly, formed the government, and Alex Campbell became premier. But, for Islanders, the deferred election outcome did not prove patronage fails to pay political dividends. Quite the opposite. Having benefited to the maximum from the PC government's generosity, the district knew that it now stood a better chance under a freshly minted Liberal regime to get yet more patronage.[2] I had to factor this same mindset into my every decision as local political baron in the handling of federal patronage on the Island. Like Walter Shaw, I learned that one does, indeed, "live by the sword, and die by the sword."

All this patronage-related power, or perceived power, might appear to give the minister a huge political advantage in recruiting workers, raising campaign funds, motivating partisans, attracting election talent—the whole nine yards. The truth was, however, for every individual who received patronage, many more had to be denied. And even the blessed were not always grateful, let alone to their political benefactor. Either the recipient thought he or she should have received something better in light of his or her political contribution or, as often as not, the partisan considered the patronage a just reward, not a gift. There's a reason that, over the years, politicians in power have steadily restricted patronage, making the awarding of government jobs and contracts less political and more merit-based. That reason is not public virtue but self-preservation. Nothing threatens a politician's re-election more than unhappy partisans. Even when handled with skill, patronage is the surest way to cause their unhappiness. Patronage is all about emotion and ambition and, in some cases, avarice. It's a messy business. Terribly messy.

A Conservative prime minister, Sir Robert Borden, did the most to create a professional, non-partisan public service at the federal level, not because he was an especially virtuous man—though, undeniably, he was that—but because, during the First World War, he headed a coalition government, and he realized patronage was creating too much squabbling among his disparate supporters. My own experience is that virtue and self-interest go hand in glove on patronage. The Stephen Harper government paid a substantial price on both counts when it ignored the party's pioneering record on patronage reform and failed to build on it. This point might strike the reader as strange, if not hypocritical, made as it is by one who himself received a patronage appointment, as consul general in Boston. But I am not arguing that all such appointments are bad. It's a question of good judgment and the public interest. Whether this standard was applied in my case is not for me to say. In any event, patronage is fraught with peril. A government party needs to handle it carefully—if not out of virtue, then, as in Borden's case, out of self-interest.

I find it ironic that the very people who most loudly demanded Senate reform when they were with the Reform/Canadian Alliance Party did more damage to the Senate's reputation than any previous government once they were elected to power as Conservatives and able to make Senate appointments themselves. Like Pamela Wallin's, former Conservative senator Mike Duffy's name has become a punchline. Both senators (former celebrity TV journalists) were suspended from the Senate for allegedly improperly charging to the taxpayer personal and travel expenses. A less famous senator, Patrick Brazeau—an Aboriginal leader when appointed at age thirty-five—was also suspended for the same reason and, to boot, for alleged domestic violence and sexual assault. Many other senators were ensnared in the "travelgate" scandal. Mike Duffy's court case received massive media coverage and public interest. Even though Justice Charles H. Vaillancourt of the Ontario Court eventually found Duffy's expense accounting not criminal, the whole business has levelled a powerful blow against the Senate's reputation. No doubt, the scandal contributed to the Harper government's electoral defeat in October 2015. As noted earlier, I have known Mike Duffy since we grew up in the same neighbourhood in Charlottetown. I have always liked him and consider him a friend. But he has tarnished public life and embarrassed all Islanders, whose best interests he was supposed to represent in the upper house. That body is now a lot lower for his having been a member.

As an integral part of our governmental system and political culture, the Senate deserves better. And the Conservative Party's brand deserves better. Sir Robert Borden could have warned Stephen Harper and his political operatives about the dangers of patronage. Given my own horrible experiences with Senate and other patronage appointments as a Cabinet minister, I also could have warned them. Below are my tales of woe.

# Senate Appointments

My thorniest patronage decision concerned one of the four Island Senate seats. A vacancy had occurred with the death of Elsie Inman on May 31, 1986, in the middle of my time as federal Cabinet minister for the Island. Inman, a Liberal, had been appointed to the Senate by Louis St-Laurent in July 1955. Though ninety-five, the woman was still a senator when she died. (This was before mandatory retirement at age seventy-five was legislated.) I once ran into Senator Inman on a plane between PEI and Ottawa, one of the few such trips she took. The old lady had no idea who I was, a parliamentary colleague from her own province. Talk about the need for Senate reform!

The fly in the ointment for me in recommending Inman's replacement to the prime minister was that the late Mrs. Inman had been not only the Island's first woman senator, but also the only one ever. To have replaced her with a man would have been politically untenable, certainly a backward step in women's equality. Accordingly, Brian Mulroney directed me to recommend only a woman. "Tommy, there's not a single damn vote to be won with this or any other Senate appointment," he said. "The only way the PEI appointment serves any partisan purpose is if it is made as part of a package that sends a strong message to voters." The message Mulroney wanted to communicate was his powerful commitment to narrowing the gender gap that favoured men in federal appointments. It was a cause about which the prime minister felt deeply and often lectured Cabinet. When I was appointed environment minister, the PM also selected a woman, Geneviève Ste-Marie, to be my deputy minister, the first for the Environment portfolio and one of only a handful in the entire government. For maximum political impact, the PM intended to announce the Island Senate appointment at the same time as he filled two other Senate vacancies. All three Senate seats were to go to women. (The two others were Mira Spivak of Manitoba and Ethel Cochrane of Newfoundland.) So, I had received my marching orders: only females need "apply" for the PEI vacancy.[3]

I faced a major problem. The competition was fierce among Island Senate aspirants, with each individual lining up supporters and lobbyists. Almost all the seekers were men. None was more eager or campaigned harder or had more supporters to land the Big Prize than Jim Lee. He had just lost both the premiership and his own seat in the legislature in the previous provincial election. The man was now unemployed. Lee's former legislative district, 5th Queen's, constituted half my federal riding. His most rabid Senate-appointment boosters were among my own most active poll and campaign workers. And yet, in light of the prime minister's instructions, I could not recommend him to fill the upper house vacancy—the XY chromosome factor. To compound the problem, the second-strongest claim to the Senate seat, at least in her own mind, was that of Marion Reid. She was a revered Tory member of the legislature for 1st Queen's, a largely rural district about twenty kilometres west of Charlottetown. Reid had been the first female Speaker of the PEI Legislative Assembly, and Mulroney would later appoint her as the first woman lieutenant governor of the Island (1990–95). Despite the woman's sterling qualifications, I could not possibly suggest her to the PM for the Senate, either, as that would have involved passing over Jim Lee for his political junior in both service to the party and time served in the legislature. There would have been hell to pay for that insult in certain quarters politically important to me, not least in 5th Queen's, the heart of my riding. What to do?

I decided to recommend Eileen Rossiter, instead. She was the widow of Conservative realtor Pete Rossiter and brother-in-law of Leo, one of the most formidable and colourful and controversial Island Tory politicians, a former long-time provincial Cabinet minister and member of the PEI legislature from Morell. For many years, Eileen had been a Tory farmhand in her own right, was as shrewd as the Island soil is red, was popular with rank-and-file Tories, and had (albeit by marriage) a quintessential Island Tory family name. Moreover, she had played a pivotal behind-the-scenes role as a senior party functionary in my winning the PC nomination in Hillsborough when I first ran, in 1979. Eileen's supporting me over two other well-qualified candidates demonstrated that this woman would bring to the Senate sound political judgment! Even if all the above had not weighed heavily on my mind, I was convinced that Eileen Rossiter would make a good senator by non-partisan criteria. Certainly, she met every requirement that Islanders consider important to ensuring all three counties (Prince, Queens, and Kings) and the two major religions of the province (Catholic and Protestant) are fairly represented in the Senate. In this case, it was the turn of a Kings County Catholic. Eileen couldn't have met those two criteria better had she been crowned the county's monarch and been beatified by the pope. Most important of all, she was the right sex for the prime minister's purposes—and, therefore, my own. Like the XX chromosomes, the stars were aligned. Or so I thought.

Two problems with Eileen Rossiter's nomination needed to be solved. First, she did not want the appointment. This was one of the few times in Canadian history (certainly in PEI's) that a living body did not want to be appointed to the Senate.[4] Second, Eileen was then serving as Marion Reid's assistant in the Speaker's office. It was bad enough that Marion's appointment would have leapfrogged over Jim Lee's aspirations; Eileen's would have pole-vaulted over Marion's. But, to my mind, it had to happen, the least of all evils—or elevations. The worst day of my life as a Cabinet minister was the Sunday afternoon I had to drive to the Hunter River area to tell Marion Reid—most of whose eight children my father had delivered—that she was not going to get the appointment she had lobbied so hard to get and that she thought I had driven all that way to tell her she was about to get. Indeed, every member of her extended family was seated around the walls of her large country kitchen—dressed to the nines and awaiting my arrival—to celebrate. As I entered the room, I felt my heart stop, sweat coat my entire body, and my nerves seize like a truck engine deprived of oil. How in hell did I ever get myself into this mess? I asked myself. God, give me strength! Upon delivering the distressing news to Marion, privately in a side room, I was abruptly shown the door with nary a "by your leave." All the way back to Charlottetown, I felt like I had just fled a crime scene in which I myself had committed the offence: capital murder.

Returning home sullied by the dirty deed I had just completed, I phoned Eileen's nephew, lawyer Eugene Rossiter, operative of the hard-nosed Morell school of politics, and got him both to convince his aunt to accept the appointment and to sit with her when the prime minister phoned to ensure that she did not fold. And so, that dirty deed got done, too. In the subsequent election, in 1988, I could not get Senator Eileen Rossiter to lift a finger to help me. She told me she was too depressed.

# PEI Supreme Court Appointments

And then there was the biggest lottery prize of all: the PEI Supreme Court vacancy. This body is not a federal court—the administration of justice is under provincial jurisdiction—but the senior government appoints justices to the provincial high court. All this constitutional filigree, however, is irrelevant to the game of landing oneself a seat on the highest bench in the province. It's all about the prestige and pay and perks—and political payoff. And these, at the time, were in the gift of the Mulroney government—which, for all practical purposes, meant your humble and besieged servant of the people. And, more to the point, of the party.

There were then seven seats on the Court (now eight). Not one had ever been held by a woman. This time, I did not need to be instructed by the prime minister. It was well past time for a woman to be appointed. Alas, among other minimum requirements, a nominee had to have practised law for at least eleven years. In the mid-eighties, however, few women lawyers on the Island met that requirement. Even fewer of the Tory variety did, the right politics also being a "qualification." One of the few women who did meet these criteria was a legal advocate with the Department of Veterans Affairs' national headquarters in Charlottetown. That woman was— yet another Rossiter! She was Jacqueline Rossiter of the same Morell Tory family dynasty of the aforesaid notoriety. Her brother was the self-same Eugene Rossiter who had played a pivotal role in the Senate appointment of his aunt. This time, however, Eugene, soon president of the PC Association of PEI, was no ally of mine. Indeed, he opposed the appointment of any woman to the PEI Supreme Court. He especially objected to his own sister's getting the nod. I presume he did so because Jackie's elevation to the bench would preclude his own, either then or, should he not get it currently, the next time—there being some limits to nepotism on the Island, even if not many. Over his objections, I proceeded, with Justice Minister Ray Hnatyshyn, to execute Jackie's appointment anyway. Today, Jacqueline Rossiter is chief justice of the Court's Trial Division, where she is serving with distinction. But I paid a gargantuan political price to put her there, not least within the Rossiter family itself. Politics on the Island was the gods' way of making the rest of the world laugh uncontrollably—and me cry.

Two members of the same prominent Tory family getting the juiciest patronage appointments of all—enough already, right? Not exactly. Not on the Island. My political life, depressing enough as it was, soon got even worse. Behind my back, Eugene Rossiter conspired with my fellow PEI Tory MP Pat Binns—a future PEI premier and also from the general Morell area—to get Eugene's father, Leo, appointed to the federal Labour Relations Board, an independent, quasi-judicial tribunal that administered various collective bargaining and adjudication systems for the public service. Though not a seat in the Senate or on the Supreme Court, it was, nonetheless, a plum appointment that paid well. Certainly, it did so by Island standards, to say nothing of Morell's. Leo had been dean of the Island legislature, from the 2nd Kings district (1955–81). He had served controversially in various Cabinet positions (Natural Resources, Fisheries, Municipal Affairs) in the Walter Shaw era. After retiring from provincial politics, he landed, as his local patronage reward, the chairmanship of what is now called the Workers Compensation Board of PEI. With that sinecure now ended, it was onto yet more patronage, this time federally. That is, until Senator Lowell Murray, minister of federal-provincial affairs, casually mentioned to me, outside the Cabinet chamber, that the Privy Council was about to do the deed. He assumed that I had approved it through the party's normal patronage vetting process. But I had not: that process had been circumvented to avoid me in this case. Was every Rossiter in the province to be appointed by the Mulroney government to something, the richer the better? Eugene himself had the highest federal government billings of any lawyer in the province. To my mind, some limit had to be placed on the Rossiter family's Mulroney government windfalls.

Around this time, the *Globe and Mail* had been running a series of front-page exposés in which a crack team of reporters was connecting the many big black dots that established a pattern of patronage appointments from the Mulroney government, not just to PC partisans, but also, in some cases, to a close-knit select few, including members of the same family. I thought it was just a matter of time before reporters exposed such federal patronage appointments in PEI on my watch. Leo Rossiter's name would draw major attention if the story broke, so I had to pre-empt the scandal. After all, Mulroney had won the 1984 federal election largely by promising to reform corrupt federal patronage practices. In PEI, I would be the scapegoat in any patronage brouhaha, should it erupt. Accordingly, I vetoed Leo Rossiter's appointment. In doing so, I incurred the wrath of every single Rossiter, not least Leo's son Eugene. On the eve of the 1988 election, he was quoted in Len Russo's column, in the *Eastern Graphic,* as promising "a prime steak dinner" to any Tory who, in my Hillsborough riding, would vote against me. All the while, he was president of the PEI Progressive Conservative Association! Only on the Island! The gods were having a field day. But I was getting mowed down.

The most "interesting" of my PEI Supreme Court appointment woes concerned Charlottetown Tory lawyer Horace Carver, whose lifelong ambition had been just such a position. He is the man whom Kennedy Wells of *MacLean's* magazine had characterized as a "prissy Protestant fundamentalist." At a minimum, this Supreme Court aspirant was an "Island Way of Life" cultural zealot who had aggressively opposed me and the Mulroney government on the Fixed Link issue. For years, Carver positioned himself for a seat on the bench and actively campaigned for it as though a judicial robe was the dress code on the other side of the Gates of Heaven. When the vacancy occurred while I was in the federal Cabinet, he asked to see me about his celestial ambitions. I met with him at my Charlottetown constituency office and gave the lawyer ample time to make his case, as it were. For almost an hour, he extolled his professional qualifications, personal virtues, and superior claims to the post. Horace Carver had been PEI attorney general during the federal-provincial constitutional conference that took place between 1980 and 1982. The conference's work led to Pierre Trudeau's major constitutional reform and patriation measures. Carver's main spiel to me was that all the other attorneys general involved in that process had received judicial appointments. To Carver's mind, each of them was a latter-day Father of Confederation. In his view, as a "Father" himself he ought to be accorded the greatest reverence—and, specifically, rewarded.

Horace Carver's exaggerated sense of his own importance astounded me. I thought it alone disqualified him for the high post he was seeking. The petitioner did not mention party loyalty among his claimed virtues. It was just as well, for he had been one of my most unrelenting critics from the time I was first elected to Parliament. I once gave the major speech at a rousing political rally for a former parliamentary colleague, Wilbur MacDonald (MP for Cardigan from 1979 to 1980). Wilbur was now a member of the provincial legislature for the 4th Queens district. On that occasion, as was my practice for partisan remarks, I did not use a prepared text. But I did speak from a pile of foolscap on which I had scribbled crib notes, most of which I only skimmed while speaking. At the end of my twenty-five-minute oration, Horace, whose 3rd Queens legislative district bordered Wilbur's, followed me as a speaker. The would-be Supreme Court justice proceeded to the podium where I had left my notes, lifted the pages high in the air, looked at my henpecks with exaggerated contempt, unceremoniously dropped them to the dais like a cement block, ignored the ones that scattered under foot, and exclaimed: "Well, I didn't expect to be subjected to all this tonight!" Wilbur MacDonald, a farmer, is one of the finest individuals ever to grace the political landscape on the Island—a true gentleman. His wife, Pauline, long a partner in his political and farming careers, is a special person, too.

They brought credit to politics—and to farming—as a profession. After Horace Carver's boorish behaviour, Wilbur was worried that my feelings might have been shattered. "Tom, Horace is just not a very nice person," he said to me when the rally ended. "Don't take his comments personally." My consoler was right on the first count. It was hard for me to heed his counsel on the second. But I tried. And now Horace Carver, so rude to me on a public platform, was petitioning me in private to support his candidacy for the plumpest plum in the gift of the Mulroney government on the Island. His palpable lack of common sense was yet another disqualifier to my mind.

I did not intend to consider Horace Carver's candidacy seriously, much less recommend him to the justice minister. But, as it turned out, the gods were squarely on my side for once. I was relieved of the need to deny Carver the post he so coveted. He would have to find another way to honour Heaven's sartorial requirements. Across the province, Islanders massively opposed Carver's elevation to the bench. Women's groups were apoplectic about the prospect of a Mr. Justice C. Horace Carver. They viewed Carver as a misogynist and, therefore, a threat to their interests. Catholics, too, feared their fate if the perceived religious fundamentalist of Protestant persuasion were put on the bench. "Horace Carver is, quite simply, intolerant," one letter to me put it. Still other community leaders and groups joined the chorus for these or similar reasons. Nowhere else was hostility to Carver's Supreme Court ambitions stronger than within the Island's legal community, across all partisan divides. One prominent lawyer said to me, "I wouldn't stand a chance representing a client before a Justice Horace Carver. He'd have made up his mind about the case before I even opened my mouth." Unofficially, I was informed that the PEI Bar would rebel if Carver were appointed. I did not necessarily agree with the most extreme things said about the applicant. Could any serious candidate for the post possibly be *that* bad? I had too many reasons of my own for thinking him unqualified for the bench to make room for the most vituperative views I was hearing concerning this Supreme Court aspirant.

Before long, the chorus of opposition to Horace Carver's elevation would have drowned out a Rolling Stones concert at the Halifax Common. Islanders of every political stripe, and of no stripe at all, let the government know their low regard for Horace Carver's judicial credentials and aspirations. Not one Carver critic questioned the man's competence as a lawyer. I can't recall anybody's doubting his professional or personal ethics, either. In almost every case, people were concerned about the candidate's personality or perceived bias. It was all about whether he had the judicial temperament required. Clearly, the jury was not out on that score. The verdict was guilty and the sentence a public lynching. Justice department officials in Ottawa thoroughly investigate every individual seriously considered for a federal judicial appointment. In an applicant's community, both geographic and professional, they fan out like a Truth Squad to unearth every conceivable skeleton in his or her closet, right down to the third bone of the three ossicles in the middle ear. When consul general in Boston—months after leaving Cabinet—I was interrogated, for example, about David Jenkins's candidacy for the bench (he later became PEI's chief justice). It was as though he were being vetted for a papal knighthood. Assessments from this process are kept secret. But, as PEI's Cabinet minister, I was told discreetly—seemingly as much to caution me as to inform—that Horace Carver had scored badly in peer assessments on "judicial temperament" grounds. As if I did not already know that.

Faced with this massive opposition, Horace B. Carver, QC—self-styled Father of Confederation, militant opponent of the Confederation Bridge—retreated from the race for a Supreme Court seat in the birthplace of Confederation. His surrender just made political life a tad easier for me. I would have taken the Court seat myself before giving it to him. And I was not even a lawyer! The serendipity of Carver's withdrawal helped me avoid alienating yet another segment of Island society that would have mobilized against me to avenge an aggrieved family member. Without question, the man's campaign to land himself a seat on the PEI Supreme Court was not going to go anywhere as long as I was the gatekeeper. Not once throughout all this process was I influenced by Horace Carver's opposition to the Fixed Link per se. As we have seen, Joe Ghiz's plebiscite demonstrated that 40 percent of Islanders were also opposed. My beloved elder sister, Eileen, was in that camp. So were many other members of my extended family, and I wasn't sure about some of the rest. What weighed heavily on my mind, instead, were the intellectual dishonesty, the truth-stretching, the unfairness, and the stridency that Carver brought to the issue. These are hardly qualities one would want in a Supreme Court judge. Moral of the story: if you want a top position in the gift of the government, be very careful about how you attack its priority project in the relevant jurisdiction. For certain, do not expose your character flaws while on the warpath lest you give the government's principal champion of that project reason to think ill of your temperament. He likely has a long memory. As the saying goes, "The wise forgive but do not forget."[5] I might not have been able to live up to the nobility of Sir Robert Borden. But I was fast learning the wisdom of his ways on patronage.

---

It was bad enough that I had made enemies of supposedly loyal Tories by not delivering anything close to the amount of patronage they sought. Even worse, I incurred the lasting enmity of their hordes of friends and supporters. Among them were whole families, such as the Lees and the Reids and the Rossiters, many of them now committed to avenging their honour by ensuring my defeat, even if the principals themselves were disinclined, at least publicly. The self-styled dispossessed included even my mother's second cousin, Mel McQuaid of Souris, her birthplace. Mel was a former PC leader in the province and federal Tory MP for Cardigan from 1968 to 1974. He had been richly rewarded with a PEI Supreme Court appointment after leaving politics. Following his lordship's retirement from the Court, the Mulroney government appointed him to the National Parole Board. When the term ended, I had to phone my relative to say he could not be reappointed. It was nothing personal, I stressed; just that I was trying to distribute the few patronage plums in my orchard among as many loyal party supporters as possible, rather than limit the fruit to just a few through reappointments. But no explanation, however valid, would have satisfied him. He hung up on me! Before doing so, however, he said: "Didn't I do a good enough job on the board? Other board members are getting reappointed" I replied: "Yes, Mel, but most of the board members are from Ontario and Quebec, and ministers from those provinces have thousands of patronage appointments to dispense, whereas I have only a handful." Mel McQuaid's son, John, a neighbour of mine in Keppoch, coordinated the four Tory riding campaigns in the 1988 federal election. John himself was later appointed to the PEI Supreme Court. (On the Island, we like to keep things within the family.) I would like to think that John never held against me the grave injustice his father went to his own grave believing I had committed towards him. But John's wife (née Power) is the sister of Eugene Rossiter's wife. Was there no end to this clan, by birth or by marriage? To that whole clan, I was now the

Devil incarnate. It did not take long for their view to infect still others. With Mel McQuaid now in the enemy camp, the virus was striking dangerously close to my own family. Yet again, Robert Borden was right on the money. Unfortunately for me, there was not enough money to go around.

# Lieutenant Governor Appointment

Even former premier J. Angus MacLean got into the patronage game. Or, at least, he tried. This was a man who, true to the Scottish stereotype, was said to have saved almost every penny he ever earned. By now, MacLean had several hefty government pensions. One of them was his indexed parliamentary pension from having served a quarter-century in the Commons (1951–76), six years as John Diefenbaker's fisheries minister (1957–63). Moreover, his family blueberry farm in Lewis, to which he returned after leaving the PEI premiership (1979–81), was an active operation and, by all accounts, profitable. He, therefore, didn't need a federal patronage job either to fill his coffers or to occupy his time. And yet, the former premier summoned us three PEI federal Tory MPs (Pat Binns, Mel Gass, and me) to his farm in the summer of 1988 primarily for this very purpose. It was close to the calling of the fall federal election. This was the first time I had ever been asked to meet with the man personally, let alone at his home. Our host had two items he wished to discuss with us. Patronage was the first. The second was his concern about free trade. Never an admirer of Brian Mulroney or his government, MacLean expressed alarm about the PM's pursuit of a formal free trade agreement with the United States. He worried that the policy might catch fire for the Liberals, spread wildly, scorch the government and PC Party, and "topple everybody," especially in Atlantic Canada. This wily old political warhorse was proven prescient on the issue. At a minimum, he was right regarding the issue's eventual devastating political impact on us Tories throughout our province and region, even though we won the 1988 election on it nationally.

I devote attention to Angus MacLean for two reasons. The first is that his case is Exhibit A for how fraught with political danger patronage is and, therefore, how right Robert Borden was to launch major reforms. The second is that MacLean contrasts sharply with the kind of politicians I believe best represent the Conservative Party's noblest traditions in the spirit of Robert Stanfield: men and women who embrace progress with an eye not only to the present, but also to the future—"sustainable development." To my mind, this is the clinical core of classic conservatism. MacLean's political life, particularly when he was premier, was not in that tradition.

Angus MacLean was a diehard supporter of John Diefenbaker, and remained so long after Diefenbaker lost the national PC Party leadership to Robert Stanfield in 1967. After the PCs lost power in 1963, some of MacLean's policy stands became enmeshed in internecine warfare between Diefenbaker loyalists and opponents—"termites," Diefenbaker called them—like Island Tory MPs David MacDonald and Heath Macquarrie. It wasn't always easy to divine MacLean's motivation on particular issues. The man's opposition to free trade was probably genuine, as it was with many Tories of his generation. This was particularly true of war veterans and people of old English or Scottish stock with United Empire Loyalist ancestry. That is the reason, for example, that the large ribbon of Loyalist territory all the way east of Toronto down to Cornwall voted massively against the Tories and free trade in 1988—causing Flora MacDonald's defeat in Kingston and the Islands, to cite one casualty among many. In any event, Binns, Gass, and I felt the former premier was taking us to the woodshed on the free trade issue as surrogates for the Mulroney government. As a Cabinet minister, I was especially suspect in MacLean's eyes. My high-profile speeches and media interviews on the subject throughout the province surely didn't help my personal standing with this Island political icon. Nor did my appearance only a little while earlier on the CBC's weekly flagship game/public affairs show, *Front Page Challenge*. As a hidden "challenger," I had represented the environmental dimensions of the free trade news story, then one of the hottest facets of the issue across the country, as we have seen.

Patronage—the pending lieutenant governor vacancy, in particular—was obviously the main reason Angus MacLean had urgently called us to his home. Governor Lloyd MacPhail's term would not expire for two years. Premier Jim Lee's finance minister, MacPhail had been appointed by the Mulroney government in 1985 to the standard five-year term.[6] It would, therefore, end in mid-August 1990. And yet, individuals interested in succeeding MacPhail were already lining up support and beginning to lobby. Even the names of people not necessarily interested in the post were being bandied about from one end of the Island to the other. Angus MacLean fretted that his name was not being mentioned. "I'm not saying I *am* interested in being governor," MacLean told us, "but I am disturbed that, after all I have done for the party, both nationally and provincially, I am not on anyone's list." Translation: *I want to be governor. It looks as though I am not being considered for the post. I want you three MPs to ensure that I am.* MacLean had lobbied Jim Lee and his Cabinet hard to support him for the position in 1985. Lee told me for this book that the former provincial PC Party leader's relentless lobbying had made him and all his Cabinet colleagues "extremely uncomfortable." Now, it was the aging blueberry farmer's last chance to land the post, and we were his last targets. US Civil War general William Tecumseh Sherman said, "War is hell." Could war possibly be worse than patronage? At my worst moments, I would have settled for a bad war and a long sentence in Hell, rather than have to dispense patronage on the Island. But this was part of the job, and, given the system, somebody had to do it. Alas, at the time, that somebody was me. And yet, did the system need to be so messy—or exist at all, for that matter?

I was shocked by the former premier's brazen ambition. Why wouldn't he have been content to live out his political retirement in dignity as an elder statesman? That is how PC supporters and Islanders generally viewed him. Angus MacLean was, in fact, one of the province's most revered figures. Part of the reason is that, as a long-serving public servant and war hero, he deserved to be. It's also because the man was a master grassroots politician and, like any of that species, knew how to masterfully create and perpetuate his own mythology. Why, though, would he want a patronage plum now, even to the detriment of partisans who had worked hard for him in election campaigns over the years? Was it just about ambition? Prestige? Power for its own sake? Remuneration? Generous pension benefits? Angus MacLean was too high-principled to be motivated by mere greed. On the Island, a public-spirited individual like him can do a great deal of good representing the Crown as lieutenant governor. I have no doubt that MacLean saw the position at least partly in this way. All three of us MPs, however, left MacLean's home as much dazed as chastened. We did not discuss the former premier's concerns with one another either then or later. Pat Binns had served in MacLean's Cabinet in various portfolios and was a political protégé of his.

But even he did not lobby me for MacLean on the eventual lieutenant governor vacancy. Nor did anyone else—not even MacLean himself again. From then on, the former premier was civil to me but no longer friendly.

My fan club was shrinking rapidly with every passing patronage appointment, especially among those who felt denied—a fast-growing number as the election approached. Was nobody on the Island active in politics for the sheer opportunity to serve—or, at least, for the enjoyment of the game? As time advanced, I could think of fewer and fewer people in either category. As I left his farmhouse in Lewis, I was not certain that Angus MacLean was necessarily among them. In retrospect, I believe he was. At the time, though, my doubts were as wild as a Bruins hockey fan at a playoff game in Boston against the Canadiens. And that's as wild as it gets.

Towards the end of our meeting at his farm, Angus MacLean complained bitterly to Pat Binns, Mel Gass, and me about Alan Scales. I was never sure how this topic related to either the governorship or free trade, ostensibly his express main concerns. But this topic, too, weighed heavily on the man's mind. Scales was Charlottetown's— indeed, the entire Island's—most successful and prosperous lawyer. His last name was the "Scales" of the multi-lawyer law firm of Scales, Ghiz, Jenkins and McQuaid (now part of McInnes Cooper). Alan was the son of Austin Scales, who founded Island Fertilizers Ltd. in 1928. By the time the elder Scales died at age 103 in 1989, his company had made him one of PEI's wealthiest residents. Peter Newman gave Austin Scales honorable mention in the first volume of his two-volume blockbuster *The Canadian Establishment.*[7] Because of the province's small economy, Newman considered the senior Scales one of only a handful of Islanders who merited the "Canadian Establishment" moniker. From both his own professional success and now inherited wealth, Austin's son, Alan, was well positioned to become the foremost fundraiser for the PC Party on the Island and possibly the single most generous contributor to it. At the height of Liberal premier Alex Campbell's popularity, the Island PC Party was so broke it had no money to fight a provincial election—not a fart or a farthing. Scales signed a personal bank note for $50,000 for the campaign—equivalent to more than a quarter of a million dollars today. He generously, and selflessly, supported my own campaigns over the years, as he did those of many other individual PC candidates across the province, federally and provincially. Often, as in my case after I left Parliament but was still in electoral politics, he did so confidentially. I am a big fan of Alan Scales, just as I was of his father, who, to my knowledge, gave little or no money to any of my campaigns. The elder Scales was, however, free with his advice about certain verbiage in my campaign literature. I remember his taking particularly strong umbrage to my use of the phrase, "I want to take this opportunity to...." Over a hundred by then, he lectured me: "Get to the point, lad. Don't waste words saying you're going to." Such advice lasted endlessly longer than any cash contribution would have done. The whole extended Scales family are just solid Islanders and, to boot, quality Tories to the marrow. Old Man Scales was a fine patriarchal model for all of them. Without exception, his progeny followed the model.

In the late 1960s, Alan Scales and Angus MacLean feuded. The feud affected Island politics for a full generation. The circumstances are as follows. Scales graduated from Dalhousie University law school in 1961. Only seven years later, he became president of the Hillsborough PC Association. "Hillsborough" was the name of the new single-member federal riding that, along with another new single-member riding, Malpeque, was carved from the previous dual riding of Queen's, following redistribution based on population shifts. Angus MacLean and Heath Macquarrie had both been representing the Queen's dual riding—MacLean since 1951, Macquarrie since 1957. During the overlapping period, the two men were electoral running mates and, once elected, joint MPs for the dual riding.[8] For the 1968 federal election, however, each man would be on his own, in one or other of the two new ridings.[9]

The questions torturing the minds of MacLean and Macquarrie alike were these: Which of the two MPs would run in Hillsborough, essentially the Charlottetown area and a Tory stronghold? And which would have to run in Malpeque, mostly rural? Malpeque would be a much bigger challenge for either man, since it had absorbed a lot of Liberal voters from the old Queen's riding. Both MPs had their hearts set on the safer Hillsborough seat. Macquarrie, fearing with good reason that he would lose in Malpeque, stubbornly refused even to consider running there. As Hillsborough's PC Riding Association president, Alan Scales rightly calculated that the party stood a stronger chance of winning both seats if MacLean, a stronger vote-getter among rural voters, were to run in Malpeque. Macquarrie's obstinacy paid off. He got his way—and the new Hillsborough riding. Angus MacLean ran, and won handily, in Malpeque, just as Macquarrie did (albeit more narrowly) in his new riding. But to the day he died, MacLean never forgave Alan Scales for siding with his former running mate on who would run in Hillsborough.

By the time MacLean left federal politics and assumed the PEI Progressive Conservative Party leadership in 1976, Scales controlled party fundraising, both federal and provincial, throughout the Island. This did not sit well at all with the new leader. He refused to meet with the party's fundraiser, who traditionally reported exclusively to the leader, sharing donor names and amounts contributed only with him. MacLean complained angrily about Scales to almost anyone in the party who would listen. He accused him of using his fundraising position for self-interested purposes of every malevolent sort. Privy to MacLean's calumny, the fundraiser insisted on a meeting with his accuser. The meeting went poorly, prompting Scales to resign as provincial PC Party bagman. The leader had given him no other option with honour. But the Charlottetown lawyer continued to raise (not to mention donate) huge amounts for the federal party in the province. His doing so grated on MacLean, who, at his farm, urged all three of us federal MPs to shun Scales for fundraising or any other purpose. I have no doubt that, had MacLean said publicly about Alan Scales what he said privately about him to Pat Binns, Mel Gass, and me, the wealthy lawyer would have had strong grounds for a libel suit. And he likely would have won; for MacLean's charges, as before, were as untrue as they were malicious. Why would the Island's most successful lawyer and one of its wealthiest individuals need a political party to line his pockets? The man was giving more money to the party than he could ever have robbed from it, even if he were to do nothing else but devote all his time and energy to the task? And, as noted, had not Scales personally signed a bank note for the party to fight an election at one point, there would not have been a ha'penny in the party's coffers to steal. All this was sliding dangerously close to fruitcake territory. The former premier had morphed into a truth-stretching, angry, and vindictive codger. To my knowledge, neither of my colleagues acted on MacLean's exhortations about Alan Scales any more than they seemed to have done on his lobbying for the governorship. Apparently, they had no bigger appetite for fruitcake than I.

For my part, I continued to value Alan Scales as a unique party resource, not to mention a reliable source of funds for my own campaigns. Moreover, I respected and liked the man, even though he had publicly opposed me for the Hillsborough PC nomination the first time I offered in 1979. Instead, he actively supported (and, presumably, helped bankroll) one of my two opponents, wealthy businessman Al MacRae. The two men were close personal friends who had invested together in various local enterprises (including Northumberland Broadcasting Co. Ltd., which owned CHTN Radio). Nor did Alan Scales support me in my only other nomination contest on the Island, this time against Henry Phillips, for the 1993 federal election. (I won my three other election nominations on the Island by acclamation.) Like MacRae, Phillips had much closer personal ties with Alan Scales than I.

As mentioned in a previous chapter, both on the Island and in Atlantic Canada as a whole, Scales was one of Brian Mulroney's strongest and earliest supporters for the PC Party leadership The Charlottetown lawyer has continued to be close to Mulroney through the years to this very day. Unlike me, Scales also supported Kim Campbell when she successfully ran for the party leadership in 1993. He personally donated a lot of money to her campaign and raised still more from others. His own hopes for a PEI Senate seat, about which he made no secret, were dashed when the party was all but wiped out in the 1993 election under Campbell. But even these hopes were rooted in his belief that the Senate would be the best platform for him to serve the Island and help make the PC Party stronger in the province and across the region. The man needed neither the income and privileges nor the prestige that the position would have provided. Angus MacLean's view of Alan Scales notwithstanding, one can bet the mortgage that Scales—unlike fellow Islander Mike Duffy—would not have gamed the system from the upper house. Even without a Senate seat, this party stalwart remained loyal to the PC cause and financially generous to it. His virtues, however, were lost on J. Angus MacLean to the end of MacLean's life. I can only surmise how much money the provincial party missed raising under MacLean's leadership to indulge a vendetta against its best fundraiser and most selfless benefactor on the part of a man who went to his grave embittered about a riding nomination dispute three decades earlier. That's politics in PEI. Robert Borden was not alive to warn *me* about such things. If only he had been! I had to learn the hard way.

After retiring as PEI premier, Angus MacLean became increasingly critical of the federal PC Party. He disliked Brian Mulroney almost as much as he did Alan Scales, sparing no verbal vitriol to condemn either man. As he got older, MacLean aligned himself with David Weale and other ultra-idealistic romantics—some would say "reactionaries"—who longed to return the Island, economically and culturally, and quite literally, to its agrarian roots. This closed circle of serious-minded Islanders constituted a virtual cult with distinctly religious fundamentalist overtones. Kennedy Wells's "Prissy Protestant Fundamentalist" Horace Carver was a charter member of this cult. Angus MacLean was widely seen, including by himself, as the cult leader. Political scientist Nelson Wiseman, quoted earlier in this chapter, has summarized a phenomenon he accurately says characterizes PEI as much as it does Newfoundland: "A similar physical separation [from the Canadian mainland] nourished an inward-looking parochialism in Prince Edward Island, where a pastoral setting generated a romanticized illusion of an idyllic past and the valorization of the family farm."[10] With the exception of David Weale, no one gave louder voice to this illusion than J. Angus MacLean. Throughout his career in Ottawa, MacLean, a devout Presbyterian, was known to be a man of rectitude and self-discipline in public and personal conduct alike. But he was not thought to be unduly judgmental or sanctimonious towards others, publicly or privately. In the company of Weale and Carver and their insulated and close-knit ilk, however, MacLean, with each passing year, became steadily more a quasi-religious cultural figure than a politician in the traditional mould or even as he himself once had been. In perception and in fact, the man assumed the mantle of moral conscience of Islanders against the perceived evils of modernity. The former premier was not a Christian fundamentalist in the mode of Preston Manning or Stockwell Day. In his later years, however, MacLean was in many ways indistinguishable from either Manning or Day as a standard-bearer for Islanders opposed to what they viewed as modern secular society's amoral character.

Opposition to federal tax credits for films with perceived objectionable content (Bill C-10), to same-sex marriage, to federal funding for Gay Pride Day, to federal support for abortion services in international maternal health care aid—all such religiously tinted policy stances were used by the Stephen Harper government to pander to its "moral values" base, as political scientist Jonathan Mallow has noted.[11] I have no doubt that, if Angus MacLean had been alive and active in politics when the Harper government was in power, he would have supported its measures in these and similar areas. As it was, he focused his own government's "social conservative" efforts on curtailing modern urban development and, by implication, the evil intrinsic to it in his eyes. As premier, he emphasized rural community life, banned new shopping malls, established a Royal Commission to examine land use and urban sprawl, and cancelled the Island's equity participation in the Point Lepreau nuclear power plant in New Brunswick. Breaking the Lepreau contract cost Islanders dearly in cancellation fees, forgone energy-cost savings, and lost economic opportunity from a cheaper and more secure energy source for local businesses and industry. Whatever moral principle it advanced in the cathedral of ideology, this action had no bearing whatsoever on the viability of the plant itself. The change just reduced the province's energy self-sufficiency—a high price to indulge one politician's ideology.

Non-Islanders might be inclined to view Angus MacLean's policies as admirable, as quintessentially conservative and, consequently—for those so inclined—as praiseworthy, even ahead of their time. After all, didn't those policies anticipate, and reflect the need to discipline, urban sprawl? Such an interpretation would be wildly off the mark. The man's positions were neither conservative in the classic sense nor praiseworthy in any sense. It's worth dwelling on the point because, to me, it strikes at the heart of what it means to be a conservative in the modern era. Concerning shopping malls, for example, Islanders were going to shop at them, anyway. Indeed, they were already doing so—in droves, principally at Champlain Place in Moncton. Islanders were also being drawn to the stores and malls of Halifax, a manageable car drive from anywhere in PEI. On the Island, local entrepreneurs such as Frank Johnston of Charlottetown were eager to capture some of that market by building malls on the outskirts of the capital, only to be stymied by MacLean. Meanwhile, city retailing was perishing because local store owners were not adapting quickly enough to fast-changing consumer demands and expectations. Before long, every single retail store along the full length of Charlottetown's most prominent commercial block was boarded up. In 1973, six years before Angus MacLean became premier, a major study—largely funded by the federal Department of Regional Economic Expansion and conducted by consultants Stevenson Kellogg—found that the city was deteriorating rapidly and that "decay had already set in."[12] The study strongly recommended major new commercial infrastructure be built in the provincial capital.

Partly because of the premier's strictures on mall development, the hemorrhage of retail dollars from the Island to the mainland was undermining the province's retail sector in communities across the province, not just Charlottetown. The premier's proscriptions against local development were also depriving the provincial government and municipalities of sales or property tax revenues badly needed to fund local facilities and services, particularly in health and education. The revenue was vital to community life across the province—MacLean's stated pre-eminent cause. A classic conservative needs to use not only his or her brain but also common sense. MacLean was using neither. His small but militant band of followers was exercising no more smarts than he. Islanders paid the heaviest price—quite literally—for this ideological extremism. The anti-development policies had the diagonally opposite effect of what was intended: communities withered across the province in no small measure because the government was preventing them from adapting.

As a long-time Island champion for the built environment and cultural property, I, like many other Islanders, would normally have been viscerally pulled towards Angus MacLean's battle banner. But the man carrying it high in the air was marching himself and his followers right over the cliff of reality. What we needed to do was not oppose the march of history—in this case, the inexorable direction consumers everywhere were going in lockstep. Instead, we should have focused on ensuring that the march in our own province did not trample upon the precious features and values that make us what we are. This meant taking two major practical steps: first, approving mall building projects on a select basis; and, second, instituting every law or regulation or covenant necessary to protect "the Island way of life" at each step. The success other communities had achieved in balancing development and heritage protection could have served as our model; we did not need to take a stab in the dark.

Islanders were not well served by being told, in effect, "*You* cannot have it." It would have been far nobler and wiser, and more classically conservative, had the leadership said, instead, "This is how *we* ought to have it and, working *together*, let *us* get it right." Such was not done on the aforementioned issues when Angus MacLean was premier. In the absence of judicious planning by the entire community over an extended period, sticking the finger in the dike of societal change eventually caused the floodgates to break from pent-up local consumer and retail demand. And now, as I publicly warned at the time, there is not a single entrance to Charlottetown, Canada's Confederation City, unmarred by indiscriminate urban sprawl.

On no other issue more than the PEI-NB Fixed Link were MacLean and his cult following zealously against modernity. MacLean himself was an outspoken critic of the project. He all but pronounced *ex cathedra* that, if built, the bridge would destroy the province both physically and morally. He must have once thought this stand was utter bunk himself, for he had won several elections in the Diefenbaker era with his fellow Island PC candidates—including Heath Macquarrie, as his running mate—campaigning for that very project. "The Party of the Causeway" was the Tory campaign slogan in successive elections at the time. A progressive he might have been in those days. But, wallowing in everything archaic and anachronistic, Angus MacLean had become a certified reactionary by the time I, as a federal Cabinet minister, needed to deal with him. It pains me to use such a term against anyone, especially an individual whom I admired and liked and for whom my father had the highest regard and affection. Too often, terms like "reactionary" are hurled as personal insults, rendering them meaningless except as epithets. My battle, though, is not against the man. Rather, my battle is against a view of conservatism that is antithetical to its classic meaning and, if practised in public policy, does great damage to the community.

In 1980, towards the end of his premiership, Angus MacLean appeared as a hidden challenger on CBC-TV's *Front Page Challenge*. He represented the story "Provinces Challenge Pierre Trudeau's Unilateral Patriation." In a verbal duel with veteran media curmudgeon Gordon Sinclair, a regular panellist, MacLean stated that his first allegiance was not to Canada but to his own province. How does one build a national community when allegiances are primarily to the parish, not to the entire nation? Canada would never have been created had the Fathers of Confederation shared this narrow mindset. No Conservative Maritime premier in my time in politics was more unlike Robert Stanfield than J. Angus MacLean in understanding the need to lead followers to the future, but in a way that builds upon the best of the past. Walter Shaw, Jim Lee, Hugh John Flemming, Richard Hatfield, Ike Smith, John Buchanan—all such Conservative premiers in the different Maritime provinces over the years strove to build a future for their people. They did not try to return their followers to a bygone era, let alone one idealized out of all proportion to how it actually was (an "illusion," as Professor Wiseman put it).

As a devoted public servant and war hero and individual, Angus MacLean merits everyone's utmost respect and positive remembrance. He has mine unreservedly. As a model for Canadian Conservatives in contemporary times, however, it is an entirely different matter. In that sense only, and not the other, I would say about Angus MacLean what Hamlet said to Horatio about his deceased father, "I shall not look upon his like again." To my mind, that is decidedly for the better.

# Patronage Epilogue

I well recall Robert Stanfield's saying that political patronage was an acceptable part of governing if done right. He said some patronage is in the public interest and the rest not. It was, to him, a matter of distinguishing the good from the bad. In my own case, the position (consul general in Boston) already existed; it didn't have to be created for me personally. The post had to be filled by a qualified person and the PM believed I was such a person. If he had been proven wrong, the decision could have been quickly reversed, for I served at the pleasure of the Crown (in effect, him). Moreover, for the post in question, no bogus process invited people to apply ostensibly in a search for the best candidate when, in fact, the winner had already been chosen beforehand. The prime minister's choice was totally transparent and generally accepted on that and other grounds. Not a single Opposition MP criticized the PM's choice and, to my knowledge, no journalist or media commentator did so, either. Indeed, many in both categories praised the appointment. To my eyes, the bogus route—"We're considering every candidate to find the best one," wink-wink—is still too often followed in government recruitments. That's especially the case with internal promotions, not necessarily executed by politicians but by fellow bureaucrats—a form of patronage rarely understood as such but inarguably exactly that.

Political patronage plays a valuable function in a democracy. For one thing, it gives a government leader flexibility to run things with the help of individuals whom he or she most trusts and respects. Patronage also makes it easier for the leader to move pieces on the chessboard—and, if necessary, demote bishops to pawns humanely. Just as patronage is worthwhile when practised judiciously, so also it is inevitable as long as elected politicians are in charge of governing. Because there is so much abuse in Atlantic Canada, however, no other region would benefit more than our own from a better system of the kind favoured (and, while premier, practised) by Robert Stanfield. As he emphasized, what is needed is a process designed to distinguish between acceptable patronage and the corrupt type to ensure that the public interest is advanced, rather than subverted, when discretionary appointments to government jobs are made and contracts for public services awarded. Another great Nova Scotian, Robert Borden, set the country on that path. As the Mike Duffy scandal demonstrated all too well, the journey has yet to be completed, least of all by us in PEI.

# Chapter 28

# THE
# 1988 FEDERAL
# ELECTION

The 1988 federal election is now part of history and, for me, a distant memory. It is amazing how in life what strikes one as all-important turns out to be, long after the fact, much less significant in the total universe of things. Any part of history, however, is important, for it allows us to draw lessons for the present and for the future. A classic conservative is intrinsically history-oriented—linked to, and required to respect, both the past and the future, while being grounded in the present. To the classic conservative, there is more to life than meets the eye, let alone caught only through one's own narrow lens, processed from one's exclusive vantage, and then used for a selfish purpose without regard for anyone else's interests. That's what liberals are for! This broader vision helps to capture with clarity the sense of *community*. For Edmund Burke, the concept meant a seamless web from the past to the present to the future; from people's forebears to themselves to their descendents; from the planet as it was to how one would want it to be. It's all about interconnectedness. For me, that is the true conservative *family value*.

Seeing the world as composed of interdependent parts causes a person to be judicious when seeking to change any one part lest the rest be damaged unintentionally, even unknowingly until much later, if at all. That's why a holistic or systemic approach to development is inherently conservative. The antithesis, in the standard metaphor, is to see only the individual trees, not the total ecosystem of the forest. The classic liberal, for whom liberty is everything, would view it as his or her right to chop down trees—other people's interests be damned. Individual freedom is, indeed, a righteous concept. But, as too often happens in contemporary society, when LIBERTY is brand-ironed onto the trunk of a tree, the consequence can be dire for more than that lone tree. Translated into policy terms, the liberal, in the name of personal liberty, demands every right for himself—from brandishing a firearm to rejecting the tax collector. Such a person—it tends to be male—identifies his interests with those of others only to the extent he sees in them a reflection of himself and their ability to help him advance what he considers his own rights, not necessarily anybody else's. To the "John Wayne" old-fashioned liberal, concern about the community consequences is for sissies. But there is nothing manly about myopia, nothing effete about farsightedness.

As I reflect on what once was—but, happily, has not been for a long time—one of the most painful parts of my personal history, the 1988 election, I sometimes upbraid myself for having once taken it so seriously. I was being distinctly *unconservative* in seeing that event and my role in it in isolation. Other times, when more contemplative—more *conservative*, as it were—I gain through the lens of this experience a sharper vision about a lot of things: about politics as a profession or calling; about public life more generally; about human nature, at both its best and its worst; and about myself, but only as a work in progress and in relation to others. After my defeat, I received a lot of advice from family, friends, campaign workers, even complete strangers, about how best to proceed professionally and personally. One close family friend suggested I take time just to think. He recommended, in particular, that I read "those one hundred books you always wanted to read but never had the time to." I actually did—*more* than a hundred, as it turned out. Some of that reading made me appreciate more fully than I ever had realized before, even at political studies grad school, what a sound value system classic conservatism is as a certain set of principles that wraps everything in life together in one overarching vision: the interconnectedness of all nature's creatures and the inextricable link between humanity's fate and the planet's. Just as Tom Sloan insisted—at the Stanfield seminar at Trent University—that liberals do not have a lock on liberty as the core of their value system, so also conservatives should not be allowed to monopolize their particular philosophical vision, either. But neither should any conservative refuse to lay claim to it as central to his or her sense of self as a citizen.

Politics is the most personal of professions. As David Brooks has said, "the politician is the product." As such, that profession, which places such a high premium on conquest, has a way of turning the practitioner inwards, onto himself (or herself), not outwards towards others except in the most superficial of ways. The individual is conditioned to believe that the world—or, at least, his survival in it—revolves around him…his thoughts, his words, his every action. The ferocity of political competition renders it extremely challenging for the politician to differentiate between his or her own interests and the public interest—"I have to win in order to save the world." For the politician, electoral survival is the name of the game. Towards that end, he or she, therefore, tends to view everyone as either an ally or an adversary. This is a form of objectifying people every bit as degrading, not to mention insidious, as the sexual kind. Typically, it is only after politicians escape that form of egocentrism, either through retirement or, as in my case, defeat that they realize how much politics can warp their perspective, distort their priorities, and alienate them from others and from themselves. When, over time, politicians come to view themselves as products, instead of people—as, indeed, the system, forces them to do to avoid defeat or even just public embarrassment, forget humiliation—the warping, the distortion, the alienation are complete. Politics in your past might not open doors to professional opportunity. But it helps open your eyes to reality.

Over the generations, many federal general elections have been held. Tens of thousands of candidates have run. Fewer—but still thousands—have won. Some winners proceed to make a big mark on the political landscape, whether in government or Opposition or (given enough time) in both. Others leave a much smaller mark. Too many make none at all. With rare exceptions, most individual politicians, even good ones, can be easily replaced by someone else just as qualified and eager to serve. But each politician is unique—as Helen Doyle would say, each is "God's creature." For my part, I think I did make a mark. Of this I am sure: I did my best. My unexpected loss in the 1988 election pained me personally, just as it did my family and friends and supporters. But, in the total scheme, as my youngest daughter, Emily, would say, it was "no big deal." I do believe, however, that the circumstances of that loss have some broader relevance from which I, at least, learned certain lessons and gained important insights. Perhaps those would interest and benefit other politicians, would-be politicians, and anyone else who believes politicians—good, bad, or indifferent—count in a democratic society. To the extent my narrative exposes any residual sense of loss or pain, it is because the words flow from real life—mine. Nobody's life is devoid of such emotion. I hope the reader will forgive the emotion while benefiting from the telling of that experience—my small part of history.

The narrative is intended to broaden the peripheral vision so as to capture four perspectives: (1) the media's proper role in public affairs and society as a whole; (2) the fact that every office holder is vulnerable to defeat, no matter how confident he or she might be of victory; (3) the office holder's age-old challenge of respecting opposing views while acting decisively on issues important to him or her; and (4) the steady decline of civility in public life and the threat this poses to our democracy.

Most people who acquire any degree of wisdom in life do so towards the end of their time on earth, when—it could be argued—"a fat lot of good that's going to do me now!" Politics, though, particularly when one wields real power (as a Cabinet minister does), is an intense human experience that tends to accelerate life's normal wisdom-generating process at warp speed. A politician—or former politician—might not end up wise, but he or she will have gained more wisdom from defeat than from victory. Winning causes us to reach for champagne. Losing forces us to search for answers. The headiness from *answers* lasts a lot longer. The search itself can be satisfying.

No matter his or her particular circumstances, significant or not in the broader constellation, all politicians are subject to the same laws of politics. The causes and effects might be different from one protagonist to another; the fundamental forces, though, are not. For a politician, a win is a win, a loss a loss. All candidates should want their candidacies to be win-win—for themselves and for the country. The balance tipped in my own case in different ways from one election to another over the years—some wins, some losses—but either way I now believe that I won for having been part of a wonderful thing: democracy and public service. Politicians and their supporters must be equipped intellectually, emotionally, and organizationally to advance their causes and convince others to join them. Just believing is not enough. History does not merely happen—people make it happen. Conservatives, by definition, seek to make history happen in the interests of everyone and every creature and every facet of our marvellous planet, animate and inanimate. I am one Conservative who felt like a winner merely by being part of the political game. Here I tell how the game, for all practical purposes, ended for me. But a new—and, in many ways, better—game began.

# The Election Lead-up

As the 1988 election loomed ever closer, I felt I had done everything I could, with the talents and time given me, to represent my constituents and province in Cabinet and in Parliament. When I first ran, in 1979, my slogan was "Tom McMillan: He'll Represent You Well in Parliament." In my subsequent campaigns in PEI, including the 1988 contest, the slogan was "Tom McMillan: He's Representing You Well in Parliament." To my mind, the latter slogan involved much more than a change in verb tense. It reflected what I thought was true: I had been delivering on the promise to do well by my constituents, both nationally and at home, and by implication would continue to do so if re-elected.

In my own riding and province, a bullet list of accomplishments filled a dense, six-page brochure that my campaign team released at the outset of the 1988 election under the caption: *Tom McMillan, He Gets Things Done*. Among them, notably, was the establishment of the Atlantic Regional Veterinary College in Charlottetown, following my incessant lobbying in concert with local community leaders. For that cause, I fought so relentlessly, from the Opposition benches, that I think I just wore down the resistance of the principal federal minister, Agriculture's Eugene Whelan. The tactic had worked for me before when I had fought, from the same side of the House, to have the Trudeau government keep open the CN Express Office in Charlottetown, which it planned to eliminate. I had made such a parliamentary nuisance of myself on the issue that, when the government announced it was closing all but two of these offices in Atlantic Canada, one of the exceptions was in my riding, the other in Deputy Prime Minister Allan MacEachen's. He had Cabinet clout. I had the next-best thing: Irish stubbornness.

Across the province, I have to confess to having shamelessly raided the budgets of both Tourism Canada and Environment Canada, the two ministries I headed at different times, to feather the Island's nest. Sometimes, it was major—to wit: a multi-million-dollar heritage-sensitive redevelopment of Anne of Green Gables in the PEI National Park at Cavendish to reflect the totality of Lucy Maude Montgomery's spirit of "Avonlea," not just, as it stood, a golf course (as magnificent as it was) and a late-nine-teenth-century farmhouse (as authentically showcased as it was). In my own riding, I worked with Jacques Dalibard of the Heritage Canada Foundation to bring its Main Street program to Charlottetown. Working with such community leaders as Mayor Jack Ready, built-heritage specialists Catherine Hennessey and Irene Rogers, and the small business community, we transformed the facades of Old Charlottetown. Now, thanks to that effort, Charlottetown looks and feels like what it is: the "Confederation City" of Canada.

Other times, the favouritism to the Island was just dear to my soul, even if the achievement itself might have been lost on most voters. The National Historic Sites and Monuments Board, which reported to me, declared Charlottetown City Hall a national historic site as one of the finest representations of period municipal architecture in the country. For the official designation ceremony, it bothered me that the Island lacked a major image of Queen Charlotte Sophia (1744–1818), wife of George III, after whom the Island's capital city had been named. So I commissioned the country's best copyist, Dusan Kadlec, to replicate the famous life-sized painting in the United Kingdom of Queen Charlotte wearing her coronation crown and robes. My Environment Canada officials found the $10,000 for Kadlec's commission within a tight budget—more to say "we owe the minister this one" than to reflect any departmental priority. Bless them all! For a similar reason, my Tourism Canada officials had earlier freed up the money for our ministry to cost-share with the Jim Lee provincial government (75 percent to its 25 percent) the purchase for the Island of tens of thousands of dollars' worth of original paintings by PEI native Robert Harris, Fathers of Confederation portraitist.[1] Had we not acquired the best of them, they would have been dispersed worldwide and likely lost forever to PEI's patrimony. Those paintings now adorrn heritage sites across the province for Islanders and their visitors to enjoy. I personally commissioned the foremost authority on Robert Harris,

Montcrieff Williamson—then curator of the Confederaton Centre of the Arts Gallery in Charlottetown—to fly to Halifax, view the paintings being sold in a gallery there, and grab the best of them with a blank cheque from us in his back pocket. Montcrieff chose wisely. Maybe all this was no big deal to some. But, to the present day, I am proud of what my co-conspirators and I did for the cultural heritage of the Island and the entire country.

No doubt, it was the big-ticket, bricks-and-mortar projects that meant the most to my voters. For me, those began—in partnership with the Island's federal Cabinet minister, David MacDonald—when Joe Clark was briefly the country's prime minister. Together, David and I successfully beat back a strong push from some arch-conservative Tory Caucus members to reverse the Trudeau government's plans to relocate Veterans Affairs national headquarters from Ottawa to Charlottetown. What a fight! And what a sweet victory it was when David and I won. The relocation brought to my riding the salaries and spending power of some six hundred public service employees and their families while enriching our population with added cultural diversity. A large government building also needed to be built in downtown Charlottetown. The new headquarters continues to boost local employment and sales of goods and services to this very day.

But, in PEI, I am most proud of my pivotal role in the decision to build the Confederation Bridge, the longest over frozen water in the world. This structure constitutes the Island's strongest and most secure link to the rest of Canada, and to other Canadians, since the Island's interprovincial railway connection was completed as a term of Confederation. The Confederation Bridge reflects the spirit of Sir John A. Macdonald, spanning the Northumberland Strait as his National Dream lives on. Of one thing I am certain: had I not spent much of my political capital fighting to bring the bridge to the Island, in the face of Joe Ghiz's obstruction, Islanders would still be waiting long hours in interminable lineups to catch—and often miss—car ferries. I do not think I could ever have contributed, to the country or to my beloved province, in any other field as substantially as I was able to do in government and politics in this and countless other such ways.

And now for the four *perspectives* in light of my reflections on the 1988 election, beginning with the lessons I learned about the media's proper role in public life and society more generally.

# Politics and the Media

Among the many low points of the 1988 campaign for me was a major front-page story in the *Evening Patriot*—Charlottetown's historically Liberal-leaning afternoon daily, now defunct—just days before the vote. Spread across six columns above the fold and headlined in big black print, "Four Seats, Tories Topple," the story all but declared every one of us three Progressive Conservative incumbents defeated (and the sole Liberal incumbent re-elected) before a single vote had been cast. The story added to the growing sense of a Liberal tide across the province, as elsewhere in Atlantic Canada. Clearly, that was the intent of the story in the first place. The *Patriot* based its "analysis" exclusively on the predictions of political scientist Gary Webster of the University of Prince Edward Island. He was presented as an independent and disinterested academic observer. In fact, he headed a virulent anti–free trade group in the province whose stated purpose was to defeat all four PC candidates in the election. Webster had conducted no poll, assembled no focus group, relied only on his own wishful thinking, and devoted much of his commentary to venting personal animus towards me. (He did concede, however, that I was an excellent MP, "sort of.") Over my years in and out of politics, I have seen both some superb journalism and some simply terrible reportage. This was the worst. I think the editors realized as much themselves, for they published a puff piece on me the next day, with considerably less prominence, seemingly to help make amends and appease outrage in some quarters, not least among PC partisans. But irreversible damage had been done to the entire Tory campaign in the province, not just my own.

As if to enter the fray, CBC-TV in Charlottetown could not contain its excitement about the plunge in the national PC Party's poll numbers immediately after the party leaders' English-language debate late in the campaign. It played up the numbers as though final election results. The local newscast stated unequivocally that the national numbers, in effect, applied to the four seats on the Island. All four PC candidates would, therefore, lose. And yet, in no federal election in memory had the results in PEI's four federal ridings—least of all in my Hillsborough riding—corresponded with national party polling, let alone ultimate countrywide party standings. Over the years, the Island consistently bucked national trends, often dramatically. It would, in fact, do so election night in 1988, but, unfortunately for us PC candidates, not in our favour. The PC Party was able to reverse the post-debate plunge in its national poll numbers, thanks largely to Brian Mulroney's frenetic campaigning and to the corporate community's rallying around the government to save the free trade agreement. The reversal was reflected in one national poll within a few days of the plunge. The last national polls, over the weekend prior to election day, showed the Mulroney government marching towards a strong majority government. Having given so much attention to national polls during the brief period in which they went against the PC government, local CBC all but ignored them when they reversed direction towards the government. For the remainder of the campaign, CBC Charlottetown stuck to its original line that all four PC candidates on the Island would likely lose. The station did so even when local and regional polls indicated, right up to election day, that would not happen in my own case. The fact that all four of us did lose—but in my case by such a slim margin that any prediction either way would not have vindicated anyone's prognosis—proved nothing, except the power of self-fulfilling prophesies.

Such was the media coverage across the Island throughout the election. On voting day itself, I awoke to see splashed across the front page of the *Guardian* (the Island's morning daily) a big bold banner headline, "Election a Referendum on Free Trade." It was exactly how the Liberals had sought to frame the entire campaign everywhere across the country. Equally, it was what I did not want to be the central question on my voters' minds. I preferred, instead, that Hillsborough electors judge primarily all the positive things I indisputably had done for them and for the Island as their MP and through Cabinet. As committed as I was to my duties as Canada's environment minister, I felt that any national success and profile I achieved in that portfolio would reflect well not just on me, but also on my riding and province, and that my constituents would see things that way, too. So, my campaign also stressed this dimension of my overall record. But, in the end, fear of free trade—and, to a lesser extent, of the Fixed Link—trumped everything else, including my record as both an MP and a Cabinet minister.

At the beginning of the campaign, someone close to the enemy camp had warned me confidentially that the anti–Fixed Link forces were planning thirty-five traps for me. I should have taken those warnings much more seriously than I did. Instead, I decided to conduct my campaign as I had always done: staying largely above the fray while meeting voters at their homes and workplaces, one voter at a time. I never did learn what all the traps were, having avoided most of them, I presume. The ringleader of the subterranean political shenanigans was Jack MacAndrew, who had been hired in 1965 by fabled performing arts impresario Mavor Moore to be executive producer of the Charlottetown Festival. MacAndrew ran unsuccessfully as a Trudeau Liberal against Heath Macquarrie on the Island in the 1968 federal election. He left the Confederation Centre in 1974 to head CBC-TV's variety programming at the network's headquarters in Toronto. In 1985, he returned to the Island to establish his own small marketing and communications company in Charlottetown. In that capacity, MacAndrew performed work for anti–Fixed Link activists, whose cause he militantly embraced. His company, for example, produced for the PEI Fishermen's Association an apocalyptic video about the proposed transportation project.[2] Just as "one should avoid the man who has read one book," as the saying goes, so, I learned, as far as journalists are concerned, one should also "avoid the man with one axe to grind." Brian Mulroney always lectured Caucus and Cabinet: "Never pick a fight with someone who buys ink by the barrel and paper by the ton." In the 1988 election on the Island, MacAndrew's axe was aimed squarely at my head, his ink and paper exclusively at the Mulroney government's and my own re-election. Now, years later, following his death at age eighty-one in May 2014, I think Jack was actually a colourful and captivating curmudgeon in the journalistic tradition of Gordon Sinclair. At the time, though, not so much.

I have always suspected that Jack MacAndrew's animus towards me began when I delivered, at the Charlottetown Rotary Club, a high-profile speech on the free trade agreement then being negotiated by Canada and the United States. I had referred to MacAndrew's presentation at a local public hearing as one example, among others, of how I thought some critics were being unduly alarmist about free trade. My future nemesis had said that the agreement would "literally rob Islanders of food from their kitchen tables." MacAndrew routinely did not distinguish between making news himself in the guise of a private citizen and reporting and commenting on it afterwards as a journalist. For him, "conflict of interest" was like jaywalking: against the rules but of no consequence and the shortest route to where he wanted to go. No doubt, I hit a nerve with the Rotary speech, for the offended one wrote an entire column in the subsequent issue of the *Eastern Graphic* attacking me for, in his eyes, attacking him. I learned from such experiences that the media like to shoot arrows at others but hemorrhage at the mere sight of an arrowhead pointed at them. Jack was hemorrhaging, and now out for my own blood.

Jack MacAndrew was a ubiquitous presence in the PEI media: besides his column in the *Eastern Graphic*, he aired a regular political commentary on radio station CFCY; he hosted an hour-long, weekday phone-in show at the same radio station; he appeared on local CBC-TV and radio public affairs programs and panels; and he wrote a back-page opinion column in *IslandSide*, a now-defunct monthly magazine about Island issues. And all this was happening in a tiny media market. As if that weren't enough journalistic hegemony, this media entrepreneur/personality browbeat other reporters to toe his political and ideological line. The chill factor was real. Young reporters were especially vulnerable. They told me so. Give the Devil his due: he was a media master.

From the beginning of the 1988 campaign till the end, Jack MacAndrew devoted his ubiquitous media appearances to lambasting me. No other politician except Brian Mulroney, whom he also detested, was in Jack's crosshairs throughout the election. It was as though I were the only candidate running in the federal election in PEI and he alone stood between me and the destruction of civilization that I was hell-bent on causing. I learned that many of the political traps set for me by the anti–Fixed Link forces were of his direct doing. Among the most annoying was his arranging for CFCY's front door to be locked when I tried to enter the building for a Hillsborough all-candidates radio debate he was moderating for that station. I characteristically arrived on time but at the last minute. So, it was predictably easy to target me without barricading the other candidates. I eventually gained entry, but only after a great deal of distress—no doubt, the purpose of the hijinks in the first place.

Yet another trap set for me in the election was far worse than annoying. It was disastrous for my campaign. It concerned my entire radio commercial "buy" for the last day before voting that a candidate was allowed by federal election law to advertise (Friday before Monday). My campaign purchased expensive thirty-second spots—about sixteen for each radio station in all—to appear at regular intervals throughout the day on both CFCY and CHTN. The same radio ad for both stations was produced professionally, and featured me making my final appeal directly to the voters. The reel containing the message was delivered to CFCY with the understanding that the station would give it to CHTN, a common reciprocal practice between the two stations then. When the ad aired the first time on CHTN, at around 6:45 A.M., one of my most trusted political advisors and closest friends, David Jenkins, heard it. To his horror, the ad had been professionally doctored, post-production, to elevate my voice by at least an octave. I was made to sound like a eunuch if not a schoolgirl. The handiwork of MacAndrew himself? He would have had both the technical skill and the access. David contacted both radio stations immediately and yanked the ad. It was too late for our campaign team to replace it, so we lost our total radio buy for the most important day of the whole election. It was bad enough that I was forced to lose this most important opportunity to speak to voters. My campaign, like that of all other candidates, was also subject to strict spending limits under federal election laws. So, even though the ads couldn't be used, we had to include the costs of producing and airing them as though they had been, in a budget that allowed no room for error.

When not setting such traps for me, MacAndrew vented his animus on air. One of my radio ads cited a profile of me by the *Wall Street Journal*. The feature front-page article incorporated a graphic artist's dead-on likeness of me somehow created as though an engraving. The writer alerted Americans that they could expect to hear a great deal more from me as Canada's environment minister, particularly concerning acid raid. Our radio ad quoted the *Journal* that I was "one of the government's most effective performers in the House of Commons."[3] MacAndrew denounced the ad on CFCY, saying, "Who cares what the *Wall Street Journal* says about Tom McMillan?" An hour later, while campaigning from door to door in an apartment building, I overheard a young resident say to his roommate, "Who cares what the *Wall Street Journal* thinks about Tom McMillan?" MacAndrew's incessant attacks on air, as in print, were having the intended effect. By the end of it, even I might not have voted for that bastard McMillan! John McQuaid, the coordinator across the Island for the four PC candidates' campaigns, eventually complained to the CFCY's manager, Ron Lewis, later Liberal appointee as PEI lieutenant governor, still in office as I write. But John's effort was for naught—good for the station's ratings? Liberal loyalties? intimidation from MacAndrew? all of the above?

Not just Jack MacAndrew, but most other CBC reporters and producers and other journalists in PEI were hostile to the Fixed Link. They openly supported my independent anti–Fixed Link opponent, David Weale, in the 1988 election. As earlier noted, he was a regular *Them Times* history commentator on the local CBC radio station, so was one of their own. Moreover, the principal on-air TV political reporter, Kathy Large, was so widely considered cozy with the Liberals—Joe Ghiz, in particular— as to be the subject of unfounded rumours, a perception that caused the CBC to transfer her to Halifax after the election. Meanwhile, I considered CBC Charlottetown's hostility to me and the Mulroney government a much greater threat to my re-election in Hillsborough than either of my two main opponents, Liberal George Proud and NDP Dolores ("Dody") Crane.

Independent candidate David Weale participated in very few high-profile all-candidates debates. He did not have to: the media, especially the CBC, gave him disproportionate access to their cameras and microphones and notebooks. That privileged access included a full hour with Jack MacAndrew on his CFCY radio phone-in show to discuss the Fixed Link—in effect, to promote Weale's own candidacy. This kind of courtesy was not extended to me or to any other Hillsborough candidate or, for that matter, to any candidate running in any of the other three ridings. Arguably, the discrimination violated the relevant provisions of federal election law, but who would have raised the matter? Certainly not the Island media, least of all CFCY or the CBC. Early in the campaign, Jack MacAndrew was listed as Weale's official media spokesman for the election campaign in Hillsborough. When my campaign team protested this blatant conflict of interest and violation of media ethics, MacAndrew's name—but, obviously, not his role—was struck from the list.

Local CBC massively covered Liberal Opposition leader John Turner's overnight visit to my riding in the last week of the campaign. National Liberal Party campaign strategists must have calculated that, at this point, they might be able to knock off a high-profile Tory Cabinet minister while enhancing their countrywide effort by appearing to be doing so. (A national leader does not normally visit one riding for two days in the dying days of a national election just to win a single seat, even a Cabinet minister's.) By sharp contrast, the CBC gave short shrift to Brian Mulroney's day-long visit to the Island a couple of weeks earlier in the campaign. During the Charlottetown leg of his campaign visit, the PM's announcement of a half-million-dollar grant to the Confederation Centre, which I had arranged with Communications Minister Flora MacDonald, received a mere two-sentence mention and no video footage on the CBC's flagship evening newscast. (That was a lot of money then for a local institution, even one, like the Confederation Centre, with a national mandate.)

The last week of the campaign, the federal government employees' union issued a news release calling on all Islanders to vote against government—that is, Progressive Conservative—candidates. The local CBC news anchor read the release as though it were a paid political commercial for the Opposition parties. The same week, the provincial Chamber of Commerce's news release supporting free trade and, by inference, candidates who supported it was shamelessly underplayed. (I have no record of its having been mentioned at all in the main local CBC newscasts.)

At the climax of the election campaign, some dozen members of the media from across PEI placed their names on a list, organized and released by Jack MacAndrew, publicly declaring their opposition to the Fixed Link and, by implication, their support for anti–Fixed Link candidate David Weale. The names included Jack MacAndrew himself; Barbara MacAndrew, Jack's wife, a local and national freelance journalist in her own right, published in *Maclean's* magazine and elsewhere; Jim MacNeil, publisher and chief editorial writer at the *Eastern Graphic* (though dropped from a later list); and Martin Dorrell, primarily of the *Globe and Mail* and CBC, but additional outlets as well. It was astounding that such a large number of journalists would have been so indiscreet—some would say professionally irresponsible—as to have allowed their names to be used in this barefaced exercise in partisanship and occupational malpractice. The list is now part of the historic record. The document stands as one of the worst cases of unethical media behaviour—to say nothing of bad judgment and personal indiscretion—in the history of modern Canadian journalism.[4]

Members of the PEI media (among them Martin Dorrell) both sponsored and actively conducted a highly unscientific local public opinion poll on the Fixed Link. The poll results were accompanied by an "analysis" that claimed widespread opposition to the project among Islanders. The same people then widely reported the results of the poll, including on the local CBC newscasts, without fully revealing their own involvement in it, let alone the methodology employed or the motivation for the poll's having been conducted in the first place. All this was done at the end of the campaign to maximize voter impact and minimize opportunities for Fixed Link supporters to respond.

My concerns about CBC Charlottetown's one-sided coverage of issues and candidates throughout the election in PEI parallel Brian Mulroney's comments in his memoirs about the CBC Ottawa bureau's biased reportage on the Meech Lake Accord. When a critical mass of a community's communications professionals align themselves publicly with one side of a political debate, what chance is there that the electorate will hear both sides of the story? It is vital for democracy that public issues be fully vented, everyone participate, each person have his or her say, all opinions be considered, and the media report it all, including their own opinions and perspectives, with equal measures of professional dispassion and fairness and balance. Then, as the saying goes, "Let the Devil have the hindmost."

Never before in my experience—in Prince Edward Island or anywhere else in the country—had the media demonstrated more political bias than the Island media did during the 1988 federal election. Put simply, the media (with admirable exceptions) got caught up in the emotional contagion of highly controversial issues around which the election pivoted—in particular, free trade and, locally, the Fixed Link. Instead of reporting and commenting upon the action, reporters became actors themselves— never their acceptable role in any circumstance. In the Cabinet's post-mortem of the campaign after the Mulroney government was re-elected, all my colleagues, one by one, reported they had experienced the same kind of media hostility to the government in their respective regions. Mostly the hostility stemmed from our pursuit of free trade with the United States. At the time, I was too shocked, busy, and distracted to process all this, still less be bitter. Now, many years later, it is even more difficult for me to define exactly what was at play. It is likely inaccurate to say, as I felt when everything was happening, that CBC Charlottetown, for example, *deliberately* undermined, for garden-variety partisan purposes, my own campaign and the Mulroney government's local efforts to get re-elected. It is probably closer to the truth to state that a more subtle and less traditional form of partisanship applied. Individual CBC reporters and producers, as well as personnel at other media outlets, felt so strongly about the aforementioned election issues that they communicated, directly or indirectly, personal views at the expense of a more balanced airing of those issues. This alternative perspective is a more complex and worthwhile question for society to explore than conventional media partisanship. For sure, the two forms are different, even if they are closely related and can lead to the same or similar result. The relevant ethical implications merit reflection and analysis not just by media outlets and individual journalists directly implicated, but also by everyone who, like me, cherishes the role of the media—including public broadcasting—as watchdogs of democracy.

Journalists have the right—indeed, duty—to criticize candidates for public office when the facts merit such treatment. After nearly a decade as an elected office holder, half as a high-profile Cabinet minister in a controversial portfolio, I had developed a thick skin in the face of media and Opposition attacks. Truth be known, I enjoyed a political brawl as much as anyone, and I believe I gave as strong a punch as I took. Criticism sharpened my game, kept me honest, helped me learn from mistakes, alerted me to my limitations and vulnerabilities, showcased my verbal and physical and mental strengths, and accorded with my view of how democracy is supposed to work—all to the good. What was happening in the "case study" at hand, however, was on an entirely different plain. Journalists were standing between candidates and voters, blocking—and, in some cases, sabotaging—candidates' communications with the electorate. It is imperative that every candidate have an opportunity to communicate his or her qualifications and policies to voters and generally make the best-possible case for why the political office seeker deserves the electorate's support. A journalist, however defined, should not impede the democratic process by going beyond fair reportage and commentary, positive or negative, to engage as a player himself or herself in electoral competition. The "engagement model" violates the most fundamental principle of journalism: *Don't be part of the story.* I fully expected political opponents and their respective teams to try to knock me down, and possibly out cold, as I threw my fists. I was doing the same to them when they lunged at me. But I did not anticipate that a referee would strike me. Unfortunately for me, a number of referees—not just Jack MacAndrew—were engaged in the fight. "I'm struck by how many sportswriters now think *they* are the story, their thoughts more interesting than the game they were sent to cover," wrote esteemed writer, editor, and Yale University English professor William Zinsser in a classic guide to writing non-fiction.[5] What Zinsser said of sportswriters could also be said of political reporters: "You are doing a job that has its codes of honor. One of them is that you are not the story."[6]

The media's political impact in tiny jurisdictions such as PEI looms disproportionately large because there is so much of it relative to the size of the market. It's like putting a giraffe in a birdcage. Nowhere else in all Canada is the disproportion more extreme than with the CBC in PEI—all that state-provided budget, high technology, programming, reporting staff, technical talent, and professional experience to cover a population one-fifth the size of the Toronto suburb of Scarborough. When a media outlet strays from sound journalistic ethics by the profession's own widely accepted standards, the effect on local politics, and on the political culture more broadly, can be devastating in such a jurisdiction. All of us can understand how individual journalists and other media personnel can get swept up in the emotional adrenalin of a highly competitive single-issue election campaign like 1988's focus on free trade—and, in PEI, also on the Fixed Link. Young and inexperienced reporters are especially vulnerable to the powerful forces at play. This is particularly true when they're in thrall to older and more seasoned practitioners of the craft who are themselves disinclined to respect journalistic standards for being zealously engrossed in the issues of the day, as happened with Jack MacAndrew in PEI. Every time a member of the media does not understand and practise his or her proper role as a professional, much more than the profession suffers. Liberty writhes in pain.

Freedom of the press does not mean exclusively the media's own *right* to report upon and analyze public events without unreasonable stricture. It also means the concomitant *responsibility* the media have to allow other voices to be heard—and to help provide outlets for them to be heard. One has the right to speak but not to silence others. As with every other civil or human right—the right to life, the right to privacy, the right to religious practice, the right to assembly, the right to an impartial judicial process, and so on—freedom of the press is not absolute. In exercising their freedom-of-expression rights, the press must be careful not to violate either other fundamental rights or other people's rights. One of the stalest of clichés still captures one of the freshest of truths: freedom of speech does not bestow the right to falsely shout "Fire!" in a crowded theatre.[7] As in this classic example, everybody without exception must always balance rights and responsibilities. The PEI media did not respect this principle when covering either the free trade debate or the Fixed Link during the 1988 federal election. And the democratic process suffered. It was as though the offenders thought the nobility of their views gave them license to act ignobly—the "end justifies the means."

Some of the examples of media malpractice I have cited might appear exceptional or extreme, reflecting the fact that 1988 was one of those times in Canadian history when a federal election was fought mostly on a single, emotionally charged issue. But, to the extent that such abuses of press freedom are commonplace in Canadian journalism, the profession itself must provide the necessary reforms. Any restriction on press freedom from without, especially involving government, would defeat the very purpose of reform: making our democracy more perfect. Physician, heal thyself. That is, in fact, what Canada's sixth prime minister, Dr. Charles Tupper, literally did for medical ethics in Canada while serving as the first president of the Canadian Medical Association (CMA) in the late 1860s. This towering Nova Scotia Conservative politician and statesman (a Father of Confederation) was an active medical practitioner himself. He headed the group that instituted the system that exists to this very day by which the Canadian medical profession rigorously regulates itself against every form of medical malpractice. Shouldn't Canadian journalists take a page from Tupper's handbook and give their press councils real authority to devise a clear and tough Media Code of Ethics and then enforce it with powerful sanctions? Nobody could reasonably say that such a system operates anywhere in Canada today. Mike Duffy, as one of Canada's most famous broadcast journalists, was able to use his privileged access to three successive prime ministers (Brian Mulroney, Jean Chrétien, and Stephen Harper) to lobby publicly for a Senate seat—ultimately with success in the case of Harper. And yet, everyone concerned, including Duffy's fellow journalists, treated the matter as amusing at the time. Given the scandal that subsequently engulfed the PEI senator, none of this is so amusing now. If enforcement of media ethics were taken more seriously in Canada, isn't it likely that the consequent damage to the Senate's reputation—not to mention the millions of dollars the relevant investigations and litigation cost the taxpayers—would have been avoided?

My experience with the species convinces me that the vast majority of Canadian journalists, including in PEI today, are committed to a high standard of professional ethics. But Charles Tupper felt the same about his fellow medical doctors when, as CMA president, he insisted that the conscience of individual practitioners was not nearly enough to protect the public interest. Like laws, professional standards seek to guard against the worst in human nature, not acknowledge the best. Journalism schools teach that the reporter must step back and look at all sides of a story. If he or she writes or airs a story before knowing, or even caring about, all the pertinent facts, the bedrock of sound journalism is violated. That bedrock is honesty—ensuring that "the most obtainable version of the truth" is told, as Carl Bernstein (of Watergate fame) frequently puts it. Metaphysics holds that truth is "that which conforms to reality." Journalism is not philosophy. Least of all is it science. But, like those two intellectual fields, it requires a degree of detachment to capture and then reflect reality. If journalists don't bring to their craft some degree of dispassion, if not neutrality, but simply impose their own predetermined version of reality on what they report, they're not engaged in the business of truth—just words. And, however artfully assembled, words devoid of truth are no substitute for the real thing.

CBC Charlottetown's unprofessional behaviour contrasted markedly with how I experienced the corporation's modus operandi elsewhere across Canada throughout my time in politics. Both its national and local journalists and producers invariably treated me with utmost courtesy, respect, and professionalism even when I might not have deserved such treatment in my own right. It was, appropriately, all about the public office I held and the democratic role I was playing, not necessarily the person I was or was perceived to be. These professionals were able to make this distinction and act accordingly. Good for them! Not bad for me, either. Best of all for democracy. I especially appreciated the treatment I received on the baker's half-dozen occasions I appeared, as either a hidden "challenger" or panellist myself, on *Front Page Challenge*. The moderator, Fred Davis, was the ultimate professional—and charmer.

The CBC plays an essential role in our country's cultural life. It provides a forum in which we Canadians can reflect and explain and interpret Canada and ourselves to one another in all our wondrous complexity and diversity. The private sector media market either cannot or will not perform this role nearly as well. In pursuit of ratings, market share, advertising dollars, and profit, it too often does not play that role at all. The CBC is especially invaluable in smaller and more remote communities, such as in the North, where my niece Elizabeth McMillan was long a reporter for the corporation before relocating with it to Halifax. Without the CBC at its best, Prince Edward Island, for example, would be virtually a media wasteland. I have always found that the corporation does an especially good job of covering agriculture and the fishery across the province. Not only are these our most important primary industries; they also help shape and preserve our unique identity and culture. Few native Islanders—whether urbanites or rural dwellers—lack red soil in their pores or saltwater in their veins. In my own case, though the son of a surgeon, I spent chunks of my boyhood as a farmhand in Vernon River, thirty-two kilometres east of Charlottetown. The experience helped mould my character, especially a profound appreciation of nature in all its marvellous forms. Hugh Segal has said that national institutions such as the CBC constitute the "muscular structure of the modern Canadian state."[8] That is why a Conservative prime minister, R. B. Bennett, created the CBC in the first place. When the CBC gets embroiled in the form of indirect partisan politics that I believe it did in covering the 1988 federal election in PEI, the corporation violates its mandate, defeats its purpose, and shortchanges the country. The same principle applies to journalism in general. Partisanship is an important part of Canadian democracy. It is, however, not one that the CBC was established to play, directly or indirectly. The corporation can end up playing a partisan role, even if not as a matter of deliberate corporate policy, when personnel at the ground level "become part of the story," rather than chroniclers and analyzers of it. This concern is not so much a conservative value—though it is certainly that, too—as it is a Canadian democratic value.

Now, for the "every politician is vulnerable" perspective.

# Strategies and Tactics

I should have foreseen, and responded better to, the hostility some PEI media were demonstrating towards me and the Mulroney government in the 1988 election. At the beginning of the campaign, I might have been lulled into a false sense of security by the fact that some other Island media outlets and reporters were acting professionally. Radio station CHTN, for example, was unfailingly fair to all candidates and political parties from beginning to end, never showing either favouritism or antipathy. The same was true of the *Journal Pioneer*, a daily newspaper published in Summerside for mostly a Prince County market, in the western part of the province, well outside my riding, which was in dead centre. The paper had little impact on my campaign, however, except to underscore how fair it was compared to, for instance, the weekly *Eastern Graphic*, which was virulently opposed to the Fixed Link. Though published in Kings County, at the other end of the Island, the *Graphic* had a big readership across the province, including in my riding, particularly among opinion leaders. In previous elections, I fared well—or, at least, not badly—with all Island media. But the 1988 election was the first one in which I ran as a Cabinet minister. In the 1979 election, I was a first-time candidate seeking an open seat where the incumbent (Heath Macquarrie) had decided not to reoffer. In both the 1980 and 1984 elections, I was the sitting MP but defending my seat from the Opposition benches. In 1988, by marked contrast, I was not only the incumbent MP but also the principal face of the political party in office. So, I had to defend my seat *and* the government's record. What I did not realize is that this fundamental change—from Opposition to government, from challenger to defender—required that I campaign in a fundamentally different way, too.

Instead of retooling my mind and mechanics to adapt to the new political realities, I campaigned in my riding in 1988 much as I always had: relying heavily on generally perceived personal assets while doing my best to compensate for my limitations. Among my strongest political assets was a first-rate constituency office that delivered for everyday folks and the community as a whole. The credit belonged mostly to a terrific riding staff, headed by my long-time trusty assistant, Jeannétte Arsenault, who was popular and respected by everyone. But, now, I personified every negative about the Mulroney government—large or small, real or perceived—while rarely getting political credit for the things people liked about it. My strategy to float above the controversies and personal attacks proved naive. Not only should I have anticipated the negative campaign my media and other well-placed detractors would run against me. I should also have organized my campaign to defend the government and the party and myself from attacks. It was not in my nature, however, to campaign in that way. I believed it was best to ignore attacks lest fuel be fed to the fire. I was also partly influenced by Tory titan Dalton Camp. When I interviewed him for my politics master's thesis in 1969, a decade before I entered electoral politics, he told me: "A politician who responds to his attackers lends credibility to both the attackers and the attacks." I think he was generally right. But a politician has to take a different approach when opponents impugn his or her character based on certain positions he or she takes on controversial issues, especially ones central to a campaign. Such was the case in the 1988 federal election for most Tory candidates across Canada on free trade—and for me in PEI, also on the Fixed Link.

As a Cabinet minister, I should have been the strongest exponent and defender of the free trade agreement on the entire Island, not just in my own riding. I chose not to be. This was a huge mistake. In a post-mortem of the election conducted for the prime minister—and summarized for Cabinet by Deputy Prime Minister Don Mazankowski—it was revealed that Mulroney Cabinet ministers and backbench MPs who had aggressively defended the government on the issue as a major part of their respective campaign strategies fared significantly better than those who had not. I was in the latter category. I have only myself to blame. That said, my campaign team and I had the damnedest time trying to obtain, from the national PC party, free trade material usable on the stump at the local level. Every time we asked for help with arguments and data that would show Islanders and Maritimers as a whole how the agreement would improve their lives and region, some operative would refer us to stock material from Foreign Affairs. Invariably, it was dry and abstract and, therefore, worthless for our purposes. To the many voters who requested a brochure on the subject, we were reduced to distributing a *Globe and Mail* editorial that both summarized the agreement and endorsed it enthusiastically. Unfortunately, like the *Wall Street Journal* profile of me, this editorial could be too easily dismissed as irrelevant to the province and region—and, more to the point, my own re-election.

As for my principal opponent, George Proud, the Liberal strategy was to keep him out of sight, out of mind, and out of trouble. It was an approach in which the media were generally content to be complicit. They never pressed him on the issues, as they did me, especially ones about which they themselves felt strongly and that others used against me—the Fixed Link above all. Liberal string-pullers knew that a direct voter comparison between a well-entrenched incumbent and a challenger who had been living out of province for many years preceding the election would have worked to their disadvantage in efforts to beat me with George Proud. Even their billboards did not mention his name. To this day, the website *Canada Votes* refers to my having been beaten in 1988 by "the unknown George Proud." The closest Liberals came to promoting their candidate directly was a billboard slogan, "Proud Liberal," implying pride in party, not the candidate's last name. But, as my youngest brother, John, noted after my loss, the Liberals probably had chosen the ideal "man of the people" to challenge an incumbent whom they set out to characterize as too national to be personable and too busy as a federal minister to be locally accessible.

Years earlier, George Proud had been active in organized labour. He made his living running the gamut from driving taxis and manning the gaming tables at local fair grounds to quasi-managerial work at Maritime Electric, the province's privately owned and operated power utility. For a time, he had served in the provincial legislature and in Alex Campbell's Cabinet. The premier was rumoured not to have had a high regard for his minister or much regret when he was defeated in his own district. Yet George did have an easy manner with people. He spent a lot of time at Tim Hortons shops across the riding, drinking coffee and eating donuts and, more important, being seen. I found him likeable myself. And I had no quarrel, fundamentally, with how he or his team ran their campaign. Even their anti–free trade scare tactics, around which they organized everything, were more Alfred Hitchcock's *North by Northwest* than the famous director's *Psycho*. The Liberals succeeded in marketing their Hillsborough candidate as more imbued with the *Helen Factor* than—as I see it—the real thing by virtue of the actual record. That said, any candidate is vulnerable when a powerful national trend is blowing the opponent's way. A politician might be highly regarded locally, but, barring ridings so safe they would elect a cactus plant, a strong national tide almost always trumps local factors. This reality played out for us Tory candidates in 1988 in ridings throughout Atlantic Canada. *Jail* for us, *Boardwalk* for them.

I did not enter the 1988 campaign overconfident of winning. And yet, polls showed that I was as invincible in the riding as any incumbent on the Island had been for a long time. It was a fairly safe Tory seat, anyway. The Liberals and NDP acknowledged both facts, as did the media. But three weeks before the vote, on November 21, John Turner scored what was generally considered a knockout punch against Brian Mulroney on the pivotal election issue of free trade in the nationally televised English-language debate. This went over well for the Liberals in Atlantic Canada, and my electoral fortunes, and those of other PC candidates in the region, tanked overnight. Lacking the business support that helped reverse the party's slide elsewhere in the country, we Atlantic Canadian Tories found ourselves abandoned faster than a voter could say, "Free trade will steal my unemployment insurance cheque! my Mom's welfare cheque! and granny's old age pension cheque!" Chequemate! Throughout the region, where federal government cheques are as blood to vampires, Tory plasma hemorrhaged like an uncapped water hydrant. Most PC candidates in the four Atlantic provinces, including popular Cabinet ministers, crashed to defeat. We won a mere twelve out of thirty-two seats, down from twenty-five in 1984—a loss of more than half our regional Caucus. Free trade defenders, particularly in PEI, where the premier campaigned against us almost full time, could no more hold back the political tide than King Canute could the real one.

Until all this struck in the middle of the campaign, I greatly underestimated Island voters' opposition to the Mulroney government—and, by association, to me— on the overarching issues of free trade and the Fixed Link. Opposition to the Fixed Link in my own riding was generally less militant than in the more rural parts of the province. And yet, opponents from across the Island aimed their guns at me as the most vocal champion of the project and the person best positioned, as a Cabinet minister, to make it happen. As residents of other ridings, they might not have been able to vote against me legally (illegally is another matter, discussed below). But they could—and did—work against me at the grassroots level. Their opposition, together with Island-wide hostility to free trade fomented by Premier Ghiz, added to the growing impression that I was under siege from all quarters. By the end, I was.

I had always resisted campaigning with a supporter (an "advance person") in door-to-door visits with voters, not wishing to have anyone stand between me and the elector while also slowing me down. What worked before, however, proved wrong now that I was much better known and, as a Mulroney Cabinet minister, endlessly more tired than in previous campaigns.[9] I discovered too late that I could no longer rely on the bountiful reserves of energy that had served me so well before. This time, those reserves steadily diminished with each passing doorstop visit—and with mounting assaults from all quarters, including, for the first time, at the doorsteps themselves. The anger was aimed not just at Brian Mulroney and the government because of our stands on free trade and the Fixed Link, but also, now, against me personally.[10] One voter I met at home was a Marine Atlantic ferry worker who feared for his job should the Fixed Link be built. He was so verbally abusive and physically threatening towards me that his teenage son felt compelled to intervene. Nothing remotely like that had ever happened to me in any previous election. Even activists in other parties had always been unfailingly courteous—"Good luck, anyway" being what every candidate soon recognizes as the perfunctory adieu of an opponent's committed supporter.

It takes a certain type of person to want to enter electoral politics at a level beyond the local school board and to thrive once there. It's not just that you have to conduct yourself largely in public, every elector is your boss, the job security is uncertain, each day is long and the work both heavy and endless, and the remuneration is paltry when calculated on an hourly basis. It's also a rough-and-tumble enterprise and getting more so all the time. The ubiquitous tabloid media culture—now the norm, rather than the niche it once was—renders it almost impossible for office holders to retain zones of security and privacy for themselves or their families, no matter how hard they try. Diverse forms of modern social media, enabled by the Internet, are exacerbating their vulnerability. Anyone can tweet your whereabouts and goings-on any time to anyone anywhere. Why would someone in his (or her) right mind want to subject himself to all that? The question begs the answer. Perhaps only the psychologically damaged now enter the fray. Which would explain why the political class is so disrespected these days—they're all nuts! Or, at least, enough of them are to create that impression. Tom Symons was pressured by the PC party to run for election in Peterborough, Ontario, at various times in the late 1960s and early 1970s. Robert Stanfield periodically broached the subject with him. But it was not in Stanfield's nature to ask anyone to turn his or her life upside down for him—or for the party—as running for office inherently would. I sometimes wonder whether the Trent University president, tough as nails but genteel by nature, would have survived the kind of take-no-prisoners politics I had to defend myself against in the 1988 election, my roughest-ever campaign. And, pre-Internet, that was a much simpler time, and politics a relatively more civil business, than is the case today. For his sake, I am glad my former boss/colleague/friend never decided to run for office. I suspect he is, too. I would recommend public service to anyone, just not necessarily this form, particularly for a person like him—a lamb and not a tiger, in Blakean terms.

Is a country well served when politics becomes so cutthroat that the idea of seeking public office repels everyone but the type of person mentally programmed to play the game that way, but ill-equipped to act wisely and competently and compassionately once elected? Aren't the two skill sets becoming mutually exclusive? Should a capacity to "win ugly" be considered the main, let alone the only, qualification for holding office? It is virtually the case now in the United States. With better statutory controls on election spending and more generous public subsidies for campaigns, Canadians running for national office have it better than their American counterparts. But, on both sides of the border, getting oneself elected or staying elected requires, at a minimum, a level of professionalism—media savvy, polling, analytics, micro-targeting, the whole nine yards—unheard of when I was first elected a Member of Parliament back in 1979. Politics nowadays is fast excluding not only the faint of heart, but also the community-spirited amateur.

For my part, given what I know now that I did not know before entering electoral politics, I have trouble reconciling two sentiments about the nature of the game as it increasingly would be played with each passing election cycle: the "winning ugly" factor. On the one hand, I would not trade for any other conceivable experience the political career I had. On the other, I would not choose the same career path if I were a young man today and just setting out. I most certainly would not want one of my daughters to select that path these days. And yet, if it happened, I can think of no more effective way she could make her life purposeful, even if generally unpleasant. Politics, thy name is paradox. In any event, a man or woman entering the political arena needs to be prepared for the worst, avoid getting inured to the best, accept with equanimity every defeat and with humility every victory; but assume defeat is inevitable for most practitioners. And it is no fun when it happens.

# Balancing Consultation and Decisiveness

## THE FIXED LINK: A CASE STUDY

A couple of days after the 1988 election, I ran into Jim Larkin, a young Charlottetown entrepreneur, tourism leader, and sometime PC member of the provincial legislature for 6th Queens. His district was the other half (along with 5th Queens) of my federal riding. "Tom, I think Jack MacAndrew's incessant media attacks against you contributed enormously to your defeat," Larkin said to me. No doubt. Opponents of the Fixed Link genuinely believed its construction would destroy the Island's character, though time has proved them wrong. These people didn't always act properly, but they cared about their cause and acted out of idealistic spirit. I now realize that my opponents and I were equally committed to our Island homeland and eager to advance its interests. We just differed on how to achieve our shared goals. I should have tried harder to understand their perspective and to seek common ground, if that were possible given a binary choice: the Fixed Link was either going to be built or it was not. Such an approach is the essence of politics—and of rational civic discourse, to say nothing of common sense, let alone a politician's self-interest. "You turn foes into allies by reaching out, not closing in," Hugh Segal has written.[11]

That principle was lost on Stephen Harper and his government. They did not just disrespect their adversaries; they despised them. John Diefenbaker also demonstrated that very mindset, in his case towards the "termites," who, at the end of his life, were virtually everyone. The guiding principle of the classic conservative is inclusivity, not alienation. If I disrespected my adversaries in the 1988 election, particularly on the Fixed Link issue, I now reject that attitude as not part of who I am as either a man or a conservative. As Joe Clark wisely counselled me, behind the House of Commons curtain back in the day, a politician should never take opposition personally. I did not always heed Clark's wisdom.

All the features that make Prince Edward Island a special place, including the very fact that it is an island, contribute to Islanders' inherent "conservatism," to which opponents of the Fixed Link appealed. But this perspective failed to account for Islanders' strong desire—as it were, their "progressive" side—to advance their economic welfare by embracing beneficial change. Where is the balance between these two sets of values, each precious and eminently defensible? And on what side of the equation should one place the Fixed Link, if that calculation would help weigh the options? Opponents could—and did—argue that the project should not be considered progressive if it threatened the environment. Supporters could—and did—argue that the Fixed Link expressed conservative values by advancing the economic interests of Island families and strengthening the community as a whole. It's all a matter of *perspective*. The conservative/progressive argument can be made every which way, depending on the person's vantage—typically the product of his or her life experience, not the indisputable logical conclusion from natural law. But such is what politics and elections entail: exposing every relevant fact, and every possible point of view, to the bright and unforgiving light of debate and discussion. The voters, and their duly elected representatives, decide. Nothing should be allowed to undermine a community's efforts to find the right balance between conflicting (and frequently ambiguous and confusing) sets of values. That is, essentially, what the political process is intended to do. For democracy to function, nobody should be permitted to tip the scales unfairly on one side of the balance or the other. This is what the Fourth Estate does when it injects itself into a story.

In the case of the Fixed Link, I had no doubt where common sense and balance lay: approve the project in principle, then subject it to the most rigorous cost-benefit analysis possible to determine both its viability and its potential impact—the course that, in fact, was followed. Indisputably, the progressive/conservative balance was found—and found to be right—for the Island, for Atlantic Canada, and for the country. Between the completion of the Confederation Bridge in 1997 and 2000 alone, Prince Edward Island's exports to the United States, its principal foreign market, more than doubled to $500 million. The number of tourists soared from an average of 760,000 pre-bridge visits a year over the period between 1993 and 1997 to an average of 1.2 million in each of the first ten years after the bridge opened. Indeed, in 2014, during celebrations of the 150th anniversary of the 1864 Charlottetown Conference that gave birth to the nation, all previous PEI visitation records for the high season (July and August) were smashed. The record was broken again in 2015 and yet again the summer of 2016.

For local industry and businesses, the bridge has slashed costs, accelerated transport, and made deliveries and orders more reliable. The markedly reduced time and cost of transporting bulky and perishable goods to market—potatoes and other farm products and fresh fish, in particular—have been a boon to PEI's primary industries and light-manufacturing sector. Total exports as a share of the Island's gross domestic product have climbed steadily every single year since the bridge opened. The positive impact of the bridge was immediate in the wholesale and retail sector. The Island experienced a 40 percent increase in retail sales between 1996 and 2004, from $957 million to $1.4 billion. What a contrast to Angus MacLean's efforts to stop retail store development in the province.

The bridge has also brought many non-economic benefits. Among them is the speed with which Islanders are now transported in medical emergencies to major centres such as Moncton and Halifax for care not available in their own province. Put simply, the structure is helping to save lives. Our education and training, our performing and fine arts, our sports and athletics, and many other areas of our cultural life have also benefited from easier and more reliable contact with our fellow Maritimers and people well beyond the region, particularly Quebecers and New Englanders. By enlarging our world, and in the process our minds, the bridge is greatly enriching Islanders' quality of life. PEI is a better place to live and we are a stronger people for it. Moreover, not one of the environmental fears of the bridge's opponents has materialized.

Brian Mulroney's government executed the relevant constitutional amendment, legislation, and private sector contracts for the bridge. Mulroney, consequently, has the right to the sentiment he expresses in his memoirs: "[The Confederation Bridge] is an accomplishment that continues to give me real pride and satisfaction." He notes: "Many of the Island's canny politicians...kept their cards close to the vest until late in the process."[12] He says "canny." I would say "cowardly." Most politicians on the Island—federal and provincial and municipal alike—were so afraid of the issue they treated it like a communicable disease. And yet, these milksops were among the first to preen before the cameras when the bridge opened with great ceremony and public pride. For sure, Joe Ghiz, whose "canniness" the former PM cites specifically, was not one of the courageous, even as he sought to claim maximum credit for the bridge at the expense of those who were. As the Island politician who led the fight for the Fixed Link, both in power circles and with the public, I share the former prime minister's pride in this historic achievement.

A few months after the bridge was officially opened on May 31, 1997, then-premier Pat Binns wrote me a personal letter on behalf of the PEI government and all Islanders to thank me for the "tremendous contribution you made in enabling the bridge to become a reality." He presented me with an Island Confederation Bridge commemorative edition licence plate for my car "as a reminder of this historic event." In his "Dear Tom" note affixed to the plate, the premier mentioned the many benefits he thought would accrue to the Island from the bridge: speedier and more direct access to the rest of Canada, increased tourism, greatly improved marketing and shipment of Island goods and services, among many others. But I think he captured the import of the project best when he said in his note: "The Confederation Bridge is also symbolic of a new sense of optimism among Islanders." Optimism—isn't that the very spirit that gave birth to Canada in our capital city, Charlottetown, way back in 1864 in the first place?

Government is not a business. Nor is it a charity. But it does contain elements of both. Its custodians, therefore, must be both competent and benevolent. In many ways, Ottawa is a one-industry town. That industry is the national government. The longer I served in Cabinet, the more I realized that I was one of about three dozen executive vice-presidents, reporting to the prime minister as CEO. Anybody who thinks a Cabinet minister doesn't wield real power knows nothing about how the system works. Every waking minute on the job requires the individual "vice-presidents" to make decisions, many of them involving millions of dollars and affecting thousands (if not millions) of people across the country. It is vital that every politician seek and respect the views of others, whether or not they accord with his or her own—indeed, especially if they don't. Nobody has a monopoly on knowledge or a corner on experience or a stranglehold on wisdom. A Cabinet minister needs to factor into decisions what others think about problems that require his or her attention. Democracy demands it, good governance requires it, the public deserves it. And yet, at the end of the day, the office holder must rely on his or her own best judgment when making an official decision, however large or small. Tasks can be delegated, responsibility and accountability can not. This was the theme Edmund Burke struck in his defining message as a conservative politician to his constituents of Bristol in 1774. In that classic treatise, Burke said that, ultimately, the elected official must govern based not on popular sentiment, but on his own "unbiased opinion, his mature judgment, his enlightened conscience." When all the studies have been completed, the recommendations made, the consultations conducted, and the discussions held, and the time comes for the decision-maker to act, that individual is left with only two things: what he or she *knows* and what he or she *believes*. "It's lonely at the top," "The buck stops here," "It's time to fish or cut bait"—whatever the leadership cliché, at some point the decider has to decide.

As Prince Edward Island's federal Cabinet minister, I knew in my head and felt in my gut that the anti–Fixed Link militants were wrong on the fundamentals. I had given a great deal of thought to the issue, so I was driven neither by romanticism nor by fantasy. Nor was I unaware of how politically explosive the issue was. But my staff and I did our homework before proceeding, and felt confident that any explosion of opposition could be contained. Accordingly, as the Mulroney government's 1984 mandate was fast ending, I thought we needed to act on Islanders' historic dream of a fixed crossing to the mainland. Or else the opportunity would be lost for another generation.

What threatened the Island, I believed, were poverty and the exodus of the province's brightest and best-educated young people from lack of economic opportunity. PEI's population has not grown appreciably since the mid-nineteenth century. Wade MacLaughlan, former president of UPEI and now PEI's Liberal premier, summarized the principal challenge the Island has faced over the years and generations: "P.E.I.'s history has been more about outmigration than about growth and prosperity."[13] (The premier's father, entrepreneur Harry MacLaughlan, was one of the most passionate and outspoken—not to mention eloquent and convincing—champions of the Fixed Link during the Ghiz government's plebiscite and right up until the bridge was built.) We Islanders are a resilient, adaptable, and vibrant people. But I felt strongly that we required sound and visionary public policies to prevent further population decline and economic and cultural stagnation. To me, the Fixed Link would help modernize the economic base of the province—its transportation route to and from major markets, in particular. As Helen Doyle used to say, "God helps those who help themselves." I also thought the Fixed Link could symbolize Islanders' confidence in the province's future, much the way the Golden Gate Bridge did for St. Francisco and all Californians. Even that motivation of mine was hard-nosed, not romantic or fanciful. Built in 1937, the iconic bridge over St. Francisco Bay was fraught with controversy, opposed by unions and powerful business interests, and subjected to often frivolous lawsuits—shades of our own bridge politics. Today, the Golden Gate Bridge is one of the most internationally recognized symbols of not only San Francisco, but also the entire United States. It has been declared one of the "Wonders of the Modern World" by the American Society of Civil Engineers. And it is the most photographed bridge in the world. I asked myself, "Why couldn't the longest bridge of its kind in the world do the same for us Islanders?" But PEI has yet to appreciate fully what a "golden bridge" it has across the Northumberland Strait.

A permanent connection between the Island and the mainland was always opposed by a minority of Islanders, some of them militant. And yet, neither major political party in PEI (Conservative or Liberal) ever officially opposed the idea in principle. In modern times, both favoured it in practice. (The NDP has only rarely had a major impact in the province.) Joe Ghiz alone played both ends against the middle for raw partisan purposes. But Robert Morrissey, his blunt-spoken minister of transportation and public works, strongly supported the bridge. "If the bridge is built, everyone will wonder what all the fuss was about," he once told me. "The [Northumberland] Strait will then be so easy to cross that it will look as small as a mud puddle." Morrissey has been proven right on both counts. What *was* all the fuss about? And how narrow the Strait now seems!

As a student of PEI history, I knew Islanders' dream of a fixed link (by whatever mode: causeway, bridge, or tunnel) was never going to vaporize into the ether. I believed—in the spirit of Edmund Burke in his message to the electors of Bristol—that the federal government should, once and for all, just get on with it. In the 1988 election, I carried many people with me on this issue, but not enough—and not nearly enough on free trade, another cause dear to us Islanders throughout our history.

# The Election Results

As voting day, November 21, 1988, approached, I sensed that the race between me and my Liberal opponent, George Proud, was tightening. At the doorstep, I could see the concern on the faces of supporters and well-wishers alike. I was getting the message that people thought they could vote Liberal to protest free trade or the Fixed Link or both, and yet somehow retain me as their Member of Parliament and Cabinet minister. Election night, I still felt I would win, albeit by a narrower margin than ever before. I hadn't realized how much the tide had turned for the Liberals. For me, the coup de grâce was a visit to the riding by my former Ottawa staffer Elizabeth May during the last week of the campaign. She came to stump for David Weale, the Independent candidate opposed to the Fixed Link. Weale's slogan, "Save the Environment," was aimed squarely at my support in that area. He hoped to siphon it to help elect Proud and thereby, he thought, scuttle the project. From the time her feet hit the tarmac in Charlottetown, Elizabeth was never more than a bellow away from CBC and CFCY air time. And she got more column inches in local daily and weekly papers during her few days on the Island than my candidacy received throughout the entire campaign. Her non-stop and ubiquitous PEI media interviews, the platoon of reportage and commentary those interviews sent off to do battle against me, her massively covered Sunday-night public rally and speech at the Charlottetown Hotel only days before the vote—all that had a powerful impact on the Hillsborough campaign at the most critical juncture. Her eleventh-hour intrusion into the contest placed me on the defensive and demoralized not just me, but also my campaign workers.

Before Elizabeth's visit, a week prior to voting day, I was leading in every public opinion poll by as much as 11 percent—by that exact margin in my own campaign's $10,000 privately commissioned Environics poll. A respected media-sponsored regional poll out of Fredericton during the last week showed I would be the only one of the three PEI Tory incumbents who would survive the anti–free trade Liberal tide sweeping Atlantic Canada. But I *would* survive.

And then, the deluge. Elizabeth May swooped into PEI on a mission to wreak havoc—with me squarely in her crosshairs. She succeeded spectacularly. My former staffer masked her political salvos in high environmental principle. But the purpose could not have been more transparent had she draped herself in my opponents' campaign colours instead of green. Without exception, all the candidates running against me in Hillsborough—even those who favoured the project—appeared at her anti–Fixed Link public rally stage-managed by David Weale's campaign organizers. Why not pile on the incumbent in common cause to unseat him? For their part, most of the Island media (the CBC most of all) shamelessly covered all this as environmentalism, not the naked political grandstanding everyone knew it to be. The game-playing all around was as transparent as it was shameless. Elizabeth May's "environmental" rally not only dominated media coverage at the climax of the campaign; it also provided that climax. To heighten the orgiastic drama, Elizabeth had arranged for environmental icon David Suzuki, a close friend of hers, to denounce me publicly from his home base in British Columbia for championing the Fixed Link.

Most of the media ignored my detailed written response to May and Suzuki's joint attack, except to reframe the duo's charges and give them added currency. Her sham claim that she had resigned from my staff over the Fixed Link—

what about the Rafferty-Almeda Dam excuse?—was accepted without challenge despite my denial. CBC Charlottetown, in particular, did everything it could to fire up the controversy, affording the environmentalist rock-star status two decades before she actually attained it as the country's Green Party leader. My ill-tempered response to Elizabeth's mischief-making, in a CBC radio interview with Craig Ainsley, compounded the political damage she inflicted on me. The CBC played the clip repeatedly long after it had lost whatever legitimate news value it might have contained. Succumbing to Ainsley's goading was my worst error of the campaign. It gave Fixed Link opponents in the media, both at the CBC and elsewhere, a fig leaf to hide their naked eagerness to perpetuate the controversy even after my nemesis had left the province—in fact, right up to election day. Throughout the last weekend of the campaign, they reported (as though in one voice) that my campaign had gone off the rails and I was losing my cool. Talk about groupthink.

Without knocking on a single door or spending much money or having any kind of traditional political organization behind him, David Weale, with most of the Island media in his back pocket, had hijacked the campaign as voters were making up their minds. Even if Weale were not to win a single vote—hardly the goal of all this, anyway—the "Anybody but Tom McMillan" message missile was hitting its mark. Just when I thought the entire business could not get more surreal, or for me more out of hand, I found myself having to answer reporters' questions as to why I had not attended Elizabeth May's "environmental" rally. After all, they said, I was the country's environment minister and all the other riding candidates had gone. But, of course, none of them was the target of the missile; each was a party to its launching. It was bad enough that the anti–Fixed Link forces and their media enablers had formed a posse to hunt me down and hang me. I now stood condemned for refusing to help build the scaffold for my own lynching.

As I listened in an upstairs bedroom in my Keppoch home to the results pour in on CBC-TV and radio on election night—"All four PC candidates are trailing"—I was stunned. In a retrospective of the 1988 election in PEI, *Canada Votes* said my defeat was a "shock" to everyone.[14] Recovering almost immediately from my own shock, I went down to the kitchen, where I joined my eldest brother, Colin, whose tradition it was to be with me every election night. We poured ourselves stiff scotches; proceeded to the headquarters of my Liberal victor; then visited my own packed headquarters to thank and console crestfallen supporters. My opening comment at George Proud's victory rally—"Unaccustomed as I am to addressing Liberal rallies..."—brought great laughter, broke the ice, and led to much graciousness and magnanimity from all present, including my victorious opponent. What his first words lacked in proper English grammar—"I could not be more humbler"—they compensated for in apparent sincerity. At my own headquarters, I spoke for about fifteen minutes without a note, surprising myself by how deeply I was able to draw on reserves of strength that I scarcely knew I possessed. Local CBC radio covered my remarks live and uninterrupted. It was one of the few times in two months—the entire course of the election campaign—they had given anything I said a sympathetic hearing or, most times, even a hearing at all.

The final results: George Proud, 8,897 (43.68 percent); Tom McMillan, 8,638 (42.41 percent). Only 259 votes separated us. Among the 295 ridings across the country, in which a total of 1,573 candidates ran, ours had the eighth-closest result. David Weale got 569 votes, by general consensus skimmed right from my base, particularly environmentalists. It was exactly what his single-issue candidacy was devised to accomplish.[15] In his college textbook on Canadian federal politics, Carleton University political scientist Rand Dyck cites the anti–Fixed Link organization's contribution to my defeat as a classic case of pressure group politics: "National or local pressure groups sometimes target particular politicians or ministers for defeat…as those opposed to a 'fixed link' between PEI and New Brunswick did to then Environment minister Tom McMillan."[16] I was later asked why, given the tiny margin of my defeat, I had not sought a recount. The main reason is that it never occurred to me. I was just too tired. In any event, the margin was slightly larger on election night than it ended up being some days later, after military and absentee votes were included in the grand total. Meanwhile, I had both conceded defeat and become resigned to it. Apart from a recount, the principal ground on which some people urged me to contest the official results concerned a rumour that many of the six hundred Marine Atlantic ferry workers had voted against me in my riding, instead of where they actually lived and could legally vote. The voter-registration drive this would have entailed was allegedly orchestrated by the Canadian Auto Workers union, of which the ferry workers were members. The union had sent professional organizers into the province at the outset of the campaign. True or not—and I am not certain either way—the rumour was far too serious, and too fraught with legal complexities, for me to pursue at a time when I just wanted to proceed with my life. My oldest daughter, Kelly, was only four; my other daughter, Becky, just two (Emily would be born two years later). They were my priorities now.

The total number of votes Elizabeth May's visit cost me? It's hard to know exactly, but, undeniably, her visit represented the difference between victory and defeat—a switch of 130 votes from my Liberal opponent to me would have flipped the outcome. Elizabeth's dagger was the decisive factor that killed me politically, even if it was I who actually plunged the weapon into myself. I alone take full responsibility for not foreseeing the crisis or, at a minimum, for not handling it better after the brouhaha erupted.

After my defeat, I was deluged with thoughtful phone calls and letters, including from well-wishing Cabinet colleagues who had survived the election. I appreciated all such good wishes and commiserations. One call, however, was a classic of how *not* to commiserate. "Despite your defeat, Tom, you're not a loser," Elmer MacKay told me. Until he called, it never occurred to me that I was! The communication that I appreciated most was from Ed Lumley, who had held various Cabinet portfolios in both Pierre Trudeau's and John Turner's governments. Lumley had lost his Cornwall-area seat (Stormont–Dundas) in the 1984 Tory sweep. I did not know him, had never met him, can't recall ever having before communicated with him, except (possibly) from across the aisle in Question Period. And yet he, a Liberal, took time from a busy corporate career to phone me. His "I know what it's like to lose" comments were as heartfelt as they were welcome. What sheer class!

The PEI business community, mostly centred in my riding, was worried about the consequences for the Island economy of my defeat and that of the other three government party MPs. Based on this concern, the Charlottetown Chamber of Commerce invited me to address its annual meeting some weeks following the election. The newly re-elected Mulroney government had just brought down its first budget the night before (April 27, 1989). Finance Minister Michael Wilson had announced harsh austerity measures, including the closure of the air force base at Summerside, one of the Island's largest employers. As was my practice, I began the speech with levity: "Ladies and gentlemen, I want you all to know that I had absolutely nothing to do with the federal budget brought down last night," I deadpanned. The audience laughed in the spirit that I had intended. Local CBC-TV, true to form, reported the statement not as a joke, but as a personal defence. Interviewed later that week by local CBC radio about the base closing, I stated the obvious: the measure was included in a federal budget; it was, therefore, part of the country's fiscal framework; the plan was not in a White Paper, so was intended as settled policy, not as a subject for discussion; and, as such, it would not likely be reversed by public pressure from Islanders. CBC radio reported my remarks in a tone that all but said that I had told Islanders, "Tough luck, fools. Suck it up."

Premier Joe Ghiz wanted to exploit the Liberals' Island federal-election sweep and to capitalize on Islanders' anger about the budget—the base closure, in particular. So he called a snap provincial election for May 29, only three years into his government's five-year mandate. The Liberals used in their campaign advertising not what I had actually said about the base closing, but, instead, the CBC's blatant distortion of what I had said. The Ghiz government was re-elected in a landslide (30 Liberals, 2 PCs, with PC leader Mel Gass losing in his own district of 2nd Queens).

I decided it was time for me to move on, both from PEI public life and probably from the province itself. It had been five months since my defeat. And yet, I still could not escape the CBC's animus towards me.[17] Apart from my position on the issues—the Fixed Link, in particular—personnel there had never forgiven me for the aftermath of my beating Liberal candidate Gerry Birt, their TV news anchor, in the 1984 election. My campaign team had discreetly suggested—through an emissary, David Jenkins, now chief justice of the PEI Supreme Court (trial division)—that it would be inappropriate for Birt to be reading, on air, stories about the Island's new principal newsmaker, me, after his appointment to the Mulroney Cabinet. Birt had then been transferred to a CBC station elsewhere in the Maritimes. Nor did I think the CBC's hostility would stop anytime soon. In such a close-knit community, where 70 percent of residents watched the corporation's newscasts—its highest market share in the country at the time—I felt trapped, not just by the local CBC, but also by the political culture it both reflected and was fast helping to mould in the province under the management of the day.

# Public Life and Civility

There was a mysterious and bizarre footnote to the 1988 election in PEI. Several Island personalities most heavily involved in the media and political skulduggery dropped dead or were killed. Craig Ainsley, the CBC radio reporter referred to earlier, had been a heart patient of my brother Colin. He collapsed and died, only in his late twenties or early thirties. Another fatality was Martin Dorrell—of the CBC, *Eastern Graphic*, and the *Globe and Mail*—who, at a similar young age, died in a violent car accident. The premier himself was soon stricken with terminal colon cancer. There were other casualties, including avid supporters of mine—among them, PEI heritage scholar and champion Irene Rogers, who was also killed in a car accident. The deceased were good people. It's the political/media game that is too often bad.

This brings me to my final perspective on the 1988 election: a lament about the sharp decline of civility in Canadian politics in recent years, particularly since Stephen Harper ascended the political mountain. To my mind, it is this dimension of his government—even more than its regressive policies—that has corrupted what it means to be a Conservative ever since Harper planted a flag in the party's name on that mountain's summit. By its very nature, politics is a blood sport. It has always been. However much "politics" might enter into every domain of ordinary life—a university or school, a hospital, a not-for-profit organization, a business, a factory, a police or fire department or, for that matter, a family or even a marriage or alternative form of romantic partnership—actual politics is like no other form. The stakes there are far higher than in those mundane domains—the dollars bigger, the impact farther-reaching, the number of people affected larger, and the consequences longer-lasting. Correspondingly, the payoff is greater, the victory sweeter, the loss more painful. And, therefore, the players are less likely to obey the rules of the game. Still less are they inclined to extend player courtesy. It's not that politicians are a species different from other human beings. It's just that the nature of the game tends to bring to the fore certain undesirable traits in everday people who, for whatever reason, end up in politics and then cease to be what they once were.

In modern times, however, this process is fast shortcircuiting. More than ever before, politics is self-selecting people who excel at the blood-sport dimension of the game while repelling almost everybody who could put points on the board for the community at large. As much as I might have regretted my own fate in the 1988 election at the hands of certain political actors, they were simply playing the game. I was naive not to realize that, in the eyes of my political adversaries, I was a far more alluring target in 1988 as a Cabinet minister than I had ever been as just the local MP or, at one time, a rookie candidate. So the ammunition used against me—not to mention the vastly larger number of people aiming it—was inevitably going to be more lethal than before.

Harry Truman is famously credited with having said: "If you can't stand the heat, get out of the kitchen." It's good advice for anyone either already in politics or aspiring to enter. Politics is not for everyone. There are much easier ways to make a living while contributing to one's community professionally. "Politics is not for anybody who can't stand the sight of his own blood," former Arkansas governor Mike Huckabee has counselled.[18] But, for a person so inclined and able to withstand the assaults on his or her very being, there is no opportunity greater than politics for improving other people's lives. Every community would benefit if the "kitchen" were made more inviting in Canada than it is today. An improved political environment—which every citizen could help achieve—would increase the odds that better people would run for public office and would want to stay longer if elected. No one should hold his or her breath waiting for the political culture to be transformed. But every true democrat would breathe more easily if it happened.

It hardly advances the public interest when politics is populated by individuals not committed to community, but, instead, desperate to fill some dark personal hole they think elected office can fill. For self-affirmation, people of sound mind don't require public approbation, let alone adulation. It comes from within, not from with-out. Is the dumbing-down that we see in American politics happening in Canada? As either a government leader or politician, Stephen Harper was no Robert Stanfield, still less a Sir John A. Macdonald. Will Justin Trudeau prove to be a patch on his father—set aside Mackenzie King or Wilfrid Laurier? When the public's expectations are modest, as I sense they are for the younger Trudeau, they tend to be self-fulfilled. Canada is no less great than it once was. If the political class is so, perhaps what's wrong is not the nation itself but the political culture that dissuades potentially great people from seeking public office. And at the top, at least the promise of greatness, if not actual greatness, is badly needed, for the very pursuit of it will ensure that the nation will benefit. To paraphrase Robert Browning, our reach should exceed our grasp, or what's a Canada for?

Did the Canadian Conservative Party in its post-2003 incarnation, under Stephen Harper's leadership, contribute to the same political disaffection in our own country that is happening in the United States? Frank Bruni of the *New York Times* says a major impact of this phenomenon is the "culling [of] the herd, not in favor of the strongest candidates but in favor of those so driven or vacuous that the caress of the spotlight redeems the indignities of the process."[19] Voter turnout in 2011, at 61.4 percent, was the third lowest in Canadian history (the lowest, at 58.8 percent, was for the 2008 election). The turnout in 2015, at 69.1 percent, bounced back to the historic norm, which suggests that Canadians might have been not only eager to fire the Harper government, but also optimistic that Justin Trudeau could usher in a better grade of politics in Canada.

I am not the only Conservative (or former Conservative) who believes that our party (or former party) has betrayed both its own best traditions and the Canadian people by practising a quality of politics unworthy of the country. Interviews and correspondence I conducted with a large number of my former Cabinet colleagues and ministerial and political staff for this book revealed to me, in private, a shocking level of discontent with the party. Joe Clark, in his book quoted a number of times here, has gone public with his own dissatisfaction. So, with his memoirs, has another luminary from the Conservative Party's recent past: retired Ontario chief justice Roy McMurtry.

Roy McMurtry was once as strong and respected a Tory as existed anywhere in the country. But, like me, he no longer supports the federal Conservative Party because of its changed behaviour and values since the dawn of the Stephen Harper era. As Ontario's attorney general (1975–85), under Premier Bill Davis, McMurtry helped broker the federal-provincial agreement that created the 1982 Constitution and the Charter of Rights and Freedoms. In his *Memoirs and Reflections*, McMurtry criticizes the Stephen Harper government for its "intense lack of compassion." He laments the government's "obvious political partisanship," which, he says, "has deeply divided Canadian society." And he denounces the prime minister himself for "fuelling a poisonous partisan atmosphere"…in Parliament, in particular.[20] Is Harper's record in this context the stuff of political greatness? Or even of routine competence?

I have known Roy McMurtry from my earliest days in politics, well before either of us held public office. We worked together in Robert Stanfield's policy-development process. McMurtry's years on the bench, including as Ontario's chief justice, never diminished his commitment to the values he championed and embodied in a long career in political trench warfare. Those values include moderation, civility, respect for opponents, policy and ideological flexibility, and willingness to compromise with adversaries for the greater good, to say nothing of McMurtry's deep-seated progressive instincts on the issues. Generally considered one of the pre-eminent Canadian public servants of his generation, McMurtry now describes himself as a "disillusioned former federal Progressive Conservative."[21] When a man of his unquestioned sound judgment and integrity and public repute is estranged from the political party in which he not long ago was among its brightest stars, one can be certain that something has gone terribly wrong. The Conservative Party's resounding defeat in the

2015 election was a powerful message from Canadian voters that they will not welcome the party back into their good graces until it changes what it stands for and how it operates.

After licking my wounds from the 1988 defeat, I was eager to rebuild my life outside politics. And, for the first time, although it took a while, I realized there was, in fact, such a life. Helen Doyle always said, "Everything happens for a reason—God's will." She had instilled in me enough of her version of Catholic religion and homespun predestination philosophy to help get me through the worst of it all. Now, I was eager to discover, in Helen's terms, what next He had in store for me. Little did I know at the time that it would be so much—and such great fun.

# Part III

# OUTSIDE LOOKING IN: CONSERVATISM FROM A NEW PERSPECTIVE

*The Canada–US border is the world's longest undefended cliché in history.*

—attributed to Margaret Atwood

# Chapter 29

# WORKING FOR THE "VATICAN"

After leaving political office, I found life deadly slow compared to the pace I had maintained as a Cabinet minister, even though I kept myself busier than most people would consider normal. I decided not to take much time to recuperate from the stress and strain of the campaign. By nature, I thrive on work, can enjoy leisure, but become restless when not challenged both mentally and physically. Income wasn't a concern, but my mental and emotional well-being was. I knew that, unless I soon threw myself into something major, I would be unhappy. You can read only so many books about other people's lives before wanting to live your own life again. The fact I received many job offers and consultancies was reassuring. Still, with a wife and two young children, I couldn't just pack my bags and relocate off-Island to where the best opportunities lay—at least, not yet. Furthermore, I made a pact with myself not to become some company's environmental front man. That was, in effect, the nature of many of the first offers. And I was not the type of person who would thrive as a private consultant, constantly chasing contracts and assignments and someone else's deadline. I wasn't sure what I wanted to do. But I sure knew what I wanted to avoid.

When the Canadian Chamber of Commerce asked me to head a blue-ribbon task force on the economy-environment partnership, I leaped at the opportunity. It was right up my alley, would be challenging, and seemed a great way for me to bide time until I could sort out my future beyond the next paycheque or deadline. (It also paid a per diem and personal expenses.) The task force—formally titled *Focus 2000 Task Force on the Environment*—decided the production of a public report would be its principal task, and entrusted me with writing it. It would recommend how the Chamber could help the country integrate economic and environmental decision-making in the spirit of the UN World Commission on Environment and Development (the Brundtland Commission). As impressed as I was with my own scientists and officials at Environment Canada, I wished I'd had the task force's first-rate members at my side while minister.[1] Each proudly signed the report, for which I had recruited former *Globe and Mail* reporter Michael Keating as my drafting and policy partner. The document received excellent reviews from both journalists and environmentalists. The Chamber itself was delighted.

Meanwhile, Trent University recruited me as a part-time special advisor to President John Stubbs on the environment. The university was planning a big expansion of facilities for teaching and research in this field. It was a terrific opportunity for me to continue advancing my environmental interests while assisting a university that had played a large role in my life through Tom Symons. What's more, I always loved Peterborough, continued to have many friends there, and welcomed the chance to escape periodically the dark clouds back home that still hung over me from the election. I also accepted a heavy round of paid speaking engagements, most of them to private sector groups eager to be told how to "go green." I wrote articles for local and regional and national publications alike and for a few international journals as well. I did some private sector consulting. Plus, responding to, and in a few cases actively considering, longer-term job offers and opportunities became itself almost a part-time job.[2]

Busy as I kept myself—travelling virtually as often as when in Cabinet—life had now changed for me. I now realized what an insane pace I had kept as a Cabinet minster. It was like being a rat on a treadmill at high speed when the machine suddenly stops: the disorientation was enough to drive you almost insane. For the first time in my life, I could not sleep, or at least not easily or for long. Upon my doctor's advice, I started taking the sleeping pill Halcion, never having taken even aspirin before. Unbeknownst to most medical prescribers at the time, including my own doctor, apparently, Halcion either causes or contributes to depression and, in the worst cases (not mine), to thoughts of suicide. It is now banned in some countries, including the United Kingdom. After several weeks, I flushed all the little famously called "blue bombs" down the toilet.

The prime minister was never too busy just to phone me to ensure himself that I was okay. Charley once told me that Brian Mulroney had a system that enabled the government switchboard to contact anyone in the world, anywhere in the world, anytime in the world. I soon discovered that the system worked. On one occasion, a few weeks after the 1988 election, I had told nobody except Kathy that I would be visiting Tom and Christine Symons in Peterborough. Mulroney tracked me down there late at night. At the time, Kathy was in Montreal on a buying trip for her retail clothing store, so she couldn't be reached easily about my whereabouts. To this day, I have no idea how the PM was able to contact me. I would not want to be hiding from this man. I will always remember with gratitude his continuing concern for my emotional health and general well-being, including professional progress. Anyone who thinks Brian Mulroney has no heart has no brain. In late July 1989, he called me in PEI to invite me to become consul general to New England, based in Boston. I have never since had trouble sleeping.

# Brian Mulroney and Patronage

It is worth pausing here to reflect on Brian Mulroney's modus operandi concerning patronage for defeated Tory colleagues. Soon after I lost my Commons seat in Hillsborough, my brother Charley told me not to expect any job offer from the prime minister for a while, if at all. Mulroney's style, he said, was to let the dust settle after a colleague had been defeated to see how well he or she might bounce back professionally and personally without the PM's help. Only when his intervention seemed advisable would he consider acting. Meanwhile, like a wise parent wishing to help an adolescent son or daughter without meddling, he would monitor the individual's progress with equal measures of care and discretion. True to Charley's insights and experience gained while one of Mulroney's closest confidants over a long time, the prime minister followed this formula with me in every detail—to wit: his calling me at the Symons home in Peterborough for no reason other than to ask, "Tommy, how're things going with you?" As with every other matter, it was not enough for him to rely on second-hand information; he needed to hear "from the horse's mouth." In this case, the horse was me.

By late spring 1989, I had let my successor as environment minister, Lucien Bouchard, know that I was finding life depressing in PEI. Everyone was treating me as though I were still the minister, making the same impossible political demands. One case, for example, concerned a young Charlottetown man I knew from a local gym. He had been caught at the Canada-US border in Calais, Maine, with hypodermic needles and anabolic steroids. The illegal possession of this performance-enhancing drug is a serious crime in the United States. My former constituent had been visiting his family on the Island for Christmas from California, where he worked as a personal-fitness trainer. His paraphernalia and drugs were confiscated. Worse, he was accused of (but not formally charged with) a crime, denied entry to the United States, and ordered not to return. The young man's personal and professional life was in shambles. He and his father, whom I did not know, contacted me for help. I did help, but this was no longer my job. Nor were the numerous other requests for my assistance. Most of them required many hours of my time, costly long-distance phone calls, and other out-of-pocket expenses. To all such people, I was still the man who could pull rabbits out of a hat. The difference now, however, was that, without the actual job and the resources that went with it, the magic was no longer as magical. And the magician was becoming increasingly worn down by the act.

When I communicated my unhappiness on the Island to the PM through Bouchard, Mulroney decided it was time to act (the "formula"). Not long afterwards, he offered me the Boston consul general post. The suppleness of Brian Mulroney's approach to the human factor in his relations with people—whether colleagues or friends or anyone else whose welfare he is directly committed to—impressed me. It contrasts starkly with his public image: arrogant, if not egomaniacal. Not for nothing has he absorbed the Catholic social teaching that so permeated his St. Francis Xavier University alma mater. I felt as though my welfare was in the hands of a benevolent parish priest, rather than a fellow partisan, still less the ruthless, self-seeking *arriviste* Mulroney's detractors often accused him of being.

Even when Brian Mulroney called me at home in Keppoch that late July evening to offer me the Boston diplomatic post, the human element loomed large with him. I said that I was delighted with the offer but would have to consult Kathy. The PM right afterwards told Charley that he understood my need to discuss the matter with my wife. But he said he was puzzled that I had not seemed more enthusiastic about the offer itself. My brother told him what I had not: that Kathy was pregnant with our third child (Emily) and, consequently, we were coping with much more than my own professional future. The PM's first concern then was the impact any geographic separation between Kathy and me might have on our marriage, should I have to move to Boston before she herself could go while pregnant. Mulroney seemed always thinking, always caring. The man's mind was like a turbojet engine incapable of being turned off. The PM told me that he would phone the next night to obtain my answer. He did. I responded yes. And he appeared happy for me and Kathy and our two young children. "You're going to *love* Boston," he said. "I hear the official residence there is one of our finest." I did. And it was.

The way Brian Mulroney appointed me consul general in Boston was eerily similar to how he moved me from Tourism to Environment. Before accepting the Boston post, I consulted Tom Symons. He was enthusiastic about the idea, encouraged me to accept, and offered one specific suggestion: that the announcement state I would be the first Atlantic Canadian ever to head the country's consulate in "the Boston states" (the historian in him, no doubt). I thought this suggestion excellent. It had struck me as odd that no one from Atlantic Canada had ever been selected to head the very diplomatic operation outside the country always considered our region's principal port of call.[3] When I suggested this to the prime minister, he said, "Tommy, the point does not need to be made in the announcement. It should be obvious to everyone." By then, I knew how to translate such Mulroney-speak: *As of now, you're in charge of the country's affairs in New England. How you package yourself publicly is up to you.* In the time it takes a man to shower and shave, the prime minister of Canada had appointed me the country's minister of the environment. In the time it takes a man to floss and brush his teeth, I was now made consul general for Canada in Boston—a clean start. Not only had my world changed; my place in the world had, too. I was moving to Boston.

# A Canadian Abroad

As an Opposition MP, I was active to some extent in international affairs. The House of Commons Sub-committee on Acid Rain, for example, required me to travel with other members to many parts of Europe, including Scandinavia, to explore different nations' solutions to acidic precipitation. While tourism minister, I had travelled widely outside Canada, especially to the United States, to elevate our country's profile and promote its attractions. Kathy and I visited, for example, West Berlin, where, among other high-ranking public and industry officials, I conferred with the city's mayor, Eberhard Diebgen, at the world's largest annual tourism fair. The fair seemed bigger than my own province! The Environment post I held later was, in many ways, as much an international one as domestic. I helped negotiate diverse multilateral or bilateral treaties and protocols and agreements and memoranda of understanding on a wide variety of issues—acid rain, global warming, Great Lakes water quality, endangered species, wildlife, among others.

While environment minister, I flew to distant places almost as often as to locales in Canada. In all such foreign travels, I was typically met by local Canadian embassy or consular or trade officials who chaperoned me in their territories. Frequently it was the ambassador or high commissioner or consul general himself or herself. That was the case in Washington, where I got to know Ambassador Allan Gotlieb well. It was also true in London, where I had already known Roy McMurtry, Canada's high commissioner, through policy work for Robert Stanfield. When I was tourism minister, Gotlieb and I appeared together at a very liquid dinner hosted jointly by American and Canadian journalists at the Washington Press Club. There, we were each expected to be light and witty as after-dinner speakers. Substantive remarks were far from the order of the day. I began by thanking my hosts for making me feel at home in the US capital by surrounding this small-town PEI boy with so many drunken Canadian reporters. After that remark scored well, it didn't much matter what else I said, which wasn't nearly as hilarious as Gotlieb's entire routine.

As frequently as I had been abroad on government business, I really had no coherent view of the world or substantial knowledge of international affairs beyond the particular issues with which I had to deal in my portfolios. I had travelled fairly widely privately before entering politics, especially when my brothers Colin and Charley were studying in the United Kingdom at different times. Around the same time (the early to mid-1970s), as senior research associate of the Commission on Canadian Studies, under Tom Symons's chairmanship, I spent several weeks in London, Paris, and Rome. The purpose was to conduct research for our report's substantial section on "Canadian Studies Abroad." This is the closest I ever came to actually studying in Europe. But it did enlarge my international experience and perspectives.

To the extent I had any world view by the time I became consul general in Boston, I had been influenced by Robert Stanfield's internationalism. Most Maritime premiers over the years, irrespective of party label, have seen the world pretty much the same way he did. Stanfield was, as Richard Clippingdale put it, "firmly and proudly in the broad constructive internationalist Canadian tradition of Borden, St. Laurent, Diefenbaker, and Pearson."[4] He staked this ground at the Priorities for Canada policy conference in Niagara Falls in 1969. I remember, as I listened to Stanfield's speech there, agreeing wholeheartedly as he emphasized the value to Canada of forging strong links with other countries. He said those links maximized our influence on the world stage. Without them, he argued, ours would be a much smaller and weaker country. His warnings of the dangers of "negative nationalism that attacks other countries or traditions" hit a particularly strong chord with me; I have always been suspicious of "isms" of any kind (other than my own!). All this said, I arrived at the Canadian consulate in Boston with no preconceived international notions, much less vision, and with hardly any knowledge of Boston. I had visited it only once—by car, eight years earlier with Kathy. We had not even stayed overnight, preferring a nearby coastal town with great heritage charm and less expensive accommodations. I did not know, therefore, what to expect regarding the consulate as my toes hit the tarmac for the first time at Logan Airport.

Whatever I expected in Boston sure wasn't what I found. Nobody had warned me that the consulate was nearly in shambles. No wonder the prime minister was concerned when I had not appeared enthusiastic about the appointment: maybe he thought I knew. Was he partly motivated to select me by the hope I would end the chaos there, as I had done at Environment Canada? I have no doubt he was primarily motivated by concern for the welfare of a fallen comrade. But, as Charley reminded me, Brian Mulroney never based a decision on one factor alone. Everything he did fit into a broader plan. Typically, a particular decision advanced more than one end, with the complexities not necessarily apparent to anyone but Mulroney himself. In this case, the plan must surely have had something to do with his wanting to have a trusted former Cabinet colleague whip into shape a diplomatic post that had been badly neglected by the previous occupant, also an appointee of his. The more I got to know Brian Mulroney, the more I marvelled at the complexity of the man. The more I got to know the consulate, the more I asked myself, "What the hell have I gotten myself into?"

The Canadian consulate in Boston operates throughout the six New England states: Massachusetts, Rhode Island, Maine, New Hampshire, Vermont, and, to some extent, Connecticut, which it shares with the consulate in New York. In my time as consul general, prior to the consulate's being downsized by half, the post promoted Canada's interests in the region in areas as diverse as trade, tourism, the fishery, immigration, customs, culture and the arts, education, and our country's overall image. The consulate itself occupies the entire fifth level of one of four huge office towers of Copley Place, at 100 Huntington Avenue, smack dab in the heart of the most upscale retail and business district of the city, in Back Bay. Copley Place bills itself as the "most distinctive shopping district in Boston." Translation: *Bring your American Express Platinum card, and we have valet parking for your Bentley.* The consulate is surrounded by a Who's Who of prestigious international brand-name stores such as Tiffany & Co. and Louis Vuitton. The Government of Canada did not intend to slum. Clearly, even in such elite company, the landlord, Simon Properties, considers its Canadian tenant the top of the heap. On a towering pole at its front entrance, Copley Place flies the Canadian flag virtually around the clock. Take that, Christian Dior!

At least I was no longer suffering from PEI cabin fever. But the early period sometimes made me long for my days in Cabinet, when I was surrounded by competent, motivated support personnel. The situation at the consulate was far different. I had a big job to do. Throughout my career as an MP and Cabinet minister, I, like my political colleagues, was conscious that External Affairs was a department like no other—in prestige, in grandeur, in self-importance, in perks and high-fallutin' titles (always "officer" or "attaché," never merely "civil servant" or "government employee," no matter how low the rank or inconsequential the work). Nobody can read Brian Mulroney's memoirs without realizing how fully he perceived this department's sense of its own superiority throughout his period as prime minister. The department was largely untouchable in times of austerity and budget-slashing. It operated in a world of its own. Like the Vatican, it was connected more to God than to man. Indeed, my own job description, Head of Mission, had a distinctly religious ring to it. I soon needed to send packing some of the missionaries under my divine command.

Don Mazankowski was always frustrated that those who held the highest and most backbreaking government jobs—in his case, deputy prime minister and minister of finance—had to room with colleagues in Ottawa to economize while separated from their families back in the ridings during parliamentary sessions. And yet, as Mazankowski travelled abroad on government business, he saw foreign service officers well down the pecking order living in government-subsidized deluxe housing in upscale neighbourhoods such as London's Mayfair. In Boston, in addition to the nine-bedroom official residence of the consul general, External Affairs had no fewer than five spacious houses, one each for five such officers. Four of the five houses the government owned were in Wellesley, a tony millionaires' enclave. The fifth was a sprawling townhouse rented in Beacon Hill, Boston's most prestigious downtown residential neighbourhood. It was on Chestnut Street, only doors from the five-storey mansion of John Kerry and his billionaire wife, Teresa Heinz. Each four- or five-bedroom residence was usually occupied by only one person—or, in an exceptional case, also by a spouse; rarely by a child. Either the officers were young and not established enough to be spouses and parents or, more often than not, they had decided to commute between home base and Boston while their familes stayed put. Upon arrival in Boston, I was thunderstruck by the incongruity between the residential and other extravagant perks available to garden-variety civil servants (notwithstanding the fancy titles) and the poor state of the consulate operations themselves, ostensibly the purpose of all these lavish expenditures in the first place.[5]

I began my position as consul general in early September 1989. Before departing for Boston, I spent about ten days in Ottawa and Washington being briefed (and, in a sense, trained) for my new job. I met with every manner of functionary in all imaginable areas: from human resources to diplomatic credentials to budget to security to specific policy areas such as trade and immigration. (Everyone assumed I already knew as much as I needed to about tourism and the environment.) The most senior

External Affairs official in Ottawa I met as part of this process was Raymond Chrétien, cousin of Jean and soon to be appointed ambassador to Belgium. I had been told he was raised in Shawinigan with the future prime minister, more like a brother than a cousin. Among all the people who briefed me, he was by far the most helpful. "Tom," he advised, "I urge you not to become a desk man in Boston. Don't be a bureaucrat—the worst thing you could do with your time. Get out of the consulate, travel widely, meet New Englanders, show the Canadian flag, be Mr. Canada everywhere you go, promote the country, advance our country's agenda." It was the best advice I could have received. It became my modus operandi, my agenda, my goal. I did all the things he recommended, and then some. I paid courtesy calls to New England movers and shakers in business, government and politics, education, culture, and other key areas. I gave public speeches and media interviews to advance Canada's interests through-out the region. (Our country's constitutional reform effort was a hot topic at the time. So was acid rain.) I hosted receptions, dinner parties, luncheons, and smaller social occasions, including one-on-ones with central players. I followed a heavy schedule of giving university and college lectures and participating in seminars to promote greater knowledge and awareness of Canada, including through formal Canadian Studies programs. I was in especially heavy demand at law schools because of the Meech Lake and Charlottetown Accords. And I wrote prolifically on Canadian topics in a wide variety of regional and US-wide forums—learned journals, book chapters, newspaper guest columns and editorials, trade publications, non-governmental orga-nization house organs, among others.[6] In all such ways, whenever possible I sought to raise Canada's flag—sometimes literally.

During my four-year term as Canada's consul general in Boston, I dealt with some fascinating people. One of the most likeable was Massachusetts senator Ted Kennedy. The senator had received an honorary degree from my PEI alma mater, St. Dunstan's University, in 1964, just six months after JFK's assassination. At SDU, the senator gave an outstanding commencement address in which he thanked Canadians for supporting the entire Kennedy family so heartily after his brother was slain. My own oldest brother, Colin, graduated and was class valedictorian at this very convocation. I told Kennedy he and Colin had been photographed together on that occasion as, I joked, the two stars. He replied, "Tom, get me the picture. I'd love to sign it for Colin." I reported Kennedy's comment to my brother, one of the least vain creatures—man or beast—God ever made. Characteristically, he liked the picture as it was, nicely framed and discreetly hung on his medical clinic office wall.

The annual Maple Leaf Ball raises a ton of money for Canada-New England student exchanges and other hands-across-the-border causes focused on youth. For the $300-a-ticket black-tie dinner and dance with a live orchestra, I borrowed two horses from the Boston police force, parked them at the hotel entrance, and flew from Canada a couple of RCMP officers to take the reins mounted in full dress uniform—red tunics and all. Car and pedestrian traffic was jammed for blocks as shocked onlookers did double-takes and marvelled at the sight. The New England-Canada Business Council, which sponsors the event, couldn't have been happier. The next year, ticket sales broke the record.

But all such details of my time as consul general are for a separate book, now almost completed. Suffice it to say here that one of the most impressive individuals I got to know in New England was not a native at all, but a Canadian who has long made his home in Boston: hockey great Bobby Orr. Bobby lived down the street from my official residence, in the town of Weston, a twenty-five-minute drive from the city.

Our paths crossed often not only in our neighbourhood, but also at different official and informal events. As with so many well-known people, this man's public image is remarkably different from his true personality. Brian Mulroney—whose public persona resembles reality as little as molasses does milk—is the only famous person I have come to know who surprised me more than Bobby Orr in this respect. Just as, despite the fame and fortune, Mulroney remains deep down the "boy from Baie-Comeau," so also Orr, for all that he has achieved in life, is still humbly "the boy from Parry Sound." The hockey legend is also endlessly more intelligent, thoughtful, and philanthropic a man than I ever would have realized had I not gotten to know him personally. Among many other characteristics Mulroney and Orr share, they both live exuberantly, laugh boisterously, joke easily, tease shamelessly, and respond quickly and wittily to life's whimsies. And have big chins! Seeing Mulroney (the political titan) and Orr (the sports legend) up close and personal caused me to reflect more generally on the celebrity image-versus-reality phenomenon. Robert Stanfield could not have been more different from Mulroney had he been born Australian instead of Canadian, lived in the nineteenth century instead of the twentieth, and chosen gold prospecting instead of politics. But like Mulroney, as with Orr, Stanfield also helped change my view of well-known individuals relative to how they likely really are. Stripped of the gauze of fame, such people are like the rest of us—human. Just with bigger bank accounts. And sometimes bigger chins.

# The Americans

As a long-time resident of the United States—not just as Canada's consul general in Boston but also as a university lecturer, writer, private consultant, and Canadian expatriate—I would make two generalizations about that country. One concerns American versus Canadian values, the other the relationship between the Maritimes and New England.

## TWO NATIONS, TWO SETS OF VALUES

We Canadians should be extremely cautious about importing American political and economic values. Those values can be easily idealized and romanticized, but, when closely examined, they are found to be deeply flawed. Canadian Conservatives should be especially wary of values described in the United States as "conservative," but that are fundamentally different from what Canadian Conservatism has traditionally stood for. It's not just that those values often transplant poorly to another country or culture (in an extreme case, Iraq). However nobly or poetically expressed in sacred constitutional documents and Federal Papers, some of the most revered and heavily touted American values are mere myths, if not shams. Some are outright lies, generally told to advance ideological or special-interest agendas that would go nowhere without being draped in the flag.

The greatest US myth of all is the so-called *American Dream*. Essentially, it holds that every citizen—no matter his or her cultural, economic, or personal background—has an equal opportunity to succeed if the individual applies himself or herself sufficiently to the task. Not equality of *outcome*; equality of *opportunity*. If any single word describes the American Idea, it is "egalitarianism." Indeed, among the first words of the Declaration of Independence are: "We hold these truths to be self-evident, that all men are created equal, that they are endowed by their Creator with certain unalienable Rights, that among these are Life, Liberty and the pursuit of Happiness." As George Orwell writes in *Animal Farm*, however, "All men are created equal but some men are created more equal than others."

We Canadians do not preach the concept of equality nearly as sanctimoniously as our American neighbours are wont to do. But we practise it more faithfully. Sanctimony is not righteousness. Good practice honours the true faith. An issue soaring on the American agenda is income inequality. By the standard measure economists use to determine income inequality among countries, the United States ranks forty-second, behind Tunisia, Yemen, and Egypt. According to the US government's own data, the bottom 80 percent of Americans own a paltry 15 percent of the nation's wealth while the top 20 percent of earners hold 85 percent of the wealth. The top 10 percent of earners take home half the income of the country. An American born and raised poor is also likely to remain impoverished for life: a smaller percentage of people escape childhood poverty in the United States than in most other major wealthy countries, including Canada, Australia, France, Germany, and Japan.[7] So much for the American Dream.

The so-called Gilded Age, spanning the last three decades of the nineteenth century, was a period of scandalous extremes of wealth and poverty in the United States. Now, Nobel Prize–winning economist Paul Krugman has lamented "America's return to Gilded Age levels of inequality."[8] This grotesque state of affairs didn't just happen. It was *made* to happen by deliberate public policy. Much of that policy was the product of conservative ideology, identified most closely with the Republican Party. The George W. Bush administration's steep income tax cuts, which disproportionately favoured the rich, accelerated trends set in motion by the Reagan administration in the 1980s. Other Bush fiscal measures—for example, huge fiscal subsidies to big oil and gas corporations and to agribusiness heavily tilted towards the largest and richest producers—widened the income gap still further. Such policies are justified in the name of private enterprise: helping the "job creators" build the economy. Help for the poor, though, is deemed "socialism." Along with "taxes," that is the worst curse word of all to the American right.

Income inequality in Canada is significantly less than in the United States, mostly because our social safety net is much stronger and has been for decades. Among the seventeen wealthiest industrialized countries, by this standard Canada ranks around the middle (eleventh); the United States ranks dead last. Our Fathers of Confederation built a country based on a set of values fundamentally different from those on which the American Republic was founded. Our National Dream flowed from the noblest of human instincts: a desire to form a community, with one for all and all for one…in our case, from "sea to sea." Though a work in progress, our nation-building experiment is succeeding. The American Dream has proven to be a nightmare for far too many people not born swaddled in silk and satin.

Canadian Conservatives seduced by the American right's preferred model for economic growth ought to examine what the relevant policies—pursued in the cause of "supply-side" economics—have done to create real growth where they have actually been tried. The theory is that, by making the wealthy wealthier, gains will "trickle down" to the non-wealthy, rendering everyone wealthier in the end. The wealthy are the chief proponents of trickle-down economics because they overwhelmingly benefit from it. But consider the practical impact of this approach on the working poor and the indigent. Some Canadian Tory leaders over the years have deemed appropriate, in moderation and in limited circumstances, individual policies integral to this overall approach. Robert Stanfield did as Opposition leader, in favouring targeted tax cuts and select deregulation; so did Brian Mulroney as prime minister, in privatizing certain federal assets and imposing fiscal discipline, particularly on discretionary spending. But neither man, nor any Canadian Conservative Party leader before them, ever embraced an economic philosophy that could be remotely described as (in American terms) "Reaganomics." Advocates of this philosophy in the current Canadian Conservative Party—and there are many, not least Stephen Harper himself when he was prime minister—need to make a much stronger case that this is right for Canada or for any other place, for that matter.

The problem isn't just that supply-side, trickle-down economics has never been proven to work—a lot of "supply" (mostly to the rich), precious little "trickle" (least of all to the poor). It's that its practitioners have selectively implemented the theory to favour the rich: massive tax breaks for top income-earners, much lower ones, if any, for the rest; little fiscal discipline at the expense of the wealthy, who have enjoyed deep regressive tax cuts and generous corporate subsidies, but frugality on the backs of the poor, as seen in cuts in everything from statutory entitlement programs to food-stamp payments. A key premise of Reaganomics was that lower tax rates at the top would stimulate economic growth, create jobs, boost consumer spending, thereby increase tax revenues, and end up saving the government money, rather than draining the treasury. George W. Bush drove the supply-side gravy train much faster and farther for the wealthy than Reagan himself did by making much steeper tax cuts targeted primarily at them. Whether this economic theory is followed in a way faithful to its own internal logic or twisted out of shape for political advantage (as Bush, especially, did) is beside the point. Either way, that approach has not narrowed the income gap between rich and poor in the United States, but widened it substantially. All the while, government revenues have plunged, not increased, as the champions of this approach predicted.

Why, then, would we want to try the same thing in Canada? If conservatism in the Canadian tradition means anything, it's that the lessons of the past should inform current and future decisions in the interests of the total community. Lessons from Americans' experience hardly tell us to follow their path wearing not so much rose-tinted glasses as blinkers and blindfolds.

## THE MARITIMES AND NEW ENGLAND

Ties between New England and Canada, particularly the Maritimes, were once close (two-way immigration, trade, tourism, blood relatives). Love of Boston must be in my own blood. My maternal grandmother, Mary McKenzie, was born and raised in Boston. As a young woman, not yet twenty, she travelled to East Bay, Nova Scotia, to attend business college. She met my grandfather (James McQuaid) in the general area, married him, remained in Canada, raised three children, and died in Charlottetown when I was a toddler. My mother told me that her classy mom spoke with a pronounced Boston Irish accent, in the mode of the Kennedys, till the day she drew her last breath. I played up my strong Boston bloodline to the hilt as consul general.

I was less forthcoming about my United Empire Loyalist bloodline on Dad's side. For sure, I did not mention that my paternal forebears fought for the Crown against the rebellious Yankees—and, apparently, killed quite a few of them in the act.

Ties between the Maritimes and New England are, however, weakening with every passing decade. I notice a big difference even between my arrival in September 1989 and now, a generation later. Americans demonstrate much goodwill towards Canadians. Their knowledge of our country, though, is not generally commensurate with that sentiment. While consul general, I got myself into deep trouble with the PEI travel industry. I had criticized the province's "We're akin to Ireland" marketing campaign, aimed primarily at New Englanders. The sales pitch was that the Island had the same kind of natural appeal and culture as the Emerald Isle—all that bucolic greenery and Celtic heritage, and so on. I had said it was foolish to be selling ourselves on the basis of some other vacation or business destination's appeal. I argued that we should, instead, be proud to market what we have on its own merits. I stated that we were making the same mistake as when, years earlier, the Island promoted itself to Americans as "the Kentucky of Canada." My main point, though, was that a Bostonian, for example, could fly to Dublin and back for a fraction of the cost of a return flight to Charlottetown. So, if a Yankee was in the market for all things Irish, he or she could get more easily and more cheaply the real thing than "something akin." They hadn't thought of that angle. Canadians generally don't.

An American who has a reason to know about Canada—say, a business involvement—likely knows more about the relevant facts than most Canadians themselves would. We Canadians are proud of what we consider our superior knowledge of the United States relative to what we think Americans know about us. Both halves of the equation, however, are misleading. We don't know nearly as much as we think we do about the United States and about Americans. And, for their part, they know more about Canada and Canadians than we credit them. As consul general, I knew better than to be unprepared when meeting a Yankee business leader with commercial or investment interests in Canada. He or she could usually match my knowledge of the Canadian factors at play. Most other Canadians, including even our ambassador, would fare no better. Yankee traders: there's a reason they long ruled the world and, in many areas of commerce, still do.

# From Diplomacy Back to Politics

The expression "it's in your blood" applies not just metaphorically, but also literally, to people for whom politics is a passion. I doubt even psychiatrists and physiologists could figure it all out. But, to me, it has to do with the adrenalin and the endorphins and all such things that rush through one's bloodstream or brain whenever the gun is fired to start a political race. Or even just whenever the subject comes up—Pavlov's dog and all that. So, a former politician appointed to a diplomatic post is not likely to become a political eunuch just by the mere fact of his appointment. Politics is not drained from his blood—or gonads. You can take the boy out of politics, but you can't take politics out of the boy. While consul general in Boston, I remained, at heart, a political animal, however much I tried (fairly successfully, I think) to be a diplomat, and not a partisan. It was not easy, especially with former political colleagues still in power regularly traipsing through Boston like movie directors drawn to a film festival.

In my time as consul general, many Canadian politicians visited Boston to enjoy its splendours, often in the guise (but not always the reality) of official business. Some had children studying in the area. Brian Mulroney's daughter, Caroline, was at Harvard. Governor General Ray Hnatyshyn's son also attended university in Boston. His Excellency's visit, though unofficial, required almost as much of the consulate's attention as the prime minister's. I hosted, for example, a dinner in the governor general's honour at the official residence. I hosted and chaperoned and tour-guided in Boston a legion of Canadian politicos of every partisan stripe and rank. Some of these individuals also visited other major centres in New England. In the region, though, there is really Boston and then all the rest—like Einstein and then all those other smart people.

In May 1993, Joe Clark accepted my invitation to come to Boston. It was the tail end of the Mulroney government's constitution-making high season. The purpose of the visit was to speak to American opinion leaders and academics and students about the Meech Lake and Charlottetown Accords. As constitution minister, Clark was the government's point man for the file. It was a coup for me to have landed such a senior minister, especially at this hectic time. The first part of the schedule required Joe to spend the afternoon at Harvard after his noontime arrival. At that renowned centre of learning, the former prime minister would make some remarks and respond to questions in a tutorial format with faculty, advanced students, and outside guests under the auspices of the Mackenzie King Canada Seminar.

I picked up Joe and his wife, Maureen McTeer, in the consulate's official car, at Logan Airport. By then, yet another PC leadership campaign was well under way, this time to choose Brian Mulroney's successor. History moves at warp speed. Defence Minister Kim Campbell from British Columbia was considered the unbeatable front-runner. I was thunderstruck by how passionately both Joe and Maureen opposed not only Kim Campbell's candidacy but also the woman herself. It is all the two wanted to discuss throughout the thirty-minute drive from the airport to their downtown hotel in heavy traffic. To both of them, Campbell would be a disaster as leader. It was, they thought, not because she was incompetent, but because she lacked progressive credentials. In their eyes, the prime ministerial aspirant was a Social Credit retread who would knock the party off the enlightened path it had taken under Robert Stanfield's and Brian Mulroney's successive leadership—and, although they did not say it, but clearly implied, under Joe Clark's as well.

I was puzzled by their militancy. Kim Campbell had been a Social Credit member of the BC legislature when elected as a federal Progressive Conservative MP in 1988. I was defeated in that election, so Campbell and I did not serve together in Parliament. I did not even meet her until she, too, visited Boston around the same time as Joe and Maureen's visit. Campbell was Mulroney's justice minister then, just before she announced her leadership ambitions, at which point Mulroney promoted her to the Defence portfolio. Kim Campbell impressed everyone who met her in Boston, including faculty and students she addressed at Harvard—not an easy audience to captivate in any circumstance. For my part, I was struck by her obvious intelligence, knowledge, eloquence, quick wit, charm, and winsome appearance. The provincial Progressive Conservative Party hardly existed in British Columbia. To me, therefore, Campbell's Social Credit background did not disqualify her to lead the national Tory party. But Joe knew Campbell much better than I. Unlike me, he had been able to see her up close and in action as a Caucus and Cabinet colleague. His impression could scarcely have been more negative had she been a serial killer. The former Tory prime minister saw the British Columbian as a certified reactionary unworthy of following in the footsteps of Sir John A. Macdonald and Robert Borden and Arthur Meighen, set aside those of more recent giants who had led the party and country.

Joe Clark would soon publicly support Jean Charest against Campbell in the 1993 PC leadership race, campaigning vigorously (some would say fanatically) for his choice. At the beginning of the leadership convention, I attended a strategy meeting of about a hundred of Charest's key supporters. Joe personally urged me to go to the podium to inspire the troops by extolling Jean's talents as a campaigner from my perspective as a nominated candidate in PEI for the coming federal election. I was glad to do so. Joe's behaviour at the convention was unusual, if not unprecedented, for a former prime minister and party leader, who is expected to stay above the fray in internal party affairs of this kind. But Clark sensed that we Tories were about to jump off a cliff by choosing, in Kim Campbell, a leader outside the mainstream of the party's progressive tradition. For him, that sense trumped precedent, political etiquette, discretion, and propriety. It was the same principled commitment to progressive values that would cause Joe to urge voters to support the Liberal, Paul Martin, rather than Stephen Harper, in the 2004 election, after the PC Party had merged with the Canadian Alliance Party a year earlier. Clark thought the merger killed the Conservative Party as it had traditionally existed, so he had license to break ranks. Indeed, he did not think he was breaking ranks at all; the Conservative Party had broken ranks with him concerning fundamental beliefs and the policy direction the party signalled it would be taking in future. How prescient he proved to be! Now Joe Clark thought he had license to throw caution to the wind in backing Jean Charest. Clark felt in his bones that Charest represented Tory values far more faithfully than Kim Campbell could or ever would.

The Mackenzie King Seminar at which I had arranged for Joe Clark to speak was part of the Mackenzie King Chair, Canada's main academic footprint at Harvard, endowed by David Rockefeller and other corporate giants in both the United States and Canada. Over the years, the Chair has been filled by such luminaries as Claude Bissell (University of Toronto), Alain Cairns (then at Waterloo), Tom Axworthy (Queen's), and Allan Gotlieb (then teaching at Harvard Law School). Guest speakers at the Canada Seminar had included prime ministers Pierre Trudeau and Jean Chrétien and a veritable Who's Who of other leading politicians, scholars, artists, and experts in various fields. So Clark's engagement under those auspices was a big deal. And he made a big deal of it. His topic was "Reflections on Canada and the Constitution Challenge." The former prime minister enthralled everyone. I had rarely seen him in better form. As with Brian Mulroney's public appearance at Harvard five months earlier, something about the place caused the Canadian visitor to reach deep inside himself to be the best the man could be.

That night, I hosted a dinner at my official residence in Joe Clark's honour. Accompanied by his wife, Maureen, Clark reprised his performance at Harvard before a different audience but with some overlap. This time, renowned economist John Helliwell, Mackenzie King Chair at the time, helped me assemble a diverse group of blue-ribbon guests, about twenty in all. It was to be a totally off-the-record, no-holds-barred format. I told my guests that they could ask the former PM "anything you want, in any way you want, about anything you want"—Canada-focused or not. The guest of honour wowed everyone with his knowledge, mastery of language, and—in this kind of informal setting, even if not on a larger stage—charm and presence. I could not help but compare his triumph with the many such occasions on which I had seen Robert Stanfield at his best—alas, as with Joe in this case, far from the view of Canadian voters. Why must the criteria for judging our political leaders be so narrow? Is a talent for theatrics and self-promotion, which both Clark and Stanfield lacked, actually more important than personal integrity and intelligence and level-headedness, which the two men had in abundance and exuded? Joe Clark was second only to the prime minister himself in government seniority and precedence. Political smarts and personal wisdom had eluded the Albertan as PM a decade earlier. Before an extremely discerning audience at my table in Boston, however, he demonstrated the qualities of a considerably more mature—not to mention greyer and heavier—statesman. To the public, Joe Who had not suddenly become Joe Wow! But, at Harvard, the man certainly was Joe Wonderful.

By January 2, 1993, Brian Mulroney had indicated to a small number of close confidants that he intended to retire as prime minister and PC Party leader, after serving almost a decade. He made the official announcement on February 24. In his memoirs, Mulroney notes that, "up to this point [early January]," the only people to whom he had mentioned his forthcoming resignation—besides his wife, Mila, of course—were two senior Cabinet colleagues: Don Mazankowski and Michael Wilson.[9] Mulroney also says he unofficially informed Governor General Ray Hnatyshyn. I think that the memoir of my former boss is a great read. I was surprised to discover how often he put himself in a harsh and unflattering light, when soft backlighting must have been almost irresistible to this proud man. In only one place, in the thousand-page tome, did I spot a factual error. It concerned that small circle of confidants (four in all) with whom Mulroney said he shared his resignation secret. There were, in fact, two others. One was Governor Bill Weld of Massachusetts. The other was me, as an unintended confidant, when I served as consul general in Boston.

As governor, Bill Weld spent much of the early part of his first term travelling abroad to promote trade for the state in countries such as Japan, South Korea, China, and, closer to home, Mexico. I got to know Bill on a first-name basis early in my posting. I liked and admired him a lot, and the feeling seemed mutual. On one occasion, I chided him for not visiting Canada and reminded him that one of our provinces alone (Ontario) conducted more trade with Massachusetts than did all of Japan. He said, "Good point, Tom. Set something up, and I'll be on the plane the next day." Calling his bluff, I arranged a prestigious speaking engagement for him at Toronto's Empire Club for April 30, 1992. There was to be an official visit the next day with the prime minister in Ottawa, including a private luncheon at 24 Sussex. The governor would also view Question Period. And my old friend John Fraser, the Speaker, would introduce him in the Special Visitors' Gallery. True to his word, Weld was on a plane to Canada, not the next day, but darn soon after I showed him my proposed agenda. Mulroney would lay a long thick red carpet in Ottawa for the governor, whom he had not previously met.

Brian Mulroney's and Bill Weld's backgrounds are vastly different, except for the law degrees and similar age. The red-headed Weld is a certified patrician, Mulroney a high-achieving plebeian. But they liked each other from the first handshake. Were Mulroney's self-identification with the Maritimes and that region's historic close ties with New England the reasons for the instant bond? They seemed to me part of the explanation. Another part is that both men are political junkies who couldn't get enough of each other's stash. Mulroney's staff had to drag him away from the Weld luncheon in Ottawa to attend to other business. Reciprocating the PM's hospitality, the governor pulled out all the stops—and created a few more, so he could pull them out, too—

when Mulroney accepted his invitation to visit Boston in early December 1992. That included greeting the prime minister with a fife-and-drum band at the foot of the grand entrance to the gilt-domed State House. The massive double doors of the edifice, built in 1798, are traditionally opened ceremonially only when a governor leaves office. But they were sprung wide open to welcome the electrician's son from Baie-Comeau. If Brian thought he had gilded the lily for his new-found friend Bill in Ottawa, Bill gilded a greenhouse full of lilies for his new friend Brian in Boston. The benevolent one-upmanship was shameless. But delightful.

In the same spirit, the two men, while conducting business in their two-hour meeting in the governor's private chambers, chatted and gossiped like two giddy schoolgirls. I was the only other person present—far more a fly on the ceiling than an actual participant. The principals seemed mindless that I was even there. But what this fly heard! He heard the Right Honourable Martin Brian Mulroney, eighteenth prime minister of Canada, tell the Honourable William Floyd Weld, sixty-eighth governor of the Commonwealth of Massachusetts, that he was going to retire early in the New Year. You could have knocked me off my chair with a broken fly swatter. There had been much speculation everywhere about Mulroney's leaving office. Even so, hearing the most secret of state secrets in such an authoritative and privileged way stunned me. It demonstrated the strong bond and mutual trust Mulroney and Weld had forged in only eight months, both as government heads and as friends. I doubt that the prime minister, caught up as he was in the moment, remembered this historic detail long enough to include it in his memoirs. But the Honourable Fly now remembers it in writing his.

Just as Brian Mulroney and Bill Weld were inveterate competitors, they were also consummate showmen—Albert Ringling meets P. T. Barnum. Politics is often as much about circuses as bread. Nobody knew that principle, and practised it more assiduously, than Franklin Roosevelt. By far the best American retail politician of his era, FDR told fabled actor and director Orson Welles, "You and I are the best actors in America."[10] Indeed, the link between politics and showmanship is unmistakeable: P. T. Barnum was not only a world-renowned circus impresario, but also an elected politician—a multiterm member of the Connecticut legislature. Successful politicians such as Brian Mulroney and Bill Weld rarely perform in anything but a three-ring circus. The same with Jean Chrétien. Had Robert Stanfield had a little more sawdust in his blood, he might now be described as "the best prime minister Canada ever had" instead of "the best prime minister Canada never had." In Nova Scotia, voters tend to gravitate towards politicians more stolid than splashy, more steady and dependable than charismatic or, for that matter, particularly personable. On a bigger stage, however, showmanship is required. To demonstrate through the media how clean Boston Harbor water had become as a result of federal and state government action, Bill Weld jumped into the Charles River (a harbor tributary) fully clothed— suit, shirt, tie, belt, shoes, socks, watch, wallet, and all!

In the Boston tête-à-tête between Brian Mulroney and Bill Weld, the prime minister told the governor an extraordinary story about Mulroney's great friend Margaret Thatcher. It was in the context of his retirement plans. In his memoirs, Mulroney says that, while he thought he could beat Jean Chrétien in the coming election, he would likely win only a minority government. But he did not think that his winning a third term was worthwhile—whether with a majority or a minority—either for the country or for his party or for himself. "The reason I will not run is…if [I] run again and win…what do [I] want to achieve? And my answer simply is 'more of the same.'

I do not believe that honest answer to be adequate, so I will step aside."[11] I am certain that this statement expressed *part* of the reason Mulroney retired from politics. In that sense, the memoirist was being truthful. But I know the stated rationale is incomplete. Mulroney informed Weld that he intended to resign "to avoid Margaret's torment happening to me before it's too late." Thatcher had been ousted from office by her own Cabinet and parliamentary colleagues in a November 1990 palace coup while she was attending a multilateral meeting in Paris of the Conference on Security and Co-operation in Europe. Sometime afterwards, Thatcher had confided to Mulroney that she was having a brutally painful time "decompressing" from public to private life. In the Weld meeting, Mulroney quoted her as saying, "Brian, when I was PM, I would take thirty important phone calls before completing breakfast and reading the morning papers and getting to the office. Now, I would not have that many in a month." Clearly, the trauma for Margaret Thatcher was not that, now out of politics after so long in it, she found herself a fish out of water. Rather, in her own reality, she was still in the water but, sadly, no longer a fish—and drowning.

Based on what I heard Brian Mulroney confide to Bill Weld, I am certain that the primary reason the prime minister did not seek a third term was the PC Party's plunging poll numbers, which were then the lowest for any Canadian national governing party on record. Mulroney's own public-approval rating was an anemic 21 percent in February 1993, when he stepped down. The PM feared not so much defeat in an election as insurmountable pressure from the party, and his Cabinet colleagues in particular, to resign—the Margaret Thatcher Factor. As we have seen, Mulroney had reversed the party's fortunes when they sank following the party leaders' English-language debate in the 1988 election. He did so by immediately hitting the election trail harder than ever before and campaigning as though his life depended on it. The man's political life did, in fact. According to the Bible, Jesus restored Lazarus of Bethany to life four days after the future saint died. Mulroney took no longer to restore his party's fortunes. In his own eyes, he was a political miracle worker. Few Tory candidates outside Atlantic Canada would have doubted him on that score at the time. The electoral comeback *was* miraculous. Mulroney's private conversation with Weld revealed that he felt confident he could repeat the miracle in the next election, due later that year at the end of his government's five-year mandate. He knew, however, that Cabinet and Caucus colleagues lacked his supreme confidence. Indeed, rumblings of discontent in those quarters were getting louder with each passing week. Mulroney was neither tone-deaf nor delusional. Master politician to the end, he acted before being forced out, as Thatcher had been. In his memoirs, Brian Mulroney hints that avoiding Thatcher's "indignities" at the end of her career loomed large in his mind when he decided to step down.[12] But he does not come close to making the point unambiguously. He did so in his private meeting with Governor Weld of Massachusetts—in the presence of the "fly."

---

While winding down my career as a diplomat in Boston, I, too, felt a sense of decompressing. In some ways, however, the consul general post had not been substantially different from my job as an MP and high-profile Cabinet minister. I had either purposely or subconsciously performed almost identically in all three theatres, albeit before a smaller audience in the case of Boston. Likely, I did so because I brought to these different roles the same personality and skill sets, and the same limitations as well.

Bridgewater State University, the second-largest state college in Massachusetts, bestowed on me an honorary Doctorate of Letters at its 1993 spring convocation—in the words of university president Dr. Adrian Tinsley, for "significant accomplishments on behalf of [Canada] in support of strong, enduring Canadian-American cooperation and ties." No previous Canadian consul general in Boston had been so recognized by any New England university. As the first Atlantic Canadian to hold the post, I felt especially honoured by this unique distinction. With all my strengths and weaknesses, I am who I am. So, no matter how much I might have needed to retool myself professionally to serve Canada as consul general, I was inevitably going to remain a politician while a diplomat, just as I had been an unofficial diplomat while a politician—always seeking the middle ground, as befits the Libran I was born. Pierre Trudeau, also a Libran, never stood accused of being a diplomat. Nor, despite two decades in politics, did he see himself as a politician, either—more a citizen statesman than a pol. But, astrology hooey aside, no one—whatever his place in the universe—becomes a different person just because destiny deals him a new hand. As I put down my own cards as consul general in the early summer of 1993, I needed to discover what hand I was to play next. Having done my best to serve my country as a diplomat, I sensed I had one more game in me as a politician.

# Chapter 30

# THE LAST
# HURRAHS

M y transition from diplomat back to politician, in the early summer of 1993, was made easier by the fact Prime Minister Brian Mulroney had announced in February he would be retiring. A leadership race was under way to succeed him. Tory Cabinet ministers were lining up supporters. Many of them courted me as a potential ally while visiting Boston on government business. The "Pavlov's dog" political juices began to kick in and pulse through my veins. Kim Campbell, Mulroney's defence minister from British Columbia, won the Tory leadership and thereby became prime minister at the party's leadership convention in mid-June.

In April 1993, just before the national leadership convention, in a hotly contested race, I captured the PC nomination against local entrepreneur Henry Phillips in my old riding of Hillsborough for the fall election. I had lost the seat five years earlier, in the 1988 election, by 259 votes in the anti–free trade tidal wave that swept across Atlantic Canada and drowned most Tory candidates throughout the region. Now, I was attempting a political comeback. Soon after my nomination, Kim Campbell, having just won the national PC party leadership, did some main-streeting with me in downtown Charlottetown before the election writ was dropped in late summer. She was the most natural and engaging street campaigner I ever saw in my decade alongside some of the best. The next best was the first black Member of Parliament, Lincoln Alexander of Hamilton, later Ontario's lieutenant governor. He had main-streeted with me in my first race, in 1979. Charismatic, funny, tactile, profane, physically imposing, Lincoln encountered a hostile voter on the streets of Charlottetown, possibly motivated by the MP's race. I still smile when recalling the advice this veteran politician gave me: I should wait until I had a few years behind me as an incumbent before telling a voter to do something with himself anatomically impossible.

Brian Mulroney was a natural campaigner, too, but even better with crowds at a podium than on the street. Joe Clark was surprisingly good with voters, one on one. Seemingly genuinely interested both in their views and in them as individuals, he radiated sheer niceness. I once stranded Clark at a constituent's house while we were campaigning together, from door to door, in the Charlottetown suburb of Lewis Point Park. It was the day after he spoke at my nominating convention for the 1984 election, which John Turner had just called. At the very moment one constituent responded to our door knock, my brother Colin, a cardiologist, cell-phoned from the hospital to alert me that my wife, Kathy, had just gone into labour with our first daughter, Kelly. I rushed off, but Joe, no longer party leader, continued to campaign along the street without me. He shocked many a homemaker who responded to the doorbell not expecting to find at the stoop—the former prime minister of Canada.

While main-streeting with me in Charlottetown, Kim Campbell provided some drama of her own. Unlike Joe Clark's experience, the incident had nothing to do with childbirth. "Cows," the brand name of a local but widely marketed ice cream, is so rich and decadent that one scoop calls for a stroke test, which one would likely fail. At the corner of Queen and Grafton Streets is the flagship retail outlet of Cows. As our entourage passed it, a young female employee dashed out and handed the new Tory leader and PM a cone of double-butterscotch ice cream—good for two strokes. A huge ice-cream cone in the hot mid-afternoon sun is conventionally the last thing a politician wants in hand while handshaking and glad-handing. After walking a safe distance from the benefactor, so as not to hurt her feelings, I discreetly reached to relieve Campbell of the burden. She shot me a look as though I had kicked her in the shin. "Hell, no, McMillan! Shove off!" she barked. "This is for me." The new PM licked the cone all the way to the waterfront, clearly enjoying the threat to her decorum—and arteries. The crowd roared its approval.

Alas, Campbell was not nearly as impressive in the election campaign itself, stumbling from one disaster to another, including in PEI. When she came to Charlottetown in the heat of the campaign, we held a joint news conference at the Prince Edward Hotel, on the same waterfront where she had finished her butterscotch ice cream four months earlier. For the conference, I had thoroughly briefed the new prime minister on the Fixed Link issue, which by this time had become even more controversial than it was in 1988. I'd heard rumours from within the higher echelons of the national campaign that the prime minister was often more preoccupied with her male partner at the time than with either matters of state or the campaign. Was this the explanation for what happened next? Despite my detailed briefing, Campbell responded to the first question at the Charlottetown news conference by saying that she knew nothing about the Fixed Link. The media event skidded downhill from there. So did my own campaign, for a variety of reasons, not just that major snafu.

It is only natural for a new leader to want to put her own mark on the party. That's especially true if, as with Kim Campbell, she heads a government. When that government has been in office for nearly a decade, as the PC government had by 1993, the desire is not only understandable but also imperative. Otherwise, the risk is that the public will seek change and elect a different government. I understood this political reality. But I was slow to realize something more fundamental was at play as the freshly minted prime minister proceeded to renew the government and restore and reshape the PC party's image heading into the federal election: she was changing the nature of the party itself. As both a long-time Progressive Conservative farmhand and now a candidate again for the party, I was concerned less about certain new party policies themselves than about the shelving of traditional Tory values. I was especially concerned about the implications of one measure: the government's procurement of some $5 billion worth of helicopters to replace the aging (and increasingly accident-prone) Sea Kings of the Canadian Navy, used for defence, coastal surveillance, and rescue missions.

The helicopter procurement, especially the enormous price tag at a time of mounting federal deficits and near-record high unemployment, was hugely unpopular across the country. Campbell had been responsible for the file as defence minister before winning the party leadership. Eventually, the new PM bowed to intense pressure, both from the public at large and from within the party, to reduce the purchases from fifty to twenty-eight aircraft and the total price tag from $5.8 billion to $4.4 billion. But the political damage to her own and the new government's image had already been inflicted and proved irreparable. The problem was that voters saw the issue exclusively in defence and profligate-spending terms. Liberal Party leader Jean Chrétien was running away with the issue on those bases. He framed it totally as one of callously misplaced priorities. I made urgent calls about my concern to people I knew close to the PM. Among them was Nova Scotian Peter McCreath, Kim Campbell's new veterans affairs minister, whose department's national headquarters was in my riding. I told these Campbell insiders that the helicopter issue was "killing us at the doorstep." I argued that we needed to sell the policy in a completely different manner, one that emphasized nation building and job creation, not shopping for military hardware. What weighed heavily on my mind was not so much the policy itself (though that, as well) as what it said about our party's overall priorities and values and how the public was judging us on that basis: harshly. Specifically, we risked being caricatured as US Republican-style defence hawks, interested in military and defence matters but not in the deep-seated concerns of struggling Canadians, especially the jobless, whose numbers were expanding alarmingly at the time. Worse, we were coming across, far beyond defence matters, as cold and heartless right-wing ideologues.

In 1993, following a decade in office, our party needed to be renewed. But it did not need to be transformed in the mould of the US Republican Party, with which Canadians would have little truck. A generation earlier, Robert Stanfield, with Tom Symons at his side, had restored the party's progressive policy traditions following its flirtation with prairie populism during John Diefenbaker erratic leadership. Changing the party into something it had never been before—a vehicle for right-wing ideologues of the Reagan/Thatcher variety—would be an affront to the institution's very being. It is one thing to modernize an institution. It is quite another to kill its soul. In the past four decades, hurling tax sops to the rich, demonstrating indifference to the disadvantaged, and subjugating the public interest to powerful corporate interests: that has been the American and British conservative stereotypes. The perception in both countries is rooted in actual public stances taken not only by leading politicians of this persuasion but also by think tanks of the same ideological hue closely aligned with them. None of this is what Canadians traditionally have voted for over the generations. And, as it turned out, they would not in 1993. The debate over helicopters was a touchstone moment in the modern history of the Canadian Conservative Party. It helped crystallize for Canadians a change in the nature of a great national institution, still familiar but no longer recognizable.

I urged the party strategists to emphasize government's central role in nation building and in fostering the best interests of the total community. I said they should downplay, in particular, the arcana of military hardware. And they should discuss the long-term defence requirements of the country only in broad terms, not in the context of defence contracts, let alone specific weaponry. Otherwise, I argued, struggling Canadians would think we were more interested in military equipment than in helping them and their families cope with their fears and uncertainties. The PC Party brass listened to my concerns respectfully. But my argument was largely lost on them. I sensed they thought I was communicating in a dead language. Initially, I wondered whether maybe I had just been out of politics too long and theirs was some new poll-driven way of framing issues with which I was not familiar. I soon realized that the "new way" wasn't new at all. It was, on a host of issues—not just the helicopter purchases—merely the same old ideological snake oil Republicans in the United States had been peddling for years: that the primary, if not sole, function of government is to protect national security from external threats, ensure law and order at home, get out of the way of the private sector so that it can maximize wealth (mostly for the already rich), and hope that crumbs from the banquet table of the tax-unburdened rich would "trickle down" to the tax-burdened poor and middle class. I could tell that my idea of appealing to Canadians' sense of common cause in the face of soaring unemployment and attendant social and economic uncertainty struck the Campbell team as effete. The emphasis, instead, was to be on something they deemed much more muscular, no doubt in the style of Reagan and Thatcher: individual citizens taking responsibility for themselves; fiscal realism; the limits of government, particularly in times of high annual federal deficits and mounting accumulated public debt; and suppressing public expectations about both their individual futures and national economic progress overall. To them, the last tenet meant candidly telling Canadians both what the government was incapable of doing for them and how unlikely it was that their economic circumstances would improve any time soon, *least of all because of government action*. It was the equivalent of a family doctor telling a patient that he not only couldn't, but also wouldn't, do anything about her breast cancer. The Campbell team's message to voters was not so much a cold shower as a deep freeze.

The PC Party's "new" theme might have helped the prime minister distance herself from her unpopular predecessor—the intent of it all, no doubt. But the message flew in the face of what it meant to be a Tory: a concern for the entire community, not just for certain sectors, however important—in the case at hand, defence. Instead of appealing to Canadians with a "we're all in this together" message, Campbell's theme sounded more like, "sorry, you're on your own—except for defence contractors." I had heard quite enough of that kind of refrain while consul general in Boston: defence contracts are a huge boondoggle for politicians everywhere in the United States.

Canadians outside the Campbell inner sanctum massively resisted the disproportionality of the new Conservative government's proposed spending on helicopters. Unlike Americans, Canadians don't attach more importance to military hardware and marching bands than to ensuring all our citizens—not just the wealthy—are safe, healthy, housed, fed, educated, and trained. We revere our Vimy Ridge, Dieppe, and Normandy heroes, not our tanks and warheads. Moreover, in contrast to Americans, we don't celebrate fighting men and women just when they're on the battlefield. At least until recent times, we have mended their broken bones, damaged brains, and lonely hearts upon their return home. The military culture in the two countries is one of the most marked differences between the two peoples. It's the difference between romanticizing war as a badge of national honour and honouring the warrior as the finest expression of national service. The helicopter procurement, particularly on such a grand scale, symbolized for Canadians that the Campbell government was out of touch with their problems, concerns, and priorities at a time of profound economic and emotional stress. More fundamentally, the government was violating core Canadian values. The issue, consequently, affected the dynamics of the 1993 election far beyond the helicopter contract itself. Like the aging helicopters threatened to do, the PC Party's election campaign crashed to earth. Most Canadians believed that its fate was deserved. Kim Campbell herself was the biggest casualty, the prime minister losing her own Commons seat in Vancouver Centre.

To me, the government's handling of the helicopter contract laid bare the party's new and different ideological direction. It was as though I had stumbled into the wrong church on a Sunday morning. Little did I realize until later that, under Kim Campbell's leadership, I was not only in the wrong church, but perhaps in the wrong religion. I recalled Joe Clark and Maureen McTeer's indictment of Campbell during that car ride from Boston's Logan Airport. Then skeptical, I was now starting to think that they had been both accurate and prescient. The party leader was, after all, as they had warned, an American-style, right-wing wolf in progressive Tory sheep's clothing. Had we all been fleeced? It was not long before my growing suspicions squashed any hope I had of winning back my seat in Hillsborough. It was going to be, for me and all PC candidates across the country, a long and tortuous election—but, for the national PC Party, a quick short trip to annihilation.

# National Campaign Disaster

The 1993 national general election was Jean Chrétien's first electoral test as national Liberal Party leader. Up to the last week, the PC campaign had been a disaster across the country. Having entered the campaign competitive in the polls, we were now trailing, with the trend steadily downward. For us Tory candidates, the fateful final week of the campaign made the disastrous weeks before seem a model of military precision. In an effort to reverse our sharp decline in the polls, the party's national campaign team threw a desperate, high-stakes Hail Mary pass by running an unbelievably tasteless TV commercial attacking Chrétien. It sought to characterize the Liberal leader as a lightweight rube incapable of garnering international respect. It did so by highlighting his facial paralysis in unflattering photos. The revulsion people felt towards the Tory commercial was total. It was like what my siblings and I would have felt had someone posted an image of our beloved Helen on street utility poles exaggerating the hint of facial hair that cancer-treatment hormones caused towards the end of her life. As Helen would have said, "It's past talking about."

Has there ever been a more inept ploy in the history of political marketing than ours against Chrétien? The Tory campaign strategists had neither the time nor the creative ingenuity nor the class to reverse the damage. The personal assault on *le petit gars* caused the already-listing Tory ship to take on more water than it could possibly bail out with all hands on deck. In the Hall of Shame for in-house wreckers of the Tory party, however unintentional, the creators of the anti-Chrétien ad should be admitted automatically on the first ballot. When I saw the ad, I was stunned. I knew immediately that any chance I had of winning back my seat—Liberal national or regional tide or not—had vanished. My Liberal opponent, George Proud, was so confident of the converse impact on his own campaign that he did not bother to participate in the last all-candidates debate, at Holland College. He, like most others, knew that the election was already over.

The *Helen Factor* in Jean Chrétien's appeal was obvious to me on the doorstep as I campaigned throughout my riding. *Le petit gars* had it, people liked it, and they voted for it. He possessed the rarest of qualities in a leader: the capacity to connect with people as one of their own. Without that quality, a leader cannot inspire, cannot lead, cannot succeed. Other things being equal, it is what separates good from great political leaders. On April 12, 1945, the patrician US president Franklin Delano Roosevelt died in Warm Springs, Georgia, at age sixty-three. His body was transported by rail to Washington, DC. The funeral train then travelled from the nation's capital to Hyde Park, New York, FDR's final resting place. On both treks, thousands of people lined the tracks to mourn their beloved leader. A journalist saw an old man crying as the funeral train passed. The reporter asked him if he had known the president.

The old man replied: "No, but the president knew me."[1] *That* is the essence of great leadership. Lincoln had it, FDR had it, Winston Churchill had it. And Jean Chrétien had enough of it to make him, if not great, then at least greatly successful. A story that made the rounds in Ottawa (possibly apocryphal) concerned a flight that Pierre Trudeau and Jean Chrétien took together on government business. The story, true or not, reflects how differently the public perceived the two men. As they were landing at the Toronto International Airport, Chrétien looked out the plane window and remarked to Trudeau: "It's raining outside." Correcting his seatmate's English, Trudeau replied: "Jean, when it rains, it always does *outside*." For average Canadians—even if not for professional linguists or logic sticklers like Pierre Trudeau—certainly for Jean Chrétien, "it rains outside."

For the first time in the history of Canada's oldest political party—over a century from Sir John A. Macdonald to Kim Campbell—the Conservative Party of Canada was all but wiped off the electoral map. The party lost its official status in Parliament, having failed to win the required twelve seats to qualify. Of 295 candidates, only two—Jean Charest in Quebec and Elsie Wayne, virtually an Independent, in New Brunswick—were victorious. The Kim Campbell phenomenon I will never understand: so much natural talent, promise, and brainpower; so much personality, wit, and presence; so much girlish sex appeal reflected in her blonde-haired, blue-eyed, bright-smile prettiness; so much application when she put her mind to it. But so little deliverance in the end. She was not so much a comet flashing brilliantly and then crashing dark. She was more a flashlight just slowly but steadily losing power with each use until, finally, at the worst time, when you need it most, the beam goes dead. Give me a meteor over a flashlight—any day, any time, any election.

As a candidate, I thought Kim Campbell's biggest failure throughout the campaign was her inability, or unwillingness, to project hopefulness as the country's leader. Like the rest of the industrialized world, Canada was still in a deep recession at this time. The unemployment rate was above 11 percent; between 1976 and 2013, the rate was higher only once, at 12 percent in 1983. When Canadians went to the polls in 1993, voters were terrified for themselves and for their families. National polls found that one Canadian in four feared he or she or a family member would be thrown out of work within a year.

The federal election years of 1984 and 1993 had more in common than just double-digit jobless rates in the snare of a recession. The government party of the day in each case (one Liberal, the other PC) suffered the worst electoral shellacking in its history, and for the same reason: a new prime minister's inability to communicate to anxious voters that change was on the way. Like John Turner in 1984, Kim Campbell did not need to be a political genius to mastermind a winning campaign. She just needed to employ the successful "politics of hope" formula practised by politicians from many different liberal democracies who, over the generations, had been geniuses.

But instead of instilling optimism in fearful Canadians, the new prime minister, on the very first day of the election campaign, warned that they should not expect the high jobless rate to drop appreciably for four years. Indeed, Kim Campbell predicted, likely not till the turn of the century. She might as well have said "till eternity," as far as Canadians struggling to keep their heads above water were concerned. Before some Tory candidates had even hit the campaign trail, Campbell had all but handed the election to Jean Chrétien, the master peddler of hope and optimism. Prime Minister Campbell could easily, and credibly, have said that her new government, like FDR's in the 1930s, had a Big Plan to slash unemployment. She then could have rhymed off a long list of major job-intensive government projects already on the pike.

Brian Mulroney has said, in private and in different ways in his memoirs, that he handed to his successor a full policy program—the makings of a Throne Speech—on which to both govern and campaign. And, he says, Campbell could have hit the ground running with that program the first day she inherited the leadership from him to become prime minister. This is not just *post facto* defensive patter aimed at shifting blame from himself to Campbell for the party's electoral rout. It has the merit of being true. The PEI-NB Fixed Link alone would create over two thousand jobs during the course of construction. At this very time, the federal government had at least a half-dozen other mega-projects in the works across the country. They included, in the PM's own province, the construction of so-called Super Ferries to ply the waters between Vancouver Island and the BC mainland: *Spirit of British Columbia* (being built in 1993) and *Spirit of Vancouver Island* (to be built in 1994). The construction of these two large ships, like that of the Fixed Link at the other end of the country, would directly employ thousands of workers. At the same time, these projects would generate substantial industrial and service spinoffs, fostering still more employment.

The new PM could even have mentioned the multi-billion-dollar Canadian Navy Sea King helicopter replacement program so dear to her as defence minister and now as government leader. For the election, it was irrelevant whether the helicopters might eventually be built elsewhere, as in fact they were. The government party needed to win an election, not points for technicalities. Jean Chrétien did not hesitate to demagogue the issue. He did so even after the election. His government cancelled the urgently needed helicopters for partisan politics—not austerity, as claimed. It cost Canadian taxpayers $500 million in cancellation fees—equivalent to half the entire cost of the Fixed Link. Kim Campbell mentioned none of these job-intensive federal projects in her disastrous first news conference of the election. That media event set the tone for the entire election. It was less the beginning of the campaign than the beginning of the end of the Progressive Conservative Party of Canada.

Kim Campbell should not bear all the blame for either the 1993 electoral disaster or for killing the PC Party as it had existed for generations. Her predecessor as prime minister and party leader, Brian Mulroney, helped dig the political grave where she and the party were later buried. Hugh Segal, Mulroney's chief of staff in 1991–92, has noted that "Campbell was defeated in 1993 by a mix of forces that pre-dated her winning of the leadership of the party as well as some she launched herself."[2] At the time, I myself would have assigned to the two leaders about equal blame. Ultimately, though, history will likely fault Campbell more than Mulroney. And with good reason. Her strong poll numbers for several weeks after she won the national PC Party leadership indicated that the 1993 election was eminently winnable for the Tories despite the public's earlier disaffection with Brian Mulroney. Indeed, in August 1993, a Gallup poll showed Campbell with a 51 percent approval rating, making her Canada's most popular prime minister in three decades. By the end of the summer, her personal popularity had far surpassed Jean Chrétien's. Support for the PC Party itself had increased to within a few points of the Liberals—within or near what pollsters call the "margin of error." All the while, the Reform Party had been reduced to single digits. The new PM alone squandered this strong advantage entering the election campaign. *That* can't be blamed on Brian Mulroney.

In retrospect, in choosing Kim Campbell to succeed Mulroney as its leader and automatically Canada's prime minister, the Progressive Conservative Party did not conduct due diligence. Neither did the media until Campbell's limitations as a national party leader became obvious without investigative journalism. Almost everybody got caught up in the excitement of the country's having its first woman prime minister. That the media are less intrusive into the lives of public figures in Canada than in the United States is both a blessing and a curse. It was a curse in the case of Campbell, for Canadians were provided little information about the woman, except that which was largely positive, before she became their prime minister. Kim Campbell, for example, either claimed or never disabused anyone of the myth that she had learned to speak fluent Russian during an extended period in the Soviet Union. However well she might have been able to muddle through a basic conversation in the language, she was not, in fact, fluent—an important distinction for voters when choosing a prime minister for the world stage. The media, however, were uninterested. Queen's University political scientist Dr. George Perlin, whom I have known since my graduate student days, once remarked to me how strange he thought it was that Campbell's false claim to speak Russian had gone unchecked by the Canadian media. He likened the media's neglect to another case: Flora MacDonald's printed material for her PC Party leadership run in 1976 falsely claimed that she had been an instructor in the politics department at Queen's, in addition to her job as administrative secretary there. As a former student in that department, I remember being puzzled at the time by Flora's claim. I could not recall her ever having taught anyone I knew. In many ways, the media then were as bedazzled by Flora as they were by Kim. In the latter's case, the seduction lasted only until the new leader's missteps at the beginning of the 1993 election threw her into a downward spiral. By that time, it was far too late for Conservatives to correct their mistake. The buyers' remorse was as sudden as it was widespread.

Brian Mulroney's reputation is finally showing signs of light after mostly darkness since he retired from politics more than two decades ago. That is unlikely to happen for Kim Campbell. Whether she would have risen to the job had she won the 1993 election can never be known. But Joe Clark's assessment of Campbell is instructive. It suggests that, had the media plunged into the political waters where Kim Campbell had been swimming throughout her previous public life, they would have discovered for Canadians a simple fact: she had never before swum far enough from shore to have developed a stroke better than a dog paddle. When thrust into deep water and required to swim freestyle against the current, she drowned. And, in the 1993 election, she pulled to their watery deaths all but two of her 295 fellow swimmers, including me.

Again, I believe that Brian Mulroney will rise steadily in any ranking of Canadian prime ministers, especially for his vision on free trade, acid rain, and national parks like South Moresby. But, reflecting his own distinguishing personal and leadership limitations, he, like Joe Clark, failed to render the Progressive Conservative Party a permanently credible alternative to the Liberals after Robert Stanfield placed it firmly on that path. Mulroney likely tried to do too much as prime minister while doing too little as PC Party leader after winning re-election in 1988. Meech Lake, the Charlottetown Accord, the goods and services tax, the Free Trade Agreement, governmental administrative reform, fiscal austerity—together, all such measures were more than Canadians could bear after some point (probably early in the second mandate). Mulroney's accelerated pursuit of a government and personal legacy in the final months of his primeministership took an especially high toll not just on his own popularity, but also on his party's—in the latter case, irreparably in parts of the country, including almost all the West. Canadians were suffering from two conditions:

Mulroney Fatigue and, to coin a medical term, RRS (Reform Resistance Syndrome). In their minds, the only antidote to both conditions was to elect a new government with a different party label and policy agenda.

Towards the end, Brian Mulroney, for all his natural political and communications skills, proved a poor salesman for himself, for his government, and for PC policies. Hubris might have gotten in the way, as it so often does with politicians in the sunset of their careers. To be widely accepted, a heavy reformist agenda requires the public to trust the purveyors. With each passing month during the government's mandate, especially after the 1988 election, the prime minister was trusted by fewer and fewer Canadians. Put simply, the messenger and the message became less and less a fit as Mulroney approached retirement—indeed, well before he entered Rideau Hall to tender it. By the time the PM departed, Canadians were glad to see the back of his head. Party focus groups revealed that the mere sight of Brian Mulroney caused voters to grab their TV remotes and change the channel or turn the boob tube off altogether. Having elected Mulroney in 1984 with the biggest parliamentary majority in Canadian history, the vast majority of Canadians wanted no further part of him nine years later. His approval ratings had sunk so low (11 percent in a 1992 Gallup poll) that more Canadians believed Elvis Presley was still alive than wanted Mulroney to be their prime minister.

Like Brian Mulroney, Kim Campbell possessed many natural gifts as a retail politician. And early in her leadership, she was personally popular. But she paid a high price for her predecessor's unpopularity. Her own missteps, once the 1993 election got under way, reminded voters of why they had become disaffected with having the PC Party in power in the first place. The highest price of all, for both Mulroney's and Campbell's mistakes, was paid by the Progressive Conservative Party. It was left politically bankrupt by the failings of two successive trustees of the party's heritage and future. By the end of 1993, more than a century after its founding, the PC Party of Canada still had its rich heritage. But little remained of its future.

The hand fate dealt me in the 1993 election proved a bust. Ironically, among all the campaigns I fought in PEI, this one was my best in terms of organization, fundraising, volunteer recruitment, advertising, and door-to-door canvassing alike. It was competently managed by local lawyer Ron Profit. His wife, Donna, would run well but unsuccessfully for the Tories in Hillsborough in 2011. My sister-in-law Sandra (married to my brother Colin) did a masterful job, with Charlottetown local Janet Wood, organizing pre-election neighbourhood barbecues to reintroduce me to voters following my four-year sojourn in Boston. They then mobilized a huge team of volunteers to go from door to door with me during the election itself. It was the first time I had ever been accompanied at the doorstep in such a comprehensive way. But, given the national collapse of the PC party in the campaign, I could have been accompanied by God and it would not have made an ounce of holy water's bit of difference.

After my defeat, I had to get on with life again. This time, defeat was not a new experience. I bounced back easily. First, I accepted a Canadian Studies teaching position at Bridgewater State University, near Boston, which, as mentioned earlier, had bestowed an honorary doctorate on me not long before. In addition to lecturing, I wrote more articles, for both academic journals and other publications. In the summer of 1996, I became a student again, enrolling in Université Laval's summer program to improve my French. There, most students were young enough to be my children, if not grandchildren. In seven summer credit courses, I got higher marks than I had ever received at university as a much younger man, let alone for French.

Indeed, I led the largest class and neared the top in the others. I say that not so much with pride as with a message of hope and inspiration for my fellow fogies. Perhaps, "mature student" means more than age.

With politics seemingly in my past, I made my top priority being a dad. Following Emily's arrival in February 1990, I now had three beautiful girls. Three years later, Kathy and I separated and, much later, divorced. Her goal, as always, was to be a good mother while also focusing more than ever before on Katherine's Ltd., her high-end women's clothing store in Charlottetown. The business had remained successful during our time in Boston. But it was time for Kathy to make up for lost ground from having to manage it from the United States for long stints. My own goal was to continue being a good father but to live and work anywhere except PEI.[3] Faced with other such personal and occupational factors, we found that never the twain shall meet. But Kathy and I, together, have succeeded as parents. The three girls, now happy and successful and confident and grounded young women, are proof of that. Ours is a broken marriage—not a broken family. I am an extremely lucky man. For me, this is one hand the gods of fortune stacked with Aces in a no-trump game.

# Jean Charest: A New Leader

Only twenty-eight at the time, Jean Charest became in 1986 the youngest Canadian Cabinet minister in history, appropriately as minister of state for youth. After Lucien Bouchard bolted the Mulroney government, Robert de Cotret succeeded him for a year as environment minister (1990–91). Charest was appointed to the portfolio when de Cotret was made secretary of state. Towards the end of my time as environment minister, I said to Charest while chit-chatting with him in the House of Commons: "Jean, this would be a great portfolio for you." Now environment minister for a few weeks, Jean said to me: "I didn't understand your comment at the time, but you were absolutely right: it *is* a great portfolio for me!" Clearly, he loved the Environment territory as much—or almost so—as I did. In 1998, he left federal politics, won the Quebec Liberal Party's leadership that year, and became premier of Quebec in 2003. When Charest's government was defeated in 2012, he lost his own seat in Sherbrooke. Meanwhile, Jean and I cultivated over the years as close a friendship as I had with anyone through Cabinet.

I was one of the first to urge Jean Charest to seek the PC leadership vacated by Brian Mulroney in 1993. Jean visited Boston on ministerial business soon after Mulroney announced his resignation in February. He was still only in his mid-thirties. I took the young Quebecer out to dinner in the city's tony Back Bay to make the point that his youth should not deter him from entering the race to succeed the prime minister, despite the misgivings I knew he had on that score. I stressed that other candidates would have much more serious drawbacks; he should run now rather than the next time, for it might never come; and, if he ran, he should do so to win, not to position himself for later, least of all merely to ensure that Quebec had a candidate in the race. He seemed to hang on my every word. I thought to myself: "His tongue is saying no to the leadership, but his eyes are saying yes." A few days later, his eyes having gotten the better of his tongue, Charest entered the 1993 PC leadership race. I am proud to have been one of his first and most active supporters from the Maritimes. One of my greatest regrets as a Tory partisan is that Jean Charest did not win then. Despite his youth,

Jean would have risen to the job and done endlessly better in the subsequent election, especially in Quebec, than did the actual leadership winner, Kim Campbell. Unlike Joe Clark, who won the PC Party leadership in 1976 at around the same age as Charest was in 1993, Charest had government experience and was endlessly more gifted than Clark as a political campaigner, strategist, and politician generally.

As we have seen, Joe Clark and his wife, Maureen, had convinced me that Campbell would be a terrible leader. They thought her reactionary. How prescient they were. Everything I knew about Jean Charest from our time together in Cabinet underscored his progressive instincts. At the June 1993 leadership convention, Jean gave by far the best speech ("The Bloc is a crock!"). But it was, apparently, not yet his time. His time came in 1997, and it drew me back to politics as a candidate after my 1993 defeat.

In the 1997 federal election, I sought a seat in Peterborough as a "carpetbagger," though I had lived there for a decade when working with Tom Symons and Robert Stanfield on PC Party policy. The impetus for my running came from a core group that had long operated the Peterborough PC Riding Association. I had made it clear publicly that I was not interested in reoffering anywhere in PEI, least of all in my old Hillsborough riding. Elements of the local media—the CBC, in particular—were still too hostile to me for that to be a realistic option. The 1997 election was called for June 2, only two days after the Confederation Bridge between PEI and New Brunswick was to be officially opened. Memories of my leading role in getting that project built were still raw among the anti–Fixed Link forces, including (perhaps especially) certain journalists. In 1997, I felt I had gone to the electoral stake twice for the Fixed Link (1988 and 1993). "Third time lucky" didn't seem my fate.

One of the Peterborough Tory ringleaders urging me to run in their riding was Marty Murphy, a beloved local lawyer. Marty and his group phoned me in PEI to broach the subject. They then flew me, not once but twice, to the riding to urge me in person. Upon returning to the Island after the second time, I decided not to run and phoned to tell them so. Two Peterborough locals I knew especially well from my Stanfield days, lawyer Alexander (Sandy) Fleming and Provincial Court judge Sam Murphy, later elevated to the Superior Court, were ambivalent about my running. As Sam put it, "If I were a betting man, I'd say don't do it. But, from my long experience in the riding and in politics, I think anything could happen, so don't rule it out." The "anything could happen" factor weighed heavily on my mind. As did the relentless persistence of my pursuers, who flew me to the riding a third time to get me to reverse my decision not to run. I told the PC contingent that my heart was just not in it, but they refused to take no for an answer. Like the McQuaids on my mother's side, I am a sucker for lost Tory causes. Accordingly, I had a change of heart.

Jean's Charest's phoning me was the decisive factor. No doubt he had been asked to do so by the local plotters. He later told me that he had intended to call anyway. Jean's pitch to me was that my running would help silence the steadily louder media drumbeat that his nominated candidates lacked government experience, as in fact they did. I knew in my bones, though, that my offering in Peterborough was doomed from the beginning. The Liberal incumbent, Peter Adams (1993–2006), a Trent University geographer, was well entrenched, considered a first-rate MP, and also widely viewed as a true gentleman. Moreover, the recently launched Reform Party would almost certainly split the traditional Conservative vote in Peterborough. The new party was wedded to extreme right-wing principles and policies that especially appealed to the rural parts of the riding. But, having helped talk Jean into seeking the PC leadership, albeit two leadership races earlier, I could hardly then refuse to assist my friend in any way I could now that he was leader, needed my help, and asked for it. Besides, I reasoned, Jean Charest was such a gifted campaigner that, despite the polls, which showed Chrétien's Liberals solidly in the lead, he might win. And, miracle of miracles, I might also if the tide turned sharply enough.

As I expected, Peter Adams won handily in Peterborough. As I also expected, the Reform Party candidate, Nancy Branscombe, and I split the traditional Conservative vote between us. She got marginally more than I, reflecting the national trend towards Reform at the PC Party's expense. But I have no regrets about having run— none whatsoever. I have always loved Peterborough and still had many friends there. Spending a few weeks back in my old stomping grounds, this time stomping for votes, didn't seem like the worst thing I could do for a limited period. I enjoyed being back on the campaign trail, especially for Jean. I will be forever indebted to the many friends and strangers alike who worked tirelessly for me.

Though my running in Peterborough in 1997 was for naught electorally, I found this campaign my most intellectually satisfying of the six I had fought as a candidate. It helped that Peter Adams, a thoughtful academic, elevated the debate at the many all-candidate forums sponsored by diverse groups. The most spirited one was at the very end of the campaign (Sunday night before election day). It was a live debate among all the Peterborough candidates on CBC Radio's *Cross Country Checkup*. The host, as always, was razor-sharp and witty Newfoundlander Rex Murphy. I thought Adams and I were in especially good form. An intelligent, personable, level-headed candidate like Peter Adams brings the best out of his opponents. The contest in Peterborough demonstrated that political combat can be vigorous without being bloody, competitive without being underhanded, and triumphant for one candidate without being humiliating for any of the others.

My respect for Peter Adams did not extend to Nancy Branscombe, the Reform Party candidate. From the beginning of the campaign, she presented herself as a long-time Tory activist who had joined the Reform Party with great regret about abandoning her traditional political home. In our first all-candidates debate, before a downtown high school audience, Branscombe claimed she had slaved for John Crosbie in a previous election, a statement discredited by Crosbie's own political team. But her "I'm too pure to be a Tory anymore" shtick appealed to some Peterborough voters. The other candidates and I, however, found both it and her exhausting before long. At public events, she often wore a baseball cap to appear one of the people, a ploy as phony as her remark about having worked for Crosbie. Branscombe is the only candidate among all the many opponents I faced in six federal elections whom I neither respected nor liked. When a political party is founded on a lie—in Reform's case, that the West was being shafted by the rest of Canada—it should not surprise anyone that many of its candidates are prepared to play fast and loose with the truth. During the campaign, Nancy Branscome and the truth rarely crossed paths.

## Preston Manning and the Reform Party

Reform leader Preston Manning had a preachy public image, as befit the ideological zealot, policy wonk, and religious fundamentalist he was. In an effort to appear more modern, however, he put himself in the hands of style experts for the 1997 national campaign. The owlish eyeglasses were replaced with contact lenses, the ill-fitting suits with expensive custom-tailored ones, and the 1950s haircut with a spiffy modern coiffure. In my speech for the PC nomination in Peterborough, I said that Manning's cosmetic makeover would not fool anyone because Reformers still embraced policies more characteristic of the American Republican Party than of traditional Canadian political parties, including the Progressive Conservative Party. We Tories, I said, were much more sensitive to the plight of the socially and economically disadvantaged. I also said that, despite Manning's "Hollywood transformation," the Reform Party leader and his followers remained "just the Social Credit in an Armani suit and with a sixty-dollar haircut." That crack, or a variation, always drew laughs and applause on the campaign trail and led Tory partisans to encourage me to lay it on even thicker. It was advice I sometimes took, escalating the comedy routine yet higher—to everyone's enjoyment, including my own.

Despite Jean Charest's own progressive instincts, under his leadership the national PC platform was far different from what it had been under Robert Stanfield, Joe Clark, or Brian Mulroney. To outflank the Reform Party, the PC Party's policy against gun control, for instance, was much more strongly stated than I personally would have preferred. I wouldn't have cared if every single gun in the country were kept under lock and key or thrown in the Otonabee River, for that matter, except for the environmental implications. During the 1997 federal election in Peterborough, I fairly successfully navigated around those treacherous policy shoals. In the case of gun controls, I did so by stressing the need to respect the rights of hunters and target shooters to keep and bear arms. I also criticized the federal government's incompetent initial efforts to establish a national gun registry. The Reform Party policy on health care stressed replacing Canada's government-funded universal health insurance system with a two-tier private/public health insurance plan. That approach would have blasted the guts out of the country's single-payer health insurance regime—sacred to all progressives, including me. Our own policy in this area was muddled but struck me as dangerously close to the Reform Party's and, therefore, anathema to what I held dear. Whether or not our plank was actually similar to the Reform Party's in this area, I found myself having to defend the party against that charge on public platforms and at the doorstep.

I sometimes couldn't believe my ears as I tried to explain and defend policies of these kinds in the party's national platform. It was as though I were running for a party not my own, perhaps even in a foreign country. I couldn't remember when any significant segment of the population had last found controversial such matters as the principles that buttress Canada's health insurance system. And yet, I now found myself embroiled in debates over something as basic as whether or not all Canadians should be covered for health care irrespective of income. Hadn't this question been answered, affirmatively, once and for all in the mid-1960s with the introduction of medicare? But years of working with Robert Stanfield and Tom Symons on the PC Policy Coordinating Committee had equipped me with policy dexterity that would have made Machiavelli proud, even as it left me ashamed. In retrospect, it is clear that the hard-right minority that had always populated the PC Party presaged the Reformers. At this point, the Reform Party was not only influencing our official policy positions, but also drawing our extremists to its banner as many of them abandoned the PC Party altogether. A mere family squabble was becoming a full-fledged schism.

Earlier, we saw how political scientist Gad Horowitz had described ideology in the Canadian tradition as a circle in which Tories and socialists were joined at each end of the circumference in seeing the role of government in fundamentally the same way:

as an instrument to advance the common good and express national character. In the late 1990s, for the Canadian Conservative Party, the circle was disintegrating. What once looked like the round outline of the sun at sunrise was looking increasingly like the distant horizon at dawn, stretched in a flat line across a hazy plain from left to right with the ends no longer meeting. As a lifelong Conservative and now candidate again, I found myself on the left of that plain looking towards the right, at the other end, and desperately wanting to fall off. I had lost my Axis of Symmetry.

In the 1970s and 1980s, more than 75 percent of Prince Edward Islanders opposed abortion on any ground. The Island's Queen Elizabeth Hospital was one of the only hospitals in the country, and PEI the only province, that refused to perform abortions for any reason—not even rape, incest, or the mother's survival, still less health. The province remained a backwater in this respect until the spring of 2016. As an MP, I consistently received more correspondence hostile to abortion than on any other issue. Sometimes, I would get dozens in one day. Each was personally written, not mass-produced or orchestrated by some special interest group, as so often happens on certain issues. So, I had no trouble toeing the anti-abortion line in Peterborough, where it was virtually state policy, just as I had always felt I needed to do in my Island campaigns. Today, I think government has no business mucking around in such personal/philosophical/theological territory. Decisions relating to women's reproductive rights should be left entirely up to them and their doctors. Government has no legitimate role except in the rarest of circumstances. On abortion, my position evolved over time. I eventually found my original stand untenable, even long before I hypocritically held firm to it on the campaign trail. I shudder when thinking of the things I said, and the sanctimony with which I said them, to curry voters' favour. Ironically, my Halifax-based daughter, Kelly, with her law partner Nasha Nijhawan, successfully sued the PEI government over its abortion policy on behalf of the Abortion Access Now PEI advocacy group. Facing almost certain defeat on "equal protection under the law" constitutional grounds, pursuant to the Charter of Rights and Freedoms, the PEI government has instituted a women's reproductive health centre that will offer a range of abortion services, including counselling.

For me, such enlightenment came too late. The moral superiority I exuded in advancing my former position on abortion soon characterized the post-merger Conservative Party's orthodoxy right across the board on issues, not just abortion. I found the party's attendant hypocrisy revolting—demanding a smaller and less intrusive role for government while insisting that government control a whole range of wholly private matters. The party's conservatism has been transformed into an American Republican–type ideology foreign to the Conservative Party's traditional bedrock of values and policies. That "new" ideology holds that government is typically bad except to force everybody to be good, and is rarely good when trying to prevent anybody's life from being bad. Where is a sense of community in that? When did the federal government's role become moral hector and enforcer for the self-righteous few, and cease being an agent of the common good? The New Puritans had arrived and were setting up camp, not at Plymouth Rock in Massachusetts, but in the Reform Party of Canada. My paternal forebears had not fired rifles and drawn swords south of the border in the 1770s, as United Empire Loyalists, to fight for *those* kinds of values. They launched new lives in Prince Edward Island to escape them and to nourish and preserve their own values—Tory community-focused values symbolized by the Crown. With their blood pulsating in my veins, I felt the same. And still do. To this day, I see in my extended family, including my three daughters—

maybe especially them—a similar mindset. Now, with the historic Progressive Conservative Party tossed into the dumpster of history, more than the national coalition it constituted has been shattering—East and West, English and French, conservative and liberal. A community within the community—my grand old Tory party—is hanging in the balance. Maybe it has already been hanged—and drawn and quartered. In the 1997 federal election, not just in Peterborough but across the land, the sun was, indeed, setting on the traditional Conservative Party of Canada. Its very soul was on the line. As the election ended, I sensed my own political soul was edging ever closer to that line—and not just wanting to fall off, but needing to hurl itself off.

On election night, I went to Peter Adams's campaign headquarters to congratulate him and his workers on their fine campaign and convincing victory. Peter and I hugged. That had never happened between me and an opponent in any of the other five elections I had fought. This was my last campaign as a candidate. I was never tempted to run again. Nor would I play a major role in anyone else's campaign, as I had often done before. I did not feel this way because I was embittered or jaded or because my options had expired; even if true, that could not be farther from my mind. I was now fifty-two years old. I had been first elected to Parliament almost two decades earlier. Now I felt I needed to take a different path while still young enough, energetic enough, and motivated enough to seek and handle new challenges. Most of all, I wanted to retrieve a degree of anonymity and privacy in those parts of the country where I had become especially well known. A high-profile Cabinet minister, as I was, is exposed to hundreds of thousands of people in a single parliamentary session. In name and face recognition, I was not a Brian Mulroney or a John Turner or an Ed Broadbent, but everywhere I went across Canada, strangers recognized me, particularly from TV coverage of the Commons. Fewer and fewer did with each passing month after I left Parliament. As consul general in Boston, however, I had maintained a high profile in Atlantic Canada and in certain circles elsewhere in Canada, too. In PEI, one's profile never diminishes even after death! To proceed to the next stage of my life, whatever that might be, I now wanted the public not to know me at all. I needed the time and space to get to know myself.

After failing to beat Jean Chrétien in the 1997 election, Jean Charest asked me to explore, on a top-secret basis, opportunities for him to come to Harvard University to boost his academic and business credentials, for he told me he was contemplating leaving politics for the corporate world. After much research, including personal inquiries on campus, I assembled a substantial dossier of options and sent it to him through confidential back channels. Soon afterwards, I discovered that he had announced his intention to seek the leadership of the Liberal Party of Quebec. I thought, good for him; good for Quebec. Despite later political problems, he was the right premier at the time for Quebec. The two were a great fit; unfortunately for him, he and the provincial Liberals much less so. This incompatibility was, I think, at the root of his later difficulties and ultimate defeat, both as premier and in his own Sherbrooke riding. Alleged illegal backroom wheeling and dealing and collusion by government and party operatives stalked the premier throughout his fateful last campaign.

No doubt, the 2012 Quebec election outcome dashed any hope that Jean Charest might have had of one day becoming prime minister of Canada. I suspect that, deep down, he had set his sights on eventually residing at 24 Sussex Drive. With such natural talent and obvious commitment to public service—advancing Canadian unity, in particular—he would not have been true to himself to rule out that possibility. Many a less talented politician had sought the post, and at least one (Kim Campbell) had won it, albeit only briefly. Whatever his long-term future, in or out of politics—my bet is the latter—federalists across the country, especially in Quebec, should never forget this about Jean Charest: he was the leading champion in that province for a united Canada for more than two decades. I am proud to call him a former colleague and, more important, a personal friend. Canadian Tories need to remind themselves of the role their party played over many generations in founding and building our country and in keeping it united. Jean Charest is in that venerable Tory tradition. If the merger of the Canadian Conservative Party of old and the Reform/Canadian Alliance Party extinguished—or even just diminished—this tradition, a vital part of the Tory Party's soul disappeared. In which case, the country also lost something precious: a strong force for federalism and national unity. That fact is no less true in light of the sovereigntists' humiliating defeat and the Liberals' landslide victory under their leader Philippe Couillard in the April 2014 provincial election. Like death and taxes, the national unity issue will always be with us. Whether the Conservative Party of Canada will ever again be a central player in keeping the country intact is, alas, far less certain.

# Experience, Wisdom Gained

By the end of the 1997 federal election, I had fought six campaigns as a PC candidate, half of them successful. From my first in 1979 (in PEI) to my last in 1997 (in Peterborough), almost two decades of my life had passed. I spent most of this period either in Parliament (including Cabinet) or as a candidate. I learned a lot in that period about politics and, I hope, about life. I also learned a great deal about party policy *in politics* that I did not learn either at all or not nearly as well *in political science*.

I have described the Stanfield/Symons partnership—between a national party leader and a university president—as transforming the policies, and thereby the public image, of the Progressive Conservative Party of Canada. One of the things I learned in a long career as a PC Party policy functionary and later as a politician is this: in voters' minds, any political party's policies are typically inseparable from the personalities of its leader and MPs and candidates, even spouses. Any one such factor in a party's success, or lack of it, gets inextricably mixed with many others in a witch's brew then impossible to separate. The impact of policy might well be the most difficult of all ingredients to isolate and assess. Like dry-cleaning fluid, policy tends to absorb, and then make part of itself, everything within reach.

Until the early 1990s and the rise of the Reform/Canadian Alliance Party and the Bloc Québécois, all major national political parties in Canada sought the support of many of the same voters, or "demographic targets." They were accessing, basically, the identical polling information about what voters thought and wanted. In light of polls and other sources of political intelligence, they tried to avoid taking extreme positions, whether on the left or right. None of the major parties wanted to alienate the swing voters—those not part of its own, or another party's, entrenched base. In a political environment of this kind, traditional voting patterns, how well a particular party or candidate is organized and funded, the standing of the party in power, and the popularity of the individual riding candidate relative to that of competitors—all such factors, rather than policy per se, tip elections in one direction or another. As often as not, barring some burning issue of the day, policy constitutes only one factor among many that motivate voters to support or oppose a political party or candidate. Even when policy or an issue dominates a campaign (for example, wage-and-price controls in the 1974 election), it is enmeshed in other factors (in that case, primarily leadership). Ultimately, getting elected depends on the candidate's ability to convince voters that he or she shares their values, is on their side, will advance their interests, and, in general, is more competent or reliable or likeable than the alternatives. Policy can advance or retard any of these objectives, but rarely does it elect or defeat anyone on its own.

The complex array of factors that influences how most people vote is embodied in a party's leader. The leader symbolizes the party as a whole. Like policy, those who stand with the leader—principally, the MPs or candidates whom the voter sees on TV—can enhance or hurt the leader's appeal and, therefore, the party's. At the end of the day, though, a party's success or failure rests largely on the leader's shoulders. In 1968, for example, Robert Stanfield assembled, to that point, the strongest team of candidates in the history of the PC Party—the so-called Dream Team. It included, in Quebec alone: Marcel Faribault, president of Montreal's Trust Général; André Gagnon, president of the Montreal School Board; Yves Ryan, brother of the editor of *Le Devoir* and a political catch in his own right; Julien Chouinard, Quebec's deputy minister of justice; and Paul Trépanier, the president of the Conservative organization of Quebec. In Ontario, business tycoon Wallace McCutcheon resigned from the Senate to run; Earl Brownridge, president of American Motors (Canada), ran; and brilliant advertising guru Dalton Camp moved from the party's backrooms to the campaign trail as a candidate himself (in Toronto). In Manitoba, Duff Roblin resigned as premier to seek a seat in Parliament for his former leadership rival. E. Davie Fulton, another 1967 leadership rival, reoffered in British Columbia. And so forth. That extraordinary team of PC candidates in 1968 helped compensate for Stanfield's own lack of electoral appeal compared to Pierre Trudeau's. It was not nearly enough, however, to overcome the Trudeaumania that swept the land. Indeed, every one of the aforementioned candidates was defeated, most of them badly. A baseball maxim says that managers are only as good as their players. In politics, leaders have to be *better* than their "players." At the end of the day, the voter's decision comes down to leadership and his or her overall political mood, which itself, like a Rorschach test, gets reflected in the voter's response to leadership choices. If a leader can't connect with voters on the "shares my values" level, how he or she tries to do so on other levels is doomed to fail before a single speech is given, an ad aired, or a hand shaken after the writ is dropped. Irrespective of how well it is marketed, a dog food that dogs don't like won't sell.

Ultimately, Canadians want in their national leader, at a minimum, competence and sensitivity to their concerns. Qualities such as great oratory and charisma are not what voters necessarily demand, however integral those qualities can be to a leader's capacity to inspire. Likeability is highly desirable, but overrated when competence and caring are projected. Besides his mother and dog, who ever loved Mackenzie King? But I have been told by contemporaries of mine whose parents knew King personally that he had considerable charm in private. Canadians, however, hardly ever saw that side of the man, and it wasn't why they voted for him. And yet, loveable or not, he was the country's most electorally successful national party leader. People want to like their leaders, but, to them, it's more important that they and their families be fed, housed, kept healthy, educated, trained, and protected from lawlessness at home and wars abroad. Citizens look to their leaders for help, not hugs. They certainly do not seek ideological purity, least of all the sort they do not themselves embrace or possibly even understand. The Conservative Party of Canada went badly wrong when it ignored this tenet of politics while entrusted with the governance of the land from February 2006 to November 2015.

In 1984, once voters decided they wanted to change government, after an entire generation of Liberal power (save the nine-month Joe Clark interregnum), the decisive factor was not that Brian Mulroney's candidates were superior to John Turner's. They were not. But Mulroney's fellow MPs had projected competence and caring in the lead-up to the election, especially in Question Period. Our perceived reliability made it easier for voters to act on their eagerness for change. That the PC Party championed progressive policies—or, at least, avoided extreme positions that would have spooked voters—advanced the same end. That said, the Tory Party did not seal the deal with Canadian voters in 1984 through sound policy any more than it did so with first-rate candidates. Rather, Canadians judged that Brian Mulroney—all things considered (including his platform and running mates)—was an acceptable alternative to John Turner as prime minister in a throw-the-bums-out election. The election pivoted around the shepherd more than the flock, the apostle more than the creed, the herald of miracles more than the belief by either disciples or potential converts that they would actually be saved any time soon. No wonder Albert Einstein said politics is more difficult than physics. Human nature always is. Unlike relativity, political phenomena cannot be reduced to a mathematical formula, much less simple verbal explanations. Sometimes, it just comes down to who the voters feels in their gut is most like them, if not in personality then in values.

Did most Canadians really see in Stephen Harper and the government he headed either themselves or their vision of and for the country? That Canadians ended up with a certain kind of government between 2006 and 2015—possibly by default—doesn't necessarily mean that the voters chose the ideological and policy road the Harperites proceeded to follow. It could be argued that, in successive elections, until voters became wise to the deceit, Harper and his people engaged in a bait-and-switch by appropriating the Conservative Party's illustrious name following the 2003 merger. And then, the new party proved not to be anything like the old. In light of the Harper government's record, it would have been far more politically honest had the Progressive Conservative name been scrapped altogether—not just the "Progressive" half. Now, the Conservative Party—through new leadership, new policies, and a new slate of candidates—must seek to restore Canadians' faith in this once-great national institution by selecting a far different direction and, I argue, by restoring the dual name that expresses it.

As a politician, I had a good run with the cards fate dealt me—basking in success when the cards were good and I played them well, struggling with defeat when the cards turned bad or I played them poorly, or both. After my last run, in 1997, I became politically dormant. I was not afraid that future cards would be deuces: I just lost interest in playing the game. Perhaps the greatest gift that politics bestowed on me is the maturity to understand that there is much more to life *than* that game. I was beginning to appreciate fully the benefits of having a real life, especially with my three daughters. This personal epiphany was the strongest set of cards the gods could ever have placed in my hand.

# Chapter 31

# CONSERVATIVES IN THE THIRD MILLENNIUM

*Before I was married, I had three theories about raising children.*
*Now I have three children and no theories.*

—John Wilmot, Earl of Rochester (1647–80)

## The Conservative Party Merger

I am not a male equivalent of *Sunset Boulevard*'s Norma Desmond, the fictional former silent-screen star pining for the return of a bygone era of pantomime movies and Tinsel Town glamour. I was not a political superstar, just a fast-rising one whose light was snuffed out by a combination of factors: bad luck (the anti–free trade Liberal sweep in Atlantic Canada in 1988); bad timing (John Turner's savaging of Mulroney in the free trade debate at the end of that campaign); some bad personal missteps (principally, not anticipating the lethal shot from spoiler candidate David Weale in my own riding); and, perhaps, certain inborn personality drawbacks, not least an inability to reach out for help when in trouble.

My world now is not the Orpheum but the orphanage. My once-great Progressive Conservative Party has been hijacked by, essentially, the latter-day hard-right Social Credit. The new entity is more a US Republican-style conservative party than the Canadian conservative-liberal coalition that survived for generations long after its original incarnation under the visionary leadership of Sir John A. Macdonald and Georges-Étienne Cartier. What survives today of the traditional Canadian Conservative Party mixes an American-type right-wing ideology with fundamentalist religious values in the mode of Social Credit founder William "Bible Bill" Aberhart and his successor and disciple, evangelist Ernest Manning. The latter was Social Credit premier of Alberta from 1943 to 1968 and father of Preston Manning, who wrought all this. The new Conservative Party is nothing I recognize as part of either my own political tradition or that of my family. Now, it is no longer my party. I am an orphan; I no longer have a political home. Not this one, anyway. The party of Stephen Harper was to that of Sir John A. Macdonald—and Robert Borden and Arthur Meighen and, yes, even "Rogue Tory" John Diefenbaker and, certainly, Robert Stanfield and Joe Clark and Brian Mulroney—what weak tea is to tequila: a thin brew for any Tory who wants his or her party to represent more than an aggregate of private vested interests removed from any sense of community or of commune with Canadian generations past and those yet born.

In 1987, Preston Manning founded, and became the only leader of, the Reform Party of Canada. Manning had run unsuccessfully as a Social Credit candidate in the 1965 federal election. In 2000, Reform evolved into the Canadian Alliance Party (formally, the Canadian Reform Conservative Alliance). In 2003, that party merged with the Progressive Conservative Party to form today's Conservative Party. The rationale for the merger was to unite the right under a single party banner using this historic name. When the merger occurred, more than the Progressive part of the dual PC name was dropped: the progressive tradition reflected in that name was dumped, too. I could understand not wanting the conservative vote split, virtually ensuring Liberal Party hegemony far into the future. Indeed, soon after Jean Charest became PC leader for the 1997 federal election, I urged him to pursue that very merger idea. But, even in a marriage, one partner should not subsume his or her soul in the other's essence, as my party did in its impetuous Nevada-style marital plunge with the Canadian Alliance Party. Jeffrey Simpson, in the *Globe and Mail*, described the current Conservative Party as "warmed-over Reform Party."[1] That's it in an oven mitt. I have said that Robert Stanfield, despite the staid exterior, was unpredictable. He invariably exceeded expectations, beat the odds, confounded the odds-makers. But I am certain that he would have hated what his Conservative Party has become. I do.

The last year I was Canada's consul general in Boston, Preston Manning, as Reform Party leader, spoke at the Mackenzie King Seminar at Harvard University. It was the spring of 1993. A national election would be held six months later. In that election, Manning's party would fall short by only three parliamentary seats of forming the Official Opposition, with him as Opposition leader. It is a distinction he would gain in the next election, in 1997. All this happened primarily at the expense of the pre-merger PC Party, which saw much of its hard-right faction bolt ranks and join the insurgents. As a regular at the Mackenzie King Seminar, I attended to hear the new Reform Party leader. Manning was charming, eloquent, informative, and, to the surprise of many, urbane and intellectually agile. He easily held his own with the "Hahvahd" attendees. Manning's message, basically, was that (a) western Canada had gotten a raw deal from Confederation; (b) over the generations, Quebec and Ontario had dominated the country's decision-making and hoarded its wealth at the expense of the West (the other regions didn't seem to exist in his mind, let alone count); (c) a revolution was needed in how the country had been governed for over a century; (d) a completely new team of men (no mention of women), especially from the West, had to take over; and, (e) until all that and more happened...well, the apocalypse. And, worse, continued socialism.

As I listened to Preston Manning bemoan his own region's exclusion from national political power in my country, I started to count privately the number of westerners in the federal Cabinet in which I myself had served. Out of thirty-nine, excluding the prime minister, there had been thirteen—one-third the total. What's more, seven of them constituted almost half the Cabinet's fifteen-member all-powerful Priorities and Planning Committee—in effect, the inner Cabinet. Harvard's Canadian guest was describing a country—my own—that sounded more foreign to me than the actual foreign country in which he was speaking. His political description of Canada was false. I asked myself, is this man delusional, or does he just not know what he is talking about?

I was periodically asked to give lectures and seminars at Harvard or serve as a resource person. I was invited to do so both as consul general and as Canada's former environment minister with a residual reputation and profile in the United States. At the Mackenzie King Seminar, however, unless giving the presentation myself, I typically remained silent, yielding the floor to others, especially students. I would sometimes pose a question if the discussion lagged or needed a new direction. But usually I remained mute. This time, I sat through Manning's remarks in a simmer, then a burble, and, finally, as my blood pressure rose and vessels risked bursting (the Irish in me!), a high boil—with the top ready to fly in every direction. I had heard enough. I just could not take any more. Let External Affairs—or the prime minister, or whoever—fire me. The consul general job just wasn't worth a stroke. I needed to speak up—now.

I began my response to Preston Manning—the first among all the others—by reminding him that the Reform Party had launched itself with the slogan "The West Wants In." The party had shelved the slogan to broaden its appeal outside western Canada, but Manning's message at Harvard, as across Canada, was still essentially the same. That message, like the slogan, implied that, in Canada, the Reform Party leader's region was kept "outside the tent," as I translated it. The Reform leader nodded affirmatively, with a nervous smile, obviously wondering what I had in my arsenal. I looked across the room at the professors and students and other attendees, about half of them American, and said: "I am Canada's consul general here in New England. But before that, I was a minister of the Crown in the Government of Canada in an important portfolio, the Environment." And then I named every single westerner in a senior portfolio in the Cabinet of which I had been a member—by heart in alphabetical order, and with their respective portfolios, committing just one error in the sequence: Harvie Andre, Pat Carney, Joe Clark, Ray Hnatyshyn, Bill McKnight, and on and on and—stopping momentarily for dramatic effect—"the finance minister and *the deputy prime minister of Canada*, Don Mazankowski of Alberta, your own province, Sir! He, who, with the prime minister, runs the whole damn show!" Then I added, as if my Irish dander had not ventilated enough: "When I was minister of the environment, the chairman of one of the two most powerful committees of Cabinet, *Social*, whose boots I had to lick every day to get one measly penny for my programs or the door opened an inch for my legislation, was none other than Jake Epp of your sister province of Manitoba, Sir—yet another westerner!" And, for good measure: "If that kind of western power at the Cabinet table is what it means to some westerners to be 'outside the tent'—well, as a Maritimer, from one of Canada's two poorest provinces and from the most impoverished region, I'll take being 'outside the tent' any damn day of the year!"

The room fell silent. More silence. Then guarded applause. Finally, loud sustained applause (and is that a "here, here!" I hear?). It was the first time I had ever heard the crowd at the Mackenzie King Seminar erupt. The ovation was not for me. Nor for anything in particular I had said. Nor even for how I had said it. The ovation was for the fact I had said it at all. That's because I expressed what everyone else in the room—especially the westerners, and there were several—felt in the gut: Canada did not deserve this ideological dung from the Reform Party leader. Manning's polite, but subdued, response—the most pathetic I had heard in a long time from any politician—was: "Well, all those senior ministers you mentioned might be from western Canada. But they aren't really westerners anymore, because they've 'gone Ottawa, gone native.'" The Reform Party leader was now condemning westerners for being at the centre of power—in effect, selling out. Manning had moved the goal posts so far that they were right off the playing field.

And this is what the grand old party of Sir John A. Macdonald and Georges-Étienne Cartier was becoming? It is one thing to oppose a particular government party's policies. Or, for that matter, its overall program and direction. A democracy could not exist, let alone thrive, without vigorous debate about policy and, yes, ideology. It is a completely different animal, however, when the attack is launched against "Ottawa" as an institution allegedly hostile to one part of the country or one community of Canadians. The federal government was created to advance the interests of all Canadians and to represent the country as a whole. Attacking it as an institution is far different from attacking any specific government or political party or its policies. Attacks against "Ottawa" are, in effect, attacks against other Canadians communally. And that is the case no matter how many votes this practice might harvest in the attacker's own patch based on a narrow ideological vision.

If the Preston Mannings of the country wish to oppose either a particular government or the way a succession of governments has governed Canada, they have every right. Running candidates to convince voters that their position is correct is also their right. Voters then decide. If the party elects enough candidates to form a government, it can change the country's direction based on its platform. That's provided sufficient support can be garnered in Parliament and, in the case of constitutional change, among the provinces and territories as well. But pitting one region against another, or one cultural or linguistic community against another, by demonizing "Ottawa" as the enemy of the particular sub-community being appealed to— that is not the hallmark of a democrat; it's the refuge of a demagogue.

Let's call a spade a spade here. The Reform/Canadian Alliance Party had its roots in ethnic hostility. The initial shoots came from anti-French, anti-bilingual, anti-metric (read European), and anti-Quebec pockets of resentment in Alberta and, to a varying extent, elsewhere across western Canada. Any Conservative leader can ride a mechanical bull of political emotional fever—against big government, against Ottawa, against the rest of Canada, against other Canadians, against other regions, or against a particular province (usually Quebec). Throw in opposition to bilingualism, gay rights, gun control, and environmentalism for good measure. Or whatever else turns the crank of ditto-heads who get their political wisdom from ranting radio talk-show hosts, rather than from reading or, better still, from becoming truly engaged in the political process. And by political engagement, I don't mean the world of wing-nuts in the blogosphere. Such a leader, by pandering to the hard core of fellow zealots, by focusing resources on a limited number of ridings (typically in one region), by pedalling a toxic agenda fuelled with hate, and by riling up emotions against an artificially created enemy, can be almost guaranteed the sixty or seventy parliamentary seats required to make him or her national leader of the Opposition. But, under normal circumstances, a leader of this sort will get no more parliamentary seats than that—certainly, not enough to become prime minister, as Manning and the Reform Party discovered.

In 2000, Stockwell Day defeated Preston Manning for the leadership of the Canadian Alliance Party. That party replaced the Reform Party in the Canadian hard-right's effort to repackage itself following the movement's failure to appeal to Canadians beyond its original ideological and regional base. Ironically, Day took even more extreme positions on issues than Manning had taken while Reform Party leader, particularly against multiculturalism, immigration, and bilingualism, with predictably disastrous results outside true believers, mostly in western Canada. The Canadian Alliance Party's failure to improve on Reform's electoral record—in vote-rich Ontario, in particular—prompted the principals to dissolve the new party, seek a merger with the PC Party, and form the current Conservative Party as a united right-of-centre political force. Within a decade or so, then, this political species mutated three times in hopes of thriving in a generally hostile jungle.

From the start, Robert Stanfield knew that he could always win a certain minimum number of parliamentary seats by firing up right-wing extremists across the country on hot-button issues like immigration and bilingualism. That was especially the case—but not exclusively—within his own party. And yet, he was never tempted to ride that mechanical bull. Nor would Tom Symons ever have agreed to help intellectualize or articulate or give academic credibility to an electoral strategy or appeal based on this sort of tribal ideological extremism. Memo to Conservative Ground Control: start with your hard-core base, but if you don't expand it through policies broadly supported across Canada, as opposed to extremist political theology with limited appeal only in parts of the country, you'll end up like Preston Manning—in political exile. Political and ideological extremism is a losing formula for the long term in liberal democratic countries such as Canada.

Unbeknownst to me, present in the room for the Preston Manning seminar at Harvard was a Foreign Service officer from Ottawa in training at the university. He transcribed my remarks as I spoke, transmitted them to External Affairs headquarters in the capital, praised my performance, and expressed wonder why more people didn't confront Manning in such a way. I did not get fired.

# Conservative Party Tradition

If one theme is clear from this book, it should be my respect—indeed, affection—for the Conservative Party of Robert Stanfield and Tom Symons and all the countless others who fought throughout the generations to keep it loyal to the best values and traditions of its founder and greatest leader, Sir John A. Macdonald. Brian Mulroney frequently and rightly describes Sir John A. as "in a class of his own" among Tory chiefs. The reason my family, on both the McMillan and McQuaid sides, were Tory since the beginning of time is not that we blindly followed that path regardless of where it led or who led it. It is because, allowing for a wrong turn now and then, the path was where we wanted to go and where we wanted our fellow citizens to travel as a community. Until now.

To understand how far and fast the grand old Conservative Party of Canada has fallen, an observer need look no farther than my three daughters—a revealing case study if ever there was one. Kelly, Becky, and Emily are the daughters of a former federal Tory Cabinet minister. They are nieces of the former senior policy advisor to a Tory prime minister. They are paternal granddaughters of a distinguished PEI doctor described in a Canadian national magazine as the television face and voice of the Tory Party throughout a generation of federal elections in PEI. They are maternal grand-nieces of a number of Tory candidates in various provincial elections in years past in PEI. And yet, despite this long and rich Tory pedigree, since becoming eligible to vote not one of my girls has ever cast a single Conservative Party ballot in a national election following the PC/Reform or Canadian Alliance Party merger in 2003.

My girls continue to say they do not intend to vote Conservative in any future election. I did not influence them. They decided on their own. Love me as they do, love them as I do, I can't influence them to stop slamming the doors on my aging Nissan Altima. Like the Earl of Rochester (quoted at the beginning of this chapter), I have no theory about managing three children, least of all how they think. Intelligent, already well educated and read and travelled, in my girls' case, and getting more so all the time, they have minds of their own—and political antennae of their own, too. Those antennae are *not* catching signals from what passes as the Canadian Conservative Party in their time. The reason is not that the new generation of McMillans (or of the equally passionate Tory McQuaids, on my mother's side) have changed. The reason, instead, is that the *Conservative Party* has changed—beyond recognition. And beyond our ability to see in the party either ourselves or our values and what we believe are our country's historic values.

Just as I do not view myself as a Norma Desmond–type romanticist, yearning for the return of a bygone era, neither do I wish to play the tiresome role of "former Mulroney Cabinet minister turned Conservative Party critic." But I am proud of the contribution that the traditional Conservative Party of Canada made to Canada over the generations. And I am equally proud now to stand up for the values and kinds of policies that my former party consistently represented, under different leaders throughout its storied past, to make the country and the Canadian community strong for everybody. More as a *cri de coeur* than an attack, what follows is intended as a plaintiff message to all Tories who believe as I do that the party needs to correct course towards—in the words of Abraham Lincoln in a different context—"the better angels of our nature." I hope my message will also resonate with other Canadians who might never have supported the party, and might never do so in the future. But perhaps they share my belief that the entire country loses when one of its great national institutions is damaged the way the historic Conservative Party has been since the 2003 merger with the Reform/Canadian Alliance Party. I know I am not alone, among either Conservatives or other Canadians, in believing that the party's soul has been sullied from the merger. My cry is that other Conservatives, and indeed other Canadians, will add their voices to this message from the heart. Then, I will have done my job, my final one for the party that I supported all my adult life until recently—my retirement from "stardom."

·

———————

The fundamental question that the Canadian Conservative Party has to ask itself is how it views the proper role of government in society. The question is not whether there should be bigger government with more public services or smaller government with fewer. The question is even more basic than that. It is whether government is, by nature, good or bad. In Ronald Reagan's first Inaugural Address, he said: "Government is not a solution to our problem, government *is* the problem." Ever since Reagan uttered those words, in 1981, his message has been the mantra of American conservatives and of far too many Canadian Conservatives as well.

Those who make a virtue of hating government, big or small, are happy with their stance until their own house catches fire and they need the fire department, they are robbed or assaulted and need the police, are injured or sick and need medical care, have a school-age child and need a teacher, fear terrorists and demand tighter security—all provided, directly or indirectly, by government. Then, government isn't a problem.

It's the solution. But no one ever accused the anti-government zealots of consistency, let alone intellectual honesty. William Cohen is a former Republican senator from Maine who, in the name of bipartisanship, later served as Bill Clinton's defense secretary. "Government is the enemy until you need a friend," said Cohen.[2] That's true of every liberal democratic society, including Canada. Is such an anti-government ideology and mindset inspiring the grand old Canadian Tory party in its new incarnation? This is the party that gave birth to Canada. It's the party that mobilized public resources to harness the country's vast geography and energy to realize great national goals and ambitions. It's the party that, under successive Conservative prime ministers, helped knit together Canada's sprawling demi-continent, which Mackenzie King said has "too much geography, just as some countries have too much history." It's the party that, in creating such supranational institutions as the Canadian Pacific and Canadian National Railways and the Bank of Canada and the CBC and the RCMP and the Canadian Wheat Board and the National Research Council, benefited every Canadian through state activism. And the party did so, not as an exercise in either fiscal indiscipline or socialist excess, but in the spirit of classic conservative values articulated by pioneering thinkers through the centuries. Those thinkers include the eighteenth-century conservative politician and philosopher Edmund Burke. Towering Conservative politicians who acted on those values at home and abroad include Benjamin Disraeli, Winston Churchill, Harold Macmillan, and, in our own country, Sir John A. Macdonald, Sir Robert Borden, Arthur Meighen, and R. B. Bennett right through the generations to John Diefenbaker and Brian Mulroney closer to our own time.

The concept that society needs shared institutions and resources to advance and protect the interests common to everyone—not just the rich and powerful—is so ingrained in the political culture of liberal democracies throughout the world, including Canada, that one could say this principle links classical political philosophies of diverse kinds, conservative and liberal and socialist alike. John Stuart Mill (1806–73), the great British liberal philosopher and economist and moral and political theorist, said: "The idea is essentially repulsive of a society only held together by the relations and feelings arising out of pecuniary interests."[3] Conservative John A. Macdonald said much the same thing—and often. What's more, he acted on his words.

Nowhere has the Conservative Party of Canada nowadays been more disloyal to this rich tradition of conservative thought and political activism than in the environmental area. Let it serve as another case study of how far and fast the party has fallen from the high plateau on which it had operated for over a century. Brian Mulroney used to say that US action on acid rain was urgently needed not only for the sake of our natural heritage—the health of our lands, the purity of our waters, and the cleanness of our air. But action was also needed, he said, as a "litmus test" of good will towards Canada by the United States, then the source of half our environmental degradation from this lethal pollutant. Mulroney could have said with equal truth that a litmus test of a *Conservative* government's loyalty to *conservative* principles is its approach to the environment—in fact, whether it has a *conservation* ethic at all. The environmental ethic is captured in the seven "R's"—reduce, reuse, recycle, renew, respect, recreate, and reform." Aren't these principles classically *conservative*?

In his *Reflections on the Revolution in France* (1790) and in other writings and in public addresses, Edmund Burke articulated the virtue of organic development— what he would term on occasion *sustainable practice*. It's the principle that society governs itself best by gradual and moderate reform, rather than by immediate and total replacement. The principle draws, he said, on the wisdom of experience with an eye to future progress. Indeed, Burke argued, such is needed to ensure progress and avoid "regress," for the sake of future generations as much as for one's own. "[A] progressive practice requires not only the yields of past effort but also the intelligent application of mind to their further development if progress, rather than regress, is to result." The proper way to avoid "shakes to civil society," Burke counselled, was to "consult and follow your experience," for experience is a condition of continuity of mind, and, on the basis of mind, of a "sustainable practice."[4] This conservative thinker produced that seminal insight two centuries before the landmark World Commission on Environment and Development (the Brundtland Commission) in the late 1980s articulated the identical principle in its own way. The Commission urged decision-makers around the world to apply the principle to global and national and local environment-and-economy planning in our own time. This UN-sponsored body expressed Burke's principle as *sustainable development*, which it defined as "development that meets the needs of the present without compromising the ability of future generations to meet their own needs." Pope Francis said, in a Twitter post in early April 2015: "We need to care for the earth so that it may continue, as God willed, to be a source of life for the entire human family." The man who took his papal name after St. Francis of Assisi, the patron saint of nature and environmentalists, could not have expressed classic conservatism any more succinctly—or on higher moral ground. By such a standard, the Stephen Harper government failed miserably as a true conservative government. And Conservatives under his leadership failed equally miserably as a true conservative party. I am not alone among traditional Canadian Conservatives in believing this. A few months ago, I received a personal e-mail from a former Cabinet colleague of mine. My correspondent had held senior portfolios, and been in the inner sanctum, of both the Clark and Mulroney governments. He wrote: "I grow more alarmed every day at the perversion of our former political party, but realize my capacity to do something about that is sharply limited now." *Former* political party, he said! Clearly, I am not the only Tory, nor the only former national Conservative Cabinet minister, who feels orphaned.

A sense of collective purpose and responsibility and commitment, over the generations and among governments and citizens, was essential to progress on the environmental front in such areas as acid rain. At pivotal times in our country's history, the Conservative Party was the instrument of that collective sense, not only in the environmental field, but also in many others—indeed, in creating and expanding and developing the country itself. As Canada faces some of its greatest challenges in the environment, as in other fields, both domestically and globally, is that role for the Conservative Party itself now but history?

# The Environment and Conservative Politics

When Brian Mulroney plucked me from the Tourism portfolio to serve as environment minister in 1985, the PM was appalled by the reputation his government had earned on the environment in its first year in office. He demanded change, both in the Environment portfolio and in the government's record. The prime minister acted swiftly to right his government's course, not only because to have done otherwise would have been politically calamitous, but, even more important to him, because he believed the country urgently needed to do better in this critical area of our national life.

The prime minister sensed I could rise to the challenge of setting the government, and the country, on a new course for the environment. Almost four years later, I had held the portfolio longer than any other person except Liberal John Roberts, who served the same length of time as I did, almost to the day.[5] Around this time, I was grilled on CTV's *Canada AM* public affairs program by journalist Nancy Wilson. It was at a godawful early-morning hour—too early for a politician on live television. One false step by a minister could doom the government, at least in Question Period later in the day. In the face of what seemed a major breakthrough on acid rain with the Reagan administration, Wilson attacked Mulroney as a Johnny-come-lately to the environment. I shot back with a litany of environmental issues on which the PM had led the government, not just followed me. "I have had more support from this prime minister on the environment than any previous environment minister has ever had from any previous prime minister," I told Wilson. Bruce Phillips, the PMO's director of communications, phoned me at CTV's Ottawa studio faster than I could whip off my microphone: "Why isn't every single one of our ministers talking like that about the PM?" he exploded on the line. The truth of my statement on *Canada AM* was validated when, in April 2006, Brian Mulroney was named the greenest prime minister in Canadian history by a broad-based politically independent panel of environmentalists from across Canada. The Conservative Party then went from being led by the greenest prime minister in Canadian history *in protecting the environment* to being led, in the person of Stephen Harper, by one of the "greenest" prime ministers in Canadian history in his commitment to the federal government's Almighty Dollar *at the expense of the environment.*

In the spring of 2010, United Nations Secretary-General Ban Ki-moon scolded the government of Stephen Harper for using worldwide economic and financial difficulties as an excuse not to act on global warming. Pressed by the Opposition parties to make climate change a theme of the G-20 meeting that Harper hosted in June 2010, Harper responded that climate change would be discussed but "the main issue will be the economy, the global economy." It was as though, to him, the economy and the environment had nothing to do with each other. That perspective flouted what the Brundtland Commission argued. It also violated the tenets of Burkean conservatism. The Conservative Party has come so far since Brian Mulroney was leader—downhill.

In 2002, in a letter to Canadian Alliance Party members, Stephen Harper called the Kyoto Protocol on global warming a "socialist conspiracy." Prior to Harper's arrival on the political scene, what Canadian Tory prime minister ever expressed himself in such terms, least of all about protecting the planet from environmental Armageddon? I was horrified when the Harper government announced, at the end of 2011, its decision to withdraw formally from the International Kyoto Protocol on greenhouse gas emissions that scientists around the world almost unanimously agree cause climate change. Global warming is the single greatest threat to the planet's survival and, therefore, to Canada's. It is worse than even terrorism or nuclear holocaust. The danger is compounded by its insidious nature, like a poisonous snake whose skin texture and colour blend seamlessly with the landscape from which it springs and pounces to inflict its mortal blow. Indeed, on February 22, 2016, scientists associated with the Potsdam Institute for Climate Impact Research in Germany released studies that showed that climate change–causing emissions primarily from the burning of fossil fuels are causing oceans to rise at the fastest rate since at least the founding of ancient Rome. It has been widely documented that the years 2013, 2014, and 2015 were the warmest on record, each one warmer than the previous year in large parts of the planet.

On September 21, 2014, over 400,000 people (many of them mothers with their children) marched in the streets of New York City to demand action on climate change. Similar protests were held in other major cities throughout the world, including my hometown, Charlottetown—not historically known for crowds storming the barricades with shovels and pitchforks. In his encyclical on the environment, Pope Francis warned of an "unprecedented destruction of ecosystems" and "serious consequences for all of us" if humanity fails to act on climate change.[6] In releasing this papal document, the Vatican called climate change "a dominant moral and ethical issue for society." Irrefutable science, growing public concern, universal moral authority—how can the climate change deniers, including of the Harper variety in the Canadian Conservative Party, so cavalierly buck all three such powerful forces? That China should condemn Canada for reneging on the Kyoto Protocol—China, of all countries!—is a measure of how badly our country has now lost the world leadership it provided on the environment under governments of different political labels and ideologies, both federal and provincial, over many decades, until Stephen Harper began to work his black magic. On this issue, Green Party leader Elizabeth May and I agree. She told the media that the decision to quit Kyoto would cause Canada to be seen around the world "as a country that deals in bad faith." My former staffer has been proven right. Canadians under the thumb of the Stephen Harper government acted in bad faith as citizens of the world. It is what that government did. It is not what Canadians do. It is not what the historic Conservative Party represented. But it is what the party has stood for since the 2003 merger. In this, as in so many other ways, the Conservative Party of Canada is no longer what it once was. The environment is the political MRI that reveals how sick this patient has become. Reneging on Kyoto, however, is hardly the only cancerous spot the screening has shown on the patient's lung, to wit:

- The United Nations Convention to Combat Desertification (UNCCD) is—as the name states—an international agreement (by over 190 countries) to combat desertification and mitigate the effects of drought. Its purpose is achieved through national action programs that incorporate ten-year strategies supported by international cooperation and partnerships based on cutting-edge science. In short, UNCCD is designed to prevent parts of the planet from becoming deserts as the planet's temperature rises at an alarming rate from pollution. Increasing world food security is one of the major benefits— 60 percent of Canada's cropland is in dry areas frequently subjected to drought. In 2013, the Stephen Harper government withdrew Canada from the desertification Convention. It was the first (and, as I write, the *only*) country to do so. Can one possibly imagine any previous Canadian federal government—no matter the party or prime minister—acting in such an irresponsible, shortsighted, and reckless way?
- In a 2012 article in *World Affairs*, award-winning journalist and politics expert Jordan Michael Smith noted that, since the end of the Second World War, Canada's wealth, strategic location, and history have allowed it "to punch above its weight in international forums."[7] Smith says multilateralism,

especially the United Nations, was a sacrosanct commitment for previous Canadian governments, regardless of political stripe. But, he observes, in Stephen Harper's first speech to the United Nations, in September 2006, the prime minister signalled a dramatic shift by questioning the international body's value "in language that might just as easily have been used by someone like Jeane Kirkpatrick, President Reagan's ambassador to the UN."[8] Indeed, much about Canada's foreign policy under Harper could have come from the Reagan administration. Under Harper, Canada's military spending reached its highest levels since the Second World War. Defence is important. So are our military alliances. But, at a time when the federal government's annual deficits were running around $37 billion, should placing our military spending on steroids have been the priority among all the pressing demands on our overstretched treasury? And was this the best way for us Canadians to meet our obligations to fellow citizens of the planet? When climate change is causing our own country's icecaps to melt, sea levels to rise, wildlife to seek refuge, shorelines to shrink, and lands to become parched, what did ignoring this issue while juicing up military spending say about the government's basic values as it decided how best to spend Canadian taxpayers' hard-earned money?

- No other province is more vulnerable to global warming than my own. That's because Prince Edward Island is, basically, a low-lying sandbar in the North Atlantic. No part of the Island is farther than 16 kilometres from the sea or higher than 142 metres above sea level, with most parts only about 50 metres in elevation (equivalent to a sixteen-storey building—that's substantially lower than one might think from glancing up the side of a skyscraper). Researchers at the University of Prince Edward Island and Simon Fraser University—including Nobel Prize–winner Adam Fenech (director of the Climate Research Lab at UPEI)—have jointly investigated the impact of climate change on PEI through CLIVE (the Coastal Impact Visualization Environment) project. These scientists discovered that 20 square kilometres of the Island have vanished since 1968 because of rising sea levels attributed to global warming. Vanished! A recent annual study conducted by UPEI's Climate Research Lab showed that the Island's coastline receded an average of 46 centimetres in 2014. Even bigger and accelerated losses are expected by 2100, during the lifetime of our youngest children today. Nothing symbolizes the impact of climate change on PEI more than the fate of the West Point Lighthouse. This historic landmark is under increasing threat of falling into the sea. Only a few metres currently separate the lighthouse from the shore, once far from this iconic structure but no longer. At one point, three snowstorms that struck the Island within a month tore away more than a metre of sand dune. So, none of this is just wild futuristic imaginings by white-coated mad scientists. It is real. What observer could reasonably think that the Harper government had the scales anywhere close to equilibrium in the military-versus-environment weighing of priorities? What purpose was served by escalating military spending in the name of defending territory that is fast shrinking for lack of attention to the most urgent issue of all—planetary and world population survival?

- The Mulroney government established the National Round Table on the Environment and the Economy to ensure that economic decisions by Canadians—government, industry, non-governmental organizations, and individuals—protected our lands, our waters, and our air for the health and well-being of Canadians now and forever. Our government's expectations for the Round Table were gloriously met in its twenty-five years of operation under successive chairs and governments. But, in its 2012 budget, the Harper government squashed the institution's $5 million budget as a camper would a mosquito at lakeside. In a $276 billion federal budget and a $1.5 trillion Canadian economy, is $5 million too high a price to help ensure our country gets its economy/environment link right? The Stephen Harper government consistently demonstrated how little it was committed to the principle of sustainable development and to ensuring Canada's capacity, through research and public involvement, to make that principle real. Canada was the first country to show the world how to act in the spirit of the Brundtland Commission. The Harper government telegraphed to the world that we no longer even cared. The Justin Trudeau government has signalled that it is eager to send a far different message to the world. Renaming the federal Environment portfolio to include "Climate Change" is literally part of that message. A good start. It also serves to highlight the terrible results from the Conservative Party's MRI.

# Canadian International Leadership

In late January 2013, at the Public Policy Forum's annual Testimonial Dinner and Awards in Toronto, former prime minister Joe Clark said: "As power disperses in the world, so does the capacity to lead....[The] most effective leadership will have to be shared....It is what we [Canadians] have so often done, and it helps make the world more stable." On environmental matters, as on others, the Harper government not only failed "to share leadership"; it also undermined the efforts of other countries to work with one another on vital global issues such as climate change and desertification. Joe Clark was an exemplary minister of external affairs. In his book, he laments that, with the exception of an activist role in Afghanistan and Haiti, the government of Stephen Harper was disengaged in international areas where our country traditionally had been a leader—for instance, on relations between rich and poor countries, on official development assistance, on Africa, and on the global environment. On the few occasions the Harper government was engaged internationally, Clark says, its actions were "obstreperous." The former prime minister cites, for example, the spoiler role Canada played at the Copenhagen climate change conference in December 2009.[9] The Canadian government at the time did all it could to undermine the Copenhagen Accord. This agreement expressed a clear political will and intent by the 115 nations that met in Denmark to constrain carbon dioxide emissions. With some 40,000 people seeking accreditation in one capacity or another, this was one of the largest meetings of world opinion leaders ever held. There, Canada stuck its foot out trying to trip the world community. It was hardly the time, if ever there is one, for Canada to be on its worst behaviour. And to be something we historically have not been, and are not by nature: "Little Canadians."

It's as though the Harper government was running a country whose stances and ways of doing business, both domestically and abroad, were in a completely different tradition from our own. In fact, the government was managing the country in a manner that risked changing our very nature as a people in the eyes of the rest of the world—and, worse, in our own eyes. And it was doing so to the point where

Canada was becoming, in effect, a foreign country compared to what it traditionally had been. Good governance is a never-ending effort by the state to brighten people's lives. During the Harper decade, the shades were subtly pulled down. By the end, the darkness was palpable. The Conservative government's approach to the environment resembled that of previous Canadian governments less than a beetle looks like a buffalo. And a beetle has five legs, a buffalo four! As Canada's environment minister, I devoted a part of my life to negotiating for Canadians, at the behest of the prime minister and his entire Cabinet, major binational and international environmental pacts. I am despondent—as a Canadian, as an environmentalist, as an erstwhile Conservative—that such leadership was not a priority of Canada's national government and, therefore, of Canadians when the Tory party was last in power. How could the Harper government have abandoned our traditional national values so blatantly in an area that, more than any other, helps define us as Canadians? And how could a political party that labels itself "Conservative" have so casually turned its back on the party's own rich tradition of environmental leadership at home and abroad?

----

In 1885, a small group of developers were hell-bent on exploiting and commercializing and profiting from the hot springs discovered by accident in Banff. It took extraordinary vision for Sir John A. Macdonald to found our nation. It also took his vision to build the original instruments of nationhood without which there could not have been a Canada. Those instruments included a transcontinental railway required to open and settle lands to make the new Dominion real. Otherwise, the country would have been only seventy-two resolutions on a page drafted in my hometown in 1864. Sir John A. applied the same vision to the threat he saw to the Banff hot springs and later to preserving the millions of acres of magnificent landscape beyond them. The Old Chieftain stepped in and blocked private exploitation of the Banff hot springs. He said, in effect: "This special natural feature of our homeland is not for the few. It is for all Canadians and their visitors, now and forever." And thus was born Canada's first national park and our national park system. This Conservative prime minister acted to protect Banff almost a century before the birth of the modern environmental movement with the publication, in 1962, of Rachel Carson's milestone book *Silent Spring*, which warned about the health dangers of chemicals.[10] Macdonald's environmental and conservation ethic and vision predated those of US president Theodore Roosevelt by more than a generation. A Canadian prime minister—a Canadian *Conservative* prime minister!—invented North American political environmentalism. How could the gods of fortune have so blessed our country with such a prophet? And why would Canadian Conservatives now want to trash the noble cause he launched in their name?

At the time, Banff was one of only two national parks on the entire continent (the other was Yellowstone, primarily in Wyoming), and one of only three on the entire planet. Canada now has more national parks or wildlife preserves (forty-six) than any other country except the United States (fifty-eight). As of 1987, ours is undeniably the world's finest national park system. South Moresby (Gwaii Haanas), Canada's Galapagos, was created in the face of the same kind of "resource exploitation versus conservation" battle fought in Banff over a century earlier. It makes a world of difference whether the prophets or the profiteers control a nation's affairs. Sir John A. Macdonald was the greatest of our prophets. Because of measures like South Moresby,

I believe historians will someday credit Brian Mulroney's visionary leadership in this and other areas, too.[11] Meanwhile, the government of Stephen Harper flouted the venerable tradition of such Canadian Conservative Party environmental leadership. How could the party have taken this terrible turn in the road? Can the Conservative Party under new leadership, following Stephen Harper's resignation, right its course? Will it even try? The extent of the challenge merits further review. Certain questions need to be answered first.

# Stephen Harper's Conservatism

As prime minister and Conservative Party leader, was Stephen Harper a prophet or a profiteer? Did Harper view Canada as a community, one much greater than the sum of private vested interests, however worthy each might be in its own right? Or was he, mindfully and wilfully, an individualistic and free enterpriser conservative, a free market fundamentalist, an economic libertarian? Did he harbour an American-inspired distrust of government and devotion to private profit, even at the expense of the commonweal? If he was that kind of ideologue, how far down the road did he pull the Conservative Party? Can the party reverse direction now? Classic conservatives, in the Burkean tradition, have always believed that society is what political scientists term a "corporate entity," not in the business sense, but meaning that society possesses a single-nation organic identity composed of many different socially cohesive parts. In this view, the parts contribute to the whole, just as they are made better by it. But, expressed in the vernacular, the tail does not wag the dog. The true follower of this tradition rejects the hyperindividualistic and atomistic social view. For the classic conservative, the dog does, indeed, wag the tail and not the converse. Was Stephen Harper a conservative in this traditional sense? Or, did his "dog" get wagged by its tail? As I followed the Harper government's environmental record at every stumbling step along the way, I dreaded the answer to all these questions. And there was only one answer to them all. Canadians answered the question their way by shellacking the Conservative government with their ballots on October 19, 2015. Voters did not seek a change of government just for the sake of change. They hated the direction the country was headed. The amount of strategic voting—the "anybody but Stephen Harper" coalescing behind the Liberals—demonstrated that fact. My own daughters told me that's how they voted, in one case for a candidate and party she otherwise would not have supported in her particular riding.

In his famous book *Bowling Alone*, Harvard University political scientist Robert Putman supports in dense empirical detail his groundbreaking thesis that, steadily over recent decades, Americans have become disconnected from one another in their families, in their friendships, and in their democratic structures. In the process, he argues, the very fabric of the country has frayed, impoverishing communities, the lives of everyone in them, and the country as a whole. Putman laments the loss of sense of community, "of shared identity and reciprocity."[12] His greatest lament is that rugged individualism has caused Americans to "be pulled apart from one another and from our communities."[13] He says this trend is reflected in the decreasing role Americans see for their national government as an instrument of the total community. Putman argues that the United States has disintegrated into discrete tribes and individuals with a tenuous common culture linking them politically, economically, or socially. Is Canada experiencing this same worrisome trend? If so, did the Harper government both reflect and accelerate it? The government's reneging on Canada's commitments under Kyoto and the Desertification Convention, along with many other parts of its overall record, particularly in the environmental field, indicates that the answer to these two questions is yes. Under Harper's leadership, we increased the risk of no longer being a "commonwealth"—with "common" being separated from "wealth" and taking a back seat to it. Far back.

In current times, the interests of the community are at greater risk in the environmental field than in any other. No institution can play a more pivotal role in protecting those interests than a country's national government. Indeed, in many ways, it is the only institution that can act for the total community and for all its constituent parts. This is true not just on the environment, but on it most of all. Without a healthy environment, all else, including life itself, risks perishing. And yet, this is the area where the Harper government repeatedly signalled that it saw most clearly a diminishing role for the state both across Canada and, even more alarmingly, in the world at large. Every genuine Conservative should lament this abandonment of traditional national and party values at the heart of who we are not only as Canadians, but also as partisans with a proud political heritage. The Harper government changed official national *values* as much as it did official national *policies*. The latter express the former and make them concrete, not just conceptual.

There is no state religion in Canada—sectarian or civic. We're a land of pluralistic values and diverse political beliefs. It's what makes us strong and free and keeps us that way. But a national community must stand collectively for more than promoting the prosperity of its individual citizens or even of the country itself. Neither per capita personal income nor gross national product makes a country great. Visionary leaders such as Sir John A. Macdonald and Georges-Étienne Cartier—Thomas D'Arcy McGee as passionately as any—believed in a larger vision: a set of values that extended beyond mere dollar signs and was as large as the country itself, from "sea to sea." These visionaries, in fact, were prepared to pay a high price, including in dollars and cents, to pursue that vision and make it happen. McGee, for one, left behind in New York and Boston virtually everything he had worked for to do so. These patriots defined what it meant to be Big Canadians. Why would any Canadian today want to be a centimetre smaller? Why would we want our country to be? As the national Conservative Party seeks to rebuild after its October 2015 election loss, it would be well advised to seek guidance from the party's own illustrious record, including at the provincial level.

Another visionary Tory politician not afraid to use the levers of government to advance the common good, in the spirit of Sir John A. Macdonald, was Leslie Frost, premier of Ontario from 1949 to 1961. "Old Man Ontario"—as he was affectionately known—was the architect of the province's postwar economic and social revolution: in education (massive investment, growth, quality reform); superhighways (notably, the 401); hospital insurance (OHIP); the public service (huge expansion, in size and professionalism); human rights (the Ontario Human Rights Commission and Code, the gold standard for the rest of the world); women's equality (including pay equity); Aboriginal rights (the franchise for the first time); municipal development (consolidation, rationalization). Frost embodied the Canadian Conservative tradition at its best and most admirable and most successful. The masterful way he almost seamlessly managed the dramatic transition of Ontario from rural prewar Upper Canada to the modern Golden Horseshoe is one of the most important, if least appreciated, stories in Canadian political history—and in Canadian Conservative Party history.

By sharp contrast to Ontario's Leslie Frost, a conservative leader of a distinctly unprogressive type was premier of the sister province of Quebec in much the same period: Maurice Duplessis, a man that only his mother and Conrad Black could love. Except for a brief period after the 1939 election, Duplessis held virtually unchallenged political power in the province from 1936 to 1959. Duplessis, who led the Union Nationale Party, was a Conservative partisan in all but name. Indeed, he and his formidable electoral machine pulled out all the stops for John Diefenbaker and PC candidates in that province in the 1958 federal election. Originally elected premier on a progressive platform, Duplessis soon abandoned many of his reformist instincts and policies. Instead, he chose to advance a highly reactionary agenda aimed at maximizing provincial autonomy from the national government and from the rest of Canada. With this agenda, Duplessis rejected federal-provincial fiscal arrangements, rejected federal Trans-Canada Highway grants, rejected federal hospital insurance grants, rejected direct federal grants to universities, and on and on. He acted on constitutional grounds or any other he could concoct. Duplessis coupled the isolation of Quebec from the rest of Canada and North America—and, in fact, the world—with staunchly conservative stands in social and economic affairs.

Most historians view Duplessis's long anachronistic period in office as corrupt and stagnant. He sold Quebec's resources to the highest bidders, many of them American. He trampled on human rights. He prevented the province from evolving as rapidly as many other jurisdictions were doing in the postwar period—in Quebec's case, from an inward-looking Church-dominated agrarian society to a modern competitive industrial state based on scientific innovation, on an educated professional middle class, on entrepreneurial spirit and competence, and on futuristic infrastructure. Most historians now acknowledge that Duplessis actively fostered industrial development in some major sectors. It is incontrovertible that Duplessis invested heavily in education and that the bureaucratic class in Quebec expanded dramatically while he was premier. But Premier Duplessis did these constructive things while perpetuating a hidebound, paternalistic, patronage-based approach to politics. He sought to create and then exploit irrational fears about external threats—mainly communism, Jehovah's Witnesses, and Ottawa, sometimes all lumped together as one big bogeyman. Duplessis and his henchmen also employed thuggish, corrupt electoral practices to eliminate opposition and entrench themselves in power. The premier himself was almost indistinguishable from corrupt American politicians of the 1920s and 1930s such as the legendary Governor Huey Long of Louisiana (later, a US senator from that state). The parallels between Stephen Harper and both Maurice Duplessis and Huey Long are much stronger than one might think.

Maurice Duplessis aligned himself closely with the Catholic Church. He campaigned on the slogan, "Heaven is blue [Union Nationale]; Hell is red [Liberal]." The new national Conservative Party formed in 2003 followed basically the identical path of mixing politics and fundamentalist religious values as that taken by Duplessis. In its case, though, the religion was not Roman Catholic. As scholar Jonathan Malloy has noted, "This religious dimension [of party politics]…carried over to the Canadian Alliance [from the Reform Party] under the even more outspokenly religious Stockwell Day and has been maintained and even increased under the reunited Conservative Party of Stephen Harper."[14] Scary but true. As Malloy has observed, the Conservative Party has been focusing on "social conservatives" and evangelicals as part of forging a larger conservative ideological coalition. It has been doing so, he says, with so-called family issues messages carefully targeted to this particular demographic.

He argues that, in such a way, the Conservative Party has turned its back on the role it had historically played in unifying the country. "[It] goes against the traditional understandings of Canadian brokerage politics that suggests the two major parties avoid and downplay divisive ideological stances in their pursuit of electoral majorities and/or national unity."[15]

To my mind, the mixing of politics and religion—and a fundamentalist form of it, to boot, whether Catholic or Protestant—most distinguishes the new Conservative Party from the historic one. It does so to the point where—along with other distinctions (most notably, in the environmental field)—the two entities are fundamentally different. The philosophical corruption of the once-great Canadian Tory party is undeniable. The comparative experiences of Canada's two most populous provinces, Quebec and Ontario, suggest that, when this kind of thing happens to a major political party, especially when it holds power, the damage extends well beyond the party itself. It impacts the wider community. Political parties are not private clubs; they constitute an integral part of society and the total culture. Their tax-exempt status as not-for-profits and the donations deductibility provisions of the *Income Tax Act* alone impose on these institutions both a community status and a concomitant responsibility to the general public. Advancing a particular set of religious values—as opposed to Judeo-Christian ethical principles that most people can support irrespective of sectarian allegiance—is not part of an officially recognized political party's civic mandate. Nor should it be. God, guard us against politicians hell-bent on inflicting their religious dogma on the rest of us in this life because they're convinced they know more than anybody else about You and Your plans for us in the next.

Quebec's path under Duplessis contrasts starkly with Ontario's under Leslie Frost's inspired and principled but resolutely secular leadership. Only upon Duplessis's death in 1959, near the end of Leslie Frost's vastly more progressive period in office in Ontario, was Quebec able to escape from *l'ancien régime*. It did so by electing as premier Jean Lesage, whose Liberal government launched the province's Quiet Revolution in the 1960s. The new government exponentially built upon the real but limited progress the previous government had made in modernizing the province in key areas. By then, however, Quebec's challenge was to catch up with Ontario, which had a full generation's head start. Leslie Frost, "Old Man Ontario," showed Canadian Conservatives how to think and act young—and get ahead. Canadian Conservatives today should learn from such history. But, first, they must know it.

The Duplessis/Frost contrast demonstrates that it matters what kind of government leaders a society has. I do not liken the Stephen Harper government to the Duplessis government in the latter's worst practices (moral corruption, human rights violations, snubbing its nose at the rest of Canada). But, when Canadian Conservative governments, national or provincial, betray Burkean principles, as the Duplessis government undeniably did, the harm to society can be disastrous. Those principles ("sustainable practice") are not hostile to development or wealth. Quite the contrary, they embrace development, but of the kind that respects the total community organically linked to past and future generations. By definition, it is development in which government has a legitimate role. Indeed, that role is necessary. It bears repeating that only government serves as the agent of the total community entrusted with the pursuit of the commonweal. As such, only it can ensure development is, in fact, sustainable in the interests of all Canadians—past, present, and future. True classic conservatives think BIG: they embrace change, pursue progress, support and engage in development, celebrate and reward success, look to the future, and help build it. But they do all those things while being prudent about the possible harm specific actions might cause to their own and others' future. Being BIG first means thinking big. Sustainable practice (or development) is a BIG IDEA. The Stephen Harper government thought small, acted small, and, not surprisingly, left a small legacy. The word "big" can be attached to that government only in describing the damage it did to the country—and to the Conservative Party. The country will recover. But will the Conservative Party? The party's current "before" MRI does not lead one to believe that the "after" magnetic resonance imaging will reveal a marked improvement without major surgery. History, both positive and negative, shows us how huge the challenge ahead is.

# Progressive Tory Tradition

Just as Duplessis started as a progressive, so John Diefenbaker conducted his victorious 1957 and 1958 campaigns with a progressive vision—of northern development, "Roads to Resources," social services for all (hospitalization, in particular), increased Old Age Security pensions, lifting disadvantaged regions (Atlantic Canada and the North especially), expanding markets worldwide (selling wheat to China), enshrining human and civil rights (the Bill of Rights), extending the vote to Aboriginal peoples, and much more. Any fair assessment of John Diefenbaker's years in power would have to acknowledge that, for the first time in a very long while, the Canadian West was brought into the PC Party and, thereby, into the priorities of the national government of the day. This Tory leader did the same for many other parts of Canada, not least my own region, as well as for certain groups of Canadians who had felt alienated from their country (among them, people of non–western European heritage). Introducing simultaneous translation to Parliament advanced bilingualism well before the Trudeau government's *Official Languages Act* made that principle official state policy and practice. A number of Alvin Hamilton's initiatives (as northern resources minister and, later, at agriculture) have stood the test of time. Justice Minister E. Davie Fulton's efforts at constitutional reform and patriation, with his Quebec counterpart Guy Favreau (the "Fulton-Favreau Formula"), laid the groundwork for Trudeau's breakthroughs on this front in the early 1980s. And the Diefenbaker government followed an expansionary fiscal policy to combat what in those years was considered a serious recession—a policy fatally undermined by Governor James Coyne's tight-money measures at the Bank of Canada.

In my own province, the PC "Diefenbaker candidates"—and they called themselves that—ran under the banner, "The Party of the Causeway." They tore a page from Sir John A. Macdonald's book, which envisioned Canadians linked, both in spirit and by transportation networks, from sea to sea. To this day, I recall as though yesterday Diefenbaker's spellbinding oratory in Charlottetown about how a permanent link between PEI and the rest of the country was part of Canada's National Dream. "Ah, there are the doubters," he thundered. "But I am not one of them." So much promise! But John Diefenbaker eventually lost his way in government and then in Opposition, particularly the latter. He retreated into a reactionary cocoon as dark as Duplessis's cave. Paranoia will do that to a leader who feels continually under siege, as Diefenbaker did—not always without cause.

Even national Canadian Tory leaders perceived over the years to have been hostile to government activism in the public interest were not, in fact, of this nature. John Diefenbaker's predecessor, George Drew, for all his matinée-idol good looks, is typically caricatured as a rock-ribbed Colonel Blimp reactionary. Perhaps the image emanates from the fact he was a lieutenant-colonel in the Royal Canadian Artillery and liked to be called "Colonel." But, as Heath Macquarrie noted in his memoir, George Drew's record as premier of Ontario (before Drew became national PC leader) "is one of enlightened, progressive and sometimes daring leadership."[16] Macquarrie, the quintessential scholar-politician, took so much pride in being a Red Tory himself that he included the term in his memoir's title. When Drew won the 1943 election that made him premier, he and his party campaigned on a demonstrably progressive platform. But, unlike Duplessis and Diefenbaker (particularly later), Drew did not abandon his progressive instincts once in office. On the contrary, he created the foundation for the reformist Tory regimes that followed, including Leslie Frost's. In energy, the Drew government linked Ontario to the North American power grid and greatly expanded capacity, investing almost half a billion dollars towards that end—many billions in today's dollars. In transportation, Drew built a huge network of roads and highways. He invested massively in schools, increasing the province's share from only 15 percent to more than 50 percent. With both direct and indirect measures, he laid the base for the province's postwar industrial complex. And he promoted such visionary antipoverty social programs as universal health coverage and free dental care. Leslie Frost and two later Ontario Tory premiers, John Robarts and Bill Davis, built on the powerful economic and social structure that Drew had constructed. The Drew/Frost/Robarts/Davis Progressive Conservative dynasty lasted, without interruption, for nearly half a century—a testament to the electoral appeal of competent, fiscally responsible, but activist and compassionate Tory government.

As national PC leader, Drew was not nearly as sensitive to Canada's French Fact as every other national Progressive Conservative leader after Diefenbaker would be—from Stanfield to Clark to Mulroney to Charest, and as Stephen Harper mostly was as prime minister even if not remarkably before then. But Drew and other leaders who pre-dated the Quebec Quiet Revolution, particularly by many years, should not be judged by today's standard. (All the more reason to be awed by Sir John A. Macdonald's enlightenment a century earlier, notwithstanding his mishandling of the Manitoba Schools Question and the hanging of Louis Riel.) In fairness to Drew—and to John Diefenbaker, for that matter—it was not as easy for a national Tory leader in that era to anticipate the Quiet Revolution as it was for, say, Lester Pearson. The Liberals had a strong electoral and organizational base in Quebec and among francophones. The Tories did not. This was their wasteland. So, the Liberals had far better access to sound advice on French language and cultural issues than the Tories, especially from within their respective parliamentary Caucuses. Robert Stanfield began to redress that imbalance as a top organizational and policy priority immediately upon becoming leader in late 1967. By then, however, the Quiet Revolution was well under way. It was worse than our slamming the barn door after the horse had fled. Concerning Quebec, the Tory Party at this time did not have much of a barn to begin with. The point here is that, setting aside his tone-deafness on the French Fact, George Drew's stance on most issues after he entered federal politics reflected the progressive instincts he had brought to the premiership of Ontario. Drew did not morph from Modern Man to Neanderthal while being driven in a black sedan fewer than five hundred kilometres from Queen's Park to Parliament Hill.

Almost without exception over the decades, Canadian national Conservative Party leaders caricatured as right-wingers in the conventional meaning have, in fact, been, like George Drew, progressives and reformers. Put simply, they were eager to use the instruments of the state to "brighten" people's lives. Before the First World War, Sir Robert Borden introduced the national income tax system, based on the ability-to-pay (or progressive) principle; he established the National Research Council (the most undercelebrated of all our major national institutions); and, most important of all, he secured from Britain Canada's right to sign international treaties as an independent and sovereign Dominion (impossible to underrate). Arthur Meighen (in the 1920s) introduced universal suffrage, fought the banks in the interests of everyday Canadians, and created the Canadian National Railway. And R. B. Bennett (1930–35), so often wrongly viewed as our Herbert Hoover, was really our FDR. He promoted Canada's "New Deal," an ambitious agenda of major economic and social reforms from minimum wage to health and unemployment insurance to tighter regulation of banking and trade (echoing Meighen). He also created the precursor to the current CBC, the greatest benefits from which accrued to the outlying parts of the country, poorly served (or not served at all) by the private market.

After his defeat in 1935, the extremely wealthy R. B. Bennett was made a British peer, as Viscount Bennett. Like Robert Stanfield almost four decades later, Bennett practised noblesse oblige. Both men were "Red Tories" before the term gained wide currency—in Bennett's case, two generations before. Bennett used his wealth to bankroll the rebuilding of the Canadian Conservative Party as a truly national institution. He almost single-handedly created, from practically nothing, a Canada-wide political machine that not only rivalled that of the Liberals but surpassed it, even in large parts of traditional Liberal strongholds—the West and Quebec. In the latter, the Conservative leader won twenty-four seats in the 1930 election that made him prime minister. The future viscount was a thoroughly modern political strategist and tactician—a sort of early-day Barack Obama. He employed the mass media—especially radio, but also newspaper advertising and printed fliers—as effectively as Franklin Roosevelt did in the United States. Bennett's voice was custom-made for radio—rich and vibrant and zealous. And he mastered this medium two years before the American president's famous "fireside chats" on the same medium. So much for stereotypes of traditional Canadian Conservative Party leaders! They were typically risk-taking pioneers, not stodgy reactionaries; believers in state activism, not rigid laissez-faire ideologues; compassionate and humanitarian devotees of their fellow human beings, not cold-hearted plutocrats. In general, Canadian Conservative prime ministers and premiers over the generations believed in government that serves the people's needs. They sought to be—and most of them were—great practitioners of the craft of governing. What they stood for, individually and collectively, constitutes a model that the Conservative Party of Canada should proudly embrace as it seeks new leadership—and, presumably, a fresh direction—after being routed in the October 2015 federal election for following a far different model: one that demonizes government, rather than embraces it enthusiastically to achieve noble public goals.

Former Conservative senator Hugh Segal has described the essence of what Conservatism traditionally has represented in the hands of most such Tory leaders over the generations. He says our Conservatism is unique to Canada, not identical to that of either Britain or the United States. He states it is "deeply indigenous to our geography, history and culture."[17] He notes it reflects the principle that "the whole [of the community] is better than the sum of its parts."[18] According to him,

Conservatives seek a balance between public and private interests to advance both. This principle holds that government has an indispensable role as the instrument of the public interest and of "national development and patriotism."[19] And, he says, it is rooted in a profound sense that members of the community feel an obligation to one another. Far from high-sounding generalities that any national or ideologue could embrace, the Canadian set of Conservative values, Segal argues, contrasts markedly with American conservatism—indeed, with the fundamental overarching *American Idea* itself. Rather than the deep-seated Canadian conservative belief in the value of community, which respects its constituent parts but does not exalt them at the expense of all else, including the wider community, the American conservative route, he says, has "led inexorably to an individualistic, arms-bearing, anti-government and self-centered 'life, liberty and the pursuit of happiness' vision of governance." The former senator observes that, in contrast, "[t]he Canadian conservatism of accommodation, of dealing respectfully with what people believed in and cared about and the institutions that protected those beliefs, led naturally to a constitutional process structured around the remarkably more [classic] conservative notion of 'peace order and good government'."[20]

Hugh Segal has it all substantially right. Canadian Conservatives who believe in the ethos he describes, and who consider it better for Canada than the set of values that enthrall American conservatives, need to be vigilant. And they should oppose, in their own country, public policies that reflect the worst of the American zeitgeist, rather than the best of the Canadian. The environment is one area where the Harper government's record cried out for Conservatives to be especially watchful. But they were not. With their voices and votes, sustainable development-minded Conservatives, like all other such Canadians, should strike as soldiers would against invaders when any Canadian government, regardless of political stripe, treats environmental programs and funding, and anything else essential to our national well-being, as disposable either in hot pursuit of the fiscal bottom line or from misguided notions of individual rights and liberties.

# The Harper Conservative Record

Despite a most promising beginning, John Diefenbaker reversed a long and distinguished Tory tradition of progressive leadership based on the kinds of principles Hugh Segal expresses. In this sense, as in others, Diefenbaker was, truly, a "rogue." It took two men, Robert Stanfield and Tom Symons, in partnership and with shared vision, to help the Progressive Conservative Party find its way back to its traditional path. That path embraced the great potential of Canada, its magnificent complexity, its multicultural character, its rich linguistic duality, its youthful energy and passion, and its limitless possibilities as a community of resourceful and hard-working people. These two men envisioned a community whose members were committed to and organically linked with both one another and the totality. In this vision, the community was not simply an aggregate of individuals pursing their own separate self-interests independent of the interests of the whole. Stanfield and Symons helped restore their party's traditional conservatism in the spirit of Sir John A. Macdonald and Georges-Étienne Cartier's partnership. The Founding Fathers' National Dream sought to forge a new country that stretched all the way from the Atlantic to the Pacific. Successive Canadian dreamers—

notably John Diefenbaker, in the 1950s—would enlarge this vision to embrace the country's northern frontier: a Canada not just from sea to sea but *from sea to sea to sea*. For none of Canada's visionaries was the National Dream a lust for territorial expansion for its own sake. For them, Canada represented a set of political and societal values symbolized by the Crown they were eager to preserve and perpetuate in the face of an imminent threat. That threat was the new republic to the south and the continental imperialism it transparently and boastfully championed: "Manifest Destiny." Our Founding Fathers did not want British North America to become just another Oregon or California. They dreamed bigger and bolder and better—not of becoming a new star or stripe on the American flag, but of building a different kind of country on the winter half of the North American continent. The Harper government allowed Manifest Destiny to sneak near our back door, ideologically and culturally, after we had so successfully bolted the front door with Confederation and added a night lock with each additional province and territory thereafter.

I met Prime Minister Stephen Harper only once. It was on April 20, 2006. The occasion was the gala dinner in Ottawa at which Brian Mulroney was honoured and feted as the "greenest Canadian prime minister in Canadian history." The organizers invited me to travel from Boston to attend the celebration as Mulroney's longest-serving environment minister and the one most closely identified with the programs and policies they thought qualified him for this unique distinction. My dinner partner was Dr. Sean Riley, then-president of St. Francis Xavier University. He had no doubt been invited because of Mulroney's close association with, not to mention massive fundraising for, St. F. X. At the event, Stephen Harper and I chatted, mostly about the state of the Conservative Party in PEI at the time (not good). The PM especially lamented, to him, the generally poor quality of candidates the party had been nominating in recent years on the Island. All three of the principal speakers (Mulroney, Harper, and Quebec premier Jean Charest) delivered major speeches on this occasion. Mulroney's address, much longer than the others, was a detailed and technical—but eloquent and highly personal and passionate—exposition on the environment-economy partnership. He linked the two in the context of the Brundtland Commission and, I thought, in the spirit of Edmund Burke. Clearly, it was both from the heart and from his own pen. The other two addresses were excellent, too. I found Stephen Harper charming, intelligent, shrewd, well-informed, public-spirited—and tall.

Stephen Harper was not a Conservative prime minister in the tradition that ran from Macdonald to Mulroney. His conservatism was more in the American tradition, not our own. The Conservative Party of Canada at its best—even before it added "Progressive" to its name in 1942—was fundamentally different from the US Republican Party. The PC Party was consistently progressive, reformist, enlightened, and modern. It was no less so—quite the contrary—for its allegiance, when appropriate, to "the tried and true." As Segal has noted, it would be intrinsically not a conservative practice to shunt tradition aside, for "to do so is to deny our history and to dilute our sense of identity."[21] The party built its progressive tradition over many years, in many elections and administrations, throughout many generations and on many diverse issues and party policies. Can any Canadian Tory today see in the Conservative Party's current incarnation, following the PC marriage to the Reform/Canadian Alliance Party, any link to the party's rich history and heritage? I abhor the party's post-2003 record on the environment, especially in government. But the party failed the country, and itself, across a broad spectrum of issues and policy areas, and not just on the domestic front, let alone only the concerns I have highlighted as of special interest to me.

The Stephen Harper government's linking of foreign aid to quasi-religious opposition to family planning is but one example in the international sphere where the post-merger Conservative Party parted company with the historic Conservative Party. Joe Clark's recent book is filled with examples—including this one—that the author cites to contrast Harper's and Mulroney's respective approaches to foreign affairs. Like some others, the foreign aid example might not have affected many Canadians directly. But it bespoke the Harper government's penchant for blending private morality and personal religious beliefs into public policy in the manner of Maurice Duplessis, Ernest and Preston Manning, and Stockwell Day. American Republicans have favoured such a practice ever since Ronald Reagan made it his signature style. But, until recently, most Canadian national political parties have scrupulously avoided acting in this way. Not coincidentally, the notable exceptions have been Social Credit and the Reform/Canadian Alliance parties.

Do Canadians really want a blend of politics and religion to form a party's signature style when it's in power? In which case, how could a vast and diverse and pluralistic country like ours ever achieve the kind of national consensus on priorities and solutions required to keep the country whole and its future secure? One only needs to look at what is happening in the United States to understand how destructive this approach can be. It has made it impossible for Americans to reach agreement on such thorny issues as gun control, family planning, reproductive rights, marriage equality, voter registration, climate change, a core public education curriculum, and the list goes on. When a society is wrenched over whether humanity was created by a supreme being in seven days only a few thousand years ago or evolved over millions of years as a result of forces every citizen, guided by science, has the right to determine for himself or herself—one fact remains certain: that society is deeply troubled. Americans are not just losing their consensus on basic civic values and priorities; they are losing their *capacity* to reach a consensus—a far more serious failing. A nation to which that happens ceases to be a people; it becomes merely a land of persons.

Did the government of Stephen Harper set Canada on that same course? All the evidence suggests that the answer is yes. Why would any of us want religious values—or absolute values of any sort—to come between one Canadian and another as our magnificent Dominion governs itself? When secular politics is treated as religious warfare in another form—a cosmic conflict between the forces of good and evil—neither God nor Caesar is well served. Canadian Conservatives eager to follow the American Republican Party's model in this respect need to know that, myth to the contrary, the US Founding Fathers never intended to establish an officially Christian nation. As well-known American theologian Gregory Boyd has written, the Declaration of Independence "proclaims truths that the founding fathers thought to be 'self-evident' to natural reason...not truths that are scriptural...[Our constitution]...owes more to John Locke than it does to the Bible."[22] The word cloud of Canada's National Dream says "Peace, Order and Good Government," not "In God We Trust," let alone does it advocate the specific religious values a Canadian must embrace, still less ones of a fundamentalist sort. The Harper government's completely different mindset, particularly on social issues, was so much smaller than our Founding Fathers' vision and utterly unworthy of it.

Each of us arrives on the planet as an individual—even, as in my case, when a twin. But, if we depart exclusively in that singular state, our time here has been wasted. Just as one does not automatically have a family by being born into one, but must earn that distinction by being a loving son or daughter and being loved in return, so also citizens of a country are not a community merely by living within the boundaries of the same jurisdiction. They, too, must demonstrate to one another a shared commitment. The very word "community" is derived from the Latin preposition *cum*, which means *with* or *together* or *together with*. People don't come together by taking separate buses. It is not in the tradition of Canadians to ride alone. Everything about Canada is BIG—its mountains, its icecaps, its ice shields, its forests and trees, its prairies, its lakes, its shorelines, its open skies, its wildlife, even its islands. Our citizens want to be Big Canadians and part of a Big Canada *together with* other Big Canadians. Otherwise, how to explain all the big things we have done together? A Canadian government that does not share this big vision of the country is small-minded, and renders Canadians and their nation smaller and the world a diminished place.

# Facts and Government

More so than any other federal government department, the Environment portfolio depends on scientific research and facts and intellectualism generally. Without reliable scientific information, that part of government cannot achieve its mandate, certainly not well. In my time as minister, many senior officials at Environment Canada had doctorates in one field of the natural or physical sciences or another. Geneviève Ste-Marie, the deputy minister, for example, had a doctorate in biology. Robert Slater, the senior assistant deputy minister, had a doctorate in chemistry. It was not unusual for me to be advised by a large group in which almost everyone had a PhD. I knew better than to attend a briefing unprepared. The subject was invariably freighted with complex scientific policy and technical detail. There are some things in life one can fake. Science is not one of them. As environmental problems become ever more global and complex and threatening to planetary and human survival, science must be viewed as the *sine qua non* of public policy in this domain. Not far back in our past, very little was known about the nature of environmental threats and, in some respects, even about their existence. Science, and only science—driven by public concern and organized activists—changed all that. The Harper government's apparent anti-intellectualism, therefore, was of particular concern to me as an environmentalist. The government's Luddite instincts were sadly reminiscent of John Diefenbaker's descent down that road late in life. Such dark instincts alarm me as a disciple of Robert Stanfield and Tom Symons. Their entire policy process was predicated on the importance they attached to evidence as the bedrock of PC Party positions on the issues. Indeed, they applied elements of the scientific method to that process. The numerous physical, natural, and social scientists they recruited to the process certainly did.

The federal government traditionally has tried to apply intellectual rigour to public policy—no matter the party in power, however imperfect the execution at times. The Harper government's decision to shift from a mandatory census to a voluntary system of Statistics Canada surveys, in the name of privacy rights, fundamentally departed from this tradition. The government's new approach rejected the spirit that inspired Stanfield and Symons to reform the PC Party's way of developing policy. The national census change caused the head of Statistics Canada, Munir Sheikh, to resign in protest. The Canadian Medical Association, the Canadian Chamber of Commerce, and the Canadian Catholic Council of Bishops were among the nearly five hundred organizations across the country that also protested the government's regressive action. In the age of information, they argued, the government was destroying Canada's capacity to gather basic facts about itself. Many opponents of the measure argued that it reflected the Harper government's subtle but palpable darkening of Canadian life more broadly. I myself am decidedly of that view. Inarguably, the federal government cannot plan well and make rational decisions without reliable and comprehensive data. Only a mandatory survey ensures that the government has access to such data. A voluntary system makes the public sector captive to personal discretion and even caprice. It levels a body blow to the scientific integrity of census data, casting doubt on the soundness of policy decisions based on the information. If knowledge is power, this marked change in information-gathering robbed the government of power it needed to achieve its purpose—serving the people and brightening their lives. Was an anti-government ethos, in fact, what really motivated the decision, as officially claimed, not the nobler-sounding cause of privacy? It is difficult to think otherwise.

Robert Stanfield and Tom Symons's elaborate process to develop Progressive Conservative Party policy based on research and facts replaced the gut-instinct approach Diefenbaker took on most issues. The Harper government's decision to establish a voluntary census turned back the party's clock to a time when politics and rhetoric and high emotion trumped research and facts and thoughtfulness. This turn away from evidence-based policy would have shocked Stanfield. An intellectual, he would have found the change anathema to sound public policy-making. The man would have been right. Hugh Segal refers to Sir John A. Macdonald as a reflective man, "a man of ideas."[23] The Old Chieftain was nothing if not that. Indeed, Canada itself was originally but an idea—his and that of a handful of individuals who shared his vision. Ideas, especially in today's complex world, cannot be spun from bolts of air. They are woven from experience, observation, evidence, experimentation, trial and error, informed consensus-building, collective judgment, and objective facts based on all those things. In the contemporary world, public policy needs to be generated and debated and agreed upon on the strongest-possible base of facts—what can be known rationally, not just felt emotionally; established with maximum certainty, not just surmised with minimal investigation; and regularly updated, and even changed or supplanted, in light of new information and insights, not etched in stone as absolutist ideological or religious belief. This is the twenty-first century, not the Middle Ages; our country is Canada, not North Korea; we are Canadians, not fools.

Throughout the federal system, the Harper government's anti-intellectualism created a breeding ground for ideology-fuelled bias unencumbered by facts. The government's assault against a mandatory census paralleled efforts in the United States by hard-right Republicans to kill or at least curtail vital surveys by the Census Bureau. Credible information is the most important single requirement for responsive government, for a strong economy, and for building a nation in which people can live their lives safely and healthily and well. We Canadians can hardly expect to compete head-to-head with other countries if we hobble ourselves with ignorance about elementary facts concerning our society and economy so essential to making rational public policy decisions. The absence of credible data forces decision-makers to rely on guesswork, gut instincts, raw emotion, untested conventional wisdom, popular prejudices, ideology, and (worst of all) divisive religious beliefs as they try to navigate through often stormy waters. One would have thought that this approach had ended for the Canadian Conservative Party when it dumped John Diefenbaker a half-century ago because Tories knew the country's challenges were complex and, therefore, not amenable to being solved with mere rhetoric and sloganeering. After all, the late 1960s was a period of extraordinary social upheaval and change both at home and abroad—in our case, with the country risking rupture over language and culture.

It was not for nothing that, in choosing its new leader back in 1967, the Conservative Party replaced a narrow-minded man with a big-minded one, an impulsive demagogue with a grounded intellectual, a highly partisan political warrior uninterested in policy with a true statesman for whom thoughtful policy was paramount. The party knew that the times called for a leader as big as the challenges the country faced: Robert Lorne Stanfield. Unlike his predecessor, Stanfield was passionately interested in keeping himself fully aware of, and well informed about, everything within his intellectual reach. To that end, he was eager to exchange knowledge and insights with others just as intellectually curious as he. The Tory leader did not want to lead a political party, much less a nation, in which facts and information did not matter, the wisdom of the ages was considered irrelevant, and the only views that counted were one's own.

As Conservative Party leader and prime minister, Stephen Harper embodied one of Robert Stanfield's greatest strengths (a fertile mind) and one of John Diefenbaker's worst weaknesses (harsh partisanship and political and moral sanctimony), with ideological rigidity thrown in for bad measure. The result was a most unfortunate amalgam that produced a net negative substantially more harmful to the country than the sum of the parts. Did Stephen Harper's sense of political and ideological and moral superiority get the best of his brains to doom Canada's mandatory long-form census when he was prime minister? The pages of history are filled with examples of such smart people who did and said stupid things because they believed and emoted more than they thought and considered. Esteemed American psychologist Robert J. Sternberg, Professor of Human Development at Cornell University, edited a book on this very phenomenon.[24]

Being a Little Canadian is never a good thing. No wonder the Harper government's legacy was so small after three terms and nine years in office. None of its major policy goals was achieved. Elevating Canada to petro superpower status—the centrepiece of the government's economic strategy—went aground among Keystone XL pipes stockpiled somewhere in a Nebraska cornfield. Expanding the ranks of "job creators" by being nice to the wealthy and mean to the poor while letting the big corporations operate unrestrained—that strategy was discredited as Canada, unlike most of its major trading partners, slid into recession and the loonie took a nosedive. Modernizing public institutions and eliminating political misconduct and corruption, particularly through Senate reform—those shiny baubles were dumped in a cesspool at Mike Duffy's PEI summer cottage. Jettisoning Canada's world environmental leadership in such areas as climate change was, however, "mission accomplished," to the Harper government's everlasting discredit.

Stephen Harper headed two parliamentary minorities and one majority. From this power trip, all Harper brought back for Canadians were the shirts he ripped from their backs. Now, with the man effectively gone from public life, Conservatives have the opportunity to regain the trust Canadians had placed in the party to run the country between 2006 and 2015. But, first, the Conservative Party must reflect hard on how it so seriously abused that trust while Stephen Harper was their leader and led the nation to decline and widespread disappointment. The party should begin the renewal process by understanding the nature of public policy and embracing its proper role.

# Assault on Reason

Allen Gregg, the well-known and widely respected political analyst and former Progressive Conservative pollster and senior strategist, is, like me, a homeless Tory, tossed out on the street by a party that no longer seems to want in its ranks people of our sort—people who hold progressive, communitarian values. On September 5, 2012, at Ottawa's Carleton University, Gregg delivered a scathing critique of the Stephen Harper government in a speech he called "Assault on Reason." He said: "More than anything else, societal progress has been advanced by enlightened public policy that marshals our collective resources towards a larger public good. Once again it has been reason and scientific evidence that has delineated effective from ineffective policy. We have discovered that effective solutions can only be generated when they correspond to an accurate understanding of the problems they are designed to solve. Evidence, facts and reason therefore form the sine qua non of not only good policy, but good government." Gregg could not have described better what Robert Stanfield and Tom Symons also believed when they set out, after the 1968 election debacle, to ensure "reason and evidence" inspired and girded national Progressive Conservative Party policy in Parliament, in elections, between elections, and across the land. In an attack against the Harper government's allegiance to the opposite approach, Gregg said: "I have spent my entire professional life as a researcher, dedicated to understanding the relationship between cause and effect. And I have to tell you, I've begun to see some troubling trends. It seems as though [the Harper] government's use of evidence and facts as the bases of policy is declining, and in their place, dogma, whim and political expediency are on the rise."

In the late 1950s and the mid-1960s, John Diefenbaker's oratory and whims and ambitions were often the only things that passed for Conservative Party policy. The current incarnation of the Conservative Party has stood on a stool, reached for the clock, turned the hands back, and circumvented the party's period of enlightenment under Robert Stanfield's leadership. In doing so, the party has returned to the dark years of Diefenbaker, rendering it once again unacceptable to many of the kinds of people Stanfield sought and worked so hard, with Tom Symons's personal help and policy team, to attract to its banner: voters who were progressive, knowledgeable, thoughtful, community-minded, future-oriented, and youthful-thinking though not necessarily young. If the term "reactionary" serves any practical purpose in Canadian politics today, it applies to the people responsible for inflicting this damage on the great national institution that was once the Conservative Party of Canada in more than just name. In the process, they have done great harm to the country's political culture and to the nation itself.

American conservatives generally give precedence to ideology over independent thinking and to individual freedom over the public interest. Canadians need to ask themselves a fundamental question: Did American conservatism inspire the Harper government's approach to decision-making and governance? Growing evidence suggests it did. Concerning Statistics Canada's national surveys, the Harper government placed a higher premium on extending to the citizen a right not to share vital data with the government, on a confidential basis, than on the demonstrable fact it serves the public good for the government to obtain that information. The Conservative government's approach turned on its head the classic Tory principle that favours the interests of the community over those of the individual when the two conflict, especially when, as in this case, the former overwhelmingly outweighs the latter.

But Tories do not have a lock on this principle. It has long girded public policy across the board. For example, income tax law, though introduced by a Conservative prime minister (Sir Robert Borden), has been supported by every government and major political party since. The *Income Tax Act* requires individual citizens to share information about their income and, through taxes, to forfeit some of their private wealth to the government for the public good based on that mandatory information.

Apart from principle, as a practical matter public policy needs to be based on objective facts. Obtaining the facts after mistakes are made is not the stuff of rational statecraft. Ironically, that is exactly what happened in the case of the census misfire. The very way the change from a mandatory to a voluntary census was mismanaged, based on incomplete information about the new policy's likely practical impact, demonstrated how misguided it is for government not to base every decision on reliable data. A mandatory census makes common sense to everyone but the hard-right libertarian ideologue who demonizes the state and consecrates the individual. A government of this sort ties the public sector's hands and is not being true to Burkean conservatism as practised in every liberal democratic society since Burke's time. Nor is it true to conservatism in the uniquely Canadian historical model Segal describes. The implications are as profound as they are alarming—not only for the Conservative Party but also for the country.

I would not be nearly as alarmed as I am about the Statistics Canada situation, worrisome as it is on its own merits, if it were not for the fact that it reveals so clearly the mindset the Harper government brought to bear on a broad swath of public policy, including the area dearest to me—the environment. Repeatedly, the Harper government demonstrated it was willing—indeed, too often eager—to allow private interests to prevail over the interests of the total community. As a case in point, it abandoned the Kyoto Protocol expressly because action against climate change would have imposed costs on the energy sector and *select* energy consumers—not on users of alternative energies, from solar to wind to geothermal to biofuel to other sources, to say nothing of the best interests of the country as a whole, still less of the planet. What in all that reflects the conservative principle that "the whole community is greater than the sum of the parts," as Segal puts it? Here, some few minority parts were equated with the total community. And the interests of those minority parts were deferred to at the expense of the majority. This policy approach was not rooted in traditional Canadian conservative values, large-"C" or small-"c"— or, indeed, in any traditional Canadian values. Sir John A. Macdonald was both founder of Canadian political environmentalism and father of the country. In the two roles alike, he applied certain values to all he did. Are contemporary Canadian Conservatives comfortable with abandoning the venerable tradition he began and the values he embodied? Are they even aware that the offenders were doing these awful things in their party's name?

# Whither the Canadian Conservative Party?

Nomenclature aside, is the Progressive Conservative Party of old dead? Or has it simply reinvented itself in a new guise to meet the requirements of the modern era? I lean markedly towards believing that the pre-2003 Conservative Party is not dead. But it is on life-support. One does not have to be a labellist to hold that some categories matter in politics. If a Canadian political party worthy of the name "Conservative" stands for anything, in the classical tradition, its First Principle—its Starting Point— must be that the state by definition is not a necessary evil, but, rather, an essential good, even if it might sometimes decide and perform badly. The state both expresses the community and serves as an instrument of the community—its shared values and common purposes. The antithetical position, in the classical tradition, is liberalism. This principle is noble, too, just as it is eminently defensible. But it is fundamentally different. Small-"l" liberals, and even many Canadians who today call themselves Conservatives, start, not from the community (the "commonweal") as the First Principle, but from the individual. They do not embrace the state. Instead, they fear it as the enemy of the individual and his or her rights, including economic and property and privacy rights. They see those rights as independent of community and, therefore, of the state—indeed, threatened by the state. Anyone who sees *classic liberalism* as the driving force behind the record of successive Canadian Conservative political leaders and their respective governments over the decades and generations, from Sir John A. Macdonald through to Brian Mulroney, does not know his or her history well. Anyone who believes that *classic conservatism* in the Canadian tradition was the driving force behind the Stephen Harper government has been living in an alternate universe.

For Sir John A. Macdonald, as for Conservative Party leaders who succeeded him, the state in a parliamentary democracy—when constrained by all the checks and balances built into the total political culture—was not the enemy. Rather, in Canada's case, it was the means by which a country with "too much geography," many and diverse and disperse regions, and a dual linguistic and multicultural reality could harness itself, mobilize itself, and express itself to realize collective ideals and achieve shared goals. The state made it possible to have a community—from sea to sea to sea to sea. Had Sir John A. Macdonald and the other founders of our nation viewed the state as an enemy, rather than as an instrument to pursue a great National Dream, the enormous expanse of real estate we now call Canada would long since have ended up part of the private property portfolio of Uncle Sam.

University of Calgary political scientist Tom Flanagan helped make Stephen Harper prime minister. He began as director of policy, strategy, and research for Preston Manning and the Reform Party. For the June 2004 election, he served as national campaign manager for the new Conservative Party following the 2003 merger. And then he was a war-room communications guru leading up to the June 2006 vote that elected Stephen Harper prime minister and defeated Paul Martin's government. Flanagan is honest and outspoken and articulate about his strategic mindset for the Conservative Party, including in his excellent book *Harper's Team: Behind the Scenes in the Conservative Party Rise to Power.*[25] Flanagan makes clear that he and his fellow ideological combatants in the post-merger Conservative Party had not been interested in building a wide coalition or consensus. In their view, every voice added to the governing coalition beyond what was necessary to win would have required compromising their political catechism. The strategic objective was to win whatever minimum number of individual parliamentary contests was required to gain and then retain power, preferably with the strongest-possible majority government, without their needing to dilute the Conservative Party's ideology-based agenda. They did not consider themselves obligated to consider anybody else's wishes or views, or those of cultural or linguistic communities or areas of the country, outside the winning coalition. Building a wider Canadian community, or sharing power with anybody they didn't have to share it with to win or hold power, did not interest them. Indeed, it was antithetical to their political modus operandi and ethos. Such a small-tent mentality for the party—and, ultimately, for the country—was also antithetical to what it has meant over the generations to be a Conservative in both the classic and Canadian traditions, though it was very much in the American conservative or libertarian tradition.

When a political party appeals only to people who will drink the ideological Kool-Aid, when it builds a governing majority (or, failing that, a minority) based exclusively on true believers, and when it then implements public policies that reflect this "state religion," it undermines Canadian democracy. The contrary political party model (called "brokerage politics") has provided one of Canada's strongest sources of national cohesiveness—what Pierre Trudeau called, in the 1972 election, our country's "integrity." The unity of the country is threatened by political exclusiveness. Had small-tent politics prevailed in the 1860s, before Confederation, there would never have been a Canada in the first place. Nor would Canada have survived its greatest crises in subsequent years—conscription, depression, separatist threats—if inspired Canadian political leaders of all political stripes had not embraced wholeheartedly a substantially larger vision of and for the country. Small-tentism in Canada was foreshadowed by American libertarian movements in the 1940s. But that kind of tent was not successfully pitched electorally in the United States until Richard Nixon made it the natural habitat of the Republican Party.

Is the Republican Party's political strategizing in recent decades around race the kind of playbook the Canadian Conservative party should be using on language and cultural identity issues to consolidate the gains it has made since the 2003 merger in challenging the Liberal Party's status as the "natural governing party"? I do not know whether Tom Flanagan, a Calgarian born and raised and educated in the United States, imported his political stratagems to Canada from the political backrooms of our southern neighbour. But such a mindset has no place in the Conservative Party of Canada or, for that matter, in any Canadian political party. It is immaterial whether the thinking came from the United States or from Ottawa's Sparks Street Mall. It is just dead wrong. I am not accusing the Harperites of having practised blatant Nixon-style politics of bigotry. I am saying, however, that it is utterly wrong for a Canadian national party that calls itself "Conservative" to craft its electoral strategy on anything less than a three-ocean, ten-province, every-territory, and every-Canadian appeal. To do otherwise would be disastrous for Canada, a country that simply could not survive ugly divide-and-rule politics. The Conservative Party would be among the first casualties, and would deserve to be. Didn't the party lose the 2015 election in large measure because it tried to appeal to the dark side of some voters, rather than the bright side of all of us? Foolishness over whether Muslim women should be allowed to wear a niqab during official citizenship ceremonies hardly reflected enlightenment. I don't mean that the Canadian Conservative Party should dilute, let alone abandon, the principles and traditions that help distinguish it from other political parties in order to broaden or maximize its popular appeal. Indeed, the need to restore those historic constants is what this book concerns. Becoming an entity that stands for nothing or that constitutes a facsimile of another party to avoid offending voters—that is a prescription for irrelevance. But the party need not make a Hobson's choice between principles and popularity. "We can resolve the clash of interests without conceding our ideals," John Kennedy wrote in *Profiles in Courage*. "Indeed, it is frequently the compromisers and conciliators who are faced with the severest tests of political courage as they oppose the extremist views of their constituents."[26] Those words could well serve as guideposts for the Canadian Conservative Party as it chooses new leadership and—one would hope—a fresh direction.

# Big Versus Small Tent

The now-silent voice of one of the Canadian Conservative Party's wisest leaders should echo in the memory's ear of every Conservative today as the party faces the greatest-ever threat to its identity and soul. When Robert Stanfield transferred the Conservative Party leadership to his successor, Joe Clark—at the Ottawa Civic Centre in February 1976—he told delegates, in his last major address as leader, how they must view their party and country. It was a vision he himself had always had—as a provincial premier, as a national party leader, as a Canadian, and as a Conservative. The departing leader had said the same thing before but never with greater passion and clarity than now. He would often reprise the theme as an elder statesman long after leaving politics. Not only was the theme quintessential Stanfield; it also captured the essence of a classic Canadian Tory. Stanfield told the packed gathering of delegates from across the country that their first allegiance as individuals and as a party should not be to their own interests or to those of the particular economic or social class or region with which they identified. Instead, he stressed, their strongest loyalty should be to the total Canadian community. As the leader said his farewell to the party and it thanked him, "a crest of emotion swept over the Civic Centre," says Joe Clark biographer David Humphreys.[27] If I myself were to title that outstanding address today, it would be "Conservatism, Community, and Trust." The retiring leader admonished his fellow Conservatives:

> Our national mission and our political self-interest coincide. **We must see our country and her people as one.** This is not a matter of trying to be all things to all people. It is rather a matter of understanding, responding to and reconciling the aspirations, the hopes and the longings of Canadians in all walks of life and in all parts of our land. **That is the way to serve our country.** It requires acceptance in our hearts, and not merely on our lips, of our country in all its diversity. **Some of us do not do that, and others notice it and do not trust us.**

In its long and storied history, never more than now, as it seeks new leadership, has the Conservative Party needed to heed such sound advice. Ideology-driven positions on the issues have forced the US Republican Party, in effect, to write off whole segments of the electorate, such as Latinos, African-Americans, and increasingly Asians as well. Is that what's in store for the Canadian Conservative Party if it continues to march on the ideological warpath it chose following the 2003 merger? Indeed, in the October 2015 federal general election, did the party experience a public backlash against small-tent policies of this very kind? How can a party reasonably expect to win elections when its extremist policies not only fail to appeal to, but demonstrably offend, whole categories of voters? A small-tent party might be able to whip up an electoral wave based on getting its diminishing core vote to the polls in a low-turnout election or in other such abberant circumstances favourable to it at a given time. Stephen Harper was able to form three governments by winning only between

36 percent and 40 percent of the total votes cast because vote-splitting among the three major national parties enabled him to win the largest number of seats in Parliament. But a political party cannot count on unreliable circumstances of this kind as a long-term winning formula. In Harper's time, in no sense was the Conservative Party able to build a true majority consensus behind his agenda for the country. Still less was the party able to create an electoral coalition among diverse segments of the Canadian population that would have enabled Conservatives to become what they historically have sought to be: "the natural governing party of the country."

As an analysis by Queen's University political scientist John Meisel shows, the same types of demographics that currently constitute the electoral base of the American Republican party, particularly for presidential elections, comprised the fast-shrinking base of the Canadian Conservative party in the dying days of John Diefenbaker's leadership for essentially the same reason: the lack of broader trust among electors of which Stanfield spoke. The Republican Party's atrophying core support is steadily becoming too small to craft a winning coalition outside territory electorally safe for the GOP. In this one respect, don't Canadian Conservatives have something to learn from their nominal counterparts south of the border about the electoral dangers of appealing to too narrow a base? A party prepared to kiss off segments of the electorate with policies not devised to serve the interests of the community as a whole will, in the long term, be unloved by anyone but that narrow and shrinking part of the electorate to which its policies appeal. As Stanfield warned the Canadian Conservative Party, voters at large notice such things and will "not trust us." However successful a more restrictive approach might be for a while or in some areas, without a big-tent strategy a major national party in either country will eventually find itself outside the tent looking in. The Canadian Conservative Party ignores Robert Stanfield's prescient warnings at great peril. A course different from the one he urged would risk killing the party. As Stanfield said, "Our national mission and our political self-interest coincide." In his book, Joe Clark discusses what he calls "a sea change" in the way Canada's political parties win national office. He notes that, from 1957 to 1993, every party had to compete everywhere across the country because its base was rarely large enough to win it national office as a legitimate and representative government. In 1993, he says, "that model broke." Clark means that the Official Opposition (the Bloc Québécois) and the next-largest party (Reform) "owed their victory to their narrow focus....[The] lesson for the parties was that being inclusive was a luxury they need not indulge."[28] Clearly, the Conservative Party under Stephen Harper's leadership followed this same "non-inclusive" model. When Joe Clark says the trend is "troubling," he pays homage to the appeal Robert Stanfield made to the PC Party membership when turning the leadership over to him in 1976. Stresses Clark: "Canada needs national conversations that reach across interests that might divide us, or regions that might confine us, or silos that are inevitable in a vast and diverse country."[29]

At this late stage in my life, I am much less concerned about the Canadian Conservative Party's electoral fortunes than about its future as a great national institution. Its pivotal role in founding and developing the country and keeping it united is as important to Canada's history and identity as that of any other of our national institutions—more so when it is the government of the land. For the country to lose this institution in its traditional and historically faithful form would be unfortunate, if not catastrophic. The country would risk being a substantially diminished place for everyone, not just Tory partisans.

I do not want the Conservative Party of Canada to survive simply for survival's sake. Least of all do I want the Conservative Party to survive in name only—albeit, already having lost half of that. For the party's survival to mean anything, the party itself must mean something, and that can't be just its own narrow purposes. The party must mean what it historically has meant: a vehicle to bring us Canadians together to dream Great Dreams and achieve them in the interests of our shared homeland and in pursuit of a better life for everybody—a civilized and humane life. That is the mission of the Conservative Party of which Robert Stanfield spoke so passionately at a packed stadium in Ottawa almost five decades ago. To him, the integrity of the Conservative Party's soul required this great national institution to be big and welcoming and trustworthy and committed to the well-being of all Canadians. To me, only then can the party be said to have survived—and to be worth surviving.

Rod McQueen, Robert Stanfield's press secretary for six years, distilled succinctly his boss's fundamental belief in the proper role of a national political party. In his 2004 remembrance of Stanfield, McQueen wrote: "Inclusiveness was the bedrock of Stanfield's being. He believed that a political party was a powerful means by which to build a national consensus."[30] It was in this very way that the Conservative Party helped found the country and, over the years, build the institutions and structures that made it a true nation, not just a chunk of geography on a map. The party, therefore, does a great disservice both to its own history and to all Canadians when it embraces divisive policies and employs confrontational divide-and-rule political strategies and tactics devised to win at any cost—including, most alarmingly, to the fabric and integrity of the country itself. Stephen Harper's governing style violated the traditional nature of the party and what it has historically meant to be a Canadian Conservative. If Robert Stanfield had been alive then, of this I am certain: he would have wept.

I weep.

# PC Party Transformation

The tectonic plate-shifting of the Conservative Party from a modern, progressive, enlightened, and all-inclusive nation-building political force under the leadership of Robert Stanfield, Joe Clark, Brian Mulroney, and Jean Charest to the very different party it is today did not happen in one step when Stephen Harper became leader after the party's 2003 merger with the Reform/Canadian Alliance Party. The PC Party had always harboured Reform Party–style elements, well before Reform was formed. In my time, ideologues of this type included Dan McKenzie, a Manitoba MP from 1974 to 1988. In Caucus, McKenzie once called the 1984 *Canada Health Act* communism. Another of this sort was Alberta rancher Jack Horner. He was a Tory MP from 1958 until 1977, when the man sold his political soul for a Trudeau Cabinet post. Before bolting PC ranks to become a Liberal, Horner described Stanfield as "a very, very sad choice" as leader. Stanfield's biographer notes that Horner told the PC leader to his face that "he considered him to be a Socialist."[31] Horner also called Joe Clark "a sheep herder," the ultimate insult from this rancher. Jack Horner came fourth on the first ballot in the eleven-candidate race for the PC Party leadership in 1976. On that ballot, this ideological extremist placed only forty-two votes behind the eventual winner, Joe Clark, out of 2,360 votes cast. So, within the party, Horner's Reform Party–type views must have had a substantial following within the national PC Party as far back as the mid-1970s, and likely long before.

Mel Gass, Malpeque MP in my own province from 1979 to 1988, was of a similar ideological hue, though endlessly more constructive and likeable than Jack Horner.[32] The same was true of Bill Domm, Peterborough MP from 1979 to 1993. He was militantly anti-metric and anti-abortion, even if progressive on the environment. Most of his views, except on the environment, were indistinguishable from those advocated by the typical Reform Party–style Conservative MP in the Stephen Harper era. When I ran in Peterborough in the 1997 federal election, I encountered substantial support throughout the riding, particularly in the rural areas, for policies of this sort. Many of the people supporting those views were Progressive Conservatives. Some would later join the Reform Party. This political phenomenon was erupting all over the country, not just in the West.

Robert Stanfield, Joe Clark, and Brian Mulroney were usually able to contain right-wing Caucus extremists with cajoling, bribery, or threats. Mulroney also did it with charm and flattery. He used his Irish gifts to great effect to keep ideological rebels in line. This PC leader did so even while in Opposition, and not yet prime minister, without all the sticks and carrots only a PM possesses to threaten or bribe or beat followers into submission on policy or any other front. Rarely were Mulroney's uncommon gifts for Caucus "persuasion" more severely tested, and demonstrated, than during the crisis he faced at the beginning of his party leadership over the Trudeau government's *Health Care Act* trap, detailed in an earlier chapter. But the most extreme Caucus "arch-conservatives"—for lack of a better term—made life difficult for all three leaders even at the best of times. John Diefenbaker and his Caucus cabal's rebellion against the *Official Languages Act* in 1969 was for Stanfield the worst of times. Whether John Diefenbaker was a forerunner of Preston Manning, Stockwell Day, and Stephen Harper within the Conservative Party is a fertile field for research. I believe he was. People close to MPs with a distinct Reform-type ideological orientation in the current Conservative parliamentary Caucus have told me that John Diefenbaker is the most admired PC leader in recent generations in their ranks. Stephen Harper's major address about Diefenbaker at the Albany Club's annual Sir John A. Macdonald Dinner in Toronto on January 11, 2007, demonstrated that he shares this affinity for Canada's thirteenth prime minister. His speech about the late Tory chieftain was much more a paean to a kindred ideological spirit than a pro-forma tribute to a primeministerial predecessor. Since my mid-twenties, as an Albany Club member, I used to regularly attend that annual celebration of Sir John A.'s birthday, including when Robert Stanfield gave the keynote address on January 8, 1990. Harper's worshipful remarks were unlike those I ever read or heard any previous Tory leader make about Diefenbaker at this event or, to my knowledge, anywhere else.

Was the transformation of the Progressive Conservative Party from what it once was to what it is today an evolution, a revolution, or, as I believe, a hostile takeover of the traditional Conservative Party by the Reform/Canadian Alliance Party? The question cries out for rigorous scholarly attention by historians and political scientists alike. However the weed grew, the seed was planted at least a decade and a half before its own pollen filled the air. I think the seeds were created, if not yet planted, as far back as when John Diefenbaker was ousted as leader in 1967 and replaced by Robert Stanfield, the first of three Red Tory leaders in a row. The Jack Horners of the party, in all parts of the country, but especially the West, could not stomach, let alone support, those leaders except when beaten, threatened, bribed, charmed, or flattered to do so. This was especially the case with Stanfield and Clark. Mulroney's two hefty majorities in Parliament between 1984 and 1993, particularly the first, caused the dynamic to slow but not stop. Mulroney's strong hand on the PC Party's helm enabled the ship to ride the waves. The seas, however, remained turbulent. Eventually, the waves engulfed the ship and sank it. Only a replica of the ship—and a bad one, at that—exists in the form of the current Conservative Party.

By the time Brian Mulroney departed the leadership in June 1993, his brand of progressive politics, like the man himself, was sufficiently out of favour within the party that the route was opened for Kim Campbell, a substantially more "conservative" politician, to succeed him. In fact, the writing was on the wall much earlier. Reform candidate Deborah Grey, who had finished fourth in the Alberta riding of Beaver River in the November 1988 federal general election, won a by-election in the same riding, viewed as the PC Party's strongest of strongholds, by a hefty 4,200 votes only five months later. Within only four years, in the 1993 election, the PC candidate, Dave Broda, came third behind Grey in this riding, beaten by 13,876 votes! Kim Campbell herself was not progressive by the standard I applied to Stanfield in an earlier chapter. Joe Clark and Maureen McTeer were proven right on that score. Nor was Campbell politically astute enough to know the danger to the party its extremists posed. Let alone was she committed, as her three predecessors had been, to containing them before they could tarnish the party's brand. Brian Mulroney's plunge in popularity and then retirement, the PC Party's electoral collapse under Kim Campbell in 1993, Jean Charest's failure to do substantially better in 1997 (a gain of only eighteen seats, from two), and the subsequent abdication of key party positions and roles by progressives to reactionaries—all of that, combined, rendered the party vulnerable to a hostile takeover by Reform/Canadian Alliance Party ideologues. The takeover happened from both within and without the party, not just in traditional Tory territory such as Alberta.

When I reluctantly ran in the 1997 federal election in Peterborough, the PC Party was already beginning to head in a policy direction far different from that in which Robert Stanfield had led the party. Stanfield would have as likely approved the party's strong anti-gun-control plank, for example, as agreed to become a male stripper. My sister Eileen and her husband, George Taylor Fulford III, both avid hunters, had the largest collection of guns in private hands in PEI. They needed a whole room in their spacious four-bedroom home, just outside Charlottetown, to rack them all. One rifle cost $25,000 in the 1980s. George's 1980 wedding gift to Eileen was a $9,000 hunting gun—giving new meaning to "shotgun marriage." As a 1997 PC candidate, I had to defend the party's policy that federal law should not require people such as George and Eileen to secure their weapons under lock and key or register each one, in the name of its owner, as part of a national database. To the extent I could understand the party's position, for lack of details provided by campaign organizers, our anti-registry rationale was that a national inventory would make it easier for potential thieves to know who owned guns across the country and, therefore, burglaries would increase. As if government could not manage proprietary information of this kind! (When was the last time a Canadian's tax return was leaked?) But such is not about logic or facts or common sense, much less the public interest. It's about American-style conservative/libertarian ideology, which sanctifies the private interest and demonizes government, while not requiring followers either to think for themselves or engage in any form of rational debate. How do you have a rational discussion with someone whose T-shirt reads, "Guns don't kill, government does"? This mindset is so fundamentally at odds with traditional Conservative Party values as to qualify as heresy.

With more than 300 million guns in circulation in the United States, with mass shootings (four or more victims) occurring at a rate of nearly one a day there, and with some 40,000 Americans killed every year in gun-related acts of violence (homicide and suicide combined), what Canadian, of any political stripe, would oppose reasonable gun-control measures to prevent such conditions in our own country? The answer: the Harper government, which abolished the long-gun registry in 2012 and took other measures to weaken Canada's gun laws. That government also refused to adopt the United Nations convention requiring every legally produced, exported, and imported weapon to be marked with identifying information. In addition, the convention also requires proper licensing and authorization procedures for commercial firearm exports. The Harper government fell short of calling the convention socialism—but not by much. Whose interests was the government protecting? Certainly not the public's.

Under Stephen Harper, the Conservative party resembled what it was under John Diefenbaker's leadership, before the Stanfield/Symons counterrevolution. The anti-intellectualism, the regressive policies, the domineering leader, the sheer meanness and spite that characterized the Harper style—all that was reminiscent of the last stages of the Diefenbaker era. In December 2011, former PM Jean Chrétien, commenting on the Harper government's steady march to the far right on such contentious issues as abortion and gay marriage, noted that the Conservatives had already bolted in that direction on Kyoto and gun control. He remarked: "Then might come capital punishment. And, one by one, the values we cherish as Canadians will be gone." It would be all too easy to dismiss these comments as partisan boilerplate, expressed as they were in a Liberal Party fundraising letter by a Liberal icon. But that would be a mistake, because the former prime minister's comments had the ring of truth. If, as Shakespeare said in *King Lear*, "Many a true word hath been spoken in jest," so also many a truth is said in partisanship. This is one such case. At a minimum, Conservatives should not make themselves vulnerable to charges of that kind. Journalist and author Lawrence Martin put it this way: "Could anyone imagine a dignified Tory like Robert Stanfield coming out with some of the venom that his party does today...he'd roll over in his grave."[33] Stanfield would do more than roll over; he would spin like a top. Not yet in my own grave, I am spinning. I know from correspondence with many others for this book, including former Cabinet colleagues and friends who were once Tories but no longer consider themselves Conservatives for reasons similar to my own, I spin not alone.

In the conclaves of the PC Party, Robert Stanfield always had to deal with partisans who pushed what was considered lunacy in his time but is party orthodoxy now: anti-intellectual, anti-science, anti-common–sense ideology. To watch Stanfield being subjected to this kind of proselytizing in the Policy Coordinating Committee (by aberrant Caucus members, in particular) was like seeing a child being forced by his mother to eat boiled spinach. I would notice Stanfield's legs stiffen under the board table, a sure sign of his anxiety. In the face of such minority elements in his Caucus, Brian Mulroney was no more comfortable than Stanfield, just better at masking his concern. Mulroney was a master of finesse, smothering the extremists with ego-boosting bromides, all the while pretending in their company that, deep down, their views were his own. Not even close. The right-wing contagion, however, remained in the party, albeit boxed in. Eventually, the contagion escaped and consumed the box. The reactionaries took over. Instead of managing these types and bringing them onside, as Stanfield and Clark and Mulroney had done with varying degrees of success, Stephen Harper not only sympathized with them but also enabled them. Indeed, he was one of them. Unlike Mulroney in the private conclaves of the PC Party, Harper wasn't acting. He was the real McCoy. Former Stanfield aide Rod McQueen has said: "I cannot imagine that Stanfield could possibly have approved of the [2003] merger that not only caused the 'Progressive' portion of the party's name to disappear but also brought to the fore so many midgets with extremist minds....The number of narrow-minded politicians seems greater now than in Stanfield's day. There were bigots back then, of course, but when they railed against him in Caucus, tried to hijack his social policy plans, or plotted his ouster, Stanfield always steered a thoughtful course without ever selling out his principles."[34] Stephen Harper did far worse than fail to steer the Conservative Party towards "a thoughtful course." He revved up the engines and sped the craft at full throttle in the opposite direction.

# Social Change

Just as the ideological transformation of the traditional Progressive Conservative Party described above did not occur in a short time span, but over an extended period under different leaders, so also the change did not occur in a social vacuum. The PC Party was reincarnated both simultaneously and in tandem with profound socio-economic shifts in the population at large. These have transpired roughly in the post-Diefenbaker period, 1967 to the present. In their insightful book, *The Big Shift*, Ipsos pollster Darrell Bricker and *Globe and Mail* journalist John Ibbitson argue that the Conservative Party's charge to the far right can be explained by demographic changes that are drawing much of the entire country's population in that ideological direction. The authors suggest that federal government immigration policy has created a new suburban, ethnically diverse, upwardly mobile, and fast-burgeoning category of citizens. According to this thesis, these citizens are demanding taxes be slashed, bureaucracy streamlined, public spending tamed, criminals punished, and traditional family values advanced and protected. Bricker and Ibbitson say that the traditional conservative core of Canadians—actually old-fashioned, classic, or unreconstructed "limited government" liberals—have been joined by these suburban immigrants to constitute a powerful new force in Canada. That force, they say, has been pushing the country markedly away from the collectivist or communitarian values that shaped Canadian politics and public policy over previous generations. In their view, this immigrant-influenced ideological trend started to occur at the very time a newly ascendant energy sector was shifting the political epicenter of the country to the conservative West and away from central Canada, traditionally more progressive. The dual shift in power towards immigrant-heavy suburbia and a soaring western Canada—in effect, a power alliance—"will make Canada inexorably a more conservative place."[35]

To my mind, the Bricker-Ibbitson thesis holds up despite the outcome of the October 2015 federal general election; any Canadian government would have been vulnerable to defeat after nearly a decade in power. What is important is the voting trend over many years—not election results, much less public opinion polls, at any given time. The Harper government's militant targeting of the immigrant vote lends credence to Bricker and Ibbitson's case. The government moderated its opposition to immigration, multiculturalism, and cultural diversity for a reason, and that was not sudden enlightenment. Academics Inder Marwah, Triadafilos Triadafilospoulos, and Stephen White note that the Harper government crafted, and then followed, an "ethnic outreach strategy" based on a "conservative ideology that includes immigrants and builds on their perceived ideological predispositions."[36] Among the wedge issues that the Conservative government used to achieve that end, these academics state, is opposition to same-sex marriage.

Though demographics help explain Canada's rightward direction in the past several decades, something even more fundamental underpins that transformation. I am referring to the phenomenon detailed by Robert Putnam in *Bowling Alone*. According to Putman's complex thesis, in the United States—and I would argue in Canada as well—(a) social links (among individuals, families, groups, neighbourhoods, and communities alike) have been breaking down; (b) a sense of "shared identity" and "reciprocity" has been weakening; and (c) people have, consequently, become less attached to all institutions, including government, that represent and foster community interests for the "mutual benefit" of all. Putman ascribes increased sectarianism, ethnocentrism, and rugged individualism to this "breakdown of community." These values, he argues, decrease people's trust in government and support for state involvement in their lives, economic and "civic." Putman argues that all this explains the strengthening hold of conservatism on voting patterns in recent decades in the United States. Canadian society is massively influenced both by America's traditional mass media and by American content on the Internet. And, like the economy of every other highly industrialized country, ours has rapidly become globalized through free trade, the increased mobility of capital, the boundary-free integration of the industry supply chain, and the fact a country's exchange rate is now driven more by world markets (for example, the price of oil) than by domestic conditions. All such factors render every Canadian a citizen of the world, not just of Canada. So, could our country possibly have escaped the social forces, including the escalating popularity of US-style conservatism, that Robert Putman identified? Surely not. Putman's book was published in 2000, three years before the Reform/Canadian Alliance/Progressive Conservative Party merger. Whole chunks of Putman's book read as though the author was describing the political realities in Canada that led to this merger.

It cannot be a coincidence that Canada and the United States—to say nothing of the United Kingdom and many other European countries, notably France, Denmark, the Netherlands, and Greece, among others—have been sprinting to the far right contemporaneously across all age groups. In the hyperindividualized "smartphone" culture of our times, the traditional conventional wisdom that the young tend not to be conservative because they have less than their elders to conserve no longer holds true in most such countries, including Canada. Stephen Harper himself, born in 1959, was but forty-one when elected leader of the Reform/Canadian Alliance Party. His chief of staff—until the Mike Duffy scandal forced him to depart the Prime Minister's Office—was Nigel Wright, a brilliant Harvard law school graduate. Wright had been instrumental in drafting Harper for the Canadian Alliance Party leadership. Born in 1963, Wright was only thirty-seven when he helped launch that far-right conservative party with many others of his age group and even younger. Kelly Pullen, in a *Toronto Life* profile of Nigel Wright, notes that Wright took a break from law school at the University of Toronto to work as a speech writer and as an assistant to my twin brother, Charley, in Brian Mulroney's PMO.[37] Later, Wright was active as a lawyer in the PEI Confederation Bridge project. I remember him well from those days and connections. But, at the time, I did not know that his ideological orientation was that far right;

Charley himself was never so inclined and still isn't. In retrospect, however, all this fits together. A lot of very bright young people like Wright were eager either to pull the Canadian Conservative Party much farther to the right than it traditionally had been or, failing that, to form a new party altogether with such a rightward orientation. But why were they so right-leaning in the first place?

# Hi-tech's Impact

The gadgets and processes the Internet is spawning—smartphones, tablets, social networks such as Facebook and Twitter, and so on—are fast atomizing society, young people especially. Tweens and teens use social media, on average, between eight and nine hours a day. Pre-adults tap more than they sleep. The digital technology revolution has transformed more than how people communicate with one another, manage their lives, and keep records. It has fundamentally changed how individuals view society—whether their local community, their province or state or county, their country, or the world population. Social bonds of every type are disintegrating. How long will be it before, for all practical purposes, all that's left of society are individuals texting one another at the same time? Two people linked fleetingly online do not so much bond with each other as simultaneously join the same world of unreality. The apparent modernity of social media is an illusion, for this is actually a primitive mode of communicating. It is utterly incapable of conveying nuanced non-verbal messages so vital to communicating what people actually think and feel as opposed to what they say they do—or, at best, believe they do—in 140 characters. Social media are to communication what Paint by Number is to art—quick, easy, and efficient, but untextured and ephemeral. In his book, Joe Clark says: "Ironically, the easy access to a wider world [through technology] can narrow our sights rather than broaden them and, in that process, erode our sense of connection to our actual neighbours and environment."[38] Someone who believes otherwise either does not have young children or hasn't noticed what they spend most of their time doing, how they're doing it, and with whom they're doing it. Though the Internet has improved all our lives in countless ways, the harm it is doing to the genuine social skills of young people—indeed, of everyone—is as inarguable as it is incalculable.

David Brooks has described this phenomenon as "the fraying of the social fabric and the rise of people who are so individualistic in their outlook that they have no real understanding of how to knit others together and look after the common good."[39] One has only to see almost everybody plugged into individual iPhones on a gym floor—blanking out everything and everyone except their own private source of sound or image ("bowling alone," as it were)—to appreciate how isolating these new forms of technology can be. Ships passing one another silently on the high seas will never form a fleet. I agree with Brooks that, as people increasingly retreat into their own private orbits in such technology-related ways, they begin to view the total world in a certain manner: "[It's] the solitary naked individual and the gigantic and menacing state." Even more to the point, he says, "This [high-tech] lens makes you more likely to share the distinct strands of libertarians that are blossoming in this fragmented age....the assumption that individual preferences should be supreme."[40] Brooks believes that the phenomenon in question is largely why young people constituted the core of libertarian Ron Paul's—the father's, not the son's—

presidential campaigns in 2008 and 2012. Might it not also explain the Reform/Canadian Alliance/Conservative Party's appeal to many youth in our own country? It is hard to believe the contrary.

If, as a young person, you have been reared in a world dominated by communications technology designed on the predicate that the individual is a stand-alone unit—and, by implication, the individual rises and falls totally on his or her own strengths—the consequence is inevitable: you likely do not value government programs such as Old Age Security, medicare, and employment insurance (let alone financial regulation and banking oversight) that seemingly advance the interests of others or the community as a whole but not necessarily your own interests, at least not in the foreseeable future. Such a perspective fundamentally distorts what it traditionally has meant to be a Canadian and how our particular form of democratic society operates and was devised to operate: on the principle that individuals succeed not only because of their own talents and skills and ambition and hard work, but also because of support from the total community we create together as a society, from one generation to another. The emergence and continuing strength of the new Canadian Conservative Party, notwithstanding its loss of power in 2015, cannot be understood outside the broader social forces that surround the party and to which, under Stephen Harper's leadership, I think it contributed—not necessarily positively.

# Can the Conservative Party Be Restored?

Those who think the Canadian Conservative Party has lost its way, want it to reverse direction, and are prepared to help set it on a truer course will need to devise a map and use a trusty compass. Destiny is not what a person hopes for and gets. It is what he or she strives for and earns. The political player—whether the candidate, the organizer, the supporter, or the voter—must first *believe* that the desired result can happen. And then everything possible needs to be done to make it happen. That is the mindset Robert Stanfield brought to bear when he—with Tom Symons and the skilled and committed team they assembled—revolutionized the policies and image of the Progressive Conservative Party back in the 1960s and 1970s. As we have seen, their work followed a decade of John Diefenbaker's leadership when the PC Party lost its way, just as it was to do with Stephen Harper and his fellow hard-right ideologues in charge. What cause could be more worthy than rescuing the political party that founded and built our nation? The party of Sir John A. Macdonald, the party of Georges-Étienne Cartier, the party of Sir Robert Borden, the party of Arthur Meighen, the party of Leslie Frost, the party of Joe Clark, the party of Brian Mulroney—*the party of Robert Lorne Stanfield*. People who believe as I do in that kind of Conservative Party, and who want to rescue its soul, must come together and be—in the words that Lord Tweedsmuir used to describe political activists—"honourably adventurous."

Must Canadian conservatives of the progressive persuasion be resigned to the existing order as far as their political party is concerned? Can the bell be unrung? Can this once-great national institution again be a force for communitarian values in its policies, in public discourse, in the federal or provincial governments it runs, and in its overall contribution to the political culture of the land? Religious-like passion—and, for many partisans, actual religious passion—drove those responsible for corrupting the Conservative Party by setting it on a far-right ideological and quasi-sectarian course more than a decade ago. That same level of passion will be required of others to reverse the consequent loss of the Conservative Party's soul and to return the party to its truer philosophical path. The Conservative Party has been an integral part of the country's history ever since the party's progenitor was founded as Canada's first "national" political party in 1854, before Canada itself was born. Restoring its soul will require a sufficient number of people to act with all the vigour of religious zealots.

Political battles (especially close ones) are won by getting to the ballot box more of one's own known committed supporters than the other side does. That requires organizational skill and effort—including aggressive fundraising—at ground zero. *Progressive* conservatives are going to have to out-hustle supporters of the status quo if their people and issues are to prevail. They should begin by looking at a certain model that is the latter-day equivalent of the careful step-by-step planning Robert Stanfield and Tom Symons employed in the pre-computer era for the PC Party more than a political generation ago.

Barack Obama and his formidable tech-savvy campaign team demonstrated how modern means of communication ("analytics") can be employed to win political battles. The relevant principles and techniques apply to contests both *within* a party (in Obama's case, to capture the Democratic Party's presidential nomination) and *between* parties (to wit: Obama's trouncing of GOP nominees John McCain and Mitt Romney in the 2008 and 2012 presidential elections, respectively). From voter research—unprecedented in quality and scope and sheer predictive power in the history of politics—the Obama team identified its actual *and* potential political and ideological supporters. It continually tailored and transmitted messages to those supporters based on their likely individual policy interests as extrapolated from demographic data, historic trends, survey results, correspondence or e-mail exchanges, and other forms of political intelligence. The team raised huge amounts of campaign funds from the same supporters, often through small individual donations made online multiple times over many weeks. Obama's people tracked the strength of supporters' commitment over time in response to different and varying issues and types of messages and appeals. They tweaked communications and other tactics accordingly. And, most important of all, at the end they both motivated their targets to vote and got them out to the polls in far greater numbers than the opposition did employing less sophisticated, more traditional methods. Nothing was left to chance, everything done to ensure victory.

At the heart of the overall election strategy that operated so well for Barack Obama was charting changes in the electorate's makeup since the previous election and focusing on one's own supporters most likely to vote in light of those changes. American political analyst and journalist Ron Brownstein has called the approach in Obama's case "creating the coalition of the ascendant"—specifically minorities, the millennial generation, and college-educated whites, especially women.[41] If Canadian conservatives of progressive persuasion are to carry the day for their own cause, they will need to employ sophisticated hi-tech campaign and election techniques of such a kind to create their own winning coalition, both within the Conservative Party and in the electorate at large. Like a great wall, that coalition will require placing many "bricks" one atop or aside another, one at a time, with great precision over a long course. Now is not too soon to begin construction.

# A Note of Personal Optimism

*[Sir John A.] Macdonald's profoundest purpose in political life was to preserve [the autonomy of British North America]…against the United States. Confederation, his most ambitious political project, was in essence a design for the defence of that separateness.*

John A. Macdonald: The Young Politician *by Donald Creighton*

---

I myself believe a once-great national institution is in ruins, or will be if the Conservative Party membership at large does not soon come to its senses and act. I know from years of working in the political trenches, and now from corresponding with countless Conservatives across Canada for many months for this book, that a broad swath of the party is progressive but went underground during the Stephen Harper leadership years. They were intimidated to the point of paralysis by the power that the prime minister and his tight inner circle ruthlessly wielded over both the party and the government and, ultimately, the country. Many Tories just gave up. Others were hoping change would happen without their effort. Still others were waiting for someone to lead the charge, and then they would follow. Will change finally happen now that Harper has resigned the leadership, setting the stage for a new leader and possibly a new party direction? Where will the new leader head— along the same route as before or on a markedly different one? I pray the latter. A course that does not involve restoring the progressive values of the Conservative Party will lead to failure. If the 2003 merger experiment proved anything over the course of over a decade, it is this: the market in Canada for an American-style conservative party has a 36 to 40 percent ceiling. It is no higher than that even in the best of electoral circumstances, as was the case during much of the 2006–15 period, when the other political parties were undergoing considerable change, including in leadership. Does the party that stretched the boundaries of Canada by thousands of miles in every direction—as far as a railway could steam across an entire continent— want to settle for so little electoral territory? And for what? To impose on Canada a type of ideological and policy agenda that the country was established to pre-empt in the first place? The Manifest Destiny of the Conservative Party of Canada is to check American Manifest Destiny at the Forty-ninth Parallel.

I am, essentially, an optimist. As a Maritimer in Parliament and, for a while, in government, I always had to be. Now, despite the obstacles, I want my political party back. I want the party to return to its progressive roots. I want it to restore the spirit of the conservative/liberal coalition that gave it, and the country, birth under prophetic anglophone and francophone leadership nearly a century and a half ago. I want the party to recommit itself to the total community that is Canada, not just those parts that make for a winning electoral coalition. All Canadians win with a larger vision. I want the party to believe truly in nation building, not just nation-management—or what Joe Clark has termed "house building," as opposed to mere "housekeeping."[42] I want the party to celebrate the country's linguistic duality, not just strategize around it. I want the party to emblazon over its front door the country's Latin motto, *a mari usque ad mare* ("from sea to sea"). That way, every person, regardless of Canadian postal code or of national or cultural origin or race, knows that he or she is warmly welcome inside. I want the party to believe every Canadian is worthy of public support when his or her luck takes a vacation. The person's congenital characteristics—from eye colour to sexual orientation—should not count. Just as the community is more than the sum of its parts, so also it is stronger when all its parts are stronger. I want the party to appeal to our better nature and to educate and uplift, rather than exploit and stoke our fears and self-ishness. I want any current or future Conservative government, federal or provincial, and the Conservative Party itself, to practise generosity in the spirit of Robert Stanfield. We are all nobler when we meet our obligations to fellow community members in greatest need—"the needful," as Sir John A. Macdonald called the poor and disadvantaged. Who among us is not just one stroke of bad luck removed from being needful ourselves, no matter how economically or socially strong we might currently be or think we are?

I also want the party to embrace proudly Canada's historic leadership in the international community as a full partner. This role has to include the natural environment, beginning with good stewardship of our own habitat. Surely, a Conservative prime minister, Sir Robert Borden, didn't seek an independent and sovereign role for Canada in world affairs so that we could play the spoiler, as the Harper government too often did on such issues as climate change. We own the planet's second-largest land mass. We, therefore, have a vested interest, to say nothing of a moral obligation, to be wise stewards of the bountiful natural resources that fate has bestowed upon us. If Canadians abdicate leadership on the environment, we shortchange not only ourselves—bad enough as that is—but also our fellow human beings and creatures. A commitment to defending the natural treasury of the planet has always been integral to who we are as a people. Canada established the world's first national park service in 1911. We also protect more square kilometres of land and water in national parks than any other country in the world. These are not answers to obscure questions in *Trivial Pursuit*, though two Canadian journalists created that board game. They are facts of planetary life that reveal much about who we Canadians are and what we hold dear. Nature is our brand. Everything else, including life itself, depends on it. A Canadian political party that does not represent and fight for every such precious value that helps both distinguish and elevate us as a people is unworthy of the name Conservative. Otherwise, what is its mission to conserve?

Above all, I want the party to have a soul and a heart and a passion for Canada beyond the ballot box, beyond public opinion polls, beyond the political calendar, beyond its electoral ambitions, and beyond its own narrow ideological agenda. I want it to have more of what I have called the *Helen Factor*. Again, by that I mean simple qualities of goodness that Helen Doyle, like Robert Stanfield, exemplified. Ones that, at our best, we Canadians generally manifest and that the Conservative Party could once again help Canadians continue to reflect in their very marrow. Like me, most people personally know somebody—perhaps a family member, a close friend, a teacher, a faith leader, a personal counsellor—who embodies values widely considered among the best in human nature. In routinely living their own lives, they make other people's lives substantially better. I have been fortunate to know several people, both within and outside my own family, who fit that description to a tot and tittle. Among them, pre-eminently, is the individual I have described as my second mother: Helen Doyle. I have highlighted her in this book not only because she has had a profound impact on my life, including my political life, but also because she represents, for me, the apogee of humanity writ humble in selfless service to others—her own family, her adopted family, her church, her community, and her God. She had no agenda in life other than to be a good person and, without necessarily being self-aware in these terms, to make the world at least a little bit better than it would have been without her. She succeeded masterfully, even if in countless small ways, day in and day out throughout her eight decades on the planet. This unpretentious woman lived a life of purpose. In an e-mail to me, my younger sister, Maura Davies, once mentioned the impact Helen Doyle had on our extended family: "Few people will ever know what a profound and lasting influence Helen has had on all of us." Shouldn't the Conservative Party, through its values and policies and actions, have that kind of benevolent impact, writ large, on the country as a whole? At one time, under leaders such as Robert Stanfield, it did. It no longer does. But it could again. I desperately want it to.

----

The essence of politics is conflict. That of government is power. Politics and government constitute a system or process by which a community allocates scarce shared resources. At least in theory, the purpose is to advance the common interest. *New York Times* columnist Gail Collins has said that politics is a question of "who gets what first."[43] The system also chooses the people (politicians) to carry out that mandate. Those political actors decide not only "who gets what first" but also where when and how. ("Why," so important to Robert Stanfield, is too rarely addressed.) By nature, politics can be a nasty and ruthless business. Nineteenth-century military theorist Carl von Clausewitz famously said "war is the continuation of politics by other means." For many politicians, politics is a form of *undeclared war*. To them, no value—least of all a sense of fair play—is more important than winning. In their type of politics, as in love and real war, "all is fair." Because politics by its very character is highly adversarial, if not literally warlike, it too frequently brings out the worst in people. This is true not only of the politicians themselves, but also of their partisan supporters. But politics can and sometimes does bring out the best in people, too. I believe that Robert Stanfield exemplified an intrinsically good person who was made even better by politics and who made politics better by having been in it. Either from history or from direct experience, I know that countless other Canadian politicians, in all political parties, fit the same description. Far too many do not.

The Conservative Party of Canada today does not embody values at either end of the moral spectrum between Robert Stanfield and, say, Richard Nixon. But it could and should do so at the Stanfield end. It's the end at which individuals stand for certain principles. Exemplars place service to others above their own interests. They hold strong views of what constitutes right and wrong. But they do not slam the door shut on those who hold contrary views. They exude optimism and good will and humour towards friends and adversaries alike. They value harmony with others while avoiding unnecessary conflict. They seek to make the world a better place than they found it. Towards that goal, they work in common cause with people of like mind or ones they think could be brought onside through dialogue and persuasion. They face life's challenges and setbacks with equal measures of strength and courage and dignity and grace. And throughout their lives, they position themselves to depart the stage, at whatever time the gods deem right, each able to say, "I did my best." Along life's journey, they earn other people's trust. *Trust*—it's the value that Robert Stanfield exhorted Progressive Conservatives to earn from every Canadian when, in February 1976, he said his farewell to them as their national leader. Why should a *politician* be held to a lower standard of trust than any other individual whose job it is to serve the public? Even more to the point, why should society not hold a *political party* to as high a standard of trust as it applies to other service institutions—from hospitals to schools and colleges to banks to accounting and law firms to police and fire departments to airlines to the courts right through to churches and mosques and synagogues?

Rod McQueen, in his 2004 remembrance of his former boss, describes what he calls "the "bedrock of [Robert] Stanfield's being": "Among Stanfield's remarkable traits were patience, integrity, decency and fortitude in the face of failure, all of them marks of a man to be much admired. He expected loyalty, and rarely received it, but he gave loyalty freely to all. No matter who you were, you never had to worry about turning your back on Robert Stanfield. He would never do you in—no matter what you might have done to him."[44] McQueen could have been describing Helen Doyle when he mentioned patience, integrity, decency, fortitude, and loyalty as among Robert Stanfield's finest personal qualities and public virtues. This is the essence of the *Helen Factor*. Robert Lorne Stanfield, like Helen herself, personified it. Does any reasonable person truly believe the *Helen Factor* characterizes the Conservative Party today? Would he or she have applied it to any Cabinet minister, including the prime minister himself, during the Stephen Harper era? If the answer is either *no* or *not completely*, Conservatives have a big job to do: restore the ideals and human qualities that their party represented when Robert Stanfield and its other great leaders not only met the highest standards of humanity, but also helped set those standards for the Canadian political class.

As we have seen, Robert Stanfield launched his national political career with a powerful opening address at the policy session of the 1967 Progressive Conservative convention that elected him leader. In that address, Stanfield called for a "broadly based party" that would eschew extremism in favour of addressing the concerns of all Canadians and bringing them together as a united nation. In departing the leadership, Stanfield returned to this theme, hitting it even harder in light of his decade-long experience as Tory leader. That chilly February 1976 evening, he warned of dire danger for the party. The warning rings even truer at present than it did then in light of the destructive, ideology-driven policies and practices and hyperpartisanship of the Conservative government under Stephen Harper's leadership: "Some Progressive Conservatives would rather fight than win," he said. "Some of us wish to elevate a legitimate concern for individual self-reliance and individual enterprise into the central and dominating dogma and theme of our party. Why do we spoil a good case by exaggeration? Why do we try to polarize a society that is already taut with tension and confrontation?"

Robert Stanfield fell short of becoming prime minister of Canada by only one parliamentary seat in 1972. The prize eluded him. But Rod McQueen has said something of himself and of Robert Stanfield that every Canadian Conservative should ponder: "If you're going to lose, far better to do it alongside a good and gallant man than be with connivers who will do anything and say anything in order to win at any cost to the country."[45] Like McQueen, I believe that, if forced to choose between winning and hurting the country, one should choose, as Stanfield always did, what I have called the *Helen Factor*. But I do not think the Conservative Party needs to make this Hobson's choice in seeking office. Canadians typically reward principled leadership of the sort Robert Stanfield championed and provided, even if he himself did not prevail over his political adversaries nationally. Indeed, Canadians typically elect as prime minister strong moral leaders—from Sir John A. Macdonald and Sir Wilfrid Laurier and Sir Robert Borden in the nineteenth and twentieth centuries to such paragons of public virtue as Louis St-Laurent, Lester Pearson, and Joe Clark closer to our own time. And Canadian voters more often than not have made these good people their leader with parliamentary majorities. So, my calling on the Conservative Party to restore the kind of principled and moral leadership it traditionally has had is not devoid of political realism or potential partisan advantage. As Stanfield himself said, the party's nation-building mission and political self-interest "coincide." As this wise man also counselled, however, the party must stand for more than just its own electoral chances or its own restricted dogma or the interests of only its own electoral base. It must stand for the total Canadian community. This is the lesson and example of Robert Stanfield's life and political career. In our own time, it's the one I want the Conservative Party to learn anew—and, once again, to act on proudly. I want it to *believe* again—in Canada and in itself. I want the Conservative Party of Canada to be, now and forever more, the party of the *Helen Factor*.

## The Path Forward: Our Better Angels

Finally, and in the same spirit, I want the Conservative Party of Canada to restore "Progressive" to its name. "Progressive" was added to "Conservative" to form the dual name "Progressive Conservative" in 1942, almost nine decades after the party was founded. But the addition earned a rich patina over the years. What's more, "Progressive" is rooted in a venerable tradition of populist protest in the West— legitimate protest, not the kind artificially stoked to win votes by divide-and-conquer political tactics of the sort Stephen Harper and his minions embraced and prac- tised. Most significant of all, "Progressive," when linked to the equally illustrious "Conservative" name, expresses—much better than "Conservative" alone could— what the Conservative Party of Canada, at its best, traditionally has stood for: *progress*. Not progress for its own sake, but progress based on both a respect for "the tried and true" *and* a commitment to making things better for every member of the Canadian community, living and yet born. That principle includes embracing enthusiastically the role of government as an agent for the total Canadian nation: for every part of our great country, and for every individual.

"Progressive Conservative"—now, that's one label I revere!

As an eternal optimist by nature, I live in hope that the Conservative Party—nay, the "Progressive Conservative Party of Canada"—will someday soon stand again for all the above, and much more. I want the party to regain its progressive and populist traditions, including the dual name that expresses that venerable political heritage. Now is the time, with Stephen Harper no longer leader, for the party to reverse course and follow its true North Star. My hope will be realized, however, only if enough like-minded Conservatives act urgently to make it happen. Non-Conservatives sym- pathetic to the cause of restoring a great national institution can also help with their voices and goodwill. Tory partisans can advance the cause by taking over local party riding associations, at both the executive and grassroots levels. They can run for, and win, national party office. They can nominate progressive individuals or, for the truly motivated, offer themselves to represent the party in actual elections, federal and provincial alike. They can raise and donate money for select candidates and campaigns. They can make their views known in every available forum, within the party and outside. Those forums include local and regional and national party policy and organizational meetings. They also include—more publicly—letters to the editor, op-ed columns, talk radio phone-in shows, social media such as Facebook and Twitter, and political blogs. To win back their party from the right-wing ideologues who have hijacked it, Conservatives of progressive persuasion can chat up their fellow partisans and friends and neighbours positioned to affect candidate nomination or election outcomes. And then everyone involved should vote to ensure that the desired result in every one of these contests, small or large, happens. Moreover, they can directly pressure the existing Conservative parliamentary Caucus in Ottawa and other centres of party power, including Conservative provincial governments (there is only one as I write—in Newfoundland). And they can write books! Those recently written by Roy McMurtry and Joe Clark have helped the cause. I hope my own will help it, too. May there be many more—the sooner, the better.

For the longer term, progressives can join, or even form, institutes and associations geared to influencing public policy while cultivating a strong core of thoughtful and informed people able to explain and defend the relevant perspectives beyond their own ranks. These bodies don't need to be formally linked to the Conservative Party, merely committed to its historic values and traditional overall policy direction. Since the Second World War, the American right has been employing this strategy with outstanding success. Canadian progressive conservatives should study the American right's model and shamelessly steal the mechanics most adaptable to our politics while rejecting the extremist ideological fuel that makes the engine run. Reform Party–style ideologues used just these methods to hijack the traditional Tory party and transform it into its current "neoconservative" form, aping the American right-wing's model for insidiously proselytizing and organizing at ground level. Stephen Harper headed the National Citizens Coalition before succeeding Stockwell Day as leader of the Canadian Alliance Party in 2002 and then capturing the leadership of the remade Conservative Party a year later. Formed in 1972, the Coalition is a right-wing lobby that campaigns against public sector unions and for smaller government and lower taxes. Its agenda is utterly indistinguishable from that of its US counterparts. The Coalition's founder, insurance tycoon Colin Brown, was militantly hostile to public health insurance—"socialized medicine," he called it. Stephen Harper captured the national Conservative Party leadership from that very ideological command post. For a classic Canadian conservative like me, this irony is as depressing as it is cruel. The Progressive Conservative Party laid the groundwork for national public health insurance when John Diefenbaker was prime minister. In a corrupted incarnation of its former self, the party ended up being led, in the person of Stephen Harper, by the chief talent scout for a farm system for right-wing political ideologues and activists hostile to the very bedrock of Canada's social safety net. Sense here a pattern, one splattered with stars and stripes? To beat all such right-wing ideologues politically at their own game, progressives will need to be at least as strategically cunning as they.

Bob Hepburn wrote in the *Toronto Star*: "[Peter MacKay] is best known for making arguably the dumbest blunder in Canadian political history when he agreed in 2003 to merge the Progressive Conservative Party that he then headed with the Canadian Alliance led by Stephen Harper to form the Conservative Party of Canada. MacKay was totally outsmarted by Harper, who subsequently sidelined both MacKay and the progressive wing of the merged party."[46] How true. How sad. How to do something about it? Those eager to win back the Conservative Party from those who have taken the party on a far different path from the one it has traditionally followed will need to fight fire with fire. The playbook about how to light the flame and keep it eternally burning hot has already been written—by the other side. It needs to be used against them. Just wringing one's hands, without helping to produce real change, will serve only to perpetuate the status quo. Both Machiavelli and Lord Tweedsmuir should be recruited to the team. For Canadian progressive conservatives to outsmart the neocons in our own country, it won't be necessary to replicate the elaborate ideological edifice constructed in the American context. It took the other side decades of careful planning—never mind tons of cash—to build and perfect that edifice. Progressives do not have the time, and likely not the ability either, to say nothing of the money, to accomplish the same feat. But the relevant organizing principles could be applied to the task.

Ultimately, the battle lines will be drawn, and the battle itself won or lost, when the Conservative Party chooses Harper's successor as leader. So, those who want a very different leader from what he has been, and a different party from the one he was pivotal in recasting in the American mould, must act immediately. Hope, though necessary, is not alone sufficient. The legendary Chinese military strategist and philosopher Sun Tzu influenced both Eastern and Western ways of conducting what he called the "art of war" ever since he made his pronouncements a half-millennium before Christ. He said that every battle is won before it is fought. By that, he meant that the key to victory is choosing the right terrain on which to fight. Progressives eager to regain their party from the Harperites must frame their narrative wisely. Then, having chosen the terrain, they must ensure that their troops fight smartly. Here, too, the war plan has already been written—in this case, not in China but France.

Some six decades ago, the French jurist, sociologist, and politician Maurice Duverger described, in his groundbreaking book *Political Parties*, the essence of politics and the nature of effective political warfare.[47] Duverger analyzed how mass-membership political organizations must organize to compete for office in first-past-the-post (single-ballot majority vote) competitive contests in light of what he termed both "mechanical" and "psychological" factors. Duverger stressed that loyal party members, though important, are less vital to a party's electoral success than, in today's parlance, "swing voters," because the latter far outnumber the former. In certain essential respects, his analysis remains as true today as it was in his own time. The hard-core, right-wing ideologues who now control the Canadian Conservative Party would fight to the death any effort to lead the party in a different direction from the one it is now following in their hands. So, the way to change the direction relies much less on trying to convert these people than on appealing to two groups: those of progressive orientation, however underground they might be at present, and what Duverger called "wavering supporters." To my mind, it boils down to crafting a compelling message, putting forward credible and attractive messengers, organizing well around that message, exploiting every avenue and opportunity to advance it, and doing all this with unrelenting zeal. That is the way forward. For Tories of a progressive bent, the wheel does not need to be reinvented. It just needs to be spun, for the first time in too long a while, in a direction that leads the party back to its rich history and heritage, to its better angels, and to a nobler future—for itself, for the country, and for all Canadians.

I want the party to return to the path of true conservatism in the Canadian tradition. Maybe in the manner I myself returned, so many years ago, to my family's true political path after a brief flirtation with the Liberals because of a chance encounter as a boy with the great Louis St-Laurent. If and when my hope is realized, I am going to have a chat with my three daughters about how they should vote. Maybe, just maybe, a McMillan will have reason to cast a Tory vote again. Then, and only then, Mr. DeMille, will I be ready for my close-up.

# ACKNOWLEDGEMENTS

A s with any book, many people helped me write mine. In my case, the number of contributors is so large that the odds are high that I would forget mentioning somebody important. So, I shall not try to list everyone. But a few people must be mentioned. Among them are my brother Dr. Colin McMillan and my sister Maura Davies, who helped with all family-related facets of the narrative, in addition to applying their formidable intellects and vast knowledge and rich life experience to vetting large swaths of the rest. My nephew Andrew McMillan (Colin's son), the genealogist in our family, filled in details about both sides of our ancestry.

Some of my former ministerial and political staff provided recollections and insights concerning our shared path. Rob Burnett (senior assistant), Terry Collins (press secretary), and Sheila Kieran (senior policy advisor), in particular, were as helpful to me in writing this book as they always were with my public career.

A number of academics and policy specialists guided me on technical matters. Foremost among them are: political scientists Drs. Rand Dyck and Denis Smith; chemist Dr. Robert Slater (my senior assistant deputy minister at Environment Canada); and PEI built-heritage authority and writer Catherine Hennessey. The individuals who agreed to be interviewed, or otherwise communicated with me about different subjects with which they had direct experience, are more numerous than the packed entries in my big dog-eared address book. These include both former Cabinet colleagues and officials and even former political adversaries. Their sharp memories were rivalled only by their eagerness to be helpful, which they were unfailingly. Former senator Lowell Murray and Dr. Tom Axworthy, former principal secretary to Prime Minister Pierre Trudeau, were especially generous with their time. So was my twin brother, Charley, Prime Minister Brian Mulroney's "intellectual bodyguard," particularly during the pre-writing stages. The same is true of immigration lawyer and artist Jean-Yves David (of Montreal), whose friendship and help (including with this book) has meant more to me than he could possibly know.

I consulted Dr. T. H. B. Symons (and his resourceful research assistant Kathryn McLeod) only to confirm technical details and to jog my memory more generally about the PC Party policy process he and Robert Stanfield created and directed. I otherwise did not engage Dr. Symons because I wanted to maximize my objectivity about a central figure in the narrative for whom I have such great admiration and affection. My gratitude for his help with the book's facts is enormous. But "gratitude" does not come close to expressing how I feel about the benevolent impact he has had on my life as a whole. Nor would that word describe adequately the debt I owe to Dr. Ralph Heintzman of the University of Ottawa's Graduate School of Public and International Affairs. As a long-time friend and erstwhile colleague, he urged me to write this book, guided it at crucial junctures, and served as my Muse throughout. Like all the others who helped, Ralph bears no responsibility for any failings the book might have, which can be attributed largely to my having fallen short of meeting the high standards by which this extraordinary scholar and thinker operates on every front. But the target was made a lot easier for me to hit thanks to his steadying my hand on the trigger. I heartily thank, as well, the Parliamentary Library in Ottawa and the Trent University Archives in Peterborough. Without their help, I could not have even contemplated undertaking the mammoth amount of digging I was required to do into the most obscure, and dustiest, of document bins.

A memoir, by definition, relies on memory to supplement archival and other records. And memory, like every human faculty, is fallible. In the case of this book, I would welcome suggestions for improving its accuracy or fairness for any future edition. Towards that end, I invite readers to contact me through the publisher.

Finally, I thank everyone at Nimbus Publishing for providing me a voice to tell this story; I am especially thankful to freelance editor Barry Norris, who not only helped me tell my story as best I could, but also ensured it was compact enough to be bound between two covers. No one knows more than I how much better the cultural landscape of Atlantic Canada is because of Nimbus Publishing's dogged efforts to help Canadians tell worthwhile stories about themselves and their country.

# NOTES

## Chapter One

1. Barbara MacAndrew. "A formidable political family," *Macleans,* June 16, 1986, 12–14.

2. Heath Macquarrie. *Red Tory Blues.* Toronto: University of Toronto Press, 1991, 146.

3. Brian Mulroney. *Memoirs,* paper ed. Toronto: McClelland & Stewart, 2007, 34.

4. Thomas Aquinas. *Philosophical Texts,* trans. Thomas Gilby. New York: Oxford University Press, 1960, 373.

5. Anthony Storr, *Churchill's Black Dog, Kafka's Mice, and Other Phenomena of the Human Mind* . New York: Grove Press, 1988, 9.

6. One such study found an identical twin reared away from his or her co-twin has about an equal chance of being similar to the co-twin in personality, interests, and attitude as one who has been reared with his or her co-twin. This led the researchers to conclude that the similarities between twins are due to genes, not environment, and that the differences between twins reared apart must be due totally to the environment. See T. J. Bouchard Jr., David Lykken, Matthew McGue, Nancy L. Segal, and Auke Telegen, "Sources of Human Psychological Differences: The Minnesota Study of Twins Reared Apart," *Science* 259, no. 4978 (1990): 223–8.

7. Carl Burke not only founded Maritime Central Airways; he also held a large block of stock in Nordair. Among his vast real estate holdings, in PEI and elsewhere, including Florida, he owned the Charlottetown Hotel at one point, though it had been built by Canadian National Railways in 1927. The largest PEI landowner was Howard Webster of Montreal. He owned, in the eastern part of the province, Dundas Farms Ltd., which had seven thousand acres, much of it for elite Highland cattle.

8. The present-day Dundee Arms Inn has a "McMillan Room," described in the inn's literature and posting this way: "Room 28, The McMillan Room, inherits its name from the McMillan family who operated the property as a guest home [*sic*] from 1956 to 1972. This room features one queen bed, antique furnishings, private bath, and colored television with extended cablevision."

## Chapter Two

1. Ben Malkin. *Gazette* (Montreal), September 29, 1965.

2. Geoffrey Stevens. *Stanfield.* Toronto: McClelland & Stewart, 1973, 79.

3. Ibid., 79.

4. Ibid.

5. Denis Smith. *Rogue Tory: The Life and Legend of John George Diefenbaker,* paperback edition. Toronto: MacFarlane Walker & Ross, 1995.

6. Ibid., 208.

7. Ibid., 210.

8. Stevens. *Stanfield.* 26; emphasis added.

9. Peter C. Newman. "Change in Conservative style," *Regina Leader-Post.* June 20, 1968.

10. Smith. *Rogue Tory,* 329–30.

11. Ibid., 489.

12. Doris Kearns Goodwin. *Team of Rivals: The Political Genius of Abraham Lincoln.* New York: Simon & Schuster, 2005.

13. Fulton lost his bid for re-election to the House of Commons in the 1968 election and was never to return to Parliament. After serving as a British Columbia Supreme Court justice from 1973 to 1981, Fulton was appointed by the Mulroney government to a six-year term on the International Joint Commission, a Canadian-US body that implements boundary water treaties and agreements between the two countries. Fulton died, still a respected figure, in 2000.

14. Anthony Westell. "Stanfield's ideas fight party bigots." *Brandon Sun,* February 26, 1969.

# Chapter Three

1. The policy was closely linked to Quebec financier Marcel Faribault, president of Montreal Trust Général, who attended the Montmorency Conference and championed the idea there. He was to run for the Tories in Quebec in 1968 as one of Stanfield's many high-profile "dream" candidates. All were crushed.

2. Among his five university degrees, King held an economics PhD from Harvard. He served as senior staff member of the John D. Rockefeller Foundation in New York City, heading its new department of industrial research. He did so after losing, in the 1911 election, the seat the future Liberal PM had won in a by-election in 1908.

3. Stevens. *Stanfield.* 218.

4. Marshal McLuhan. *Understanding Media: The Extensions of Man,* reprint. Cambridge, MA: MIT Press, 1994.

5. John Meisel. *Working Papers on Canadian Politics.* Montreal; Kingston, ON: McGill-Queen's University Press, 1973, 81.

6. Stevens. *Stanfield.* 139.

7. Robert Stanfield, "Conservative Principles and Philosophy," in *Politics: Canada,* ed. Paul Fox and Graham White. Toronto: McGraw-Hill Ryerson, 1987, 376–81.

8. Gore Vidal. *The Second American Revolution.* New York: Random House, 1982, 160.

# Chapter Four

1. Tom Symons's professional career is the subject of Ralph Heintzman, ed., *Tom Symons: A Canadian Life*, Ottawa: University of Ottawa Press, 2011. Heintzman's own introductory chapter, "Becoming Tom Symons," details Symons's personal and family background and rise to professional stardom. Denis Smith's chapter, "Tom Symons and the Founding of Trent University," explores the early history of Trent and Symons's pivotal role in making the university the respected institution it has become. My own chapter, "Robert L. Stanfield and Tom Symons: A Public Policy Partnership," summarizes the PC Party policy process the two men devised and operated when Stanfield was leader.

2. The term "Brahmin"—coined by Oliver Wendell Holmes, Sr. in *Atlantic Monthly* in 1860—came from India. It applied to the highest Hindu caste, considered divinity personified. The term in a North American context is typically used to describe New England bluebloods. But I believe it is applicable, as well, to individuals and families throughout the Maritime provinces with the same economic and social characteristics and values. The moral rectitude, devotion to public service, and philanthropy of many Brahmins in New England and the Maritimes render the term "Brahmin" appropriate for old upper-crust families of Protestant and (primarily) English origin on both sides of the US-Canadian border. Stanfield's most distinguishing public characteristic, personal integrity, is rooted in such an identity. Nevertheless, as with most New England Brahmins, his public persona, like the real person, was devoid of self-righteousness. The Brahmin families amassed their original wealth, in the late eighteenth to mid-nineteenth centuries, from such enterprises as shipbuilding, textiles (in the Stanfields' case, woollens in the mid-1800s), and the "East Indie" import/export trade. Stanfield publicly acknowledged being a millionaire—in today's dollars, a multimillionaire (with a net worth of between $7 and $9 million, some close friends think much more).

3. While campaigning door to door in my riding in the 1984 federal general election, I ascended a steep wooden exterior fire escape to a second-storey apartment occupied by an elderly woman. She had, on her living room wall, a small primitive but exquisite painting—no doubt executed in real time—of the 1856 Tryon Stanfield factory in PEI (a family heirloom?). Four years later, during the 1988 campaign, I revisited the apartment, but she was no longer there, likely having died. To this day, I wonder what became of that precious mid-nineteenth-century artifact of PEI and Stanfield history—and of the old lady and her elephantine black-and-white cat, the biggest I have ever seen. Such is the stuff of retail politics.

4. Stevens. *Stanfield*. 15.

5. Robert Stanfield would later reside in the same neighbourhood in the official residence, Stornoway, reserved for the Official Opposition leader, and, upon retirement, in his own home; indeed, on the same street: Acacia Drive.

6. Rod McQueen. "Remembering Robert Stanfield: A good-humoured and gallant man," *Policy Options* (25, no. 2). February 1, 2004, 2. Available online at policyoptions.irpp.org/magazines/canadas-cities/remembering-robert-stanfield-a-good-humoured-and-gallant-man/.

7.  At one Press Gallery black-tie dinner, the sartorially adventuresome Trudeau wore a red silk turtleneck top with his tuxedo, instead of the conventional white dinner shirt and black bowtie. When his turn at the microphone came, Stanfield looked over at the PM and cracked, with the mock seriousness of a Jack Benny and the comic timing of a Johnny Carson: "I always knew Pierre Trudeau was a reactionary. Until tonight, I didn't know he was a redneck!" The crack broke up everyone.

# Chapter Five

1.  The name first bandied about for the conference was "Priority Canada," playing on the party's "PC" initials. Discarded in the end, it was considered too cute by half. Worse, many thought it was too much like what the Liberal government of the day slapped on every agency and service while making a fetish of dropping "Royal" and "Dominion" from them wherever the government could (for example, "Statistics Canada" for "Dominion Bureau of Statistics"). George Hees was a competent minister in two different Tory governments (Diefenbaker's—International Trade; Mulroney's—Veterans Affairs). But he was generally considered no rocket scientist. When the party's marketing professionals showed a Niagara Conference planning committee a proposed new logo for the party, Hees, alone in the "focus group," had trouble identifying the stylized "PC" lettering in the graphics. The graphics were then simplified: a red maple leaf bracketed by a bold blue "P" and "C," in a semblance of the Canadian flag. This remained the party's logo until "Progressive" was dropped from the party's name in 2003, following the PC/Reform or Alliance merger. Hees was right—much better. "Gorgeous George's" image to the contrary in some circles, Hees was no idiot. Even with considerable family wealth, he was often the voice of common sense and of "the common man" in party conclaves.

2.  The Kingston Conference was actually held (in September 1960) on Grindstone Island, just outside Kingston.

3.  Sir John A. was born in Glasgow, Scotland, not Kingston, Ontario. But, for him, Kingston was home.

4.  Frank Moores, the National PC Association president (later premier of Newfoundland), issued a news release on June 16, 1969, to announce the conference on behalf of the Executive Committee. The conference was to be held in the Grand Ballroom of the Sheraton-Brock Hotel, in Niagara, beginning at 7:00 P.M. on Thursday, October 9, and ending at 2:00 P.M. the following Monday, October 13.

5.  Quoted by John Walker, *Montreal Gazette*, June 23, 1969.

6.  W. L. Morton (1908–80), a Manitoban, was a proud Red Tory—a stupendously elegant writer/historian, specializing in the development of the West. Towards the end of his career, Morton, as Vanier Professor, was the most distinguished man on campus at Trent University apart from the chancellor, former long-time Ontario premier Leslie Frost. I had private non-credit tutorials with Morton—"readings," he called them, in the tradition of Oxford, where he had studied as a Rhodes Scholar. It was an opportunity I largely wasted for the normal pursuits of a red-blooded young buck.

7.  Smith. *Rogue Tory*. 523.

8.  L. Ian MacDonald. *Mulroney: The Making of the Prime Minister*. Toronto: McClelland & Stewart, 1984, 227.

9.  Stevens. *Stanfield*. 239.

10. All official party records, news releases, and media statements, PCC minutes, and correspondence cited throughout the book are housed at the Trent University Archives, Peterborough, ON. Unless noted, they are referenced, for clarity of context, in the chapter narrative, not individually in these end notes.

11. Throughout the book, my conversion of dollar values from a particular period in the past to current dollar values is based on the Royal Bank's "Inflation Calculator," which uses monthly consumer price index data from 1914 to the present to show changes in the cost of a fixed "basket" of consumer purchases. These include food, shelter, furniture, clothing, transportation, and recreation. An increase in this cost is "inflation."

12. Canada, House of Commons, Special Senate Committee on Poverty, *Poverty in Canada*. Ottawa: Information Canada, 1971.

13. Halifax *Mail-Star*, October 14, 1969.

14. Dalton Camp, *Toronto Telegram*, October 20, 1969.

15. Stevens. *Stanfield*. 240.

# Chapter Six

1.  Hugh Segal. *The Right Balance: Canada's Conservative Tradition*. Vancouver: Douglas & McIntyre, 2011, 136.

2.  Robert Stanfield. House of Commons Debates, First Session, Twenty-Eighth Parliament, Official Report, vol. 3. Ottawa: Queen's Printer, 1969, 2793.

3.  In 1988, Peter McCreath was elected MP for the Nova Scotia riding of South Shore. He served as veterans affairs minister in the short-lived Kim Campbell government five years later. We were classmates in graduate school at Queen's University before he switched from political studies to history, but we remained friends.

4.  James Farney. "Canadian Populism in the Era of the United Right," in *Conservatism in Canada*, ed. James Farney and David Rayside. Toronto: University of Toronto Press, 2013, 46.

5.  Ibid., 47.

6.  Walter Gordon advised successive Liberal leaders Pearson and Trudeau, but did not develop a policy process for the Liberal Party as a whole. He became a senior Cabinet minister, including at Finance, in the Pearson government.

7.  Smith. *Rogue Tory*. 330.

8.  The British "constitution" is not codified in a single document. It can be found in a variety of documents, from diverse sources, among them statutes such as the 1215 Magna Carta and the 1701 *Act of Settlement*; laws and customs of Parliament; and Court decisions and precedents written by such judicial luminaries as Walter Bagehot and A. V. Dicey. Changes to Britain's unwritten constitution require a

simple majority in both Houses of Parliament and then Royal Assent. Supporters of the British system believe it allows for maximum flexibility and change without undue procedure.

9. Sir John A. Macdonald, letter to Brown Chamberlin, editor of the *Montreal Gazette*, January 21, 1856.

10. McQueen. "Remembering Robert Stanfield."

11. Stevens. *Stanfield.* 26.

12. Storr. *Churchill's Black Dog.* 5.

13. W. A. Wilson. Syndicated column, *Toronto Star.* October 13, 1969.

14. Stevens. *Stanfield.* 238.

15. Anthony Westell. "Nationalism emerges prime policy issue," *Ottawa Journal*, July 5, 1969.

# Chapter Seven

1. Richard Clippingdale. *Robert Stanfield's Canada: Perspectives of the Best Prime Minister We Never Had.* Montreal; Kingston, ON: McGill-Queen's University Press, 2008, 4.

2. Stevens. *Stanfield.* 30.

3. Macquarrie. *Red Tory Blues.* 226.

4. I sent a draft of this chapter to one of the participants in the Stanfield seminar (not Tom Symons) to confirm my memory and records of what had transpired that extraordinary weekend at Trent University. In private correspondence, he said: "What you recall accords with my memory....What I retained at the time was admiration, and a certain feeling that Stanfield had been too reticent about his own views; but you have now given me a convincing explanation of what he was trying to achieve by holding back."

5. MacDonald. *Mulroney.* 298.

6. Gad Horowitz. "Conservatism, Liberalism and Socialism: An Interpretation," *Canadian Journal of Economics and Political Science.* 32, no., 2 (1966): 143–71.

7. Stevens. *Stanfield.* 126.

8. Segal. *Right Balance.* 147, 150.

9. Stevens. *Stanfield.* 31.

10. Segal. *Right Balance.* 17.

11. Ibid., 19.

12. Ibid., 59.

13. Ibid., 67.

14. Ibid., 81.

15. Ibid., 146.

16. Ibid., 99.

17. Ontario Human Rights Commission. *Life Together: A Report on Human Rights in Ontario.* Toronto: Queen's Printer, July 1977.

# Chapter Eight

18. Emphasis added. The statement was appended to the minutes of a two-day meeting (February 23–24, 1971) of the policy Working Committee as the Annual Meeting fast approached. Stanfield had requested the action, reflecting the priority he attached to the policy progress detailed.

19. Stephen Clarkson. "The Conservative Annual Meeting: the Four Fuses." *Canadian Forum.* January-February, 1972, 4.

20. Ibid., 5.

21. George Perlin, ed. *Party Democracy in Canada: The Politics of National Party Conventions.* Scarborough, ON: Prentice Hall Canada, 1988, 5; emphasis added.

22. Ibid.

23. Macquarrie. *Red Tory Blues.* 263.

24. Tom Flanagan. "Something Blue: The Harper Conservatives as Garrison Party" in Farney and Rayside, *Conservatism in Canada*, 91.

25. Ibid.

26. Clarkson. *Canadian Forum.* 5.

# Chapter Nine

1. McQueen. "Remembering Robert Stanfield," 4.

2. Maureen McTeer began her work as a PC Party research assistant on the staff of St. John East MP Jim McGrath. She was then hired in the summer of 1971 by the party's parliamentary Research Office. McTeer returned the following summer, and remained there throughout the 1972 federal general election while still an arts student at the University of Ottawa. (She began her law studies at the same university in the fall of 1973.) According to the only biography of Joe Clark ever written—the book covers Clark's life merely up to 1978, before he became PM—Maureen McTeer parted ways with PC Research Office director Geoffrey Molyneux over her "extracurricular [political] enthusiasms"; see David L. Humphrey, *Joe Clark: A Portrait.* (Ottawa: Deneau & Greenberg, 1978, 110). It was at this point, just after the October 1972 election, that the young woman went to work in Clark's Ottawa parliamentary office as a research assistant. McTeer and Clark began to date soon thereafter. He was then only thirty-three, she not yet twenty-one. The two were married on June 30, 1973.

3. Indeed, the Canadian Association of Former Parliamentarians' quarterly magazine, *Beyond the Hill*, revealed publicly, for the first time, a fascinating fact. The morning after election night, when the Tories were ahead in parliamentary seats, Prime Minister Trudeau phoned Norm Cafik, his Liberal candidate in the riding of Ontario, who trailed his PC opponent, Frank McGee, by thirteen votes. Trudeau told Cafik he was "ready to concede victory to Stanfield." The Liberal candidate, however, convinced the prime minister not to do so. A judicial recount a week and a half later gave the seat to the Liberals by a four-vote margin and the government to Trudeau by two seats. But it had been a near-miraculous achievement by Stanfield. The Tories had soared from 72 to 107 seats, the Liberals

plunged from 155 to 109, the NDP went from 22 to 31, Social Credit remained at 15, and there was 1 independent. Almost ten million votes had been cast. But for four votes in one riding (out of 265), Robert Lorne Stanfield would have become the sixteenth prime minister of Canada. Four votes! See Amélie L. Dugas, "The Night Trudeau Conceded Defeat," *Beyond the Hill* (Spring 2009): 10.

# Chapter Ten

1. Gail Collins. "Don't ask, don't debate." *New York Times*, September 22, 2010.

2. Frank Ledwell, one of the best teachers I ever had, would later leave the priesthood, marry Carolyn Duffy, and have six children. As a University of Prince Edward Island teacher, scholar, poet laureate, academic leader, and community activist, he did as much as any other individual to instill in Islanders an appreciation of their rich literary heritage while adding to that heritage himself through his own writings and publications. Ledwell died at age seventy-eight in August 2008.

# Chapter Eleven

1. Charles J. McMillan. *The Japanese Industrial System, Third Edition*. Berlin, New York: DeGruyter Studies in Organization, 1996.

2. T. Harry Williams. "Introduction," in Huey P. Long, *Every Man a King*. Chicago: Quadrangle Paperbacks, 1964, xxiii.

3. After her stint as external affairs minister in the Joe Clark government, Flora MacDonald wrote an article about her own experience with skewed advice from senior officials: "Do Public Servants Dominate Ministers?" in *Crosscurrents: Contemporary Political Issues*, ed. Mark Charlton and Paul Barker (Scarborough, ON: Nelson, 1994). In an article in the same publication, Mitchell Sharp responded. He had been a long-time senior federal government official (including deputy minister) before becoming a senior Cabinet minister in various portfolios (among them, Finance) in successive Liberal governments. I myself did not experience in the Environment portfolio the practice MacDonald describes, against which Brian Mulroney was always vigilant, as was I, but some of my colleagues felt they were often sold "a bill of goods" by officials, in the words of one.

4. Thomas S. Axworthy and Pierre E. Trudeau. *Towards a Just Society: The Trudeau Years*. Markham, ON: Viking, 1990.

5. Clair Balfour. "MacDonald the key to election edifice." *Globe and Mail*, January 17, 1972.

# Chapter Twelve

1. Robert Stanfield, House of Commons Debates, 3rd session, 28th Parliament, December, 9, 1971, 10316.

2. Gore Vidal, quoted by Tim Teeman in "Why Gore Vidal Refused to Identify as Gay," *Out*, January 7, 2014, 49.

3. Robert Louis Stevenson. *Familiar Studies of Men and Books: The Travels and Essays of Robert Louis Stevenson*, vol. 19. New York: Charles Scribner's Sons, 1902.

# Chapter Thirteen

1. I saved some of Tom Symons's hen-scratchings, which survive to this day in one archival file or another. To me, the man's handwritten notes are like sheet music for orchestrations whose main melodies I recall as though played on my iPhone only yesterday. What a fascinating period of my life. And what intriguing men these two were—so thoughtful, so purposeful, and so imbued with archaic idiosyncrasies even by the standards of the day.

2. In my long session with Reuben Baetz, he told me he and his wife had been wined and dined earlier in the week by the German ambassador to Canada at their official residence. There, he said, only the finest wines straight from German vineyards had been served "without any of the chemical crap injected for North American tastes." Baetz told me: "I never drank so much wine before in my life. At the end of the evening, my head was spinning so much I could hardly stand. And yet, I had to be up at five o'clock to catch a flight only hours later. When I got up, my head was as clear as a bell, as though I had not drunk alcohol at all. No chemicals, no hangover!" Moral of the story: if you're going to get inebriated, drink wine at the home of an ambassador from a wine-producing country—the best hooch, no headache.

3. Although arguably the most famous polling firm in the world, Gallup has had one of the worst track records of all over the years. In fact, it has now had three dismal US elections in a row: overestimating Obama's performance in 2008, overestimating congressional Republicans' performance in the mid-term elections of 2010, and underestimating Obama's vote in 2012. Robert Stanfield and his team recognized Gallup's unearned reputation years before anyone else did. It is part of the reason they built their own independent capacity for public opinion sampling and analysis.

4. Doug Fisher, syndicated column, March 18, 1974.

# Chapter Fourteen

1. Smith. *Rogue Tory*. 568.

2. Macquarrie. *Red Tory Blues*. 264.

3. Clippingdale. *Robert Stanfield's Canada*. 56.

4. Ibid., 71.

5. Bob Plamondon. *The Truth about Trudeau*. Ottawa: Great River Media, 2013, fn693.

6. Drew Westen. *The Political Brain: The Role of Emotion in Deciding the Fate of the Nation*. New York: Public Affairs, 2007, xv.

7. Senator Keith Davey's memoir is titled *The Rainmaker: A Passion for Politics*. Toronto: Stoddart, 1986. Robert Stanfield long resented his unfair treatment by the Liberals in the 1974 election. But he always respected Davey's "beautifully controlled campaign" and the man personally (Clippingdale. *Robert Stanfield's Canada*. 71).

8. Clippingdale. *Robert Stanfield's Canada*. 71.

9. Segal. *Right Balance*. 149.

10. "Tories need a leader," editorial. *Montreal Star*, November 23, 1974.

11. Macquarrie. *Red Tory Blues*. 264.

12. Clippingdale. *Robert Stanfield's Canada*. 4.

13. In *Memoirs* (paperback edition, 981–2), Brian Mulroney reprints the letter he received from Robert Stanfield upon the former's resignation as PC Party leader. Mulroney refers to it earlier on page 792 in the context of the Meech Lake Accord, which Stanfield proudly and actively supported.

14. See: Walter Isaacson, ed. *Profiles in Leadership: Historians on the Elusive Quality of Greatness*. New York: W. W. Norton & Co., 2010.

# Chapter Fifteen

1. Macquarrie. *Red Tory Blues*. 330.

2. Both parents, highly respected in the community, are now deceased. The oldest son, Bill, an engineer, found success with Exxon in Toronto. Doug, popular with everyone because of his winning personality, died of cancer while still only in his thirties. Wayne continues to operate the robust family business (Hambly Enterprises Ltd.) in Charlottetown. Like his father before him, he is a pillar of the community, not only in business but also in volunteerism. Among many other community services, he continues to chair the board of the Confederation Centre of the Arts and has been the district governor of Rotary.

3. Canada, Parliament, House of Commons, Sub-committee on Acid Rain, *Still Waters, the Chilling Reality of Acid Rain* (Ottawa: Minister of Supply and Services Canada, 1981).

4. George Perlin. *The Tory Syndrome: Leadership Politics in the Progressive Conservative Party*. Montreal; Kingston, ON: McGill-Queen's University Press, 1980.

5. From John Crosbie's experience with a blimp at the June 1983 PC Party leadership convention in Ottawa, I opposed certain plans from communications "experts" contracted by my officials to launch the first Environment Week, early in my time as environment minister. Like Crosbie's floor show, those plans involved a big air balloon that, true to form, malfunctioned, almost lifting MP Stan Darling into the skies. Too new in the job to feel comfortable pressing my opposition to the balloon idea, I had deferred to the "professionals." Memo to everyone: Never use as a political gimmick anything that contains more hot air than a politician.

6. Mulroney. *Memoirs*, paper ed., 281.

7. Ibid.

8. McQueen. "Remembering Robert Stanfield." 3.

9. Mulroney. *Memoirs*, paper ed. 272.

10. Margaret Trudeau. *Beyond Reason*. New York: Grosset & Dunlap, 1979.

# Chapter Sixteen

1. Lougheed's grandfather, Sir James Lougheed, a Canadian senator, was the only Albertan ever knighted by the Crown and the first Conservative from Alberta appointed to the federal Cabinet (R. B. Bennett's). The elder Lougheed played a key role in Alberta's becoming a province in 1905.

2. Mulroney. *Memoirs* paper ed. 446.

3. In March 1984, the Supreme Court ruled in Ottawa's favour in a dispute between the federal government and Newfoundland over management and control of seabed resources. In the national election later in the year, Brian Mulroney promised that, if elected prime minister, he would give the province equal say over offshore resource management and make it the "principal beneficiary" of the oil and gas industry. As PM, he honoured that commitment by signing the Canada-Newfoundland Atlantic Accord (February 11, 1985). The accord granted the province significant decision-making powers and financial benefits, with the two levels of government equal partners, in the management of offshore developments through the Canada-Newfoundland Offshore Petroleum Board. A $300 million offshore development fund was created to help prepare the province for industrial growth, to which Ottawa contributed $225 million.

    The accord allowed the province to collect taxes and royalties from petroleum resources as if it owned them. The income was protected from a dollar-for-dollar loss of equalization payments using a complex formula that enabled the province to benefit most from oil revenues in the earliest years covered by the agreement, on an inverted pyramid basis. As a result of the windfall, in 2008 Newfoundland and Labrador became a "have" province for the first time since it joined Confederation in 1949. This meant it paid into the equalization program instead of receiving money from it.

4. Mulroney. *Memoirs,* paper ed. 446.

# Chapter Seventeen

1. L. Ian MacDonald. "Minister tells provinces tourism is 'people' more than rooms." *Montreal Gazette.* April 19, 1985.

2. See *Tourism Tomorrow, Towards a Canadian Tourism Strategy.* Ottawa: Tourism Canada, 1985.

3. Laurence J. Peter and Raymond Hull. *The Peter Principle: Why Things Always Go Wrong.* New York: William Morrow, 1969, 8.

# Chapter Eighteen

1. Les McIlroy had a great flair for marketing and a natural gift for language. As Mike Wilson's chief of staff at International Trade, Les got himself into trouble over a highly stylized electronic map of Canada, part of a free trade promotion, that omitted PEI. The snafu gave ammunition to the anti–free traders, who charged it symbolized how indifferent the minister was to the geographic integrity of Canada in the trade negotiations. And yet Les, who felt ultimately

responsible for this embarrassment to his boss, had previously been the chief of staff to a minister from Prince Edward Island: me. This was a "much ado about nothing" controversy. Les did not deserve the grief he endured concerning it. A man of principle, he resigned over the controversy. My friend and former colleague died in Toronto on January 11, 2011.

2. Linda Bridges and William F. Rickenbacker. *The Art of Persuasion: A National Review Rhetoric for Writers.* New York: National Review, 1991, 8.

# Chapter Nineteen

1. A little-known fact is that a teleprompter breakdown occurred throughout Sarah Palin's boffo vice-presidential nominee acceptance speech at the Republican national convention in St. Paul, Minnesota, on September 3, 2008. So, unbeknownst to anyone in the hall, she had to ad lib a lot. Even John McCain, at the top of the ticket, didn't know until told afterwards. However little this vapid woman knows about anything, she is a formidable demagogue. For the story on the Palin "prompter mishap," see John Heilemann and Mark Halperin. *Game Change.* New York: HarperCollins, 2010, 372.

2. Mulroney. *Memoirs*, paper ed. 648.

3. Ron Reagan. *My Father at 100: A Memoir.* New York: Viking, 2011, 217.

4. Ibid., 217–18.

# Chapter Twenty

1. A transcript of my remarks was published by *Issues of the Day* 5, no. 10 (1992). Several book publishers asked me to edit the transcript and permit them to include the text in various anthologies on the environment. I declined, reserving the right to publish, as I do here, the central information in my own way with greatly expanded material.

2. Four US presidents have been assassinated: Abraham Lincoln (1865), James Garfield (1881), William McKinley (1901), and John Kennedy (1963). And there have been twenty documented assassination attempts against presidents or presidential or vice-presidential candidates, including Ronald Reagan (1981), sixty-nine days into his presidency. By contrast, the only national politician assassinated in Canada was D'Arcy McGee, a Father of Confederation. He was slain, at age forty-two, allegedly by a Fenian extremist dedicated to the establishment of an independent Irish Republic. And this happened in 1868, when Canada was but eight months young.

3. Joe Clark. *How We Lead: Canada in a Century of Change.* Toronto: Random House Canada, 2013, 181.

4. Allan Gotlieb. "Canada passes the acid test on lobbying over acid rain." *Globe and Mail.* March 12, 1990.

5. Cited in Brian Mulroney, "Acid Rain: A Case Study in Canada-U.S. Relations." *Policy Options.* April 2012, 47.

6. Ibid., 43.

7.  Gotlieb. "Canada passes the acid test."

8.  Mulroney. *Memoirs*, paper ed. 840.

9.  Brian Mulroney. "The Acid Rain Treaty at 21" (address, Ottawa, March 13, 2012), 1.

10. Ed Struzik. "An Environmentalist in Power." *Borealis* 1, no. 2, 1989, 33.

# Chapter Twenty-one

1.  L. Ian MacDonald. "How a few people with a dream can make a difference." *Montreal Gazette*, September 1, 2010.

2.  David Israelson. *Silent Earth: The Politics of Our Survival.* New York: Viking Press, 1990, 238.

3.  Mulroney. *Memoirs*, paper ed. 617.

4.  Philip Dearden. "The Fourth World Wilderness Congress." *Parks News* 23, no. 3, 1987, 15.

5.  Bill Devall. "Was it the World Economic Conference or the Economic Development Conference?" *Earth First!*, vol. 8, no. 1, November 1, 1987, 9–10.

6.  Ibid., 15.

7.  David Israelson. "The Tories are setting environmental agenda now." *Toronto Star.* January 21, 1988.

# Chapter Twenty-two

1.  Elizabeth May. *Budworm Battles: The Fight to Stop the Aerial Insecticide Spraying of the Forests of Eastern Canada.* Halifax: Four East Publications, 1982.

2.  Struzik. "Environmentalist in Power." 30–3.

3.  Ibid., 33.

4.  Carl Bernstein has often used the phrase "discovering the best obtainable version of the truth" to describe what reporters ought to consider their mandate (e.g., in an interview on CNN's *Reliable Sources* with host Brian Stelter on April 12, 2015).

5.  Bill Redekop. "Dam deals: Saskatchewan water projects and the birth of environmental law." *Winnipeg Free Press*, May 19, 2012, 1; see also idem, *Dams of Contention: The Rafferty-Alameda Story and the Birth of Canadian Environmental Law.* Winnipeg: Hartland Associates, 2012.

6.  Lisa Blackburn. "If Only Milton Had Visited South Moresby." *CM Archives* 18, no. 5, 1990, 2.

7.  Redekop. "Dam deals." 1.

8.  Struzik. "Environmentalist in Power." 33.

9.  Elizabeth May. *Paradise Won: The Struggle for South Moresby.* Toronto: McClelland & Stewart, 1990.

10. Ibid., 314.

11. Ibid., 144.

12. Ibid., 144–5.

13. Ibid., 200.

14. Ibid., 261.

15. Ibid., 239.

16. Ibid., 312.

17. Ibid., 151.

18. Ibid., 148.

19. David Hunt (address to the Churchill Society for the Advancement of Parliamentary Democracy at its Seventh Annual Dinner, Toronto, November 29, 1990), 19.

20. Struzik. "Environmentalist in Power." 33.

21. Mulroney. *Memoirs*, paper ed. 841.

22. Ibid., 908.

# Chapter Twenty-three

1. May. *Paradise Won*. 238.

2. In 1964, PEI celebrated the centennial of the 1864 Charlottetown Conference, the first meeting of the Fathers of Confederation, which led to the birth of the nation in 1867. This celebration planted the first seeds of widespread interest among Islanders in PEI's cultural heritage and property. The formation of the PEI Heritage Foundation was born of that interest. Then, in 1973, PEI's celebration of the centennial of its entry to Confederation sparked further passion on the part of Islanders for indigenous antiques and heritage furnishing of all sorts, as well as interest in Confederation-era public buildings and private homes across the province. Two Charlottetown women, Irene Rogers and Catherine Hennessey, were largely responsible for instilling in Islanders a greater appreciation of their rich built inheritance. In PEI, local antiques became a hot commodity and the preservation of older public and private buildings both a passion for some and a big economic opportunity for others. There was also a boom in local books and articles about such matters, including Irene Roger's own publications on Charlottetown's heritage buildings, neighbourhoods, and streetscapes.

3. Charles, Prince of Wales. *A Vision of Britain: A Personal View of Architecture*. New York: Doubleday, 1989.

# Chapter Twenty-four

1. Brian Mulroney. *Where I Stand*. Toronto: McClelland & Stewart, 1983.

2. Oxford University. *Oriel College Record*. 2013, 105.

3. H. Basil Robinson. *Diefenbaker's World: A Populist in Foreign Affairs*. Toronto: University of Toronto Press, 1989.

4.  Mulroney. *Memoirs*, paper ed. 235.

5.  David Humphreys. *Joe Clark: A Portrait*. Ottawa: Deneau & Greenberg, 1978, 62.

6.  The other PC senator who insisted on sitting as a Progressive Conservative was Elaine McCoy. She continues to sit in the Red Chamber with that identification as a member from Alberta. Born in 1946, she can serve until 2021, when there will no longer be a national Progressive Conservative parliamentarian anywhere unless the party restores its historic values and the dual name that reflects them.

7.  Gordon Robertson. *Memoirs of a Very Civil Servant: Mackenzie King to Pierre Trudeau*. Toronto: University of Toronto Press, 2000, 361.

8.  Ibid., 338. In a newspaper article on Meech Lake, about which Robertson commented in his memoirs, Pierre Trudeau stated that the 1982 Constitution and Charter of Rights and Freedom had given Canada "a creative equilibrium between the provinces and the central government [so that] the federation was set to last a thousand years!"

9.  Ibid., 380.

10. Mulroney. *Memoirs*, paper ed. 414.

11. Ibid., 329.

12. Ibid.

13. Cited by Robertson. *Memoirs of a Very Civil Servant*. 360.

14. Milton Friedman. *Capitalism and Freedom*. Chicago: University of Chicago Press, 1962.

15. Mulroney. *Memoirs*, paper ed. 30.

16. Robertson. *Memoirs of a Very Civil Servant*. 340.

17. Abraham Kaplan, address at a meeting of the American Educational Research Association, February 1962, published in *Journal of Medical Education* 37. June 1962, 637.

18. David Brooks. "The Republicans' incompetence caucus." *New York Times*, October 13, 2015.

19. Julianne Schultz. *Reviving the Fourth Estate*. Cambridge: Cambridge University Press, 1998, 49.

20. Mulroney. *Memoirs*, paper ed. 787.

21. Ibid., 539.

22. Ibid., 343.

23. David Brooks, interview by Fareed Zakaria, *GPS*, CNN, April 19, 2015.

24. Clark. *How We Lead*. 195.

25. Brian Mulroney. "A Tribute to Sir Winston Churchill at Blenheim Palace (Woodstock, England) on the 50th Anniversary of His Death," excerpted in the *National Post*, May 29, 2015.

26. Achim Steiner, cited by Seth Borenstein. "Scientists say ozone layer is recovering." *Associated Press*, September 11, 2014.

27. There is nothing as "past" as a past politician. I was Brian Mulroney's environment minister for virtually all his first term as prime minister, when most of his government's major environmental measures were achieved. By contrast, Jean Charest became environment minister in 1991, towards the end of Mulroney's time as prime minister. There was too little time remaining in the government's mandate for Charest to achieve much in the Environment portfolio. Moreover, the government, including Charest as a candidate, would soon be distracted by the leadership succession. And yet, in his book *The Right Balance*, then Conservative senator Hugh Segal refers to Mulroney's "[fully engaging] on the environmental file with the help of the remarkable leadership of Minister Charest" (163). Charest was premier of Quebec when the senator wrote and published those words. I was then long gone from both politics and the country itself. In politics, Segal's bouquet to my good friend Jean Charest is called "sucking up." It bothers me no more than minor—as opposed to, in this case, major—factual errors in this otherwise first-rate book. (The Liberal Kingston Policy Conference, for example, was held in 1960, not 1961, as Segal states.) Life moves on, so did I, and so also did Hugh Segal's memory of me and of my record as environment minister. *Sic transit gloria mundi.*

28. Clark. *How We Lead.* 107.

29. Flanagan. "Something Blue." 85.

30. Clark. *How We Lead.* 103.

# Chapter Twenty-five

1. Peter C. Newman. *The Canadian Establishment*, vol. 1, *The Old Order.* Toronto: McClelland & Stewart, 1975, 215.

2. Mulroney. *Memoirs*, paper ed. 574.

3. Erik Neilsen. *The House Is Not a Home.* Toronto: Macmillan of Canada, 1989.

4. Mulroney. *Memoirs*, paper ed. 456, 612.

5. Ibid., 250.

6. Dalton Camp. *Gentlemen, Players, and Politicians.* Toronto: McClelland & Stewart, 1970.

7. Mulroney. *Memoirs*, hardcover ed. 755; emphasis added.

8. Mackenzie King was the grandson of the great nineteenth-century Upper Canada rebellion leader William Lyon Mackenzie. He was as heroic as Paul Revere in the United States, but we Canadians tend not to glorify our giants of history, much less elevate them to folk-hero status the way Americans do, sometimes with very undeserving characters.

9. Jean Chrétien. *Straight from the Heart.* Toronto: Key Porter Books, 1994.

10. Mulroney. *Memoirs*, paper ed. 343.

# Chapter Twenty-six

1.  The FDR quote was cited by Frances Perkins, his Labour Secretary (1933–45) following her government service career. After the president died, Perkins taught at the New York State School of Industrial and Labor Relations at Cornell University until her own death in 1965 at age eighty-five. She wrote a highly personal account of her years with FDR (*The Roosevelt I Knew*. New York: Viking Press, 1946) in which she devotes a chapter to the man's approach to politics. Perkins said, "Roosevelt was sympathetic to a lot of new ideas that failed to get popular approval, but he knew it was important to wait for the moment when the people were ready for a program" (137).

2.  I detailed and analyzed the federal government's National Water Policy in an article I wrote after leaving the Environment portfolio: "Water Resource Planning in Canada." *Journal of Soil and Water Conservation*, 45, no. 6, 1990, 614–16. It was one of many such articles of mine published in learned journals and other publications in this post-Cabinet period.

3.  Howard Pawley, NDP premier of Manitoba, had also opposed the free trade agreement. But his numerically weak majority government was defeated in the legislature in March 1988, eight months before the 1988 federal general election, further isolating Peterson in his opposition to free trade.

4.  Allan Rankin is a well-known PEI songwriter and performer. Close to anti–Fixed Link activists, especially his long-time friend David Weale, Rankin was a high-ranking Ghiz government employee (a political appointee) in the cultural area. It was widely rumoured—and I have always assumed it true—that Rankin, with Premier Joe Ghiz's blessing, if not complicity, wrote partisan anti–free trade speeches, on government time, during the 1988 federal election for Malpeque Liberal candidate Catherine Callbeck (MP from 1988 to 1993; premier from 1993 to 1996; now a senator). Rankin was not alone in, allegedly, combining such government "service" with Liberal partisanship. In this sense, PEI at the time did not have so much democracy as "modified democracy."

5.  Joe Ghiz's widow, Rose Ellen, told PEI journalist Barb McKenna, "Joe's main concern [in opposing the Fixed Link] was always for the ferry workers; he was very concerned about the impact [the bridge] would have on the Marine Atlantic employees"; see "The Link: The Guardian Commemorative Issue," May 30, 2007, 28.

6.  The organized Fixed Link opponents gave themselves the modern-sounding, media-friendly name "Friends of the Island." The group, though, was an offshoot of an earlier political sect called "The Brothers and Sisters of Cornelius Howatt." Founded in 1973, the centennial of PEI's joining Confederation, it was named after a member of the provincial legislature in 1873 who had opposed the colony's membership in the new Dominion. Very symbolic! Howatt and his disciples resisted the introduction of both the railway and the automobile in the province, just as they had always fought the causeway/tunnel idea (on the Island's agenda ever since colonial days). The "Friends" often deviously framed their opposition in environmental terms to exploit Islanders' intrinsic love and respect for the land and water. But the true spirit that drove them was cultural; they did not want the Island to change, except to turn the clock backwards. They believed geographic isolation from the mainland was the way to resist the evils

of modernity. David Weale, an articulate and popular history teacher at UPEI, became the latter-day Cornelius Howatt. Another prominent activist was Betty Howatt, a direct descendant of Cornelius and one of the principal organizers of the reactionary sect that bore his name.

A fundamentalist lay minister, Weale preached against the Fixed Link at every turn—and against many other economic and social reforms as well. Many in the media idolized him, either because they, like Weale, were themselves Luddites; or, simply, because Weale and other Fixed Link opponents made for good copy; or because supporting Weale in his various crusades advanced their own political agendas, including defeating me. Betty Howatt, too, was a freelance CBC commentator (she on horticulture). Weale and Howatt's many supporters at the local CBC station in Charlottetown gave these two ideologues a ready bull-horn for their reactionary political views. The corporation hardly ever gave equal time, and often none at all, to people on the other side of issues that Weale and Howatt espoused.

In the winter of 2006, the University of Prince Edward Island learned that Weale—by then only a part-time history instructor—had successfully bribed many of his students to quit his course by promising them an automatic B-minus grade. His efforts to lighten his own workload succeeded spectacularly: the university fired him.

7.  Rex Murphy. "An environmental review process is an organized procrastination." *National Post,* January 30, 2016.

8.  Kennedy Wells. "An Island Not Entire of Itself." *Macleans,* August 31, 1981, 32.

9.  This was also the title of a slim book he virtually self-published; see David Weale. *Them Times.* Charlottetown: Institute of Island Studies Press, 1992.

10. Jim Brown. "Classic Contest: A McMillan-Ghiz Showdown Would Be Too Close to Call." *Atlantic Insight,* August 1988, 14–17.

11. By toppling the septuagenarian Walter R. Shaw, Alex Campbell became, at age thirty-two, the third-youngest premier in history. Brian Gallant, current premier of New Brunswick and the youngest premier in Canada, was also thirty-two when he took office in October 2014. George Edwin King (premier of New Brunswick from 1870 to 1871) was elected at age 30. To this day, King remains the youngest person ever to have been a premier. He served again from 1872 to 1878.

12. Charles McMillan. *Eminent Islanders—Prince Edward Island: From French Colony to the Cradle of Confederation.* Bloomingdale, IN: AuthorHouse, 2007.

13. The Joe/Robert Ghiz and Thane/Alex Campbell father-son combinations were not the only ones in Canadian history. William Bennett, premier of British Columba (1975–86), was the son of W. A. C. Bennett, BC premier from 1952 to 1972—third cousin twice removed of R. B. Bennett, eleventh prime minister of Canada (1930–5). Hugh John Flemming, premier of New Brunswick (1952–60), was the son of that province's premier John Kidd Flemming (1911–14). Duff Roblin, premier of Manitoba (1958–67), was the grandson (not the son) of a premier—Sir Rodman Roblin (1900–15). Leonard Percy DeWolffe Tilley, premier of New Brunswick (1933–5), was the son of Sir Samuel Leonard Tilley, a Father of Confederation and premier of the New Brunswick colony (1861–5).

# Chapter Twenty-seven

1. Nelson Wiseman. "Provincial Conservatism." Farney and Rayside, *Conservatism in Canada*, 213.

2. The politics of the Island during this period is chronicled in: Wayne MacKinnon. *Between Two Cultures: The Alex Campbell Years.* Stratford, PEI: Tea Hill Press, 2005.

3. When the Mulroney government was formed in September 1984, only about 17 percent of Privy Council–type appointments had been going to women. The percentage rose to the mid-thirties towards the end of the Tories' first term in office, very largely because of Mulroney's insistence. He had zero tolerance for perpetuating the gender imbalance, and gave offending Cabinet ministers a verbal thrashing, both alone and at Cabinet meetings. Apart from sharing his cause, I knew better than to ignore the importance he attached to it. Most other ministers did, too. So thrashings were rare.

4. Rare as the occurrence is, some individuals do decline a Senate appointment. One actually refused to serve after being appointed. Rufus Curry (1859–1934), from Windsor, Nova Scotia, was an extremely wealthy shipbuilder and shipowner. Later, he was active in furniture manufacturing, electric power, a foundry, and marine fittings and supplies. This industrial baron, an ardent provincial and federal Liberal, was appointed to the Senate in 1903. But Curry declined the appointment. Never having been sworn in, let alone seated, the appointee failed to inform the governor general (Lord Minto) of his lack of interest in the post in time to avoid being officially enrolled as a Senator. Not until March 1905 was the seat declared officially vacant. Meanwhile, Rufus Curry never set foot in the Red Chamber.

5. The full quote is: "The stupid neither forgive nor forget; the naive forgive and forget; the wise forgive but do not forget"; Thomas Szasz, "Personal Conduct," in *The Second Sin* (New York: Anchor Books, 1973).

6. When Lloyd MacPhail was appointed PEI lieutenant governor in 1985, no woman had ever been appointed to the position. (One would be five years later: Marion Reid, in 1990.) I was eager to change that dismal fact by supporting Norma Simpson instead of MacPhail for the post. MacPhail had been a long-time Tory provincial politician (member of the PEI Legislature, for 2nd Queens, from 1961 to 1982, and holder of various Cabinet posts, including Finance from 1979 to 1981). Simpson, a former nursing instructor, was from Charlottetown, but she grew up in a rural area (St. Catherine's), and was the daughter of beloved former premier Walter R. Shaw (1959–66). She had moved my nomination with a terrific speech at the convention that selected me to run for the PCs in Hillsborough for the 1979 election, my first campaign. This wonderful woman, a cancer survivor herself, was a community leader in this area and in many others. She had many of her father's gifts, including brains and charm and oratory, not to mention an imposing presence, plus many of her own special qualities. But I could not get enough PEI Tories to back my efforts to have Norma appointed governor. Some of the strongest opposition came from Island Tory women, including the president of the provincial PC Party, Anne Huestis, a Summerside realtor. Faced with such obstinacy, I had to withdraw Norma's name.

7. Newman. *Canadian Establishment*, vol. 1, 213.

8. Angus MacLean was first elected to the House of Commons in a by-election on June 25, 1951, when he defeated Liberal Cecil Miller 9,540 votes to 9,087—a plurality of 453. In the subsequent federal general election, in 1953, MacLean ran with fellow PC candidate Chester McLure in the dual riding of Queen's. There, each voter had two votes to cast for any two candidates. They could cast both votes for two PCs or for two Liberals or they could split their two votes between the parties. Heath Macquarrie told me it was not uncommon for a candidate of one party to encourage voters to vote for him but not necessarily for his running mate, of the same party. Heath did not follow the practice himself, when running with MacLean, and roundly condemned it as underhanded. In 1953, MacLean won, McLure lost. So, obviously, there had been vote-splitting. James Lester Douglas, a Liberal, represented this dual riding, as one of its two MPs, from 1940 until his death in 1950, which required the 1951 by-election that sent MacLean to Parliament the first time. My Hillsborough predecessor said Douglas made a practice of encouraging voters to split their franchise, as long as they voted for him. Heath hinted MacLean had done the same at the former's expense.

    Heath Macquarrie respected Angus MacLean, his former running mate, but they were not close personal friends. Ideologically, they had little in common, especially as MacLean became increasingly arch-conservative in later years and Macquarrie, if anything, even a "redder" Red Tory than he had been when younger.

9. At various times in Canada's history, a few federal ridings were represented by two members. In some instances, the dual-member ridings existed so that each political party could field both a Protestant and a Roman Catholic candidate in the same riding. The electoral district of Halifax was created at Confederation in 1867. Like Queen's in PEI, it returned two members until 1968. All dual ridings were terminated in 1966 before the 1968 federal general election.

10. Wiseman. "Provincial Conservatism." 211.

11. Jonathan Malloy. "The Relationship between the Conservative Party of Canada and Evangelicals and Social Conservatives." Farney and Rayside, *Conservatism in Canada*, 197.

12. See Stevenson Kellogg. *The Greater Charlottetown Urban Area Opportunities Study*, 3 v., 1973. The deterioration of Charlottetown's commercial core reflected a number of factors, not just competition from off-Island stores, let alone Angus MacLean's moratorium against malls. Some of the iconic Island retail names also suffered from what is sometimes called "Third Generation Syndrome"—management by a third generation of family members inferior to that provided by the original founders of a family-owned business and by the (second) generation that immediately succeeded them.

# Chapter Twenty-eight

1. The Robert Harris painting of the Fathers of Confederation destroyed in the Parliament building fire in 1916 had been originally commissioned in 1883 to illustrate the Charlottetown Conference of 1864. The painting was later

expanded also to represent the follow-up Quebec Conference. The final painting featured thirty-three "Fathers" and the secretary, Hewitt Bernard. The painting was installed in the original Parliament building in 1884. The Confederation Centre of the Arts in Charlottetown owns several preliminary works (including an oil sketch) done by Harris for this iconic painting. The National Gallery of Canada owns the full-scale "cartoon" (blueprint) for the painting (acquired by the Government of Canada after the 1916 fire).

2. Sometime after the 1988 election, while at the Royal Bank on Queen St. in Charlottetown, I encountered Rory McLellan, then head of the PEI Fishermen's Association. "You know, Tom, fishermen didn't really oppose the Fixed Link, despite all our vocal opposition to the project," he told me. "We just wanted to stir up as much fuss as we could to maximize compensation from the federal government for lost revenue during construction." David Weale, a historian, had no expertise whatsoever in the complex scientific and engineering factors surrounding the Fixed Link. But that did not prevent him from claiming that the project would destroy the province's environment and wipe out its fishery. Most Island journalists treated his every word as though it were *ex cathedra*, coming as it did not only from a UPEI professor, but also from a Protestant lay preacher.

3. John Urquhart. "Taking his acid-rain fight on the road." *New York Times*, October 16, 1987.

4. Journalism schools continue to debate the professional ethics surrounding a photo taken by photojournalist Doug Ball of Robert Stanfield's fumbling a football at a 1974 election stopover. The photo was splashed across the front pages of almost every newspaper in the country. Along with Stanfield's being caught on TV eating a banana while awaiting voting results at the 1967 PC leadership convention, the football photo became a defining image of the PC leader's career—and, certainly, in this case, of the Conservative Party's staggering 1974 election campaign. And yet, the media—The Canadian Press wire service, in particular—could have used, instead, photos made available by Ball of Stanfield's actually catching the football, in some shots with great athleticism. Did this selectivity reflect political bias or just a warped sense that a fumble was more newsworthy than a catch? Even when the actor knows his lines and says them well, critics can still shut down the show.

5. William Zinsser. *On Writing Well: The Classic Guide to Writing Nonfiction, 30th Anniversary Edition.* New York: HarperCollins, 2006, 184.

6. Ibid., 186.

7. The familiar metaphor "shouting fire in a crowded theatre" paraphrases Oliver Wendell Holmes, Jr.'s opinion in the 1919 US Supreme Court case *Schenck v United States.* The Court held that the defendant's speech in opposition to the military draft during the First World War was not protected free speech under the First Amendment of the US Constitution.

8. Segal. *Right Balance.* 104.

9. The prime minister ordered ministers to campaign outside their own provinces, and said he would deal personally with any who refused requests from the national organization. My campaigning for other Tory candidates included

visits to Toronto and southeastern Ontario ridings in the last days of the election, when being in my own riding might have made the difference between winning and losing, given the tiny margin of defeat. To boot, I had to attend to ministerial business, both at home and in Ottawa. Such business included travelling out West to participate in a major federal-provincial conference on the environment and wildlife. The Prime Minister's Office phoned my chief of staff to ensure that I would attend. I also had to travel to Toronto to debate high-profile Liberal Sheila Copps and each of the other parties' parliamentary spokesperson on the environment in a nationally televised special produced by the CBC's *Journal*, the corporation's main nightly public affairs program at the time.

10. Some weeks after the 1988 election, I was visiting my younger sister, Maura Davies, in Halifax. While I was ordering a beer at a local pub, a young woman bartender asked me if I was Tom McMillan. Not wishing to talk politics, I told a white lie and said no, but that I was sometimes mistaken for him. "I'm from Prince Edward Island," she said. "McMillan was a great MP. But, Jeez, what they did to destroy that poor man, after all he had done for them!" I didn't feel "destroyed." But I appreciated her concern, even if expressed "to someone else."

11. Segal. *Right Balance*. 98.

12. Mulroney. *Memoirs*, paper ed. 987–8.

13. Wade MacLauchlan. Letter to the Editor. Charlottetown *Guardian*, January 11, 2013.

14. "The long Tory drought: 17 years without a seat in Parliament." *Canada Votes.* CBC Prince Edward Island, January 16, 2005.

15. The other nominal Tory single-issue independent candidate, Baird Judson, received 281 votes. He ran on an anti-abortion platform with the "Christian Heritage" label. Most of his votes would have come from my traditional Progressive Conservative base. Some observers believe he, too, was encouraged (and possibly funded) to run by the Joe Ghiz operatives. I am less convinced of that possibility than I am of Liberal plotting behind Weale's candidacy. Judson, also a UPEI professor, was just an odd duck, quite capable of running on his own initiative, as he would again a number of times later, including when I was not a candidate. But one wonders where he got the money to run against me in 1988. Particularly puzzling was the fact all his campaign billboards were in my own campaign colours and style (presumably to confuse the voter by conflating his campaign with mine); they were placed right next to my signs in every case (the same effect); and his campaign office was adjacent to my own, on University Avenue (ditto). All too clever, and expensive, to have been the brainchild of a strange little man who was known not to possess the wherewithal to do any of this on his own.

16. Rand Dyck. *Canadian Politics: Critical Approaches, Second Edition.* Scarborough, ON: Nelson Education, 1996, 439.

17. Soon after his election to Parliament, George Proud engaged in real estate wheeling and dealing in the Ottawa/Hull area. He was rumoured to have amassed a $600,000 debt, for which his creditors aggressively pursued him. It was publicly revealed that he had borrowed heavily from a well-known Charlottetown bootlegger, a long-time Liberal partisan and poll worker. If, as one might assume, all

this extracurricular activity and personal pressure hurt his parliamentary and constituency work, the Island media weren't concerned. The CBC, in particular, mostly gave the new Hillsborough MP a pass on the matter.

18. Interview on *Fox News Sunday*, July 19, 2015.

19. Frank Bruni. "The vain and the desperate." *New York Times*, September 20, 2014.

20. Roy McMurtry. *Memoirs and Reflections*. Toronto: University of Toronto Press, 2013, 529–30.

21. Interview with Jim Coyle. "A life-time of achievement chronicled in 'Red Tory's' life story." *Globe and Mail*, September 15, 2013.

# Chapter Twenty-nine

1. The members of the task force were: Peter Pearse, professor of forestry, University of British Columbia; James Hughes, manager, energy and industry outlook, Imperial Oil; Susie Washington, president, Western Environmental and Social Affairs Trends Inc.; Douglas Bruchet, director, health, safety and environment, Canadian Petroleum Association; Charles Ferguson, director, environment affairs, Inco Ltd.; Murray Coolican, VP, government relations, National Sea Products Ltd.; Frank Frantis, VP, environmental services, Noranda Inc.; Margot Franssen, president, Body Shop Canada; Raymond Brouzes, director, environmental affairs, Alcan Aluminum Ltd.; Mark Toivanen, chairman and CEO, Sanican Group Inc.; Pierre Veilleux, manager, environmental and technical services, printing paper group, Abitibi-Price Inc.; Douglas Gregory, advisor, public affairs, IBM Canada Ltd.; and Michael Keating and Beatrice Olivastri, consultants to the task force.

2. The PEI CBC-TV station said, in its main suppertime news show, that I was unemployed for a long time after the election. This was demonstrably untrue. I phoned the station to set the record straight. On air the next day, the station retracted its "mistake." It detailed a number of my professional involvements. For my hurt to have been inflicted by personnel at an institution that I had once admired compounded the emotional pain I felt at the time and long afterwards.

3. Since my own appointment, there has been a succession of consuls general in Boston from Atlantic Canada: former Nova Scotia premier Donald Cameron, former Halifax MP Mary Clancy, former Nova Scotia finance minister Neil LeBlanc, former PEI premier Pat Binns, and, as I write, currently former New Brunswick premier David Alward. Before my time in the post, we Atlantic Canadians had never had even a senior officer at the consulate.

4. Clippingdale. *Robert Stanfield's Canada*. 54.

5. The Canadian government's current policy for Boston, as elsewhere around the world, is to lease, rather than own, property for its residential and official purposes. External Affairs (renamed Global Affairs Canada) is now required to operate much less ostentatiously and more frugally than in its golden era, the tail end of which I experienced.

6. One of the many pieces I wrote for more serious publications in the United States while consul general was a chapter titled "International Environmental Law and

Global Business Development," in *Transnational Environmental Law and Its Impact on Corporate Behaviour*, ed. Eric J. Urbani and Conrad P. Rubin. Irvington-on-Hudson, NY: Transnational Juris Publications, 1992, 73–80.

7. See, for example: Raj Chett, Nathaniel Hendren, Patrick Kline, and Emmanuel Saez. "The Economic Impacts of Tax Expenditures: Evidence from Spatial Variation across the U.S." Cambridge, MA: Harvard University, Equality of Opportunity Project, July 2013. Available online at http://web.archive.org/web/20141214131555/http://obs.rc.fas.harvard.edu/chetty/tax_expenditure_soi_whitepaper.pdf.

8. Paul Krugman, "Now that's rich," *New York Times*, May 9, 2014.

9. Mulroney, *Memoirs*, paper ed., 965.

10. Filmmaker Henry Jaglom recorded a number of conversations he had with Orson Welles shortly before the latter's death in 1985. The conversations were edited by film historian and author Peter Biskind (*Easy Riders, Raging Bulls: How the Sex-Drugs-and-Rock 'n' Roll Generation Saved Hollywood*), and published as *My Lunches with Orson Welles: Conversations between Henry Jaglom and Orson Welles* (New York: Metropolitan Books, 2013).

11. Mulroney. *Memoirs*, paper ed. 962.

12. Ibid., 844.

# Chapter Thirty

1. An excellent account of Franklin Roosevelt's funeral is: Robert Klara *FDR's Funeral Train: A Betrayed Widow, a Soviet Spy, and a Presidency in the Balance*. New York: Palgrave Macmillan, 2010.

2. Segal. *Right Balance*. 168.

3. Kathy eventually sold her successful store, Katherine's Ltd., to her sister-in-law, Eleanor Hambly, after operating it for seventeen years. By the time this classy store sold its last Jones of New York suit and finally closed, it had been the style-setter for Island women and its many customers off-Island for nearly two decades. For Kathy, as for me, it was time to move on to the next stage. She became executive director of the Charlottetown Chamber of Commerce. When, a few years later, she was offered a high-level position with the PEI government, as director of business development, she accepted it. With an MBA from Dalhousie, she later had a robust consulting business of her own on the Island. The Chamber then beseeched her to return as executive director when her replacement did not pan out. Kathy agreed to serve again, for a limited time.

# Chapter Thirty-one

1. Jeffrey Simpson. "It's same old, same old on climate change after Prentice." *Globe and Mail*, November 17, 2010.

2. Quoted by E. J. Dionne Jr. "The street on welfare." *Washington Post*, March 18, 2008.

3.  John Stuart Mill. *Principles of Political Economy with Some of Their Applications to Social Philosophy.* Book IV, Chapter 7, "On the Probable Futurity of the Labouring Classes." 1848, repr., New York: Kelley, 1961, 754.

4.  I have distilled Burke's political philosophy from two sources. The first is Ian Harris, "Edmund Burke," in *Stanford Encyclopedia of Philosophy*, ed. Edward N. Zalta (Spring 2012 ed.). The second is Edmund Burke's *Reflections on the Revolution in France: New Interdisciplinary Essays*, ed. John Whale (Manchester, UK: Manchester University Press, 2000). Burke's use of the phrase "sustainable practice" is cited in the former, but the concept itself is also analyzed (as "organic development") in the latter.

5.  John Roberts served as federal environment minister from March 3, 1980, to August 11, 1983—three years and five months. I served from August 22, 1985, to December 7, 1988—three years and four months.

6.  Francis I. *Laudato Si'.* Encyclical Letter on care for our common home. Vatican City, June 18, 2015.

7.  Jordan Michael Smith. "Reinventing Canada: Stephen Harper's Conservative Revolution." *World Affairs*, online ed., March-April 2012, 1.

8.  Ibid., 2.

9.  Clark. *How We Lead.* 93.

10. Rachel Carson. *Silent Spring.* Boston: Houghton Mifflin, 1962.

11. Such ranking by academics in the guise of scholarliness, especially of prime ministers soon after they have left office, is largely a mug's game. As often as not, it reveals more about the political leanings of the rankers than about the leadership qualities and record of the ranked—witness Norman Hillmer and J. J. Granatstein's "Best and Worst" list in *Maclean's*, April 21, 1997. The historians surveyed placed Mackenzie King above Sir John A. Macdonald. Not a single scholar acknowledged Mulroney's outstanding record on the environment. And the slam by several historians against Lester Pearson that, as one put it, "he excelled at being a civil servant and should have remained one," is pathetic. (Gordon Robertson, long-time senior advisor to prime ministers from King to Trudeau, ranked Pearson in the top six, as would I.)

12. Robert Putman. *Bowling Alone: The Collapse and Revival of American Community.* New York: Simon & Schuster Paperbacks, 2000, 18.

13. Ibid., 27.

14. Malloy. "Relationship." 186.

15. Ibid., 187.

16. Macquarrie. *Red Tory Blues.* 63.

17. Segal. *Right Balance.* 3.

18. Ibid., 59.

19. Ibid., 96.

20. Ibid., 37.

21. Ibid., 16.

22. Gregory Boyd. *The Myth of a Christian Nation: How the Quest for Political Power Is Destroying the Church*. Grand Rapids, MI: Zondervan, 2005, 101.

23. Segal. *Right Balance*. 97.

24. Robert J. Sternberg. *Smart People Can Be So Stupid*. New Haven, CT: Yale University Press, 2002.

25. Tom Flanagan. *Harper's Team: Behind the Scenes in the Conservative Rise to Power*. Montreal; Kingston, ON: McGill-Queen's University Press, 2007.

26. John F. Kennedy. *Profiles in Courage*. New York: Harper, 1956, 1.

27. Humphreys. *Joe Clark*. 206.

28. Clark. *How We Lead*. 199.

29. Ibid., 200.

30. McQueen. "Remembering Robert Stanfield." 4.

31. Stevens. *Stanfield*. 235.

32. The short-lived Clark government completed plans to transfer the national head-quarters of the Department of Veterans Affairs from Ottawa to Charlottetown. The project had been initiated by PEI Trudeau Cabinet minister Daniel J. MacDonald while veterans affairs minister before his defeat in the 1979 election. PEI Tory Cabinet minister David MacDonald and I had to fight to save the relocation plan for Charlottetown (part of my riding). The relocation was opposed by Tory Caucus right-wingers led by Dan McKenzie. Mel Gass, otherwise a fierce defender of Island interests, supported McKenzie during a heated debate on the issue in Caucus. David MacDonald beseeched me to get Mel Gass on side. Gass backed off his original position.

33. Lawrence Martin. "Anti-intellectualism: Political venom moves north." *Globe and Mail*, September 23, 2010.

34. McQueen. "Remembering Robert Stanfield." 4.

35. Durrell Bricker and John Ibbitson. *The Big Shift: The Seismic Change in Canadian Politics, Business, and Culture, and What It Means for Our Future*. Toronto: HarperCollins Canada, 2013.

36. Inder Marwah, Phil Triadafilopoulos, and Steven White. "Immigration, Citizenship, and Canada's New Conservative Party." Farney and Rayside, *Conservatism in Canada*, 111–12.

37. Kelly Pullen. "With Friends Like Harper: How Nigel Wright Went from Golden Boy to Fall Guy." *Toronto Life*, March 25, 2014, 5.

38. Clark. *How We Lead*. 200.

39. David Brooks. "The solitary leader." *New York Times*, June 10, 2013.

40. Ibid.

41. Cited in: Ezra Klein. "Obama's budget and the coalition of the ascendant." *Washington Post: Wonkblog*, April 13, 2013, 1.

42. Clark. *How We Lead*. 196.

43. Gail Collins. "Beyond the demon sheep." *New York Times*, May 7, 2015.

44. McQueen. "Remembering Robert Stanfield." 4–5.

45. Ibid., 5.

46. Bob Hepburn. "Kevin O'Leary and the Tories' sorry state." *Toronto Star,* January 17, 2016.

47. Maurice Duverger. *Political Parties: Their Organization and Activity in the Modern State,* trans. Barbara North and Robert North. London: Methuen, 1954.

# INDEX

Mowat, Farley 268

Mulroney, Brian

## N

## O

# T